Measurement and Evaluation for Physical Educators

Second Edition

Measurement and Evaluation for Physical Educators

Second Edition

Don R. Kirkendall, PhD
State University of New York at Cortland

Joseph J. Gruber, PhD
University of Kentucky

Robert E. Johnson, PhD
Kansas State University

Human Kinetics Publishers, Inc.
Champaign, Illinois

Library of Congress Cataloging-in-Publication Data

Kirkendall, Don R.
  Measurement and evaluation for physical educators.

Includes bibliographies and index.
  1. Physical fitness—Testing. 2. Physical education
and training—Evaluation. 3. Grading and marking
(Students) I. Gruber, Joseph J. II. Johnson, Robert
E., 1941-   . III. Title.
GV436.K54 1987   613.7   86-18086
ISBN 0-87322-081-1

Senior Editor: Gwen Steigelman, PhD
Production Director: Ernie Noa
Assistant Production Director: Lezli Harris
Copy Editor: Kevin Neely
Assistant Editor: Kathy Kane
Proofreader: Linda Purcell
Typesetter: Sandra Meier
Text Layout: Lezli Harris
Cover Design: Keith Blomberg
Printed By: Murray Printing

ISBN: 0-87322-081-1

Printed in the United States of America

10 9 8 7 6 5 4 3 2 1

Human Kinetics Publishers, Inc.
Box 5076, Champaign, IL 61820

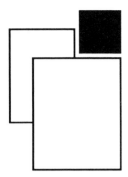

Contents

Chapter
1

Overview of Measurement and Evaluation   3

**Chapter
2**

Organizing and Analyzing Measurements for Evaluation   13

**Chapter
3**

Criteria for the Selection and Construction of Tests   53

**Chapter
4**

Writing Goals and Measurable Objectives   73

Part II Measurement in the Motor Domain   81

**Chapter
5**

Selection and Construction of Motor Performance Tests   83

■ **Chapter
6**

Components of Motor Performance   101

■ **Chapter
7**

Motor and Physical Fitness Testing   143

**Chapter
8**

Sport Skills Testing   205

Part III   Measurement in the Cognitive and Affective Domains   281

**Chapter
9**

Construction of Written Knowledge Tests   283

Chapter 10

Measurement in the Affective Domain   317

Part IV Application of Measurements in Evaluation   353

Chapter 11

Administration of the Evaluation Program   355

Chapter
12

Grading   373

Chapter
13

Evaluation of Special Populations   389

**Chapter
14**

Evaluation Programs in Preschools and Elementary Schools   443

**Chapter
15**

Example Evaluation Programs
for Secondary Physical Education and Competitive Athletics   493

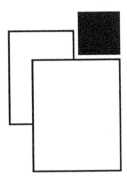

Acknowledgments

The authors are especially indebted to several individuals for their assistance in making this book possible. We thank the following individuals for allowing us to use photographs of them: Pam Baker, Diane Beauchamp, George Bell, Eric Brooks, Suzanna Folk, Jay Gruber, Lissa and Randy Kirkendall, Judy Logan, Paul McGurl, and Melody Noland. Special thanks go to Craig McVey, Steve Miller, Russell Reiderer, and Donald Shondell for allowing their testing materials to be included in the text. Similarly, Randy Kirkendall is thanked for writing the appendix on computers. Thanks also go to Lorane Goin, who greatly assisted in typing the manuscript. Finally, we are most grateful to our wives, Judy, Lorene, and Juanita, who provided the encouragement and understanding necessary for completing the manuscript.

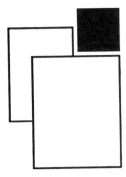

Preface

The evaluation of participants in physical activity requires exercise leaders and teachers to make many decisions. In order to make fair and accurate decisions that will help participants, the physical educator must acquire a thorough knowledge and understanding of measurement and evaluation. The material presented in this text is intended to provide prospective physical educators and exercise scientists with the knowledge and understanding necessary to make intelligent decisions about their programs and program participants.

This text is divided into four parts designed to present a comprehensive overview of measurement and evaluation for physical educators. Part I provides a general background for evaluation and then describes the technical tools that are necessary to conduct an evaluation program.

Part II is devoted to the measurement of motor performance. Procedures for selecting and/or constructing motor performance tests are described, followed by chapters devoted to tests of the components of motor performance, motor and physical fitness, and sports skills.

The techniques necessary for constructing, using, and evaluating tests in the cognitive and affective domains are presented in Part III. Following this discussion, various available tests and instruments are presented and described.

Part IV is devoted to applying the information presented in the first three parts to various physical education settings. Chapter 11 is concerned with the administration of evaluation programs. Some solutions to the ever present problem of marking and grading in school physical education programs are presented in chapter 12. Five chapters present examples of evaluation programs in a variety of physical education settings. Studying these examples should prepare the reader to apply his or her own measurement and evaluation program when given that opportunity.

Several chapters in this book contain material that is rarely, if ever, found in measurement and evaluation texts. The most notable of these unique materials are the examples of measurement and evaluation programs presented in five chapters of Part IV. Chapter 14 presents information that will greatly assist the evaluation activities of elementary physical education teachers. Issues in measurement and evaluation for physical educators who must deal with special-needs students are discussed in chapter

13. Some guidelines for evaluation in adapted physical education programs are also presented in chapter 13.

Chapter 15 presents an example evaluation program for ninth grade physical education as well as four examples of how evaluation can be applied to competitive athletic programs. Finally, chapter 16 provides examples of the application of measurement and evaluation programs in nonschool settings.

This text has been designed with several other unique features to assist the reader's study of measurement and evaluation for physical educators. Perhaps most notably, the text is written for physical educators as defined in the broadest possible sense. Throughout the text, issues are discussed and examples are given to address the needs of physical education teachers, exercise scientists, and exercise leaders in many diverse settings.

An introduction to computer utilization in measurement and evaluation is presented in Appendix D. Instead of formal summaries, chapter review questions are presented at the end of each chapter. These questions identify the important concepts to be acquired and will assist the reader in reviewing each chapter.

Exercises are also presented at the end of most chapters. Answers to the odd-numbered exercises are provided to help the reader keep on the right track. Bibliographic references are also provided at the end of each chapter for readers who desire more in-depth information on particular topics.

Throughout this text, the emphasis is on *practical application* of measurement and evaluation in physical education. To be of any value, the knowledge available about measurement and evaluation must be *applied*. The authors hope that students and physical education professionals will find this text informative, challenging, and interesting. With serious participation in the learning process, the knowledge about measurement and evaluation that readers gain from this text will make them better physical educators.

Don R. Kirkendall
Joseph J. Gruber
Robert E. Johnson

Part I

General Considerations in Measurement and Evaluation

One of the most perplexing problems facing physical educators today is how to evaluate motor performance accurately and fairly. In this age of fiscal accountability physical educators are also compelled to justify the existence and/or expansion of their programs whether they are physical education classes in the schools or corporate fitness programs. The intent of this book is to provide students and physical educators with the tools necessary for evaluating participants' performance in physical activity programs and to justify the existence of those programs. Part I of the text has been designed to help the reader to understand what is involved in these measurement and evaluation processes.

An introductory overview of measurement and evaluation is presented in chapter 1, which attempts to demonstrate the important role of evaluation in the operation of physical activity programs. Chapter 2 is devoted to the statistical tools necessary for measuring and evaluating both individual performance and program effectiveness. Procedures are presented for analyzing test scores obtained in physical activity programs. Chapter 3 contains a discussion of the criteria that should be used in the selection and construction of tests. The technical as well as practical aspects of test selection are presented. The last chapter of this section contains necessary information about developing and writing appropriate goals and behavioral objectives for physical activity programs.

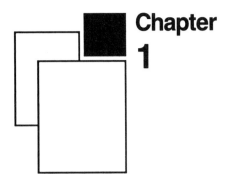

Chapter

1

Overview of Measurement and Evaluation

When many teachers and educators hear the term *evaluation*, they think only about administering tests and assigning grades to students. Although these are major aspects of evaluation, evaluation covers a much broader range of activities than testing and grading. As will be shown in this text, evaluation serves many purposes in physical activity programs.

Tests, Measurement, and Evaluation

Before continuing, we need to define some terminology. Three terms—*tests*, *measurement*, and *evaluation*—are often incorrectly used interchangeably. These terms are related, but each has a definite and distinct meaning.

- **Test.** *A test is an instrument used to gain information about individuals or objects.* These instruments may be in the form of questions asked on paper or in interviews, observations of requested physical performance, or observations of behavior through

checklists or anecdotal records. Whatever form a test takes, however, all tests should have certain characteristics. The important features of tests will be presented in chapter 3. Much of this text is devoted to discussing tests that are useful to the physical educator.

- **Measurement.** *Measurement is the process of collecting information.* We usually think of measurement as the objective determination of a numerical score based on performance. It is through measurement that the present achievement level or status of participants is determined. Administering a test is part of the measurement process. The results of measurement need to be quantifiable in terms of time, distance, amount, or number of tasks performed correctly. Unfortunately, most "measurements" in physical education are not very pure or absolute. For example, instead of saying that the time recorded for the 50-yard dash measures a runner's speed, it might be more accurate to state that administering the 50-yard dash is a measurement procedure that yields a test score indicative of a person's speed. Of course, the measurement of time in a dash may be considered a more true measurement than many other sources of information commonly used in physical education, such as subjective ratings. Our ultimate goal is to make measurements as true or pure as possible; however, the less "pure" measurements must be recognized for their worth as well as their limitations.

- **Evaluation.** *Evaluation is the process of determining the value or worth of collected data.* Evaluation includes both testing and measurement. It might be thought of as the process of qualitatively appraising the quantitative data collected through measurement. Collected data are usually appraised so that a fair and informed decision can be made. For example, Is our program accomplishing its stated objectives? Has the student or participant made satisfactory progress? These decisions may be about individuals, an entire class, program objectives, teaching methods, or a combination of these.

The interrelationship among the terms *tests*, *measurement*, and *evaluation* can now be seen. Evaluation is all encompassing; it necessarily reflects the evaluator's own philosophies, goals, and objectives. These in turn determine the tests and measurements to be used. Measurement provides the means by which information pertinent to our philosophies, goals, and objectives is collected, and tests are the instruments used to gain the information. Finally, evaluation involves the appraisal of this information against identified standards. This appraisal tells us how well we have satisfied our philosophies, goals, and objectives.

Objectives and Evaluation

Evaluation must always be conducted in terms of the general goals of the discipline. Goals and objectives determine what is to be measured and evaluated. Even more importantly, these goals and objectives provide the very *reasons* for measuring and evaluating. When determining instructional objectives, we should start with rather general goals and then advance to very specific behavioral and/or performance objectives.

Perhaps the most commonly stated general goals of physical education are the following ones expressed by Nash (1948):

- **Organic development.** This general goal refers to physical fitness and the basic components of fitness, namely muscular strength, power and endurance, and cardiovascular endurance.
- **Neuromuscular development.** This general goal refers to sports skill, balance, flexibility, agility, coordination, and speed.
- **Interpretive development.** In physical education this general goal refers to knowledge and understanding of game rules, strategies, courtesies, and equipment.
- **Emotional development.** This general goal includes psychological factors such as leadership, feelings, values, personality, attitudes, and sportsmanship.

Numerous other sets of general goals have been stated for physical education. Most of these are quite similar to the general goals stated by Nash. With the relatively recent trend toward "movement exploration" in school physical education, additional goals such as the development of creativity and/or individual awareness might also be included. In any case, the final selection of general goals and the relative emphasis given to them depends on the physical educator's philosophy, the institutional philosophy, and—above all—the needs of the people for whom a program is planned. These general goals provide the guidelines for assessing the initial level or status of participants. Initial behavioral and performance objectives need to

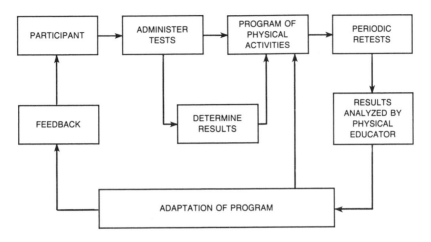

Figure 1.1 Evaluation in program planning.

be determined. Then decisions must be made about what to test, what tests to employ, and how to use the information derived from the tests. Once obtained, this information helps the physical educator to establish priorities and behavioral objectives for each participant or group. When the specific objectives have been set, the next step is to select activities for the program that will achieve those objectives. Periodic retesting of participants on the same tests will yield information about the performance level of the participants after participation in the program over a period of time. Comparing the results of each participant's tests taken before and after participation in the program enables the physical educator to determine whether each participant's performance level has improved, remained unchanged, or regressed. This process assists the evaluator in determining whether the program and its objectives should or should not be changed. Repeating this process provides the basis for continuous, ongoing modification of the program and its objectives.

This planning process is participant centered and requires a dynamic operation of tests, measurements, and evaluations from which a physical education program can be designed and continuously modified. Figure 1.1 shows a sim-

plistic model for this planning process and illustrates the interaction between the physical educator and the participant. The planning process focuses on the participant as he or she moves through the tests, programs, and retest cycles while the physical educator guides the participant through the process. The physical educator must also determine what to test and what tests to employ. The tests are then administered and the results obtained. Evaluation of the test results helps the physical educator to set objectives and design a program of physical activities that will enhance participant performance. The program is then applied. After a period of time determined by the physical educator, tests are reapplied, and the new results are compared to the results of the first test. The physical educator decides if the participant's performance level has improved, remained the same, or regressed and then gives feedback to the participant. If necessary, the physical educator may modify the objectives and redesign the physical activity program. The new program is then applied, and the cycle continues. Informally, this cycle may occur one or more times a day rather than only once in a unit, semester, or year. On a larger and more formal scale, this process should occur at the end of each unit, semester, and/or year.

Most good teachers and exercise leaders have undoubtedly used this approach without formalizing it conceptually. This discussion simply conceptualizes the process in writing so that its value can be more easily understood. Because this approach is completely participant centered, it allows for individual differences. It also provides a sensible means and rationale for changing a program to meet identified needs instead of allowing the program to stagnate. This evaluation process model is used throughout this text. More importantly, the knowledge and procedures necessary to *implement* this process are presented.

Purposes of Measurement and Evaluation

As indicated earlier, general goals determine the purposes of any measurement and evaluation program. Of course, the overriding goal or purpose of all evaluation activities must be to improve the program that is being evaluated. Within this global purpose, more specific purposes of measurement and evaluation are generally accepted. Not all of these will be appropriate for all situations at all times.

Status Determination

The most common purpose of measurement and evaluation is to determine the status, progress, or achievement of participants. This determination may be used to assign grades, exempt participants from an instructional unit, promote participants from one grade or level of instruction to another, provide feedback to improve performance, place individuals into special groups, or determine specific exercise prescriptions. In essence, status determination encompasses all of the other purposes of measurement and evaluation.

Classification Into Groups

Sometimes evaluators need to arrange participants into homogeneous or heterogeneous groups on the basis of some trait or ability. Thus one purpose of measurement and evaluation may be to *classify* participants. Some common types of classification are those made on the basis of a student's grade level or age, sex, medical condition, body size (height and weight), functional ability (skill), fitness level, or interest. In general, the goal of classification is to improve the instructional setting.

Selection of Few From Many

Measurement and evaluation are certainly useful for selecting a few participants from many based on identified criteria. This may consist of selecting varsity team members, class leaders, or participants with special physical, social, or emotional needs.

Motivation

If properly administered, evaluation can be a positive motivational process. Similarly, the unwise use of tests and evaluation can impair motivation. Evaluators can use test results to counsel participants about their present performance levels and to motivate them to improve performance through program participation. Properly conducted, evaluation and counseling can help participants to become self-motivated to participate in the physical education instructional program and other physical activities outside the program.

Maintenance of Standards

A quality evaluation program assists us in maintaining standards of performance expected of our clientele. Evaluation enables us to determine if a program is providing participants with instruction that helps and motivates them to achieve at desired performance levels. Stated another way, measurement and evaluation enable us to determine if we are meeting our objectives. If we are not, then the instructional program needs to be revised. What is taught and how it is taught must be evaluated and scrutinized as part of an ongoing process. The evaluation process can be effective only if it is planned as an integral part of the physical education program.

Furnishing Educational Experiences

Both the participant and exercise leader should learn from the evaluation process. The participant should learn about himself or herself as well as about the activity being evaluated. The teacher or exercise leader should learn something about each participant and also learn valuable information about his or her teaching methods, the activity program, and their effect upon the participants.

Conducting Research

Research can be thought of as the means by which a body of knowledge is expanded. Research is dependent upon precise and accurate information or data gathered through carefully planned measurement procedures. Information and data gathered for research purposes must be evaluated for their significance. Thus one important purpose of measurement and evaluation is to provide the necessary tools for conducting research.

Principles of Measurement and Evaluation

A principle should be thought of as a guiding rule for action. To establish and implement a successful evaluation program, we must be cog-

nizant of certain principles. Although several principles have been alluded to already, a more detailed presentation and discussion of these and additional principles follow.

A measurement and evaluation program must be compatible with the evaluator's philosophy of life and education. It is inconceivable that one would conduct a program that is at variance with his or her basic beliefs. Related to this is the principle that *measurement and evaluation must recognize an institutional philosophy.* For example, if a school policy dictates that grades must be given for all courses, then teachers must provide for grading in their programs. If this or some other policy of the school conflicts with a teacher's own philosophy, then the teacher must either change, find a way to resolve the conflict, or find another place to teach. A similar situation could occur in a health club. As a program or exercise leader, your actions, including your evaluation procedures, must be in accord with the institution's policies and practices.

In order to evaluate effectively, all measurement must be conducted in terms of program objectives. We need to identify our objectives before tests are administered in order to evaluate the results of the tests against those objectives. In all aspects of evaluation, we must constantly keep our objectives in mind. Otherwise our testing and evaluation program will have no direction or purpose.

Testing is part of measurement, and measurement is only one phase of evaluation. Evaluation includes both testing and measurement. However, evaluation is much broader than only testing and measurement; it lies at the very core of decision-making. Data collected through measurement procedures must be appraised for their value in order for intelligent decisions to be made. Tests that collect data without a planned purpose are a waste of program time and resources.

Measurement and evaluation must be conducted and supervised by trained specialists.

One of the reasons that you are enrolled in a measurement and evaluation course is to become an individual trained in measurement and evaluation. Not everyone can effectively administer an evaluation program, and evaluation is too serious and important to leave to untrained personnel. After all, evaluators make decisions about a most important aspect of life—a person's physical fitness and well-being. To administer a physical activity evaluation program effectively, a teacher must be knowledgeable and proficient both in what is to be offered in the activity program and in how to evaluate what is offered.

The results of measurement and evaluation must be interpreted in terms of the individual's whole life, including its social, emotional, physical, and psychological dimensions. If someone performs poorly on a test, the conscientious professional looks beyond the low score and tries to determine the reasons for the poor performance. The professional who cares first attempts to identify the reasons for the poor performance and then provides assistance when necessary and possible. Poor performance on a physical test may result from something other than physical causes. If the cause is physical, the competent physical educator who finds out exactly where the difficulty lies can then direct attention toward improving the performance.

Measurement and evaluation are important educational tools and play a major role in the total educational process. Evaluation is not an educational fad. It is an integral part of the educational process and must be used as a tool to facilitate the accomplishment of educational goals. It should be recognized, however, that a quality physical education program does not consist of measurement alone; other components of a total physical education program are equally important. Extreme cases of physical education programs that are primarily testing programs are just as unsound as programs that include no measurement at all. In general, approximately 10% of instructional time should be spent on measurement.

Measurement and evaluation rest on the premise that whatever exists exists in amount and hence can be measured. In other words, anything that we include in our physical education program should lend itself to sound definition and thus be measurable. Of course, some areas in physical education are not as well defined and measurable as we might like. The area of social and personal development, which includes factors such as sportsmanship, socialization, and emotional development, for example, is not precisely defined. As a result, our measurements in this area are not very precise, and caution is required in using them. This does not mean, however, that this important area should be ignored, but rather that the limitations of the measurements must be recognized. In other words, we must never lose sight of the fact that *no test or measurement is perfect.* Occasionally people acquire such confidence and "faith" in their tests and measurements that they begin to believe they are infallible. We must always use the best tests possible, but we must always realize that errors are likely. Sound judgment and caution must always prevail in using tests and analyzing test results.

There is no substitute for judgment in measurement and evaluation. This is perhaps the most important principle of measurement. In fact, evaluation *is* judgment. Sometimes people attempt to substitute judgment with objective measures. Although we should diligently strive for objectivity, objective measures can never supersede professional judgment. If there were no place for judgment in measurement and evaluation, then all teachers and exercise leaders could be replaced by technicians or machines. On the other hand, judgments made without substantiating data are also unacceptable. Measurement provides the data that allow the best possible judgments or decisions to be made.

Participants' initial abilities must be measured in order to obtain knowledge about their achievement in the physical education program. We cannot identify or provide the type of program participants need if we do not know their present ability levels. Furthermore, we cannot determine what participants have learned or achieved in a program if we do not know where they started. Measuring participants' abilities only at the end of a class, unit, or semester tells only where they are at that point; it indicates nothing about the *effects* of the program upon these participants. In other words, if we do not measure individuals' performance both before and after program participation, the impact of our program will remain unknown.

People sometimes argue that the use of tests creates a stagnant uniformity in programs and mechanizes teachers and teaching. Hopefully, it is obvious to the reader that *the use of tests need not produce deadly uniformity in teachers or teaching.* If the teacher or exercise leader fails to recognize that professional judgment plays a vital role in measurement and evaluation, then perhaps stagnant uniformity could occur. However, measurement and evaluation conducted by serious, well-prepared professionals should have just the opposite result. Through testing, measurement, and evaluation, the possibility of individualizing a program to meet each participant's needs will be greatly enhanced. The evaluation model presented earlier (see Figure 1.1) clearly emphasizes continual program change and the importance of meeting individual participants' needs.

The most valid, reliable, and objective tests possible must be utilized in all measurement activities. The terms *validity*, *reliability*, and *objectivity* will be explained further in chapter 3, but the essence of this principle is that we must always use tests that tell us what we need to know. Tests should consistently measure what they claim to measure and should be scored the same way regardless of who performs the scor-

ing. As stated earlier, no test is perfect, and no test results will be perfectly valid, reliable, and objective. Nevertheless, we must use the best tests available and continually strive to improve our measurement tools.

Types of Evaluation

Program objectives dictate the type of evaluation that should be conducted. The three classifications of evaluation strategies generally discussed in measurement and evaluation literature are introduced here and are further developed throughout the text.

Summative Versus Formative Evaluation

Grading is one aspect of evaluation that most teachers usually conduct, but unfortunately it is often conducted poorly. This is an important task required in most school situations and must be conducted seriously and fairly. Grading at the end of a unit, course, semester, or year is an example of one type of evaluation called *summative evaluation*, that is, the evaluation is based on information that is cumulative or additive over a period of time. Recognition of achievement by issuing certificates or badges in a fitness program is another example of summative evaluation.

A more important type of evaluation in the teaching-learning process is *formative evaluation*. Formative evaluation provides information about the progress of a participant each day throughout a learning unit. Daily, on-the-spot information about participant performance is obtained, evaluated, and immediately fed back to the participant so that performance can be continuously adjusted and improved. Practice with such feedback should enhance skill acquisition. Formative evaluation involves breaking a learning unit down into smaller parts to enable both the physical educator and the participant to identify the precise parts of a task or performance that are in error and need correcting. For example, a teacher or coach who films or videotapes a performance and immediately analyzes the replay with the performer is using formative evaluation.

Product Versus Process Evaluation

Based on our particular program objectives, we may be interested in evaluating the *product* resulting from physical performance, the *process* by which the product was obtained, or both. For example, in product evaluation determining the final placements in a 10-kilometer race would only require recording the amount of time a runner takes to complete the race. If we are interested in improving the running style of runners, however, then we need to analyze the process of running, including aspects such as the runner's foot plant, arm swing, length of stride, body lean, and so forth. This would be *process* evaluation. For most activities, we are interested in both process and product evaluation. Some activities, such as gymnastics, lend themselves more to process evaluation than product evaluation. Whether we choose to evaluate the product or process of performance or both dictates the kind of test we select or construct. Later in this text, chapter 3 presents procedures for making such decisions.

Criterion-Referenced Versus Norm-Referenced Evaluation

In the evaluation process it is sometimes desirable to establish formal performance standards and then evaluate individual participants' performances against those standards. For example, a physical educator might establish a grading scale for a knowledge test in which 70% of the questions must be answered correctly to pass the test. This is *criterion-referenced evaluation*.

In other situations there may be a need to compare individual participants' performances with the performance of some relevant groups. For example, a coach who selects a varsity team from a large number of students trying out for the team must determine how each participant performs in relation to the other participants. This is *norm-referenced evaluation*.

It should already be clear that each of these evaluation methods is necessary and valuable in certain situations. The type of evaluation chosen influences decisions such as the type of tests selected or constructed and is a primary consideration throughout this text.

Review Questions

1. What is a test?
2. What is measurement?
3. What is evaluation?
4. How do testing, measurement, and evaluation differ?
5. What is the main function of tests and measurements in evaluation?
6. Do testing and measuring ensure that the physical educator's decision will be accurate and fair?
7. Why should the physical educator continually assess the strengths and weaknesses of the participants under his or her direction?
8. What should be learned from an effective measurement and evaluation program?
9. Why must we consider our own philosophy of life and education, our general goals, and the institutional goals before determining what factors to test?
10. Why must measurement and evaluation be conducted and supervised by persons with specialized training?

11. Some physical educators acquire such faith in their tests and measurements that they begin to believe they are infallible. Of what have these physical educators lost sight?
12. What is the most important principle presented in this chapter?

Bibliography

Barrow, H.M., & McGee, R. (1979). *A practical approach to measurement in physical education* (3rd ed.). Philadelphia: Lea & Febiger.

Baumgartner, T.A., & Jackson, A.S. (1982). *Measurement for evaluation in physical education* (2nd ed.). Dubuque, IA: Wm. C. Brown.

Bloom, B.S. (1970). Toward a theory of testing which includes measurement-evaluation-assessment. In M.C. Wittrock & D.E. Wiley (Eds.), *The evaluation of instruction: Issues and problems* (pp. 25-50). New York: Holt, Rinehart and Winston.

Bloom, B.S., Englehart, M.D., Furst, E.J., Hill, W.H., & Krathwohl, D.R. (Eds.). (1956). *A taxonomy of educational objectives: Handbook 1, the cognitive domain*. New York: McKay.

Bloom, B.S., Hastings, J.T., & Madaus, G.F. (1971). *Handbook on formative and summative evaluation of student learning*. New York: McGraw-Hill.

Clarke, H.H. (1976). *Application of measurement to health and physical education* (5th ed.). Englewood Cliffs, NJ: Prentice-Hall.

Ebel, R.L. (1973). *Measuring educational achievement*. Englewood Cliffs, NJ: Prentice-Hall.

Ebel, R.L. (1966). The social consequences of educational testing. In C.I. Chase & H.G.

Ludlow (Eds.), *Readings in educational and psychological measurement* (pp. 26-31). Boston: Houghton Mifflin.

Harrow, A.J. (1972). *A taxonomy of the psychomotor domain*. New York: McKay.

Jewett, A.E., Jones, S., Luneke, S.M., & Robinson, S.M. (1971). Educational change through a taxonomy for writing physical education objectives. *Quest,* **15**, 32-38.

Johnson, B.L., & Nelson, J.K. (1979). *Practical measurements for evaluation in physical education* (3rd ed.). Minneapolis: Burgess.

Kibler, R.J., Baker, L.L., & Miles, D.T. (1970). *Behavioral objectives and instruction*. Boston: Allyn & Bacon.

Krathwohl, D.R., Bloom, B.S., & Masia, B. (1964). *A taxonomy of educational objectives: Handbook II, The affective domain*. New York: McKay.

McCloy, C.H., & Young, N.D. (1954). *Tests and measurements in health and physical education*. New York: Appleton-Century-Crofts.

Mager, R.F. (1962). *Preparing instructional objectives*. Palo Alto, CA: Fearon.

Mathews, D.K. (1978). *Measurement in physical education* (5th ed.). Philadelphia: W.B. Saunders.

Nash, J.B. (1948). *Physical education: Interpretations and objectives*. New York: A.S. Barnes.

Safrit, M.J. (1977). Criterion-referenced measurement: Applications in physical education. *Motor Skills: Theory into Practice,* **2**(1), 21-35.

Safrit, M.J. (1981). *Evaluation in physical education* (2nd ed.). Englewood Cliffs, NJ: Prentice-Hall.

Simon, G.B. (1969). Comments on implications of criterion-referenced measurement. *Journal of Educational Measurement,* **6**, 259-260.

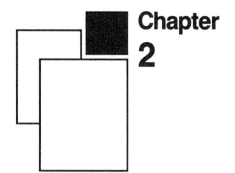

Chapter 2

Organizing and Analyzing Measurements for Evaluation

It is neither possible nor desirable to make a complete presentation of statistical techniques in this text. In order to administer a measurement and evaluation program successfully, however, some basic aspects of statistical analysis must be understood.

Studying Statistics

By itself, a score has little meaning. For example, if a student correctly answers 70 out of 95 questions on a written test, how good or poor is this performance? To answer this question, we need to answer some preliminary questions. Is the score above or below the average for the class? Is it above or below average for all classes? Is it above or below average for the district or state? We might also want to know how this score of 70 compares to a standing long jump of 75 inches or 191 centimeters. Or perhaps we wish to compare the performance of one class with the performance of another class. A knowledge of statistics helps us to answer these questions and make such comparisons.

Thus one reason for studying statistics is to facilitate the interpretation of test scores. The interpretation of test scores helps the physical educator to make informed decisions that are an integral part of planning a physical activity program.

Closely related to the interpretation of test scores is the problem of arriving at a total performance score or assigning grades in physical education. Physical educators often combine scores from various activities into one composite score. How does one determine a total performance score for a participant who puts the shot 36 feet or 11 meters, runs the 440-yard dash in 66 seconds, and scores 70% on a written test? Through the application of statistics, we can solve this problem and at the same time provide an objective basis for assigning an overall grade to this composite performance. Thus statistics can facilitate the decision-making process in assigning grades.

Physical educators must be fully able to interpret performance scores, but it is equally important for participants to know the meaning of performance scores. Physical educators often must present scores to participants and, in some situations, to their parents so that they understand them. Part of the study in this chapter involves the presentation of scores or data.

Properly constructing and/or selecting tests to be used in a measurement and evaluation program requires some knowledge of statistical techniques. We must apply statistical techniques in order to determine the validity, reliability, and objectivity of a test. Thus knowledge of statistics is necessary to select and/or construct tests properly.

If you wish to conduct research or to read professional research literature, you must have some knowledge of statistics. Although this text will not fully prepare you to do either of these, hopefully it will provide a foundation of statistical knowledge upon which you can build.

Statistics Defined

The term *statistics* has struck unnecessary fear into the hearts and minds of many students. A myth has been spread that to study statistics you must be a mathematical wizard. Although statistics is a branch of mathematics, the level at which we discuss statistics in this text requires only the ability to perform the basic mathematical manipulations of addition, subtraction, multiplication, and division.

The major goal in statistics is to describe a group or the characteristics of a group concisely and precisely. By describing a group, we can not only better understand it, but we can also better understand the individuals that comprise the group. Sometimes we have information on every individual in a group. When that is the case, the methods used to describe the group are called *descriptive* statistics. The area of descriptive statistics involves the description of a group (set) of individuals or items by means of graphic, tabular, or numerical devices. This description may take one of the following forms:

- Determining the *frequency* with which various values occur. Example 1: There are 15 girls and 29 boys in the afternoon health education class. Example 2: There are 4 boys in the ninth grade who are over 72 inches tall, 12 between 68 and 72 inches tall, 10 between 64 and 68 inches tall, and 3 who are less than 64 inches tall. Generally, a graphic representation such as a table and/or figure enhances comprehension of this type of description.

- Determining a *typical* or *usual value*. Example: The typical or most frequently occurring family size in the United States is 4 members.

- Determining the *amount of variability* in a set of scores or observations. Example: The number of chin-ups performed by a group of students ranged from 0 to 16.

- Determining the *degree of relationship* between two or more observations from a group of individuals or objects. Example: The grades students received in kinesiology may be related to the grades they will receive in anatomy.

This text will be primarily concerned with descriptive statistics, but it is important to realize that often it is desirable to make statements about an entire group when information is available about only part of the group. This process requires the use of *inferential* statistics. For example, suppose we live in a town called Wonder City that has 20,000 residents, of whom 3,000 are between 16 and 21 years of age. We wish to determine the physical condition of the persons in this age group by finding the average value of maximum oxygen uptake ($\dot{V}O_2max$). Measuring $\dot{V}O_2max$ on all 3,000 youths would be an overwhelming if not impossible task. Instead, we could carefully select a representative subgroup of the 3,000 youths, say 100 of them, measure their $\dot{V}O_2max$, find the average value, and then *infer* that this average value represents a good estimate of the average for the total group.

The group we want information about is called the *population* or *universe*. In our example, the population is the 3,000 youths in Wonder City between 16 and 21 years of age. A *population* or *universe* is defined as a set of individuals (or objects) with one or more common characteristics that are considered for a particular purpose. The population is always defined by the experimenter or inquirer either directly by choice or indirectly by what is done; direct choice is preferred. We may want our population to be quite large or relatively small. There is no such thing as a population for all situations; each particular situation that arises presents its own population.

The present example defines the population as the 3,000 youths in Wonder City between 16 and 21 years of age. Thus we have decided that the individuals in the population should have two characteristics in common: residence in Wonder City and age between 16 and 21 years. We could have defined our population to be much larger, such as all youths in the state, or much smaller, such as only those youths in Wonder City who attend a particular school.

Once a population has been defined, the purpose is to determine specific characteristics about that population. The term given to a measure of a characteristic of a population or universe is *parameter*. In other words, parameters are constant values that are used to describe populations. In the Wonder City example, we have already discussed two characteristics (age and residence). We did not, however, provide a measure of these characteristics. If we knew or determined the *average* age of our population or determined the *exact number* of those youths in Wonder City, these would constitute parameters. The main parameter of interest in this example is the average value of maximum oxygen uptake ($\dot{V}O_2$max) for the 3,000 youths.

It is advisable to determine population

Figure 2.1 Relationships among population, sample, parameters, and statistics.

parameters whenever feasible. This is exactly what is done in the area of descriptive statistics. Often, however, determining population parameters is not feasible due to time or financial constraints. In these cases, we must select a subset of our population, measure the desired characteristic of this subset, and infer this characteristic back to the population. A subset of a population is called a *sample*, and a measure of a characteristic of a sample is called a *statistic*. Thus a statistic is to a sample as a parameter is to a population.

In the present example, suppose we select 100 youths from our population and determine their average oxygen uptake. Our *sample* is the 100 youths, and the average value (of oxygen uptake) determined is a *statistic*. We might also have found other statistics, such as the range of scores of $\dot{V}O_2$max, for the sample. We use statistics of the sample as estimates of the parameters of the population. This procedure is summarized in Figure 2.1. We define a population, select a sample from that population, determine statistics of interest for that sample, and use these statistics as estimates of parameters for the population. Whenever we make inferences or conclusions on the basis of incomplete (sampled) information, we take a risk that we may be wrong. This is why the reliability of conclusions derived from inferential statistics must be evaluated objectively in terms of probability statements. Using inferential statistics allows us to make conclusions but also lets us know the risk (probability of error) involved in making them. For this reason, the theory of probability plays a fundamental role in the understanding and application of inferential statistics.

In other applications of inferential statistics we may want to compare the parameters of two or more populations on the basis of statistics collected on two or more samples. The procedures involved in these applications include (a) establishing a hypothesis, (b) collecting data from a subgroup (sample) of the group (population) to be studied, and (c) rejecting or accepting the hypothesis based on the results obtained from the subgroup and an awareness of the probability (stated as a percentage) that this hypothesis might be wrong. For example, suppose we wish to know if the "part" method of teaching soccer (i.e., instruction consisting only of fundamentals) is as effective as the "whole" method of teaching soccer (i.e., instruction consisting of playing the game). First we would establish a hypothesis, usually in a form expressing no difference between the methods.

> *Hypothesis:* There is no difference between the soccer skill achieved by students taught by the "part" method and soccer skill achieved by students taught by the "whole" method.

Because we cannot possibly use all soccer students to test this hypothesis, we might form two subgroups of our students within each class we teach and use a different teaching method with each subgroup. At the conclusion of the soccer unit, we would administer a skills test and compare the average scores of the two subgroups. Obviously, we would not expect the two subgroups' averages to be exactly the same. Through the application of inferential statistics, however, we could determine whether or not the difference between the average scores of the two subgroups is larger than could be reasonably expected by chance and, based on this find-

ing, draw the appropriate conclusions about the hypothesis and the population.

The study of inferential statistics is generally beyond the scope of this text. However, the student of measurement and evaluation must have some knowledge of the procedures involved in inferential statistics because they are frequently used in the development of the many measurement devices described throughout this text.

Scales of Measurement

Measurements obtained in physical education differ in the amount of information they provide. Some measurements may indicate whether an individual belongs to a particular group, whereas other measurements indicate the level of achievement or a quantity for a performance. The type of measurement used partly determines the type of group descriptors or parameters (or statistics) that should be calculated.

Typically, four levels, or scales, of measurement are identified: nominal, ordinal, interval, and ratio scales. The *nominal scale* is used only to identify an object or person. An example of this kind of scale would be gender; a person belongs to either the male or the female gender. One could indicate, for example, that males are assigned the numeral 1 and that females are assigned the numeral 2. These numbers or "scores" indicate identity only and do not denote order or amount; they indicate only whether various frequencies of observations are equal ($=$) or not equal ($\neq$) to one another. As a result, the only parameter or statistic that is appropriate with nominal scale scores is frequency of occurrence.

An *ordinal* scale enables us to indicate the rank or order of various scores. For example, you might record the results of the various events in a track meet by stating the contestants' order of finish. You would say that in the 100-yard dash Joe finished first, Jack second, Don third, and Bill fourth. You would assign the numerals 1, 2, 3, and 4 respectively to the four participants. In this example, the scores not only identify the contestants but also rank-order each individual's place in finishing the race. Ordinal scales enable us not only to determine if our observations of members of the population are equal ($=$) or not equal ($\neq$) but also if any observation is less than ($<$) or greater than ($>$) any other observation. Ordinal scores do not, however, permit us to determine the *amount* of difference between 1 and 2, 2 and 3, and 3 and 4; they indicate *position* only. Thus from a technical point of view, averaging these types of scores would not be appropriate because it cannot be assumed that the differences between each rank are all the same.

Interval and *ratio* scales are the highest levels of measurement. Unlike nominal and ordinal scales, these scales are *quantitative* and thus indicate *amount*. They also permit the use of the arithmetic operations of addition, subtraction, multiplication, and division. These scales have all the properties inherent in the ordinal scale, but they have a very important additional property: They measure the amount associated with an observation. An important characteristic of both interval and ratio scales is that the differences between adjoining points on any part of the scale are equal. For example, ranges of motions (measured in degrees) are measures of flexibility that are taken with a goniometer. If Student A can elbow flex 145°, Student B 150°, and Student C 155°, then we know that the difference in flexibility between Students A and B is the same as the difference between Students B and C, namely 5°. By the same token, if Student D has a range of motion in elbow flexion of 156°, then he is only 1° better than Student C. Many of the measurements used in physical education involve interval or ratio scales.

The only difference between an interval and a ratio scale is that the interval scale utilizes an arbitrary zero point, whereas the ratio scale employs an absolute zero point. In the ratio scale, zero indicates the absence of the phenomenon being measured, whereas in the interval scale it does not. In the flexibility example, degrees constitute a ratio scale, with 0° indicating no flexibility and 360° indicating maximum flexibility. We can talk about ratios of numbers in the ratio scale, but we cannot do so with the interval scale. An example that illustrates this point quite well is measuring the height of individuals. Usually we measure one's height from the floor. Therefore, if you are 70 inches tall and your younger brother is 35 inches tall, you are not only 35 inches taller than your brother, you are also twice as tall as he is. This is an example of a ratio scale with zero indicating the absence of height. If we had made our measurements from the top of a desk that is 30 inches high, then you would be given a score of 40 inches and your brother a score of 5 inches. We could still say that you are 35 inches taller (an interval concept) than your brother, but it would be erroneous to say that based on this measurement you are eight times taller (a ratio concept) than your brother. This latter measurement is an example of an interval scale where zero is only an arbitrary point of reference.

The scales of measurement, in descending order according to how much information is given by them, are ratio, interval, ordinal, and nominal. In other words, the ratio and interval scales give us more information than the ordinal or nominal scales.

Organization of Scores

When we simply record a group of scores, it is difficult to know very much about the group's performance or how good or poor an individual performance is. Table 2.1, for example, presents push-up scores for 110 freshmen. These

Table 2.1 Push-Up Scores for 110 Freshmen

30	31	30	32	36	33	31	26	32	31
34	25	34	37	32	29	28	30	29	30
22	20	26	30	30	29	31	32	34	25
36	29	26	34	26	31	26	36	30	29
28	33	27	29	33	37	32	27	28	30
33	38	32	27	27	28	30	33	31	28
22	29	31	35	29	32	30	29	27	36
30	34	28	33	25	27	31	28	26	30
35	32	35	32	30	34	29	31	23	33
31	28	29	34	28	30	25	33	30	29
38	24	24	37	27	35	40	35	23	25

scores would be more meaningful if they were organized into some form that would reveal the relative position of particular scores. A group of scores such as those in Table 2.1 is called a *distribution*. If we place scores in order and record the frequency with which each occurs, we have a *frequency distribution*. In the first two columns of Table 2.2, this has been done for the 110 push-up scores.

The next column in Table 2.2, *relative frequency*, represents the frequency with which each score occurs in relation to the total number of scores in the distribution. The relative frequency is obtained by dividing each frequency by the total number of scores, in this case 110. The *frequency percent* is obtained by simply multiplying the relative frequency by 100. In our example, we can now state that 0.14 or 14% of our students did 30 push-ups, whereas 0.11 or 11% did 29.

Using only the first few columns of the table, we begin to get a picture of the distribution of scores. More students (14%) did 30 push-ups than did any other number. Also, more students scored in the middle of the distribution than at its extremes. Thus we already have a better description of these scores than when they were presented in a disorganized array.

The numbers in the remaining columns in Table 2.2 are easily calculated and provide us with additional useful information. The column labeled *cumulative frequency* is an accumulation of frequencies starting at the lowest score (bottom of the table); that is, one person scored 20 or below, three people scored 22 or below, five people scored 23 or below, and so on. The *relative cumulative frequency* is determined by dividing each cumulative frequency by the total number of scores (110). The *percentile rank* is obtained by multiplying the relative cumulative frequencies by 100. This last column, percentile rank, is most useful in presenting performance scores to participants or their parents.

The percentile rank of a score represents the percentage of scores that are equal to or less than that score. We usually denote a percentile rank by the letter P, with a subscript representing the rank. For example, a percentile rank of 85 is represented as P_{85}. Percentile rank tells a person his or her relative standing in a class or group. In our example, a person who did 35 push-ups performed as well or better than 91% of his classmates, whereas the student who did 23 push-ups fell into the lower 5% of the class. Another way of writing these would be $P_{91} = 35$ and $P_{05} = 23$. This interpretation of a score is an easy method for most people to understand relative standing in a group. Frequently, norms for tests are presented in percentile ranks. Later in this chapter we will see that there is another way to determine percentile ranks.

Certain percentile ranks have special names. Each 10th percentile rank is called a *decile* and is represented by D. In other words, $D_1 = P_{10}$, $D_2 = P_{20}$, $D_3 = P_{30}$, and so on. Each 25th percentile rank is called a *quartile* and is denoted by Q. Thus $Q_1 = P_{25}$, $Q_2 = P_{50}$, $Q_3 = P_{75}$, and $Q_4 = P_{100}$.

Occasionally we may need to reduce a frequency distribution into a more compact picture. To do this, we group our scores into intervals. If we take the scores from Table 2.2 and group them into seven intervals with each interval

Table 2.2 Frequency Distribution of Push-Up Scores

a Push-up score	b Frequency	c Relative frequency	d Frequency percent	e Cumulative frequency	f Relative cumulative frequency	g Percentile rank
40	1	.01	1	110	1.00	100
39	0	0	0	109	.99	99
38	2	.02	2	109	.99	99
37	3	.03	3	107	.97	97
36	4	.04	4	104	.95	95
35	5	.05	5	100	.91	91
34	7	.06	6	95	.86	86
33	8	.07	7	88	.80	80
32	9	.08	8	80	.73	73
31	10	.08	9	71	.65	65
30	15	.14	14	61	.55	55
29	12	.11	11	46	.42	42
28	9	.08	8	34	.31	31
27	7	.06	6	25	.23	23
26	6	.05	5	18	.16	16
25	5	.05	5	12	.11	11
24	2	.02	2	7	.06	6
23	2	.02	2	5	.05	5
22	2	.02	2	3	.03	3
21	0	0	0	1	.01	1
20	1	.01	1	1	.01	1

Note. Total number of scores = 110. All calculations rounded to two decimal places.

containing three scores, we obtain the *grouped frequency distribution* shown in Table 2.3.

The frequency, relative frequency, frequency percent, cumulative frequency, relative cumulative frequency, and percentile rank are determined in the same manner for the grouped frequency distribution of scores as they were for the original frequency distribution. The midpoint of each interval is the score that represents the interval. All scores in the interval 38-40, for example, are represented by 39. Actually, we are collapsing our original distribution into a more compact array. By doing so, however, we lose accuracy in our scores because in Table 2.3 the different scores in any single interval are considered the same. For example, no distinction can now be made between the scores 26, 27, and 28 because they all are now represented by the score 27. Obviously, we would prefer not to lose accuracy; hence grouping data is not recommended except in situations where a compact presentation of data is necessary.

Table 2.3   Grouped Frequency Distribution of Push-Up Scores

Interval	Midpoint	Frequency	Relative frequency	Frequency percent	Cumulative frequency	Relative cumulative frequency	Percentile rank
38-40	39	3	.03	3	110	1.00	100
35-37	36	12	.11	11	107	.97	97
32-34	33	24	.22	22	95	.86	86
29-31	30	37	.34	34	71	.65	65
26-28	27	22	.20	20	34	.31	31
23-25	24	9	.08	8	12	.11	11
20-22	21	3	.03	3	3	.03	3

Graphing Techniques

After organizing scores, often it is desirable to present them via a graphic drawing. A pictorial representation of data helps readers to readily recognize the essential features of a frequency distribution or other data. Graphs may be pre-shaped or have axes. In physical education, graphs with horizontal and vertical axes are most common and are the topic of our graphing techniques discussion.

It is impossible to give specific rules for selecting the size of the scale units represented on the vertical and horizontal axes of graphs because the size of unit varies depending on the data being presented. Generally, however, a good policy is to *make the initial entry on the Y-axis zero* unless the scores for the variable being presented are always much greater than zero.

Another generally accepted rule is that *the vertical (Y-axis) should not be longer than about three fourths of the length of the horizontal (X-axis)*. This approach usually results in a better looking graph and also minimizes distortion of the data presented.

The units along each axis should be uniform throughout the scales. In other words, do not start with scale units of 10 and then suddenly switch to other units such as 1. Changing the scale units would obviously distort the data presented. *Each axis must be clearly labeled, and the scores must be marked along regular, uniform intervals.* Also, *always label a graph with a clear and concise title.*

In the final analysis, the one ironclad rule for all graphing is that *the graph must present a realistic picture of the data that assists the reader in interpreting its meaning.*

Particularly in advertising or political campaigns, graphs are often used to purposely distort data on some occurrence. This is done by altering the length of the vertical axis (ordinate, or Y-axis) and horizontal axis (abscissa, or X-axis) of a graph. For example, two different bar graphs depicting the amount of grip strength improvement after an 8-week unit on strength development are presented in Figure 2.2. The graph on the left realistically depicts the amount of strength gained, whereas the graph on the right distorts the amount of strength gained by maximizing the vertical distance between the initial strength and final strength bars. Graphic misrepresentation such as the graph on the right does not clarify the data being presented and is therefore contrary to the purpose of graphic representations.

Another example of graphic misrepresentation is presented in Figure 2.3. Each graph

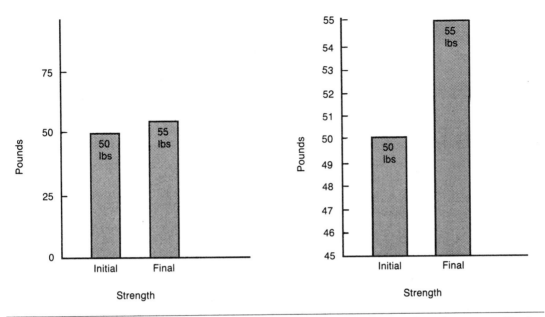

Figure 2.2 Bar graphs representing improvement in grip strengths after an 8-week program. The bar graph on the left represents strength gain accurately whereas the graph on the right distorts the data.

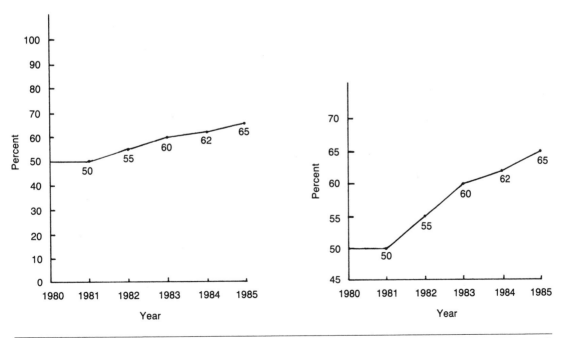

Figure 2.3 Percentage of eighth graders qualifying for the President's Council on Physical Fitness Award.

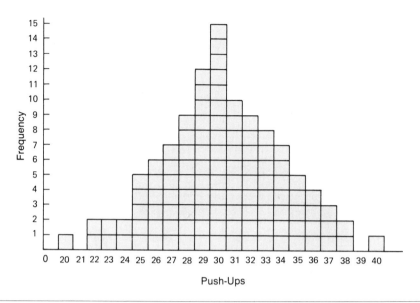

Figure 2.4   Histogram of push-up scores.

presents the percentage of eighth-grade students who qualified for the President's Council on Physical Fitness Awards during the five-year period 1980-1985. The graph on the right appears to exaggerate the significance of the percentage differences between years. A physical education teacher might be tempted to utilize the graph on the right in making a presentation before the local school board; however, this representation is not accurate, and the teacher should let the temptation pass.

Histograms, Polygons, and Ogives

The most common and useful graphic drawings used to display statistical data are the *histogram*, *polygon*, and *ogive*. These graphics illustrate frequency distributions or grouped frequency distributions pictorially.

In a histogram, each unit of measure is represented by an area on the graph. The histogram shown in Figure 2.4 represents the frequency of the 110 push-up scores from Table 2.2. Usually a histogram is made without the horizontal lines; they are presented here to emphasize that each unit of measure occupies the same area. This is true because the units of measurement along the X and Y axes are marked at equal intervals for the data characteristic they represent. A histogram can be used to present data from any of the columns in Table 2.2. In Figure 2.5, the relative cumulative frequency is presented in histogram form. Note the different placement of the scores for the cumulative representation. The scores are placed directly below the vertical lines instead of in between them because the total number of accumulated scores is not present until the interval of the graph is complete.

A polygon is another way to represent frequencies and/or cumulative frequencies pictorially. Instead of bars, a polygon uses a line drawn by connecting data points on the graph. To convert a histogram to a polygon, we simply connect the points on the histogram as illustrated in Figure 2.6. Note that at the end of the frequency polygon a line is drawn back to zero.

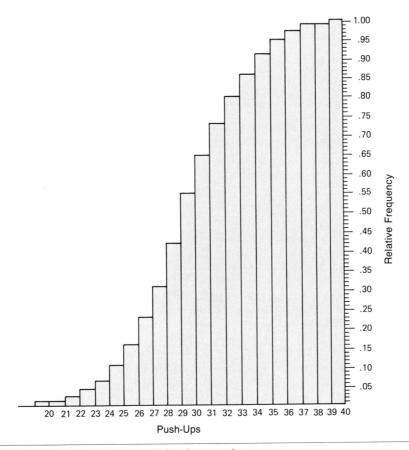

Figure 2.5 Histogram for relative cumulative frequencies.

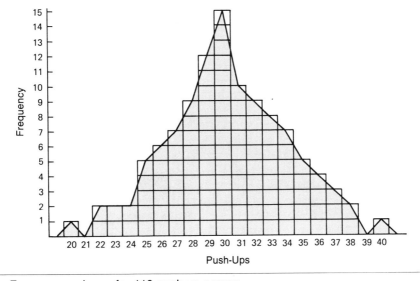

Figure 2.6 Frequency polygon for 110 push-up scores.

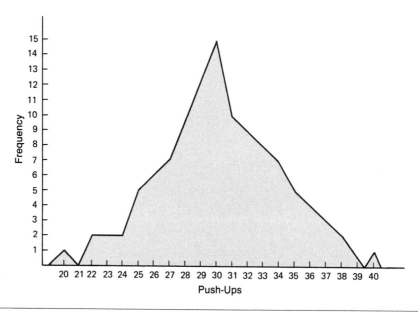

Figure 2.7 Frequency polygon for 110 push-up scores.

This is done to avoid having the polygon appear to be floating. A polygon is usually presented as connected data points rather than superimposed over the histogram (see Figure 2.7).

The ogive is also used to present a picture of frequencies and/or cumulative frequencies. In fact, an ogive is a smooth curve version of the polygon. An ogive for the relative cumulative frequency or the percentile rank of the 100 push-up scores in our example is presented in Figure 2.8. This type of graph is useful for quickly estimating percentile ranks.

As mentioned previously, all of these graphic techniques can also be applied to grouped frequency distributions. We leave that as an exercise for you.

Descriptive Statistics

The foregoing techniques are useful for presenting a group of scores and for providing some

insight into the meaning of individual scores. Frequently, however, physical educators need to describe a distribution of scores more succinctly. Two characteristics used to represent a distribution of scores are *central tendency* and *variability*.

Measures of Central Tendency

In almost any group of scores (distribution) there tends to be a greater concentration of scores toward the middle than anywhere else. This "central tendency" was quite evident in the frequency distribution example for push-ups in the previous section. Thus one of the ways to describe a distribution is to have a measure of this central tendency. Three such measures are commonly used: the mode, the median, and the mean.

Mode. The *mode* is the most frequently occurring score. If we have pull-up scores of 9, 7, 6, 6, 6, 4, and 4 for seven students, the mode for this distribution of scores is 6 because that

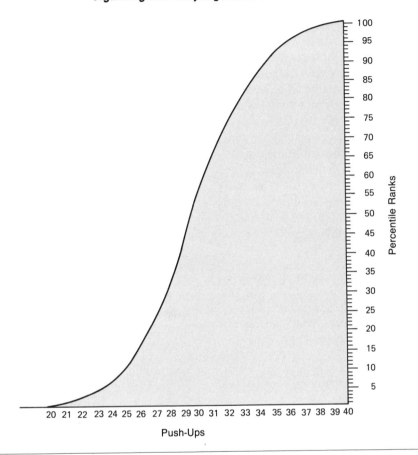

Figure 2.8   Ogive for cumulative frequency for 110 push-up scores.

score occurs more times (three) than any other score. The mode is symbolized by M_0. Thus we write $M_0 = 6$. It is possible to have more than one mode for a distribution. For example, if the distribution of push-up scores is 7, 7, 6, 5, 5, and 4, then the modes would be 7 and 5. When a distribution has two modes it is said to be *bimodal*. If it has three modes, it is *trimodal*, and so on.

The mode is not a particularly good measure of central tendency because there may be more than one mode and because not every score is involved in the mode's determination. Thus the mode may misrepresent the central tendency of the distribution and should be used only to give a quick and approximate estimate of central tendency.

Median.   Another measure of central tendency is the *median*. The median is the middle point in an ordered distribution at which an equal number of scores lie on each side of it. In other words, with an ordered array of scores, if N represents the number of scores present, the median is the $(N + 1)$th/2 score from either end of the distribution. From our earlier example of the seven pull-up scores of 9, 7, 6, 6, 6, 4, and 4, the median, denoted by *Mdn*, is the $(7 + 1)/2 = $ 4th score from either end of the ordered distribution. In this case, then, the *Mdn*

= 6. If our distribution consisted of the push-up scores 7, 7, 6, 5, 5, and 4, the median would be the $(6 + 1)/2 = 3.5$th score, or $Mdn = 5.5$ because it lies halfway between 5 and 6. The median can be a useful measure of central tendency, particularly in distributions with a small number of scores (fewer than 15) or when there are a few extreme scores at one or both ends of the distribution. The median has the drawback, however, of not being mathematically determined, which means that it cannot be used in mathematical calculations. Additionally, the median takes only the *position*, and not the *size*, of each score into account.

Mean.   The most common and useful measure of central tendency is the *mean*. The mean of a distribution is simply the arithmetic average of the scores. For example, for the scores of 9, 7, 6, 6, 6, 4, and 4, the mean is equal to

$$\frac{9 + 7 + 6 + 6 + 6 + 4 + 4}{7} = \frac{42}{7} = 6$$

We denote the mean by a capital letter with a bar over it; the most commonly used letter is $\overline{X}$. Thus we can denote the mean as $\overline{X}$, read as "X-bar." (In some professional journals, μ is used to symbolize the mean.) In our example, $\overline{X} = 6$.

We need to be able to write our definition of the mean symbolically so that it indicates how to find the mean for all situations. If we allow X_i to represent any score in a distribution and N to represent the number of scores in that distribution and if we have five scores, then $N = 5$ and our scores will be represented by X_1, X_2, X_3, X_4, and X_5. Thus

$$\overline{X} = \frac{X_1 + X_2 + X_3 + X_4 + X_5}{5}$$

In a more general expression for any size distribution,

$$\overline{X} = \frac{X_1 + X_2 + \ldots + X_N}{N}$$

To shorten the expression even further we can write

$$\overline{X} = \frac{\sum\limits_{i=1}^{N} X_i}{N}$$

where the Greek capital sigma (Σ) tells us to sum. This expression is read, "X-bar equals the sum of the X_i's for $i = 1$ through N, divided by N," which gives the definition of the mean for any distribution.

The mean is an excellent measure of central tendency because it takes into account the *value* and not just the position of every score in the distribution. This characteristic allows us to use the mean in other mathematical operations that are necessary to determine the variability in a distribution. In most situations, the mean is the measure of central tendency that should be used.

Measures of Variability

Two distributions can have equal means, medians, and modes but still be quite different. Consider, for example, the following two distributions of scores:

X			Y		
1			5		
2	$M_0 = 6$		6	$M_0 = 6$	
6	$\overline{X} = 6$		6	$\overline{Y} = 6$	
6			6		
15	$Mdn = 6$		7	$Mdn = 6$	

We see that the mean, median, and mode are equal to 6 for each distribution. However, the Y-scores are less spread out than the X-scores. Thus the other characteristic of a distribution that interests us is the *variability* among the scores, or the extent to which the scores are spread out. The measures of variability to be presented here are the range, semi-interquartile range, variance, and standard deviation.

Range and Semi-Interquartile Range. The *range* is a simple and easily determined measure of variability that is found by subtracting the smallest score in the distribution from the largest score. For example, if our distribution consists of the sit-up scores of 33, 30, 30, 25, 21, and 18, the range would be $33 - 18 = 15$. Because it is determined by only the two most extreme scores in a distribution, the range is rather unstable and is not a very good estimate of variability. For this reason the range is recommended only as a quick and *temporary* measure of variability. It is comparable to the mode in its quality of information.

Occasionally in measurement and evaluation literature, the *semi-interquartile range* is reported as a measure of variability. The semi-interquartile range is defined as one half the difference between the 75th and 25th percentiles, or

$$\text{Semi-Interquartile Range} = \frac{P_{75} - P_{25}}{2}$$

The semi-interquartile range has been used when extreme scores were present. Although extreme scores do not affect this measure to the extent they affect the range, the semi-interquartile range cannot be readily used in mathematical operations and is thus limited in its usefulness for describing data.

Variance and Standard Deviation. To be effective, a measure of variability should be large when the scores are heterogeneous, or spread out, and smaller when the scores are homogeneous, or clustered closely together. It is also desirable for each score in the distribution to be included in the determination of the measure. At first thought, the sum of the deviations between each score and the mean appears

to be a good approach for measuring variability. Symbolically, we can write this as

$$\sum_{i=1}^{N} (X_i - \overline{X})$$

Now let's use the X-scores of 1, 2, 6, 6, and 15 given at the beginning of this section. Because our $\overline{X} = 6$, then

$$\sum_{i=1}^{N} (X_i - \overline{X})$$

$$= (1 - 6) + (2 - 6) + (6 - 6) + (6 - 6) + (15 - 6)$$

$$= (-5) + (-4) + (0) + (0) + (9)$$

$$= -9 + 9 = 0$$

We thus get a value of zero. As a matter of fact, *the sum of the deviations about the mean for any distribution will always equal zero.* Therefore, this method, as presented, does not measure variability. However, if we were to square each deviation before summing, we would eliminate the cancelling-out effect of negative numbers and may have a useful measure of variability. This would be written symbolically as

$$\sum_{i=1}^{N} (X_i - \overline{X})^2$$

and substituting our X-scores again,

$$\sum_{i=1}^{N} (X_i - \overline{X})^2$$

$$= (1 - 6)^2 + (2 - 6)^2 + (6 - 6)^2 + (6 - 6)^2 + (15 - 6)^2$$

$$= (-5)^2 + (-4)^2 + (0)^2 + (0)^2 + (9)^2$$

$$= 25 + 16 + 0 + 0 + 81$$

$$= 122$$

Now the only apparent problem is that in order to have a large variability value, we would only need to have additional scores that are not equal to the mean. So, let's divide this measure of variability by the number of scores, which will give us a *mean squared deviation*.[1] We can write

$$\sigma_x^2 = \frac{\sum\limits_{i=1}^{N} (X_i - \overline{X})^2}{N}$$

This measure is called the *variance* of a distribution and is represented by σ^2.

Let's see if the variance can distinguish between two distributions that do not have the same homogeneity among scores. The X- and Y-scores we used previously should suffice for this purpose because the Xs are more dispersed than the Ys. Therefore, the variance of the Xs (1, 2, 6, 6, and 15) should be larger than the variance of the Ys (5, 6, 6, 6, and 7). For the X distribution, we have already found that

$$\sum\limits_{i=1}^{N} (X_1 - \overline{X})^2 = 122$$

So,

$$\sigma_x^2 = \frac{122}{5} = 24.4$$

In the Y distribution

$$\sigma_y^2 = \frac{\sum\limits_{i=1}^{N} (Y_i - \overline{Y})^2}{N}$$

$$= \frac{(5-6)^2+(6-6)^2+(6-6)^2+(6-6)^2+(7-6)^2}{5}$$

$$= \frac{(-1)^2 + (0)^2 + (0)^2 + (0)^2 + (1)^2}{5}$$

$$= \frac{1 + 0 + 0 + 0 + 1}{5} = \frac{2}{5} = .4$$

The variance does in fact work because $\sigma_x^2 = 24.4$ and $\sigma_y^2 = .4$.

If the mean is not a "nice" round number as it has been in our examples, the calculation of the variance could be a tedious procedure if the variance formula were used in its present form. (Imagine subtracting a mean of 8.64 from every score, squaring it, and then summing!) However, by algebraically manipulating the variance formula, we derive the following equivalent formula[2] that is much easier to use:

$$\sigma^2 = \frac{\sum\limits_{i=1}^{N} (X_i - \overline{X})^2}{N} = \frac{N\left(\sum\limits_{i=1}^{N} X_i^2\right) - \left(\sum\limits_{i=1}^{N} X_i\right)^2}{N^2}$$

where

$$\sum\limits_{i=1}^{N} X_i^2$$

tells us to square each score and then add these squared scores and

$$\left(\sum\limits_{i=1}^{N} X_i\right)^2$$

tells us to sum all of the scores and then square this sum.

Let's use this new form of the variance formula to calculate the σ_y^2 again to see if it works. The scores were 5, 6, 6, 6, and 7. Therefore,

$$\sum\limits_{i=1}^{N} Y_i^2 = 5^2 + 6^2 + 6^2 + 6^2 + 7^2$$

$$= 25 + 36 + 36 + 36 + 49 = 182$$

---

[1]The authors are fully aware that if we have a sample, the variance estimate of the population would be $s^2 = \dfrac{\Sigma(X - \overline{X})^2}{n - 1}$. However, we are assuming that inference to a population is not desired.

[2]The complete stepwise derivation of the calculating formula from the definitional formula is presented in Appendix B.

$$\sum_{i=1}^{N} Y_i^2 = (5 + 6 + 6 + 6 + 7)^2$$

$$= (30)^2 = 900$$

and

$$\sigma_y^2 = \frac{N\left(\sum_{i=1}^{N} Y_i^2\right) - \left(\sum_{i=1}^{N} Y_i\right)^2}{N^2}$$

$$= \frac{(5)(192) - 900}{(5)(5)} = \frac{910 - 900}{25} = \frac{10}{25} = .4$$

We see that this is an equivalent formula.

The variance is a most useful measure of variability and meets the criteria we suggested that a measure of variability should have. Its only drawback is that it is a value presented in squared units. In our examples, if we were working in centimeters, our variances would be 24.4 cm squared and .4 cm squared. In order to get our variability measure back into the units with which we work, we take its square root and have the most useful and commonly used measure of variability, the *standard deviation*. The standard deviation (σ) is the positive square root of the variance and is defined symbolically as

$$\sigma_x = \sqrt{\frac{\sum_{i=1}^{N} (X_i - \overline{X})^2}{N}}$$

$$= \sqrt{\frac{N\left(\sum_{i=1}^{N} X_i^2\right) - \left(\sum_{i=1}^{N} X_i\right)^2}{N^2}}$$

In our examples,

$$\sigma_x = \sqrt{24.4} = 4.94$$

and

$$\sigma_y = \sqrt{.4} = .63$$

If our scores were in centimeters, we would say that our standard deviations are 4.94 cm and .63 cm. Unfortunately, there is no exact, literal interpretation of the standard deviation. However, in order to have a sense of the meaning of the standard deviation, one can think of it as a "kind of average" deviation between the mean and the scores in the distribution. We say "kind of average" because it is not *exactly* the average but is a close approximation.

The mean and standard deviation can usually describe a distribution of scores quite sufficiently. They are the descriptive measures used throughout the remainder of this text.

Standard Scores

Many times one may want to combine or compare scores from performances that have dissimilar units of measure. For example, we might have performance scores from the shot put, the 100-yard dash, and a written test that would be useful if combined into a composite score. Suppose the respective scores from these performances for a particular individual named Jim are 38 feet, 12.2 seconds, and 79 answers correct. With these diverse units of measure, we cannot combine or compare these scores. Thus there is a need for a standard means of reporting scores from diverse measurement units. Three such methods of standardization are the standard z-score scale, the T score scale, and the 6-σ score scale.

Using Jim's example scores, if we know the mean and standard deviation for each of the activities, we have some basis for knowing the relative position of Jim's performance in each of the activities. For example, suppose the mean and standard deviation for the shot put for Jim's class were $\overline{X}$ = 42 feet, σ = 8 feet; for the 100-yard dash, $\overline{X}$ = 12.0 seconds, σ = .2 seconds; and for the written test, $\overline{X}$ = 75 answers correct, σ = 8 correct. We can see immediately that Jim performed below the mean on the shot put and higher than the mean on the written test. In the 100-yard dash his time (12.2 seconds) was greater and thus below average in terms of performance.

In order to be more exact, we find that Jim's score is 4 feet or .5 standard deviation unit below the mean for the shot put, 4 points or .5 standard deviation unit above the mean for the written test, and .2 of a second or 1 standard deviation unit below the average on the dash. These standard deviation units are called *z-scores* and are found by subtracting the mean from an individual score and dividing the difference obtained by the standard deviation.

$$z\text{-score} = \frac{X - \overline{X}}{\sigma}$$

For Jim's 38-foot shot put performance,

$$z = \frac{38 - 42}{8} = \frac{-4}{8} = -.5$$

for his 100-yard dash score of 12.2 seconds,

$$z = \frac{12.2 - 12.0}{.2} = \frac{.2}{.2} = 1.0$$

and for his written test score of 79,

$$z = \frac{79 - 75}{8} = \frac{4}{8} = .5$$

When working with activities that involve speed and have time as the unit of measure, we must always change the sign of our z-score if we wish to speak of performance. Thus in terms of performance, Jim's 100-yard dash z-score will be -1.0 instead of $+1.0$.

The z-score not only allows the comparison of an individual's performance in dissimilar activities but also allows these performances to be combined into an average performance score. The z-scores for Jim were

Activity	z-Score
Shot put	-0.5
100-yard dash	-1.0
Written test	$+0.5$

Thus his overall average performance would be $(-0.5 + -1.0 + 0.5)/3 = -1/3 = -.33$, or .33 standard deviation unit below the mean. Finding z-scores for all participants in an event is advantageous in order to standardize the reporting of performances. If we were to average all the z-scores for any particular event, we would find that the mean for z is $z = 0$ and that the standard deviation for z is $\sigma_z = 1$.

All standard scores are based on the z-score. There is some objection to working with small numbers and negative numbers that are prevalent with z-scores because the range of z-scores for most distributions is usually -3 to $+3$. Instead, many people prefer to use standard scores that are positive and larger. To obtain these scores, we could add a constant to every score in a distribution or multiply every score in the distribution by a constant. Adding a constant to every score or multiplying every score by a constant will in no way alter the shape or the relative position of the scores in a distribution. The procedures simply have the effect of placing a picture of the distribution under a magnifying glass.

If we multiply each z-score in a distribution by 10 and add 50, we obtain *T scores*. In other words,

$$T \text{ score} = 50 + 10z$$

Or, if we replace the z with what it equals, we have

$$T \text{ score} = 50 + 10\frac{(X - \overline{X})}{\sigma}$$

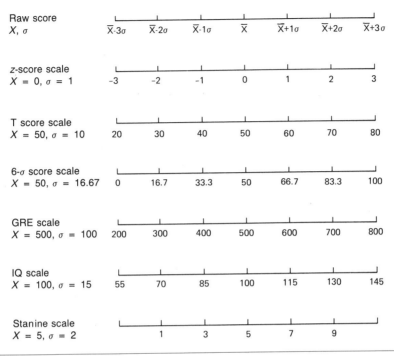

Figure 2.9   Comparisons among common standard score scales.

The mean of all T scores in a distribution is equal to 50, and the standard deviation is equal to 10. Therefore, T scores usually range from 20 to 80.

Some teachers and researchers do not like the T score range; they prefer a range of 0 to 100. The *6-σ score* scale generally achieves this range. To obtain 6-σ scores, we multiply each z-score by 16.67 and add 50, or

$$6\text{-}\sigma = 50 + 16.67z = 50 + 16.67 \frac{(X - \overline{X})}{\sigma}$$

The mean for the 6-σ scale is 50, and the standard deviation is 16.67. The graph in Figure 2.9 helps to illustrate the relationship among several common standard scores. It must be emphasized again that all of these standard scores are based on standard deviation units above or below the mean. Numerous other standard scores can be utilized. Some of these are also listed in Figure 2.9.

During the past decade or so, calculators and now computers have become commonly used tools to assist us in making calculations and storing information. Appendix C includes examples of how to utilize a programmable calculator in determining the mean, standard deviation, and T scores. Appendix D provides an introduction to these same programs that can be used on minicomputers. You are urged to acquaint yourself with these time-saving tools if you are not already well versed in their usage.

Normal Curve

Looking at the frequency distribution of push-up scores and its graphic representations presented earlier (p. 24), we notice that more scores occur toward the center than at the extremes. This phenomenon occurs in most real-life measures and certainly occurs in most performance

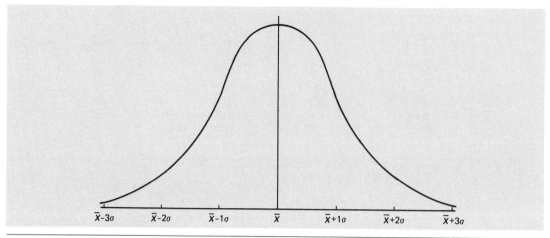

Figure 2.10 Normal curve.

measures used in physical education. Mathematicians worked with this phenomenon until they were able to define mathematically a curve that closely approximates the distribution of real-life measures. This curve is called the *normal curve* and can be very useful in working with physical education measures. The normal curve is a curve or ogive that represents a frequency distribution for a population. The normal curve is presented graphically in Figure 2.10.

The normal curve is bell-shaped and has a single peak, or mode, at the same place as the mean. In fact, in a normal distribution the mean, median, and mode fall at exactly the same point. The curve is also symmetrical, meaning that the left half is a mirror image of the right half; that is, the scores above the mean are distributed in the same way as the scores below the mean. Additionally, the curve is concave downward between the mean and one standard deviation in either direction and concave upward beyond these points.

Although very few distributions of scores *perfectly* fit the normal curve, most distributions that contain at least 30 scores will *approximate* the normal curve closely enough to warrant its use. Scores in some distributions, however, are not normally distributed. For example, if a test were extremely difficult, a disproportionately

large number of scores would fall at the lower end of the distribution. When this occurs, the distribution is said to be *skewed to the right*, or *positively skewed*. A positively skewed distribution is illustrated in Figure 2.11(a). If a disproportionately large number of scores falls at the higher end of the distribution, then the distribution is said to be *skewed to the left*, or *negatively skewed*. If an extremely easy test were given, we would expect scores on that test to be skewed to the left. An illustration of a negatively skewed distribution is shown in Figure

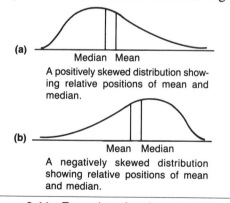

(a)

Median Mean

A positively skewed distribution showing relative positions of mean and median.

(b)

Mean Median

A negatively skewed distribution showing relative positions of mean and median.

Figure 2.11 Examples of a skewed distribution. (a) A positively skewed distribution showing relative positions of mean and median. (b) A negatively skewed distribution showing relative positions of mean and median.

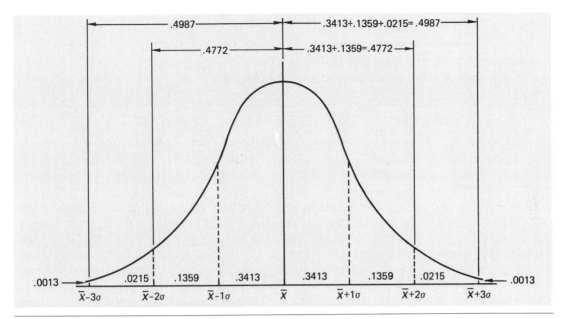

Figure 2.12 Normal curve percentages.

2.11(b). If one suspects that his or her data are skewed, the frequency data should be plotted. If the skewness appears to be severe, then the normal curve should not be used and a statistician should be consulted.

An important use of the normal curve for physical educators is in the determination of percentile ranks. Because the normal curve is mathematically defined, the percentage of scores expected between any two points can be determined. As shown in Figure 2.12, for example, in a normal distribution .3413 or 34.13% of the scores occur between the mean and one standard deviation unit; .4772 or 47.72% of the scores occur between the mean and two standard deviation units; and .4987 or 49.87% of the scores occur between the mean and three deviation units. Finally, 50% of the scores can be expected to be on either side of the mean.

Percentages of scores occurring between numerous intervals have been calculated and are presented in Table 2.4. The table presents the percentage of scores expected to occur between the mean and a specified number of standard deviation units or z-scores. For example, by using this table we can see that 19.85% of the scores will occur between the mean and .52 standard deviation units. Another example shows us that 46.25% of the scores can be expected to fall between the mean and 1.78 standard deviation units.

After working through the following examples, it should be apparent how physical educators can use the table:

Example 1. The mean on a test was $\overline{X} = 65$, and the standard deviation was $\sigma = 11$. Assuming that the scores on the test were normally distributed, if Charlene scores 72 on the test, what was her percentile rank?

Solution: To answer this question we should first diagram the position of Charlene's score on the normal curve (see Figure 2.13). Next, let's determine her z-score:

$$z\text{-score} = \frac{72 - 65}{11} = \frac{7}{11} = .64$$

This means that Charlene's score lies .64 standard deviation units *above* the mean.

Table 2.4   The Normal Distribution

Percentage area under the standard normal curve from 0
to z (shown shaded) is the value found in the body of the table.

z	0.00	0.01	0.02	0.03	0.04	0.05	0.06	0.07	0.08	0.09
0.0	0.0000	0.0040	0.0080	0.0120	0.0160	0.0199	0.0239	0.0279	0.0319	0.0359
0.1	0.0398	0.0438	0.0478	0.0517	0.0557	0.0596	0.0636	0.0675	0.0714	0.0753
0.2	0.0793	0.0832	0.0871	0.0910	0.0948	0.0987	0.1026	0.1064	0.1103	0.1141
0.3	0.1179	0.1217	0.1255	0.1293	0.1331	0.1368	0.1406	0.1443	0.1480	0.1517
0.4	0.1554	0.1591	0.1628	0.1664	0.1700	0.1736	0.1772	0.1808	0.1844	0.1879
0.5	0.1915	0.1950	0.1985	0.2019	0.2054	0.2088	0.2123	0.2157	0.2190	0.2224
0.6	0.2257	0.2291	0.2324	0.2357	0.2389	0.2422	0.2454	0.2486	0.2517	0.2549
0.7	0.2580	0.2611	0.2642	0.2673	0.2704	0.2734	0.2764	0.2794	0.2823	0.2852
0.8	0.2881	0.2910	0.2939	0.2967	0.2995	0.3023	0.3051	0.3078	0.3106	0.3133
0.9	0.3159	0.3186	0.3212	0.3238	0.3264	0.3289	0.3315	0.3340	0.3365	0.3389
1.0	0.3413	0.3438	0.3461	0.3485	0.3508	0.3531	0.3554	0.3577	0.3599	0.3621
1.1	0.3643	0.3665	0.3686	0.3708	0.3729	0.3749	0.3770	0.3790	0.3810	0.3830
1.2	0.3849	0.3869	0.3888	0.3907	0.3925	0.3944	0.3962	0.3980	0.3997	0.4015
1.3	0.4032	0.4049	0.4066	0.4082	0.4099	0.4115	0.4131	0.4147	0.4162	0.4177
1.4	0.4192	0.4207	0.4222	0.4236	0.4251	0.4265	0.4279	0.4292	0.4306	0.4319
1.5	0.4332	0.4345	0.4357	0.4370	0.4382	0.4394	0.4406	0.4418	0.4429	0.4441
1.6	0.4452	0.4463	0.4474	0.4484	0.4495	0.4505	0.4515	0.4525	0.4535	0.4545
1.7	0.4554	0.4564	0.4573	0.4582	0.4591	0.4599	0.4608	0.4616	0.4625	0.4633
1.8	0.4641	0.4649	0.4656	0.4664	0.4671	0.4678	0.4686	0.4693	0.4699	0.4706
1.9	0.4713	0.4719	0.4726	0.4732	0.4738	0.4744	0.4750	0.4756	0.4761	0.4767
2.0	0.4772	0.4778	0.4783	0.4788	0.4793	0.4798	0.4803	0.4808	0.4812	0.4817
2.1	0.4821	0.4826	0.4830	0.4834	0.4838	0.4842	0.4846	0.4850	0.4854	0.4857
2.2	0.4861	0.4864	0.4868	0.4871	0.4875	0.4878	0.4881	0.4884	0.4887	0.4890
2.3	0.4893	0.4896	0.4898	0.4901	0.4904	0.4906	0.4909	0.4911	0.4913	0.4916
2.4	0.4918	0.4920	0.4922	0.4925	0.4927	0.4929	0.4931	0.4932	0.4934	0.4936
2.5	0.4938	0.4940	0.4941	0.4943	0.4945	0.4946	0.4948	0.4949	0.4951	0.4952
2.6	0.4953	0.4955	0.4956	0.4957	0.4959	0.4960	0.4961	0.4962	0.4963	0.4964
2.7	0.4965	0.4966	0.4967	0.4968	0.4969	0.4970	0.4971	0.4972	0.4973	0.4974
2.8	0.4974	0.4975	0.4976	0.4977	0.4977	0.4978	0.4979	0.4979	0.4980	0.4981
2.9	0.4981	0.4982	0.4982	0.4983	0.4984	0.4984	0.4985	0.4985	0.4986	0.4986
3.0	0.4987	0.4987	0.4987	0.4988	0.4988	0.4989	0.4989	0.4989	0.4990	0.4990

Note. Abridged from Table 9 in *Biometrika Tables for Statisticians*, Vol. 1 (3rd ed.), edited by E.S. Pearson and H.O. Hartley, 1966, New York: Cambridge. Reproduced with kind permission of E.J. Snell for the *Biometrika* trustees.

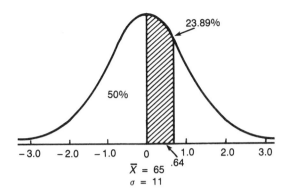

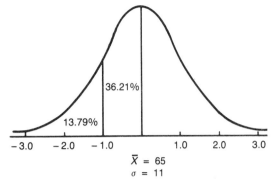

Figure 2.13   Charlene's score (72) standardized ($z = .64$) on the normal curve.

Figure 2.14   Bill's score (53) standardized ($z = -1.09$) on the normal curve.

From Table 2.4 we learn that between the mean and .64 standard deviation units lie 23.89% of the scores; however, because 50% of the scores fall *below* the mean, we must include them so that 23.89% + 50%, or 73.89%, of the scores were at .64 standard deviations or lower. Therefore, Charlene's percentile rank is 73.89. Symbolically, her score is expressed as $72 = P_{74}$.

Example 2. Given the same $\overline{X}$ and σ as in Example 1, determine Bill's percentile rank if he scored 53 on the test. Let's locate Bill's position on the normal curve.

Solution: Bill's z-score

$$= \frac{53 - 65}{11} - \frac{-12}{11} = -1.09$$

From Table 2.4 we find that 36.21% of the scores will fall between the mean and a z of 1.09. This is shown in Figure 2.14. We want to know the percentage of scores at or below Bill's score, and because 50% of the scores fall below the mean, Bill's percentile rank is 50% − 36.21%, or 13.79%; that is, $53 = P_{14}$. Drawing a graph for solving each of your problems is highly recommended because such graphs indicate what you need to know and help you to find it.

Example 3. Given the same $\overline{X}$ and σ as before, suppose we now want to find the score corresponding to the 70th and 40th percentile ranks. First, for P_{70} our graph would appear as Figure 2.15. We can then see that we must find the point at which 20% of the scores lie between it and the mean. Searching Table 2.4, we find that 20% falls between .52 and .53 but is closer to .52. Therefore, a z-score of .52 is equal to P_{70}. To get back to our test score units, we use the z-score formula that allows us to convert z-scores to raw scores:

$$z = \frac{X - \overline{X}}{\sigma}$$

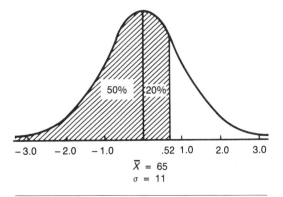

Figure 2.15   Diagram for determining P_{70}.

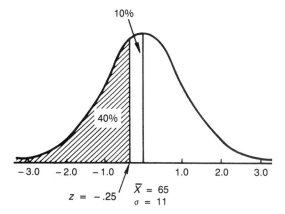

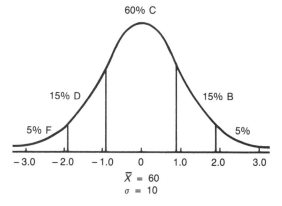

Figure 2.16 Diagram for determining P_{40}.

Figure 2.17 Sample distribution of letter grades on a normal curve.

When we solve for X, we have $X = \overline{X} + z\sigma$. In our case, then

$$X = 65 + (.52)11 = 65 + 5.72 = 72.72$$

Therefore, $P_{70} \cong 73$. In order to find P_{40}, we start again with a graph as shown in Figure 2.16. This time we are looking for the point at which 10% of the scores lie between it and the mean. From Table 2.4, we find the value to be .25. Because this point is below the mean, P_{40} is equal to a z-score of $-.25$. Finally, to find the raw test score we use

$$X = \overline{X} + z\sigma$$

$$= 65 + (-.25)11$$

$$= 65 - 2.75 = 62.25$$

Therefore, $P_{40} \cong 62$.

We commonly hear of instructors grading "on the curve." Usually, this entails the use of the normal curve, an example of which follows:

Example 4. Using the principle of normal score distribution, a teacher decides to determine 5% of the scores on a test as As, 15% as Bs, 60% as Cs, 15% as Ds, and 5% as Fs. Assume that $\overline{X} = 60$ and $\sigma = 10$ for this test. The

teacher's distribution of grade percentages is shown on the normal curve in Figure 2.17.

As we can see, this is simply a problem of determining P_{05}, P_{20}, P_{80}, and P_{95}. In order to find the test score needed for an A, we must find P_{95}. From Table 2.4 we find that $z = 1.64$, and therefore $X = 60 + 1.64(10) = 60 + 16.4 = 76.4$, or $P_{95} = 76$ and above. Similarly, for P_{80} we find that $z = .84$, and therefore $X = 60 + .84(10) = 60 + 8.4 = 68.4$, or $P_{80} = 68$. For P_{20}, we find that $z = -.84$, and therefore $X = 60 - .84(10) = 60 - 8.4 = 51.6$, or $P_{20} = 52$. Finally, for P_{05}, we find that $z = -1.64$, and therefore $X = 60 - 1.64(10) = 60 - 16.4 = 43.6$, or $P_{05} = 44$. Thus our grading distribution turns out to be

A = highest 5%   = 76 and above
B = next highest 15% = 68-75
C = middle 60%   = 52-67
D = next lowest 15%   = 44-51
F = lowest 5%   = 43 and below

Establishment of Norms

The term *norm* frequently appears in measurement and evaluation literature. *Norm* is an abbreviated form of the word *normal*, which in the context of measurement and evaluation denotes the *average* or *mean* performance of a group. Furthermore, the plural form *norms* refers to the availability of the mean, standard deviation, and percentile ranks for various performances of a comparative group, or reference group. For example, norms for different age groups and both sexes are available for the various tests of the AAHPER Youth Fitness Test. In other words, the means, standard deviations, and percentile ranks for boys and girls in each age group are available for each of the tests. These norms were established by testing approximately 10,000 boys and girls throughout the United States.

Typically, norms are utilized when applying some sort of norm-referenced evaluation, a concept introduced in chapter 1. An individual's performance is compared with the performance of some defined reference group. For example, one might state that on a sit-up test sophomore Jane scored at the 84th percentile rank when her score was compared to the national norms for female high school sophomores. One might also state that Jane scored one standard deviation above the national average (mean performance) on the sit-up test.

The most important questions to ask about norms are, What is the nature of the group on which the norms were determined, and is this group appropriate for current purposes? Although national norms for tests are frequently available for some groups, norms may not be available for a group similar to the one currently being tested. For instance, if we have just administered a cardiovascular endurance test to a group of adult women aged 25 to 40 and discover that norms for the test are available only for men aged 18 to 25, then the available norms would be of little or no value. Because of situations such as this, it is often desirable for physical educators to develop their own local norms.

To ensure that norms are based on a representative population, they must be based on a large number of scores. Thus when local norms are developed, one needs to continuously update means and standard deviations by deriving combined means and standard deviations from more than one group. One approach to this process is to constantly update frequency distribution tables and then calculate an updated mean and standard deviation. One can then determine percentile ranks and/or T scores or other standard scores. A more efficient way to update means and standard deviations, however, is provided in the following example. Suppose the mean and standard deviation on a grip strength test on a previous group of eighth-grade boys with $N_1 = 100$ students were $\overline{X}_1 = 75$ lbs and $\sigma_1 = 8$ lbs. If we just completed the test on another group of eighth-grade boys ($N_2 = 50$) with a mean and standard deviation of $\overline{X}_2 = 80$ lbs and $\sigma_2 = 9$ lbs, we would want to know the mean and standard deviation for the combined group of 150 boys. To find these values for the combined group, we must calculate the *weighted* averages, which are averages adjusted according to the size of the group. Thus

$$\text{Combined } \overline{X} = \frac{N_1\overline{X}_1 + N_2\overline{X}_2}{N_1 + N_2}$$

$$\text{Combined } \sigma = \sqrt{\frac{N_1\sigma_1{}^2 + N_2\sigma_2{}^2}{N_1 + N_2}}$$

For our example,

$$\text{Combined } \overline{X} = \frac{100(75) + 50(80)}{100 + 50}$$

$$= \frac{7500 + 4000}{150}$$

$$= \frac{11,500}{150}$$

$$= 76.67$$

$$\text{Combined } \sigma = \sqrt{\frac{100(8^2) + 50(9^2)}{100 + 50}}$$

$$= \sqrt{\frac{100(64) + 50(81)}{150}}$$

$$= \sqrt{\frac{6400 + 4050}{150}}$$

$$= \sqrt{\frac{10,450}{150}} = \sqrt{69.67} = 8.35$$

This procedure can, of course, be expanded to any number of groups.

From the combined mean and standard deviation, we can determine whichever percentile ranks we desire as long as we can assume that the scores are normally distributed, thus allowing us to use the normal curve table. Most norms list every 5th or 10th percentile rank, although some will list every percentile rank from 0 to 100. An example of norms for every 5th percentile rank is found on page 211. Of course, once the appropriate mean and standard deviation have been determined, one can also derive standard score norms. An example of a T score norm chart is given on page 128.

Correlation

We often talk about two or more occurrences or performances being related to one another. For example, we might expect performance on the standing long jump to be related to performance on the jump-and-reach because both of these skills rely heavily on leg power. In other words, individuals who score high on the one task will also score high on the other, whereas individuals who score low or average on the one will score similarly on the other. Rather than subjectively estimating whether or not and to what degree performances are related, we can use statistical techniques to determine this. These techniques involve the calculation of a correlation coefficient.

A *correlation coefficient* is the mathematically computed degree of relationship or agreement between variables and is denoted by the letter r. This coefficient also indicates the direction (positive or negative) of a relationship. For example, if people score high on one variable and low on another variable, the two variables are negatively related.

Perfect agreement between two variables in the same direction indicates a perfect positive correlation between the two variables ($r = 1.00$). This occurs if the person with the highest score on one variable also has the highest score on the other variable and the person with the second highest score on the first variable is also the second highest on the other variable, and so on. A perfect negative agreement ($r = -1.00$) occurs in the opposite direction if the person with the highest score on one variable has the lowest score on the other variable, the person with the second highest score on the first variable has the second lowest score on the other, and so on. It is extremely rare to have a perfect correlation, either positive or negative. When no relationship or agreement whatsoever exists between the variables ($r = 0.00$), the variables are said to be *independent* of one another. As with perfect correlations, it is extremely rare for variables to have absolutely no relationship. Generally, variables are related to one another to some degree, but not perfectly.

The square of the correlation coefficient (r^2) is often reported in the literature. The quantity r^2 represents the amount of overlap between two variables, or more specifically, the percentage of variance that two variables share. Figure 2.18 shows this in diagrammatic form.

The quantity r^2 is called the *coefficient of determination*. Its counterpart ($1 - r^2$) is called the *coefficient of nondetermination*. Their values range from 0 to 1. The coefficient of determination is a better indicator of relationship than r because it can be interpreted more easily.

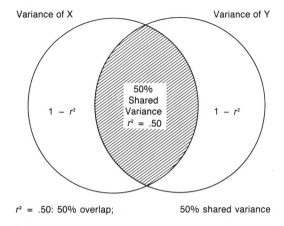

$r^2 = .50$: 50% overlap; 50% shared variance

Figure 2.18 Percentage of shared variance.

Variance of X

Variance of Y

$1 - r^2$

50%
Shared
Variance
$r^2 = .50$

$1 - r^2$

Table 2.5 Rank-Order Correlation

Student	Rank on tennis serving	Rank in ladder tournament	d	d²
A	6	5	1	1
B	9	10	−1	1
C	3.5	1	2.5	6.25
D	5	8	−3	9
E	3.5	4	−0.5	0.25
F	8	6	2	4
G	10	9	1	1
H	2	2	0	0
I	7	7	0	0
J	1	3	−2	4
			Sum =	26.5

$\sum d^2 = 26.5; N = 10$

$$\text{rho} = 1 - \frac{6(26.5)}{10(100 - 1)}$$

$$= 1 - \frac{159}{990} = 1 - .16 = .84$$

Additionally, a negative correlation of the same magnitude as a positive correlation indicates the same degree of relationship because the coefficient of determination is the same in each case. For example, a correlation of −0.80 indicates just as strong a relationship as a correlation of +0.80 because in each case $r^2 = 0.64$.

Two common techniques for determining the correlation between two variables are the Spearman rank-order correlation and the Pearson product-moment correlation. The Spearman rank-order correlation is the agreement between the *ranks* on two variables, and the Pearson product-moment correlation indicates the similarity of *position* on the normal curve for two variables. In each case, there must be a pair of scores or ranks, including one for each variable for each person. The Spearman rank-order correlation coefficient is usually denoted by *rho* in order to distinguish it from the Pearson *r*. The following examples illustrate how to determine each of these coefficients.

Example of Applying *rho*

Suppose that 10 students have been ranked 1 through 10 on their ability to serve in tennis, with 1 indicating the best server. Also assume that a ladder tournament was conducted for these

students and that the students' rankings were again recorded from 1 through 10. The results of these two rankings are presented in the first two columns of Table 2.5. It can be seen that Student D, for example, was the fifth best on the service rankings but finished eighth in the ladder tournament. Note that Students C and E tied for the third and fourth ranks on serving and were each given the rank of 3.5.

Assume that we want to determine the relationship between these two performances. In other words, we want to determine to what degree the rankings on serves are related to the tournament results. Because we have only the performance ranks available, it is appropriate to calculate the Spearman rank-order correlation coefficient.

The formula for determining *rho* is

$$rho = 1 - \frac{6(\Sigma d^2)}{N(N^2 - 1)}$$

where Σd^2 is the sum of the differences between the ranks of students on the two tests squared and N is the total number of students.

The column labeled d in Table 2.5 represents the differences between the ranks obtained by the students on the two tests, whereas d^2 simply indicates that each of these differences has been squared.

In this example,

$$rho = 1 - \frac{6(\Sigma d^2)}{N(N^2 - 1)} = 1 - \frac{6(26.5)}{10(100 - 1)}$$

$$= 1 - \frac{159}{990} = 1 - 0.16 = 0.84$$

This correlation of 0.84 indicates that a sizable positive relationship does exist between the two variables, which may have been reasonably expected.

The Spearman rank-order correlation coefficient can also be used when one or both of the variables are quantitative scores and not just ranks. To do this, one simply assigns ranks to individual performances in accordance with the performance. An exercise in doing this is given at the end of this chapter.

Example of Applying Pearson *r*

In Table 2.6, scores for students on push-ups and chin-ups are presented. Because we have actual scores on both of the variables, the Pearson *r* should be used to determine the degree of relationship between them. The definitional formula for the Pearson correlation coefficient is

$$r = \frac{\sum_{i=1}^{N} (X_i - \overline{X})(Y_i - \overline{Y})}{\sqrt{\left[\sum_{i=1}^{N} (X_i - \overline{X})^2\right]\left[\sum_{i=1}^{N} (Y_i - \overline{Y})^2\right]}}$$

An equivalent formula that is convenient for calculation purposes is

$$r = \frac{\sum_{i=1}^{N} (X_iY_i - N\overline{XY})}{\sqrt{\left[\sum_{i=1}^{N} (X_i^2 - N\overline{X}^2)\right]\left[\sum_{i=1}^{N} (Y_i^2 - N\overline{Y}^2)\right]}}$$

Table 2.6 Correlation Coefficient Calculation

Chin-ups		Push-ups		
X	X²	Y	Y²	XY
5	25	20	400	100
2	4	19	361	38
12	144	35	1225	420
8	64	17	289	136
1	1	12	144	12
7	49	23	529	161
5	25	19	361	95
9	81	29	841	261
3	9	16	256	48
5	25	22	484	110

$\Sigma X = 57; \Sigma X^2 = 427; \Sigma Y = 212;$
$\Sigma Y^2 = 4890; \Sigma XY = 1381$

$$\overline{X} = \frac{57}{10} = 5.7 \qquad \overline{Y} = \frac{212}{10} = 21.2$$

$$r = \frac{\Sigma XY - N\overline{XY}}{\sqrt{(\Sigma X^2 - N\overline{X}^2)(\Sigma Y^2 - N\overline{Y}^2)}}$$

$$= \frac{1381 - 10(5.7)(21.2)}{\sqrt{[427 - 10(5.7)^2][4890 - 10(21.2)^2]}}$$

$$= \frac{1381 - 1208.4}{\sqrt{(427 - 324.9)(4890 - 4494.4)}}$$

$$= \frac{172.6}{\sqrt{(102.1)(395.6)}} = \frac{172.6}{200.9} = .86$$

$r = .86$, hence $r^2 = (.86)^2 = .74$

All the components in this formula and how they are calculated are shown in Table 2.6, which should be sufficiently self-explanatory.

Regression

A correlation coefficient can also be used to predict performance on one variable when performance on another variable is known. If you want to predict performance on one variable from another variable, it is appropriate to use a procedure called *regression*. A regression equation is determined in the form

$$\hat{Y} = a + bX$$

which is the equation of a straight line. $\hat{Y}$ represents the variable scores to be predicted; X represents the variable scores used to predict Y; b represents the amount of change in Y associated with each unit change in X; and a represents the constant adjustment that must be made in order to put X and Y on the same scale. The value a also represents the point where the regression line intersects the y-axis; thus it is called the *y-intercept*. In other words, b is a weight and indicates the amount that the predicted Y score will increase or decrease for each corresponding change in X. The formulas for finding a and b are

$$a = \overline{Y} - b\overline{X}$$

and

$$b = \frac{\sum (X - \overline{X})(Y - \overline{Y})}{\sum (X - \overline{X})^2} = \frac{\sum XY - \left[(\sum X)\frac{(\sum Y)}{N} \right]}{\sum X^2 - \frac{(\sum X)^2}{N}}$$

Using Table 2.6, if we want to find a regression equation for predicting push-ups from chin-up scores, we find that

$$b = \frac{1381 - [(57)(212)/10]}{427 - [(57)^2/10]}$$

$$= \frac{1381 - 1208.4}{427 - 324.9} = \frac{172.6}{102.1} = 1.69$$

and

$$a = 21.1 - (1.69)(5.7)$$

$$= 21.2 - 9.63 = 11.57$$

Therefore, the regression equation is

$$\hat{Y} = 11.57 + 1.69X$$

The $b = 1.69$ in this equation means that for each additional chin-up that an individual can do, we would predict an increase of 1.69 push-ups that he or she would be able to do. The value $a = 11.57$ in this equation means that we would predict that an individual who can do no chin-ups would be able to do 11.57 push-ups. To apply this equation, if a student were to do 6 chin-ups we would predict that he or she could do $[11.57 + 1.69(6)] = 11.57 + 10.14 = 21.71$, or 22 push-ups.

A graphic representation of this example is presented in Figure 2.19. Each dot on the graph in Figure 2.19 represents a pair of scores obtained by an individual. For example, the circled dot represents the person who did 9 chin-ups and 29 push-ups. The line represents the determined regression line. This line is called the *best fit* line, which means that it is the line that allows the most accurate prediction of Y-scores from X-scores. The correlation coefficient tells us how well this regression line fits the pairs of scores; this is the connection between regression and correlation. Also note that the point representing the mean of X and the mean of Y ($\overline{X}$, $\overline{Y}$) always falls on the regression line. Thus to draw the regression line one needs only to determine the y-intercept, a, and the mean point for X and Y ($\overline{X}$, $\overline{Y}$) and pass a line through these two points.

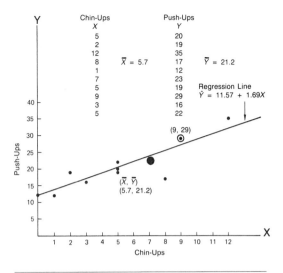

Figure 2.19 Graphic presentation of a regression equation.

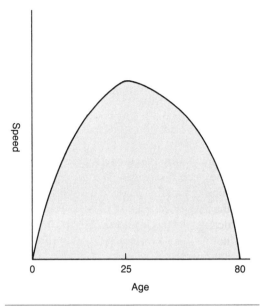

Figure 2.20 Relationship between age and speed.

Regression or prediction is important in the development of many tests in physical education. Variables that are difficult to measure can often be predicted on the basis of a variable that is not so difficult to measure. For example, $\dot{V}O_2$max has generally been shown to be an excellent indicator of cardiovascular fitness. To actually measure $\dot{V}O_2$max, however, requires a great deal of time and expensive lab equipment. Therefore, a prediction or regression equation for predicting $\dot{V}O_2$max from scores on a 12-minute run for distance or from some other more easily measured variable would be most helpful. Cooper did this in 1968 using the following original regression equation determined from 115 US Air Force male officers:

$$\dot{V}O_2max = -11.2872 + 35.9712 \text{ (Distance in}$$

miles for 12-minute run-walk)

Therefore, if we have the distance in miles that a US Air Force male officer ran in 12 minutes, we can *estimate* his $\dot{V}O_2$max. For illustrative purposes, if officer Jones ran 1.375 miles in 12 minutes, then we would predict his $\dot{V}O_2$max as

$$\dot{V}O_2max = -11.2872 + 35.9712(1.375)$$

$$= 38.1732 \text{ ml/kg/min}$$

Cooper found a correlation coefficient of 0.897 for the relationship between these two variables, so we would expect our estimated $\dot{V}O_2$max to be quite accurate.

It must be pointed out that regression equations and correlations generally should be developed for specific groups of persons. For instance, the equation given above was developed on US Air Force male officers and should be used only for similar types of persons.

Shape of Relationships

Thus far, only straight-line regression and correlation have been discussed. Sometimes, however, the relationship between two variables cannot be represented by a straight line. These relationships are called *curvilinear*. The relationship between age and speed is an example of a curvilinear relationship. We expect an average person's speed to improve with age until about the age of 25. After the age of 25, we expect speed to decline. Figure 2.20 shows this graphically.

As can be seen in Figure 2.20, a straight line does not fit this relationship very well. Although it is important to be aware of possible curvilinear relationships, the procedures for determining curvilinear correlations are well beyond the scope of this text. However, one should graphically plot his or her data to at least determine if a linear relationship is a reasonable expectation. If it does not appear reasonable, a statistician should be consulted.

Cautions in Correlation Interpretation

All linear correlations should be viewed with caution. The possible existence of a curvilinear relationship is only one reason for caution; another is that a correlation coefficient represents the relationship only for the range of scores found in the variables. For example, if we relate age with speed and our subjects range in age from 10 to 25, then our correlation can be interpreted only for that age range. To extend it beyond that range is obviously dangerous. Additionally, a correlation coefficient and regression equation should be used only for subjects who are similar to those who were used to determine the correlation and regression. This is why in our earlier example on $\dot{V}O_2$max and the 12-minute run we were careful to indicate that the regression equation was used for an individual from the same population on which the regression was determined.

The size of a correlation coefficient depends greatly on the number of pairs of scores from which it is determined. A small number of score pairs will result in a higher correlation coefficient than a large number of score pairs because it is easier to fit a line to a small number of points than to a large number of points.

A correlation coefficient indicates only the relationship between variables and does not necessarily indicate that a cause-and-effect phenomenon is in effect. For example, teachers' salaries and the amount of liquor sold in a state have been shown to be fairly highly correlated. But this does not indicate that one is a direct result of the other. Finally, the variance for each variable affects the size of a correlation coefficient. If a variable is highly homogeneous (little variance), then finding anything that is highly correlated to it is extremely difficult.

Other Statistical Techniques

Numerous other statistical techniques are used in measurement and evaluation. Because this is not a statistics text, however, only three other commonly used techniques will be very briefly introduced. For more detailed information on these topics, consult the references at the end of this chapter.

Multiple Correlation and Regression

We can extend our discussion of regression and correlation by considering the possibility of two or more easily measured variables predicting a variable that is most difficult to measure. This is precisely what is done in multiple regression: Two or more variables are used to predict some other variable. The regression equation is written as

$$\hat{Y} = a + b_1 x_1 + b_2 x_2 + \ldots b_p x_p$$

where b_i represents the weight or importance

of that particular predictor. How well the *X*-variables predict the *Y*-variable is determined by a multiple correlation coefficient, denoted by *R*, which ranges from 0 to +1.00.

This technique has been applied in physical education in determining the percentage of lean body mass in an individual. The direct methods of determining percentage of lean body mass (i.e., underwater weighing and scintillation counter) either are extremely time-consuming or require very expensive equipment. Exercise scientists have discovered that by taking several skinfold measures and calculating multiple regression equations, the percentage of lean body mass can be estimated fairly accurately. The exact nature of these equations is given in chapter 7.

Factor Analysis

Factor analysis is another method of correlation that begins with a set of correlation coefficients between many tests thought to be part of a certain domain. These tests are mathematically arranged into clusters on the basis of one or more common ingredients; that is, tests that are determined to measure something in common are grouped together. This group, cluster, or factor is then usually given a name describing the common ingredient. Usually several (4 to 10) of these factors are identified.

Factor analysis is a useful statistical tool in measurement and evaluation when we are attempting to determine the underlying ingredients in a complex domain. An example of the application of this tool is in the development of Kenyon's Attitude Toward Physical Activity Questionnaire. Kenyon (1968a, 1968b) identified six dimensions that he and other experts thought were the ingredients in people's attitudes toward physical activity. Questions were written for each of the dimensions and administered to a large number of subjects. The subjects' scores were factor analyzed, and 5 of the 6 hypothesized dimensions were found to be valid.

Kenyon's questionnaire is presented in chapter 10.

Comparison of Means

In physical education we occasionally want to compare the performance of one group with a particular standard of performance or the performance of a second group. For example, we might want to compare the performance on a 2-mile run of a group of people who used interval training along with long-distance running to the performance of another group of people who used only long-distance running for their training. In order to compare the performances of these two groups, we would compare the means of each group. However, any differences detected between the means of the two groups might not be large enough for us to conclude that the difference is larger than we would expect it to be by chance; that is, the difference may not be a *significant difference*. The procedures necessary to determine significant differences, as opposed to differences attributable to chance, are called *t*-tests. *t*-tests are beyond the scope of this text. We recommend, however, that all physical educators complete a statistics course in which *t*-test procedures are thoroughly presented.

Analysis of Variance

The term *analysis of variance* actually refers to an entire family of statistical techniques that are extremely useful in physical education research and the scientific construction of physical performance tests. These techniques allow us to compare performances across several groups, which is an extension of the *t*-test procedure. More specifically, analysis of variance techniques are particularly useful in establishing the reliability of performance tests and, to a lesser extent, in establishing the validity of tests. No attempt is made in this text to present all the details of these techniques. However, an example of an analysis of variance problem for determining test reliability is presented in Appendix E. If further study into this area is desired, the text by Safrit (1986) or the text by Dotson and Kirkendall (1974) should be consulted for excellent coverage of this topic.

Review Questions

1. What is the basic reason for studying and understanding statistics?
2. What is the major goal of statistics?
3. When one has information about every individual in a group, what statistical methods are used to describe the group?
4. When one has information about only a representative part of a total group, what statistical methods are used to describe the total group?
5. Why is it more common for the practicing physical educator to use descriptive statistics rather than inferential statistics to describe a group?
6. What is a distribution?
7. What is a frequency distribution?
8. How does one obtain the (a) relative frequency, (b) frequency percent, (c) cumulative frequency, (d) relative cumulative frequency, and (e) percentile rank of a distribution?
9. What does the percentile rank of a score represent?
10. Why is the percentile rank of a score a useful representation of that score?
11. What are histograms, polygons, and ogives?
12. What are the three most common measures of central tendency? Define each of these measures.
13. Why is the mean an excellent measure of central tendency?
14. What are the four measures of variability presented in this chapter? Define each of these measures of variability.
15. What are the three standard scores presented in this chapter? How is each determined?
16. What are the mean and standard deviation of (a) a z-score distribution, (b) a T score distribution, and (c) a 6-σ score distribution?
17. Why would one wish to change scores to standard scores?
18. The normal curve is mathematically defined and may be used to determine the percentage of scores expected between any two points. What is the relative measure usually determined by the practicing physical educator in using this concept?
19. What is a correlation coefficient?
20. What does the square of the correlation coefficient represent?
21. Why should all linear correlations be viewed with caution?

Problems and Exercises

1. A physical education teacher measured the height of 66 juniors at the local high school. The teacher measured each student's height in centimeters with a stadiometer and obtained the following results:

Student	Height (cm)	Student	Height (cm)	Student	Height (cm)
S1	183.4	S23	185.4	S45	180.1
S2	186.2	S24	172.0	S46	170.4

S3	177.3	S25	170.2	S47	186.4
S4	169.9	S26	175.5	S48	178.8
S5	171.7	S27	177.6	S49	174.5
S6	181.6	S28	180.1	S50	192.5
S7	171.2	S29	188.2	S51	174.8
S8	184.4	S30	176.0	S52	185.9
S9	171.7	S31	174.8	S53	193.6
S10	172.5	S32	174.5	S54	179.6
S11	159.3	S33	175.0	S55	177.0
S12	177.0	S34	173.5	S56	161.0
S13	164.1	S35	172.0	S57	171.7
S14	173.0	S36	172.0	S58	178.8
S15	184.4	S37	179.3	S59	182.9
S16	171.2	S38	176.5	S60	166.4
S17	175.5	S39	165.9	S61	191.3
S18	180.9	S40	171.2	S62	177.6
S19	167.6	S41	174.8	S63	187.7
S20	181.1	S42	174.8	S64	167.9
S21	183.6	S43	168.4	S65	170.4
S22	181.9	S44	179.6	S66	160.0

a. Calculate a mean and standard deviation.
b. Calculate a z-score for each student.
c. Calculate a T score for each student.
d. Calculate a 6-σ score for each student.
e. Calculate a range for the distribution.
f. Develop a frequency distribution table. Use an interval of 1 cm change in height from low to high score.
g. Construct an ogive for percentile rank and height.
h. Estimate the percentile rank of Students S1, S2, S4, S11, and S53 using the area under a normal curve. Compare this estimated percentile rank with the actual calculated percentile rank from your frequency distribution table.

Answers:
1.a. $\overline{X} = 176.3$ cm; $\sigma = 7.43$ cm

	b. z-score	c. T score	d. 6-σ score
S1	.96	59.6	66.0
S2	1.33	63.3	72.2
S3	.13	51.3	52.2
S4	−.86	41.4	35.7
S5	−.62	43.8	39.7
S6	.71	57.1	61.9
S7	−.69	43.1	38.5
S8	1.09	60.9	68.2
S9	−.62	43.8	39.7
S10	−.51	44.9	41.5
S11	−2.28	27.2	12.0
S12	.09	50.9	51.6
S13	−1.64	33.6	22.6

S14	−.44	45.6	42.6
S15	1.09	60.9	68.2
S16	−.69	43.1	38.6
S17	−.12	48.8	48.2
S18	.62	56.2	60.3
S19	−1.17	38.3	30.5
S20	.65	−56.5	60.8
S21	.98	59.8	66.4
S22	.75	57.5	62.6
S23	1.22	62.2	70.4
S24	−.58	44.2	40.4
S25	−.82	41.8	36.3
S26	−.11	48.9	48.2
S27	.17	51.7	52.9
S28	.51	55.1	58.5
S29	1.60	66.0	76.7
S30	−.04	49.6	49.3
S31	−.20	48.0	46.6
S32	−.24	47.6	46.0
S33	−.17	48.3	47.1
S34	−.38	46.2	43.7
S35	−.58	44.2	40.4
S36	−.58	44.2	40.4
S37	.40	54.0	56.7
S38	.03	50.3	50.4
S39	−1.40	36.0	26.7
S40	−.69	43.1	38.6
S41	−.20	48.0	46.6
S42	−.20	48.0	46.6
S43	−1.06	39.4	32.3
S44	.44	54.4	57.4
S45	.51	55.1	58.5
S46	−.79	42.1	36.8
S47	1.36	63.6	72.7
S48	.34	53.4	55.6
S49	−.24	47.6	46.0
S50	2.18	71.8	86.3
S51	−.20	48.0	46.6
S52	1.29	62.9	71.5
S53	2.33	73.3	88.8
S54	.44	54.4	57.4
S55	.09	50.9	51.6
S56	−2.05	29.5	15.7
S57	−.62	43.8	39.7
S58	.34	53.4	55.6
S59	.89	58.9	64.8
S60	−1.33	36.7	27.8
S61	2.02	70.2	83.7
S62	.17	51.7	52.9

S63	1.53	65.3	75.6
S64	−1.13	38.7	31.2
S65	−.79	42.1	36.8
S66	−2.19	28.1	13.4

e. 34.3 cm

f.

Height (cm)	f	Rel f	$f\%$	Cum f	Rel Cum f	%tile rank
193-193.9	1	.015	1.5	66	1.000	100
192-192.9	1	.015	1.5	65	.984	98
191-191.9	1	.015	1.5	64	.969	97
190-190.9	0	.000	0.0	63	.954	95
189-189.9	0	.000	0.0	63	.954	95
188-188.9	1	.015	1.5	63	.954	95
187-187.9	1	.015	1.5	62	.939	94
186-186.9	2	.030	3.0	61	.924	92
185-185.9	2	.030	3.0	59	.893	89
184-184.9	2	.030	3.0	57	.863	86
183-183.9	2	.030	3.0	55	.833	83
182-182.9	1	.015	1.5	53	.803	80
181-181.9	3	.045	4.5	52	.787	79
180-180.9	3	.045	4.5	49	.742	74
179-179.9	3	.045	4.5	46	.696	70
178-178.9	2	.030	3.0	43	.651	65
177-177.9	5	.075	7.5	41	.621	62
176-176.9	2	.030	3.0	36	.545	55
175-175.9	3	.045	4.5	34	.515	52
174-174.9	6	.090	9.0	31	.469	47
173-173.9	2	.030	3.0	25	.378	38
172-172.9	4	.060	6.0	23	.348	35
171-171.9	6	.090	9.0	19	.287	29
170-170.9	3	.045	4.5	13	.196	20
169-169.9	1	.015	1.5	10	.151	15
168-168.9	1	.015	1.5	9	.136	14
167-167.9	2	.030	3.0	8	.121	12
166-166.9	1	.015	1.5	6	.090	9
165-165.9	1	.015	1.5	5	.075	8
164-164.9	1	.015	1.5	4	.060	6
163-163.9	0	.000	0.0	3	.045	5
162-162.9	0	.000	0.0	3	.045	5
161-161.9	1	.015	1.5	3	.045	5
160-160.9	1	.015	1.5	2	.030	3
159-159.9	1	.015	1.5	1	.015	2
Below 159	0	.000	0.0	0	.000	0
Total	66					

   h. S1 estimated percentile rank   = 83%
      Actual calculated percentile rank = 83%
      S2 estimated percentile rank   = 91%
      Actual calculated percentile rank = 92%
      S4 estimated percentile rank   = 19%
      Actual calculated percentile rank = 15%
      S11 estimated percentile rank   = 1%
      Actual calculated percentile rank = 2%
      S53 estimated percentile rank   = 99%
      Actual calculated percentile rank = 100%

2. The same physical education teacher as in Problem 1
   measured the weight of the same 66 students. Using a
   metric weighing scale, the instructor measured each
   student's weight in kilograms with the following results:

Student	Weight (kgwt)	Student	Weight (kgwt)	Student	Weight (kgwt)
S1	78.9	S23	78.3	S45	68.6
S2	92.4	S24	69.4	S46	79.4
S3	71.9	S25	69.5	S47	71.4
S4	73.5	S26	63.4	S48	64.5
S5	77.0	S27	74.5	S49	75.6
S6	92.4	S28	86.1	S50	86.6
S7	67.0	S29	68.8	S51	77.2
S8	85.8	S30	71.4	S52	89.9
S9	69.2	S31	79.3	S53	88.0
S10	89.6	S32	69.1	S54	79.4
S11	60.3	S33	79.5	S55	68.2
S12	67.7	S34	68.6	S56	72.7
S13	60.9	S35	76.2	S57	73.4
S14	66.7	S36	74.0	S58	76.6
S15	78.4	S37	80.3	S59	81.4
S16	72.5	S38	72.2	S60	61.1
S17	92.6	S39	70.1	S61	90.7
S18	84.3	S40	77.0	S62	81.3
S19	62.9	S41	68.5	S63	82.4
S20	64.8	S42	76.5	S64	74.4
S21	95.6	S43	74.7	S65	65.0
S22	78.7	S44	94.1	S66	59.0

   a. Calculate a mean and standard deviation.
   b. Calculate a z-score for each student.
   c. Calculate a T score for each student.
   d. Calculate a 6-σ score for each student.
   e. Calculate a range for the distribution.
   f. Develop a frequency distribution table. Use an interval
      of 1 kg change in weight from low to high score.
   g. Construct an ogive for percentile rank and weight.

    h. Estimate the percentile rank of Students S1, S2, S4, S11, and S53 using the area under a normal curve. Compare this estimated percentile rank with the actual calculated percentile rank from your frequency distribution table.

3. Convert the mean ($\overline{X}$) and the standard deviation (σ) height found in Problem 1 to inches.
Answer:
$\overline{X}$ = 69.4 in.; σ = 2.9 in.

4. Convert the mean ($\overline{X}$) and the standard deviation (σ) weight found in Problem 2 to pounds.

5. Calculate a Pearson r for the paired scores of height and weight in Problems 1 and 2. Develop a predictive equation for predicting weight from height.
Answer:
r_{xy} = 0.660; $y = -53.5 + .73x$

6. What is the percentage of shared variance between height and weight of the 66 students in Problems 1 and 2?

7. A physical education teacher working with 10 early elementary children with problems in motor performance decided to run a Spearman rank-order correlation coefficient between IQ score and strength. The following rankings on the two tests occurred:

Student	Rank on IQ Test	Rank on Strength Test
S1	3	9
S2	8	5
S3	10	10
S4	2	8
S5	7	7
S6	1	3
S7	6	4
S8	9	2
S9	4	6
S10	5	1

What is the rho between these paired rankings?
Answer:
rho = 0.042

8. The same physical education teacher as in Problem 7 decided to run a Spearman rank-order correlation coefficient between IQ score and perceptual motor performance with the same 10 children. The following rankings on the two tests occurred:

Student	Rank on IQ test	Rank on Perceptual Motor Test
S1	3	4
S2	8	7
S3	10	8
S4	2	5
S5	7	6
S6	1	1
S7	6	3
S8	9	10
S9	4	2
S10	5	9

What is the rho between these paired rankings?

Bibliography

Alder, H.L., & Roessler, E.B. (1968). *Introduction to probability and statistics*. San Francisco: Freeman.

Cooper, K.H. (1968). A means of assessing maximal oxygen intake correlation between field and treadmill testing. *Journal of the American Medical Association, 203*(3), 135-138.

Dixon, W.J., & Massey, Jr., F.J. (1969). *Introduction to statistical analysis* (3rd ed.). New York: McGraw-Hill.

Dotson, C.O., & Kirkendall, D.R. (1974). *Statistics for physical education, health, and recreation*. New York: Harper & Row.

Ferguson, G.A. (1971). *Statistical analysis in psychology and education*. New York: McGraw-Hill.

Hall, P.G. (1971). *Elementary statistics*. New York: Wiley & Sons.

Hammond, K.R., Householder, J.E., & Castellan, Jr., N.J. (1970). *Introduction to the statistical method*. New York: Knopf.

Hays, W.L. (1963). *Statistics*. New York: Holt, Rinehart and Winston.

Kenyon, G.S. (1968a). A conceptual model for characterizing physical activity. *Research Quarterly, 39*(1), 96-105.

Kenyon, G.S. (1968b). Six scales for assessing attitude toward physical activity. *Research Quarterly, 39*(3), 566-574.

Marascuilo, L.A. (1971). *Statistical methods for behavioral science research*. New York: McGraw-Hill.

Minimum, E.W. (1970). *Statistical reasoning in psychology and education*. New York: Wiley & Sons.

Ostle, B. (1963). *Statistics in research*. Ames: Iowa State University Press.

Remington, R.D., & Schork, M.A. (1970). *Statistics with applications to the biological and health sciences*. Englewood Cliffs, NJ: Prentice-Hall.

Runyon, R.P., & Haber, A. (1971). *Fundamentals of behavioral statistics*. Reading, MA: Addison-Wesley.

Safrit, M.J. (1986). *Evaluation in physical education* (3rd ed.). Englewood Cliffs, NJ: Prentice-Hall.

Siegel, S. (1956). *Nonparametric statistics for the behavioral sciences*. New York: McGraw-Hill.

Winer, B.J. (1971). *Statistical principles in experimental design*. New York: McGraw-Hill.

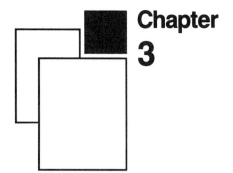

Chapter
3

Criteria for the Selection and Construction of Tests

The selection and construction of tests is one of the most important phases of a measurement and evaluation program. If poor tests are selected or constructed, the evaluation program will inevitably be weak as well. In this chapter the criteria to be used in selecting, constructing, and judging the quality of tests are discussed in detail.

Technical Criteria— Validity, Reliability, Objectivity

The three most important characteristics of a test are clearly its validity, reliability, and objectivity. These criteria are prerequisite to all other criteria for test selection or construction. *Validity* is defined as how well a test measures what it is intended to measure; *reliability* is the degree of consistency with which a test measures what it measures; and *objectivity* is the degree of agreement in scoring among different testers. No test is ever perfectly valid, reliable, and objective. However, the greater a test's validity, reliability, and objectivity, the greater the test's

usefulness and value will be. For a test to be valid, it must also be reliable and objective. In other words, a test cannot measure what it is intended to measure unless it does so consistently regardless of who administers or scores the test.

Validity

As can be seen from Figure 3.1, validity is an all-encompassing term. Traditionally, however, the term *validity* is used primarily in terms of whether a test is relevant and applicable to a particular situation. Does the test actually measure what it is intended to measure? Will the test results tell us who is best, next best, and so on? Will the test help us to determine who has mastered a unit and who has not? These are the most important questions we can ask about any test. Within this context, then, a synonym for validity might be *relevance*. If a test has poor validity, or relevance, it is a waste of time to use it. In determining the validity of a test, we are actually determining its fairness and appropriateness. Throughout the remainder of this text, we will generally use the term *validity* in its traditional sense of *relevance* but will

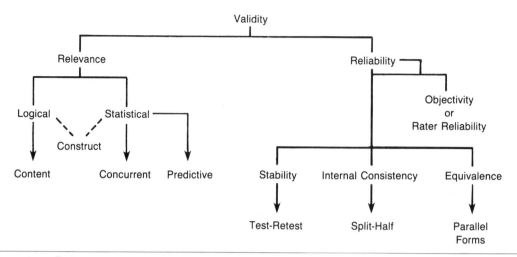

Figure 3.1 Relationship of relevance and reliability to validity. *Note.* From *Measurement for Evaluation in Physical Education* by T.A. Baumgartner and A.S. Jackson, 1975, Boston: Houghton Mifflin. Copyright 1975 by Houghton Mifflin. Reprinted by permission.

continue to remind the reader that validity is actually an all-encompassing concept.

Content or Logical Validity. One way to determine a test's validity is by using logic or professional judgment. This is usually the first step in constructing a valid test. If a test contains items that logically measure the skill or ability we wish to measure, then we say it has *logical* or *content validity.* For example, if we want to measure baseball ability, we determine the skill components in baseball and try to construct a test whose items will logically measure each component. The components of the skill might be determined by a single teacher or by a panel of experts. Suppose, for example, that the important skill components in baseball are fielding, throwing, and hitting. We would then, either on our own or through a panel of experts, devise test items that logically measure each component. As one test item, perhaps we would have the fielding of ten ground balls on a smooth infield and count the number of errors that each subject made. For the hitting component, we might have a batting test in which the batter swings at ten machine-pitched balls, scoring a

point for each ball hit. These test items appear to measure baseball skill logically and thus have content validity.

We can assess the content validity of written tests in much the same way that we do for physical performance tests: by analyzing what we wish to measure and developing test items that logically measure it. Examining course outlines, analyzing textbooks, and reviewing other tests on the same topic are methods commonly used to achieve content validity. Establishing content validity is extremely important in the selection and construction of tests. A more in-depth discussion on how to determine or ensure content validity in the construction of motor tests and written tests is presented in chapters 7 and 9.

Content validity is established by assumption or definition; hence it does not determine the *degree* to which a test measures what it is intended to measure. In other words, content validity is essential but not sufficient. If we are to determine the degree of a test's validity, we need ways to establish its numerical validity. Although test items and test scores may be determined subjectively, the degree of a test's validity must be determined objectively.

Construct Validity. As indicated in Figure 3.1, *construct validity* is a statistical method used to verify content validity. Specifically, a construct or structure of some ability or phenomenon derived from logical thought is proposed; then a statistical check is made to determine whether that construct actually exists. Generally, we are not interested in the validity of each item of the test but are more concerned about whether the test *as a whole* measures the identified components of the ability or phenomenon. We may want to measure psychological constructs such as anxiety, extroversion, or emotional stability. In the area of physical performance we may want to identify constructs such as reaction time, agility, or balance.

Three techniques commonly used to establish construct validity are factor analysis, multiple regression of test batteries, and testing differences between extreme groups. Each of these techniques is more appropriate to some situations than to others. Because the mathematical derivations and calculations of these techniques are complex and beyond the scope of this text, only a brief overview of each is presented here.

In studies using factor analysis to establish construct validity, a theoretical construct or structure of the phenomenon under consideration is established. This is usually done by dividing the phenomenon into various components. Several test items are then prepared for each component, and all items are administered to a group of subjects. The statistical technique of factor analysis is applied to the test scores, and the factors obtained are compared to the proposed components of the phenomenon. This comparison is subjective, but it does give evidence of the construct validity of the test items. Factor analysis techniques attempt to identify or confirm constructs or factors that have moderate to low interrelationships, which helps to eliminate duplicate measurement of the same phenomenon. One of the best examples of the use of construct validity in physical education

is the development of Kenyon's Attitude Toward Physical Activity Instrument (Kenyon, 1968a, 1968b). Kenyon empirically identified six constructs and then verified their existence through factor analytic techniques. This instrument, with its six constructs, or factors, is presented in part in chapter 10.

Sometimes a battery of test items is proposed as a measure of some complex skill or phenomenon. If an acceptable criterion can be determined, then multiple regression techniques can be used to determine if the proposed battery is the proper construct to measure the phenomenon. In this procedure, the standardized regression weights obtained in the multiple regression are used to indicate each test item's relative degree of importance. The validity of many of the physical fitness and motor fitness tests currently in use was established in this way.

Testing differences between extreme groups is the last method for determining construct validity. In this method, it is known in advance that two groups differ greatly in their ability levels on some variable of interest. A test is proposed to measure this ability and is then administered to each group. The average score for each group is then determined. If the average scores of the two groups differ sufficiently in the direction of known ability differences, then the proposed test is deemed to have construct validity.

Some sports tests have established construct validity through the extreme groups comparison method. Usually, the scores of varsity or professional performers on the proposed test are compared with novices' scores on the test. For example, a proposed badminton test could be administered to a group of nationally ranked badminton players and to a group of people who have just learned the game. If the difference between the average scores of the two groups on the proposed test is large enough, then the test is determined to have some validity. Also, in mastery learning the construct should differentiate between masters and nonmasters.

Determining how large the difference between the two groups' average scores must be in order to establish construct validity requires the application of inferential statistics, which are not presented in this text. Objective means to determine construct validity are available, however, and the reader is referred to the statistics references in chapter 2 for more detailed information on such techniques.

Concurrent Validity. One empirical or statistical means to determine the validity of a proposed test is to establish a criterion for the variable we wish to measure and then determine how closely the test relates to or predicts this criterion. This form of validity is called *concurrent* or *criterion-related validity*. In establishing concurrent validity, the most important step is determining what criterion will be used.

One commonly used criterion is *expert opinion*. A panel of judges rates students' abilities in the skill (variable) under consideration. Although this rating is subjective, we can provide guidelines to the raters or judges to establish some assurance that they are rating the same skill components. After an overall rating is obtained from the judges, the proposed test is given to the same students. A regression equation to predict the judges' ratings from the proposed test is then determined. The correlation coefficient associated with this regression equation is the validity coefficient. In other words, we are determining how accurately the proposed test predicts the judges' overall ratings.

Another criterion commonly used to determine concurrent validity is *tournament results*. This method is particularly effective for determining the validity of skills tests for specific sports. For example, to determine the validity of a proposed tennis skill test, first we would conduct a tournament, such as a ladder or double elimination tournament, to determine the ranking of the players' tennis abilities. We would then administer the proposed test to these same players and determine the regression equation for predicting tournament rankings from the test scores. We would also calculate the correlation between the two sets of scores. This correlation coefficient indicates the degree of validity of our test; that is, the correlation coefficient indicates the test's ability to rank the abilities of players in the same order as the tournament results.

Another means of establishing concurrent validity is to use an *established valid test* as the criterion. The validity coefficient is then the correlation between the proposed test and the established test. The regression equation accompanying this correlation coefficient predicts the scores on the established test by use of scores on the proposed test. An example of this procedure was presented in chapter 2 when the 12-minute run was used to predict $\dot{V}O_2max$. In that example, the regression equation determined was

$$\dot{V}O_2 = -11.2878 + 35.9712 \text{ (Distance in miles for 12-minute run-walk)}$$

The accompanying correlation coefficient, $r = .897$, indicates a high degree of validity.

Although the established test method is commonly used, validity coefficients determined through this method should be viewed with extreme caution. Because the established test is undoubtedly not completely valid, any relationship between it and the new test may be partially due to the new test's relationship to the invalid portion of the established test. This possibility is even greater if the established test is in its third, fourth, or later "generation."

The veracity of our initial statement that the most important step in establishing concurrent validity is the determination of the criterion to be used should now be evident. A proposed test can never be better than the criterion selected because in establishing validity we determine how well the proposed test predicts the criterion.

How large a validity coefficient is considered acceptable for validity? Although acceptable size of the coefficient depends on the particular situation, some guidelines can be given. In general, if the validity coefficient is determined on a group of 100 or more individuals, the following rating might be used:

Validity rating	Correlation coefficient
Excellent	.80-1.00
High	.70- .79
Average or Fair	.50- .69
Unacceptable	.00- .49

Again, these coefficients should be viewed with great caution. The acceptability of any validity coefficient depends on the purpose, situation, and intended use of the test as well as the appropriateness of the criterion.

Predictive Validity. If a test is to be used to predict individuals' future performances, then *predictive validity* needs to be determined. Predictive validity involves the use of a criterion to be predicted, such as later behavior. For example, if we want a test that will predict success in playing basketball, we administer the proposed test to a group of students. At a later date, we rate their success at playing the game. The correlation between the test scores and the playing success ratings indicates the test's predictive validity. If the correlation coefficient is satisfactory, we determine a regression equation for predicting success. This regression equation would then be used with a new group, and if we successfully predicted the relative success of this new group, we can then conclude that the test's predictive validity has been truly established.

Although we would be interested in the predictive validity of a test used to select members of athletic teams, usually predictive validity cannot be accurately determined. To establish true predictive statistical validity for a test to select athletic teams, it would be necessary to keep everyone who tried out for a team on the team for at least part of the season. If some people are cut from a team, we can no longer determine whether they would have contributed successfully to the team.

In actual situations, the predictive criterion (actual playing ability) is determined by a player either making or not making the team. If those who ultimately make the team tend to receive high scores on the test and those who are "cut" receive low scores, then we can conclude that the proposed test has substantial predictive validity.

Universities sometimes use written tests for predictive purposes. Examples include the Scholastic Aptitude Test (SAT) used to predict success in college and the Graduate Record Exam (GRE) used to predict success in graduate school. These tests have many of the same limitations just described, and many universities using them have been criticized for doing so.

Factors Affecting Validity. Numerous factors may affect the validity of a test. Physical educators must be aware of and consider these factors in selecting and constructing tests.

A test is valid only for a particular group at a particular time for a particular purpose. There is no such thing as a generally valid test. For example, a test that is valid for college students may not be valid for elementary students. Similarly, a skill test may be valid when used with beginners but invalid if used with advanced performers. Another test may be valid for middle-class white American girls 10 to 13 years of age but invalid for other groups. Thus the culture or unique characteristics of a group often affect a test's validity for that group.

Written tests sometimes contain inadvertent response sets or answer patterns. For example, all of the correct answers on a multiple choice test might be letter *a*. This factor could affect the responses made by persons taking the test and thus affect the test's validity. Also, if the directions given for a test are unclear or complicated, the test's validity may be adversely affected.

In testing motor performance, students' familiarity with a test may affect the validity of their test scores. For example, if the 12-minute run is to be administered as a cardiovascular endurance test and the examinees have never run 12 minutes before, they will not know how to pace themselves, and their test results will be partially invalidated. Thus individuals conducting motor performance testing should typically allow at least one practice trial of the test.

As illustrated in Figure 3.1 at the beginning of this chapter, to be valid a test must also be reliable and objective. Thus low reliability or objectivity will adversely affect a test's validity. If a test does not measure accurately or consistently, it cannot be expected to measure validly. On the other hand, if a test is valid, it must have some degree of reliability. As we shall see, however, reliability does not ensure validity.

Reliability

The second most important criterion to be considered in test construction and selection is *reliability*. Reliability is the degree of consistency with which a test measures what it measures. Another way to think of a test's reliability is in terms of whether the test measures the true average performance of an individual.

We might represent an individual's obtained test score as

Obtained score = True score + Error score

where the *true score* represents the performance level that is truly indicative of the individual's ability and the *error score* represents the part of the individual's obtained score that is due to one or more factors other than the individual's true ability. If a test is perfectly reliable, the obtained scores are equal to the true scores. When a test is measuring true scores, a person taking the test more than once will score the

same every time. Most reliability methods are based on this principle. Specifically, the total variance in the obtained scores is found, and then the amount of variance due to true performance and the amount due to error performance are estimated. Using the previous equation, we can represent this as

$$\text{Variance of obtained score} = \text{True score variance} + \text{Error score variance}$$

or

$$\sigma_{os}^2 = \sigma_t^2 + \sigma_e^2$$

Theoretically, then, reliability is the percentage of total obtained variance accounted for by the true score variance, that is,

$$\text{Reliability} = \frac{\sigma_t^2}{\sigma_{os}^2} = \frac{\sigma_{os}^2 - \sigma_e^2}{\sigma_{os}^2}$$

As might be expected, these reliabilities are expressed as correlation coefficients.

Two major areas or classifications of error contribute to the error score and error variance. These two classifications are *measurement error* and *systematic error*. Measurement error refers to changes in performance scores due to inaccuracies in equipment, scorer errors, and errors in test administration. Systematic error is the change in performance or behavior due to biological factors. Individuals are likely to perform differently on motor skills from day to day or trial to trial because precise consistency of performance is not natural to human behavior.

To illustrate these two types of errors, suppose that three trials of the standing long jump are administered to Joan and that her three scores are 62, 58, and 63 inches. These variations in performance might arise from inherent physiological and/or psychological factors or result from inaccuracies in scoring, such as a loose mat on one trial or the scorer's reading the numbers incorrectly. The physiological and/or psychological factors are examples of systematic error, whereas the other factors are measurement errors.

Both systematic and measurement error affect the reliability of a test. Measurement errors are typically controllable and should be eliminated or greatly reduced through the careful administration of tests. Systematic error is generally more of a problem in motor performance testing than it is in administering written tests because many motor performance tests consist of repeating more than one trial of the same task. Sometimes, too, these trials need to be repeated on different days. Systematic error is unlikely to occur with written tests because if a test is administered repeatedly, students are likely to remember the questions from previous administrations.

Due to this difference between written cognitive tests and motor performance tests, techniques appropriate for determining the reliability of the one may not always be appropriate for the other. In other words, reliability techniques that do not distinguish between measurement error and systematic error may be appropriate for written tests but not entirely adequate for use with motor performance tests. The first four methods for determining reliability presented in the following sections are most appropriate for determining a reliability coefficient for written tests because they make no distinction between or determination of the two types of error. It should be noted, however, that in practice these written test techniques are frequently applied to motor performance tests. Although inappropriate, this practice may not be too serious a problem provided that the test user realizes its potential limitations and practices all precautions to prevent measurement errors.

The appropriate methods for determining the different types of errors in motor performance tests require the application of statistical techniques such as analysis of variance that

are beyond the scope of this book. Thus, after the presentation of reliability techniques for written tests, only a brief overview is given for techniques to determine the reliability of motor performance tests. This introduction should be sufficient, however, to help the reader begin to select and/or construct motor performance tests intelligently.

Test-Retest Reliability. One means of estimating the reliability or consistency of a test is to administer it on two different occasions to the same group (test, then retest) and then determine the correlation between the two sets of scores. This correlation is called the *coefficient of stability*. The time interval between the two administrations of the test should be relatively short; that is, long enough that individuals are not likely to repeat error performance, but not so long that they may either forget or learn during the interval. In all cases, the conditions for the test administration should be precisely the same both times the test is administered.

It is particularly tempting for physical educators to administer physical performance tests on the same day in order to determine test-retest reliability. Baumgartner (1969), however, has shown that same-day test-retest coefficients consistently overestimate the reliability of a test. Consequently, test-retest administrations should be made on different days.

Equivalent Forms Reliability. Test reliability can also be estimated by determining the correlation between scores on two equivalent forms of a test taken by the same people. The correlation coefficient in this case is called the *coefficient of equivalence*. In this method, the two tests must be exactly the same in terms of length, difficulty, content, means, standard deviations, and validities. Such test equivalencies are difficult to obtain, however, and so this reliability method is not particularly practical, especially for motor performance tests.

Split-Half Reliability. One of the disadvantages of the test-retest method for determining test reliability is the difficulty of assuring identical testing conditions during each administration. Also, administering two versions of the same test is costly in terms of time and materials. To avoid these disadvantages, methods have been proposed to determine reliability through one test administration. The most common of these methods is the split-half technique. In this method, a test is administered to a group of students, and the test results are then split into two equal halves for scoring. Separate scores are obtained for each half. For written, objective tests, the split is often made by scoring all even-numbered items separately from the odd-numbered items. The correlation between the two scores from the even and odd halves of the test results is then determined. This technique can also be applied to motor performance tests. For example, if we conducted six trials on a tennis wall-volley test, we could take the total score on the even-numbered trials as one-half the test and the total score on the odd-numbered trials as the other half and calculate the correlation between these two sets of scores.

This correlation coefficient represents an estimate of reliability for only one-half of the test. However, the reliability of a test is greatly affected by its length: Within reason, the longer a test is, the more reliable it is likely to be. Thus a technique has been developed to estimate the reliability of an entire test when the split-half method has been used. This technique is a special application of what is called the Spearman-Brown Prophecy formula, where

$$\text{Reliability of whole test} = \frac{2(\text{reliability of 1/2 test})}{1 + (\text{reliability of 1/2 test})}$$

The two halves of the test are assumed to be identical in content and difficulty, but in practice this assumption is often ignored.

As an example of applying this technique, assume that we have administered a test, separately scored the odd- and even-numbered answers, and found the correlation between the odd and even scores to be .80. Thus the estimated reliability of the whole test would be

$$\text{Reliability of whole test} = \frac{2(.80)}{1 + .80} = \frac{1.60}{1.80} = .89$$

As you can see, the reliability of the complete test is estimated to be greater than that of half of it (.89 > .80).

In general, the longer a test, the more reliable it is apt to be. This fact, of course, could be carried to an extreme if a test were so long that fatigue became a factor affecting test results. The general Spearman-Brown Prophecy formula can be used to estimate the effects of lengthening a test by any amount, not only doubling its length. This formula is

$$r = \frac{K(r_{xx})}{1 + (K - 1)(r_{xx})}$$

where r represents the reliability of the lengthened test, r_{xx} represents the reliability determined for the original test, and K represents the number of times longer the new test is lengthened from the original test. This formula was used for the split-half reliability example above in which $K = 2$.

As an example of applying this technique, suppose that we have a 30-item test and have determined its test-retest reliability to be .70. Dissatisfied with this reliability, we add 60 items to the test that cover the same content and are of the same difficulty. The new test thus has 90 items; it is three times longer than the original test. Therefore, the estimated reliability for the new lengthened test would be

$$r = \frac{3(.70)}{1 + (3 - 1)(.70)} = \frac{2.10}{1 + 2(.70)}$$

$$= \frac{2.10}{1 + 1.40} = \frac{2.10}{2.40} = .88$$

This estimated reliability should be considered the *maximum possible* reliability, not the *actual* reliability.

You may sometimes need to determine how many times a test must be lengthened in order for it to approach a specified reliability. In this case our formula is solved for K, and we have

$$K = \frac{r(1 - r_{xx})}{r_{xx}(1 + r)}$$

For example, if we had a 20-item test with a test-retest reliability of .60, and we wanted a reliability of .90, how many items would we need to lengthen the test? To answer this we find

$$K = \frac{.90(1 - .60)}{.60(1 - .90)} = \frac{.90(.40)}{.60(.10)} = \frac{.36}{.06} = 6$$

We would need to lengthen the test a total of 6 times its original 20-item length, or $6 \times 20 = 120$ items. Because we already had 20 items we would need 100 *additional* items.

There is a need to emphasize again that the Spearman-Brown Prophecy formula must be used very cautiously. Reliability coefficients determined by using the split-half and Spearman-Brown Prophecy methods are generally higher than those determined by test-retest methods. In most physical education situations, therefore, the split-half method should be avoided. Furthermore, reported reliabilities that have been determined by these methods should be viewed with extreme caution. In general, reliabilities determined by test-retest on different days are preferred.

The following guidelines are given for possible use in determining the level of acceptable reliability coefficients:

Reliability rating	Correlation coefficient
Excellent	.90-1.00
High	.80- .89
Average	.60- .79
Unacceptable	.00- .59

These coefficients should be used cautiously because acceptable reliability depends on the particular testing situation.

Reliability of Motor Performance Tests. Special problems involved in determining the reliability of motor performance tests may not often occur in written tests. The problem of separating systematic error from measurement error was discussed earlier. In addition, the product-moment correlational techniques previously presented do not distinguish between the two types of error. Furthermore, multiple motor performance trials occurring over more than one day are not taken into consideration by these techniques.

On the surface these problems may not seem too serious, but they can be very significant. For example, assume that five students have taken a motor skill test consisting of four trials and have received the following scores:

Student	Trial 1 scores	Trial 2 scores	Trial 3 scores	Trial 4 scores
S1	2	6	10	10
S2	4	8	12	12
S3	6	10	14	14
S4	8	12	16	16
S5	10	14	18	18

The first question that might be asked is, How do we determine a reliability coefficient for this test? The answer is that with the methods given so far we cannot. However, someone might propose that correlations be determined between Trials 1 and 2, 2 and 3, 3 and 4, 1 and 3, 1 and 4, and 2 and 4. The question then would be, Which correlation coefficient is the right one? The difficulties in such a procedure may already be evident, but there are additional problems.

Suppose that you calculated all of the correlation coefficients proposed for our illustration. You would find that in every case the correlation coefficient is equal to 1.00 because each student retains his or her same relative position for all trials. (Calculate them if you doubt it.) The perfect correlation found indicates the absence of measurement error. Does it indicate perfect reliability? No, because reliability means consistency, and these measures have not remained consistent over all trials. As a check on consistency, you could calculate the mean performance for each trial. In this case, $\overline{X}_1 = 6$, $\overline{X}_2 = 10$, $\overline{X}_3 = 14$, and $\overline{X}_4 = 14$. These results indicate the presence of systematic error, such as problems in learning how to do the test. Consistency is not reached until the third and fourth trials. To assess the true performance of the students on this task, then, it might be wise to use only the third and fourth trials.

We still have the problem of tests that are administered on different days. To address this problem, the same number of trials should be administered on more than one day, and then the same checks on consistency should be made among trials and between days as indicated.

One additional note needs to be made about the number of trials. In constructing a performance test, a large number of trials should be administered in order to determine at what point the test scores stabilize. This must be done for each sex and age group for whom the test is intended. The best approach is to determine and perhaps even plot the means for each trial and use the trials where the means stabilize or plateau. For example, Baumgartner and Jackson (1970) found that in the standing broad jump, the performance of senior high school boys did not stabilize until Trials 4 through 6, whereas with junior high school boys the first three trials were stabilized, and the boys' performance became unstable on Trials 4 through 6. Thus for senior high boys, six trials needed to be administered with only the last three counting, and with junior high boys only three trials needed to be administered with all of them counting.

Formal solutions to our problems have yet to be presented. By utilizing these simple procedures, however, we can gain some insight into the problems of motor performance reliability. This discussion is intended to help the reader to be alert to these problems and realize the limitations of the Pearson correlation coefficient when selecting and/or constructing motor performance tests.

Intraclass Correlation Coefficient and Test for Trend.   An alternative to the Pearson r for determining the reliability of motor performance data is the intraclass correlation coefficient, which partially takes care of the problems indicated earlier. This coefficient is a measure of how consistent scores remain across performance trials regardless of the number of trials. Perfect positive correlation is found when scores remain constant for each individual for all trials. In addition, or actually before the intraclass correlation coefficient is calculated, a procedure called *testing for trend* should be performed to determine the severity of the differences among the trial means. Both of these procedures require the use of analysis of variance procedures. Analysis of variance procedures also help to determine if it is important to administer multiple trials of a particular test on the same day or on different days.

An example problem is presented in Appendix E for readers who wish to explore these techniques more fully. Readers may also wish to consult the references given at the end of this chapter, and chapter 2, especially the texts by Safrit and by Dotson and Kirkendall.

Standard Error of Measurement.   Whether one is working with written or motor performance test scores, it is sometimes desirable to have reliability stated in terms of the variability expected in an individual student's score. The variability may be determined by finding an estimate of the standard deviation of an individual score. This standard deviation is called the *standard error of measurement* and is found as follows:

$$\text{Standard error of measurement} = S_e = \sigma\sqrt{1 - r_{xx}}$$

where σ is the established or accepted standard deviation for the test with which we are working and r_{xx} is the reliability coefficient, either Pearsonian or intraclass. For example, if the standard deviation for a grip strength test is 10 pounds and the reliability of this test is r_{xx} = .84, then

$$S_e = 10 \sqrt{1 - .84} = 10 \sqrt{.16}$$
$$= 10(.4) = 4.0 \text{ pounds}$$

We may interpret this to mean that if one individual were to take this strength test many times, we would estimate the standard deviation of the scores for that individual to be 4.0 pounds.

Let us further assume in our example that a person's score on this strength test was 78 pounds. By using the normal curve, we could estimate that this person's performance, if repeated many times, would be between 74 and 82 pounds 68% of the time or between 70 and 86 pounds 95% of the time. To calculate these estimates, we found the intervals for $\pm$ one standard deviation from the score and $\pm$ two standard deviations from the score. Another way to state what these intervals mean is that we are 68% confident that this person's true score will be between 74 and 82 pounds or 95% confident that the true score is between 70 and 86 pounds.

Factors Affecting Reliability. Several factors may affect the reliability of a test. Some of these include the length of the test, the nature of the students taking the test, the administration of the test, and the testing environment.

The nature of the students taking a test will affect its reliability. In general, the more heterogeneous, or variable, the group, the greater a test's possibility for high reliability. If the students taking a test are not motivated, the reliability of the test is adversely affected. Related to this is the fact that boredom and fatigue have a negative effect on reliability. The level of the student's skill and familiarity with the test will also affect the test's reliability. In general, higher reliability can be expected with higher-level performers.

It is critical that a test be administered exactly according to its instructions. Unclear or inconsistent test administration will lower a test's reliability. The order in which test items are administered may also affect the reliability of various items. For example, if a standing long jump test were administered immediately following a 600-yard run, subjects' performances on the standing long jump would probably be adversely affected and thereby affect the reliability of the test. Obviously, too, if cheating occurs on a test, the reliability of the test declines. In physical performance tests, warm-ups tend to increase a test's reliability. When administering a test, the environment should be as free as possible from distractions. If students' concentration is disrupted by noise, visual distractions, uncomfortable temperatures, or other factors, the reliability of the test performance will decline. The test administrator must try to eliminate as many of these distractions as possible.

Objectivity

The *objectivity* of a test is defined as the degree of agreement among testers. In other words, a test that is completely objective is one that will be scored identically by different scorers. Some written tests, such as multiple choice or true and false, obviously have high objectivity. Other written tests and many physical performance tests are not as objective.

A synonym for objectivity might be *rater reliability*, that is, the consistency with which different raters score or judge a performance. To determine rater reliability for a test, two individuals score the test or judge the performance of all tested students, and a correlation coefficient is determined. This coefficient indicates the degree of agreement between the two judges' scores or ratings. An alternative method that is sometimes used but not nearly as reliable involves having the same individual score the tests or judge the performances on two different occasions and then finding the correlation between the two scorings. This latter procedure gives an inflated value for the degree of objectivity and is much less desirable for determining objectivity.

The use of the analysis of variance procedures briefly mentioned in our discussion of reliability is also often appropriate for determining objectivity. Consistency of ratings by three or more judges and consistency of ratings by the same judge can be assessed simultaneously through analysis of variance. Although detailed discussion of these procedures is beyond the scope of this text, the reader should be aware that such procedures are available.

A guideline for rating the objectivity of a test follows. Again, remember that these are only guidelines and must be viewed with extreme caution. The particular situation will determine the adequacy of an objectivity coefficient.

Objectivity rating	*Correlation coefficient*
Excellent	.95-1.00
High	.85- .94
Average	.70- .84
Unacceptable	.00- .69

As with validity and reliability, several factors can affect the objectivity of a test. Awareness of these factors can help one to prevent problems. In physical performance tasks in which ratings are involved, for example, it is critically important for the criteria used to judge the performance to be very well defined. Considerable discussion is devoted in chapter 8 to developing checklists of criteria for assessing performance. Checklists greatly improve the objectivity of the judgments made. Gymnastics and diving are excellent examples of motor performance tasks for which objective checklists have been developed.

Individuals who are judging or rating performance must be well trained. Poorly trained judges adversely affect objectivity. Judges or raters must be familiar with the activity as well as with the test to be administered. In addition, the positioning of a rater or judge in relation to the performer can affect the rating that the judge is likely to give. Therefore, if only one rater is to be used, it is imperative that the rater assume the same position to observe each performer. This is also the reason that the three or more judges at gymnastics and diving competitions are positioned at different angles to the performers.

The order of performers can also affect the objectivity of ratings and/or judgments. If a good performance follows a very poor performance, the good performance may seem better than it actually is. Related to this is the effect that individuals' past performances may have upon current ratings. To overcome these difficulties, two earlier solutions apply again: the judge or rater must be well prepared, and the criteria for judging the quality of performance must be well defined. Randomizing the order of the individuals' performances for each event and/or trial is also helpful.

Additional Selection/ Construction Criteria

Unquestionably, the three most important criteria for selecting and constructing tests are validity, reliability, and objectivity. Several other criteria, however, must also be met if a test is to be useful. Sometimes a test that is valid, reliable, and objective will not be utilized because it fails to meet some of these additional criteria.

Economy

Among these additional criteria for selecting and constructing tests is the issue of *economy*, or the economic feasibility of implementing a proposed test. Is the test economical in terms of time, money, and personnel? The answer to this question may determine the viability of implementing a proposed test. Regardless of how valid, reliable, and objective a test is, if it is not economically feasible to administer in the available setting, it is useless. For example, the $\dot{V}O_2$max test, which uses gas analysis to determine cardiorespiratory endurance, has been shown to be satisfactorily valid, reliable, and objective. However, thousands of dollars' worth of equipment is needed to conduct the test, and only one person can be tested at a time. The test takes about 45 minutes and requires two or three highly trained individuals to administer it. In a school setting with 500 students, one physical education teacher, and none of the equipment, even considering implementation of this test is impractical; it simply would not be economically feasible.

Ease of Administration

Another important criterion for a test is its *ease of administration*. A test must be relatively easy to administer if it is to be used with large numbers of participants. The directions for administering a test must be standardized so that the results will be the same regardless of who administers it. The directions must be explicit and leave nothing to doubt. (Does a ball landing on the line, for example, count as a good or poor toss?) At the same time, directions must be simple enough that, with a clear explanation, students will understand them.

A test must be reasonable in terms of its demands on the students. If a test is so rigorous that it causes sore muscles and joints, perhaps it is not appropriate. Similarly, if a test requires an inordinate amount of preparation time by either the students or the teacher, its use may not be warranted.

Developmental Value

In selecting or constructing a test, there is also a need to consider its *developmental value*. A test should be a learning experience for the students if at all possible. In taking a test, students should learn something about themselves from which they may benefit. Hopefully, students will learn skills or knowledge from the test itself. On a written test, a student may learn a fact or concept by missing a question or by answering it correctly. If physical performance tests are administered properly, test results can often motivate students to improve. It is questionable whether the use of a test can be justified if its only function is to determine grades.

Interest

In order to produce an accurate appraisal of a student's performance, a test should provide *interest* and challenge to its participants. If a test is boring, excessively repetitive, too easy, or too difficult, students may lose interest and not show their true ability. Physical performance tests are particularly vulnerable to problems in maintaining participant interest.

Norms

Norms may be thought of as representative values for a particular population. These values are usually the mean, standard deviation, and percentile ranks. If any comparisons between your participants and a larger population are to be made for some test, the use of norms is absolutely required. Such comparisons can provide valuable information to the physical educator as well as to the test participants. If your participants consistently score well below the national average on most items of a physical fitness test, you should consider revising your program.

To be meaningful, norms must be based on a population appropriate for comparison with your participants. Most physical performance norms should be based on body size because this factor generally plays an important role in performance. Certainly, norms on a physical fitness test for college-aged women would not be appropriate for seventh-grade boys.

Before using norms, consider the following important points:

1. How large a group was used to establish the norms? Although the number of subjects will not solve other problems a test may have, the sampling of a population must be large enough to ensure that the normative values are representative of the total population. Even in the smallest population, several hundred scores should be available if norms are to be established and used.

2. What is the nature of the group for which the norms were established? In addition to sex, age, height, and weight, additional factors such as geographical region, intelligence of subjects, physical conditioning level of subjects, type of school, and so on may be relevant for a particular test. Generally, you will want to compare students to a population that is quite similar to them.

3. Are the test directions explicit enough to ensure that you are administering the test precisely as it was administered when the normative scores were gathered?

4. How current are the norms? Because society is constantly changing, norms established in 1939 may not be appropriate in 1986.

Perhaps the most meaningful norms are ones that are established for a particular school, institution, or region. Such norms are a means for determining the progress made toward

the achievement of local program objectives. Establishing local norms simply requires keeping records on standardized tests and updating the statistics calculated from students' scores. Rather reliable norms can be established within 2-3 years. However, it is important to keep these norms up-to-date.

Criterion-Referenced Standards

Formal performance standards against which individual performances are evaluated are *criterion-referenced standards*. If this approach to evaluation is used, it is important to establish appropriate standards of allowable performance for various mastery states. As with norm-referenced evaluation, criterion-referenced standards are typically more useful when they are established at the local level where the needs and purposes of the particular setting can be considered.

The establishment of standards is the most crucial aspect of criterion-referenced evaluation. It requires professional physical educators to be knowledgeable about the activities under consideration as well as the participants involved in the activities. One must rely on past training and experiences and other expert guidelines for determining these standards of expected performance. Once initial standards are established or accepted, they must be reviewed and revised periodically.

Duplicate Forms

Although having duplicate forms of a single test is generally not an important criterion for a test to meet, occasionally it is critical to have more than one form of a test available. This is particularly true for knowledge, personality, and attitude assessment tests that are administered before and after a program in order to assess changes in behavior. Duplicate tests should be carefully scrutinized to ensure that they are actually duplicates. For different tests to be similar is not adequate in most cases; the tests must be the same in content, length, and difficulty.

Summary

The relationships among the validity, reliability, and objectivity of a test emphasized throughout this chapter illustrate a clear hierarchy. Validity is actually an all-encompassing term that includes relevance, reliability, and objectivity. A test can never be valid if it is not first reliable and objective. Furthermore, a test can never be reliable if it cannot be scored objectively. Thus any factors that affect the objectivity of a test will also affect its reliability, which in turn will affect its validity. Finally, no degree of objectivity ensures reliability, and no degree of reliability ensures validity or relevance.

Remember that the relevance or validity of a test is the *most* important characteristic to consider. For example, one might propose hat size as a measure of intelligence. There is no question that hat size can be measured objectively and reliably. However, hat size has no relation or relevance to a person's intelligence. Consequently, although the proposed test can be shown to be objective and reliable, it is completely useless for the proposed purpose because it does not measure what it purports to measure (validity). Without validity, a test has no value regardless of how reliable or objective it may be.

A checklist for evaluating a test is presented in Figure 3.2 to assist the reader in applying the criteria for the selection and construction of tests discussed in this chapter. This checklist will be applied in later chapters of this text. Of course, no test is perfectly valid, reliable, and objective, nor is it likely to perfectly satisfy all other criteria for selecting/constructing tests. Therefore, it is important to remember two of the most important principles of measurement and evaluation: First, there is no such thing as a perfect test, and, second, there is no substitute for judgment in measurement and evaluation. Our task is to select or construct the best possible test for the particular situation by applying the criteria just presented. In order to select or construct the "best" test, you should use the information discussed in this chapter to make sound professional decisions instead of poorly informed judgments.

Finally, although a test must possess the characteristics and meet the criteria presented in this chapter, the competence of the test administrator or user is also crucial. Regardless of how well a test meets the identified criteria or characteristics, to be useful and valuable it must be administered and interpreted by a competent professional.

Review Questions

1. What are the three most important characteristics of a test? Define each of these three characteristics.
2. In what ways does one obtain content or logical validity?
3. In what ways does one obtain concurrent or criterion-related validity?
4. In what ways does one obtain predictive validity?
5. In what ways does one obtain construct validity?
6. What factors affect the validity of a test?
7. In what way does one obtain test-retest reliability?
8. What is equivalent form reliability?
9. One of the disadvantages of the test-retest method is that it is most difficult to ensure identical testing conditions in the two administrations. What method is used to overcome this disadvantage?
10. What factors affect the reliability of a test?
11. How does one determine the objectivity of a test?

Test Evaluation Checklist

Test name _____

Test objective _____

Reported validity _____

   How determined _____

   Valid for whom _____

Reported reliability _____

   How determined _____

Reported objectivity _____

   How determined _____

Special equipment needed _____

_____

Time required to administer (minutes) _____ per person _____ per group of 30

Special training needed for testers _____

_____

Clarity of directions _____ Clear and precise
                  _____ Inexact

Norms available for what groups _____

_____

_____

Participants learn from test _____ Yes _____ No

Participants find test interesting _____ Yes _____ No

Duplicate forms available _____ Yes _____ No

Figure 3.2 Checklist for evaluating a test.

Problems and Exercises

1. A physical education teacher in a large high school developed a new test for measuring service skills in tennis. She wanted to establish the concurrent validity of her test and decided to use an established valid test as the criterion. She measured her 150 students on the established valid test and then measured the same students with her new test. The following results were obtained (X = data from established test, Y = data from new test):

   $N = 150$

   $\overline{X} = 14.43$ $\overline{Y} = 5.49$

   $\Sigma X^2 = 32,583.7$ $\Sigma Y^2 = 4858.5$

   $\Sigma XY = 12,357.6$

   What is the concurrent validity of the new test? According to the guidelines in this text, is this result excellent, high, average, or unacceptable?
   Answer: $r = .703$; high

2. The same physical education teacher in Problem 1 decided to run a test-retest so that she could estimate the reliability of her test. Two days after she measured the students with her test, she administered the same test again with the following results:

   $N = 150$

   $\overline{X} = 5.49$ $\overline{Y} = 5.58$

   $\Sigma X^2 = 4,858.5$ $\Sigma Y^2 = 5,156.5$

   $\Sigma XY = 4,933.3$

   What is the coefficient of stability? According to the guidelines in this text, is this excellent, high, average, or unacceptable?

3. A physical education teacher administered a 100-item written test on gymnastics techniques. He made the odd and even items identical in content and difficulty. He found a reliability correlation coefficient of one-half the test to be .64. What is the reliability of the whole test?
   Answer: .78

4. A physical education teacher was dissatisfied with a test-retest reliability on a test of football rules. The coefficient of stability on the 30-item test was .75. He wanted a correlation coefficient of .85. How many items must be added to secure this desired correlation coefficient?

5. The physical education teacher in Problem 4 was interested in the correlation coefficient that would be obtained
if he tripled the length of his 30-item test. What would
the reliability coefficient be if he tripled the length of his
test?
Answer: $r = .90$

6. The number of full-length push-ups performed by each
student in a ninth-grade physical education class was used
as a test-retest on endurance. The standard deviation for
the class was 6, and the test-retest reliability coefficient
was .86. What is the standard error of measurement?

7. A ninth-grade student did 30 push-ups. What would be
the estimated performance of this student 68% and 95%
of the time if he repeated the performance many times?
Use the standard error of measurement found in Problem
6 to determine your answer.
Answer: It is estimated that 68% of the time he would
perform 28-32 push-ups and 95% of the time he would
perform 26-34 push-ups.

Bibliography

Ahmann, J.S., & Glock, M.D. (1971). *Evaluating pupil growth* (4th ed.). Boston: Allyn & Bacon.

Alexander, H.W. (1946). A general test for trend. *Psychological Bulletin, 43*, 533-557.

Alexander, H.W. (1947). The estimation of reliability when several trials are available. *Psychometrika, 12*, 79-99.

American Psychological Association. (1966). *Standards for educational and psychological tests and manuals.* Washington, DC: American Psychological Association.

Baumgartner, T.A. (1968). The application of the Spearman-Brown Prophecy formula when applied to physical performance tests. *Research Quarterly, 39*, 847-856.

Baumgartner, T.A. (1969a). Estimating reliability when all test trials are administered on the same day. *Research Quarterly, 40*, 222-225.

Baumgartner, T.A. (1969b). Stability of physical performance test scores. *Research Quarterly, 40*, 257-261.

Baumgartner, T.A., & Jackson, A.S. (1970). Measurement schedules for tests of motor performance. *Research Quarterly, 41*, 10-18.

Baumgartner, T.A., & Jackson, A.S. (1975). *Measurement for evaluation in physical education.* Boston: Houghton Mifflin.

Dotson, C.O., & Kirkendall, D.R. (1974). *Statistics for physical education, health, and recreation.* New York: Harper & Row.

Ebel, R.L. (1951). Estimation of the reliability of ratings. *Psychometrika, 16*, 407-424.

Ebel, R.L. (1962). Measurement and the teacher. *Educational Leadership, 20*, 20-24.

Henry, F.M. (1959a). Reliability, measurement error, and intra-individual difference. *Research Quarterly, 30*(1), 21-24.

Henry, F.M. (1959b). Influence of measurement error and intra-individual variation on the reliability of muscle strength and vertical jump tests. *Research Quarterly, 30*(2), 155-159.

Henry, F.M. (1970). Individual differences in motor learning and performance. In L.E. Smith (Ed.), *Psychology of motor learning* (pp. 243-256). Chicago: Athletic Institute.

Henry, F.M., Cureton, T.K., Hewitt, J.E., & Jarrett, R.F. (1949). Errors in measurement. In M.G. Scott, T.K. Cureton, R. Abernathy, C.W. Bookwalter, K.W. Bookwalter, H.H. Clarke, F.M. Henry, L.A. Larson, & A.H. Steinhaus (Eds.), *Research methods applied to health, physical education, and recreation* (pp. 459-477). Washington, DC: American Association for Health, Physical Education, and Recreation; National Education Association.

Kenyon, G.S. (1968a). A conceptual model for characterizing physical activity. *Research Quarterly, 39*(1), 96-105.

Kenyon, G.S. (1968b). Six scales for assessing attitude toward physical activity. *Research Quarterly, 39*(3), 566-574.

Kroll, W. (1962a). A note on the coefficient of intraclass correlation as an estimate of reliability. *Research Quarterly, 33*, 313-316.

Kroll, W. (1962b). Reliability of a selected measure of human strength. *Research Quarterly, 33*, 410-417.

Kroll, W. (1963). Reliability variations of strength in test-retest situations. *Research Quarterly, 34*, 50-55.

Safrit, M.J. (1973). *Evaluation in physical education.* Englewood Cliffs, NJ: Prentice-Hall.

Safrit, M.J. (1977). Criterion-referenced measurement: Applications in physical education. *Motor Skills: Theory into Practice, 2*, 21-35.

Safrit, M.J. (Ed.). (1976). *Reliability theory appropriate for motor performance measures.* Washington, DC: American Association for Health, Physical Education, and Recreation.

Schmidt, R.A. (1970). Critique of Henry's paper. In L.E. Smith (Ed.), *Psychology of motor learning* (pp. 256-260). Chicago: Athletic Institute.

Symonds, P.M. (1928). Factors influencing test reliability. *Journal of Educational Psychology, 19*, 73-87. (Reprinted in D. Payne and R. McMorris [Eds.], *Educational and Psychological Measurement—1967* [pp. 46-54]. Waltham, MA: Blaisdell.)

Thorndike, R.L. (1951). Reliability. In E.F. Lindquist (Ed.), *Educational Measurement* (pp. 560-620). Washington, DC: American Council on Education.

Thorndike, R.L., & Hagen, E. (1955). *Measurement and evaluation in psychology and education.* New York: Wiley & Sons.

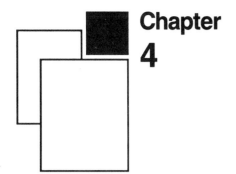

Chapter 4

Writing Goals and Measurable Objectives

A proposed program of physical activity must have one or more formal goals and measurable objectives in order to accomplish what is intended. Formal, explicit goals give direction to a program, and measurable objectives provide the means to determine whether and to what extent a program's goals are being accomplished.

Program Goals

Goals are general statements that specify the desired outcomes that a program is intended to accomplish. Stating a formal goal for a physical activity program is no simple matter. A well-stated and well-written goal will provide clear direction to a program. Well-stated goals prevent confusion among the individuals involved in the program about the program's purpose and desired direction. On the other hand, a poorly stated goal will create confusion, disagreement, and conflict among the individuals involved in the program about the program's direction and desired outcomes. In other words, a well-stated and well-written goal will communicate the de-

sired direction and attainable aims of a program, and a poor one will not.

A well-stated goal facilitates successful decision making in a physical activity program. Important decisions about what factors to test and, subsequently, about what tests are good indicators of those factors can be reached more easily and with better results if the program's goals are clear and well-stated. The purpose or purposes for testing are often stated or at least implied in a well-written goal. Testing procedures become apparent because a well-stated goal indicates a program's desired accomplishments and attainable direction for evaluation. A well-stated goal is the foundation for clear and logical decision making.

A goal should be stated and written in terms that

- are clear and unambiguous,
- delineate observable and measurable behavioral objectives, and
- give clear, attainable direction to the program.

Let's look at some examples of written goals for programs in physical education, athletics, and health clubs. After stating each goal we will use these three criteria to determine whether each goal communicates desired outcomes and provides clear direction for the program.

Physical Education Program

Goal 1. To appreciate, know, and understand the joy of physical fitness.

The words *appreciate, know, understand*, and *joy* are open to many interpretations. These terms are ambiguous and therefore violate our first criterion for developing well-stated goals. Furthermore, it would be difficult if not impossible to break down the words *appreciate, know, understand*, and *joy* into behavioral objectives that are observable and measurable. Thus this goal is poorly stated.

Goal 2. To improve the physical fitness level of each student enrolled in a physical education course.

Physical fitness is defined in this text as muscular strength, muscular endurance, cardiovascular endurance, power, and flexibility. Each of these elements of physical fitness can be observed and measured. Keep in mind that if each student is to improve his or her physical fitness level through participation in the course, then each student's physical fitness level at exiting the course must exceed what it was when entering the course. The entry and exit levels of physical fitness for each student for each element are observable and measurable. Thus this goal communicates the desired direction and specifies attainable outcomes for the program. Thus this is a well-stated goal.

Athletic Program

Goal 1. To execute the proper skills for a pass receiver in the "down and out" pass pattern in football.

Some words in this goal are ambiguous, but in football terminology the words "down and out" have precise and specific meaning. In football, "down and out" means to sprint down the field and then break to the outside (sideline). After years of coaching experience, attending football coaching clinics, and reading materials written by established football authorities, the football coach who wrote this goal developed a sequential set of physical performance standards for the proper skills in the "down and out" pass pattern. These physical performance skills are written as criteria that are observable and measurable. This goal does communicate desired direction and attainable accomplishments for the program and is therefore a well-stated goal.

Goal 2. To develop the participants into well-rounded individuals so that each can become an integral part of the school.

The words *well-rounded individual* are open to many interpretations. For example, does *well-rounded* mean that each participant should become fat? The words *integral part of the school* are also ambiguous. The language of this goal conveys little information about what the program is intended to accomplish or what direction it should take. Thus this goal is poorly stated.

Health Club Program

Goal 1. To increase the aerobic work capacity of the participants in an aerobic program.

What constitutes *aerobic work capacity*? It is the efficiency of an individual's oxygen transport and utilization system while that individual is performing more difficult work such as pedaling a bicycle ergometer or running on a treadmill. These elements are observable and measurable, and several valid and reliable methods for measuring aerobic work capacity have been developed. Increases in participants' aerobic work capacities can be measured by testing each individual both before and after program participation and comparing each individual's pre- and postprogram test results. Thus the elements of this goal are observable and measurable, and this is a well-stated goal.

Goal 2. To grasp the significance of anthropometric measures in developing a beautiful body.

What are *anthropometric measures*? Anthropometric measures are measurements of the body and body segments of individuals. Examples of such measurements include height, upper arm girth, calf girth, waist girth, chest girth, and so on. Are these elements observable and measurable? Yes, they are because the various measures of length and girth have been well-defined in anthropometric measures. What does it mean to *grasp the significance of anthropometric measures in developing a beautiful body*? The words *significance of* and *beautiful body* are ambigu-

ous. This immediately fails the criterion that program goals must avoid ambiguous terms. We need go no further; this is a poorly written goal. What did the directors of the health club want to accomplish when they wrote this goal? What they actually wanted was to train five individuals to become judges of a "body beautiful contest" to be held at the club. If that is what they wanted, then they should have said so and developed an appropriate goal to meet the desired outcome. If they wanted to include anthropometric measures as a standard in the judging process, they could have stated the goal as follows:

Goal 2. To train five individuals to take anthropometric measurements and to compare these measures to standards established by individuals with a high degree of expertise regarding what anthropometric measures constitute a beautiful body. These five individuals will serve as judges of a body beautiful contest to be held at the club.

Are there any ambiguous words in this goal? No, there are not; we have clearly defined what the experts will do to help us determine what measures constitute a beautiful body. Can the words used in this goal be broken down into elements that are observable and measurable? Yes, they can. Does this goal give attainable directions that the program should take? Yes, it does because it calls for designing a training program for taking anthropometric measures and comparing these measures to standards established by experts. The goal also tells us the purpose for which the training will be used.

Goals give direction, whereas behavioral objectives provide means to determine whether and when goals have been attained. A well-written goal indicates in rather broad terms the intended outcome of a program, but it does not indicate *when* the intended outcome has been achieved. A well-written behavioral objective will tell *when* an intended outcome has or has not been achieved.

Behavioral Objectives

Motor tests or academic examinations are useless unless they measure a participant's performance in terms of behavioral objectives. Stating behavioral objectives allows the participant to evaluate his or her own progress and allows the instructor or coach to evaluate the amount of successful achievement each participant has attained. Stating behavioral objectives also gives the decision-maker accountability in the decision-making process of classification, selection, grading, and diagnosis because comparisons can be made to specific standards. Stating behavioral objectives allows the instructor or coach to

- select appropriate teaching methods, skills, and strategies,
- choose needed equipment and suitable materials, and
- select an appropriate time schedule for program presentation.

Mager (1975, p. 5) pointed out that

The machinist does not select a tool until he knows what operation he intends to perform. Neither does a composer orchestrate a score until he knows what effects he wishes to achieve. Similarly, a builder does not select his materials or specify a schedule for construction until he has his blueprints (objectives) before him.

Mager goes on to say,

I cannot emphasize too strongly . . . that an instructor will function in a fog of his own making until he knows just what he wants his students to be able to do at the end of the instruction.

In other words, stating and writing behavioral objectives allows one to know when the intended outcomes of a program have been achieved. What standards should be applied to determine whether we have indeed stated or written an appropriate behavioral objective? Behavioral objectives should

- be stated in terms that can be measured,
- describe an outcome that is observable, and
- describe a standard of excellence expected of a participant.

Let's apply these standards for effective behavioral objectives to our example of Physical Education Program Goal 2, "To improve the physical fitness level of each student in a physical education course." We previously defined the elements of physical fitness as muscular strength, muscular endurance, cardiovascular endurance, power, and flexibility. Now we must decide what tests are good indicators of these elements of physical fitness.

For the elements of muscular strength and muscular endurance, let's use the norm-referenced AAHPER Youth Fitness Tests (1976) of (a) pull-ups for boys and flexed arm hang for girls, both of which are indicators of muscular strength and endurance of the arms and shoulders; (b) sit-ups for both boys and girls, which is an indicator of trunk strength and endurance; and (c) standing long jump for both boys and girls, which is an indicator of leg strength.

For the element of cardiovascular endurance, let's use the norm-referenced AAHPERD

Health-Related Fitness Test (1980) of the 1-mile run, and for the element of power, let's use the norm-referenced AAHPER Youth Fitness Test (1976) of the 50-yard dash. The sit-and-reach test of the AAHPERD Health-Related Fitness Test (1980) can be used for the element of flexibility.

Note that all of the above tests are norm referenced and have percentile ranks recorded for given scores. We will test each student at the beginning of the semester and record an *entry-level percentile rank* on pull-ups (boys), flexed arm hang (girls), sit-ups (boys and girls), standing long jump (boys and girls), 1-mile run (boys and girls), 50-yard dash (boys and girls),

and sit-and-reach (boys and girls). We will also administer the same tests to each student at the end of the semester and record an *exit level percentile rank* for each student. The exit level percentile rank minus the entry level percentile rank equals the change in percentile rank, which in turn represents the improvement. We know that entry-level students who score in the low percentile ranks have a better chance of improvement than those who score in the higher ranks. To offset this inequity, we set the procedural standards presented in Table 4.1.

Now that our procedural standards have been established, let's write our behavioral objective.

Table 4.1   Improvement and Grading for Physical Fitness Testing

Student entry level percentile rank	Improved percentile rank[a] and grade[b] received for each test				
Equal to or below the 20th	25 or above Grade A	20 to 24 Grade B	10 to 19 Grade C	5 to 9 Grade D	4 or below Grade F
Between 20th and 41st	20 or above Grade A	15 to 19 Grade B	8 to 14 Grade C	4 to 7 Grade D	3 or below Grade F
Between 40th and 61st	15 or above Grade A	10 to 14 Grade B	3 to 9 Grade C	1 to 2 Grade D	0 or below Grade F
Between 60th and 81st	10 or above Grade A	7 to 9 Grade B	3 to 6 Grade C	1 to 2 Grade D	0 or below Grade F
Between 80th and 96th	5 or above Grade A	4 Grade B	2 to 3 Grade C	1 Grade D	0 or below Grade F
Equal to or above the 96th	0 or above Grade A	−1 Lacks improvement Grade B	−2 Lacks improvement Grade C	−3 Lacks improvement Grade D	−4 Lacks improvement Grade F

[a]Top score in each cell represents change in percentile rank.
[b]Represents grade for change in percentile rank.

Behavioral objective: A student must be able to pass 5 of the 7 tests given with a grade of C or better.

This behavioral objective is stated in terms that are measurable and observable, and it describes a standard of excellence expected of a participant. Our goal told us in rather broad terms what our intended outcome should be, and this behavioral objective tells us how to know *when* that intended outcome has been achieved.

We used norm-referenced tests to formulate our behavioral objective in the above example. Must we write goals and objectives if we use criterion-referenced tests? The answer to this question is an emphatic *yes*. With criterion-referenced tests, we must still provide program direction and know when intended outcomes have been achieved. As an example, let's examine our example of Athletic Program Goal 1:

Goal 1: To execute the proper skills for a pass receiver in the "down and out" pass pattern in football.

The coach has developed a criterion-referenced test for comparing a participant's actual movement patterns to the proper skills required of a pass receiver in the "down and out" pass pattern. The following criteria were established for the "down and out" pass pattern along with a task analysis for immediate feedback to the participant concerning areas of weakness.

When placed at the end or flanker back position to the right side, upon the snap of the ball a participant will sprint toward a defensive back with the shoulders squared and both eyes fixed on the defensive back. The participant will continue to sprint toward the defensive back until the defensive back takes a

step backward to cover deep. At the instant the defensive back steps backward to cover deep, the participant will plant the left foot on the ground and drive off this foot at a right angle to his present direction. At the same time of the foot plant, the participant will rotate the face and trunk toward the sideline. Once the face and trunk have rotated, the participant will look for the football and will visually follow the ball into the hands for a catch.

A simple form used for task analysis of this criterion-referenced test is presented in Figure 4.1.

Now that the criteria have been established and a task analysis developed for immediate feedback to the participant, we can state the behavioral objective.

Behavioral Objective: During each practice day before being released from practice, a participant for right end or right flanker must be able to perform the "down and out" pass pattern five times with no check marks against the performance as analyzed by the offensive coach using the task analysis for the "down and out" pass pattern.

This behavioral objective is stated in terms intended to ensure that the participant masters the skills necessary to perform the task. It is stated so that the participant must practice the skills and perform them correctly five times each day before he is released from practice.

Practice does not make perfect; *correct* practice makes perfect. That is why we conduct the task analysis to provide immediate correctional feedback to the participant. The behavioral objective is stated in terms that are measurable in that it delineates specific skills that a partici-

Task Analysis Checklist

Name of participant _____

Date _____

Task _____

(Place check mark to indicate error in performance.)

1. ☐ Does not sprint toward defensive back.
2. ☐ Dips shoulders toward ground.
3. ☐ Twists shoulders from side to side.
4. ☐ Does not keep eyes on defensive back.
5. ☐ Telegraphs move by looking in direction he is going to cut.
6. ☐ Telegraphs move by leaning toward direction of the cut.
7. ☐ Does not plant left foot for drive force.
8. ☐ Runs curved patterns rather than straight line patterns.
9. ☐ Does not turn trunk, shoulders, and face toward sideline on the cut.
10. ☐ Does not look football into hands on the catch.

Comments:

Figure 4.1   Task analysis for right end or right flanker in down-and-out pass pattern right.

pant either does or does not perform correctly. The behavioral objective also describes an outcome that is observable through a criterion-referenced task analysis, and it describes a standard of excellence expected of a participant in that five pass patterns must be done correctly each day of practice.

Summary

A well-stated goal and behavioral objective give a program attainable direction and allow us to know when an intended outcome has been achieved. In addition, a well-stated goal assists us in the decision-making process of (a) determining what to test, (b) determining what tests are good indicators of the factors to be tested, (c) selecting appropriate testing procedures, and (d) establishing desired directions and outcomes of a program.

A well-stated behavioral objective will assist us in the decision-making process of (a) designing a program of activities that is designed to attain the stated goal; (b) selecting appropriate teaching methods, skills, and strategies; (c) selecting appropriate equipment and materials; (d) selecting an appropriate time schedule for program presentation; and (e) determining if the program of activities, teaching methods, skills, and strategies is in fact achieving the stated behavioral objectives. Last but not least, well-stated goals and behavioral objectives provide an instructor or coach with accountability for his or her decisions in conducting a program and evaluating the performance of program participants.

Review Questions

1. Name the three criteria that may be used to determine if a goal is well-written.
2. Name the three criteria that may be used to determine if a measurable objective is well-written.
3. What is the relationship between goals and measurable objectives?
4. How do well-stated goals and measurable behavioral objectives give the instructor accountability? To whom and for what is the instructor accountable?

Problems and Exercises

1. Write a goal for a physical education class. Describe the testing procedures. Write a behavioral objective to attain the goal.

2. Write a goal for some phase of an athletic event. Describe the testing procedures. Write a behavioral objective to attain the goal.

3. Write a goal for a health club. Describe the testing procedures. Write a behavioral objective to attain the goal.

4. Write a goal for a therapeutic recreation program. Describe the testing procedures. Write a behavioral objective to attain the goal.

5. Write a goal for a coronary rehabilitation program. Describe the testing procedures. Write a behavioral objective to attain the goal.

6. Write a goal for an exercise prescription program. Describe the testing procedures. Write a behavioral objective to attain the goal.

7. Write a paper showing the relationships between evaluation, goals, and behavioral objectives.

8. Conduct a class discussion about how an instructor and/or coach would be accountable in each of the following situations:
   a. An instructor gives a student a grade of D for the semester. The student and her parents feel that this grade is unjustified.
   b. A high school basketball coach cuts a young man from the chance to be on the school's basketball squad.

Bibliography

American Alliance for Health, Physical Education, and Recreation. (1976). *Youth fitness test manual* (3rd ed.). Washington, DC: Author.

American Alliance for Health, Physical Education, Recreation, and Dance. (1980). *Health-related physical fitness manual.* Reston, VA: Author.

American College of Sports Medicine. (1980). *Guidelines for graded exercise testing and prescription* (2nd ed.). Philadelphia: Lea & Febiger.

Falls, H., Baylor, A., & Dishman, R. (1980). *Essentials of fitness.* Philadelphia: Saunders.

Heyward, V. (1984). *Design for fitness.* Minneapolis: Burgess.

Loovis, E., & Ersing, F. (1979). *Assessing and programming gross motor development for children.* Cleveland Heights: Ohio Motor Assessment Associates.

Mager, R. (1975). *Preparing instructional objectives* (2nd ed.). Belmont, CA: Fearon.

Safrit, M. (1980). *Evaluation in physical education* (2nd ed.). Englewood Cliffs, NJ: Prentice-Hall.

Ulrich, D. (1984). Domain (criterion-referenced testing) in adapted physical education reliability study. *Adapted Physical Activity Quarterly,* **1**(1), 52-60.

Vort Corporation. (1979). *Action words directory: An index to verbs for setting objectives.* Palo Alto: Vort Corp.

Part II

Measurement in the Motor Domain

In 1956, B.S. Bloom published a taxonomy of the cognitive domain that exposited intellectual functions as they relate to educational objectives. In due time there followed a taxonomy of the affective domain (Krathwohl, Bloom, & Masia, 1964), and by 1985 at least 12 separate models or taxonomies of motor performance had appeared (Gilchrist & Gruber, 1983-84). Many different attempts to define motor performance appear in the professional literature because each of the domains—cognitive, affective, and motor—actually encompasses several subdomains that should be classified somewhat independent of each other. The affective domain, for example, is composed of personality, interests, values, attitudes, social adjustment, and other emotional dimensions. In the domain of human motor performance, we find physical educators concentrating on dimensions such as physical fitness, development of fundamental motor skills, and specific sport skills, to name only a few. Each of these areas should be viewed as a separate domain of motor activities.

The measurement of motor performance involves using a few test items to adequately sample a defined area of interest that has been referred to in measurement literature as a *domain, universe, fund of information*, or *population* of abilities. The most recent literature (Brennan, 1983; Hopkins & Stanley, 1981; Martuza, 1977; Safrit, 1981; Ulrich, 1984) has concentrated on the terms *domain* or *universe* to represent the carefully defined behaviors that are sampled by a test. We shall follow this trend in the remaining chapters of this text.

Obviously, care must be taken to carefully define the domain behaviors that are the basis for writing specific instructional or behavioral objectives. This in turn will lead to more effective testing and measuring, which provide necessary information that practitioners can use as a basis for decision-making.

The first chapter in this section deals with constructing tests that sample a defined universe or domain of motor performance. Principles and problems in constructing both norm-referenced and criterion-referenced tests are discussed and are followed by relevant examples. Criteria for evaluating motor performance tests are also presented. Chapter 6 presents tests for measuring underlying components of motor performance, and chapter 7 deals with motor and physical fitness testing. The last chapter of this section presents tests to be used in assessing skills in specific sports.

Selection and Construction of Motor Performance Tests

Motor performance tests assess how well an individual performs defined motor tasks. Many types of motor tests have been developed. Some assess fine motor skills such as handwriting, watch repairing, and piano playing. Physical educators, however, are more familiar with gross motor skill tests that concentrate on tasks requiring movement of the limbs and body through space. The testing literature in physical education is replete with strength and physical fitness tests, motor fitness tests, motor ability tests, perceptual-motor tests, and sports skills tests. Unfortunately, however, many of these tests were not subjected to rigorous standards of quality test construction. Hence we must be careful in appraising the motor performance tests we intend to use. Tests are comprised of items that sample and represent a larger, well-defined universe of items. In order to select and/or construct quality tests, certain steps must be followed.

As a physical educator you will sometimes find that no valid and reliable test exists in the testing literature to provide you with the information you need for decision-making. When this situation arises you must construct your own test. Thus all physical educators must be familiar with the steps in constructing or appraising a motor performance test. If you follow these steps in constructing a test, you will have developed an adequate test that provides you with relevant information. If you choose to consider an existing standardized test, you must carefully examine the test manual to determine if the authors followed these steps when they constructed the test. If these steps were not followed, the test must be suspect in your mind and you should not use it. These basic steps for constructing quality tests include the following:

1. Determining the purpose of testing and selecting either a norm-referenced or criterion-referenced format depending on the purpose of the test.
2. Identifying the abilities to be assessed.
3. Selecting or developing motor items that test these abilities according to certain criteria.
4. Securing necessary facilities and equipment.

5. Conducting a pilot study on a group of examinees.
6. Revising test items and directions.
7. Administering test items to a large number of examinees.
8. Determining internal and external validity of the test where feasible.
9. Securing test reliability information.
10. Developing norms for a norm-referenced test or establishing appropriate levels for pass/fail cutoffs for a criterion-referenced test.
11. Preparing a test manual.
12. Periodically revising the test based on evaluative data.

Determining the Purpose of Testing

What is the purpose of the test you want to construct? How will you use the test data? What decisions will you make about the participant and/or the program based on the test results? How crucial is the decision to the welfare of the participant? These questions must be answered before constructing a test or selecting an existing standardized test. In the broadest sense, testing should provide effective feedback to participants, instructors, administrators, and parents so that instruction and the instructional setting can be continuously improved.

Formative or Summative Evaluation

The techniques for constructing tests and the criteria for selecting tests differ slightly depending on how the test data are to be used. Therefore, it is important to determine if we will use the test data as the basis for formative or summative evaluation decisions. Recall that formative evaluation provides the learner with daily, on-the-spot feedback about performance. Flaws

in technique or performance routines are indicated, and the participant uses this information as a basis for subsequent practice. Summative evaluation occurs at the end of an instructional unit or when a larger block of material has been covered. A summative test, for example, might include a variety of basketball skills given after 6 weeks of instruction for input into determining a student's grade.

Motor skill testing can be utilized to satisfy the formative or summative evaluation needs of the physical educator. When formative evaluation is desired, however, specific skills must be identified and utilized. These skills are usually the fundamentals that must be practiced daily for skill development. An operational definition of each skill component (i.e., the correct process of performance) must be known by the physical educator and utilized as the basis for a task analysis. This operational definition of each skill component may also be reflected in a rating scale that provides frequent feedback to the learner so that performance adjustments can be achieved.

Criterion-Referenced or Norm-Referenced Tests

Another important determination to be made in constructing or selecting a test is whether a norm-referenced or criterion-referenced test is more conducive to the testing purpose. For example, if we want to compare individual participants' performances with the performances of other participants at the end of an instructional unit, we need a norm-referenced test developed for summative evaluation purposes. Other decisions concerning pupil achievement, classification, prediction, and selection can be made based on norm-referenced test data. These decisions, however, are all relative to the performances of other individuals in the norm group. The norm group is the appropriate standard for status comparison in this case. An example of how a norm-referenced test may be used in pupil achievement would be to compare a student's physical fitness score with the scores of other students in a national norm group at the start of the instructional unit by determining the student's percentile rank. Periodically, as well as at the end of the semester, one can see if any improvement in fitness is reflected in the student's percentile rank.

Criterion-referenced tests can also be very useful to physical educators. One use of criterion-referenced testing involves identifying those participants who have attained a predetermined level of skill, such as the ability to swim 50 yards while demonstrating two strokes, one on the front and one on the back or side. Rather than comparing participants' performances to others, the goal here is for the participant to pass this skill requirement so that he or she may advance to the next level of skill instruction. A second use of criterion-referenced tests is to determine the percentage of items or tasks that a participant can perform correctly within a particular level of difficulty. In this process, one establishes a *cutting score*, that is, the level of performance at which a participant has mastered a sufficient percentage of items to warrant being promoted to a more advanced level of instruction.

The type of standard selected (norm- or criterion-referenced) depends on the nature of the decisions the physical educator needs to make based on the test data. We must also consider the extent to which the physical educator might make an erroneous decision. What are the repercussions to the participant, society, and the profession if we set the cutting score too high or too low? In other words, how critical is the decision to pass or fail a participant? In a beginning swimming class, if we erroneously pass a participant on a specific skill, we can go back and provide more instruction until the participant passes that item, and little harm is done.

Let us consider, however, a more critical situation such as a test to certify lifesaving skills. If six lifesaving skills are identified, then to en-

sure that all certified lifeguards have acquired all necessary skills the cutting score will be six out of six, or 100% mastery. Society cannot afford to have certified lifeguards who can perform only four out of six critical lifesaving skills. Society and professional aquatics safety personnel justifiably expect lifeguards to master all lifesaving skills required in the job description. We would certainly not use a norm-referenced approach in this situation because what is important is not how well one participant's skills compare to others' skills but rather that every certified lifeguard possesses all lifesaving competencies stated.

It is important to note that criterion-referenced tests may also be used in a summative evaluation situation. For example, we may want to determine if a student has mastered 80% of beginning-level basketball skills before we promote that pupil to an intermediate class.

Teachers must be aware that they are held accountable for the decisions they make based on test data. If their decision adversely impacts on the pupil or other members of society, teachers are open to legal repercussions (Bayless & Adams, 1985; Henderson, 1985). Hence we introduce the concepts of *false positive* and *false negative decisions* and the cost-effectiveness of establishing a certain criterion or cutoff score. In his analysis of the concept of cost-effectiveness, Martuza (1977) indicated that if the overall cost of erroneously passing nonmasters (a false positive decision) is greater than the overall cost of retaining or failing masters (a false negative decision), then raising the cutting score will tend to minimize losses. This is exemplified in the lifesaving skill test previously described. Conversely, if false negatives are more costly than false positives, then lowering the cutting score will minimize losses. This is exemplified in the beginning swimming skill test just discussed. The problem is one of minimizing costs or repercussions due to erroneous decisions of the teacher, coach, or administrator. Later, in chapter 17, we will see that false negative decisions can be extremely costly or even fatal in the operation of an exercise rehabilitation program for heart patients.

Finally, one test can serve a number of purposes. For example, an achievement test in basic volleyball can provide some of the information that is used to determine a physical education grade and at the same time diagnose weak areas in certain tested skills. These same test scores can also be used to develop local norms for certain basic volleyball skills at various stages of learning. This latter point is an example of how a teacher can develop norm-referenced standards to judge an individual's performance in relation to the performances of all students previously tested under similar conditions in the same grade at a particular school.

Process or Product Evaluation

Inherent in determining the purposes for testing is the concept of *process* and/or *product* evaluation. In *product* evaluation, we are usually concerned with a summed score (product) such as the number of baskets made in 30 seconds on a basketball skill test. We could also evaluate the *process* of making a basket by examining skill components such as hand position on the ball, mechanics of the shot, spin on the ball, and so on. In baseball batting, the number of contacts with the ball can be counted (product), and/or the mechanics of the swing can be rated (process). The evaluation of other skills, such as gymnastics routines, primarily involves assessing the process or quality of sequential movements. For these skills, the process *is* the product, and both must be evaluated jointly. The instructor must decide which type of evaluation will provide the most effective feedback at a particular stage in learning. The physical educator must consider the type of skill, the way it is to be performed in actual use, and the skill level of instruction (beginning, intermediate, or advanced) when arriving at this decision before an appraisal instrument is constructed or selected.

Standardized or Self-Made Tests

One final decision to be made is whether to construct your own test or to select a test from a pool of existing standardized tests. This decision is made after you have determined how the test scores will be used. If you want to determine how well a participant or the class has achieved in terms of program objectives, a self-made criterion-referenced test will probably be superior to a standardized test. Using a standardized test may subject the physical educator to the charge of testing for what has not been taught, especially if there is a gap between the content of the test and the content of the instruction. On the other hand, if you wish to compare class or program data with scores from other regions of the country, then you will logically select a standardized norm-referenced test with the appropriate normative data.

Statewide competency testing is being adopted in many states. Standardized tests are being employed to determine how well local units meet state or national standards in teaching subject matter in various fields. These efforts are intended to stimulate local schools to improve their programs if necessary. In terms of refinement in test construction, standardized tests are probably superior to self-made tests because standardized tests are usually developed by persons who specialize in both test construction and the subject matter covered in the test. In addition, the constructor of a standardized test usually has financial and logistical resources available that will enhance appropriate validity and reliability studies, including the development of norms or appropriate criterion-referenced standards.

Identifying Abilities to be Assessed

Motor skills are classified in several ways based on the nature of the skill and the way the skill is projected in the environment. Schmidt (1975) differentiates between *discrete* skill performance and *serial* skill performance as well as between *open* performance environment and *closed* performance environment. If a task has a discrete beginning and end, it is termed a *discrete* skill. Examples of a discrete skill include a ball throw or standing long jump. On the other hand, if the skill involves stringing a number of different discrete skills together to form a sequence of specified movements, it is a *serial* skill. When the shortstop moves in to field a ground ball, straightens up, and throws the runner out at first base, he or she is performing a serial skill. The hop, step, and jump and the pole vault are other examples of serial skills.

Serial skills that are projected for a long period of time, such as playing basketball or bicycling for 40 minutes, constitute a long-term continuous performance. A situation in which the environment is not changing and the performer can plan movements well in advance without fear of the situation changing, as in bowling or archery, is termed a *closed performance environment*. A situation in which the environment is constantly changing, such as a basketball game or tennis match, is termed an *open performance environment*. In an open performance environment, each individual's performance is affected by changing environmental stimuli furnished by teammates, opponents, audience members, noise level, and so forth. Thus environmental conditions and the way the skill will be used by the performer in the physical education class should influence the type of skill test item that the teacher constructs. Specificity of testing, or content validity, will thus be assured to some degree.

Activities can also be categorized according to their method of pacing. In a *self-paced* movement, such as bowling or archery, the performer initiates movement when he or she is ready and performs at his or her own rate. In *externally paced* tasks, such as basketball or soccer, the performer is paced by others in the environment; that is, other people stimulate the performer's movement response and in some cases dictate how fast or how often the performer responds.

Both Stallings (1982) and Schmidt (1975) provide further insight into the nature of motor skills that teachers must consider in constructing tests. Skills that are important in the early stages of learning often change in complexity and movement pattern or become subordinate skills at intermediate or advanced levels. Cognition and information processing are quite important in the early stages of learning but become less important as skills become more automatic at the advanced levels. At advanced levels of skill performance, cognition may be turned toward strategy instead of toward the correct way to execute a skilled movement. Hence a motor skill test that is appropriate at the beginning of an instructional program may be inappropriate at the end of the program if students' motor abilities have changed markedly in the course of instruction. Discrete skills tests may be appropriate for beginners, whereas complex serial skills tests are usually more suitable for intermediate and advanced performers. Aquatics skills provide a good example: beginners are tested on skills such as floating, gliding, and breath holding, whereas intermediate and advanced swimmers are tested on 25- or 30-yard swims for time in the various strokes.

Characteristics of the learner, including age, grade level, present physical functioning level, and previous background in skill acquisition, must also be considered when identifying the skills to be tested. Young children in elementary physical education or those being diagnostically tested in a remedial motor skills laboratory will probably be tested on many simple, discrete motor tasks such as jumping, hopping, throwing, catching, turning, twisting, and rolling to assess their strength, flexibility, balance, eye-hand or eye-foot coordination, speed, and agility. These discrete motor tasks are tested in order of difficulty and may become serial in nature as they increase in complexity. Again, the items selected must satisfy a relevant rationale for testing but be specific to the testing purpose with the test performance simulating the performance expected in the game or activity situation at each stage of learning.

Selecting or Developing Motor Items

Let us assume that we want to construct a criterion-referenced test of advanced sidestroke skills to evaluate student achievement after 3 weeks of instruction in an advanced swimming class that met for three 50-minute periods a week. Thus our purpose in testing is to estimate the percentage of advanced achievement. Our expert knowledge of the component sidestroke skills that comprise advanced ability must be used in constructing the test. To have good content validity, the test items should reflect the skills in the appropriate ability or domain level.

First we must identify the essential skill components for the advanced ability domain. We may wish to consult other swimming experts to establish a consensus on which skills belong to the advanced sidestroke level. A thorough review of the literature in swimming manuals and teaching texts would also assist us in identifying the relevant skills in the advanced ability level.

Next we must identify the skill elements that we wish to test within each component of proper advanced sidestroke swimming. For example, we may want to test the leading arm pull element in the arm coordination component. In other words, we need to determine *what* and *how* to measure based on input from our own expert opinion, the opinions of other swimming instructors, and a review of pertinent literature. We must now develop an operational definition of the skill to be tested, namely advanced sidestroke swimming. This definition must reflect the components and elements of the skill as used by advanced sidestroke swimmers. Skill perfor-

mance can be measured in terms of time, distance, accuracy, force, or form. We must carefully think through the movement sequence of the skill and devise the most appropriate way to measure it, that is, to measure the way the skill is actually used in swimming the sidestroke properly. Safrit (1981) provides an excellent discussion of the problems inherent in measuring skills in units not related to the way the skill is projected in actual practice.

Components and elements of skills can be assessed by using the task analysis method as a follow-up to criterion-referenced testing. Task analysis is particularly useful in formative evaluations. The elements in each component of a skill are identified and listed, and an identifying mark is made next to each element on the list to indicate proper or improper execution. A word description of each element for each component of the skill appears on the criterion-referenced test for ready reference. It is essential that this word definition describe and accompany the degree of skill observed. Physical educators can distribute task analyses so that individual class members can see where their weaknesses lie. Pupils with similar faults can be grouped together for remedial practice. Figure 5.1 is an example of a criterion-referenced test and task analysis for the advanced sidestroke skill.

The procedures for developing test items for a norm-referenced test of motor performance are generally similar to the ones described for a criterion-referenced test with one main exception: Norm-referenced test items must be difficult enough to maximize the items' capacity to discriminate among different levels of ability. All items in a norm-referenced test should contribute to the identification of individual differences in levels of ability. In other words, we must be able to rank-order our pupils based on their test scores. For example, we might propose that the time required to swim 50 yards using various strokes (sidestroke, backstroke, crawl, and breaststroke) be our norm-referenced test for measuring swimming ability. Note that this test could likely be used for various levels of performers because the time required to complete each test item is in fact a function of skill level.

After selecting or developing the items to be tested, detailed directions for the administration and scoring of the test items need to be written. This aspect of the test construction must not be taken lightly. The validity of measurement heavily depends on accurate and consistent testing procedures. For example, if two people take a test under different conditions, we do not know if differences in their scores are due to actual differences in their abilities or differences in the way we administered or scored the test. We may exemplify this with a pull-up test: One pupil uses a forehand grip, the other pupil uses a backhand grip and receives a different score. Is the difference in their scores due to the type of grip used or to differences in the muscle group endurance we want to estimate?

Sidestroke Task Analysis Sheet

Name of performer _____ Name of analyzer _____

Criterion for passing at the end of the unit for sidestroke: The participant must have acceptable form as rated by the instructor in 4 out of 4 components tested by the end of a 3-week unit on the sidestroke. The components are: 1. body position during glide; 2. arms; 3. legs; 4. coordination and breathing. Once a participant has passed a component, he or she does not have to repeat the test for that component. A participant may request to be tested at any swimming lesson.

Component I. Body Position During Glide
    Criterion: The participant must score 4 points to achieve acceptable form. Score 1 point for each element passed and 0 points for each element failed.

Form Rating—Glide

Score _____ Arms and legs fully extended

_____ Legs together

_____ Body stretched and straight

_____ Body on side

_____ Head turned toward upper shoulder to facilitate breathing

Task Analysis for Immediate Feedback

The form was not acceptable (check appropriate error):

_____ Arms and legs not fully extended

_____ Legs are not together

_____ Body not stretched and straight

_____ Body turned toward back-down position

_____ Body turned toward stomach-down position

_____ Head not turned toward the upper shoulder to facilitate breathing

Total score _____

Form is acceptable _____
Form is not acceptable _____

(Cont.)

Component II. Arm Coordination

Criterion: The participant must score 4 points to achieve acceptable form. Score 1 point for each element passed and 0 points for each element failed.

Form Rating—Arms	Task Analysis for Immediate Feedback
Score _____ Pull of the leading (lower) arm long and smooth	The form was not acceptable (check appropriate error):
_____ Pull of the leading arm just below water surface	_____ Pull of the leading (lower) arm too short
_____ Leading arm recovered with fingertips leading	_____ Pull of the leading arm too deep
_____ Elbow of leading arm brought to ribs before recovery of that arm	_____ Leading arm not recovered with fingertips leading
_____ Trailing (upper) arm pulls to thigh	_____ Elbow of leading arm not brought to ribs before recovery of that arm
Total score _____	_____ Trailing arm (upper) does not pull to thigh

Form is acceptable _____
Form is not acceptable _____

Component III. Leg Coordination

Criterion: The participant must score 6 points to achieve acceptable form. Score 1 point for each element passed and 0 points for each element failed.

Form Rating—Legs	Task Analysis for Immediate Feedback
Score _____ Legs perform scissors kick	The form was not acceptable (check appropriate error):
_____ Legs bend at knees during recovery	_____ Legs separated vertically; resulting in a breaststroke kick
_____ Knees brought up to stomach during recovery	_____ Inverted scissors kick used
_____ Legs recover slowly	_____ Legs do not bend enough at knees during recovery
_____ Legs straightened before the squeeze	_____ Knees brought too far in front of stomach during recovery
_____ Strong effort during squeeze	_____ Legs recovered too vigorously
_____ Ankles extended to point toes during late part of squeeze	_____ Legs not straightened before the squeeze
	_____ Too little effort during squeeze
Total score _____	_____ Ankles not extended to point toes during last part of squeeze

Form is acceptable _____
Form is not acceptable _____

_____ Legs pass each other at end of squeeze

(Cont.)

Component IV. Coordination and Breathing

Criterion: The participant must score 5 points to achieve acceptable form. Score 1 point for each element passed and 0 points for each element failed.

Form Rating—Coordination and Breathing

Score _____ Upper arm pulls toward thigh while lead (lower) arm thrusts toward knee

_____ Leading arm glides with body and does not pull immediately after recovery

_____ Leading arm does not pull at same time kick is delivered

_____ Kick is delivered as leading arm ready to recover

_____ Exhalation during leg kick or glide

_____ Inhalation follows immediately after exhalation

_____ The duration of the glide is held until the body slows in the water

Total score _____

Form is acceptable _____
Form is not acceptable _____

Task Analysis for Immediate Feedback

The form was not acceptable (check appropriate error):

_____ Both arms pull toward feet at same time

_____ Leading arm begins pull immediately after recovery

_____ Leading arm pulls at same time kick is delivered

_____ Kick delivered before leading arm ready to recover

_____ Exhalation is at a time other than during leg kick on glide

_____ Inhalation does not follow immediately after exhalation

Figure 5.1 Criterion and task analysis sheet for the sidestroke. Adapted from *Teaching Aquatics* (p. 211) by J.A. Torney and R.A. Clayton, 1981, Minneapolis: Burgess. Copyright by Burgess Publishing Company. Reprinted by permission.

Securing Facilities and Equipment

The instructor must specify and secure the facilities and equipment needed to administer the test items. The manner in which courts, pools, and playing fields are to be measured and marked must be noted and exact dimensions specified. These details will facilitate accurate administration of the test items. The area must be free of any safety hazard or obstruction that may hinder safe and accurate testing. All equipment (stopwatches, weights, calipers, scales, etc.) must be carefully calibrated, and all testing personnel must be thoroughly trained in the use of the facilities and equipment in order to eliminate measurement error.

Conducting a Pilot Study and Revising Items

Conducting a pilot study on a small group of participants should help to identify problems in the administration and scoring of the test items. We should be able to determine if our operational definitions of skill components are relevant to the level of abilities we need to assess. In addition, our method of scoring can be scrutinized. Do the test items identify participants with performance difficulties? If mastery learning is one of our goals in testing, have we set realistic levels for mastery cutoff scores for each item? Revise items and procedures if necessary. Pilot testing is crucial in the development of criterion-referenced tests so that content validity can be determined. This is the most important type of validity in criterion-referenced testing because the criterion measure for validity is not an external measure or rating but rather the established cutoff points.

Pilot testing is also crucial in the development of norm-referenced tests. Problems in administration and scoring of items should be identified. It is also essential to determine if items are sufficiently difficult to distinguish among ability levels. Any problems that are discovered should be eliminated in item revision prior to subsequent usage of the test. It is important that teachers set up the testing stations early and calibrate all equipment prior to testing.

Administering Test Items

With pilot testing completed, we are ready to secure more validity and reliability information on groups that represent physical education classes. The test must be administered with care taken to follow directions for test administration and scoring. There is no "magic number"

of people needed in testing. However, there must be enough individuals involved to allow for various ability levels to be projected in a norm-referenced test. In other words, test enough people who represent above average, average, and below average ability levels. Depending on the nature of the test item, between 25 and 100 participants may be necessary to allow differences in natural abilities to be displayed. Hopefully, the distribution of scores from pilot testing should closely resemble a normal curve, although this is not absolutely essential. An important consideration is to have sufficient variability in subjects' ability levels to allow their test results to be rank-ordered. Approximately 30 to 100 people should also be involved in the pilot testing of criterion-referenced measures. We want to be able to calculate the percentage of people who pass the test or meet the criterion the first time they attempt the test item. We also want enough subjects so that we can estimate item and test validity. Several hundred people must be involved in the final test validity and reliability study.

Determining Internal and External Validity

In order to approximate the concurrent validity of a norm-referenced test, a group of experts should rank the participants on the motor skill under consideration. These experts must all use the same definition of ability in their ratings. Other physical education teachers, coaches, and even members of a varsity team may serve as effective judges. The ratings of these experts may now be correlated with each item score as well as the total score the participants made on the test. In order to compute a total score, all part scores will need to be converted to a common scale such as a T score. Examine the correlations between each skill item and the criterion of expert ratings; the higher the correlation, the better the item estimates ratings of ability. Items should generally have fairly low correlations among themselves in order to avoid having two items providing the same information, which wastes testing time. Retain items that correlate well with the criterion and low with one another. An efficient norm-referenced skill test should probably not have more than four or five items of optimum difficulty in order to have economy of testing time. You can compute a multiple correlation between the five items combined and the criterion score. This technique permits the items to uniquely combine their contribution when estimating the criterion. It also permits one to determine the weight or influence (degree of importance) each item has in the multiple relationship. Generally, a multiple correlation (R) of .80 or above is quite acceptable for a skill test.

In criterion-referenced testing, the construct validity refers to the extent to which a test places pupils into correct categories or mastery levels (Safrit, 1981). Two extreme groups can be established: one that receives instruction and one that does not. The majority of students attaining mastery should be in the instructed group, whereas the majority of nonmasters should be in the group not receiving instruction. When this happens the test (item) is sensitive to instructional outcomes.

item as well as for the total test. These reliability coefficients should exceed .80 for a norm-referenced test.

Ulrich (1984) has shown that two different reliability coefficients can be computed for criterion-referenced tests to estimate domain status. He was able to consistently classify students on two different occasions as masters or nonmasters of fundamental motor skills using either an 85% mastery as the criterion cutoff score or the 70% mastery level.

The test-retest reliability procedure may also be used to assess the stability of the pass/fail decision for each skill in a criterion-referenced test. The extent to which a test and the testing procedures produce consistency in pass/fail decisions is an indication of the test's freedom from random measurement error. One can also estimate the objectivity of scoring or rating of performance with one or with several experts.

The teacher must consider the role of fatigue, boredom, and practice when estimating the reliability of test data. All of these factors will cause changes to occur in test-retest data collected in the same day's class period. To avoid this situation, administer the retest on a separate day. Test directions often specify that at least six trials are allowed. Which trial score do we use for our decision? Plot the means for all trials on graph paper. Use the scores from those trials where the mean scores are similar.

Determining Reliability

Several methods of determining test reliability were presented in chapter 3. The preferred method is some form of test-retest. In order to obtain a reliability coefficient using this method, we test our group of participants on the items we have developed. Then we retest the same group a few days later. Now we have two sets of scores for the same participants, which allows us to estimate test-retest reliability for each

Developing Norms or Establishing Appropriate Levels for Pass/Fail

It will be desirable in time to develop local standards for both criterion- and norm-referenced tests. This can be done by testing a number of groups of participants. Thus participants can compare their test scores with the scores obtained by all other participants tested in the same type group or class. If other physical educators are going to use the test, it is important to develop a test manual that contains all of the relevant information concerning testing procedures. We must again stress that over 200 individuals should be tested for purposes of establishing normative data that represent the local group.

Writing a Test Manual

The purpose of a test manual is to thoroughly acquaint a potential test user with all of the essential qualities of the test. In most cases the contents of the test manual will be the basis for a decision either to adopt the test or continue searching for a more appropriate one. The criteria used in developing the test must be addressed in detail and validation procedures described in the test manual. The methods of establishing content validity and actual reports of validity and reliability studies should also be included, as well as descriptions of the age, sex, race, and cultural background of subjects.

Detailed instructions for the administration and scoring of the test must be included in the manual with a list of necessary facilities and equipment and instructions for their use. If norm charts are included in the manual, the participants in the normative data sample should be described. Procedures for combining separate test items into a composite score must be included, along with a description of how the professional can interpret the test results. Also, one should provide a discussion on how to construct and interpret a profile of students' scores from different test variables.

Evaluating the Test

As we evaluate a test, we should use an operational checklist similar to the one in Figure 5.2. Notice that the checklist includes all of the steps for test construction/selection presented in this chapter. An example application of the checklist for a norm-referenced summative evaluation test designed for grading purposes in a physical fitness unit is presented in Figure 5.3.

Skill Test Construction Checklist

Activity _____ Proficiency level: Beginner _____ Intermediate _____
Advanced _____

Description of group to be tested: Age _____ Sex _____ Race _____

School or setting _____

Purpose of test: Achievement _____ Classification _____ Diagnosis _____
Promotion _____ Prediction _____ Selection _____

Evaluation mode: Formative _____ Summative _____

Reference focus: Norm referenced _____ Criterion referenced _____

Type of validity: Content _____ Construct _____ Concurrent _____ Predictive _____

(Cont.)

Content of domain of skills: _____

_____

Selected skills for testing: _____

_____

Operational definition of performance for each skill: Yes _____ No _____

Procedures for administration and scoring of skills: Yes _____ No _____

Facilities and equipment needed to conduct test: _____

_____

Type of scoring: Pass/Fail _____ Quantitative _____ Process scoring _____
              Product scoring _____

Pilot study conducted: Yes _____ No _____

Problems in administration and scoring of test items: _____

_____

Reliability of testing: Test-retest ___ Split-half _____ Adequate _____

              Inadequate _____ (list items)

Skills and number of trials to achieve consistency: _____

_____

Revise items and procedures where indicated: Yes _____ No _____

Revise test format (list items in order of difficulty): Yes _____ No _____

Establish or adjust criterion for pass/fail: Yes _____ No _____

Figure 5.2 Checklist for construction of skill test.

Skill Test Selection Checklist

Selection or construction (circle one)

Description of group to be tested: Age: _13-14_ years Sex: M F

Name of test: _AAHPER Youth Fitness Test 1976_

School or setting: _Carter Middle School_

(Cont.)

Purpose of test: Achievement _____ Classification _____ Diagnosis _____
Promotion _____ Prediction _____ Selection _____

Evaluation mode: Formative _____ Summative _____
           Comment: A summative evaluation will be made at the end of unit.

Reference focus: Norm referenced _____ Criterion referenced _____

Types of validity: Content _____ Construct _____ Concurrent _____ Predictive _____
Comments: AAHPER Youth Fitness Test provides estimates for a number of factors. The AAHPER Youth Fitness Test possesses factorial validity.

Content of domain: To test the fitness status of youth.

Selected skills for testing: Dynamic and/or static strength and endurance of arms and shoulders, trunk strength and endurance, speed and change in direction, explosive strength of legs, explosive strength of legs and speed of lower extremities, and cardiorespiratory endurance.

Facilities and equipment needed to conduct test:

Pull-Up (boys): A metal or wooden bar approximately 1-1/2 in. in diameter. A doorway gym bar can be used, and if no regular equipment is available, a piece of pipe or even rungs of a ladder can also serve the purpose.

Flexed-Arm Hang (girls): A horizontal bar approximately 1-1/2 in. in diameter is preferred. A doorway gym bar can be used; if no regular equipment is available, a piece of pipe can serve the purpose. A stopwatch.

Sit-Up (flexed leg) (boys and girls): Clean floor, mat, or dry turf and a stopwatch.

Shuttle Run (boys and girls): Two blocks of wood, 2 × 2 × 4 in. and a stopwatch. Pupils should wear sneakers or run barefooted.

Standing Long Jump (boys and girls): Mat, floor, or outdoor jumping pit, and a metric or English tape measure.

50-Yard Dash (boys and girls): Two stopwatches or one with a split-second timer.

9-Minute Run for Distance or 1-Mile Run for Time (boys and girls): Track area marked off in known distance segments in yards or meters; stopwatch; score sheets and pencil.

Types of scoring: Pass/Fail _____ Quantitative _____ Process scoring _____
           Product scoring _____

Pilot study conducted: Yes _____ No _____

Problems in administration and scoring of test items: None, the test is easily administered by the instructor with very little equipment required. National norms are presented in the test manual. Conducted over a two day period. Two days are recommended for conducting the test.

(Cont.)

Reliability of testing: Test-retest _____ Split-half _____ Adequate _____
Inadequate _____ (list items)
Comments: Reported reliability coefficients: Pull-Ups .82 to .89, Flexed-Arm Hang .74, Standing Long Jump .83 to .98, 50-Yard Dash .83 to .94, Sit-Ups .57 to .68, Shuttle Run .68 to .75, 12- or 9-Minute Run .98.

Factors and number of trials to achieve consistency:

Pull-Ups (boys): Dynamic strength and endurance of arms and shoulders. Allow 1 trial unless it is obvious that a participant has not had a fair chance.

Flexed-Arm Hang (girls): Static strength and endurance of arms and shoulders. Allow 1 trial unless it is obvious that a participant has not had a fair chance.

Shuttle Run (boys and girls): Speed and change of direction. Allow 2 trials, record the better.

Standing Long Jump (boys and girls): Explosive strength of legs. Allow 3 trials, record the best of the three.

50-Yard Dash (boys and girls): Explosive strength of legs and speed of lower extremities. Allow 1 trial.

Sit-Ups (boys and girls): Trunk strength and endurance. Allow 1 trial unless the instructor believes the participant has not had a fair opportunity to perform.

9-Minute Run for Distance or 1 Mile Run for Time (boys and girls): Cardiorespiratory endurance. Allow 1 trial. Record the time or distance.

Revise items and procedures where indicated: Yes _____ No _____
Comments: No revision necessary in this test.

Revise test format (list items in order of difficulty): Yes _____ No _____
Comments: It is recommended that testing be conducted over a two-day period with pull-ups or flexed-arm hang, sit-ups, and the shuttle run being administered the first day; and the standing long jump, 50-yard dash, and 9-minute run for distance or 1 mile run for time being completed on the second day. This process is recommended to reduce possible fatigue of participants.

Establish or adjust criterion for pass/fail: Yes _____ No _____
Grading standard for each test given:
80 percentile or above = A
60 to 79 percentile   = B
40 to 59 percentile   = C
20 to 39 percentile   = D
19 percentile or below = F
Based upon national norms; an average percentile rank will be calculated and a summative grade will be assigned at the end of the fitness unit using the above grading standard for each participant.

Figure 5.3 Steps in selecting a motor performance test.

You should now recognize the care and detailed steps that are necessary in constructing and/or selecting a test. These steps are essential if you are to have valid test data upon which to base the decisions you make about participants in your physical education programs.

Review Questions

1. What are the steps involved in constructing a test of motor performance?
2. What differences between norm-referenced and criterion-referenced tests must we consider in constructing a motor test?
3. Define *discrete skill, serial skill, open environment*, and *closed environment*. What role does each play in the construction of tests?
4. Give an example of a false positive and false negative decision resulting from test data.
5. What is the difference between process evaluation and product evaluation?
6. What are the advantages and disadvantages of using either a standardized or self-made test?
7. What procedures should be followed in developing items for a motor test?
8. What do we mean by *task analysis*? Give an example.
9. Why is it necessary to adhere to standardized directions in test administration?
10. How can you establish the validity and reliability of a norm-referenced and a criterion-referenced test?
11. What information should be included in a test manual?

Problems and Exercises

1. List the physical education activities that you teach or would like to teach. What are your daily, weekly, or grading period objectives? Indicate which objectives can be met by utilizing formative and summative evaluation techniques.
2. Describe how you can establish and implement both criterion-referenced and norm-referenced standards for a sport. What decisions can you make using these standards?
3. Describe how you would establish skill mastery levels for beginner achievement in swimming.
4. Develop a table of skill requirements for a volleyball skill test at the intermediate level. Use the checklist illustrated in Figure 5.2 as an outline for constructing the skill tests.
5. Define the fundamental skills relative to the beginning, intermediate, and advanced ability levels for basketball, gymnastics, and swimming. Define the components of each skill by writing an operational definition of each skill. Use the checklist for constructing tests presented in Figure 5.2.

6. Devise ways to test for the skills listed in Problem 5. Develop appropriate record forms, checklists, and rating scales. List facilities and equipment needed.

7. Administer one of the sport skill tests from Problem 5 on two different days to the same group of students. Compute the reliability coefficient for each test item.

Bibliography

American National Red Cross. (1981). *Swimming and aquatics safety.* Washington, DC: Author.

Barrow, H.M., & McGee, R. (1979). *A practical approach to measurement in physical education* (3rd ed.). Philadelphia: Lea & Febiger.

Bayless, M.A., & Adams, S.H. (1985). A liability checklist. *Journal of Physical Education, Recreation and Dance,* **56**(2), 49.

Bloom, B.S. (1956). *Taxonomy of educational objectives: The cognitive domain.* New York: David McKay.

Brennan, R.L. (1983). Some statistical procedures for domain referenced tests. In L.D. Hensley & W.B. East (Eds.), *Proceedings of the Fourth Measurement and Evaluation Symposium* (pp. 90-130). Cedar Falls, IA: University of Northern Iowa and the American Alliance for Health, Physical Education, Recreation, and Dance.

Cowell, C.C., & Ismail, A.H. (1961). Validity of a football rating scale and its relationship to social integration and academic ability. *Research Quarterly,* **32**(4), 461-467.

Gilchrist, J.R., & Gruber, J.J. (1983-84). Psychomotor domains. *Motor skills: Theory into practice,* **7**(1-2), 57-70.

Henderson, D.H. (1985). Physical education teachers, how do I sue thee? Oh, let me count the ways! *Journal of Physical Education, Recreation and Dance,* **56**(2), 44-48.

Hopkins, K.D., & Stanley, J.C. (1981). *Educational and psychological measurement and evaluation* (6th ed.). Englewood Cliffs, NJ: Prentice-Hall.

Krathwohl, D.R., Bloom, B.S., & Masia, B.B. (1964). *Taxonomy of educational objectives: The affective domain.* New York: David McKay.

Martuza, V.R. (1977). *Applying norm-referenced and criterion-referenced measurement in education.* Boston: Allyn & Bacon.

Safrit, M.J. (1981). *Evaluation in physical education* (2nd ed.). Englewood Cliffs, NJ: Prentice-Hall.

Schmidt, R.A. (1975). *Motor skills.* New York: Harper & Row.

Stallings, L.M. (1982). *Motor learning, from theory to practice.* St. Louis: C.V. Mosby.

Torney, J.A., & Clayton, R.D. (1981). *Teaching aquatics.* Minneapolis: Burgess.

Ulrich, D.A. (1984). The reliability of classification decisions made with the objectives-based motor skill assessment instrument. *Adapted Physical Activity Quarterly,* **1**(1), 52-60.

Washburn, R.A., & Safrit, M.J. (1982). Physical performance tests in job selection. A model for empirical validation. *Research Quarterly for Exercise and Sport,* **53**(3), 267-270.

Chapter
6

Components of Motor Performance

This chapter is intended to acquaint the physical educator with practical tests that can be administered to a large number of participants in a minimum of time. Emphasis is also placed on presenting tests that do not require expensive equipment. Tests that require expensive equipment or that can be administered to only one person at a time are discussed only briefly.

Most physical educators agree that the fundamental abilities and components of motor performance necessary for effective performance in sports and games include muscular strength, muscular endurance, muscular power, cardiovascular endurance, balance, flexibility, agility, speed, body awareness, eye-foot coordination, eye-hand coordination, and whole body coordination. Early developmental levels involve additional motor performance components, including simple motor responses, reflexes, sensory input, and awareness of space and tempo. These components are illustrated as a developmental hierarchy in Figure 6.1. An examination of these components reveals that some of them comprise what we call motor fit-

ness, physical fitness, basic motor development, or general motor ability. We must also consider cognitive abilities involved in learning and executing motor acts, such as visual factors, timing, sensory rhythms, and concentration. Thus some general motor ability tests may also serve as perceptual motor tests.

Motor learning research has indicated quite conclusively that all sports and games do not require the same components for effective performance and that each component does not exist by itself in a motor performance. Instead, each sport or activity requires its own rather unique interplay of certain aspects of the various motor performance components. Individuals, for example, will not score well on an agility test if their balance and coordination are poor. Tests of motor fitness and physical fitness are covered in the next chapter of this book. In this chapter, those test items that are thought to measure the important motor performance *components* utilized in sports and games are identified, beginning with strength and concluding with agility.

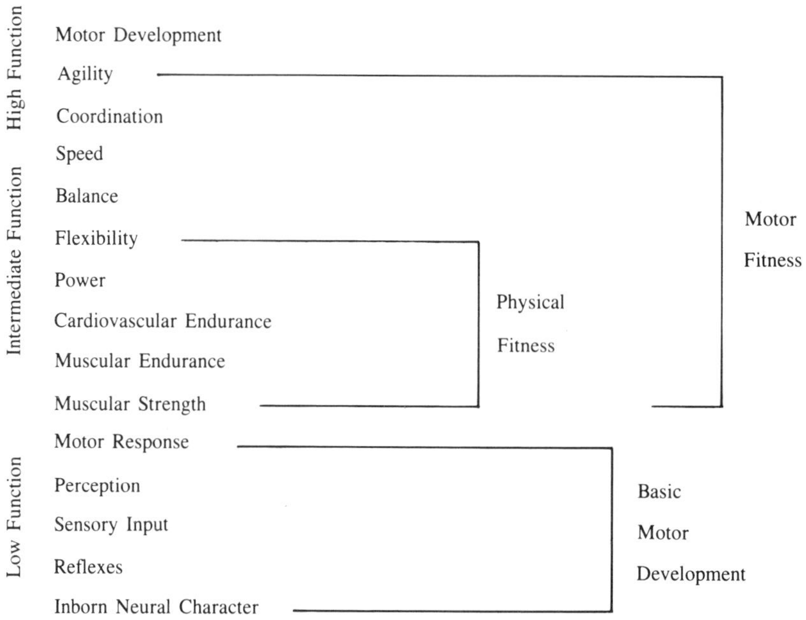

Figure 6.1   Chart of motor development elements.

The main purposes of testing to measure the presence of the components or basic abilities underlying motor performances are to

• diagnose an individual's strengths and weaknesses in the components so that developmental needs can be identified, individual objectives established, and a realistic remedial program designed in a motor diagnostic clinic;
• classify participants into instructional groups, especially for activities that are heavily dependent on strength, speed, power, and endurance;
• motivate participants to improve their physical condition and abilities;
• demonstrate the effectiveness of a prescribed program; and
• prepare the participant for future instruction in motor activities and the performance of more complicated motor patterns in sports and games.

Each of the fundamental components of motor performance can be tested many different ways. Indeed, Oxendine (1984), Singer (1980), and Sage (1984) provide evidence that the relationships among various tests of balance, kinesthesis, reaction time, movement time, strength, and flexibility are generally low, which indicates that unique aspects of each ability are measured by their various tests. In addition, results of these tests do not correlate well with success in sports and games. However, when the motor performance component to be measured is expressed and tested in a manner similar to the way it would be used in a specific sport, the correlations between test results and success in sports and games increase substantially. This evidence again supports the concept of specificity of skill; that is, one must doubt the existence of "general" speed, "general" balance, "general" kinesthesis, and so forth to predict successful performance in a specific sport. Each activity requires a unique aspect and amount of various motor abilities to effect a skillful performance. Thus one should select or develop a test of each motor ability that closely resembles the manner in which it will be used in actual sport situations.

Because no motor ability exists by itself in physical education and athletic activity, we will present the abilities as a complex of components that subjectively appear to function together when employed in sports and games. Thus sample tests are presented that may be used to estimate muscular strength/endurance ability, power, agility/coordination ability, and flexibility/balance ability.

Muscular Strength and Endurance

The muscles of the body generate the energy required to apply the force of muscular contraction needed to hold the body in a particular position, move the body from one place to another, and push or pull objects away from or toward the body. Sufficient muscular strength and endurance are required to enable us to perform even routine daily tasks. The intensity and type of strength required will by necessity be related to the specific nature of the task to be performed. Thus the specific strength requirements of a shot putter will be quite different from the requirements of an office worker, although both individuals need sufficient general body strength and endurance to prevent muscular-skeletal problems that may be reflected in low back pain, abdominal ptosis, and other orthopedic problems. Thus strength is an important element of motor performance and health and fitness status.

Sufficient muscular strength and endurance prepares the individual to participate in future activities requiring strength and endurance for an effective performance. For example, we have observed preadolescent boys who were unable to support their bodies properly with their arms and shoulders as they attempted to learn simple tumbling stunts. After testing revealed that these young boys could not perform one pull-up, it was apparent that strength conditioning of the upper body was required to enable them to effectively learn simple tumbling stunts.

Strength development is a fundamental prerequisite for success in many sports and games. McCloy and Young (1954) found a correlation of .91 between Athletic Strength Index scores and a battery of six track and field events. Clarke (1976) conducted another extensive review of the logical and empirical validity of strength tests when administered singly and when combined into a test battery. Clarke found that athletes in school consistently scored higher in strength measures than nonathletes in the same schools.

Many measurement texts and various strength-testing manuals are currently on the market. If you were to review these texts and manuals, you might become confused by all the different types of strength that are measurable. Additional confusion can arise when in some cases you see the same test item being used to measure supposedly different types of strength. This problem is illustrated in Bosco and Gustafson's (1983) historical analysis of 25 different tests developed since 1897. They found that similar tests were designed to measure endurance, physical fitness, motor fitness, static strength, and dynamic strength components of the arm and shoulder girdle musculature. They also determined that the terminology of motor performance components has changed substantially over time.

You should remember that any measurement score is only an indirect and rather crude estimate of the type of strength assessed. A measurement score reflects a certain mechanical efficiency of the muscle groups involved, but measurement scores are never perfectly precise. The maximum tension or contractile force that a muscle can exert in a measurement test is rarely transferred completely during actual useful work. Stated another way, maximum tension is rarely tested because the tension against the resistance is not the same tension that occurs in the muscle group. Indeed, de Vries (1986) determined that for any given strength of a muscle, physical educators should consider three practical issues when estimating external force produced by the muscle, including (a) angle of pull of the muscle, (b) length of the muscle at any given time, and (c) the velocity of muscle shortening. It should be obvious that these conditions will vary continuously as muscles are used to do any kind of work. In other words, the number we record from a test score relates to a particular situation and does not represent the absolute strength of the muscle groups involved. Nor does the strength score represent an ability of the individual to use the "tested strength" effectively in a particular activity. Thus strength application is specific to an activity; the pole vaulter and baseball pitcher may have the same strength test score, but they apply their strengths in different ways. In fact, many physical education and athletic activities do not require maximal muscular contraction but instead call for repeated submaximal contractions of the muscle groups involved.

In order to eliminate some of the confusion over terminology in the literature and to put us all in the same frame of reference, Heusner and Van Huss (1978) provide us with the following definitions of strength and endurance that are relevant for testing:[1]

- *Static strength* is the maximum effective force that can be applied only once to a fixed object by a person in a standardized immobile position. The object cannot be moved

[1]Adapted from "Strength, power, and muscular endurance" by W.W. Heusner and W.D. Van Huss, 1978, in H.J. Montoye (Ed.), *An Introduction to Measurement in Physical Education* (pp. 55, 56). Boston: Allyn and Bacon. Reprinted by permission.

through a range of motion. The force applied to a leg lift dynamometer is an example of static strength. Static strength is also referred to as *static contraction* or *isometric contraction*.

- *Dynamic strength* is the maximum load that can be moved once through a specific joint range of motion with the body in a particular position. The military press in weight lifting is an example of dynamic strength. Dynamic strength is also referred to as *dynamic contraction* or *isotonic contraction*.

- *Static muscular endurance* is the length of time a given intensity of contraction can be maintained. The timed flexed-arm hang is an example of static muscular endurance.

- *Dynamic muscular endurance* represents a continuum of activity ranging from moving a heavy resistance through a range of motion at least twice to moving a light resistance through a range of motion for many repetitions. Dynamic muscular endurance can be divided into three aspects, including (a) short duration (high-intensity work for up to 30 seconds; e.g., chin-ups, dips, and push-ups); (b) medium duration (moderate-intensity work that can last up to 4 minutes; e.g., 400- and 800-meter dashes); and (c) long duration (low-intensity work; e.g., distance running, cycling, and swimming).

- *Power* is the amount of work that can be performed per unit of time. Strength and speed are involved in projecting a body at a maximum rate of movement. In physical education and athletics, explosive movements such as the shot put, 50-meter dash, vertical jump, standing broad jump, and the lineman's charge in football are considered power movements. Exercise physiologists also consider tests of dynamic muscular endurance (short, medium, or long duration) to be power tests if as much work as possible is completed in the shortest time. You must determine what type of power is needed for an effective performance in a specific sport or position in a sport. Vertical jumping ability is quite important in volleyball, but a volleyball player's time in a 100-meter dash is not as important in playing volleyball.

Relative Dynamic Strength

Strength is a basic component of motor fitness as well as of physical fitness. As such, each individual's strength score must be related to the person's body weight. A person who weighs 160 pounds (72.57 kg) and can pull 185 pounds (83.91 kg) up to the chinning position over a horizontal bar should be considered stronger per unit of body weight (1.156) than an individual who weighs 215 pounds (97.52 kg) and can pull-up 220 pounds (99.79 kg) over the bar (1.023). The first person lifted 1.156 kg for each kilogram of body weight, whereas the other individual pulled up 1.023 kg for each kilogram of body weight. The calculations are as follows:

$$\text{Relative dynamic strength} = \frac{\text{Strength score}}{\text{Body weight}}$$

$$= \frac{83.91 \text{ kg}}{72.57 \text{ kg}}$$

$$= 1.156;$$

$$= \frac{99.79 \text{ kg}}{97.52 \text{ kg}}$$

$$= 1.023$$

The first person has a greater strength-to-weight ratio and is thus considered the stronger person from that point of view. This is what we call *relative dynamic strength*. In the absolute sense, the second person would appear to be stronger because that person can lift more actual weight. In certain sports, games, and fitness survival activities, the first person would perform better. For example, when two wrestlers compete in the same weight class, the odds would favor the wrestler with the higher strength-to-weight ratio. You can estimate relative dynamic strength by having students do *one* chin-up, dip on parallel bars, bench press, standing vertical arm press, or bench squat test. The resistive force is determined by attaching enough weight to the body so that the participant can perform only one chin-up or dip. In weight lifting, sufficient weight is placed on the barbell so that only one repetition of the task can be performed (Johnson & Nelson, 1979).

Muscular Strength and Endurance Test Batteries

The goal of many conditioning programs for athletes and physical education students is to improve the strength and endurance of the body's major muscle groups. Individuals enroll in weight-lifting or weight-training programs in order to enter bodybuilding contests, compete in weight lifting, or increase performance capability and prevent injuries in other sports and games. An individual's general muscle strength and endurance should not be estimated based on one measurement in a single muscle group. The correlation between strength measures from different parts of the body (e.g., arm versus leg) is a rather low .40 or less (Åstrand & Rodahl, 1977). Thus a battery of tests should be selected that will measure the strength of the major muscle groups of the body. Because the correlation between the dynamic and isometric strength of the same muscles is rather high (.80) in muscles not previously conditioned by either method (Åstrand & Rodahl, 1977), dynamic strength testing is recommended when possible due to the ease of test administration and the lower cost of equipment involved with dynamic strength tests.

Roger's Strength and Physical Fitness Index

Roger's Strength and Physical Fitness Index is one of the oldest individually administered strength tests and has been very widely used since it was developed in 1926. We discuss it briefly here for its historical relevance. Sixty years ago strength and physical fitness were viewed as being equivalent variables. In addition, tuberculosis was a high-incidence disease. This may explain the presence of a pulmonary function item on the test. The items in this strength and fitness index tax an individual's anaerobic energy system but not the aerobic energy system. Today, muscular strength is regarded as one of several components of physical fitness which also includes flexibility, cardiovascular endurance, muscular endurance, and power. Hence, a critique of the test not only reveals several shortcomings inherent in calculating strength and fitness but also shows problems inherent in older tests that do not meet current standards of test construction.

The Strength Index (SI) is the sum of six strength tests plus lung capacity. Strength items included in the index include right grip strength, left grip strength, back strength, leg strength, and arm strength. Note that most of these items measure anaerobic work. Arm strength is determined by the following formula:

$$(\text{pull-ups} + \text{push-ups}) \times (\frac{\text{weight}}{10} + \text{height} - 60)$$

The scoring system for the arm strength score unduly penalizes the short boy and rewards the tall boy. If you are 72 inches tall, the physical stature element of the above formula is a larger multiplier than if you are 60 inches tall. Also, no rationale is given for dividing the weight by 10 or for multiplying the endurance performance by physical stature. The test requires access to a spirometer to measure lung capacity, a hand dynamometer, and a back-leg lift dynamometer. Also note that the formula is calculated with lung capacity, which is not a strength measure. The Physical Fitness Index (PFI) is determined by the following formula:

$$PFI = \frac{SI}{\text{Norm for age, height, weight}} \times 100$$

This estimate of physical fitness is not valid today because no measures of cardiovascular endurance, muscular endurance, flexibility, and power are included. Thorough historical reviews of this and other early strength tests appear in Clarke (1976) and Bosco and Gustafson (1983).

Cable-Tension Strength Test Batteries

A battery of 25 static strength test items measured with a cable tensiometer was described by Clarke and Munroe (1970). These items are designed to measure the strength of individual muscle groups in boys and girls that may have been weakened due to some disability. Smaller test batteries of three items were developed to predict a person's score on all 25 items. The batteries can be administered to students in upper elementary, junior high, and senior high schools and colleges. A tensiometer and cable must be utilized. A padded strength test table needs to be constructed so that the person can be placed in proper position and immobilized if necessary when tested. Only the particular muscle group of interest in each test item is allowed freedom of movement to pull on a cable attached to the tensiometer. This battery of cable tension tests is well suited for adapted physical education programs so that the effects of corrective exercises for specific muscle groups may be demonstrated. Only one person at a time can be tested, which is appropriate for individually prescribed corrective exercise programs but a drawback in large classes.

Weight-Lifting Strength Testing

If you have access to a well-equipped weight lifting room, a number of dynamic strength tests

Figure 6.2 Bench press strength test.

can be administered using free barbell weights or a Universal Gym. Johnson and Nelson (1979) indicate that some experimentation needs to be done to determine the maximum weight that can be lifted. The bench press, standing vertical arm press, half-squat, and curl are some suggested strength testing positions. One may also attach a spring scale to a bar and push or pull the bar to determine force of contraction on the scale.

Two problems confound the weight-lifting test score. The first occurs when the examinee must do a few lifts in order to determine when he or she is approaching the point of maximal effort. In doing this, some muscle fatigue occurs, and the actual test score may underestimate the correct value. The second problem involves the effect upon the test score of the subject's

learning *how* to lift weights. In weight-lifting classes, the amount of weight a participant can lift usually increases rapidly. Much of this "strength" gain is likely due to the participant's learning to lift correctly rather than to an actual gain in strength. After learning has occurred and the examinee has been lifting weights for some time, however, weight-lifting tests can provide good estimates of dynamic strength.

Sensible supervised weight training programs may be established for prepubescent boys and girls in school or agency programs. Duda (1986) dispels many of the old myths concerning damaging young children with weight training programs. Indeed, when trained appropriately both sexes respond in an equal manner to training with no harmful aftereffects.

Figure 6.3 Weight lifting strength test.

Dynamic Muscular Endurance Test— Short

Yuhasz (personal communication, 1976) proposed a 5-Minute Muscular Endurance Test as a simple and economical measurement of the endurance of the major muscle groups using the body as the resistive force. The test is easy to explain and administer individually or to a group. One half of a group can perform the test while the other half counts production and records the score. The test requires no equipment other than a pencil, scorecard, and gym floor. The test is applicable to persons of both sexes and most ages. The test items can also be used as the core items of a muscular endurance workout, with the participants keeping track of weekly progress on their own record forms.

The physical educator should determine local test-retest reliability for each of the test items and in time can construct norms for the various ages of participants. When testing elementary school children, you may also wish to experiment with reducing the time limit for each item from 60 to 40 seconds for boys and from 30 to 20 seconds for girls, but *only* if the younger children cannot do the items in the regular time span or if girls cannot keep up with boys. However, with some conditioning activity most young children will probably be able to perform the items without a time modification.

Measurement Technique. For high school boys and men, time limits of 60 seconds for four

Figure 6.4 Push-up.

of the six exercises and 30 seconds for the chest raise and the double backward leg raise are imposed. With younger boys, girls, and women, each exercise is performed for 30 seconds only, except for the side leg raise, which is performed for 30 seconds on each side. A 10-second break is allowed between the exercises in order to score the results. The performer attempts to repeat each exercise as frequently as possible within the time limit but may perform them at his or her own pace and rest whenever he or she wishes. The items are illustrated in Figures 6.4 to 6.8.

Description of Test Items

1. *Push-ups* (males, 60 seconds; females, 30 seconds). A front lying position is taken with the hands at the sides of the chest. The body is raised by extending the arms completely while keeping the body in a straight line. The principal muscles involved are the pectorals and the triceps.

2. *Sit-ups* (males, 60 seconds; females, 30 seconds). The knees are flexed at 90° with the feet held flat on the floor. The hands are placed behind the head. From the back lying position, the performer sits up and touches both elbows to both knees. The principal muscle involved is the rectus abdominis.

3. *Side leg raise* (males and females, 30 seconds on each side). A side leaning rest position is taken with the right side down. The weight of the body is balanced above the right arm and the extended right leg. The left leg is repeatedly lifted laterally to the horizontal and lowered. At the end of 30 seconds, the movement is performed with the left side down. The pectorals, deltoids,

Figure 6.5   Side leg raise.

Figure 6.6   Chest raise.

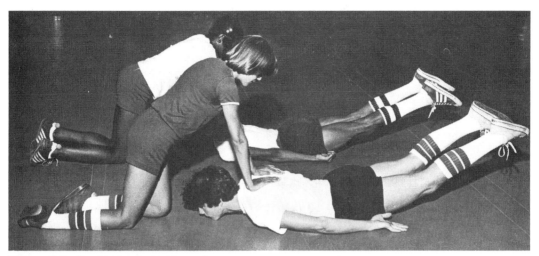

Figure 6.7 Double backward leg raise.

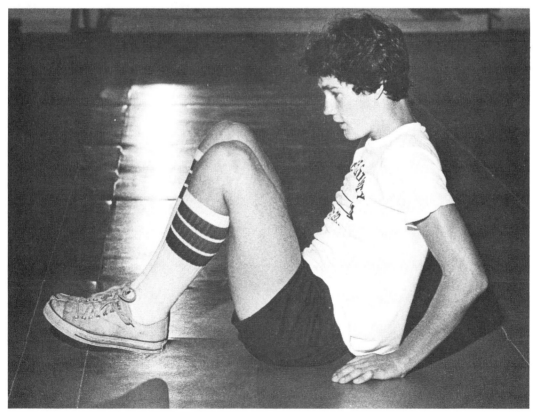

Figure 6.8 Sitting tucks.

trapezius, and rhomboid muscles fix the balancing arm and shoulder. The sartorius, glutei, vastus lateralis, and tensor fasciae latae are involved in the leg raise.

4. *Chest raise* (males and females, 30 seconds). A front lying position is taken with the hands behind the head. The legs are held. The performer raises the chin as high as possible from the floor and then lowers the chest to the floor. Muscles of the neck and shoulders are involved, as well as the erector spinae, sacrospinalis, glutei, and hamstrings.

5. *Double backward leg raise* (males and females, 30 seconds). A front lying position is taken with the arms along the sides and the palms facing downward. The chest is held down. Both legs are lifted upward with the legs held straight to clear the thighs from the floor. The muscles used are the erector spinae, sacrospinalis, and the gluteus maximus.

6. *Sitting tucks* (males, 60 seconds; females, 30 seconds). A long sitting position is taken with the arms placed palms down behind the hips. The heels are lifted 6 inches off

Name _____ Age _____ Date of Birth _____

School _____ Height Nearest Inch (cm) _____

Grade _____ Weight Nearest Pound (kg) _____

Test data _____	Date of test _____		Date of test _____		Date of test _____		Date of test _____	
	Age Yrs.__ Mos. __		Age Yrs.__ Mos. __		Age Yrs.__ Mos.__		Age Yrs.__ Mos.___	
	Raw score	Centile rank	Raw score	Centile rank	Raw score	Centile rank	Raw score	Centile rank
5-Minute Muscular Endurance								
1. Push-ups								
2. Sit-ups								
3. Side leg raise								
4. Chest raise								
5. Double backward leg raise								
6. Sitting tucks								

Figure 6.9 Muscular strength and endurance score sheet.

the floor. Both legs are flexed to bring the knees to the chest, heels together, and then the legs are straightened, keeping the heels off the floor. The muscles involved in flexing the leg are the psoas major and minor and iliacus, and the quadriceps and rectus femoris are utilized in extending the legs.

Strength and endurance testing data may be recorded on the score sheet illustrated in Figure 6.9. Standard scores and norms for the Yuhasz Muscular Endurance Test developed on male and female college physical education students as well as secondary school boys are presented in Tables 6.1 through 6.5.

Table 6.1 Yuhasz 5-Minute Muscular Endurance Test Norms for Physical Education Men

Classification	Standard score	Push-ups (60 sec)	Sit-ups (60 sec)	Chest raises (30 sec)	Double leg raises (30 sec)	Side leg raises (60 sec)	Sitting tucks (60 sec)
Excellent	100	66	59	69	69	131	137
	95	64	57	67	67	129	133
	90	63	56	65	66	127	129
Very good	85	61	54	63	64	125	125
	80	60	53	62	62	122	121
	75	58	51	60	60	120	117
Above average	70	57	50	58	58	118	113
	65	55	48	56	57	116	109
	60	54	47	54	55	114	105
Average	55	52	45	53	53	112	100
	50	50	44	51	51	110	97
	45	49	42	49	49	108	93
Below average	40	47	41	47	48	106	89
	35	46	39	45	46	104	85
	30	44	38	44	44	101	81
Poor	25	43	36	42	42	99	77
	20	41	35	40	40	97	73
	15	39	33	38	39	95	69
Very poor	10	38	32	36	37	93	65
	5	36	30	35	35	91	61
	0	35	29	33	33	89	57

Date

Note. From Dr. Michael Yuhasz, University of Western Ontario, Canada. Used with permission.

Table 6.2   Yuhasz 3-1/2-Minute Muscular Endurance Test Norms for Physical Education Women

Classification	Standard score	Push-ups (30 sec)	Sit-ups (30 sec)	Chest raises (30 sec)	Double leg raises (30 sec)	Side leg raises (60 sec)	Sitting tucks (30 sec)
Excellent	100	33	32	50	68	145	75
	95	32	30	48	66	140	72
	90	30	29	46	64	134	68
Very good	85	28	28	45	62	129	65
	80	26	27	43	60	123	62
	75	25	26	42	58	118	59
Above average	70	23	25	41	56	112	56
	65	21	24	39	54	107	53
	60	20	22	38	52	101	50
Average	55	18	21	36	50	96	47
	50	16	20	35	48	90	44
	45	15	19	34	46	85	41
Below average	40	13	18	32	44	79	37
	35	11	17	31	42	74	34
	30	9	16	29	40	68	31
Poor	25	8	15	28	38	63	28
	20	6	14	27	36	57	25
	15	4	13	25	34	52	22
Very poor	10	3	11	24	32	46	19
	5	1	10	22	30	41	16
	0	0	9	21	28	35	13
Date							

Note. From Dr. Michael Yuhasz, University of Western Ontario, Canada. Used with permission.

Table 6.3 Yuhasz 5-Minute Muscular Endurance Test Norms
for 17- and 18-Year-Old Secondary School Boys

Classification	Standard score	Push-ups (60 sec)	Sit-ups (60 sec)	Chest raises (30 sec)	Double leg raises (30 sec)	Side leg raises (60 sec)	Sitting tucks (60 sec)
Excellent	100	61	63	67	69	128	115
	95	58	60	65	66	122	110
	90	55	58	62	63	116	105
Very good	85	52	55	59	60	110	100
	80	49	53	56	57	104	95
	75	46	50	54	54	98	90
Above average	70	43	48	51	51	92	85
	65	40	45	48	48	86	80
	60	37	43	46	45	80	75
Average	55	34	40	43	42	74	70
	50	31	38	40	39	68	65
	45	28	36	37	36	62	60
Below average	40	26	33	35	33	56	55
	35	23	31	32	30	50	50
	30	20	28	29	27	44	45
Poor	25	17	26	27	24	38	40
	20	14	23	24	21	32	35
	15	11	21	21	18	26	30
Very poor	10	8	18	19	15	20	25
	5	6	16	16	12	14	20
	0	3	13	13	9	8	15

Note. From Dr. Michael Yuhasz, University of Western Ontario, Canada. Used with permission.

Table 6.4 Yuhasz 5-Minute Muscular Endurance Test Norms for 15- and 16-Year-Old Secondary School Boys

Classification	Standard score	Push-ups (60 sec)	Sit-ups (60 sec)	Chest raises (30 sec)	Double leg raises (30 sec)	Side leg raises (60 sec)	Sitting tucks (60 sec)
Excellent	100	61	63	65	68	121	115
	95	58	60	62	65	115	110
	90	54	57	59	62	109	104
Very good	85	51	55	56	59	103	99
	80	48	52	53	56	97	93
	75	45	50	50	52	91	88
Above average	70	42	47	47	49	85	82
	65	39	44	44	46	79	77
	60	36	41	41	43	73	71
Average	55	32	39	39	40	67	65
	50	29	36	36	37	61	60
	45	26	34	34	34	55	55
Below average	40	23	31	31	31	49	49
	35	20	28	28	28	43	44
	30	17	26	25	25	37	38
Poor	25	14	23	22	22	31	33
	20	11	20	19	19	25	27
	15	7	18	16	16	19	22
Very poor	10	4	15	13	13	13	16
	5	1	12	10	10	7	11
	0	0	10	7	7	1	5

Note. From Dr. Michael Yuhasz, University of Western Ontario, Canada. Used with permission.

Table 6.5 Yuhasz 5-Minute Muscular Endurance Test Norms
for 13- and 14-Year-Old Secondary School Boys

Classification	Standard score	Push-ups (60 sec)	Sit-ups (30 sec)	Chest raises (30 sec)	Double leg raises (30 sec)	Side leg raises (60 sec)	Sitting tucks (60 sec)
Excellent	100	56	63	63	67	109	100
	95	53	60	60	63	103	95
	90	50	57	57	60	98	90
Very good	85	46	53	53	56	92	85
	80	43	50	50	53	87	80
	75	40	47	47	49	81	75
Above average	70	37	44	44	46	76	70
	65	34	41	41	42	70	65
	60	31	33	38	39	65	60
Average	55	28	35	35	35	59	55
	50	25	32	32	32	54	50
	45	22	30	30	29	49	45
Below average	40	20	27	27	25	43	40
	35	17	24	24	22	38	35
	30	14	21	21	18	32	30
Poor	25	9	18	18	15	27	25
	20	6	15	15	11	21	20
	15	3	12	12	8	16	15
Very poor	10	1	10	10	5	10	10
	5	0	7	7	2	5	5
	0	0	4	4	0	0	0

Note. From Dr. Michael Yuhasz, University of Western Ontario, Canada. Used with permission.

Power Tests

Power is defined as work output per unit of time. Chemical energy developed as a result of metabolic processes is expended in the mechanical process of external work. Work is done when contracting muscles move an object some distance through space. When the force of muscular contraction moves an object such as a book from one desk to another desk in the room, work has been performed. The amount of work done over time constitutes power. Power may be calculated using the following formula:

$$\text{Power} = \frac{\text{Force} \times \text{Distance}}{\text{Time}}$$

or

$$\text{Power} = \frac{\text{Work}}{\text{Time}}$$

where Work = Force × Distance. It also follows that because Distance ÷ Time = Velocity, then Power = Force × Velocity.

Thus we see that *power* is the term used to describe how fast one performs work. Coaches often refer to the "explosive power" required to perform certain activities such as the lineman's charge in football and the power thrust of the leg in high jumping. Force of contraction is accompanied by speed of contraction. Theoretically, this one contraction or application of force, if done maximally, would move the athlete a maximum distance. In physical education and athletic activities, we are concerned with how much work is done in a given time span.

Vertical Jump

Measuring the distance between a person's standing reach and the height he or she can jump and reach has been proposed as a test of leg power. If the person's body weight and speed of muscular contraction in performing the jump are not a part of the measurement, we cannot regard this test as a true estimate of leg power. Thus a 170-pound (77.27 kg) boy who vertically jumps 2 feet (60.96 cm) produces less power than a 180-pound (81.81 kg) boy who vertically jumps the same distance. Fox and Mathews (1981) present a nomogram that takes into consideration body weight when performing the vertical jump-and-reach test. The nomogram in Figure 6.10 may be used as follows for a 170-pound (77.27 kg) boy who jumps and reaches 22 inches (55.88 cm): Lay a ruler across the nomogram connecting 170 pounds (right column) and 22 inches (left column). From the center column, read the corresponding foot-pounds per second (ft-lb/sec) as the power output. Note that the measurements may be in either English or metric units. In the latter units, the power output would be 130 kilogram-meter/second (kg-m/sec). Directions for administering the vertical jump-and-reach test are as follows:

Record the performer's weight. Have the individual assume a standing position, facing sideways to the jump board with the hand away from the board placed behind the back at the belt line. The arm nearer the board is to be raised vertically with the hand turned outward and fingers extended. The fingers should be chalked. The performer stands as tall as possible on the toes and touches as far as he or she can reach with the middle finger. The performer adopts a full squat position and while maintaining good balance jumps as high as possible to touch the board at the maximum extension of the arms at the height of the jump. Three trials are allowed. Record the best score, which is the distance between the two chalk marks.

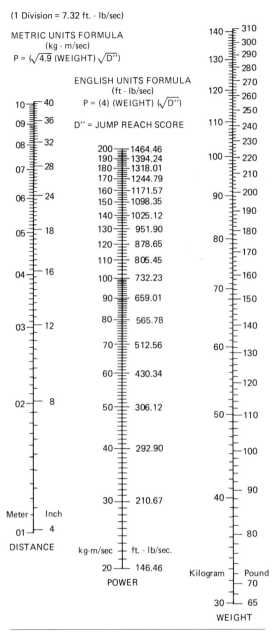

(1 Division = 7.32 ft. · lb/sec)

METRIC UNITS FORMULA
(kg · m/sec)

$P = (\sqrt{4.9} \text{ (WEIGHT)}) \sqrt{D''}$

ENGLISH UNITS FORMULA
(ft · lb/sec)

$P = (4) \text{ (WEIGHT)} (\sqrt{D''})$

D'' = JUMP REACH SCORE

Figure 6.10 The Lewis nomogram for determining anaerobic power from jump-reach score and body weight. *Note.* From *The Physiological Basis of Physical Education and Athletics* (2nd ed.) by D.K. Mathews and E.L. Fox. Copyright © 1976 by W.B. Saunders Co. Reprinted by permission of CBS College Publishing.

The standing broad jump and the 50-yard (45.73 m) dash are also proposed in the literature as tests of leg power. These tasks become more accurate tests of power when body weight is included in the calculations. Nomograms should also be developed.

Margaria-Kalamen Power Test

The Margaria-Kalamen Test has also been proposed to estimate leg power. It is used rather widely due to its ease of administration and scoring. Directions for administering and scoring this test are as follows (Fox & Mathews, 1981):

> The student stands 6 meters (19.68 feet) in front of a staircase and approaches and runs up the stairs as rapidly as possible, three stairs at a time. A switchmat is placed on the third and ninth stairs (an average stair is 174 mm or 6.84 inches high). A clock starts as the person steps on the first switchmat (on the third step) and stops as he or she steps on the second mat (on the ninth step). Time is recorded to a hundredth of a second. Permit three trials and record the best score in which power output is computed using the following formula:

$$P = \frac{W \times D}{t}$$

where P = power, W = weight, D = vertical height between the two switchmats (3rd and 9th stairs), and t = time from first to second switchmat.

An example test is scored as follows: W = 75 kg, D = 1.05 meters, and t = .49 seconds. Hence,

$$P = \frac{75 \times 1.05}{0.49} = 1.61 \text{ kg-meters per second}$$

Table 6.6 Guidelines for the Margaria-Kalamen Test (Kilogram Meters per Second)

Classification	15-20	20-30	Age groups (years) 30-40	40-50	Over 50
Men					
Poor	Under 113	Under 106	Under 85	Under 65	Under 50
Fair	113-149	106-139	85-111	65-84	50-65
Average	150-187	140-175	112-140	85-105	66-82
Good	188-224	176-210	141-168	106-125	83-98
Excellent	Over 224	Over 210	Over 168	Over 125	Over 98
Women					
Poor	Under 92	Under 85	Under 65	Under 50	Under 38
Fair	92-120	85-111	65-84	50-65	38-48
Average	121-151	112-140	85-105	66-82	49-61
Good	152-182	141-168	106-125	83-98	62-75
Excellent	Over 182	Over 168	Over 125	Over 98	Over 75

Note. From *The Physiological Basis of Physical Education and Athletics* (2nd ed.) by D.K. Mathews and E.L. Fox. Copyright © 1976 by W.B. Saunders Co. Reprinted by permission of CBS College Publishing.

Norms for this test are reproduced in Table 6.6. Teachers may wish to experiment with this test by using stop watches if switchmats are unavailable. Also, if the height of the stair is different, the norms in Table 6.6 should not be used.

Fox and Mathews (1981) indicate that a correlation of .974 was obtained between the 50-yard (45.73 m) dash time with a 15-yard (13.72 m) running start and the Margaria-Kalamen Power Test. The high correlation indicates that substituting the 50-yard (45.73 m) dash for the Margaria-Kalamen Test yields similar results and at the same time eliminates the need for expensive equipment. Kalamen also reported an insignificant relationship between the 50-yard (45.73 m) dash and the vertical jump-and-reach test when body weight was not considered. If timing equipment and a staircase are available, the Margaria-Kalamen Power Test is superior; if not, the 50-yard (45.73 m) dash with the 15-yard (13.72 m) running start may be substituted.

Anaerobic Versus Aerobic Power Tests

The power tests described earlier qualify as anaerobic tests because they measure explosive or maximal expenditure of energy very quickly in the absence of oxygen. One cannot prolong performance by ingesting oxygen during normal respiration while taking the test. On the other hand, tests of aerobic power measure an individual's ability to utilize oxygen efficiently during longer bouts of work. For example, one's best performance time in a mile run would be a crude estimate of aerobic power. In a controlled laboratory setting, we can measure maximal oxygen consumption per kilogram body weight during an exhausting run on a treadmill, pedaling to exhaustion on a bicycle ergometer, or stepping up and down a bench.

Aerobic power can be measured directly or indirectly in the laboratory. A direct test is one in which the person's maximal oxygen uptake (aerobic power) is estimated during an exercise routine carried to exhaustion. An indirect estimate of aerobic power is made from an exercise test terminated before exhaustion. Oxygen uptake at a predetermined submaximal work load is used as an indirect estimate of maximal aerobic power. Values of maximal oxygen uptake measured on an inclined treadmill are usually 5 to 15% higher than those obtained with a step test or bicycle ergometer because more active muscle tissue is utilized in running, whereas cycling or bench stepping leads to localized thigh muscle fatigue. This fatigue usually occurs before maximally stressing the circulatory and respiratory systems, resulting in a smaller maximal oxygen uptake (Fox & Mathews, 1981).

Direct Assessment. A direct assessment of maximal oxygen uptake will be illustrated with a treadmill protocol. Work loads are increased during the run on either a continuous or discontinuous basis. In the latter mode, a rest period is allowed before increasing each load. There are no differences in the maximum oxygen uptake values for the two types of loading. The continuous method is recommended for most subjects because it saves time.

A continuous test may begin with a 5- or 10-minute walk-jog on the treadmill at 0% grade to familiarize the subject with the test environment. The initial work load is 6 miles per hour at 0% grade for 3 minutes. Every 2 minutes thereafter, the treadmill incline increases 2.5% with the speed held constant. The subject works to exhaustion. Oxygen consumption is monitored each minute during later stages of work. Maximal aerobic power is determined when a leveling off or decrease in oxygen uptake is noted with increasing work loads. Other criteria for terminating the test are volitional exhaustion and, in young subjects, heart rates in excess of 190 beats per minute. For a further discussion of the rationale for different types of continuous or discontinuous test protocols available for subjects of varying physical conditions, consult Heyward (1984).

Indirect Assessment. The administration of direct measurements requires expensive laboratory equipment, considerable amounts of time, and a high level of motivation on the part of the subject. Direct measurements may also be dangerous depending on the age and health status of the subject. For these reasons, indirect tests involving bench stepping, bicycle ergometry, and treadmill running have been developed. We shall illustrate an indirect protocol (Åstrand & Rodahl, 1977) with a bicycle ergometer test suitable for both males and females. A work load is selected on the bicycle ergometer that produces a heart rate between 130 and 150 beats per minute. The initial work load is usually 450 to 600 kilogram meters per minute for women and 600 to 900 kilogram meters per minute for men. The subject pedals for 6 minutes at a pedaling frequency of 50 complete pedal turns per minute. During the test, the heart rate is taken every minute (last 30 seconds $\times$ 2), and the average heart rate for the 5th and 6th minute is recorded. If these two heart rates differ by more than five beats per minute, the work session is prolonged until a steady state heart rate is reached. If the heart rate is less than 130 beats per minute after 6 minutes, another 6-minute bout is performed after increasing the work load by 300 kgm/min.

A nomogram is used to estimate maximum oxygen uptake from the submaximum heart rate at the work load for the bicycle ergometer. The correlation between actual maximal oxygen uptake and the predicted maximal value is .74, with a standard error of prediction ranging from $\pm$ 10 to $\pm$ 15% for trained and untrained persons respectively (Heyward, 1984). Oxygen consumption is only one of the variables in fitness testing. Field tests that estimate aerobic power are described in detail in chapter 7, "Motor and Physical Fitness Testing."

Agility and Coordination

Coordination may be defined as the harmonious interplay of muscle groups during a motor performance that indicates some degree of skill. *Agility* is defined as the ability to change direction of the body or parts of the body rapidly. It is apparent that to be agile one must also be well coordinated. Thus it is difficult to speak of or measure agility and coordination as two separate abilities. Therefore, the tests presented here measure both agility *and* coordination. It should also be obvious that individuals must also possess sufficient strength, endurance, balance, and flexibility in order to score well on tests of the agility-coordination ability.

Two tests of *whole body agility/coordination* are the squat thrust described by McCloy and Young (1954, p. 75) and the modified Edgren side step (1932). Because these tests do not involve running, they can be administered to several people simultaneously in a small area. Directions for the administration and scoring of these tests are as follows:

1. *Squat Thrust Test.* From an erect standing position, lower the body to a squat-rest position, leaning forward and placing the hands on the floor in front of the feet. Thrust the legs backward as far as they will go to a front leaning-rest position with arms fully extended. Return to the squat-rest position and then to the standing position. The test is scored in terms of the number of performances completed in 10 seconds. A complete performance is scored as 1. Scores for a partial performance are 1/4 for touching the hands to the floor, 1/2 for thrusting the legs backward, and 3/4 for returning to a squat-rest position.

2. *Edgren Side Step.* Three parallel lines are drawn on the floor 4 feet (1.22 m) apart. The student stands astride the middle line. On the signal *go*, the pupil *side steps* to the right (using any variation of the side step without crossing the feet) until the right foot touches across the line to his right. The student then side steps to the left until the left foot touches across the outside left line, repeating this movement to the right and left between the outside lines as rapidly as possible for 30 seconds. Each trip from the center line to an outside line and back to the center line counts one point. Each complete round trip counts two points. Three trials are allowed. Count the best score.

Several tests of whole body agility/coordination that do involve running include (a) the Shuttle Run item on the AAHPERD Youth Fitness Test, (b) the Right-Boomerang Run, (c) the Dodging Run, and (d) the Auto-Tire Test. Directions for administering and scoring the AAHPERD Shuttle Run item are presented in chapter 7 on "Motor and Physical Fitness Testing," p. 152. Directions for the other three tests appear in McCloy and Young (1954) and are reproduced here:

1. *Right-Boomerang Run.* A cone marker is placed 17 feet (5.18 m) from a starting line, and another marker is placed 15 feet (4.57 m) beyond the first marker. Additional cone markers are placed 15 feet (4.57 m) on each side of the first marker (17 feet or 5.18 m) from the starting line. The performer follows the course indicated in Figure 6.11. The student makes quarter right turns at the middle marker and half turns at the corner markers. The pupil's

score is the time required to complete the course.

2. *Dodging Run.* A starting line 6 feet (1.83 m) long is drawn on the floor. One hurdle is placed 12 feet (3.66 m) in front of the starting line; a second hurdle is placed 6 feet (1.83 m) in front of the first hurdle; and a third hurdle is placed 6 feet (1.83 m) in front of the second hurdle. The performer follows the course indicated in Figure 6.12. The score is the time required to run the complete course.

3. *Auto-Tire Test.* A starting line 6 feet (1.83 m) long is drawn on the floor. Five auto tires with their centers 6 feet (1.83 m) apart are placed in each of the two columns 4 feet (1.22 m) apart. The center of the first tire in the column at the left is 6 feet (1.83 m) from the starting line, and the center of the first tire in the column at the right is 3 feet (.91 m) from the starting line. The performer begins behind the starting line, steps with the right foot into the first tire in the right column, then with the left foot into the first tire in the left row, and continues similarly until he has stepped into all the tires. He then turns to the left and returns similarly to the starting line as in Figure 6.13. The score is the time required to make the round trip.

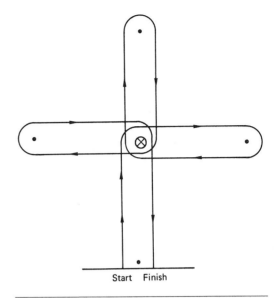

Start   Finish

Figure 6.11 Right-Boomerang Test floor markings. *Note.* From *Tests and Measurements in Health and Physical Education* (3rd ed.) by C.H. McCloy and N.D. Young, 1954, Appleton Century Crofts.

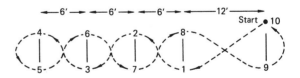

Figure 6.12 Dodging-Run Test floor markings. *Note.* From *Tests and Measurements in Health and Physical Education* (3rd ed.) by C.H. McCloy and N.D. Young, 1954, Appleton Century Crofts.

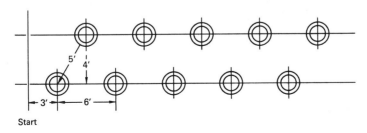

Start

Figure 6.13 Auto-Tire Test floor markings. *Note.* From *Tests and Measurements in Health and Physical Education* (3rd ed.) by C.H. McCloy and N.D. Young, 1954, Appleton Century Crofts.

Eye-hand coordination/agility can be estimated by utilizing the *softball repeated throws test*. Eye-foot coordination/agility can be estimated by using the *soccer wall volley* and/or the *soccer dribble test*. All three of these test items involve movement of the total body. Gruber (1964) provides the following directions for administering and scoring these tests:

1. *Softball Repeated Throws Test*. This test purports to measure eye-hand coordination, whole body coordination, and agility. On a flat wall space, mark a target area 5.5 feet (1.69 m) wide and at least 10 feet (3.05 m) high at a distance of 6 inches (15.24 cm) from the floor. A throwing area 5.5 feet (1.69 m) square is marked on the floor at a distance of 10 feet (3.05 m) from and parallel to the target. The student stands at any place that he or she chooses inside the throwing area. At the command *go*, the student throws a 12-inch (30.48 cm) softball at the target area using an overhand throw. The student continues successive throws until the signal *stop* is given. The balls may be received from the target either on the bounce or on the fly. The pupil must recover the balls that get out of control without assistance. A 10-second practice trial is allowed. Next, two 15-second trials are given for the test. Each good hit is worth one point. The total number of points is recorded for each trial. Line hits do not count. Count the best trial score as the pupil's score. (*Note:* This test can be made more difficult for older children by increasing the distance from the wall and/or centering a 2-foot square (.61 m) inside the larger target area. Award two points for a hit in the smaller area.)

2. *Soccer Wall Volley Test*. This item is proposed to estimate eye-foot coordination, whole body coordination, and agility. A target area 8 feet (2.44 m) long and 4 feet (1.22 m) high from the floor is drawn on the gym wall. An area 12 feet (3.65 m) by 14 feet (4.23 m) is marked off on the floor in front of the target area. A restraining line is placed 6 feet (1.83 m) between the baseline and the base of the wall. The ball is set on the restraining line, and the student stands back of the ball ready to kick on the command *go*. The student continues to kick as many times possible, with either foot, by immediately kicking the ball or blocking and steadying it, soccer style, before rekicking. Use of the hands at *any* time is prohibited, and one point is deducted from the pupil's score for each infraction. Three 20-second trials are taken, and the pupil's score is the best of the three trial scores. A student's score is determined by the number of times within the 20-second time limit that he or she successfully propels the ball against the wall. The ball must be directed by the foot, knee, or leg only. The pupil must remain behind the restraining line at all times. If the pupil kicks in front of the line, falls forward, or steps over the restraining line during the follow-through, that kick does not count.

3. *Soccer Dribble Test*. This is another item that can estimate eye-foot coordination, whole body coordination, and agility. The pupil starts to dribble the soccer ball in and out of the markers with the feet from behind the starting line as illustrated in Figure 6.14. The examiner times the student from the moment the signal *go* is given until the

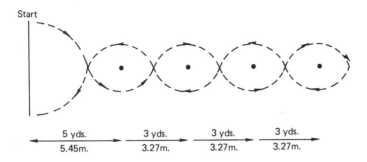

Figure 6.14 Diagram of Soccer Dribble Test.

student returns to the starting line. No practice trials are allowed. Three trials are allowed for the test. The student must finish with the ball in his or her control. The score for the best trial is recorded to the tenth of a second.

Flexibility and Balance

The ability of the body and its segments to take various positions, either stationary or moving, requires varying degrees of flexibility and balance responses. The amount and type of flexibility and balance response required are task-related. The specific flexibility and balance responses required by a gymnast performing on a balance beam differ from that required by an individual with cerebral palsy walking up a flight of stairs. Both individuals need to learn well-defined neuromuscular responses resulting in sufficient flexibility and balance to protect them against injury. Flexibility and balance are important components of motor performance but as stated are task-specific.

The tests presented in this section are practical in that they can be administered to a large number of students in a relatively short time and do not require expensive equipment. The results of these tests are not absolutes and should be used only as guides in establishing realistic objectives for program planning. The following tests of flexibility and balance with norms will assist the practicing physical educator in establishing these objectives and planning physical education activities to meet these objectives.

Flexibility

Most measurement texts on the market today are in fair agreement about the definition of *flexibility*. For example, Barrow and McGee (1979) and Baumgartner and Jackson (1982) define flexibility as the range of movement in a joint. From a scientific viewpoint, testing flexibility is a quite long and tedious process. Only one person at a time may be tested. Special restraining gear must be used to hold one segment stationary while the angular range of movement of the adjoining segment is measured in various planes. Special equipment for measuring angles must be utilized.

From a practical viewpoint, we test flexibility by observing and recording the stretching ability of muscles. In other words, most tests that physical educators apply to test flexibility involve some form of stretching of muscles, reaching, or bending the segments of the body and recording the distance moved. An example of a trunk flexibility test (Corbin, Dowell, Lindsey, & Tolson, 1974) follows.

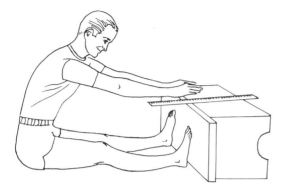

Figure 6.15 Trunk Flexibility Test. *Note.* The meterstick or ruler or yardstick extends 15 in. (38.1 cm) over the end of the bench nearest the student.

Table 6.7 Trunk Flexibility Test Norms

| | Trunk flexibility | | | |
| | Females | | Males | |
Percentile	cm	in.	cm	in.
100	63.5	25.0	61.0	24.0
90	56.4	22.2	54.9	21.6
80	53.1	20.9	51.8	20.4
70	50.5	19.9	49.8	19.6
60	48.3	19.0	47.5	18.7
50	46.5	18.3	45.2	17.8
40	44.4	17.5	43.4	17.1
30	41.4	16.2	40.1	15.8
20	37.6	14.8	36.3	14.3
10	30.5	12.0	29.7	11.7
0	10.2	4.0	15.2	6.0

Note. From "Physical Fitness Norms for College Freshmen" by W.B. Zuti and C.R. Corbin, 1977, *Research Quarterly,* **48**, p. 502. Copyright 1977 by American Alliance for Health, Physical Education, Recreation, and Dance. Reprinted by permission.

Trunk Flexibility Test. This sit-and-reach test is designed to test the stretching ability of the hamstring and lower-back muscles. The student sits on the floor with the knees together and the feet flat against a bench turned on its side. With a partner holding the knees straight, the student reaches forward with the arms fully extended. Measure and record the distance the reach of the fingertips on the meter or yardstick fixed on the bench (see Figure 6.15). Face validity is assumed, and no reliability coefficients were given.

The mean value for males is 45.1 centimeters (17.75 inches) with a standard deviation of ± 9.7 centimeters (± 3.81 inches). The mean value for females is 45.85 centimeters (18.05 inches) with a standard deviation of ± 9.99 centimeters (± 3.93 inches). The norms in Table 6.7 represent over 3,000 subjects ranging in age from 17.6 to 19.5 years.

When we speak of flexibility, it should be emphasized that the points of contact and ligaments crossing at joints along with the protective reflex muscular actions make a stretching

movement distinctive in each individual. Because the stretching ability of each individual may differ, unnecessary strain to the muscle attachments and joints should be avoided in testing. Corbin and Noble (1980) have written an excellent review of flexibility in which they discuss flexibility as a major contributor to physical fitness, athletic performance, health, and injury prevention.

Balance

Franks and Deutsch (1973, p. 125) define *balance* as "the ability to maintain equilibrium at rest and during a series of prescribed movements." Barrow and McGee (1979, p. 113) define balance as "the ability of the individual to maintain his neuromuscular system in a static condition for an efficient response or to control it in a specific efficient posture while it is moving.'' Essentially, balance is the ability to control our bodies when staying still or when moving. It should be emphasized that balance is a complex phenomenon that involves eyesight, tactile sensations, proprioceptors, and the vestibular system located in the inner ear. Our brains interpret the complex input of signals and send return signals that result in various motor responses to the particular balancing situation.

From a scientific viewpoint, testing balance is also a complex process. To test and measure the various responses of the vestibular system to both angular and linear acceleration requires very special equipment. To test and measure conflicting stimulation of the visual, vestibular, tactile, and proprioceptive systems would require very special equipment. In other words, the *scientific* testing and measuring of balance are beyond the scope of the practicing physical education teacher.

From a practical viewpoint, however, balance can be tested by observing an individual's various responses to a given physical situation. Typically, we apply two physical situations to test balance. One situation involves the ability of an individual to maintain a stationary position, which is called *static balance*. The other involves the ability of an individual to maintain balance during movement, which is called *dynamic balance*. In other words, most tests that physical education teachers use to test balance involve the motor responses necessary to hold a stationary position or to move. The teacher uses either a time element and/or number of errors to score the test. Sample tests for static and dynamic balance follow.

1. *The Stork Stand: A Static Balance Test.* The *Stork Stand Test* is designed to test a student's static balance. The student stands on the foot of the dominant leg. He or she places the toes of

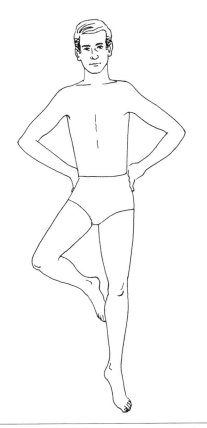

Figure 6.16 Stork Stand for testing static balance.

the nondominant leg against the knee of the dominant leg and places the hands on the hips. Upon command, the student raises the heel of the dominant foot from the floor and attempts to maintain balance as long as possible without removing the hands from the hips and without the heel touching the floor or the ball of the foot moving from its original position. The best time of three attempts is recorded in seconds (see Figure 6.16).

In a test-retest check on the Stork Stand balance test, Johnson and Nelson (1979) reported a reliability coefficient of .87. Face

Table 6.8　Stork Stand—Static Balance Test Norms

College men				College women			
T score	Raw score[a]	T score	Raw score[a]	T score	Raw score[a]	T score	Raw score[a]
80	73	57	36	90	62	63	30
79	71	56	34	89	61	62	29
78	70	55	32	88	60	61	28
77	68	54	31	87	59	60	27
76	66	53	29	86	57	59	25
75	65	52	28	85	56	58	24
74	63	51	26	84	55	57	23
73	61	50	24	83	54	56	22
72	60	49	23	82	53	55	21
71	58	48	21	81	52	54	20
70	57	47	20	80	50	53	18
69	55	46	18	79	49	52	17
68	53	45	16	78	48	51	16
67	52	44	15	77	47	50	15
66	50	43	13	76	46	49	14
65	49	42	12	75	44	48	12
64	47	41	10	74	43	47	11
63	45	40	8	73	42	46	10
62	44	39	7	72	41	45	9
61	42	38	5	71	40	44	8
60	41	37	4	70	38	43	6
59	39	36	2	69	37	42	5
58	37	35	1	68	36	41	4
				67	35	40	3
				66	34	39	2
				65	33	38	1
				64	31		

Note. From *Practical Measurements for Evaluation in Physical Education* (2nd ed.) (p. 198) by B.L. Johnson and J.K. Nelson, 1974, Minneapolis, MN: Burgess. Copyright 1974 by Burgess Publishing Company. Reprinted by permission.

[a]In seconds.

validity is assumed. The norms presented in Table 6.8 represent 99 male subjects and 114 female subjects of college age.

2. Modified Bass Test for Dynamic Balance. The *Modified Bass Test* is designed to test a student's dynamic balance. The student stands on the right foot on the starting point and then hops to the first tape mark on the left foot and attempts to hold a static position for 5 seconds. After this, the student hops to the second tape mark on the right foot and attempts to hold a static position for 5 seconds. He or she continues to alternate feet hopping and holding a static position for 5 seconds until the course is completed. The ball of the student's foot must completely cover each tape mark so that it cannot be seen. A successful performance consists of covering each tape with the ball of the foot, not touching the heel or any other part of the body to the floor, and holding a static position on each tape for 5 seconds while keeping the tape mark covered. Five points are earned for landing and covering a tape mark successfully, and an additional five points may be earned for each second the student can hold a static balance position. A student can earn a maximum of 10 points on each tape mark or a total of 100 points for the complete course. Each 5-second balance attempt should be counted aloud, with one point allowed for each second and a score recorded for each tape marker. (The student is allowed to reposition himself or herself for the 5-second balance attempt after landing successfully.) The equipment and materials needed include a stopwatch or watch with a second

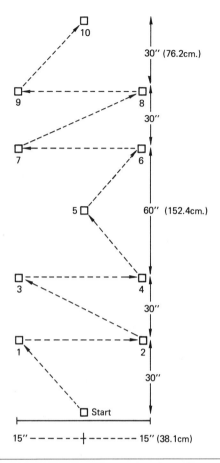

Figure 6.17 Diagram of Modified Bass Test of Dynamic Balance.

hand movement, eleven 1 × 3/4-inch (2.54 by 1.9 cm) pieces of marking tape, and a tape measure, meterstick, or yardstick. (See Figure 6.17 for the proper placement of each tape marker.)

A test-retest reliability coefficient of .75 was found, and a validity correlation coefficient of .46 was found when the Modified Bass Test was compared to the Bass Test of Dynamic Balance. The norms presented in Table 6.9 were based on the scores recorded on 100 college women.

Table 6.9 Modified Bass Test
for Dynamic Balance Norms

T score	Raw score	T score	Raw score
67	100	40	60
66	98	39	59
65	97	38	57
64	95	37	56
63	94	36	54
62	93	35	53
60	91	34	51
59	90	33	50
58	88	32	48
57	85	31	47
56	84	30	45
55	82	29	44
54	81	28	42
53	79	27	41
52	78	26	39
51	76	25	38
50	75	24	36
49	73	23	35
48	72	22	34
47	70	20	32
46	69	19	30
45	67	18	29
44	66	17	27
43	64	16	26
42	63	15	24
41	62	14	23

Note. From *Practical Measurements for Evaluation in Physical Education* (3rd ed.) (p. 234) by B.L. Johnson and J.K. Nelson, 1979, Minneapolis, MN: Burgess. Copyright 1979 by Burgess Publishing Company. Reprinted by permission.

General Motor Ability

For almost half a century physical educators have clung to the belief that performance in a variety of select motor tasks can indicate a child's general motor ability. Information from such testing is thought to enable teachers and coaches to quickly identify the successful athlete, predict which pupils will do well in a physical education class, or classify pupils into different ability groups in order to enhance instruction. Before investigating the credibility of this traditional belief, we should first distinguish between the terms *ability* and *skill* as used by motor learning specialists (Schmidt, 1975; Stallings, 1982).

A *motor ability* is thought to be a general quality that can facilitate future performance in a more specific task. Thus motor ability is viewed as an underlying contributor to future success in more specific motor tasks. For example, from birth through early childhood, an individual learns to grasp, manipulate, and throw an object. Gradually, the child develops the necessary strength, flexibility, and coordination of appropriate muscle groups to throw a ball a certain distance. We observe the child and indicate that the child possesses throwing ability at a certain level. A number of children may exhibit the same motor pattern of throwing and throw the same distance. Later, however, if these same children become interested in different sports their throwing patterns become more specific to meet the demands of the specific sport. One becomes a catcher in baseball and must develop a new throwing pattern from a squatting position—a specific throwing *skill* for a specific sport. Another pupil trains to throw the javelin instead of a ball, and yet another student becomes a quarterback in football and learns to pass the unusually-shaped football. Thus different, specific throwing patterns or skills are unique to their respective sport or game. This same concept of *specificity of skill* also applies to strength, flexibility, coordination, balance, speed, timing, and so forth as uniquely expressed in particular sports. Hence if a pupil lacks a skill it may be due to a lack of an underlying motor ability that may be discovered through testing.

General Motor Ability and Educability Tests

Many general motor ability (GMA) and general motor educability (GME) tests have been proposed that authorities in the past have claimed measure the fundamental general motor abilities thought to be important for successful participation in sports and games. These fundamental general motor abilities are thought to be determined by both genetic factors and early environmental stimulation. The concepts of GMA and GME were presented to physical educators in much the same way as the idea of Intelligent Quotient (IQ) was presented to psychologists; that is, GME and IQ tests are thought to assess components that are necessary for future success in motor and cognitive skills respectively. According to this logic, if a child cannot play a game well, he or she has not yet developed general motor abilities. Similarly, a psychologist might claim that a boy or girl who is doing poorly in reading and arithmetic may have an IQ score below normal. To some degree one certainly cannot fault this logic, especially when it is applied in an individualized diagnostic setting. To have diagnostic potential, however, the test must have a sufficient number of motor items that estimate the important motor components at each developmental level. A task analysis format is quite appropriate in diagnostic work.

Most of the general motor ability tests described in the measurement literature consist of test items that estimate many of the motor performance components described in this chapter and whose performance scores are summed into a single composite score. Thus these GMA tests actually provide no information about single motor performance components such as flexibility. For example, an individual may need to be somewhat flexible in order to perform well on a zigzag run, but the zigzag run does not measure flexibility.

Once we define the important components of motor ability, we must use a test item designed to measure that component. In recent years a transition from the use of general motor ability tests to specific skill testing has occurred. The following discussion is provided to acquaint you with the historical evolution from general to specific skill testing as well as the evidence to support this transition.

General motor ability tests are thought to assess the motor abilities of speed, muscular strength and endurance, power, kinesthesis, eye-hand coordination, eye-foot coordination, agility, flexibility, timing, and sensory motor rhythm. A test item is developed to estimate each of these components, and then a composite score is computed for all test items. This composite score becomes the criterion for test validity. Through the data reduction technique of multiple correlation, a relationship is determined between the composite score and a subset of three to five items.

Two example tests of GMA are the Scott test for high school and college men and the Barrow test for high school and college men. These and other tests of GMA can be found in measurement texts by Barrow and McGee (1979), Clarke (1976), Meyers and Blesh (1962), and Mathews (1978). The test items for the Scott and Barrow tests are as follows:

Scott GMA Test	*Barrow GMA Test*
Obstacle race	Standing broad jump
Basketball throw	Softball throw
Standing broad jump	Zigzag run
Wall pass	Wall pass
4-second dash	Medicine ball put
	60-yard dash

Tests of general motor educability are proposed to disclose the rapidity with which a child learns motor skills. GME test items are supposed to be unfamiliar motor tasks that the child performs. If a child performs these unfamiliar tasks correctly, he or she is thought to be an individual who will experience little difficulty in learning future motor skills. These tests can also be termed *motor aptitude* tests or tests of *motor learning potential*. A number of motor educability tests have been developed and are reviewed in the same sources cited for general motor ability tests. The Iowa Brace Motor Educability Test is presented here as an example of an early GME test. It consists of 21 items, some of which are included in motor proficiency or perceptual-motor tests currently used in special physical education programs.

Iowa Brace Motor Educability Test
1. From side leaning rest position on the right side, raise left arm and leg and hold for 5 seconds.
2. Hold a one-knee balance on floor for 5 seconds with arms sideward at shoulder level.
3. From balance position in #2, touch head to floor and recover.
4. Standing on one foot, eyes closed, take five hops backward, maintaining position.
5. Three push-ups.
6. Jump, swing legs forward, and touch toes with hand, not bending more than 45°.
7. Full left turn.
8. Double heel click.
9. Move arms in a circle 1 foot in diameter with arms horizontally to the side while bouncing up and down from a full squat position for 10 seconds.
10. Loop jump.
11. Standing on the left foot, jump and make a half left turn.
12. Swing left leg to the side, jump up with right leg, clap feet, and land with feet apart.
13. Foot-touch-head.
14. Grapevine.
15. Full right turn.
16. Kneeling jump.
17. Crossed leg sit.
18. Stork stand.
19. Do a Russian dance step by alternately raising legs forward, twice on each side; heel of extended leg may touch the floor.
20. From a sitting position with lower legs flexed and on the floor, arms under knees, and hands grasping ankles, roll like a top onto right knee, right shoulder, back, left shoulder, and knee and recover. Do twice to complete circle.
21. While squatting on either foot, hands on hips, raise other leg forward and hold for 5 seconds.

Tests of general motor ability and general motor educability are usually proposed to predict learning potential and athletic ability, select athletes from a large number of team candidates, and classify students into different groups for physical education instruction. During the past 20 years, much research has been conducted on the effectiveness of general motor measures as related to testing purpose. This research has been well reviewed in the motor learning texts by Stallings (1982), Schmidt (1975), Singer (1980), Lawther (1977), and Kerr (1982), to mention a few. We can summarize this research with the following basic points:

• General motor ability test scores usually do not correlate well enough with bowling, tennis, basketball, and track and field scores to justify use of the GMA test to predict future performance. This is also true of tests of general motor educability. They correlate about .40 to .60 with tests of athletic ability, as well as rate of learning water skills, tennis, volleyball, field hockey, and wrestling. Correlations of this magnitude are also obtained with general motor ability tests and a sport-specific skill test such as a volleyball test. As a general rule, tests of general motor ability do not correlate well with specific skills because the manner in which sport-specific skills are expressed is not present in the general motor ability test items.

- If a general test is used to classify pupils into discrete ability groups at the beginning of an instructional unit, the classification would soon be of little value. This is due to the fact that the performance variability (differences) among individuals within each group would increase as instruction progresses, indicating that differences increase with the rate and amount of pupil learning over time.
- Motor skills used at the beginning of instruction change in terms of complexity and pattern of execution at more advanced stages of learning. This factor, in addition to increasing performance variability among participants as instruction progresses, partially explains the generally low relationships found between initial and final skill test scores.
- The use of the composite score as a criterion for test validation is inadvisable because you are essentially correlating the GMA test score with one component. In addition, these multiple correlations are generally inflated because the same items appear in both the test and the composite score (Cumbee & Harris, 1953).

In summary, the use of general motor measures to classify students for instruction, predict athletic ability, or predict rate of learning is highly questionable and appears to be unwarranted based on current research. Indeed, some researchers question even the existence of general motor ability. However, it is true that future learning of any type is always based on a foundation of prior experiences. As children progress through the many motor tasks of childhood and later physical activities in school, their skills become more and more specific. This in-

crease in specificity of skills is apparent in the low relationships between students' initial and final scores. If you want to classify students for instruction, select a test that simulates the specific sport or activity to be learned. It is important to remember that you may need to intermittently reclassify some students into different ability groups as instruction progresses and you observe the various rates of students' improvement taking place. Make changes when so indicated and do not "pigeon hole" or "type" a person into a category for long periods of time based on a preinstruction test score. Keeping a student in the wrong group may result in low achievement levels and could have unfavorable emotional repercussions on the pupil. Remember, no test is perfect!

This does not, however, mean that the general motor measures are of little value to practitioners. On the contrary, they may be of great value when utilized in a motor diagnostic clinic to assist in detecting motor deficiencies that may be the cause of a child's lack of motor development.

Review Questions

1. When you conduct a test for flexibility/balance ability, would you also involve elements of the other motor components such as strength/endurance? Explain your answer.
2. List the components of motor performance.
3. Relationships between various tests of motor performance are generally low. In addition, these tests usually do not correlate well with success in sports and games. What does this indicate?
4. The intensity and type of motor components developed will be task-related. Explain what this means.
5. In the testing of strength, the test score we obtain is only an indirect and rather crude

estimate of a student's actual strength. Why?

6. State the various definitions of strength and endurance listed in this chapter. What is the basic difference between testing for strength and testing for endurance?

7. Why are the tests for power performed by a student only a crude indicator of the student's power?

8. From a scientific viewpoint, why is it impossible for a practicing physical education teacher to measure flexibility and balance?

9. From a practical viewpoint, what do we observe and record when we test a student's flexibility and balance?

10. Why would tests of coordination/agility be considered the higher order of testing of motor components?

11. What problems are involved in using the composite score as a criterion for test validation?

Problems and Exercises

1. Twenty-five females performed the Yuhasz 3-1/2 minute endurance test and achieved the following scores:

Subject	Push-ups 30 sec	Sit-ups 30 sec	Chest raises 30 sec	Double leg raises 30 sec	Side leg raises 30 sec	Sitting tucks 30 sec
S1	18	18	37	50	112	57
S2	8	18	31	37	79	31
S3	12	21	38	54	94	62
S4	31	27	46	63	130	67
S5	7	16	30	35	79	28
S6	13	23	33	53	112	47
S7	3	12	23	36	52	16
S8	23	27	40	57	108	62
S9	16	21	34	48	96	41
S10	32	30	46	68	134	74
S11	4	15	26	39	51	25
S12	17	22	41	55	90	52
S13	18	19	37	52	85	41
S14	21	27	40	53	100	52
S15	9	18	35	46	89	44
S16	21	22	40	51	100	59
S17	15	21	39	46	90	44
S18	28	26	43	62	118	68
S19	3	8	14	31	34	25
S20	17	20	37	46	79	37
S21	16	21	36	48	90	43
S22	14	19	32	45	87	40
S23	30	28	48	62	125	69
S24	16	21	37	49	95	46
S25	10	19	32	43	70	36

a. Determine the approximate percentile rank of each student in each event and calculate a mean percentile rank for each student across all events.
b. Calculate an $\overline{X}$ and s for each event.
c. Calculate a z and T score for each student in each event.

Answer 1a.

	Percentile rank push-ups	Percentile rank sit-ups	Percentile rank chest raises	Percentile rank double leg raises	Percentile rank side leg raises	Percentile rank sitting tucks	$\overline{X}$
S1	55	40	60	55	70	70	58.3
S2	25	40	35	25	40	30	32.5
S3	40	55	60	65	55	80	59.2
S4	95	80	90	90	85	90	88.3
S5	25	30	35	20	40	25	29.2
S6	40	60	45	65	70	55	55.8
S7	10	40	65	55	60	5	39.2
S8	70	80	70	75	65	80	73.3
S9	50	55	45	50	55	45	50.0
S10	95	95	90	100	90	100	95.0
S11	15	25	20	30	15	20	20.8
S12	55	60	70	70	50	65	61.7
S13	55	45	60	60	45	45	51.7
S14	65	80	70	65	60	65	67.5
S15	30	40	50	45	50	50	44.2
S16	65	60	70	60	60	75	65.0
S17	45	55	65	45	50	50	51.7
S18	85	80	80	85	75	90	82.5
S19	5	25	0	10	0	20	10.0
S20	55	50	60	45	40	40	48.3
S21	50	55	55	50	50	50	51.7
S22	45	45	40	45	45	45	44.2
S23	90	85	95	85	80	90	87.5
S24	50	55	60	55	55	55	55.0
S25	35	45	40	40	30	40	38.3

(Cont.)

Answer 1b.

	Push-ups		Sit-ups		Chest raises		Double leg raises		Side leg raises		Sitting tuck	
	$\overline{X}$	s	$\overline{X}$	s	$\overline{X}$	s	$\overline{X}$	s	$\overline{X}$	s	$\overline{X}$	s
	16.08	±8.78	20.76	±4.79	35.8	±7.33	49.16	±13.24	91.96	±23.59	46.64	±15.12

Answer 1c.

	Push-ups		Sit-ups		Chest raises		Double leg raises		Side leg raises		Sitting tuck	
	z	T	z	T	z	T	z	T	z	T	z	T
S1	.21	52.2	-.58	44.2	.16	51.6	.06	50.6	.85	58.5	.69	56.9
S2	-.92	40.8	-.58	44.2	-.65	43.5	-.92	40.8	-.55	44.5	-1.02	39.8
S3	-.46	45.4	.05	50.5	.30	53.0	.37	53.7	.09	50.9	1.02	60.2
S4	1.7	70.0	1.3	63.0	1.39	63.9	1.05	60.5	1.61	66.1	1.35	63.5
S5	-1.03	39.7	-.99	40.1	-.79	42.1	-1.07	39.3	-.55	45.5	-1.23	37.7
S6	-.35	46.5	.47	54.7	-.38	46.2	.29	52.9	.85	58.5	.02	50.2
S7	-1.49	35.1	-1.8	32.0	-1.75	32.5	-.99	40.1	-1.69	33.1	-2.03	29.7
S8	.79	57.9	1.3	63.0	.57	55.7	.59	55.9	.68	56.8	1.02	60.2
S9	-.009	49.9	.05	50.5	-.25	47.5	-.09	49.1	.17	51.7	-.37	46.3
S10	1.81	68.1	1.9	69.0	1.39	63.9	1.42	64.2	1.78	67.8	1.81	68.1
S11	-1.38	36.2	-1.2	38.0	-1.33	36.7	.77	42.3	-1.74	32.6	-1.43	35.7
S12	.10	51.0	.26	52.6	.71	57.1	.44	54.4	-.08	49.2	.35	53.5
S13	.22	52.2	-.37	46.3	.16	51.6	.21	52.1	-.30	47.0	-.37	46.3
S14	.56	55.6	1.3	63.0	.57	55.7	.29	52.9	.34	53.4	.35	53.5
S15	-.81	41.9	-.58	44.2	-.19	48.9	.24	47.6	-.13	48.7	-.17	48.3
S16	.56	55.6	.26	52.6	.57	55.7	.14	51.4	.34	53.4	.82	58.2
S17	-.12	48.8	.05	50.5	.44	54.4	.24	52.4	-.08	49.2	-.17	48.3
S18	1.36	63.6	1.09	60.9	.98	59.8	.97	59.7	1.10	61.0	1.41	64.1
S19	-1.49	35.1	-2.66	23.4	-2.97	20.3	-1.37	36.3	-2.46	25.4	-1.43	35.7
S20	.10	51.0	-.16	48.4	.16	51.6	-.24	47.6	-.55	44.5	-.64	43.6
S21	-.009	49.9	.05	50.5	.03	50.3	-.09	49.1	-.08	49.2	-.24	47.6
S22	-.24	47.6	-.37	46.3	-.52	44.8	-.31	46.9	-.21	47.9	-.44	45.6
S23	1.59	65.9	1.51	65.1	1.66	66.6	.97	59.7	1.40	64.0	1.48	64.8
S24	-.009	49.9	.05	50.5	.16	51.6	-.01	49.9	.13	51.3	-.04	49.6
S25	-.69	43.1	-.38	46.3	-.52	44.8	-.47	45.3	-.93	40.7	-.70	43.0

2. Twenty male students in a kinesiology class ran a flight of stairs and were timed with a stopwatch. The vertical height of the run was 10 feet. Based on the data below,
   a. Calculate the work in ft lbs/sec for each student.
   b. Calculate the work done in kg • wt • m/sec for each student.
   c. Calculate an $\overline{X}$ and s in both systems for the class.
   d. Develop a frequency distribution and graph the results (work versus frequency).
   e. Develop a percentile ranking for the class in both systems.

Subject	Wt. (lbs)	Time (sec)	Vertical height = 10 ft
S1	160	1.9	
S2	185	2.2	
S3	160	1.8	
S4	162	1.9	
S5	170	1.8	
S6	175	1.8	
S7	168	2.0	
S8	143	1.6	
S9	210	2.3	
S10	173	2.0	
S11	156	1.6	
S12	162	1.7	
S13	174	1.9	
S14	201	2.0	
S15	193	2.0	
S16	184	1.9	
S17	156	1.8	
S18	144	1.7	
S19	162	2.1	
S20	170	2.2	

3. Thirty female high school seniors performed the Trunk Flexibility Test with the following results:

Student	Trunk flex (cm)	Student	Trunk flex (cm)
S1	51.2	S16	44.3
S2	47.0	S17	43.0
S3	42.2	S18	49.2
S4	46.0	S19	46.8
S5	38.5	S20	55.5
S6	56.0	S21	37.2

(Cont.)

Student	Trunk flex (cm)	Student	Trunk flex (cm)
S7	47.8	S22	45.8
S8	53.0	S23	46.5
S9	41.2	S24	53.2
S10	37.5	S25	43.0
S11	46.0	S26	50.6
S12	44.8	S27	57.0
S13	51.2	S28	45.6
S14	53.0	S29	41.0
S15	46.4	S30	47.4

a. Determine the approximate percentile rank of each student.
b. Calculate an $\overline{X}$ and s for the whole group.
c. Examine the $\overline{X}$ and s for the college freshmen presented in this chapter and determine if the $\overline{X}$ for college freshmen plus or minus the s captures the mean for the high school seniors.

Answers

3a.

Student	Approximate percentile rank	Student	Approximate percentile rank
S1	70	S16	40
S2	50	S17	40
S3	40	S18	70
S4	50	S19	50
S5	20	S20	90
S6	90	S21	20
S7	60	S22	50
S8	80	S23	50
S9	30	S24	80
S10	20	S25	40
S11	50	S26	70
S12	40	S27	90
S13	70	S28	50
S14	80	S29	30
S15	50	S30	60

3b. $\overline{X} = 46.93$ cm; $s = \pm 5.3$ cm

3c. Yes, it does capture the $\overline{X}$ for the high school seniors.

4. A physical education teacher wanted to test the static balance ability of her beginning gymnastic class. The 20 girls were in the ninth grade and were timed as follows for the Stork Stand Test.

Subject	Time (sec)	Subject	Time (sec)
S1	12	S11	12
S2	8	S12	21
S3	10	S13	11
S4	6	S14	8
S5	18	S15	7
S6	5	S16	4
S7	14	S17	13
S8	12	S18	3
S9	9	S19	12
S10	6	S20	12

a. Calculate a percentile rank and graph the results.
b. Calculate an $\overline{X}$ and s for the group.
c. Calculate a T score for each student. Compare the ninth-grade girls' T scores with the T score norm raw scores in seconds for college women.

5. A high school physical education teacher decided to run a test-retest reliability correlation coefficient on the Modified Bass Test of Dynamic Balance. She tested 20 10th-grade girls on one day and waited a week and tested them once again with the following results:

Subject	Score 1	Score 2
S1	66	69
S2	75	66
S3	67	63
S4	82	79
S5	74	81
S6	57	53
S7	84	88
S8	81	76
S9	53	60
S10	76	78
S11	70	64
S12	72	81
S13	60	57
S14	62	70
S15	75	76
S16	88	79
S17	64	60
S18	58	60
S19	73	75
S20	66	68

a. Calculate a product moment correlation coefficient using the ungrouped data.
   Answer .997

6. A junior high school coach wanted to test the agility of his gym class. He decided to use the Right-Boomerang Run Test. He ran 40 seventh and eighth graders through the test with the following results:

Subject	Time (sec)	Subject	Time (sec)
S1	13.5	S21	15.1
S2	13.7	S22	14.8
S3	13.8	S23	14.6
S4	13.4	S24	13.7
S5	13.3	S25	13.6
S6	13.9	S26	13.6
S7	14.0	S27	14.2
S8	14.0	S28	12.0
S9	14.1	S29	11.2
S10	13.2	S30	15.6
S11	13.1	S31	14.2
S12	14.2	S32	13.6
S13	13.1	S33	13.4
S14	14.3	S34	13.9
S15	13.0	S35	13.8
S16	12.4	S36	15.5
S17	14.9	S37	11.1
S18	14.8	S38	13.0
S19	12.1	S39	14.0
S20	12.9	S40	13.7

a. Calculate an $\overline{X}$ and s for the group.
b. Establish local T score norms for the seventh- and eighth-grade boys.

Bibliography

Åstrand, P.O., & Rodahl, K. (1977). *Textbook of work physiology, physiological basis of exercise* (2nd ed.). New York: McGraw-Hill.

Barrow, H.M., & McGee, R. (1979). *A practical approach to measurement in physical education* (3rd ed.). Philadelphia: Lea and Febiger.

Baumgartner, T.A., & Jackson, A.S. (1982). *Measurement for evaluation in physical education* (2nd ed.). Dubuque, IA: William C. Brown.

Bosco, J.S., & Gustafson, W.F. (1983). *Measurement and evaluation in physical education, fitness, and sports.* Englewood Cliffs, NJ: Prentice-Hall.

Clarke, H.H. (1976). *Application of measurement to health and physical education* (5th ed.). Englewood Cliffs, NJ: Prentice-Hall.

Clarke, H.H., & Munroe, R.A. (1970). *Oregon cable-tension strength test batteries for boys and girls from fourth grade through college.* Microcard publications in health, physical education, and recreation. Eugene: University of Oregon.

Corbin, C.B., Dowell, L.J., Lindsey, R., & Tolson, H. (1974). *Concepts in physical education with laboratories and experiments* (2nd ed.). Dubuque, IA: William C. Brown.

Corbin, C.B., & Noble, L. (1980). Flexibility: A major component of physical fitness. *Journal of Physical Education and Recreation,* **51**(6), 23-24, 57-60.

Cumbee, F.Z., & Harris, C.W. (1953). The composite criterion and its relation to factor analysis. *Research Quarterly,* **24**(2), 303-321.

deVries, H.A. (1986). *Physiology of exercise* (4th ed.). Dubuque, IA: William C. Brown.

Duda, M. (1986). Prepubescent strength training gains support. *The Physician and Sports Medicine,* **14**(2), 157-161.

Edgren, H.D. (1932). An experiment in the testing of ability and progress in basketball. *Research Quarterly,* **3**(1), 159-171.

Espenschade, A.A. (1963). Restudy of relationships between physical performance of school children and age, height, and weight. *Research Quarterly,* **34**(2), 144-153.

Fox, E.L., & Mathews, D.K. (1981). *The physiological basis of physical education and athletics* (3rd ed.). Philadelphia: W.B. Saunders.

Franks, B.D., & Deutsch, J. (1973). *Evaluating performance in physical education.* New York: Academic Press.

Gruber, J.J. (1964). *Tests and measurements laboratory manual.* West Lafayette, IN: Purdue University, Department of Physical Education for Men.

Heusner, W.W., & Van Huss, W.D. (1978). Strength, power, and muscular endurance. In Henry J. Montoye (Ed.), *An introduction to measurement in physical education* (pp. 55-56). Boston: Allyn and Bacon.

Heyward, V.H. (1984). *Designs for fitness: A guide to physical fitness appraisal and exercise prescription.* Minneapolis: Burgess.

Ismail, A.H., & Cowell, C.C. (1961). Factor analysis of motor aptitude of preadolescent boys. *Research Quarterly,* **32**(4), 507-513.

Johnson, B.L., & Nelson, J.K. (1974). *Practical measurements for evaluation in physical education* (2nd ed.). Minneapolis: Burgess.

Johnson, B.L., & Nelson, J.K. (1979). *Practical measurements for evaluation in physical education* (3rd ed.). Minneapolis: Burgess.

Kerr, R. (1982). *Psychomotor learning.* Philadelphia: Saunders College Publishing.

Lawther, J.D. (1977). *The learning and performance of physical skills* (2nd ed.). Englewood Cliffs, NJ: Prentice-Hall.

Mathews, D.K. (1978). *Measurement in physical education* (5th ed.). Philadelphia: Saunders College Publishing.

McCloy, C.H., & Young, N.D. (1954). *Tests and measurements in health and physical education.* New York: Appleton Century Crofts.

Meyers, C.R., & Blesh, T.E. (1962). *Measurement in physical education.* New York: Ronald Press.

Oxendine, J.B. (1984). *Psychology of motor learning.* Englewood Cliffs, NJ: Prentice-Hall.

Sage, G.H. (1984). *Motor learning and control: A neuropsychological approach.* Dubuque, IA: William C. Brown.

Schmidt, R.A. (1975). *Motor skills.* New York: Harper and Row.

Singer, R.N. (1980). *Motor learning and human performance* (3rd ed.). New York: Macmillan.

Stallings, L.M. (1982). *Motor learning from theory to practice.* St. Louis: C.V. Mosby.

Zuti, W.B., & Corbin, C.R. (1977). Physical fitness norms for college freshmen. *Research Quarterly,* **48**(2), 499-503.

Chapter
7

Motor and
Physical Fitness Testing

The improvement of human physical functioning has always been a primary goal of physical education programs. When programs have primarily addressed themselves to increasing the participants' muscular strength, endurance, and cardiovascular efficiency and to reducing adipose tissue in the body, they have been called "conditioning programs," "fitness programs," or "physical training programs." Some practitioners have adopted more exotic names for their programs, such as "slimnastics," "figure improvement," or "body styling" in an effort to attract participants.

Physical educators, exercise physiologists, and physicians have proposed many tests to demonstrate the effects of such programs. These tests have generally been labeled "motor fitness tests," "physical fitness tests," and "cardiovascular tests." Additional tests have been developed by state departments of physical education as well as many colleges and universities. With so many groups and individuals promoting different fitness tests, the practitioner may easily become confused, especially when the same items appear on both motor and physical fitness tests. Thus one might ask whether there is a difference between motor fitness and

physical fitness. Are the dimensions of fitness equally relevant to all people of all ages? Are the specific importance and meaning of fitness taken into account when tests of motor and/or physical fitness are developed? Obviously, the nature of fitness—what it means to the participant, the type of fitness activities selected, the intensity and duration of exercise—varies among school children, young adults, the middle-aged, and senior citizens. In other words, fitness is specific to the needs of different populations. This is reflected in the perennial question, "Fitness for what?"

Definitions of Motor Fitness and Physical Fitness

The term *motor fitness* became popular during World War II as the military services developed tests to evaluate the capacity of military personnel for vigorous work (Mathews, 1978). Motor fitness is thought to be a limited dimension of general motor ability. Elements of motor fitness include muscular endurance, muscular strength, power, flexibility, coordination, balance, and agility. These elements of motor fitness are usually reflected in motor performances such as running, jumping, dodging, climbing, swimming, lifting weights, and carrying loads for a prolonged period of time. The President's Council on Physical Fitness and Sports defines physical fitness as "the ability to carry out daily tasks with vigor and alertness, without undue fatigue, with ample energy to enjoy leisure time pursuits, and to meet unforeseen emergencies" (Clarke, 1971, p. 1). Implicit in this definition of fitness is the ability to withstand the stress of life and persevere under difficult circumstances. The President's Council (Clarke, 1971) goes beyond the components of motor development identified earlier in chapter 6 (see Figure 6.1) by identifying the primary components of physical fitness as muscular strength, muscular endurance, and cardiorespiratory endurance. Other physical fitness components identified by the President's Council include agility, speed, flexibility, and balance. Some of these components become increasingly important when designing physical fitness programs for senior citizens or members of certain occupations. When working with atypical groups, the importance of each component may vary. Senior citizens, for example, require more activities designed to develop and preserve flexibility and balance than activities to develop muscular strength and power.

The importance of an optimal level of physical fitness as a reflection of certain aspects of health was demonstrated by the work of Kraus and Raab (1961) on hypokinetic diseases, or diseases directly related to a lack of exercise. These physicians identified low back pain, foot problems, abdominal ptosis, obesity, hypertension, and degenerative cardiovascular diseases as conditions produced by sedentary life-styles in our affluent, tension-producing society. Thus the concept of physical fitness does

convey a meaning of healthful living that is partly reflected in the new Health-Related Fitness Test described later in this chapter. Because heart disease, stroke, and circulatory disorders are still primary causes of death in affluent parts of the world, the cardiovascular component of physical fitness is highly relevant for all people. Sedentary people suffer a higher incidence of coronary heart disease than active persons (Morris et al., 1973; Paffenbarger & Hale, 1975). Thus attaining a desirable level of physical fitness is an important aspect of preventive medicine because physical inactivity appears to be related to coronary heart disease. Recent longitudinal data shows that Harvard alumni who expend 2,000 calories a week in vigorous exercise during their life span will increase the quality of life as well as live one or more years longer than sedentary persons (Paffenbarger et al., 1986). Several special physical fitness programs are described in chapter 16 on "Evaluation in Nonschool Settings." For most young participants, however, a physical fitness test is one that attempts to measure the efficiency of both the muscular and cardiovascular systems.

Identification of Fitness Components

Several researchers have applied the correlational research technique of factor analysis to the many fitness test items in an effort to eliminate some of the confusion surrounding the many tests and test items that authorities in medicine, physical education, and physiology have proposed as measures of motor and/or physical fitness. Factor analysis is used to identify basic components found in a large number of test items believed to measure fitness. The analysis identifies the items that contribute the most to each fitness component (factor) and thereby enables the researcher to eliminate unimportant items from the measurement scheme. Once the important test items for each factor are identified, the researcher names the factor based on his or her judgment of the physiological performances inherent in the test items. The research of Fleishman (1964) and Falls et al. (1965) contributed significantly to current understanding of physical fitness. The factors and relevant items identified by Fleishman and Fall are summarized as follows:

Fleishman's Analysis (nine factors identified with relevant items)

Factors	Items
1. Extent flexibility	Twist and touch, abdominal stretch, toe touching
2. Dynamic flexibility	Lateral bend, one foot tapping, bend-twist and touch for time
3. Explosive strength	Shuttle run, 50-yard dash (45.73-m), standing broad jump
4. Static strength	Hand grip strength, medicine ball put, arm pull-dynamometer
5. Dynamic strength	Pull-ups, bent-arm hang
6. Trunk strength	Leg lift, half-hold sit-ups
7. Gross body equilibrium	Stand on a stick with preferred foot for time
8. Gross body coordination	Jump through a rope without tripping, falling, or releasing the rope
9. Stamina (cardio-vascular endurance)	600-yard (548.78-m) run-walk for time

Fall's Analysis (nine factors identified with relevant items)

Factors	Items
1. Athletic fitness	Percentage lean body mass, 50-yard (45.73-m) dash, standing broad jump, pull-ups, shuttle run
2. Maximum metabolic rate	Maximum O_2 uptake/kg lean body mass, maximum O_2 uptake, maximum minute volume ventilation
3. Respiratory capacity	Submaximal minute volume ventilation/kg body weight, submaximal minute volume ventilation
4. Basic height of blood pressure	Recovery diastolic blood pressure, resting diastolic blood pressure
5. Heart rate response to exertion	Exercise increase in pulse, maximum heart rate
6. Expiratory capacity	Forced vital capacity
7. Pulse pressure	Postexercise pulse pressure, resting pulse pressure
8. Force efficiency (balance)	Force platform (vertical score), force platform (frontal score)
9. Resting heart rate	Standing heart rate, resting heart rate

Note that the items analyzed by Fleishman included flexibility measures as well as several strength items, whereas Fall's analysis included many items that physicians and exercise physiologists use to measure the pulmonary and cardiovascular components of physical fitness. This illustrates the point that a factor analysis can show relationships only among the kinds of components that were selected for the analysis originally.

A more recent factor analysis conducted on both men and women by Zuidema and Baumgartner (1974) identified four fitness factors that are common to both sexes. Zuidema and Baumgartner summarized the factors and relevant items as follows:

Purposes of Fitness Testing

Physical fitness tests can be used for one or more of the following purposes:

- *Classification*, or placing similar participants into instructional groups on the basis of a physical fitness score. Classifying participants of similar abilities into the same group allows the instructor to address the needs of all participants in an instructional group at the same time. Thus all those who have an initially high test score can be placed in a class that begins at a high level of exercise intensity, and those who score low on the test can be placed into a class that begins at a low level of exercise intensity.

Factors	Items for men	Items for women
1. Upper body strength and endurance	Chin-ups, pull-ups, push-ups	Modified push-ups, overhand straight-arm hang, modified chin-ups
2. Trunk strength and endurance	Half-hold sit-ups, leg raises	Bent-knee sit-ups, half-hold sit-ups
3. Leg explosive strength and endurance	Standing broad jump, jump and reach	Standing broad jump, jump and reach, 50-yard (45.73-m) dash
4. Cardiorespiratory endurance	12-minute run, 880-yard (804.88-m) run	12-minute run

In summary, one can say that the components of physical fitness identified by factor analysis are generally in agreement with the basic components presented by the President's Council on Physical Fitness and Sports. For the purposes of this text, *physical fitness* is defined as the combined performance factors of muscular strength, muscular endurance, cardiovascular endurance, power, and flexibility. *Motor fitness* is defined as all of the physical fitness factors plus balance, speed, coordination, and agility.

- *Diagnosis*, or determining participants' cardiovascular efficiency and the strengths and weaknesses of their major muscle groups. On the basis of this data, an appropriate conditioning program can be prescribed for each individual to meet his or her particular needs.
- *Achievement*, or measuring the effects of a fitness program upon each participant through initial and periodic testing during the program.

- *Motivation*, or stimulating participants to improve their level of fitness.
- *Program evaluation*, or demonstrating the effects of a physical fitness program to the participants and other interested parties such as parents and school administrators. The physical educator can also compare the mean scores of participants from his or her program against the mean scores obtained by participants of the same age in other programs in the county, state, region, or nation.
- *Norm development*, or developing average scores for each test item collected from a large number of participants so that local norms can be established. An individual's performance can then be compared to the performances of other people in the same program.

The Physical Examination

The first test administered to any individual of any age who is to participate in any physical activity program should be a thorough physical examination by a licensed physician. Specific health problems identified by the physician that contraindicate vigorous physical exercise should be recorded on an appropriate school or agency health appraisal form (Figure 7.1). Based on the medical examination, the physician should classify the individual into one of the following categories:

1. *Unrestricted Activity.* Individuals designated for unrestricted activity are fully capable of tolerating the stress of vigorous physical activity in the agency's physical education and/or competitive athletic programs.
2. *Moderate Activity.* Individuals designated for moderate activity can perform activities that are submaximal in terms of exer-

cise stress intensity. These individuals can engage in physical activity but will require frequent rest periods due to minor problems such as asthma, mild heart or lung disease.
3. *Restricted Activity.* Individuals designated for restricted activity are limited to mild forms of exercise such as walking, table tennis, or archery due to limitations required by serious physical problems.

Only those individuals who are in category #1 (unrestricted physical activity) should perform all of the items on motor and physical fitness tests because the examinee is asked to exert maximal effort to perform optimally on each test item.

Body Size and Muscular Performance

We have known for some time that taller and/or heavier people perform more poorly than lighter individuals on certain muscular performance items and perform better than shorter or lighter people on other types of items. Fleishman (1964) found direct evidence of a significant negative correlation between an individual's body weight and performance on muscular endurance items such as pull-ups, flexed-arm hang, and dips. Thus lighter people tend to score higher on endurance items. Power tests that involve moving the total body weight quickly, such as the vertical jump, rope climb for time, and the 50-yard dash, are also negatively related to body weight. You will recall from our previous discussion that in the past most fitness tests did not take body weight into account. Thus we should not expect people of different body weights to perform equally well on certain items. However, there is a positive relationship between body weight and *static strength* measures such as the dynamometer press, dynamometer

School _____   Birth Date _____   Sex _____

Name _____   Parent(s) Name _____

Address _____   Phone _____

Code: 1 = Excellent,   2 = Mild Problem,   3 = Rather Severe Problem

GRADE						Genitalia					
DATE						Nervous system					
Nutrition						Bones & joints					
Height						Muscle tone					
Weight						Posture					
Skin & hair						Type of inoculations (date)					
Eyes						Type of vaccinations (date)					
Vision test											
Ears											
Hearing test											
Nose & throat						Physician's remarks & recommendations:					
Teeth & gums											
Thyroid gland											
Lymph nodes											
Heart & lungs											
Abdomen											

PHYSICAL EDUCATION AND ATHLETIC PARTICIPATION RECOMMENDATION

1. Unrestricted activity: All vigorous P.E. and competitive athletic programs					
2. Moderate activity: Frequent rest periods; badminton, jogging, volleyball, tennis					
3. Resricted activity: Serious health problems; archery, golf, table tennis, walking, bowling					

PHYSICIAN'S SIGNATURE _____

Figure 7.1 Health appraisal (by physician) form.

arm push or pull, and medicine ball put. In these test items, unlike power tests, body weight is not the primary resistance to overcome. Correlations are high enough to justify developing norms for some of the items based on age, sex, and body weight. Unfortunately, most norm charts in use today do not include body weight in their calculations.

An excellent theoretical discussion explaining the correlations reported by Fleishman can be found in the chapter on ''Body Dimensions and Muscular Work'' in Åstrand and Rodahl's (1977) *Textbook of Work Physiology*. Other examples of the influence of body weight on muscular performance have been offered by Ricci (1974). Ricci suggests that norms should take body weight into account when they are developed and also suggests that one can look at scoring pull-ups from a biomechanical point of view. In scoring pull-ups, one would consider body weight and displacement of the body as a pull-up is performed and calculate the amount of work accomplished in kilogram-meters.

The important thing to remember is to be careful about how normative data are used. If you are going to utilize norms to classify people for instructional purposes, you probably do not need to worry much about the relationship between body weight and performance. However, if norms are to be used in making critical decisions such as predicting success, selecting team members, or assigning grades, then you must consider body weight and other factors that are known to influence performance.

The AAHPER Youth Fitness Test

Hunsicker (1958) presented the AAHPER Youth Fitness Test Battery to professional physical educators on behalf of a physical fitness research committee that developed a youth fitness test for nationwide use. The AAHPER test battery was developed as a result of a need to upgrade and assess the fitness level of American youth, which Kraus and Hirschland (1954) had reported was below that of European school children. Over a period of years, extensive test data were collected, and national norms were revised and published in the *AAHPER Youth Fitness Test Manual* (1965). The tests' items included pull-ups for boys, flexed-arm hang for girls, sit-ups to a maximum of 50 for girls and 100 for boys, shuttle run, standing broad jump, 50-yard (45.73 m) dash, softball throw for distance, and the 600-yard (548.73 m) run-walk. The AAHPER Youth Fitness Test was revised again in 1976; the softball throw for distance was eliminated, and the straight leg sit-up was changed to the number of bent-knee sit-ups performed in 60 seconds. In addition, the 9- and 12-minute run-walk (i.e., the 1-mile [1609.76 m] run and 1-1/2-mile [2414.64 m] run for time, respectively) were suggested as an alternative to the 600-yard run-walk. Current test items and factors that appear to be inherent in the items include the following:

Items	Factors
1. Pull-ups or flexed-arm hang	Dynamic strength and endurance of arms and shoulders
2. Sit-ups	Trunk strength and endurance
3. Shuttle run	Speed and change of direction
4. Standing broad jump	Explosive strength of legs
5. 50-yard (45.73 m) dash	Explosive strength of legs and speed of lower extremities
6. 600-yard (548.78 m) run-walk; 9- or 12-minute run-walk for distance; 1-mile (1609.76 m) or 1-1/2-mile (2414.64 m) run for time	Cardiorespiratory endurance

The AAHPER Youth Fitness Test is easily administered with very little equipment. An additional feature of the test is the extensive national norms available in the test manual. It is recommended that testing be conducted over a 2-day period with pull-ups or flexed-arm hang, sit-ups, and the shuttle run administered the first day, and the standing broad jump, 50-yard (45.73 m) dash, and 600-yard (548.78 m) run-walk (or the 9-minute run-walk or 1-mile [1609.76 m] run for time) administered on the second day.

Testing Procedures: AAHPER Youth Fitness Test Revised (1976) Edition[1]

1. Pull-Ups (boys)

   Equipment: A metal or wooden bar approximately 1-1/2 inches (3.81 cm) in diameter. A doorway gym bar can be used, and if no regular equipment is available, a piece of pipe or even the rungs of a ladder can also serve the purpose (Figure 7.2).

   Description: The bar should be high enough so that the pupil can hang with the arms and legs fully extended and the feet free of the floor. The pupil should use an overhand grasp with the palms facing away from the body. From the hanging position, the pupil raises the body by the arms until the chin can be placed over the bar and then lowers the body to a full hang as in the starting position. The exercise is repeated as many times as possible.

Figure 7.2 Pull-ups.

Rules: Allow one trial unless it is obvious that the pupil has not had a fair chance. The body must not swing during the execution of the movement. The pull must in no way be a snap movement. If the pupil starts swinging, check this by holding your extended arm across the front of the thighs. The knees must not be raised, and kicking of the legs is not permitted.

Scoring: Record the number of completed pull-ups to the nearest whole number.

2. Flexed-Arm Hang (girls)

   Equipment: A horizontal bar approximately 1-1/2 inches (3.81 cm) in diameter is preferred. A doorway gym bar can be used; if no regular equipment is available, a piece of pipe can serve the purpose. A stopwatch is needed.

---

[1]Testing procedures for the AAHPER Youth Fitness Test Revised (1976) Edition are reprinted by permission of the American Alliance for Health, Physical Education, Recreation and Dance, 1900 Association Drive, Reston, VA 22091.

Figure 7.3 Flexed-arm hang.

Description: The height of the bar should be adjusted so it is approximately equal to the pupil's standing height. The pupil should use an overhand grasp. With the assistance of two spotters, one in front and one in back of the pupil, the pupil raises the body off the floor to a position where the chin is above the bar, the elbows are flexed, and the chest is close to the bar. The pupil holds this position as long as possible (Figure 7.3).

Rules: The stopwatch is started as soon as the subject takes the hanging position. The watch is stopped when (a) the pupil's chin touches the bar, (b) the pupil's head tilts backwards to keep chin above the bar, and (c) the pupil's chin falls below the level of the bar.

Scoring: Record in seconds to the nearest second the length of time the pupil holds the hanging position.

3. Sit-Ups (flexed leg; boys and girls)

   Equipment: Clean floor, mat, or dry turf and stopwatch.

   Description: The pupil lies on the back with the knees bent, feet on the floor, and heels not more than 12 inches (30.48 cm) from the buttocks. The angle at the knees should be less than 90 degrees. The pupil puts the hands on the back of the neck with fingers clasped and places the elbows squarely on the mat, floor, or turf. The pupil's feet are held by his or her partner to keep them in touch with the surface. The pupil tightens the abdominal muscles and brings the head and elbows forward as he or she curls up, finally touching the elbows to the knees. This action constitutes one sit-up. The pupil returns to the starting position with his elbows on the surface before he sits up again. The timer gives the signal *Ready? Go!*, and the sit-up performance is started on the word *Go!* Performance is stopped on the word *stop.* The number of correctly executed sit-ups performed in 60 seconds is recorded as the score (Figure 7.4).

   Rules: Only one trial shall be allowed unless the teacher believes the pupil has not had a fair opportunity

Figure 7.4 Sit-up (flexed leg).

to perform. No resting between sit-ups is permitted. No sit-ups shall be counted in which the pupil does not (a) keep the fingers clasped behind the neck, (b) bring both elbows forward in starting to sit-up without pushing off the floor with the elbow, or (c) return to starting position, with elbows flat on the surface, before sitting up again.

Scoring: Record the number of correctly executed sit-ups the pupil is able to do in 60 seconds. A foul nullifies the count for that sit-up. The watch is started on the word *go* and stopped on the word *stop*.

4. Shuttle Run (boys and girls)
   Equipment: Two blocks of wood, 2 inches (5.08 cm) × 2 inches (5.08 cm) × 4 inches (10.16 cm),

and stopwatch. Pupils should wear sneakers or run barefoot.

Description: Two parallel lines are marked on the floor 30 feet (9.14 m) apart. The width of a regulation volleyball court serves as a suitable area. Place the blocks of wood behind one of the lines as indicated in Figure 7.5. The pupil starts from behind the other line. On the signal *Ready? Go!*, the pupil runs to the blocks, picks up one, runs back to the starting line, and places the block behind the line. The pupil then runs back and picks up the second block, which he carries back across the starting line. If the scorer has two stopwatches or one with a split-second timer, it is preferable to have two pupils running at the same time. To eliminate the need to return the

Figure 7.5 Shuttle run.

blocks after each race, start the races alternately, first from behind one line and then from behind the other.

Rules: Allow two trials with some rest in between.

Scoring: Record the time of the better of the two trials to the nearest tenth of a second.

5. Standing Long Jump (boys and girls)

Equipment: Mat, floor, or outdoor jumping pit and a metric or English tape measure.

Description: Pupil stands as indicated in Figure 7.6, with the feet several inches apart and the toes just behind the take-off line. Preparatory to jumping, the pupil swings the arms backward and bends the knees. The jump is accomplished by simultaneously extending the knees and swinging the arms forward.

Rules: Allow three trials. Measure from the take-off line to the heel or other part of the body that touches the floor nearest the take-off line. When the test is given indoors, it is convenient to tape the tape measure to the floor at right angles to the take-off line and have the pupil jump along the tape. The scorer stands to the side and observes the mark to the nearest inch.

Scoring: Record the best of the three trials in feet and inches to the nearest inch (cm).

6. 50-Yard (45.73-m) Dash (boys and girls)

Equipment: Two stopwatches or one with a split-second timer.

Description: It is preferable to administer this test to two pupils at a time. Have both pupils take positions behind the starting line. The starter will use the commands *Are you ready?* and *Go!* The *Go!* command will be accompanied by a downward sweep of the starter's arm to give a visual signal to the timer, who stands at the finish line (Figure 7.7).

Rules: The score is the amount of time between the starter's signal and the instant the pupil crosses the finish line.

Scoring: Record in seconds to the nearest tenth of a second.

7. 600-Yard (548.78-m) Run-Walk (boys and girls)

Equipment: Track or marked area (Figure 7.8) and stopwatch.

Description: Pupil uses a standing start. At the signal *Ready? Go!*, the pupil starts running the 600-yard

Figure 7.6 Standing long jump.

Figure 7.7 50-yard dash (start).

(548.78-m) distance. The running may be interspersed with walking. It is possible to have a dozen pupils run at one time by having the pupils pair off before the start of the event. Then each pupil listens for and remembers his partner's time as the latter crosses the finish line. The timer merely calls out the times as the pupils cross the finish line.

Rules: Walking is permitted, but the object is to cover the distance in the shortest period of time.

Scoring: Record scores in minutes and seconds.

8. 9-Minute Run or 1-Mile (1609.76 m) Run for Time

Equipment: Track or area marked off in known distance segments in yards or meters, stopwatch, score sheets, and pencil.

Description: (a) At the signal *Ready? Go!*, the pupil runs the mile distance in as short a time as possible. Administer the test to several students at one time as in the 600-yard (548.78 m) run. (b) At the signal *Ready? Go!*, the pupil covers as much distance as possible in 9 minutes. If the track or running area

Figure 7.8   Distance run finish.

is marked off every 200 yards (182.88 m), the runner's partner can count the number of laps completed and additional markers passed. Convert total distance covered to yards or meters.

Rules: Encourage pupils to run the entire distance; discourage walking.

Norms for the various items on the AAHPER Youth Fitness Test are presented on a percentile rank basis for each age and appear in Tables 7.1 through 7.11.

Evaluation of the AAHPER Test

Validity

A comparison of the items on the AAHPER Youth Fitness Test with the items that measure the various motor and/or physical fitness factors described earlier in this chapter reveals that the AAHPER Test provides estimates of several of the factors. Thus one may conclude that the AAHPER Test possesses factorial validity. This type of validity identifies the more important test contents that underlie certain fitness factors.

Table 7.1 Pull-Up for Boys—
Percentile Scores Based on Age/Test Scores
in Number of Pull-Ups

	Age (years)							
Percentile	9-10	11	12	13	14	15	16	17+
95th	9	8	9	10	12	15	14	15
75th	3	4	4	5	7	9	10	10
50th	1	2	2	3	4	6	7	7
25th	0	0	0	1	2	3	4	4
5th	0	0	0	0	0	0	1	0

Note. From the *AAHPER Youth Fitness Test Manual* (revised 1976 edition). Reprinted by permission of the American Alliance for Health, Physical Education, Recreation, and Dance, 1900 Association Drive, Reston, VA 22091.

Table 7.2 Flexed-Arm Hang for Girls—
Percentile Scores Based on Age/Test Scores
in Seconds

	Age (years)							
Percentile	9-10	11	12	13	14	15	16	17+
95th	42	39	33	34	35	36	31	34
75th	18	20	18	16	21	18	15	17
50th	9	10	9	8	9	9	7	8
25th	3	3	3	3	3	4	3	3
5th	0	0	0	0	0	0	0	0

Note. From the *AAHPER Youth Fitness Test Manual* (revised 1976 edition). Reprinted by permission of the American Alliance for Health, Physical Education, Recreation, and Dance, 1900 Association Drive, Reston, VA 22091.

Table 7.3 Sit-Up for Boys and Girls
(Flexed Leg)—Percentile Scores Based
on Age/Test Scores in Number
of Sit-Ups Performed in 60 Seconds

	Age (years)							
Percentile	9-10	11	12	13	14	15	16	17+
Boys								
95th	47	48	50	53	55	57	55	54
75th	38	40	42	45	47	48	47	46
50th	31	34	35	38	41	42	41	41
25th	25	26	30	30	34	37	35	35
5th	13	15	18	20	24	28	28	26
Girls								
95th	45	43	44	45	45	45	43	45
75th	34	35	36	36	37	36	35	35
50th	27	29	29	30	30	31	30	30
25th	21	22	24	23	24	25	24	25
5th	10	9	13	15	16	15	15	14

Note. From the *AAHPER Youth Fitness Test Manual* (revised 1976 edition). Reprinted by permission of the American Alliance for Health, Physical Education, Recreation, and Dance, 1900 Association Drive, Reston, VA 22091.

Table 7.4 Shuttle Run for Boys and Girls—
Percentile Scores Based on Age/Test Scores in Seconds and Tenths

Percentile	Age (years)							
	9-10	11	12	13	14	15	16	17+
Boys								
95th	10.0	9.7	9.6	9.3	8.9	8.9	8.6	8.6
75th	10.6	10.4	10.2	10.0	9.6	9.4	9.3	9.2
50th	11.2	10.9	10.7	10.4	10.1	9.9	9.9	9.8
25th	12.0	11.5	11.4	11.0	10.7	10.4	10.5	10.4
5th	13.1	12.9	12.4	12.4	11.9	11.7	11.9	11.7
Girls								
95th	10.2	10.0	9.9	9.9	9.7	9.9	10.0	9.6
75th	11.1	10.8	10.8	10.5	10.3	10.4	10.6	10.4
50th	11.8	11.5	11.4	11.2	11.0	11.0	11.2	11.1
25th	12.5	12.1	12.0	12.0	12.0	11.8	12.0	12.0
5th	14.3	14.0	13.3	13.2	13.1	13.3	13.7	14.0

Note. From the *AAHPER Youth Fitness Test Manual* (revised 1976 edition). Reprinted by permission of the American Alliance for Health, Physical Education, Recreation, and Dance, 1900 Association Drive, Reston, VA 22091.

Table 7.5 Standing Long Jump for Boys and Girls—
Percentile Scores Based on Age/Test Scores in Feet and Inches

Percentile	Age (years)							
	9-10	11	12	13	14	15	16	17+
Boys								
95th	6' 0"	6' 2"	6' 6"	7'1"	7' 6"	8' 0"	8'2"	8' 5"
75th	5' 4"	5' 7"	5'11"	6'3"	6' 8"	7' 2"	7'6"	7' 9"
50th	4'11"	5' 2"	5' 5"	5'9"	6' 2"	6' 8"	7'0"	7' 2"
25th	4' 6"	4' 8"	5' 0"	5'2"	5' 6"	6' 1"	6'6"	6' 6"
5th	3'10"	4' 0"	4' 2"	4'4"	4' 8"	5' 2"	5'5"	5' 3"
Girls								
95th	5'10"	6' 0"	6' 2"	6'5"	6' 8"	6' 7"	6'6"	6' 9"
75th	5' 2"	5' 4"	5' 6"	5'9"	5'11"	5'10"	5'9"	6' 0"
50th	4' 8"	4'11"	5' 0"	5'3"	5' 4"	5' 5"	5'3"	5' 5"
25th	4' 1"	4' 4"	4' 6"	4'9"	4'10"	4'11"	4'9"	4'11"
5th	3' 5"	3' 8"	3'10"	4'0"	4' 0"	4' 2"	4'0"	4' 1"

Note. From the *AAHPER Youth Fitness Test Manual* (revised 1976 edition). Reprinted by permission of the American Alliance for Health, Physical Education, Recreation, and Dance, 1900 Association Drive, Reston, VA 22091.

Table 7.6 Standing Long Jump for Boys and Girls—
AAHPER Percentile Scores Based on Age/Test Scores in Meters

| Percentile | Age (years) | | | | | | | |
	9-10	11	12	13	14	15	16	17+
Boys								
95th	1.82[a]	1.87	1.98	2.15	2.28	2.43	2.48	2.56
75th	1.62	1.70	1.80	1.90	2.03	2.18	2.28	2.36
50th	1.49	1.57	1.65	1.75	1.88	2.03	2.13	2.18
25th	1.37	1.42	1.52	1.57	1.67	1.85	1.98	1.98
5th	1.16	1.21	1.26	1.32	1.42	1.57	1.65	1.60
Girls								
95th	1.77	1.93	1.87	1.95	2.03	2.00	1.98	2.05
75th	1.57	1.67	1.67	1.75	1.80	1.77	1.75	1.82
50th	1.42	1.52	1.52	1.60	1.62	1.65	1.60	1.65
25th	1.24	1.37	1.37	1.44	1.47	1.49	1.44	1.49
5th	1.04	1.16	1.16	1.21	1.21	1.21	1.21	1.24

Note. From the *AAHPER Youth Fitness Test Manual* (revised 1976 edition). Reprinted by permission of the American Alliance for Health, Physical Education, Recreation, and Dance, 1900 Association Drive, Reston, VA 22091.
[a]To convert to centimeters move the decimal point two places to the right; 2.41 meters = 241 centimeters.

Table 7.7 50-Yard (45.73-m) Dash for Boys and Girls—
Percentile Scores Based on Age/Test Scores in Seconds and Tenths

| Percentile | Age (years) | | | | | | | |
	9-10	11	12	13	14	15	16	17+
Boys								
95th	7.3	7.1	6.8	6.5	6.2	6.0	6.0	5.9
75th	7.8	7.6	7.4	7.0	6.8	6.5	6.5	6.3
50th	8.2	8.0	7.8	7.5	7.2	6.9	6.7	6.6
25th	8.9	8.6	8.3	8.0	7.7	7.3	7.0	7.0
5th	9.9	9.5	9.5	9.0	8.8	8.0	7.7	7.9
Girls								
95th	7.4	7.3	7.0	6.9	6.8	6.9	7.0	6.8
75th	8.0	7.9	7.6	7.4	7.3	7.4	7.5	7.4
50th	8.6	8.3	8.1	8.0	7.8	7.8	7.9	7.9
25th	9.1	9.0	8.7	8.5	8.3	8.2	8.3	8.4
5th	10.3	10.0	10.0	10.0	9.6	9.2	9.3	9.5

Note. From the *AAHPER Youth Fitness Test Manual* (revised 1976 edition). Reprinted by permission of the American Alliance for Health, Physical Education, Recreation, and Dance, 1900 Association Drive, Reston, VA 22091.

Table 7.8 600-Yard (548.78-m) Run for Boys and Girls—
Percentile Scores Based on Age/Test Scores in Minutes and Seconds

| Percentile | Age (years) | | | | | | | |
	9-10	11	12	13	14	15	16	17+
Boys								
95th	2' 5''	2' 2''	1'52''	1'45''	1'39''	1'36''	1'34''	1'32''
75th	2'17''	2'15''	2' 6''	1'59''	1'52''	1'46''	1'44''	1'43''
50th	2'33''	2'27''	2'19''	2'10''	2' 3''	1'56''	1'52''	1'52''
25th	2'53''	2'47''	2'37''	2'27''	2'16''	2' 8''	2' 1''	2' 2''
5th	3'22''	3'29''	3' 6''	3' 0''	2'51''	2'30''	2'31''	2'38''
Girls								
95th	2'20''	2'14''	2' 6''	2' 4''	2' 2''	2' 0''	2' 8''	2' 2''
75th	2'39''	2'35''	2'26''	2'23''	2'19''	2'22''	2'26''	2'24''
50th	2'56''	2'53''	2'47''	2'41''	2'40''	2'37''	2'43''	2'41''
25th	3'15''	3'16''	3'13''	3' 6''	3' 1''	3' 0''	3' 3''	3' 2''
5th	4' 0''	4'15''	3'59''	3'49''	3'49''	3'28''	3'49''	3'45''

Note. From the _AAHPER Youth Fitness Test Manual_ (revised 1976 edition). Reprinted by permission of the American Alliance for Health, Physical Education, Recreation, and Dance, 1900 Association Drive, Reston, VA 22091.

Table 7.9 9-Minute/1-Mile (1609.76-m) Run for Boys and Girls—
Percentile Scores Based on Age/Test Scores in Yards/Time

| Percentile | 9-minute run (yards) Age (years) | | | 1-mile (1609.76-m) run (time) Age (years) | | |
	10	11	12	10	11	12
Boys						
95th	2294	2356	2418	5:55	5:32	5:09
75th	1952	2014	2076	7:49	7:26	7:03
50th	1717	1779	1841	9:07	8:44	8:21
25th	1482	1544	1606	10:25	10:02	9:39
5th	1140	1202	1264	12:19	11:56	11:33
Girls						
95th	1969	1992	2015	7:28	6:57	6:23
75th	1702	1725	1748	9:16	8:45	8:11
50th	1514	1537	1560	10:29	9:58	9:24
25th	1326	1349	1372	11:42	11:11	10:37
5th	1059	1082	1105	13:30	12:59	12:24

Note. From the Texas Physical Fitness-Motor Ability Test and the _AAHPER Youth Fitness Test Manual_ (revised 1976 edition). Reprinted by permission of the American Alliance for Health, Physical Education, Recreation, and Dance, 1900 Association Drive, Reston, VA 22091.

Table 7.10   12-Minute/1-1/2-Mile (2414.64-m) Run for Boys and Girls, Age 13 and Older—
Percentile Scores Based on Age/Test Scores in Yards/Time

| | Boys | | Girls | |
| | 12-minute | 1.5-mile (2414.64-m) | 12-minute | 1.5-mile (2414.64-m) |
Percentile	run (yards)	run (time)	run (yards)	run (time)
95th	3297	8:37	2448	12:17
75th	2879	10:19	2100	15:03
50th	2592	11:29	1861	16:57
25th	2305	12:39	1622	18:50
5th	1888	14:20	1274	21:36

Note. From the Texas Physical Fitness-Motor Ability Test and the *AAHPER Youth Fitness Test Manual* (revised 1976 edition). Reprinted by permission of the American Alliance for Health, Physical Education, Recreation, and Dance, 1900 Association Drive, Reston, VA 22091.

Table 7.11   9-Minute and 12-Minute Run for Boys and Girls—
AAHPER Percentile Scores Based on Age/Test Scores in Meters

| | 9-minute run | | | 12-minute run |
| | Age (years) | | | Age (years) |
Percentile	10	11	12	13 and up
Boys				
95th	2097.6	2154.3	2211.0	3014.7
75th	1784.9	1841.6	1898.3	2632.5
50th	1570.0	1626.7	1683.4	2370.1
25th	1355.1	1411.8	1468.5	2107.6
5th	1042.4	1099.1	1155.8	1726.3
Girls				
95th	1800.4	1821.4	1842.5	2238.4
75th	1556.3	1577.3	1598.3	1920.2
50th	1384.4	1405.4	1426.4	1701.7
25th	1212.4	1233.5	1254.5	1483.1
5th	968.3	989.3	1010.4	1140.2

Note. From the *AAHPER Youth Fitness Test Manual* (revised 1976 edition). Reprinted by permission of the American Alliance for Health, Physical Education, Recreation, and Dance, 1900 Association Drive, Reston, VA 22091.

We must recognize that the AAHPER test items do not include all fitness factors. Indeed, if the practitioner desires to measure flexibility or balance, specific flexibility and balance items should be included in the test.

Ismail, MacLeod, and Falls (1964) studied the relationship between composite scores on the AAHPER Test and composite scores on other fitness tests such as the Purdue Motor Fitness Test, JCR Test, Larson Muscular Strength Test, California Physical Efficiency Test, United States Air Force Test, Southern Methodist Test, and Indiana Motor Fitness Test. The correlations between the AAHPER Test and the other tests ranged from .63 to .98. This is not too surprising because similar items are found on most of these tests. Note that the longest run (cardiovascular fitness measure) on any of the tests was 600 yards (548.78 m).

In another study, Ismail, Falls, and MacLeod (1965) reported correlations ranging between .51 and .59 among the AAHPER composite scores and scores on physical fitness criterion test batteries. The criterion batteries primarily measure percent lean body mass, maximum oxygen uptake/kg lean body mass, exercise pulse rate, pulmonary ventilation, and blood pressure items. Based on these data, it is reasonable to conclude that the AAHPER Test with the 600-yard (548.78-m) run primarily measures motor fitness and is only moderately related to physical fitness as defined by the criterion test batteries. Safrit (1981) summarized correlations obtained in a number of studies on males and females aged 11 years to adult between the 600-yard (548.78-m) run and maximum oxygen uptake of $-.27$, $-.53$, $-.62$, $-.64$, $-.66$, $-.68$, and $-.71$. She reported higher validity coefficients ranging from .65 to .90, with most exceeding .80, for the 12-minute run in nine studies. It appears that the longer the run, the higher the correlations with maximum oxygen uptake will be. Earlier research by Jackson and Coleman (1976) on elementary school boys and girls and by Burke (1976) on male college students supports this contention. They found that the 9-minute run for elementary children and the 12-minute run for college men were the most valid measures of aerobic power (maximal oxygen uptake) when compared to the shorter 600-yard (548.78 m) run. They reported validity coefficients of .82 for elementary boys, .71 for elementary girls, and .90 for college men. In the elementary school study, increasing the run from 9 minutes to 12 minutes did not increase the validity of the test. Thus there appears to be little advantage in running more than 1 mile or for more than 9 minutes. Because the 1976 revision of the AAHPER Test includes runs longer than 600 yards (548.78 m), one will come closer to estimating physical fitness with the longer run and estimating aspects of motor fitness primarily with the remainder of the items.

Reliability of AAHPER Test Items

Several reliability studies on the AAHPER Test are reported in the literature. Safrit (1981) summarizes these studies, which have been conducted mostly on elementary and secondary pupils. The range of reliability coefficients for the various AAHPER Test items are as follows:

Pull-ups	.82 to .89
Flexed-arm hang	.74
Standing broad jump	.83 to .98
50-yard (45.78-m) dash	.83 to .94
Softball throw	.90 to .93
Sit-ups to maximum	.57 to .68
Shuttle run	.68 to .75
600-yard (548.78-m) run-walk	.65 to .92
12-minute run	.75 to .94

Recording AAHPER Test Results

A convenient cumulative score record for fitness testing appears in Figure 7.9, and a profile sheet is illustrated in Figure 7.10. One may use a different colored line for different testing dates to indicate changes in fitness profile.

Fitness Test Data

Name _____ Date of Birth _____

School _____ Medical Clearance for Testing Date_____

Grade _____ Sex _____

Test Items	Date of Test _____ Age:Years___ Mos___		Date of Test _____ Age:Years___ Mos___		Date of Test _____ Age:Years___ Mos___		Date of Test _____ Age:Years___Mos___	
	Raw Score	Centile Rank	Raw Score	Centile Rank	Raw Score	Centile Rank	Raw Score	Centile Rank
Height								
Weight								
Pull-up (boys)								
Flexed-arm hang (girls)								
Sit-ups in 60 seconds								
Shuttle run								
Standing broad jump								
50-yard (45.73 m) dash								
600-yard (548.78 m) run								
9-minute run or 1-mile (1609.76 m) run								
Step test								
Percentage body fat								
Body density								

Figure 7.9 Cumulative scoring record for AAHPER and other fitness items.

Physical Fitness: Semester Profile for _____   Semester 1 2 19 _____

Rank in Group	Index	Letter Grade	T Score	AAHPER Test Items						Alternate Items			Knowledge	Ratings
				Pull-Up or Flexed-Arm Hang	Standing Broad Jump	50-yard (45.73m) Dash	No. of Sit-Ups in 60 Seconds	Shuttle Run	600-yard (548.78 m) Run	1-Mile Run or 9-Minute Run	Step Test	Vertical Jump	Physical Fitness Knowledge Test Score	
99			80											
			78											
	6.5	A+	76											Excellent
98			74											
	6.0	A	72											
95			70											
	5.7	A−	68											Very Good
90	5.3	B+	66											
			64											
80	5.0	B	62											
75	4.7	B−	60											Above Average
70	4.3	C+	58											
			56											
60			54											Average
50	4.0	C	52											
40			50											
			48											Below Average
30	3.7	C−	46											
25	3.3	D+	44											
20			42											
	3.0	D	40											
10			38											Poor
5	2.7	D−	36											
			34											
2	2.0	F	32											Very Poor
			30											
			28											
			26											
			24											
			22											
1			20											

Recreational Sport Skills Acquired This Semester _____

Comments _____

Figure 7.10 Physical Fitness Profile.

1980 Revision of the AAHPER Youth Fitness Test

In 1975, a joint committee representing the Measurement and Evaluation, Physical Fitness, and Research Councils of AAHPERD studied the need to revise the AAHPER Youth Fitness Test. Based on their work, a position paper (Jackson et al., 1976) was developed that proposed the committee's recommendations. The committee's first recommendation linked physical fitness directly to health. The committee then identified the areas of health that are of national interest such as cardiovascular endurance, obesity, and musculoskeletal dysfunction, particularly low-back pain and tension. To revise the AAHPER Test, the committee recommended that

1. a battery be developed to measure the components of physical fitness as identified and defined by the joint committee. Such a physical fitness test should meet the following criteria:
   - It should measure the range of a component from severely limiting dysfunction to high levels of functional capacity.
   - The physical fitness component should be improved with appropriate physical activity.
   - Changes in functional capacity should be accurately reflected by changes in test scores.
2. a separate test battery be developed consisting of motor performance items that have historically been included in physical fitness batteries.

For the Physical Fitness Battery, the committee recommended that

1. distance run tests be used as field tests of cardiovascular endurance. The recommended test includes
   - a 1-mile (1609.76-m) run-walk for time or
   - a 9-minute run-walk for distance.
2. a national study be conducted to estimate the body composition of American boys and girls by the use of appropriate statistical procedures and that these results be used to determine desirable levels of body fat;
3. the maximum number of flexed-leg sit-ups performed in 1 minute be the test to measure abdominal strength. This test is currently part of the 1976 revision of the AAHPER Youth Fitness Test.

For the Motor Performance Battery, the committee recommended that

1. the present AAHPER Test items of pull-ups for boys and the flexed-arm hang for girls be retained except that the grip be changed from the forward grip to the reverse grip;
2. the present 50-yard (45.73-m) dash test be retained;
3. the present shuttle run be retained and, in addition, that optional tests that require more turning be considered as an alternative test;
4. the present standing broad jump be retained and that an optional vertical jump test be included due to its greater relevance to sports such as basketball and volleyball.

In 1977 a Task Force on Fitness comprised of members of the Measurement and Evaluation and Physical Fitness Councils of AAHPERD was established to consider these recommendations for revision of the AAHPER Test. After two years of work, the task force reported at the 1979 AAHPERD National Convention and delineated the rationale for revising the test as the AAHPERD Health-Related Physical Fitness

Test. The revised test was eventually approved and is now known as the 1980 Health-Related Physical Fitness Test.

The new 1980 test shifts emphasis away from sport and motor fitness performance to a primary focus on the health aspects of fitness. The task force recommended that current motor and sport performance items be examined and revisions made considering the fitness elements they are supposed to measure. In the meantime, teachers could continue to use the sport and motor fitness items if they wanted to test for those components. The new test manual includes norms for the following items that focus on the health aspects of fitness: (a) the distance run, which measures cardiovascular fitness; (b) percent body fat (body composition); (c) timed flexed-knee sit-ups and a sit-and-reach test (musculoskeletal function in the low back and hamstring muscle areas of the body).

Validity of the musculoskeletal function tests has been established by logic, clinical observations of physicians, and electromyographical tracings. Validity of the distance run has already been discussed, and the skinfold tests correlate with values of body composition obtained by the underwater weighing method. Body composition measures will be discussed more fully later in this chapter. The reliability of the four tests is well established with coefficients ranging from .68 to .98.

Testing Procedures: AAHPERD Health-Related Physical Fitness Test (1980)[2]

The Distance Run

Purpose. The purpose of the distance run is to measure the maximal function

---

[2]Testing procedures for the *AAHPERD Health-Related Physical Fitness Test* are reprinted by permission of the American Alliance for Health, Physical Education, Recreation and Dance, 1900 Association Drive, Reston, VA 22091.

and endurance of the cardiorespiratory system.

Test Description. Standardized procedures and norms are provided for two optional distance run tests, including the mile (1609.76-m) run for time and the 9-minute run for distance. The decision as to which of the two tests to administer should be based on facilities, equipment, time limitations, and personal preference of the teacher.

1. *Mile (1609.76-m) Run.* Students are instructed to run 1 mile (1609.76 m) in the fastest possible time. The students begin on the signal *Ready? Go!* As they cross the finish line, elapsed time should be called to the participants or to their partners. Walking is permitted, but the object is to cover the distance in the shortest possible time.

2. *9-Minute Run.* Students are instructed to run as fast as possible in 9 minutes. The students begin on the signal *Ready? Go!* Participants continue to run until a whistle is blown after 9 minutes. Walking is permitted, but the object is to cover as much distance as possible in 9 minutes.

3. *Optional Distance Runs for Older Students.* For students 13 years of age and older, the 1.5-mile (2414.64-m) run for time or the 12-minute run for distance may be utilized as the distance run item. Administrative procedures for these tests are the same as for the mile and 9-minute runs.

Equipment and Facilities. Either of the distance run tests can be administered on a 440-yard (402.34-m) track or on a flat measured area. Examples of appropriate measured areas are the 110-yard (100.58-m) straightaway or other outside field or indoor court.

Scoring. The mile (1609.76-m) run is scored to the nearest second. The 9-minute run is scored to the nearest 10 yards. Performances should be recorded on a score card.

Administrative Suggestions. In order to obtain valid results, students must be adequately prepared for the test.

- The school nurse should be consulted to identify students with medical problems that would indicate abstention from the test.
- Students should be allowed to practice distance running, with emphasis placed on the concept of pace. Most uninstructed students will run too fast early in the test and then be forced to walk during the latter stages. Results are usually better if the child can maintain a constant pace during most of the race, walking for short periods of time only if necessary and perhaps using a strong closing effort.
- Students should be properly motivated. Like many other physical education tests, this test is only as good as the effort the participants exert.
- Warm-up and taper down activities such as slow stretching, walking, and jogging should be encouraged prior to and following the run.

Sum of Skinfolds (triceps and sub-scapular)

Purpose. The purpose of the sum of skinfolds item is to evaluate the level of fatness in school-aged boys and girls.

Test Description. In a number of regions of the body, the subcutaneous

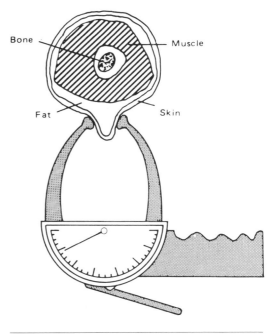

Figure 7.11   Skinfold calipers.

adipose tissue may be lifted with the fingers to form a skinfold. The skinfold consists of a double layer of subcutaneous fat and skin whose thickness can be measured with a skinfold caliper (Figure 7.11).

Two skinfold sites (triceps and subscapular) have been chosen for this test because they are easily measured and are highly correlated with total body fat. The triceps skinfold is measured over the triceps muscle of the right arm halfway between the elbow and the acromial process of the scapula with the skinfold parallel to the longitudinal axis of the upper arm (Figure 7.12). The subscapular site (right side of the body) is 1 cm below the inferior angle of the scapula in line with the natural cleavage lines of the skin (Figure 7.13). The following testing procedure is recommended:

Skinfold back of upper arm

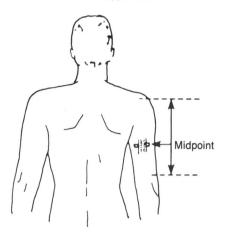

Skinfold subscapular

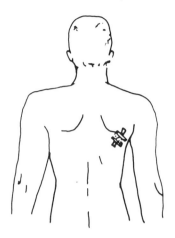

Figure 7.12 Skinfold back of upper arm.

Figure 7.13 Subscapular skinfold.

1. Firmly grasp the skinfold between the left thumb and forefinger and lift up.
2. Place the contact surfaces of the caliper 1 cm (1/2 inch) above or below the finger.
3. Slowly release the grip on the calipers to enable calipers to exert their full tension on the skinfolds.
4. Read skinfold to the nearest millimeter after the needle stops (1 to 2 seconds after releasing grip on calipers).

Equipment. Data from a large sample of children in the United States were obtained using the Lange Caliper manufactured by Cambridge Scientific Industries. Characteristics of this skinfold caliper include accurate calibration capability and a constant pressure of 10 gm/mm throughout the range of skinfold thicknesses. Care needs to be taken to ensure that the instrument is properly calibrated and that the caliper registers zero in the closed position.

Scoring. The skinfold measurement is registered on the dial of the caliper. Each measurement should be taken three consecutive times with the mean of the three scores constituting the final score. Each reading should be recorded to the nearest .5 mm. Norms are provided to interpret the sum of the skinfolds of the scapula and triceps and the triceps only. The recommended procedure is to use the sum of the two skinfolds. If only one skinfold can be secured, however, the triceps should be selected.

Administrative Suggestions. Testers who have not used these calipers before should practice locating the skinfold sites and measuring them on several children. When a reproducibility of less than 2 mm is consistently achieved, then the tester can begin evaluating skinfolds for school children. Occasionally, consecutive measurements will differ by more than 2 mm, especially in obese children, even with experienced testers. If this is the case, an additional set of three measurements should be taken and averaged with the first set of data.

Skinfold fat measures should be conducted separately for each child without comment or display. Each child has the right to share or withhold the results of this test. In all cases, interpretation of the measures should be given individually.

To measure the triceps skinfold, it is essential to locate the measurement at the midpoint of the back of the upper right arm and to avoid measuring above, below, or to either side of the midpoint as described. Whenever possible, the same tester should administer the skinfold fat test on the same persons on subsequent testing sessions. Intertester error is common and may cause interpretation of serial results to be confusing and misleading.

Sit-Ups

Purpose. The purpose of the sit-ups test item is to evaluate abdominal muscular strength and endurance.

Test Description. The pupil lies on the back with the knees flexed, feet on the floor, and the heels between 12 and 18 inches (30.48 and 45.72 cm) from the buttocks. The pupil crosses the arms on the chest, placing the hands on the opposite shoulder. The feet are held by a partner to keep them in touch with the testing surface. By tightening the abdominal muscles, the pupil curls to the sitting position. Arm contact with the chest must be maintained. The sit-up is completed when the elbows touch the thighs. The pupil returns to the down position until the midback contacts the testing surface.

The timer gives the signal *Ready? Go!*, and the sit-up performance is started on the word *Go*. Performance is stopped on the word *Stop*. The number of correctly executed sit-ups performed in 60 seconds constitutes the score. Rest between sit-ups is allowed, and the pupil should be informed of this before initiating the test.

Equipment. The standard test equipment includes a mat or other comfortable surface and a stopwatch.

Scoring. Record the number of correctly executed sit-ups that the pupil is able to perform in 60 seconds.

Administrative Suggestions.

- Because of the importance of the heel placement in relation to the buttocks, the teacher may wish to use a yardstick or precut measured yarn to determine this distance.
- The supervising tester acts as the timer.
- Partners will count and record each other's score. The supervising tester must observe each performance carefully to ensure that the sit-ups are being done correctly.
- The partner is to keep the pupil's feet in contact with the testing surface. The partner should hold the pupil's feet, ankles, or calves.
- The teacher can improve the validity and reliability of individual scores by providing sufficient instruction and practice in the correct sit-up technique prior to collecting any test data.

Sit and Reach

Purpose. The purpose of the sit-and-reach item is to test the flexibility of the low back and posterior thigh.

Test Description. The pupil removes shoes and assumes the sitting position with the knees fully extended and the feet against the apparatus shoulder width apart. The arms are extended forward with one hand placed on top of the other. The pupil reaches directly forward, palms down, along the measuring scale. In this position, the pupil slowly stretches forward four times and holds the position of maximum reach on the fourth count. The position of maximum reach must be held for 1 second with the knees in full extension while the feet are in contact with the apparatus. The pupil receives one 4-count trial.

Equipment. The standard test apparatus consists of a bench or box with a measuring scale where 23 cm is at the level of the feet. The testing apparatus should be placed against a wall or other firm vertical surface (see Figure 6.9 in chapter 6).

Scoring. The score is the maximum distance reached measured to the nearest centimeter.

Administrative Suggestions.

- The teacher can improve the validity and reliability of individual scores by providing sufficient time and instruction for warm-up. Slow, sustained static stretching of the low back and posterior thighs preceding the test is suggested.
- If the hands reach out unevenly, the test trial must be repeated.
- If the knees become flexed, the trial must be repeated. The tester can monitor this by placing his hand lightly across the pupils' knees.

Norms for these test items appear in Tables 7.12 through 7.18.

Table 7.12 Percentile Norms Ages 5-18 for the 1-Mile Run (Minutes and Seconds) for Boys and Girls

						Age (years)							
Percentile	5	6	7	8	9	10	11	12	13	14	15	16	17+
Boys													
95th	9:02	9:06	8:06	7:58	7:17	6:56	6:50	6:27	6:11	5:51	6:01	5:48	6:01
75th	11:32	10:55	9:37	9:14	8:36	8:10	8:00	7:24	6:52	6:36	6:35	6:28	6:36
50th	13:46	12:29	11:25	11:00	9:56	9:19	9:06	8:20	7:27	7:10	7:14	7:11	7:25
25th	16:05	15:10	14:02	13:29	12:00	11:05	11:31	10:00	8:35	8:02	8:04	8:07	8:26
5th	18:25	17:38	17:17	16:19	15:44	14:28	15:25	13:41	10:23	10:32	10:37	10:40	10:56
Girls													
95th	9:45	9:18	8:48	8:45	8:24	7:59	7:46	7:26	7:10	7:18	7:39	7:07	7:26
75th	13:09	11:24	10:55	10:35	9:58	9:30	9:12	8:36	8:18	8:13	8:42	9:00	9:03
50th	15:08	13:48	12:30	12:00	11:12	11:06	10:27	9:47	9:27	9:35	10:05	10:45	9:47
25th	17:59	15:27	14:30	14:16	13:18	12:54	12:10	11:35	10:56	11:43	12:21	13:00	11:28
5th	19:00	18:50	17:44	16:58	16:42	17:00	16:56	14:46	14:55	16:59	16:22	15:30	15:24

Note. From the *AAHPERD Lifetime Health-Related Physical Fitness Test Manual* (1980). Reprinted by permission of the American Alliance for Health, Physical Education, Recreation, and Dance, 1900 Association Drive, Reston, VA 22091.

Table 7.13   Percentile Norms Ages 5-18 for the 9-Minute Run (Yards) for Boys and Girls

						Age (years)							
Percentile	5	6	7	8	9	10	11	12	13	14	15	16	17+
Boys													
95th	1760	1750	2020	2200	2175	2250	2250	2400	2402	2473	2544	2615	2615
75th	1320	1469	1683	1810	1835	1910	1925	1975	2096	2167	2238	2309	2380
50th	1170	1280	1440	1595	1660	1690	1725	1760	1885	1956	2027	2098	2169
25th	990	1090	1243	1380	1440	1487	1540	1500	1674	1745	1816	1887	1958
5th	600	816	990	1053	1104	1110	1170	1000	1368	1439	1510	1581	1652
Girls													
95th	1540	1700	1900	1860	2050	2067	2000	2175	2085	2123	2161	2199	2237
75th	1300	1440	1540	1540	1650	1650	1723	1760	1785	1823	1861	1899	1937
50th	1140	1208	1344	1358	1425	1460	1480	1590	1577	1615	1653	1691	1729
25th	950	1017	1150	1225	1243	1250	1345	1356	1369	1407	1445	1483	1521
5th	700	750	860	970	960	940	904	1000	1069	1107	1145	1183	1221

Note. From the *AAHPERD Lifetime Health-Related Physical Fitness Test Manual* (1980). Reprinted by permission of the American Alliance for Health, Physical Education, Recreation, and Dance, 1900 Association Drive, Reston, VA 22091.

Table 7.14   Percentile Norms Ages 13-18
for the 1.5 Mile (Minutes and Seconds) and 12-Minute (Yards) Run for Boys and Girls

	Boys		Girls	
Percentile	12-minute run	1.5-mile run	12-minute run	1.5-mile run
95th	3297	8:37	2448	12:17
75th	2879	10:19	2100	15:03
50th	2592	11:29	1861	16:57
25th	2305	12:391622		18:50
5th	1888	14:20	1274	21:36

Note. From the Texas Physical Fitness Test (1973) as reported in the *AAHPERD Lifetime Health-Related Physical Fitness Test Manual* (1980). Reprinted by permission of the American Alliance for Health, Physical Education, Recreation, and Dance, 1900 Association Drive, Reston, VA 22091.

Table 7.15 Percentile Norms Ages 6-18[a] for Sum of Triceps
Plus Subscapular Skinfolds (mm) for Boys and Girls[b]

						Age (years)						
Percentile	6	7	8	9	10	11	12	13	14	15	16	17
Boys												
95th	8	9	9	9	9	9	9	9	9	9	9	9
75th	11	11	11	11	12	12	11	12	11	12	12	12
50th	12	12	13	14	14	16	15	15	14	14	14	15
25th	14	15	17	18	19	22	21	22	20	20	20	21
5th	20	24	28	34	33	38	44	46	37	40	37	38
Girls												
95th	9	10	10	10	10	11	11	12	13	14	14	15
75th	12	12	13	14	14	15	15	16	18	20	20	20
50th	14	15	16	17	18	19	19	20	24	25	25	27
25th	17	19	21	24	25	25	27	30	32	34	34	36
5th	26	28	36	40	41	42	48	51	52	56	57	58

Note. From the *AAHPERD Lifetime Health-Related Physical Fitness Test Manual* (1980). Reprinted by permission of the American Alliance for Health, Physical Education, Recreation, and Dance, 1900 Association Drive, Reston, VA 22091.

[a]The norms for age 17 may be used for age 18.

[b]Based on data from Johnston, F.E., D.V. Hamill, and S. Lemeshow. (1) *Skinfold Thickness of Youth 6-11 Years* (Series II, No. 120, 1972), and (2) *Skinfold Thickness of Youth 12-17 Years* (Series II, No. 132, 1974). U.S. National Center for Health Statistics, U.S. Department of Health, Education, and Welfare, Washington, DC.

Table 7.16 Percentile Norms Ages 6-18[a] for Triceps Skinfold for Boys and Girls[b]

						Age (years)						
Percentile	6	7	8	9	10	11	12	13	14	15	16	17
Boys												
95th	5	4	4	5	5	5	5	4	4	4	4	4
75th	6	6	6	7	7	7	7	7	6	6	6	6
50th	8	8	8	8	9	10	9	9	8	8	8	8
25th	9	10	11	12	12	14	13	13	12	11	11	11
5th	13	14	17	20	20	22	23	23	21	21	20	20

(Cont.)

Table 7.16 (Cont.)

Percentile						Age (years)						
	6	7	8	9	10	11	12	13	14	15	16	17
Girls												
95th	9	10	10	10	10	10	10	11	12	13	13	14
75th	11	12	12	14	14	14	15	17	18	19	19	20
50th	14	15	16	17	18	19	19	20	23	25	25	27
25th	17	19	21	23	24	25	27	29	32	34	36	37
5th	26	29	35	41	42	43	49	51	52	58	59	59

Note. From the *AAHPERD Lifetime Health-Related Physical Fitness Test Manual* (1980). Reprinted by permission of the American Alliance for Health, Physical Education, Recreation, and Dance, 1900 Association Drive, Reston, VA 22091.

*a*The norms for age 17 may be used for age 18.

*b*Based on data from Johnston, F.E., D.V. Hamill, and S. Lemeshow. (1) *Skinfold Thickness of Youth 6-11 Years* (Series II, No. 120, 1972), and (2) *Skinfold Thickness of Youth 12-17 Years* (Series II, No. 132, 1974). U.S. National Center for Health Statistics, U.S. Department of Health, Education, and Welfare, Washington, D.C.

Table 7.17 Percentile Norms Ages 5-18 for Sit-Ups for Boys and Girls

Percentile							Age (years)						
	5	6	7	8	9	10	11	12	13	14	15	16	17+
Boys													
95th	30	36	42	48	47	50	51	56	58	59	59	61	62
75th	23	26	33	37	38	40	42	46	48	49	49	51	52
50th	18	20	26	30	32	34	37	39	41	42	44	45	46
25th	11	15	19	25	25	27	30	31	35	36	38	38	38
5th	2	6	10	15	15	15	17	19	25	27	28	28	25
Girls													
95th	28	35	40	44	44	47	50	52	51	51	56	54	54
75th	24	28	31	35	35	39	40	41	41	42	43	42	44
50th	19	22	25	29	29	32	34	36	35	35	37	33	37
25th	12	14	20	22	23	25	28	30	29	30	30	29	31
5th	2	6	10	12	14	15	19	19	18	20	20	20	19

Note. From the *AAHPERD Lifetime Health-Related Physical Fitness Test Manual* (1980). Reprinted by permission of the American Alliance for Health, Physical Education, Recreation, and Dance, 1900 Association Drive, Reston, VA 22091.

Table 7.18 Percentile Norms Ages 5-18 for Sit and Reach (cm) for Boys and Girls

Percentile	Age (years)												
	5	6	7	8	9	10	11	12	13	14	15	16	17+
Boys													
95th	32	34	33	34	34	33	34	35	36	39	41	42	45
75th	29	29	28	29	29	28	29	29	30	33	34	36	40
50th	25	26	25	25	25	25	25	26	26	28	30	30	34
25th	22	22	22	22	22	20	21	21	20	23	24	25	28
5th	17	16	16	16	16	12	12	13	12	15	13	11	15
Girls													
95th	34	34	34	36	35	35	37	40	43	44	46	46	44
75th	30	30	31	31	31	31	32	34	36	37	41	39	40
50th	27	27	27	28	28	28	29	30	31	33	36	34	35
25th	23	23	24	23	23	24	24	25	24	28	31	30	31
5th	18	18	16	17	17	16	16	15	17	18	19	14	22

Note. From the *AAHPERD Lifetime Health-Related Physical Fitness Test Manual* (1980). Reprinted by permission of the American Alliance for Health, Physical Education, Recreation, and Dance, 1900 Association Drive, Reston, VA 22091.

Field Estimates of Cardiovascular Efficiency (Aerobic Power)

Distance Running Tests

The 1-mile (1609.76-m) run-walk for time or the 9-minute run-walk for distance is recommended for upper elementary and secondary boys and girls. Information concerning validity, reliability, norms, and directions for administering and scoring this test have already been presented. Due to problems encountered in motivating elementary school-aged children to run for longer distances or times, Welch (1978) recommended that the 600-yard (548.78-m) run-walk be used in the lower elementary grades.

Cooper (1977, 1982) proposed a 12-minute walking-running test, a 12-minute swimming test, and a 12-minute cycling test as field estimates of physical fitness. Age-adjusted standards are presented in Tables 7.19, 7.20, and 7.21 that permit adult men and women to determine their fitness category. Based on the category an individual is placed into an aerobic program of appropriate intensity level. Cooper strongly recommended that medical clearance be secured and that sedentary adults over 30 years of age complete a basic walking/running program for 6 weeks before they take the test. Safrit (1981) summarized the validity and reliability of the 12-minute run. Validity coefficients ranged from .65 to .90 in nine different studies where the criterion was maximum oxygen uptake. Reliability coefficients from seven studies ranged from .75 to .94.

Table 7.19 12-Minute Walking/Running Test (Distance [Miles] Covered in 12 Minutes)

Fitness category		13-19	20-29	Age (years) 30-39	40-49	50-59	60+
I. Very poor	(Men)	< 1.30[a]	< 1.22	< 1.18	< 1.14	< 1.03	< .87
	(Women)	< 1.0	< .96	< .94	< .88	< .84	< .78
II. Poor	(Men)	1.30-1.37	1.22-1.31	1.18-1.30	1.14-1.24	1.03-1.16	.87-1.02
	(Women)	1.00-1.18	.96-1.11	.95-1.05	.88- .98	.84- .93	.78- .86
III. Fair	(Men)	1.38-1.56	1.32-1.49	1.31-1.45	1.25-1.39	1.17-1.30	1.03-1.20
	(Women)	1.19-1.29	1.12-1.22	1.06-1.18	.99-1.11	.94-1.05	.87- .98
IV. Good	(Men)	1.57-1.72	1.50-1.64	1.46-1.56	1.40-1.53	1.31-1.44	1.21-1.32
	(Women)	1.30-1.43	1.23-1.34	1.19-1.29	1.12-1.24	1.06-1.18	.99-1.09
V. Excellent	(Men)	1.73-1.86	1.65-1.76	1.57-1.69	1.54-1.65	1.45-1.58	1.33-1.55
	(Women)	1.44-1.51	1.35-1.45	1.30-1.39	1.25-1.34	1.19-1.30	1.10-1.18
VI. Superior	(Men)	> 1.87	> 1.77	> 1.70	> 1.66	> 1.59	> 1.56
	(Women)	> 1.52	> 1.46	> 1.40	> 1.35	> 1.31	> 1.19

Note. From *The Aerobics Program for Total Well-Being*, by Dr. Kenneth H. Cooper. Copyright ©
1982 by Kenneth H. Cooper. Reprinted by permission of the publishers, M. Evans & Co., Inc.,
NY, NY 10017-1502.
[a]< Means "less than"; > means "more than."

Table 7.20 12-Minute Swimming Test (Distance [Yards] Swum in 12 Minutes)

Fitness category		13-19	20-29	Age (years) 30-39	40-49	50-59	60+
I. Very poor	(Men)	< 500[a]	< 400	< 350	< 300	< 250	< 250
	(Women)	< 400	< 300	< 250	< 200	< 150	< 150
II. Poor	(Men)	500-499	400-499	350-449	300-399	250-349	250-299
	(Women)	400-499	300-399	250-349	200-299	150-249	150-199
III. Fair	(Men)	600-699	500-599	450-549	400-499	350-449	300-399
	(Women)	500-599	400-499	350-449	300-399	250-349	200-299
IV. Good	(Men)	700-799	600-699	550-649	500-599	450-549	400-499
	(Women)	600-699	500-599	450-549	400-499	350-449	300-399
V. Excellent	(Men)	> 800	> 700	> 650	> 600	> 550	> 500
	(Women)	> 700	> 600	> 550	> 500	> 450	> 400

Note. From *The Aerobics Program for Total Well-Being*, by Dr. Kenneth H. Cooper. Copyright ©
1982 by Kenneth H. Cooper. Reprinted by permission of the publishers, M. Evans & Co., Inc.,
NY, NY 10017-1502. The swimming test requires you to swim as far as you can in 12 minutes,
using whatever stroke you prefer and resting as necessary, but trying for a maximum effort. The
easiest way to take the test is in a pool with known dimensions, and it helps to have another person record the laps and time. Be sure to use a watch with a sweep second hand.
[a]< Means "less than"; > means "more than."

Table 7.21   12-Minute Cycling Test (3-Speed or Less) (Distance [Miles] Cycled in 12 Minutes)

		Age (years)					
Fitness category		13-19	20-29	30-39	40-49	50-59	60+
I. Very poor	(Men)	< 2.75[a]	< 2.5	< 2.25	< 2.0	< 1.75	< 1.75
	(Women)	< 1.75	< 1.5	< 1.25	< 1.0	< 0.75	< 0.75
II. Poor	(Men)	2.75-3.74	2.5-3.49	2.25-3.24	2.0-2.99	1.75-2.49	1.75-2.24
	(Women)	1.75-2.74	1.5-2.49	1.25-2.24	1.0-1.99	0.75-1.49	0.75-1.24
III. Fair	(Men)	3.75-4.74	3.5-4.49	3.25-4.24	3.0-3.99	2.50-3.49	2.25-2.99
	(Women)	2.75-3.74	2.5-3.49	2.25-3.24	2.0-2.99	1.50-2.49	1.25-1.99
IV. Good	(Men)	4.75-5.74	4.5-5.49	4.25-5.24	4.0-4.99	3.50-4.49	3.00-3.99
	(Women)	3.75-4.74	3.5-4.49	3.25-4.24	3.0-3.99	2.50-3.49	2.00-2.99
V. Excellent	(Men)	> 5.75	> 5.5	> 5.25	> 5.0	> 4.5	> 4.0
	(Women)	> 4.75	> 4.5	> 4.25	> 4.0	> 3.5	> 3.0

Note. From *The Aerobics Program for Total Well-Being*, by Dr. Kenneth H. Cooper. Copyright ©
1982 by Kenneth H. Cooper. Reprinted by permission of the publishers, M. Evans & Co., Inc.,
NY, NY 10017-1502. The cycling test can be used as a test of fitness if you are utilizing the
cycling program. Cycle as far as you can in 12 minutes in an area where traffic is not a problem.
Try to cycle on a hard, flat surface, with the wind (less than 10 mph), and use a bike with no
more than 3 gears. If the wind is blowing harder than 10 mph, take the test another day. Measure
the distance you cycle in 12 minutes by either the speedometer/odometer on the bike (which may
not be too accurate) or by another means, such as a car odometer or an engineering wheel.
[a]< Means "less than"; > means "more than."

Cooper (1968) reported a validity coefficient of .897 between a 12-minute run-walk field
test performance and maximal oxygen consumption from treadmill testing in normal males aged
17 to 52 years. Once the distance covered in
the 12-minute run has been determined, one can
estimate maximal oxygen consumption from
Table 7.22. The values in Table 7.22 were determined from the following prediction equation:

$$\dot{V}O_2 \text{ ml/kg} \cdot \text{min} = -11.2872 + 35.9712$$
(distance in miles for 12-minute run-walk)

This equation provides an estimate of current
cardiovascular fitness. Exercise physiologists
use the maximal oxygen consumption per kilogram of body weight each minute as an estimate
of aerobic power as was described in chapter

6. We can classify individuals into aerobic
capacity categories by consulting Table 7.23.

The field tests of running are easy to administer and do not require expensive or elabo-
rate laboratory equipment such as treadmills,
bicycle ergometers, and apparatus for determining concentrations of oxygen and carbon dioxide
in expired air. Only a stopwatch, whistle, and
running area marked off in distance segments
are required. The running field tests can be administered on a group basis. The school teacher
should be cautioned against using the norms that
have been determined on adults. Local teachers
are encouraged to compute their own norms for
each age level. Pupils should practice running
for a few days prior to testing so as to learn how
to pace themselves during the test.

Table 7.22 Predicted Maximal Oxygen Consumption on the Basis of 12-Minute Run Performance

Distance (miles)	Laps (1/4-mile track)	Predicted maximal O₂ uptake (ml/kg/min⁻¹)
1.000	4	28.2
1.065	4-1/4	30.0
1.125	4-1/2	31.9
1.187	4-3/4	33.8
1.250	5	35.7
1.317	5-1/4	37.5
1.375	5-1/2	39.2
1.437	5-3/4	41.0
1.500	6	42.7
1.565	6-1/4	44.6
1.625	6-1/2	46.4
1.687	6-3/4	48.2
1.750	7	50.0
1.817	7-1/4	51.8
1.875	7-1/2	53.5
1.937	7-3/4	55.3
2.000	8	57.0

Note. Based on data from *A Simple Field Test for the Assessment of Physical Fitness* by B. Balke, 1963, Oklahoma City: Publication 63-6, Civil Aeromedical Research Institute; "A Means of Assessing Maximal Oxygen Intake" by K.H. Cooper, 1968, *Journal of American Medical Association,* **203**, p. 210; and "Energy Cost of Running" by R.P. Margaria, 1963, *Journal of Applied Physiology,* **18**, p. 367. Copyright 1968 by American Medical Association.

Step Tests

The Harvard Step Test. The Harvard Step Test was developed by Brouha (1943) to meet a need for a field test during World War II. It

Table 7.23 Aerobic Capacity Classification Based on Sex and Age

Age (years)	Maximal oxygen consumption (ml/kg/min⁻¹)				
	Low	Fair	Average	Good	High
Women					
20-29	28	29-34	35-40	41-46	47
30-39	27	38-33	34-38	39-45	46
40-49	25	26-31	30-37	38-43	44
50-65	21	22-28	27-34	35-40	41
Men					
20-29	37	38-41	42-50	51-55	56
30-39	33	34-37	38-42	43-50	51
40-49	29	30-35	36-40	41-46	47
50-59	25	26-30	31-38	39-42	43
60-69	21	22-25	26-33	34-37	38

Note. From Katch, F.I., and McArdle, W.D.: *Nutrition, Weight Control, and Exercise,* 2nd edition. Lea & Febiger, Philadelphia, 1983.

was designed to estimate the body's capacity to adjust to and recover from hard muscular work. The test was originally developed on 2,200 college men and was the first field test to estimate muscular endurance. One of the chief advantages of this and other step tests is that they can be administered to a group in a small space in a short period of time. The test does discriminate between individuals who are in good and poor physical condition such as trained athletes and nonathletes. The test consists of stepping up and down a 20-inch (50.8-cm) high bench, 30 times a minute for 5 minutes. The following testing procedures are recommended:[3]

---

[3]Adapted from "The Step Test" by L. Brouha, 1943, *Research Quarterly,* **14**(1), pp. 31-35. Copyright 1943 by the American Alliance for Health, Physical Education, Recreation and Dance. Reprinted by permission.

Equipment. Standard testing equipment includes a stopwatch and a 20-inch (50.8-cm) high bench or stool.

Description. The student steps up and down the bench 30 times a minute for 5 minutes or until he or she can no longer perform. The student steps up with the left foot and brings the right foot alongside the left foot on the bench. The student then steps down with the left foot and follows with the right foot to the floor. Using a metronome or the sweep second hand of a watch to count the cadence, every other second the timer should say *up* to pace the student's performance. The lead foot may be changed during the exercise. Immediately after completing the exercise, the student sits down and prepares for the pulse count.

Scoring. The pulse is counted three times for 30 seconds at 1 minute, 2 minutes, and 3 minutes after exercise. The pulse may be taken at the carotid or radial artery.

The *Physical Efficiency Index* (PEI) is calculated as follows:

$$PEI = \frac{\text{Duration of exercise in seconds} \times 100}{2 \times \text{Sum of pulse counts in recovery}}$$

The class must be trained in taking and recording the pulse before the test begins. Do not begin testing until accurate reproducibility of pulse counts is obtained in all students. If several benches are available, one half of the class can take the test while the other half steadies the bench, spots for the person exercising, and counts the pulse. The teacher may keep time and count the cadence.

The PEI score is interpreted according to the following standards:

Below 55	Poor physical condition
55 to 64	Low average
65 to 79	High average
80 to 89	Good
Above 90	Excellent

The following scoring scheme should be utilized for those failing to complete the 5-minute test and for whom no pulse counts were taken:

Duration of exercise	*PEI score*
Less than 2 minutes	25
2 to 3 minutes	38
3 to 3-1/2 minutes	48
3-1/2 to 4 minutes	52
4 to 4-1/2 minutes	55
4-1/2 to 5 minutes	59

A short form of the Harvard Step Test involving counting the pulse only once from 1 to 1-1/2 minutes after exercise is reviewed by Karpovich and Sinning (1972, pp. 289-292). The short form is scored and interpreted as follows:

$$PEI = \frac{\text{Duration of exercise in seconds} \times 100}{5.5 \text{ (Pulse count)}}$$

Below 50	Poor
50 to 80	Average
Above 80	Good

Both the long and short form pulse scores were correlated with counting the pulse continuously for 10 minutes after exercise. The correlations between the 10-minute pulse count and the three pulse counts was .98; between the 10-minute pulse count and the one pulse of the short form was .92. Test-retest reliability was .83 and .89 for the three and one pulse counts respectively. Thus the short form test appears to be as effective as the long form.

Modifications of Harvard Step Test. A number of modifications of the Harvard Step Test have occurred so that it may be used for both sexes at various ages—7 years through adults (Gallagher & Brouha, 1943; Skubic & Hodgkins, 1963; Hodgkins & Skubic, 1963; Skubic & Hodgkins, 1964; Meyers & Blesh, 1962). Most of the changes involve bench height, cadence, duration of exercise, and scoring scheme. Research presented in the cited references indicates that the modified step tests discriminate between individuals in good and poor physical condition. Directions for administration and scoring can also be found in these references. Test-retest reliabilities of .825 for trained testers and .820 for untrained testers are reported by Skubic and Hodgkins (1963).

Evaluation of the Harvard Step Test. One of the most extensive reviews of the Harvard Step Test and its modifications was conducted by Montoye (1978). His findings are summarized as follows:

- In general maximum work capacity or endurance, performance on the treadmill and in various distance runs including cross country is not highly correlated with heart rate response in the step test. Nor is the relationship high between maximum oxygen uptake and the step test score. Thus the step test score does not give a very precise estimate of aerobic work capacity. This is probably due to not measuring heart rate during the last 30 seconds of bench stepping.
- The step test scores will discriminate between people who are in good or poor physical condition. In addition, the effects of a vigorous conditioning program will lower the pulse count in both trained and untrained subjects.
- Reliability of administering and scoring the step test is more than adequate, especially with trained testers.
- In over 10 studies on children and young adults, it was revealed that there is almost no correlation of the step test scores with height, weight, body surface area, or lower extremity length. In general, obese people do poorly.
- The correlation between the sum of the three heart beats after recovery (long form) and the heart rate taken once (short form) is almost perfect; thus, it is wasteful to take the last two pulse counts.

The chief uses of the Harvard Step Test are classification of the participant into a fitness category and demonstration of the effects of a conditioning or fitness program to participants. In this respect its use is similar to that of the Cooper 12-minute run, cycle, or swim test. Aerobic power reflected in oxygen consumption is not estimated by these tests for people of various ages or sex. The Harvard Step Test has been modified to estimate oxygen consumption in males and females. Several of these tests are described in the next section.

Cotton Group Cardiovascular Step Test. Cotton (1971) developed a modified step test for group cardiovascular testing on college men. The test is felt to be quite applicable to school situations because one half of the class may be tested at one time by stepping up and down the bottom step of the gymnasium bleachers approximately 17 inches (43.18 cm) high. Test-retest reliability of the modified step test was .95 in college men and .75 in high school boys. Training high school pupils in taking the pulse count should increase the reliability coefficient. A validity coefficient of .84 was obtained between the step test score and time it took the heart rate to reach 180 (near exhaustion) on the Balke Treadmill Test. A description of the Cotton group cardiovascular step test[4] follows:

---

[4]From "A Modified Step Test for Group Cardiovascular Testing" by D.J. Cotton, 1971, *Research Quarterly,* **42**(1), pp. 91-95. Copyright 1971 by the American Alliance for Health, Physical Education, Recreation and Dance. Reprinted by permission.

Equipment. Standard equipment for the Cotton group test includes a bleacher step 17 inches (43.18 cm) high; test directions and cadences prerecorded on tape; a tape recorder; and a score sheet for each pupil listing innings 1 through 18.

Description. The test consists of 18 consecutive innings of stepping on a 17-inch (43.18-cm) bleacher step. Each inning consists of 30 seconds of work and 20 seconds of rest with no pause between innings. Total testing time is 15 minutes. During the 20-second rest period, the subject's pulse is taken for 10 seconds beginning with "second 5" and stopping at "second 15." A buddy system is used with one partner exercising and the other partner counting the pulse.

An increased work load is provided by the three phases of the test. Phases I, II, and III are continuous. Each phase consists of six innings. Phase I: 24 steps/minute cadence; Phase II: 30 steps/minute cadence; Phase III: 36 steps/minute cadence. An increased work load is provided in each phase.

An individual has completed the test when the heart rate reaches 150 beats per minute (25 beats in the 10-second counting period) or when 18 innings are completed. The score is the inning in which the heart rate reaches 150 beats. If the individual completes 18 innings, a score of 19 is assigned.

Test Instruction. To ensure correct timing and cadences, the commands and cadences for all 18 innings should be prerecorded on tape. Before starting the tape, the teacher gives the following instructions:

> At the command, you will step up and down in cadence with the step.

You will stop at a given command and your partner will count your pulse and record it. To acquaint you with the procedure, a complete inning will be demonstrated. Be aware of the cadence and instructions as to the exact moment your partner is to begin counting your pulse and the point at which he is to stop. When your pulse count reaches 25 for the 10-second period, the test will be terminated. The inning in which this occurs will be your score.

Administrative Suggestions.

- Prerecord commands and cadences for 18 innings. Provide a reminder prior to innings 7 and 13 that the pace is increasing.
- On the day of the test, no vigorous exercise should precede the test period.
- Divide the class into pairs.
- Have the exercising member of each pair sit on the bottom bleacher step and his partner sit behind him on the second row.
- A 15-minute rest period should precede the test. During this time instructions should be given and a complete inning demonstrated. Have each person practice finding and counting the partner's pulse.
- After the rest-practice period, the subjects on the bottom row stand and face the bleachers. The instructor says, "Prepare to exercise," and starts the tape.

Norms are unavailable for college men or high school boys. Local teachers should develop their own school norms. There is no reason that this test cannot be used for high school girls or college women. Heyward (1984) indicates that maximum oxygen uptake can be estimated from the Cotton Step Test in high school- and college-aged men by using the following prediction equation:

$\dot{V}O_2$max (ml/kg · min)

$= 1.69978 \times$ (step test score)

$- .06252 \times$ (body weight in pounds)

$+ 47.12525$

The following data obtained on a 160-pound college male who ceased exercising after the 13th inning, when the heart rate reached or exceeded 150 beats per minute, will illustrate the use of the equation.

$\dot{V}O_2$max (ml/kg · min)

$= 1.69978(13) - .06252(160) + 47.12525$

$= 22.09714 - 10.00320 + 47.12525$

$= 59.219$

In a study on 63 college males, Holland (1974) obtained a correlation of .89 between $\dot{V}O_2$ uptake estimated by a *submaximal* Åstrand-Rhyming nomogram and the Cotton Step Test prediction equation value.

Siconolfi Step Test. The Siconolfi Step Test provides an accurate estimate of maximal oxygen uptake and is safe and suitable for in-the-home assessments of fitness for individuals 19 to 70 years of age (Siconolfi, Garber, Lasater, & Carleton, 1985). This test is recommended for use in epidemiologic studies. The step test was validated against direct measures of maximal oxygen consumption obtained on a bicycle ergometer and the estimated maximal oxygen uptake from the modified Åstrand-Rhyming submaximal bicycle test. Validity coefficients for

both submaximal tests were .92. The step test estimate of maximal oxygen uptake was 12% higher than directly measured oxygen uptake values, reflecting the expected difference between stepping and cycling. The correlations between the step test and the submaximal bicycle test ranged from .89 to .98 for various age groups.

The Siconolfi Step Test protocol[5] consists of stepping on a portable 10-inch (25.4-cm) high braced box for 3 minutes per stage for a maximum of three stages. The stepping rates for each stage are 17, 26, and 34 steps per minute respectively. During the last 30 seconds of the third minute of each stage of stepping, heart rates are recorded at 2:30, 2:45, and 3:00 minutes. If the average of these three heart rates does not equal or exceed 65% of the age predicted maximum heart rate (estimated as $220 -$ age in years), then the subjects are instructed to complete Stage 2. If the heart rates did not reach the 65% target level at the completion of Stage 2, the subjects then go on and complete Stage 3. Each stage is separated by 1 minute of sitting rest.

It is recommended that test instructions and stepping rates be played with a tape recorder and that heart rate be monitored with a sensor attached to the subject with an ear clip. Maximal oxygen consumption for the last stage of the test completed is predicted with the following equations:

Stage 1: VO_2(l/min) $= 16.287 \times$ Wt(kg)/1000

Stage 2: VO_2(l/min) $= 24.910 \times$ Wt(kg)/1000

Stage 3: VO_2(l/min) $= 33.533 \times$ Wt(Kg)/1000

[5]From "A Simple, Valid Step Test for Estimating Maximal Oxygen Uptake in Epidemiological Studies" by S.F. Siconolfi, C.E. Garber, T.M. Lasater, and R.A. Carleton, 1985, *American Journal of Epidemiology*, **121**(3), pp. 382-390. Copyright 1985 by American Journal of Epidemiology. Reprinted by permission.

The value obtained from one of the above equations is then used in one of the following equations to adjust the maximal oxygen consumption for sex and age:

Males:　$y = 0.348(X_1) - 0.035(X_2) + 3.011$

Females: $y = 0.302(X_1) - 0.19(X_2) + 1.593$

where $y = VO_2(l/min)$, X_1 is the $VO_2(l/min)$ estimate of the Åstrand-Rhyming test from one of the three stages of the step test, and X_2 is the age in years. The error in predicting VO_2 uptake from a submaximal test will be somewhat larger than a prediction from a maximal VO_2 uptake test.

Queens College Step Test[6] and Oxygen Consumption. A short step test developed on thousands of college men and women that can be used to predict maximum oxygen consumption obtained with a treadmill protocol was reviewed by Katch and McArdle (1983). Following a demonstration, the subjects should be given 15 seconds of practice before the test begins. For females, the test consists of stepping up and down a bleacher step approximately 16.25 inches (41.275 cm) high at a rate of 22 steps per minute for 3 minutes. The test conditions are similar for males except that males step at a rate of 24 steps per minute for 3 minutes. Subjects remain standing after exercise, and a 15-second pulse count is taken beginning 5 seconds after cessation of exercise. The 15-second count is multiplied by 4 to record the score in beats per minute.

The concept that a person with a low recovery heart rate would have a higher predicted maximum oxygen consumption was validated in controlled laboratory studies. The equations predicting maximum oxygen uptake

in milliliters per kilogram of body weight for males and females are as follows:

Men: $\dot{V}O_2max = 111.33$
　　$- (0.42 \times$ step test pulse rate, beats/min)

Women: $\dot{V}O_2max = 65.81$
　　$- (0.1847 \times$ step test pulse rate, beats/min)

The percentile rankings for various heart rate scores as well as the predictions of maximum oxygen uptake from the equations appear in Table 7.24. We should emphasize that predicting maximal oxygen consumption from submaximal step tests or distance runs involves a standard error of estimation of about $\pm 10\%$ for trained individuals and $\pm 16\%$ for untrained individuals. Hence the best use of these submaximal tests may be for classifying individuals into the aerobic capacity categories in Table 7.23.

Estimating Percent Body Fat and Body Density

In a previous section of this chapter, the point was made that physical fitness includes not only motor and cardiovascular fitness but may also reflect the degree to which an individual is free of disease or symptoms that may indicate a pending health problem. One such problem reaching serious levels in our affluent, sedentary society is obesity. Mayer (1968) found that an increased level of obesity is positively related to mortality rates and is also one of the underlying conditions of most aspects of heart disease, including hypertension, atherosclerosis, and hypercholesterolemia. Thus physical educators must be able to estimate participants' obesity levels in order to counsel individuals into taking appropriate remedial action.

It must be emphasized that in many cases height-weight tables do not provide an accurate

---

[6]Paraphrased from Katch, F.I., and McArdle, W.D.: *Nutrition, Weight Control, and Exercise*, 2nd edition. Lea & Febiger, Philadelphia, 1983.

Table 7.24 Percentile Rankings for Recovery Heart Rate
and Predicted Maximal Oxygen Consumption for Male and Female College Students

Percentile ranking	Recovery HR female	Predicted $\dot{V}O_2$max (ml/kg/min^{-1})	Recovery HR male	Predicted $\dot{V}O_2$max (ml/kg/min^{-1})
100	128	42.2	120	60.9
95	140	40.0	124	59.3
90	148	38.5	128	57.6
85	152	37.7	136	54.2
80	156	37.0	140	52.5
75	158	36.6	144	50.9
70	160	36.3	148	49.2
65	162	35.9	149	48.8
60	163	35.7	152	47.5
55	164	35.5	154	46.7
50	166	35.1	156	45.8
45	168	34.8	160	44.1
40	170	34.4	162	43.3
35	171	34.2	164	42.5
30	172	34.0	166	41.6
25	176	33.3	168	40.8
20	180	32.6	172	39.1
15	182	32.2	176	37.4
10	184	31.8	178	36.6
5	196	29.6	184	34.1

Note. From Katch, F.I., and McArdle, W.D.: *Nutrition, Weight Control, and Exercise,* 2nd edition. Lea & Febiger, Philadelphia, 1983.

estimate of obesity. This is because an overweight individual is not necessarily obese. Football players and lumberjacks are generally much taller and heavier than the "average" values found on age-height-weight tables, but they are not obese. In fact, in most cases they are quite lean and have desirable body compositions with high lean-to-fat ratios. In other words, only a small percentage of their body weight is fat. Hence estimates of percent body fat are more accurate and appropriate indicators of obesity than height-weight tables.

Percent body fat and lean body weight are calculated after we estimate the body density or specific gravity of the individual. Physical educators must remember that two people of the same age, height, weight, and sex can have quite different body densities. One individual may have large bone development and/or proportionally more muscle tissue than fat tissue. Another person may have small bones and proportionally less muscle than body fat. Bone and muscle tissue is more dense than fat; that is, one cubic centimeter of bone or muscle weighs more than one cubic centimeter of fat. Thus the first person has a higher body density or specific gravity than the second person. When asked to float in a swimming pool, the person with greater body density would be more likely to ''sink,'' whereas the second person would float more easily.

The terms *specific gravity*, *specific weight*, and *specific density* all have the same meaning in physics, namely the comparison of the density of one substance with that of another substance. Water is the standard substance chosen by physicists with which to compare the densities of all solids and liquids (Dull, Metcalfe, & Brooks, 1949). In physics the term *specific* is used to imply ratio; hence the weight of a substance compared to the weight of an equal volume of the standard substance (water) is called its *specific weight*. In estimating the specific gravity or body density of a human being, we merely apply Archimedes' principle as follows:

1. Weigh the person to determine his or her weight in air.
2. Find the weight of an equal volume of water by determining how much less the body weighs when submerged in water.
3. Divide the weight of the body in air by the weight of the same volume of water.

Because the specific gravity of water is 1.0, a body will float (i.e., be less dense) when it has a specific gravity of less than 1.0. A person will sink when his or her body has a specific gravity of more than 1.0 (i.e., is more dense) or when the weight of the body in the air is greater than the weight of the volume of water that the body displaces (Figure 7.14).

Several laboratory methods of determining lean body weight and percent body fat have been proposed. They include weighing tissue obtained from cadaver dissection, radiography, ultrasound, computerized axial tomography, measuring body water, measuring potassium 40 levels

Figure 7.14 Underwater weighing to estimate the specific gravity (body density) of a male paraplegic athlete.

in the body, bioelectrical impedance, and body density or specific gravity. Virtually all of these methods are beyond the scope of physical education practitioners. Physical educators can, however, make a few estimated predictions of percent body fat and lean body weight. Wilmore and Behnke (1969) have developed several equations to predict lean body weight and body density that utilize anthropometric measurements such as height, weight, diameters of certain bony areas of the body, circumference of certain body parts, and skinfold measurements.

Weight and Body Circumference and Diameter Measurements

To measure body girths, a steel anthropometric tape is recommended. A Gulick tape is suggested because a spring attached to its handle allows constant pressure to be applied to the tape during measurement. Cloth tapes are not recommended because they stretch with repeated use. The following descriptions of weight and anatomical girth measurements are to be used in the prediction equations in this text. The sites are illustrated in Figure 7.15.

1. *Weight (in kilograms)*. The subject is weighed in stocking feet on a balance scale while wearing the least amount of clothing possible. A bathing suit is preferred. Weight is recorded in kilograms.
2. *Wrist diameter (in centimeters)*. Wrist diameter is measured as the distance between the styloid process of the radius and ulna.
3. *Abdominal circumference (in centimeters)*. Abdominal circumference is measured at the level of the umbilicus.
4. *Hip circumference (in centimeters)*. Hip circumference is measured at the maximum protrusion of the gluteal muscles.
5. *Forearm circumference (in centimeters)*. Forearm circumference is measured as the maximal girth with the elbow extended and the hand supinated.

The equation that practitioners can use most feasibly in the field to predict lean body weight in young adult males is as follows:

Lean body weight in kg (LBW kg)

$= 44.636 + 1.0817$ (body weight in kg)

$- 0.7396$ (abdominal circumference in centimeters)

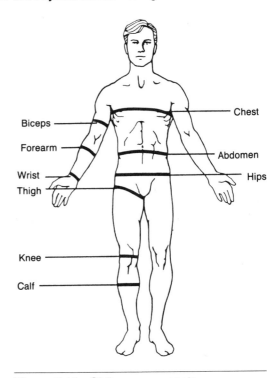

Figure 7.15   Girth measurements.

The correlation between predictions from this equation and actual estimates of lean body weight arrived at by the underwater weighing method is $R = .938$. The standard error of estimate is 2.815 kilograms. Percent body fat is then estimated from the following equation:

$$\text{Percent fat} = 100 - (100 \times \frac{\text{LBW (kg)}}{\text{body weight (kg)}})$$

The following is an example of how this technique is applied:

Name: Bill Smith
Body weight = 89 kg
Abdominal circumference = 88 cm

$$LBW = 44.636 + 1.0817(89)$$
$$- .7396(88)$$
$$= 44.636 + 96.2713 - 65.0848$$
$$= 140.9073 - 65.0848$$
$$= 75.8225 \text{ kg}$$

$$\text{Percent body fat} = 100 - (100 \times \frac{75.8225}{89})$$
$$= 100 - 100 \times .8519$$
$$= 100 - 85.19$$
$$= 14.81 \text{ or } 15\%$$

For a young adult female, the following prediction equation is used:

$$\begin{array}{l}\text{Lean body} \\ \text{weight in kg} \\ \text{(LBW kg)}\end{array} = 8.987 + 0.732\left(\begin{array}{c}\text{body wt.} \\ \text{in kg}\end{array}\right) +$$

$$3.786\left(\begin{array}{c}\text{wrist diam-} \\ \text{eter in cm}\end{array}\right) -$$

$$0.157\left(\begin{array}{c}\text{max. abdominal} \\ \text{circumference} \\ \text{in cm}\end{array}\right) -$$

$$0.249\left(\begin{array}{c}\text{hip circumference} \\ \text{in cm}\end{array}\right) +$$

$$0.434\left(\begin{array}{c}\text{forearm circumference} \\ \text{in cm}\end{array}\right)$$

The following is an example of how this technique is applied:

Name: Mary Jones
Body weight = 51.8 kg
Wrist circumference = 5 cm
Maximal abdominal
   circumference = 66.25 cm
Hip circumference = 91 cm
Forearm circumference = 23.2 cm
$$\begin{array}{l}LBW = \\ \text{kg}\end{array} \quad 8.987 + .0732(51.8)$$
$$+ 3.786(5) - 0.157(66.25)$$
$$- 0.249(91) + 0.434(23.2)$$
$$= 8.987 + 37.9 + 18.93$$
$$- 10.4 - 22.7 + 10.1$$
$$= 65.83 - 10.4 - 22.7 + 10.1$$
$$= 55.43 - 22.7 + 10.1$$
$$= 32.73 + 10.1$$
$$= 42.8$$

$$\text{Percent body fat}$$
$$= 100 - (100 \times \frac{LBW \text{ kg}}{\text{Body weight kg}})$$
$$= 100 - (100 \times \frac{42.8}{51.8})$$
$$= 100 - (100 \times .83)$$
$$= 100 - 83$$
$$= 17$$

The correlation between predictions from this equation and actual estimates of lean body weight arrived at by the underwater weighing method is $R = .922$ (Behnke & Wilmore, 1974).

Skinfold Measurements

You will need to secure a caliper to measure thickness of skinfolds. Two of the more accurate calipers are the Lange Caliper and the Harpenden Caliper.[7] These calipers are designed to provide a constant pressure of 10 gm/mm^2 over prolonged periods of use. Some of the less expensive calipers do not provide this feature, and thus one must often check their spring tension prior to use. Certain precautions are necessary in using skinfold calipers. Procedures must be standardized, and extensive practice is required to secure accurate measurements. Once the measurement site is located, the skinfold is grasped firmly between the thumb and index finger. The caliper is placed 1/2 to 1 inch (1.27 to 2.54 cm) above or below the thumb and index finger. Skinfold thickness is measured in millimeters. Readings should be taken 2 to 3 seconds after applying the caliper. Three

---

[7]The Lange Calipers are sold by Cambridge Scientific Industries, 527 Poplar Street, Cambridge, MD. Harpenden Calipers are sold by the H.E. Morse Company, 455 Douglas Avenue, Holland, MI. Other less expensive calipers are sold by Creative Health Products, Inc., 144 Saddle Ridge Road, Plymouth, MI 48170 and AAHPERD, 1900 Association Drive, Reston, VA 22091.

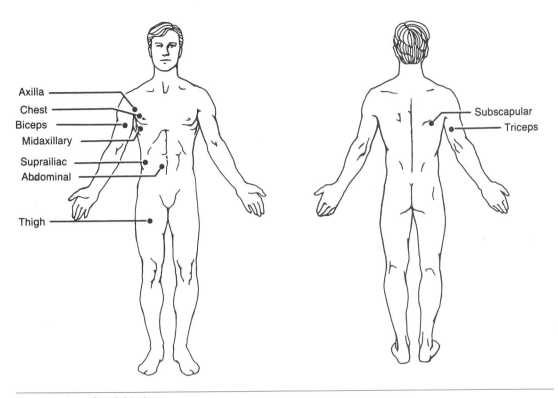

Axilla

Chest

Biceps

Midaxillary

Suprailiac

Abdominal

Thigh

Subscapular

Triceps

Figure 7.16 Skinfold sites.

measurements are taken with the skinfold released between trials. Reliability can be a problem unless measurements are taken at exactly the same site, in the same way, and at the same time of day.

Skinfolds are usually taken on the right side of the body and measured in millimeters. The following is a bodily description of the skinfold sites used in this text. These and other less common skinfold sites are illustrated in Figure 7.16.

1. *Thigh skinfold*. Vertical skinfold in the anterior midline of the thigh, halfway between the inguinal ligament and the top of the patella.
2. *Subscapular skinfold*. Skinfold running downward and laterally in the natural fold of the skin from the inferior angle of the scapula.

3. *Suprailiac skinfold*. Vertical skinfold over the iliac crest in the midaxillary line.
4. *Triceps skinfold*. Vertical skinfold on the back of the arm (triceps) halfway between the acromion and olecranon processes with the elbow extended.
5. *Biceps skinfold*. Vertical skinfold taken over the belly of the biceps brachei midway between the shoulder and elbow joints.
6. *Chest skinfold*. A diagonal skinfold taken halfway between the anterior axillary line and the nipple for men and one third of the distance from the anterior axillary line and the nipple for women.
7. *Abdominal skinfold*. A horizontal skinfold taken adjacent to the umbilicus.

A simple equation for predicting body density and total body fat utilizing two skinfold measurements in young adult men and women with accompanying nomograms has been developed by Sloan and Weir (1970). The body density prediction equation for young men 18 to 26 years of age is as follows:

$$\text{Density (gm/ml)} = 1.1043 - 0.00133 \left(\begin{array}{c} \text{thigh skin-} \\ \text{fold in mm} \end{array} \right)$$

$$- 0.00131 \left(\begin{array}{c} \text{subscapular} \\ \text{skinfold in mm} \end{array} \right)$$

$$\text{Percent body fat} = 100(\frac{4.570}{D} - 4.142)$$

For young women (aged 17 to 25 years), the following body density equation is used:

$$\text{Density (gm/ml)} = 1.0764 - 0.00081 \left(\begin{array}{c} \text{suprailiac} \\ \text{skinfold in mm} \end{array} \right)$$

$$- 0.00088 \left(\begin{array}{c} \text{triceps skin-} \\ \text{fold in mm} \end{array} \right)$$

$$\text{Percent body fat} = 100(\frac{4.570}{D} - 4.142)$$

The following example of a prediction of percent body fat for a young woman illustrates the technique.

    Name: Suzi Smith
    Suprailiac skinfold = 18 mm
    Tricep skinfold = 16 mm
    D gm/ml = 1.0764 − 0.00081(18) −
       0.00088(16)
       = 1.0764 − 0.0146 − 0.0141
       = 1.0618 − 0.0141
       = 1.0477

$$\begin{array}{rl} \text{Percent} \\ \text{body fat} \end{array} = 100(\frac{4.570}{1.0477} - 4.142)$$

       = 100(4.3619 − 4.142)
       = 100(0.2199)
       = 21.99 or ≅ 22

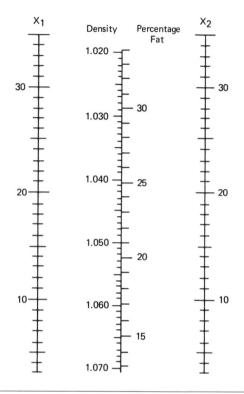

Figure 7.17 Nomogram for predicting body density and percentage of total body fat for young women. X_1 = suprailiac skinfold thickness (mm); X_2 = back of arm skinfold thickness (mm). *Note.* From "Nomograms for Prediction of Body Density and Total Body Fat from Skinfold Measurements" by A.W. Sloan and J.B. de V. Weir, 1970, *Journal of Applied Physiology,* **28**(2), pp. 221-222. Copyright 1970 by the American Physiological Society. Reprinted by permission.

To eliminate computation, use the nomograms in Figures 7.17 and 7.18 to estimate body density and percent body fat for adult men and women directly. The equations just described are used to predict the percent body fat and body density that would have been obtained using the underwater weighing method, which itself is a relative approximation of the values. Hence

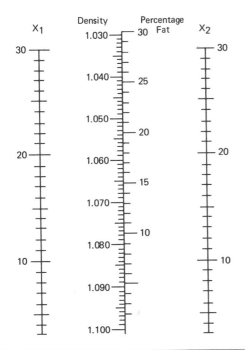

Figure 7.18 Nomogram for predicting body density and percentage of total body fat for young men. X_1 = thigh skinfold thickness (mm); X_2 = subscapular skinfold thickness (mm). *Note.* From "Nomograms for Prediction of Body Density and Total Body Fat from Skinfold Measurements" by A.W. Sloan and J.B. de V. Weir, 1970, *Journal of Applied Physiology*, **28**(2), pp. 221-222. Copyright 1970 by the American Physiological Society. Reprinted by permission.

these prediction equations provide approximations of percent body fat and body density. Montoye (1978) indicated that skinfold measures of various sites are highly correlated (.74 to .93). Furthermore, the sum of four skinfolds (triceps, subscapular, abdominal, crest of iliac) correlates .90 with the sum of two (triceps and subscapular). Hence we do not gain much more information when we use measurements of more than three or four skinfolds.

Estimating Ideal Weight and Overweight

Some individuals want to lose body fat and approach an ideal weight as one of their fitness goals. The ideal body weight for a college-aged male is thought to be about 15% or less body fat, whereas for college-aged women it is 25% or less body fat (Katch & McArdle, 1983). Suppose that Bill Smith is one of your students. He weighs 165 pounds (74.84 kg) and has a predicted 21% body fat. If we accept 15% as the ideal percent body fat for Bill, then we can calculate his desirable weight as follows (Katch & McArdle, 1983):

$$\text{Fat weight} = \frac{\text{percent body fat}}{100} \times \text{body weight}$$
$$= .21 \times 165 \text{ pounds}$$
$$= 34.65 \text{ pounds fat}$$

$$\begin{array}{l}\text{Fat free} \\ \text{body weight} \\ \text{(lean body weight)}\end{array} = \text{body weight} - \text{fat weight}$$
$$= 165 \text{ pounds} - 34.65 \text{ pounds}$$
$$= 130.35 \text{ pounds}$$

$$\begin{array}{l}\text{Desirable} \\ \text{body weight}\end{array} = \frac{\text{lean body weight}}{1.00 - \text{percent fat desired}}$$
$$= \frac{130.35}{.85}$$
$$= 153.35 \text{ pounds}$$

$$\begin{array}{l}\text{Desirable} \\ \text{fat loss} \\ \text{(pounds)}\end{array} = \begin{array}{l}\text{present} \\ \text{body weight}\end{array} - \begin{array}{l}\text{desirable} \\ \text{body} \\ \text{weight}\end{array}$$
$$= 165 - 153.35$$
$$= 11.65$$

Problems
With Prediction Equations

The practitioner must be aware of several problems in using prediction equations to estimate percent body fat. The first problem applies to all participants in a fitness program and involves counseling students about attaining a desirable body weight. Conditioning can foster a loss in body fat and a simultaneous gain in lean muscle mass. If these processes cancel each other out, then body weight remains stable. A few individuals may gain weight because muscle tissue weighs more than fat. This state is desirable because an increase in lean body mass means more metabolically active tissue in the body, which is important for weight control. Placing too much emphasis on "ideal body weight" may not be justified due to the nature of the fitness program. Participants sometimes establish unobtainable goals. Unrealistic goals can lead to negative feedback and can negatively motivate the participant to indulge in unhealthy eating and exercise behaviors in order to lose weight. Such behaviors are becoming a major problem among members of dance, cheerleading, and majorette groups (Humphries & Gruber, 1986). In addition, some coaches of long distance runners exhort their athletes to lose weight because the loss of a pound may reduce their running time by a single second. Often these runners will lose essential body fat, which is a health-threatening situation. Thus coaches and physical educators must be extremely careful in providing fitness counseling.

The second major problem lies in using these prediction equations on populations that differ from the validation group (white, college-aged males). The proportion of subcutaneous fat to internal fat is approximately 1:1 in young college-aged adults, but the proportion of subcutaneous fat tends to diminish with age. The proportion of subcutaneous fat is higher in females than in males. Wilmore (1983) indicated that for populations at extreme ages (8- to 12-year-old children and senior citizens) the equations tend to overestimate fat values by densiometric techniques. This tendency occurs because the mineral content of bones is less dense in young people due to incomplete growth, whereas in senior citizens there is a natural reduction of bone mineral content due to hormonal changes that accompany aging. Hence both groups will weigh lighter when in water, but this is not due to increased body fat. Furthermore, in special athletic populations, we tend to overestimate and underestimate fat content, depending on sport and/or racial differences among athletes (Smith & Mansfield, 1984). In addition, Lohman, Pollock, Slaughter, Brandon, and Boileau (1984) have shown that the type of calipers used, training of testers, and prediction equation used all contribute to the variability in estimating fat content in college female basketball players. This finding likely applies to other athletic groups of either sex.

Equations
for Children and Adolescents

Do not use the prediction equations previously listed in this chapter on children under 17 years of age. Pǎrízková (1961) underwater weighed and measured skinfolds on 9- to 16-year-old boys and girls. Using only two skinfold measurements (triceps and subscapular), she reported correlations between hydrostatic weighing and the log of skinfolds to be from .81 to .95. She developed nomograms based on prediction equations to estimate body density and percent body fat. The nomograms appear in Figures 7.19 to 7.22. The X scale on these nomograms represents the triceps skinfold, and the Y scale represents the subscapular skinfold. Connect the X and Y values on the nomogram with a ruler and read off the percent body fat and density values.

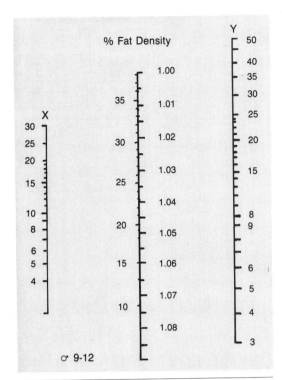

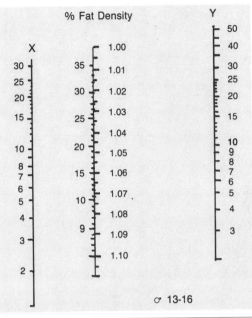

Figure 7.19 Nomogram for estimating body density or percent body fat from triceps skinfold (*X*-scale) and subscapular skinfold (*Y*-scale) in boys 9 to 12 years old. *Note.* From "Total Body Fat and Skinfold Thickness in Children" by J. Pǎrízková, 1961, *Metabolism*, **10**, pp. 794-802. Copyright 1961 by Greene & Stratton. Reprinted by permission.

Figure 7.20 Nomogram for estimating body density or percent body fat from triceps skinfold (*X*-scale) and subscapular skinfold (*Y*-scale) in boys 13 to 16 years old. *Note.* From "Total Body Fat and Skinfold Thickness in Children" by J. Pǎrízková, 1961, *Metabolism*, **10**, pp. 794-802. Copyright 1961 by Greene & Stratton. Reprinted by permission.

Generalized Equations

Gender-specific "generalized equations" have been developed for use with mature men and women. These equations account for the curvilinear relationship between skinfold fat and body density as well as for the changes in proportion of subcutaneous and internal fat that occur with age (Pollock, Schmidt, & Jackson, 1980). The generalized equations account for these differences in age and predict body density more accurately because the standard error of prediction is more constant over a wide range of adult populations. The standard errors from generalized equations range from 3.5 to 3.9% fat prediction, which compares favorably with 2.7% standard error of prediction for laboratory underwater weighing. Thus to reduce errors in predicting percent body fat in people who are not part of the young adult validation group, practitioners should use the generalized equations.

The following generalized equation (Jackson, Pollock, & Ward, 1980) is used to predict body density in women 18 to 55 years of age:

$$\text{Body density} = 1.0994921 - 0.0009929(X_3) + 0.0000023(X_3)^2 - 0.0001392(X_4)$$

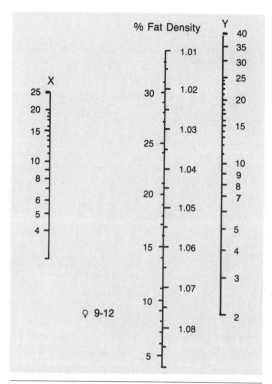

Figure 7.21 Nomogram for estimating body density or percent body fat from triceps skinfold (*X*-scale) and subscapular skinfold (*Y*-scale) in girls 9 to 12 years old. *Note.* From "Total Body Fat and Skinfold Thickness in Children" by J. Pǎrízková, 1961, *Metabolism*, **10**, pp. 794-802. Copyright 1961 by Greene & Stratton. Reprinted by permission.

where X_3 = sum of triceps, thigh, and suprailiac skinfolds and X_4 = age in years. The following generalized equation (Jackson & Pollock, 1978) is used to predict body density in males 18 to 61 years of age:

$$\text{Body density} = 1.10938 - 0.0008267(X_3) + 0.0000016(X_3)^2 - 0.0002574(X_6)$$

where X_3 = sum of chest, abdominal, and thigh skinfolds and X_6 = age in years. Pollock, Schmidt, and Jackson (1980) provide estimates

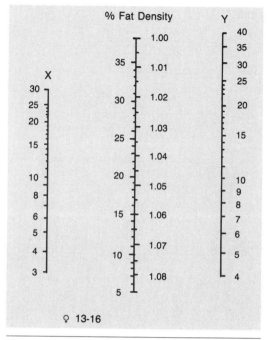

Figure 7.22 Nomogram for estimating body density or percent body fat from triceps skinfold (*X*-scale) and subscapular skinfold (*Y*-scale) in girls 13 to 16 years old. *Note.* From "Total Body Fat and Skinfold Thickness in Children" by J. Pǎrízková, 1961, *Metabolism*, **10**, pp. 794-802. Copyright 1961 by Greene & Stratton. Reprinted by permission.

of percent body fat based on three skinfold measurements for adult males and females aged 18 to 61 years (see Tables 7.25 and 7.26). These percentages were developed from generalized equations.

The generalized equations have been validated for estimating percent body fat in college-aged women athletes (Sinning & Wilson, 1984) and for analyzing body composition in college-age male athletes (Sinning et al., 1985). In addition, Thorland, Johnson, Tharp, Fagot, and Hammer (1984) have validated the generalized equations for estimating body density in adolescent male and female athletes 15 to 19 years of

Table 7.25 Percent Fat Estimates for Men (Sum of Chest, Abdominal, and Thigh Skinfolds)

Sum of skinfolds (mm)	Under 22	23 to 27	28 to 32	33 to 37	38 to 42	43 to 47	48 to 52	53 to 57	Over 58
				Age (to the last year)					
8-10	1.3	1.8	2.3	2.9	3.4	3.9	4.5	5.0	5.5
11-13	2.2	2.8	3.3	3.9	4.4	4.9	5.5	6.0	6.5
14-16	3.2	3.8	4.3	4.8	5.4	5.9	6.4	7.0	7.5
17-19	4.2	4.7	5.3	5.8	6.3	6.9	7.4	8.0	8.5
20-22	5.1	5.7	6.2	6.8	7.3	7.9	8.4	8.9	9.5
23-25	6.1	6.6	7.2	7.7	8.3	8.8	9.4	9.9	10.5
26-28	7.0	7.6	8.1	8.7	9.2	9.8	10.3	10.9	11.4
29-31	8.0	8.5	9.1	9.6	10.2	10.7	11.3	11.8	12.4
32-34	8.9	9.4	10.0	10.5	11.1	11.6	12.2	12.8	13.3
35-37	9.8	10.4	10.9	11.5	12.0	12.6	13.1	13.7	14.3
38-40	10.7	11.3	11.8	12.4	12.9	13.5	14.1	14.6	15.2
41-43	11.6	12.2	12.7	13.3	13.8	14.4	15.0	15.5	16.1
44-46	12.5	13.1	13.6	14.2	14.7	15.3	15.9	16.4	17.0
47-49	13.4	13.9	14.5	15.1	15.6	16.2	16.8	17.3	17.9
50-52	14.3	14.8	15.4	15.9	16.5	17.1	17.6	18.2	18.8
53-55	15.1	15.7	16.2	16.8	17.4	17.9	18.5	18.1	19.7
56-58	16.0	16.5	17.1	17.7	18.2	18.8	19.4	20.0	20.5
59-61	16.9	17.4	17.9	18.5	19.1	19.7	20.2	20.8	21.4
62-64	17.6	18.2	18.8	19.4	19.9	20.5	21.1	21.7	22.2
65-67	18.5	19.0	19.6	20.2	20.8	21.3	21.9	22.5	23.1
68-70	19.3	19.9	20.4	21.0	21.6	22.2	22.7	23.3	23.9
71-73	20.1	20.7	21.2	21.8	22.4	23.0	23.6	24.1	24.7
74-76	20.9	21.5	22.0	22.6	23.2	23.8	24.4	25.0	25.5
77-79	21.7	22.2	22.8	23.4	24.0	24.6	25.2	25.8	26.3
80-82	22.4	23.0	23.6	24.2	24.8	25.4	25.9	26.5	27.1
83-85	23.2	23.8	24.4	25.0	25.5	26.1	26.7	27.3	27.9
86-88	24.0	24.5	25.1	25.7	26.3	26.9	27.5	28.1	28.7
89-91	24.7	25.3	25.9	25.5	27.1	27.6	28.2	28.8	29.4
92-94	25.4	26.0	26.6	27.2	27.8	28.4	29.0	29.6	30.2
92-97	26.1	16.7	27.3	27.9	28.5	29.1	29.7	30.3	30.9
98-100	26.9	27.4	28.0	28.6	29.2	29.8	30.4	31.0	31.6
101-103	27.5	28.1	28.7	29.3	29.9	30.5	31.1	31.7	32.3
104-106	28.2	28.8	29.4	30.0	30.6	31.2	31.8	32.4	33.0
107-109	28.9	29.5	30.1	30.7	31.3	31.9	32.5	33.1	33.7
110-112	29.6	30.2	30.8	31.4	32.0	32.6	33.2	33.8	34.4

(Cont.)

Table 7.25 (Cont.)

Sum of skinfolds (mm)	Under 22	23 to 27	28 to 32	Age (to the last year) 33 to 37	38 to 42	43 to 47	48 to 52	53 to 57	Over 58
113-115	30.2	30.8	31.4	32.0	32.6	33.2	33.8	34.5	35.1
116-118	30.9	31.5	32.1	32.7	33.3	33.9	34.5	35.1	35.7
119-121	31.5	32.1	32.7	33.3	33.9	34.5	35.1	35.7	36.4
122-124	32.1	32.7	33.3	33.9	34.5	35.1	35.8	36.4	37.0
125-127	32.7	33.3	33.9	34.5	35.1	35.8	36.4	37.0	37.6

Note. Percent fat calculated by the formula by Siri. Percent fat = ([4.95/BD] − 4.5) × 100, where BD = body density. Reprinted from *Comprehensive Therapy* (1980): **6**(9), 12-27. Courtesy of the Laux Publishing Company, Inc., P.O. Box 700, Ayer, MA 01432.

age. The Jackson, Pollock, and Ward (1980) generalized equation appears to effectively reduce the error in predicting body density among various somatotypes in women. In fact, greater accuracy in prediction of body density may be achieved by using prediction equations developed on previously somatotyped samples (Bulbulian, 1984).

Paraplegic Athletes

Several equations for predicting percent body fat in paraplegic wheelchair athletes have been developed by Johnson, Bulbulian, Gruber, Darabos, and Sundheim (1986). The most efficient equation (see Equation 1) had a multiple R of .94 with the middle 50% of the residuals (over- or underestimates of percent body fat) being ± 2.9%. The second equation (2) had an R of .86 with the middle 50% residuals = ± 3.8%.

$$\text{Percent body fat} = 2.271 + 0.754 \left(\begin{array}{c} \text{abdominal} \\ \text{circumference} \\ \text{in cm} \end{array} \right)$$

$$- 0.305 \, \frac{\text{weight}}{\text{in kg}} + 0.567 \left(\begin{array}{c} \text{chest skinfold} \\ \text{in mm} \end{array} \right)$$

$$- 1.017 \, \frac{\text{chest diameter}}{\text{in cm}} \quad (1)$$

$$\text{Percent body fat} = -31.804 + 0.617 \left(\begin{array}{c} \text{abdominal} \\ \text{circumference} \\ \text{in cm} \end{array} \right) \quad (2)$$

Chest diameter is measured by placing the body caliper at the level of the fifth to sixth ribs (nipple line in men). Arms are adducted back to the side of the body for measurement.

Any prediction equation must be used cautiously in recommending specific target weights. Some measurement error is inherent in even the best regression equations, including those that estimate body density by underwater weighing. Errors of predicting body fat may range from ± 2 to ± 5%.

Obesity

Mayer (1968) defined obesity as the presence of excessive body fat. The problem for physical educators is to determine the cut-off point for obesity in individuals of different body types at various ages. If we estimate percent body fat for college-aged men and women, we can arrive at desirable values of 19 to 25% body fat for women and 13 to 17% body fat for men. These values vary depending on individuals' participation in occupational or athletic activities. Athletes and manual laborers, for example,

Table 7.26 Percent Fat Estimates for Women (Sum of Triceps, Suprailiac, and Thigh Skinfolds)

Sum of skinfolds (mm)	Under 22	23 to 27	28 to 32	33 to 37	38 to 42	43 to 47	48 to 52	53 to 57	Over 58
				Age (to the last year)					
23-25	9.7	9.9	10.2	10.4	10.7	10.9	11.2	11.4	11.7
26-28	11.0	11.2	11.5	11.7	12.0	12.3	12.5	12.7	13.0
29-31	12.3	12.5	12.8	13.0	13.3	13.5	13.8	14.0	14.3
32-34	13.6	13.8	14.0	14.3	14.5	14.8	15.0	15.3	15.5
35-37	14.8	15.0	15.3	15.5	15.8	16.0	16.3	16.5	16.8
38-40	16.0	16.3	16.5	16.7	17.0	17.2	17.5	17.7	18.0
41-43	17.2	17.4	17.7	17.9	18.2	18.4	18.7	18.9	19.2
44-46	18.3	18.6	18.8	19.1	19.3	19.6	19.8	20.1	20.3
47-49	19.5	19.7	20.0	20.2	20.5	20.7	21.0	21.2	21.5
50-52	20.6	20.8	21.1	21.3	21.6	21.8	22.1	22.3	22.6
53-55	21.7	21.9	22.1	22.4	22.6	22.9	23.1	23.4	23.6
56-58	22.7	23.0	23.2	23.4	23.7	23.9	24.2	24.4	24.7
59-61	23.7	24.0	24.2	24.5	24.7	25.0	25.2	25.5	25.7
62-64	24.7	25.0	25.2	25.5	25.7	26.0	26.7	26.4	26.7
65-67	25.7	25.9	26.2	26.4	26.7	26.9	27.2	27.4	27.7
68-70	26.6	26.9	27.1	27.4	27.6	27.9	28.1	28.4	28.6
71-73	27.5	27.8	28.0	28.3	28.5	28.8	29.0	29.3	29.5
74-76	28.4	28.7	28.9	29.2	29.4	29.7	29.9	30.2	30.4
77-79	29.3	29.5	29.8	30.0	30.3	30.5	30.8	31.0	31.3
80-82	30.1	30.4	30.6	30.9	31.1	31.4	31.6	31.9	32.1
83-85	30.9	31.2	31.4	31.7	31.9	32.2	32.4	32.7	32.9
86-88	31.7	32.0	32.2	32.5	32.7	32.9	33.2	33.4	33.7
89-91	32.5	32.7	33.0	33.2	33.5	33.7	33.9	34.2	34.4
92-94	33.2	33.4	33.7	33.9	34.2	34.4	34.7	34.9	35.2
95-97	33.9	34.1	34.4	34.6	34.9	35.1	35.4	35.6	35.9
98-100	34.6	34.8	35.1	35.3	35.5	35.8	36.0	36.3	36.5
101-103	35.3	35.4	35.7	35.9	36.2	36.4	36.7	36.9	37.2
104-106	35.8	36.1	36.3	36.6	36.8	37.1	37.3	37.5	37.8
107-109	36.4	36.7	36.9	37.1	37.4	37.6	37.9	38.1	38.4
110-112	37.0	37.2	37.5	37.7	38.0	38.2	38.5	38.7	38.9
113-115	37.5	37.8	38.0	38.2	38.5	38.7	39.0	39.2	39.5
116-118	38.0	38.3	38.5	38.8	39.0	39.3	39.5	39.7	40.0
119-121	38.5	38.7	39.0	39.2	39.5	39.7	40.0	40.2	40.5
122-124	39.0	39.2	39.4	39.7	39.9	40.2	40.4	40.7	40.9
125-127	39.4	39.6	39.9	40.1	40.4	40.6	40.9	41.1	41.4
128-130	39.8	40.0	40.3	40.5	40.8	41.0	41.3	41.5	41.8

Note. Percent fat calculated by the formula by Siri. Percent fat = ([4.95/BD] − 4.5) × 100, where BD = body density. Reprinted from *Comprehensive Therapy* (1980): **6**(9), 12-27. Courtesy of the Laux Publishing Company, Inc., P.O. Box 700, Ayer, MA 01432.

generally have less than average percent body fat. We should also remember that the nature and intensity of physical training may alter body composition (Behnke & Wilmore, 1984).

When an individual's triceps skinfold measurement lies beyond one standard deviation above the mean for his or her age, Mayer (1968) maintains that the individual is obese. Values for obesity in various age groups appear in Table 7.27. Another standard used to indicate overfatness is above 20% body fat for males and above 30% for females. In the absence of prediction equations, we may subjectively estimate fatness using one of the following procedures proposed by Mayer:[8]

- *The Mirror Test*. While naked, look at yourself in the mirror. If you look fat, you probably are fat.
- *The Pinch Test*. In people under 50 years of age, at least one half of the body fat is directly under the skin. At many locations of the body, such as the back of the upper arm, the side of the lower chest, the back just below the shoulder blade, the back of the calf, or the abdomen, a fold of skin from the underlying soft tissue and bone can be pinched and lifted between the thumb and the forefinger. In general, the layer beneath the skin should be between one fourth and one half inch thick; because the skinfold is a double thickness, it should be 1/2 to 1 inch thick. A skinfold from the back of the upper arm that is more than 1 inch thick indicates excessive body fatness, whereas one

Table 7.27 Obesity Standards in Caucasian Americans

Age (years)	Minimum triceps skinfold thickness indicating obesity (millimeters)	
	Males	Females
5	12	14
6	12	15
7	13	16
8	14	17
9	15	18
10	16	20
11	17	21
12	18	22
13	18	23
14	17	23
15	16	24
16	15	25
17	14	26
18	15	27
19	15	27
20	16	28
21	17	28
22	18	28
23	18	28
24	19	28
25	20	29
26	20	29
27	21	29
28	22	29
29	22	29
30-50	23	30

Note. From *Overweight: Causes, Cost and Control* (p. 34) by J. Mayer, 1968, Englewood Cliffs, NJ: Prentice-Hall. Copyright © 1968 by Prentice-Hall, Inc., Englewood Cliffs, NJ 07632.

---

[8]From the book *Overweight: Causes, Cost and Control* by Jean Mayer, © 1968, by Prentice-Hall, Inc. Published by Prentice-Hall, Inc., Englewood Cliffs, NJ 07632.

less than 1/2 inch thick indicates abnormal thinness.

- *The Ruler Test.* This test relates to the slope of the abdomen when an individual is lying on his or her back. If the individual is not too fat, the surface of the abdomen between the flare of the ribs and the front of the pelvis is normally flat or slightly concave, and a ruler placed on the abdomen along the midline of the body should touch both the ribs and the pelvic area. Of course, pregnancy and certain pathological conditions can interfere with this test.
- *The Belt-Line Test.* In men, the circumference of the chest at the level of the nipples should exceed that of the abdomen at the level of the navel. If the circumference of the abdomen is greater, then abdominal fat is probably excessive.

Remember: If you are fit you are not fat, and if you are fat you are not fit.

Review Questions

1. What is a physical fitness program?
2. What is a physical fitness test?
3. What are the components of physical fitness according to the President's Council on Physical Fitness and Sports?
4. What are the four physical fitness factors common to both men and women according to Zuidema and Baumgartner? What test items are indicators of these four factors for men and women?
5. For what purposes can one use physical fitness test results?
6. What examination should always precede a physical fitness test or program?
7. What are the items on the revised AAHPER Youth Fitness Test? What factors does each item indicate?
8. Why should the practicing physical educator use the AAHPER Youth Fitness Test?
9. What did Montoye's investigations reveal about step tests?
10. What two methods for estimating percent of body fat are presented in this chapter?
11. What problems exist when attempting to use one equation for predicting percent body fat in different groups such as children, athletes, young adults, and senior citizens? How can you take these problems into account in assessments?
12. What is the purpose of the Siconolfi step test? How does it differ from other step tests?

Problems and Exercises

1. A physical education teacher used the AAHPER Youth Fitness Test to estimate the physical fitness of her fifth-grade class. She conducted the test and obtained the following measurements:

Student	Sex	Age	Sit-up	Shuttle run	Long jump	50-yard dash	9-minute run	Flexed-arm hang	Pull-up
S1	M	11	35	10.6	5-5	7.9	1824	—	3
S2	F	11	30	11.3	4-10	8.2	1537	10	—
S3	F	10	29	11.8	4-8	8.6	1478	9	—
S4	F	11	29	11.5	5-0	8.3	1501	11	—
S5	M	11	33	10.9	5-2	8.0	1734	—	1
S6	M	12	39	10.5	5-8	7.5	1886	—	4
S7	F	11	30	11.3	5-0	8.2	1573	10	—
S8	M	11	34	11.1	5-0	8.0	1734	—	1
S9	F	11	22	11.7	4-11	8.4	1573	8	—
S10	F	12	24	12.0	4-8	8.5	1491	2	—
S11	M	11	37	10.8	5-2	8.0	1779	—	3
S12	M	11	31	10.9	4-11	8.3	1594	—	0
S13	F	10	33	11.2	5-0	8.3	1583	18	—
S14	M	11	38	10.5	5-6	7.7	1915	—	2
S15	F	11	32	11.3	5-1	8.2	1573	15	—
S16	M	11	30	11.4	4-8	8.5	1544	—	0
S17	F	11	33	11.0	5-3	8.1	1645	15	—
S18	F	11	29	11.5	4-8	8.4	1468	11	—
S19	F	11	30	11.9	4-7	8.5	1393	7	—
S20	F	12	28	11.4	4-11	8.0	1560	10	—
S21	M	11	33	11.1	4-10	8.3	1779	—	1
S22	F	11	35	11.0	5-1	8.0	1645	20	—
S23	F	11	29	11.7	4-11	8.3	1537	11	—
S24	M	11	37	10.6	5-6	7.9	1824	—	3
S25	F	11	28	11.7	4-8	8.4	1501	7	—

From the National Norm Tables, find the percentile rank
for each student in each event.
Answer:

Student	Sit-up	Shuttle run	Long jump	50-yard dash	9-minute run	Flexed-arm hang	Pull-up
S1	55	60	60	60-65	55	—	60-65
S2	55	55	45	55	50	50	—
S3	55	50	50	50	45	50	—
S4	50	50	55	50	45	55	—
S5	45	50	50	50-55	45	—	30-45
S6	65	60	65	70	55	—	70-75
S7	55	55	55	55	55	50	—
S8	50	40	40	50-55	45	—	30-45
S9	25	40	50	45	55	45	—
S10	25	25	30	30	40	20	—
S11	60	55	45-50	50-55	50	—	60-65
S12	40	50	35	40	30	—	0-25
S13	85	70	70	65	60	75	—
S14	65	65-70	65-70	70	65	—	50-55
S15	65	55	60	55	55	65	—
S16	35	30	25	30	25	—	0-25
S17	70	65-70	70	60	65	65	—
S18	50	50	40	45	40	55	—
S19	55	35	35	40	30	40	—
S20	45	50	45	55	50	50	—
S21	45	40	30	40	50	—	30-45
S22	75	65-70	60	65	65	75	—
S23	50	40	50	50	50	55	—
S24	60	60	65-70	60-65	55	—	60-65
S25	45	40	40	45	45	40	—

2. Calculate a class $\overline{X}$ and σ for each event in Problem 1.

3. Calculate an $\overline{X}$ and σ for each event from the results produced by the girls in Problem 1.
Answer:

	Sit-ups	Shuttle run	Long jump	50-yard dash	9-minute run	Flexed-arm hang
$\overline{X}$	29.4	11.5	4-8.6	8.3	1,537.2	10.9
σ	3.3	.3	2.4 in.	.2	67.4	4.6

4. Calculate an $\overline{X}$ and σ for each event from the results produced by the boys in Problem 1.

5. Calculate a Pearsonian correlation coefficient between the results of the shuttle run and the 50-yard dash in Problem 1. (Caution: do not use rounded values.)
Answer: $r = .86$

6. Convert the $\overline{X}$ values for the long jump and 9-minute run in Problem 3 to meters.

7. A 10th-grade high school student performed the Harvard Step Test and completed the full test. His pulse was counted three times at 1, 2, and 3 minutes after exercise with the following results: 1 minute = 72 beats, 2 minutes = 55 beats, 3 minutes = 40 beats. What is his PEI? How does he rate in physical conditioning?
Answer: PEI = 90 (Excellent)

8. Use the value of the heart beat after 1 minute of rest in Problem 7 and calculate the student's PEI using the short form of the Harvard Step Test. What is his PEI? How does he rate in physical conditioning using the short form?

9. Develop a list of physical education activities in your school for the general categories of unrestricted activity, moderate or submaximal stress activities with frequent rest periods, and restricted activities with low stress on the cardiovascular system. Consult with appropriate health authorities when compiling your list. How can you test for degree of strength and fitness in the various groups?

10. What is the relationship between the composite score on the six-item AAHPER test and a smaller battery of items such as pull-ups, sit-ups, and 50-yard dash or pull-ups, sit-ups, and 600-yard run? What conclusion can be drawn if your correlation coefficient is high or low?

11. Compute local norms for the AAHPER test items. How do they compare with national norms for children of the same age?

12. Compute correlation coefficients between scores on the 600-yard run, 9-minute run, Cotton Step Test, and Harvard Step Test? If the correlations are high (.80 or above), what does this mean? What would low correlations mean? What factors could account for high, moderate, or low relationships?

13. Using the pinch test or one of the other subjective estimates, classify your pupils into one of three groups: nonobese, obesity uncertain, obese. Which group performs better on the various strength and fitness tests? How can you best use this information? Would another teacher place the same children in the same categories that you did?

14. Norm data for the Cooper's Aerobics Tests are presented in English measurement units in Tables 7.19 to 7.21. Prepare new norm charts by converting the distances run, swum, or cycled to meters.

15. Estimate your pupils' maximum oxygen consumption from the Cotton Step Test, the Queens College Step Test, and the 12-Minute Run. Do you get the same values from the three different estimates? Compute correlation coefficients for the three different estimates.

16. Estimate pupils' percent body fat using body diameter circumference and skinfold measures. Are the values for percent body fat similar? Compute the relationship between the various ways of estimating percent body fat.

17. List the sources of measurement error in predicting body density and percent body fat. How can you reduce these errors?

Bibliography

American Association for Health, Physical Education, and Recreation. (1965). *Youth fitness test manual* (rev. ed.). Washington, DC: Author.

American Association for Health, Physical Education, and Recreation. (1976). *Youth fitness test manual* (rev. 3rd ed.). Washington, DC: Author.

American Alliance for Health, Physical Education, Recreation, and Dance. (1980). *Lifetime health-related physical fitness test manual*. Reston, VA: Author.

Åstrand, P.O., & Rodahl, K. (1977). *Textbook of work physiology: Physiological bases of exercise* (2nd ed.). New York: McGraw-Hill.

Barrow, H.M., & McGee, R. (1979). *A practical approach to measurement in physical education* (3rd ed.). Philadelphia: Lea and Febiger.

Baumgartner, T.A., & Jackson, A.S. (1982). *Measurement for evaluation in physical education* (2nd ed.). Dubuque, IA: William C. Brown.

Behnke, A.R., & Wilmore, J.H. (1974). *Evaluation and regulation of body build and composition.* Englewood Cliffs, NJ: Prentice-Hall.

Brouha, L. (1943). The step test: A simple method of measuring physical fitness for muscular work in young men. *Research Quarterly,* **14**(1), 31-36.

Bulbulian, R. (1984). The influence of somatotype on anthropometric prediction of body composition in young women. *Medicine and Science in Sports and Exercise,* **16**(4), 389-397.

Bulbulian, R., Johnson, R.E., Gruber, J.J., & Darabos, B. (1987). Body composition in paraplegic male athletes. *Medicine and Science in Sports and Exercise,* **19**(3).

Burke, E.J. (1976). Validity of selected laboratory and field tests of physical working capacity. *Research Quarterly,* **47**(1), 95-104.

Clarke, H.H. (Ed.). (1971). Basic understanding of physical fitness. *Physical Fitness Research Digest,* **1**(1). Washington, DC: President's Council on Physical Fitness and Sports.

Clarke, H.H. (Ed.). (1975). Physical fitness testing in schools. *Physical Fitness Research Digest,* **5**(1). Washington, DC: President's Council on Physical Fitness and Sports.

Clarke, H.H. (1976). *Application of measurement to health and physical education* (5th ed.). Englewood Cliffs, NJ: Prentice-Hall.

Cooper, K.H. (1968). A means of assessing maximal oxygen intake. *Journal of the American Medical Association,* **203**, 201-204.

Cooper, K.H. (1977). *The aerobics way.* New York: M. Evans.

Cooper, K.H. (1982). *The aerobics program for total well-being.* New York: M. Evans.

Cotton, D.J. (1971). A modified step test for group cardiovascular testing. *Research Quarterly,* **42**(1), 91-95.

Dull, C., Metcalfe, H., & Brooks, W. (1949). *Modern physics* (rev. ed.). New York: Henry Holt.

Durnin, J.V.G.A., & Womersley, J. (1974). Body fat assessed from total body density and its estimation from skinfold thickness: Measurements on 481 men and women aged 16-72 years. *British Journal of Nutrition,* **32**, 77-92.

Falls, H.B., Ismail, A.H., MacLeod, D.F., Wiebers, J.E., Christian, J.E., & Kessler, M.V. (1965). Development of physical fitness test batteries by factor analysis results. *The Journal of Sports Medicine and Physical Fitness,* **5**(4), 185-197.

Fleishman, E.A. (1964). *The structure and measurement of physical fitness.* Englewood Cliffs, NJ: Prentice-Hall.

Gallagher, J.R., & Brouha, L. (1943). A simple method of testing the physical fitness of boys. *Research Quarterly,* **14**(1), 24-30.

Heyward, V.H. (1984). *Designs for fitness: A guide to physical fitness appraisal and exercise prescription.* Minneapolis: Burgess.

Hodgkins, J., & Skubic, V. (1963). Cardiovascular efficiency test scores for college women in the United States. *Research Quarterly,* **34**(4), 454-461.

Holland, J. (1974, February). *The estimation of oxygen uptake from a step test.* Paper presented at the Southern District annual meeting of the American Association of Health, Physical Education, and Recreation, Norfolk, VA.

Humphries, L.L., & Gruber, J.J. (1986). Nutritional behaviors of university majorettes. *The Physician and Sportsmedicine,* **14**(11), 91-98.

Hunsicker, P.A. (1958). AAHPER physical fitness test battery. *Journal of Health, Physical Education, and Recreation,* **29**(6), 24-25.

Ismail, A.H., MacLeod, D.F., & Falls, H.B. (1964). *Evaluation of selected tests of motor and/or physical fitness.* Unpublished manuscript, Purdue University, Department of Physical Education for Men, West Lafayette, IN.

Ismail, A.H., Falls, H.B., & MacLeod, D.F. (1965). Development of a criterion for physical fitness tests from factor analysis results. *Journal of Applied Physiology,* **20**(5), 991-999.

Jackson, A.S., & Coleman, A.E. (1976). Validation of distance run tests for elementary school children. *Research Quarterly, 47*(1), 86-94.

Jackson, A.S., Franks, B.D., Katch, F.I., Katch, V.L., Plowman, S.L., & Safrit, M.J. (1976). *Revision of the AAHPER youth fitness test.* Position paper presented at the Measurement and Evaluation, Physical Fitness, and Research meetings of the annual meeting of the American Alliance for Health, Physical Education, and Recreation, Milwaukee, WI.

Jackson, A.S., & Pollock, M.L. (1978). Generalized equations for predicting body density of men. *British Journal of Nutrition, 40*, 497-504.

Jackson, A.S., Pollock, M.L., & Ward, A. (1980). Generalized equations for predicting body density of women. *Medicine and Science in Sports and Exercise, 12*(3), 175-182.

Johnson, R.E., Bulbulian, R., Gruber, J.J., Darabos, B., & Sundheim, R. (1986). Estimating percent body fat of paraplegic athletes. *Palestrae, 3*(1), 29-37.

Karpovich, P.V., & Sinning, W.E. (1971). *Physiology of muscular activity.* Philadelphia: W.B. Saunders.

Katch, F.I., & McArdle, W.D. (1983). *Nutrition, weight control, and exercise* (2nd ed.). Philadelphia: Lea and Febiger.

Kraus, H., & Hirschland, R.P. (1954). Minimum muscular fitness tests in school children. *Research Quarterly, 25*(2), 178-188.

Kraus, H., & Raab, W. (1961). *Hypokinetic diseases.* Springfield, IL: Charles C. Thomas.

Lohman, T.G., Pollock, M.L., Slaughter, M.H., Brandon, L.J., & Boileau, R.A. (1984). Methodological factors and the prediction of body fat in female athletes. *Medicine and Science in Sports and Exercise, 16*(1), 92-96.

Mathews, D.K. (1978). *Measurement in physical education* (5th ed.). Philadelphia: W.B. Saunders.

Mayer, J. (1968). *Overweight—Causes, cost, and control.* Englewood Cliffs, NJ: Prentice-Hall.

Meyers, C.R., & Blesh, T.E. (1962). *Measurement in physical education.* New York: Ronald.

Montoye, H.J. (1978). Circulatory-respiratory fitness. In H.J. Montoye (Ed.), *An introduction to measurement in physical education* (pp. 91-121; 150-177). Boston: Allyn and Bacon.

Morris, J.N., Adam, C., Chave, S.P.W., Sirey, C., Epstein, L., & Sheehan, D.J. (1973). Vigorous exercise in leisure time and the incidence of coronary heart disease. *Lancet, 1*, 333-339.

Paffenbarger, R.S., & Hale, W.E. (1975). Work activity and coronary heart mortality. *New England Journal of Medicine, 292*, 545-550.

Paffenbarger, R.S., Hyde, R.T., Wing, A., & Hsieh, C.C. (1986). Physical activity, all-cause mortality, and longevity of college alumni. *The New England Journal of Medicine, 314*(10), 605-613.

Pařízková, J. (1961). Total body fat and skinfold thickness in children. *Metabolism, 10*, 794-802.

Pollock, M.L., Schmidt, D.H., & Jackson, A.S. (1980). Measurement of cardiorespiratory fitness and body composition in the clinical setting. *Comprehensive Therapy, 6*(9), 12-27.

Ricci, B. (1974). Fitness testing. In G.H. McGlynn (Ed.), *Issues in physical education and sports* (pp. 73-80). Palo Alto, CA: National Press.

Safrit, M.J. (1981). *Evaluation in physical education* (2nd ed.). Englewood Cliffs, NJ: Prentice-Hall.

Siconolfi, S.F., Garber, C.E., Lasater, T.M., & Carleton, R.A. (1985). A simple, valid step test for estimating maximal oxygen uptake in epidemiological studies. *American Journal of Epidemiology, 121*(3), 382-390.

Sinning, W.E., Dolney, D.G., Little, K.D., Cunningham, L.N., Racaniello, A., & Siconolfi, S.F. (1985). Validity of "generalized" equations for body composition analysis in male athletes. *Medicine and Science in Sports and Exercise, 17*(1), 124-130.

Sinning, W.E., & Wilson, J.R. (1984). Validity of generalized equation for body composition analysis in women athletes. *Research Quarterly for Exercise and Sport, 55*(2), 153-160.

Skubic, V., & Hodgkins, J. (1963). A cardiovascular efficiency test for girls and women. *Research Quarterly, 34*(2), 191-198.

Skubic, V., & Hodgkins, J. (1963). Cardio-vascular efficiency test scores for college women in the United States. *Research Quarterly,* **34**(4), 454-461.

Skubic, V., & Hodgkins, J. (1964). Cardio-vascular efficiency test scores for junior and senior high school girls in the United States. *Research Quarterly,* **35**(2), 184-192.

Sloan, A.W., & de V. Weir, J.B. (1970). Nomo-grams for prediction of body density and total body fat from skinfold measurements. *Journal of Applied Physiology,* **28**(1), 221-222.

Smith, J.E., & Mansfield, E.R. (1984). Body composition prediction in university football players. *Medicine and Science in Sports and Exercise,* **16**(4), 398-405.

Thorland, W.G., Johnson, G.O., Tharp, G.D., Fagot, J.G., & Hammer, R.W. (1984). Validity of anthropometric equations for the estimation of body density in adolescent athletes. *Medicine and Science in Sports and Exercise,* **16**(1), 77-81.

Welch, H.G. (1978). Endurance. In H.J. Montoye (Ed.), *An introduction to measurement in physical education* (pp. 80-90). Boston: Allyn and Bacon.

Wilmore, J.H., & Behnke, A.R. (1969). An anthropometric estimation of body density and lean body weight in young men. *Journal of Applied Physiology,* **27**(1), 25-31.

Wilmore, J.H. (1983). Appetite and body composition consequent to physical activity. *Research Quarterly for Exercise and Sport,* **54**(4), 415-425.

Zuidema, M.A., & Baumgartner, T.A. (1974). Second factor analysis of physical fitness tests. *Research Quarterly,* **45**(3), 247-256.

Chapter 8

Sport Skills Testing

Many existing sport skills tests were developed 20 to 50 years ago. Since then, many improvements in measurement techniques, changes in rules and playing procedures, and developments in the identification and classification of skills and skill patterns have rendered many of these older tests obsolete. A major flaw of many older skill tests is that their test items and/or the way they are administered to students are not related to actual game play. The validity of such tests is certainly questionable, especially if the test scores are used for grading purposes at the end of an instructional unit.

For example, volleying a ball back and forth above a 10-foot line on a wall for 30 seconds is not the way a volley is actually played during a game. This test item may be used validly in grading wall volley ability, but its use in estimating volleyball *playing* ability is dubious. Because a volleyball player must return many different types of shots during a game, an effective volleyball skills test must measure a par-

ticipant's skill in returning these various types of shots. The wall volley is certainly a good drill for beginners and may have merit in testing beginners' skills; the items may be relevant for classification but not for other purposes. Indeed, one test item may be well suited for classifying participants into different groups for instructional purposes, but for other purposes and more crucial decisions a number of test items and/or ratings must be utilized.

Physical educators must also remember that validity, reliability, and norms are situation-specific; the applicability of tests, items, and norms should not be overgeneralized beyond the purposes and populations for which they are intended. Many skill tests and norms, for example, were developed on college students. Thus they are probably inappropriate for use in testing junior and senior high school students because of obvious differences between college and high school students' physical and emotional maturity.

Evaluation of Sport Skills Tests

When evaluating tests, you should employ the criteria of validity, reliability, objectivity, norms, standardized directions, and administrative feasibility to the tests and their items. You may find the Test Evaluation Form presented in Figure 8.1 to be useful for evaluating tests. For illustration purposes, the form in Figure 8.1 has been completed for the AAHPER Archery Skills Test. Several sport skills tests presented in this chapter are critiqued as examples of how you should evaluate the other tests discussed in the chapter as well as tests not included here. The first critiqued test is the AAHPER Archery Skills Test. Its test items are discrete tasks performed in a stationary or closed performance environment. In a second example, two early basketball skills tests for men and women (1934, 1952) are presented. They are critiqued from the frame of reference that basketball is a serial task performed in an open environment. The deficiencies found in early tests are indicated. Over the course of time, changes in rules and playing style mandate the development of more relevant tests. After these older tests are reviewed and critiqued, the new AAHPERD Basketball Skills Tests (1984) for boys and girls are examined in detail. You should again use the form illustrated in Figure 8.1 to evaluate this test.

Although it is not the intent of this chapter to present directions for administering and scoring skill tests for all sports, some tests are presented for purposes of reference and illustration. Skill tests for a few individual, dual, and team sports that are frequently offered in junior and senior high school curricula are considered and critiqued. The tests reviewed in this chapter contain performance skill items that in most cases still apply today. You must make a decision as to how you intend to use test data based on the nature of each skill item, the way the test item is performed, and the age of participants.

Archery

In 1967, the American Association for Health, Physical Education, and Recreation (AAHPER) published an *Archery Skills Test Manual* for use with boys and girls. The tests are designed to be used as practice rounds or "practice tests" to measure individuals' achievement in shooting with a bow and arrow at a 48-inch (1.22-m) target from Distance A (10 yards or 9.15 m), Distance B (20 yards or 18.29 m), and Distance C (30 yards or 27.44 m). Students in the class can be grouped into squads of four with one squad shooting at each target. Each archer shoots two "ends" (sets of arrows shot and scored as a group) of six arrows each for a total of 12 arrows. In addition, each archer can be scored on a pass/fail basis on the following items of form: bracing the bow, stance, nocking the arrow, finger placement, draw, anchor, release, and follow-through.

Test Procedures

A more detailed description of actual testing procedures with percentile rank norms established for boys and girls follows.[1] The purpose of the AAHPER Archery Skills Test is to measure accuracy in shooting with a bow and arrow at a standard 48-inch (121.92-cm) archery target from Distance A (10 yards or 9.15 m), Distance B (20 yards or 18.29 m), and Distance C (30 yards or 27.44 m).

---

[1]From the *Archery Skills Test Manual* (1967). Reprinted by permission of the American Alliance for Health, Physical Education, Recreation, and Dance, 1900 Association Drive, Reston, VA 22091.

Test Evaluation Form

Title <u>ARCHERY SKILLS TEST</u> Author <u>AAHPER</u>   Publisher <u>AAHPER</u>

Date Constructed <u>1967</u> Cost <u>$3.70</u> Time Required <u>NOT REPORTED</u>

Purpose <u>ACHIEVEMENT IN SHOOTING</u> PRACTICE TESTS OF Groups Applicable <u>12-18 YRS. OF AGE</u> BOYS AND GIRLS Forms Available <u>ONE</u>

Practical Features <u>ITEMS OF FORM AS WELL AS SKILL IN SHOOTING AT 10, 20, AND 30 YDS.</u>

Description Test Items <u>BRACING BOW; STANCE; NOCKING ARROW; FINGER PLACEMENT;</u>
<u>DRAW; ANCHOR; RELEASE; FOLLOW-THROUGH; SHOOT AT TARGET 10, 20, 30 YARDS AWAY</u>

How Items Selected <u>BY PROJECT COMMITTEE</u>

Difficulty Level of Items <u>EASY TO MODERATE FOR BOYS</u> TOO DIFFICULT FOR GIRLS Motor or Mental Functions

Sampled by Items <u>EYE-HAND COORDINATION IN AIMING AND SHOOTING AT TARGET.</u>
<u>KNOWLEDGE OF SAFETY AS APPLIED IN CLASS SHOOTING ENVIRONMENT</u>

Type of Validity Established (Describe): <u>CONTENT VALIDITY BY PROFESSIONAL</u>
<u>JUDGMENT OF EXPERTS</u>

Size of Validity Coefficient(s) <u>NO VALIDATION STUDY REPORTED</u> Describe Characteristics of

Validation Sample <u>N/A</u>

Size and Type of Reliability Coefficient(s) <u>NO RELIABILITY STUDY REPORTED</u>
<u>HOWEVER, AAHPER CLAIMS RELIABILITY OF AT LEAST .80.</u>

Comments on Adequacy of Directions for Administration and Scoring of Test Items <u>HIGHLY</u>
<u>ADEQUATE; DIRECTIONS ARE CLEAR AND EXPLICIT</u>

Special Training Required for Administration <u>CAREFUL ATTENTION TO INSTRUCTIONS</u>
<u>AND SAFETY; KNOWLEDGE OF BASIC ARCHERY</u>

Types of Norms Available <u>NATIONAL NORMS</u>

Describe Norm Group <u>BOYS AND GIRLS 12-18 YEARS OF AGE</u>

Comments of Reviewers <u>N/A; CONCURRENT VALIDITY NEEDS TO BE ESTABLISHED</u>
<u>ALSO, RELIABILITY STUDIES ARE NEEDED FOR METHODS OF BOW SIGHTING.</u>

Your General Evaluation of the Test <u>SUITABLE FOR PURPOSE VALIDITY, RELIABILITY,</u>
<u>AND NORMS NEED TO BE ESTABLISHED FOR METHODS OF BOW SIGHTING. DEVELOP LOCAL NORMS.</u>

Figure 8.1 Test evaluation form. From Baumgartner, Ted A., and Andrew S. Jackson, *Measurement for Evaluation in Physical Education*, 2nd. ed. © 1982 Wm. C. Brown Publishers, Dubuque, Iowa. All rights reserved. Reprinted by permission.

Equipment. Standard equipment for the test includes

- a shooting range on level ground of at least 200 feet long and 50 feet wide for each archery target in use;
- standard 48-inch (121.92-cm) face archery targets placed on suitable stands so that the center of the target is 48 inches (121.92 cm) above the ground;
- when the test is given indoors, a gymnasium floor at least 96 feet in length with appropriate backstops behind the targets;
- bows of assorted pull strengths ranging from 15 to 40 pounds, depending on the age and ability of the archers being tested;
- arrows of 24 to 28 inches in length to fit the bows and archers, with 8 to 10 arrows of the same color for each archer (archers may use their own equipment if it is inspected and safe);
- an arm guard, finger tab or glove, and quiver for each archer; and
- a line marker, stakes, measuring tape, whistle, squad score cards, pencils, and class composite record sheet.

Description. The standard archery target is made of straw and is usually mounted on a wooden tripod. The target face may be made of oil cloth or heavy paper with five concentric circles, with the center circle 9.6 inches in diameter and the others increasing by 4.8-inch increments (see Figure 8.2). The center circle is painted gold, followed by red, blue, and black circles with the outer circle white.

Squads of four archers shoot at any one target. Each archer shoots two ends of six arrows at each distance for which he or she qualifies. Each archer shoots one end, is scored on these arrows, and then waits his or her turn

to shoot the remaining end. The scorer withdraws the arrows and announces the score of each arrow as it is withdrawn. The recorder records the score of each arrow on the squad score card. After each archer has shot 12 arrows, the total score at the distance is recorded.

After all archers in a squad have completed shooting two ends at Distance A, the squad members move back to the second Distance B, take their practice shots, and again shoot two ends as before. After completing shooting at Distance B, the squad members (boys only) move to Distance C, and, after practicing, shoot two ends in rotation as before. Archers stand astride the shooting line while shooting. Any method of aiming can be used (i.e., bow sight, point of aim, or instinctive shooting). The archer may adjust the aim during the practice shots or during testing, but no additional practice shots are allowed for this purpose. Archers who fail to score 10 points at any distance may be disqualified from shooting from the next distance at the tester's discretion.

Rules. The following rules must be observed during the test:

- The archer must stand astride the shooting line while shooting.
- Four practice shots at each distance are allowed.
- The archer may adjust the point of aim during practice shots or during testing, but no additional practice shots for this purpose are allowed.
- Each archer shoots one end at a time and then waits his or her turn to shoot the other end.

Scoring. Arrows hitting in the center (gold) circle count 9 points; arrows hitting in the next

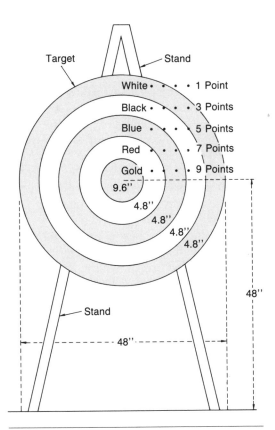

Figure 8.2 Archery target face. From the *Archery Skills Test Manual* (1967). Reprinted by permission of the American Alliance for Health, Physical Education, Recreation, and Dance, 1900 Association Drive, Reston, VA 22091.

(red) circle count 7 points; arrows hitting in the blue circle count 5 points; arrows hitting in the black circle count 3 points; and arrows hitting in the outer (white) circle count 1 point. Arrows striking in two color areas count the value of the higher scoring area. Arrows striking the target but falling to the ground count 7 points regardless of where they strike. The maximum

score for shooting from the first two distances (for girls) is 216 points, and the maximum score for shooting from all three distances (for boys) is 324 points.

Critique

The following discussion amplifies the comments noted in Figure 8.1. Validity is the degree to which a test measures what it is supposed to measure. Although there are several types of validity, any test should contain relevant content, and its content should result in test scores that correlate highly with the final standing of archers competing in a tournament. In other words, the better tournament archers should score higher on the skill test, and the archers in the lower tournament rankings should score much lower on the test. Most information concerning the criteria used to evaluate a test should be presented in a test manual. Careful examination of the *AAHPER Archery Test Manual* indicates that on the surface the test possesses good content validity as related to purpose: "These skill tests should be regarded as 'practice tests' because they are intended to be used by players as a way of improving abilities in the fundamental skills of archery" (p. 12). Because national norms based on 600 to 900 scores for each sex at each age are presented in the manual, a pupil's score can be compared to the scores of other pupils around the country. Ratings of form as well as target points provide feedback to the student. The content validity of the test in terms of the fundamental archery skills taught in basic courses appears to be well established.

A major problem, however, is that the test manual provides no information concerning concurrent or predictive validity. Thus it has not been demonstrated that scores on this archery skill test can estimate archery ability in actual competition. Teachers can and should establish this relationship in their own schools if they intend to use the test scores for grading purposes. In all likelihood, this relationship will be quite high because the test items are performed in a manner similar to and in fact probably replicate the way a class would shoot in an actual tournament. This validity should be easy to establish because there is very little variability between the way archery skills are performed in a testing versus a tournament environment. The skills are discrete; hence movement patterns in archery performance are not complex in either a testing or tournament setting. Similarly, targets and archers are stationary in an unchanging terrain. Fundamental archery skills are taught this way and are logically tested this way.

The *AAHPER Archery Test Manual* indicates that shooting from 30 yards (27.44 m) is too difficult for girls but does not indicate why. Perhaps the girls lacked sufficient strength to draw the proper bow to shoot that distance. Physical educators must recognize the fact that students must possess sufficient strength, flexibility, and balance in order to perform many skill test items. If they lack one of these components, the test becomes a test of strength rather than archery skill. Insofar as 65% of the girls tested at ages 12 and 13 and 35% of those tested at ages 17 and 18 were unable to score from a distance of 30 yards (27.44 m), it was proper not to include that distance in the norms.

As progression in archery instruction increases through intermediate and advanced levels, skill complexities and environmental conditions will change. Barrett (1969) briefly described a variety of archery sports and games such as field or range shooting, clout shooting, flight shooting, hunting, and novelty shooting. To develop an appropriate test item, the instructor should attempt to structure the test item and its administration to simulate the actual performance and environmental conditions under which the student will use the skill.

Reliability is reported in the manual to be at least .70 for event scores on the basis of accuracy and form. The AAHPER Skills Test Project Committee has adopted this standard in the *Archery Test Manual* (1967, p. 9) for all test items scored in this manner for various sports. Thus actual reliability coefficients for each distance, each sex, and each age have apparently not been computed. In addition, students are permitted to use any method of aiming (i.e., use of bow sights, use of point of aim, or instinctive shooting). One must ask if the reliability coefficient will vary among different sighting methods. In other words, will student scores be as consistent regardless of sighting method? If, for example, pupils' score variability is quite low when using bow sights but high when using the point of aim method, the former is more reliable than the latter. Hence, you can use test data with a greater degree of confidence when students are tested using the bow sight method. In summary, then, the *reliability* of the archery skill tests discussed here needs to be established. Teachers in local schools can do this, but their reliability studies must be specific and must calculate reliability coefficients for both boys and girls for each age and method of sighting.

Norms for the AAHPER Archery Skill Test appear in Tables 8.1 and 8.2 and are presented in percentile ranks that correspond to the test scores in points for boys and girls, ages 12 through 18, at the various distances. Because more than 600 pupils of each sex and age were tested, one would assume that these are adequate national norms. However, one must ask several questions at this point. First, were the data collected in a standardized way in the many schools where testing occurred? Second, will the norms vary across methods of sighting? In Tables 8.1 and 8.2, everything is pooled in the norms presented. Using the descriptive statistics

Table 8.1   AAHPER Archery Test—Boys Percentile Scores Based on Age/Test Scores in Points for 12 Arrows

	Age (years)																			
	12-13				14				15				16				17-18			
Yards[a]	10	20	30	Total	10	20	30	Total	10	20	30	Total	10	20	30	Total	10	20	30	Total
Percentile																				
100th	91	70	45	195	96	75	50	210	100	90	81	270	100	100	95	270	100	95	85	270
95th	83	53	28	156	88	61	34	179	97	77	50	215	99	78	56	220	98	78	64	222
90th	78	44	24	138	80	48	28	160	94	70	41	195	97	71	47	205	96	72	53	206
85th	73	38	22	128	78	45	24	150	90	66	35	187	96	67	43	197	93	67	47	197
80th	70	34	18	122	75	41	21	146	88	63	31	177	91	63	40	189	90	63	42	190
75th	67	31	16	112	72	38	18	143	84	58	28	167	90	59	36	181	88	59	39	184
70th	64	28	14	103	70	36	16	139	80	54	25	158	88	56	32	173	86	55	37	176
65th	61	26	12	98	68	33	15	136	78	51	22	149	86	54	30	163	84	52	35	166
60th	59	24	11	93	67	30	13	130	76	47	20	140	84	51	28	160	82	49	31	158
55th	57	23	9	87	65	28	11	124	73	42	17	130	80	48	25	154	79	46	28	151
50th	54	22	8	81	63	26	10	119	69	39	15	120	79	46	23	148	77	43	26	144
45th	50	20	7	74	60	24	8	114	65	36	14	114	77.	43	22	142	74	40	24	136
40th	48	18	6	67	57	22	7	110	62	34	13	107	75	41	20	136	71	37	21	130
35th	45	16	4	60	55	20	5	106	59	31	12	100	72	39	18	129	68	34	20	125
30th	42	14	0	54	52	18	4	98	55	28	11	94	70	36	16	123	63	32	17	119
25th	38	12	0	47	45	16	0	87	51	24	10	87	67	33	13	117	59	29	16	112
20th	34	10	0	38	40	14	0	77	48	21	9	79	61	28	11	110	55	25	11	109
15th	31	8	0	28	36	12	0	69	43	18	7	70	51	25	9	103	48	20	9	96
10th	26	6	0	21	31	10	0	61	36	15	6	62	50	20	6	80	40	17	6	86
5th	16	3	0	15	25	6	0	43	25	9	2	43	40	14	2	61	27	11	3	65
0	0	0	0	0	0	0	0	0	0	0	0	0	0	0	0	0	0	0	0	0

Note. From *Archery Skills Test Manual* (1967). Reprinted by permission of the American Alliance for Health, Physical Education, Recreation, and Dance, 1900 Association Drive, Reston, VA 22091.

[a]10 yards = 9.15 meters; 20 yards = 18.29 meters; 30 yards = 27.44 meters.

Table 8.2 AAHPER Archery Test—
Girls Percentile Scores Based on Age/Test Scores in Points for 12 Arrows

	Age (years)														
	12-13			14			15			16			17-18		
Yards[a]	10	20	Total	10	20	Total	10	20	Total	10	20	Total	10	20	Total
Percentile															
100th	85	60	129	89	70	159	96	81	160	100	91	161	100	95	180
95th	69	40	100	74	47	109	82	55	130	87	58	134	87	71	149
90th	60	29	89	68	38	99	75	47	112	80	50	115	80	60	129
85th	50	22	81	63	35	89	70	43	103	73	44	107	73	52	123
80th	46	19	69	58	32	84	66	39	96	67	40	100	69	47	116
75th	41	17	64	54	28	79	63	34	89	64	36	96	66	42	109
70th	38	15	60	50	25	75	60	32	85	60	32	91	62	40	104
65th	35	13	55	48	23	70	56	29	80	56	29	87	58	36	100
60th	34	12	50	46	21	66	53	27	77	53	27	80	55	32	95
55th	32	10	46	43	20	62	51	25	73	49	25	76	52	29	91
50th	30	9	42	41	18	58	49	23	70	46	22	72	48	26	85
45th	27	7	38	38	16	54	46	22	66	43	20	67	46	24	78
40th	24	6	35	35	14	50	43	20	62	41	18	63	42	21	73
35th	22	1	32	33	12	47	40	18	59	38	16	60	40	19	68
30th	19	0	28	30	10	45	37	16	55	33	14	56	38	18	64
25th	16	0	25	28	8	42	34	13	51	31	12	52	35	16	60
20th	14	0	22	25	7	40	31	11	45	29	10	47	31	14	53
15th	12	0	17	22	0	34	27	8	40	25	8	41	28	12	45
10th	10	0	12	19	0	28	21	6	33	21	6	36	24	9	38
5th	6	0	5	12	0	22	13	0	25	16	0	26	19	0	30
0	0	0	0	0	0	0	0	0	0	0	0	0	0	0	0

Note. From *Archery Skills Test Manual* (1967). Reprinted by permission of the American Alliance for Health, Physical Education, Recreation, and Dance, 1900 Association Drive, Reston, VA 22091.

[a]10 yards = 9.15 meters; 20 yards = 18.29 meters.

methods recommended in chapter 2, teachers can develop specific local norms that are relevant for grading purposes. The national norms presented in the AAHPER manual should only be used by individual pupils to enable them to see how their performance compares to those of other pupils around the country.

It should be pointed out that the *AAHPER Archery Test Manual* is well developed. It includes explanations of how the tests were selected and how testing data were collected; instructions for preparing the testing environment, organizing the class for test administration, and using the norm tables; a description of needed equipment and facilities; safety precautions; rules for scoring; sample scoring sheets; and class record forms. In addition, the test items are well illustrated. Indeed, the criteria of *standardized directions* and *administrative feasibility* appear to have been met.

Badminton

The two badminton tests that follow are based on two basic skills: the clear (Miller Wall Volley Test) and the short serve (French Badminton Test).

Miller Wall Volley Test

The Miller Wall Volley Test[2] (1951) was developed upon discovering that men and women consistently use "clears" (i.e., shots hit high and deep into the opponent's court) more frequently than any other shot in badminton singles play. Test procedures were developed based on movies of the various types of clears. The test requires a wall space at least 10 feet (3.048 m) wide and 15 feet (4.572 m) high, with a line marked on the wall at a height of 7 feet, 6 inches (2.2286 m). A floor line is marked 10 feet (3.048 m) from and parallel to the wall. On the signal, the pupil puts the sponge-end shuttlecock into play with a legal serve from behind the 10-foot (3.048-m) line and continually volleys the rebounds for 30 seconds. Three 30-second trials are performed with a rest period of 30 seconds between trials. A practice period of 1 minute is given before the first trial. The final score is the total number of hits made from behind the restraining line that strike the wall on or

above the 7-foot, 6-inch (2.286-m) line, including "carries" or double hits. The shuttlecock remains in play regardless of faults. A validity coefficient of .83 with a criterion of badminton playing ability in college women is reported. Reliability was estimated to be .94.

French Badminton Test

The French Badminton Test[3] (Scott, Carpenter, French, & Kuhl, 1941) consists of two items including (a) the short serve and (b) the clear. The short serve test involves serving 20 shuttlecocks either consecutively or in two groups of 10 to a target in the opposite service court by directing the bird beneath a rope stretched 20 inches (50.8 cm) above and parallel to the net as illustrated in Figure 8.3. Illegal serves are repeated. The radii of the target arcs are 22 inches (55.88 cm), 30 inches (76.2 cm), 38 inches (96.42 cm), and 46 inches (116.84 cm) respectively.

The clear test consists of returning 20 serves over a rope stretched 14 feet (4.267 m) across the court from the net and 8 feet (2.438 m) high and onto a target as illustrated in Figure 8.4. To receive the serve, the testee stands on the center line between two 2-inch (5.08-cm) squares marked on the floor 3 feet (.9144 m) either side of the center line and 11 feet (3.352 m) from the net. An experienced player serves each shuttlecock from the intersection of the short service and center lines on the target side. The serve must reach the testee and be between the squares, but the testee may move into desired position once the serve is made. The target markings consist of a parallel line 2 feet (.6096 m) toward the net from the doubles rear service line and a similar line 2 feet (.6096 m)

[2]Adapted from "A Badminton Wall Volley Test" by F.A. Miller, 1951, *Research Quarterly*, **22**(2), pp. 208-213. Reprinted by permission of the American Alliance for Health, Physical Education, Recreation, and Dance, 1900 Association Drive, Reston, VA 22091.

[3]Adapted from "Achievement Examinations in Badminton" by M.G. Scott, 1941, *Research Quarterly*, **12**(2), pp. 242-253. Reprinted by permission of the American Alliance for Health, Physical Education, Recreation, and Dance, 1900 Association Drive, Reston, VA 22091.

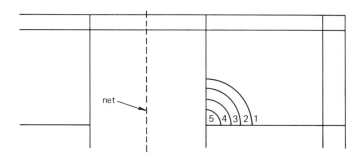

Figure 8.3 French serve target. From "Achievement Examinations in Badminton" by M.G. Scott, 1941, *Research Quarterly*, **12**(2), pp. 242-253. Reprinted by permission of the American Alliance for Health, Physical Education, Recreation, and Dance, 1900 Association Drive, VA 22091.

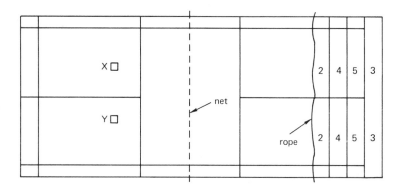

Figure 8.4 French clear target. From "Achievement Examinations in Badminton" by M.G. Scott, 1941, *Research Quarterly*, **12**(2), pp. 242-253. Reprinted by permission of the American Alliance for Health, Physical Education, Recreation, and Dance, 1900 Association Drive, VA 22091.

further from the net than the rear singles service line. Illegal strokes are given another trial. The final score for each item consists of the total number of points scored by legal hits that passed either below or above the rope as specified. A validity coefficient of .85 and reliability coefficients of .77 and .98 are reported on college women.

Basketball

Basketball skill tests for boys and girls and men and women are quite numerous in the testing

literature. Basketball skills are usually serial and continuous in nature when used in an actual game situation. A player may catch a pass, dribble the ball around a screen, and then take a jump shot many times during a game. In addition, the player does this under many varied environmental conditions. Shots are taken from different positions on the floor, against different types of defenses, and with different players acting as defenders. However, these serial movement skills performed in a varied, open environment rarely appear as such on tests purported to estimate basketball skill. Thus some of the current, standardized basketball skill tests are questionable as a basis for critical decision making.

The same problem arises with other tests that purport to estimate skill in sports such as soccer, volleyball, baseball, football, softball, and field hockey. Indeed, Kerr and Smoll (1977) argue that teachers should teach the performer to decrease his or her variability in activities (e.g., archery) in which advancement in skill level should produce greater consistency in performance. Conversely, in sports that demand a wide range of movement skills to be performed under varied conditions, the teacher should construct learning situations that develop skill variability. Thus archers should strive to minimize variability in skill performance, whereas basketball players should be able to shoot from all over the court, and infielders should be able to throw to first base from different infield locations. If teachers structure progressive learning experiences that simulate and transfer skills into actual game play, then they need to replicate game play as closely as possible in developing test items. Teachers should also remember that different test items are probably needed for beginners and advanced players.

An examination of the test items appearing on skill tests for basketball and other sports reveals that testers usually try to reduce variability in test performance so that everything is standardized. Johnson and Nelson (1979) claim that skill testing poses a choice between objective scoring versus realism and validity. In order to improve the reliability and objectivity of scoring, the influence of a second person on the performance of the person being tested is eliminated to standardize testing conditions. However, such standardization often impairs test validity by reducing the similarity of test items to actual sport situations. After all, a basketball player usually dribbles while being guarded by a defender, but most tests do not test dribbling skills under these conditions. Most basketball skill tests call for the player to dribble around stationary chairs or pylons for time. This testing procedure allows initial ball-handling, body position, and dribbling skills to be observed and analyzed, but eventually we should move to a testing mode in which the player dribbles up the floor in a defined area while being guarded by a defender. The latter point is crucial if test data are to be used to predict or estimate basketball playing ability.

Two older basketball skill tests found in many measurement texts are the Johnson test for high school boys (1934) and the Leilich test for girls and women (1952). McCabe and McArdle (1978) describe the items on these tests. They are presented below in brief.

Johnson Basketball Battery

Johnson's total test battery includes the three-item test of basic skill and four items of potential ability. The Iowa-Brace, footwork, jump-and-reach, and dodging run tests, which purport to measure potential ability, are not included here because the validity of these test items has not been established.

The validity and reliability coefficients are based on data obtained from 180 high school boys. The boys were divided into a "good" group of boys who made the basketball squad and a "poor" group who did not. There were 50 boys in the good group and 130 boys in the poor group. Johnson reported validity coefficients ranging between .73 and .88 for the items and the total battery to the criterion of the boy's ability to make the squad. Reliability coefficients ranged from .73 to .89. The test includes the following items:

1. *Field goal speed test.* The pupil stands anywhere under the basket and makes as many baskets as possible in 30 seconds.
2. *Dribble test.* Chairs are placed in a straight line over a 54-foot course with 8 feet between chairs. The pupil dribbles the ball in a weaving fashion around the chairs for 30 seconds. The number of chairs passed is the score.

3. *Passing test.* A target similar to an archery target is placed on the wall. From 40 feet away the pupil performs 10 trials with either an overhand or hook pass at the target.

Basketball Tests for Girls and Women

The Professional Studies and Research Committee of the Midwest Association of College Teachers of Physical Education for Women reported achievement levels in basketball skills for women physical education majors (Miller, 1954). To obtain data for these skill norms, the committee selected three tests on the basis of a factor analysis study by Leilich of all basketball tests appearing in the literature. The three tests selected to measure these factors were the Johnson Half-Minute Shooting Test, the Push-Pass Test, and the Bounce and Shoot Test, a description of which follows:

1. *Half-Minute Shooting Test.* The subject takes any position under the basket she desires. The object is to make as many baskets as possible in 30 seconds.
2. *Push-Pass Test.* From a spot 10 feet from a wall, the subject makes as many two-handed chest passes as possible in 30 seconds at a target on the wall. Points are given for each pass depending on the area of the target in which the ball lands.
3. *Bounce and Shoot Test.* Two chairs are placed 18 feet away from the basket at a 45° angle. The chairs are set outside the free throw area but are extended out from the free throw line. A ball is placed on each chair. The subject picks up the ball, bounces it once and shoots, recovers the ball on the rebound, and passes it back to someone behind the chair. The subject then runs to the other chair and repeats the process for a total of 10 shots. A timer keeps track of the time the subject takes to complete the test. A second score consists of 2 points for each basket and 1 point for hitting the rim.

The original source for this test indicates a reliability coefficient of .82 for 51 college women. A method of combining the speed and accuracy scores into a composite score is also indicated, but no norms are given.

Critique

Both of these basketball skill tests contain items that test what are considered to be fundamental skills in the game, namely basket shooting, passing or throwing for accuracy, dribbling, and the bounce and shoot. Thus one is tempted to say that the tests achieve content validity. Unfortunately, however, the test items are not performed in ways that these skills are used in actual play. One does not dribble around chairs, throw or pass a ball 10 times at a stationary target, or make as many lay-up shots in 30 seconds as possible during game play. Also, a serious criticism of the Leilich test is that the time and accuracy elements are both variable. A student taking such a test is apt to ask which is more important, the number of baskets made or the time it takes to perform 10 trials. Attempting to get a very low time score could result in sloppy skill execution and no baskets, whereas total concentration on accuracy could produce a slow, nongamelike pattern of skill execution. These items are, however, skills that players should learn before advancing to effective game play.

The Bounce and Shoot Test comes a bit closer to game-like shooting; the student receives the ball, takes a dribble, and then shoots. The Johnson Test was validated against an extreme groups criterion, that is, 50 high school boys who made the basketball squad and 130 who did not. The construct validity coefficients are adequate; thus the test can be used to classify boys into "good" and "poor" groups in performance of these test items. Note that the 130 boys in the poor group are typical of many students in our physical education classes. The relationship between the basketball ability of these 130 boys and their scores on the Johnson Basketball Battery is the crucial point to determine if we intend to use these test scores as part of a grading system. Physical educators should use videotape equipment if available and record games played in their classes. Use the videotaped performances to rate each pupil on basketball game playing ability and then compute a validity coefficient between these ratings and the scores on the Johnson test. If the coefficient is above .80, instructors can place confidence in the test scores as part of a pupil's grade.

In an attempt to use game results as a criterion for validating basketball skill tests, Stroup (1955) found that team average skill scores on the three items of goal shooting, wall passing, and dribbling around stationary obstacles were highly related to the teams' ability to win 10-minute games in men's physical education classes. Forty-one games were played, and the team average skill scores correctly predicted the outcomes of 84% of the games. Thus these items can be validly used as a quick and practical way to equate teams for intramural competition. But because each team was composed of players with varied skills in each of the items, these test scores should not be used to estimate individual pupils' grades in a basketball unit.

The content validity of the women's basketball test was established by selecting items to represent factors identified in a large number of basketball skill test items appearing in the literature. Nearly all of these test items represent fundamental components of skills performed in a stationary (closed) environment and do not simulate the performance of skills in actual play. Other validity information is unavailable.

Norms for these two tests were developed more than 30 years ago. At best, these norms are quite obsolete and not applicable to most school teaching situations today.

Reliability of testing the passing, shooting, and dribbling items on the Johnson test appear to be adequate because the coefficients are .80,

.73, and .78 respectively. Reliability of the bounce and shoot test for college women is .82.

Standardized directions for administering and scoring these test items are more than adequate. Administrative feasibility is also apparent in terms of the items' simplified testing procedures and economy of administration time. However, the usefulness of any sport skill test score depends on how its validity was determined. In other words, how do you intend to use the test scores? Has this intent been verified by adequate validation study?

AAHPERD Basketball Test for Boys and Girls

A well-constructed, norm-referenced basketball skill test for boys and girls was developed by AAHPERD in 1984. The test is applicable to both sexes and consists of items that measure speed spot shooting, passing, control dribble, and defensive movement skills. Content validity was established by a committee of measurement experts who identified the essential skills of basketball. A survey was conducted of male and female basketball coaches representing professional, college, high school, and elementary levels. The coaches were asked to identify four essential basketball skills and suggest performance tests to measure those skills. Twelve ways to measure the four skills were identified. Pilot studies were then conducted on fifth- and sixth-grade boys and girls, seventh- and eighth-grade boys, and college men. Based on these and subsequent studies, four items that measure essential skills and can be administered in two school class periods were selected.

Construct validity was established by identifying test performance differences among groups of varsity and nonvarsity players. Hence this type of validity permits us to classify pupils into instructional levels or use the test as part of a selection scheme. Concurrent validity was established by correlating test item scores with ratings of each skill and game performance. This should permit us to use this test as input in grading decisions.

The 32 test-retest reliability coefficients for the four test items obtained on males and females in elementary, junior high, and senior high school and college ranged from a low of .84 to a high of .98. Concurrent validity coefficients on both sexes in all four grade levels were quite acceptable. The multiple correlations between the test battery and ratings of performance ranged from .65 to .95, with the majority of the eight coefficients exceeding .77. Objectivity of raters of performance of males and females was also acceptable. The eight coefficients ranged from .62 to .87, with only two coefficients below .78. Norms developed on 10,000 pupils are available. Percentile rank and T score norms

for each sex from ages 10 through college are presented in the test manual. Abbreviated percentile norms are illustrated in Tables 8.3 through 8.6. Directions for administering and scoring each item are illustrated in Figures 8.5 through 8.8 and are described in the following text.[4]

Speed Shot Shooting

The purpose of the speed shot shooting test item is to measure skill in rapidly shooting from specified positions and, to a certain extent, agility and ball handling.

[4]From *Skills Test Manual: Basketball for Boys and Girls* (1984). Reprinted by permission of the American Alliance for Health, Physical Education, Recreation, and Dance, 1900 Association Drive, Reston, VA 22091.

Table 8.3 Speed Spot Shooting—Percentile Norms for Females and Males Ages 10 to College

Percentile	10	11	12	13	Age (years) 14	15	16-17	College
Females								
95th	18	19	22	22	25	23	23	35
75th	11	11	13	13	15	15	14	21
50th	8	8	10	10	11	11	11	17
25th	5	5	7	8	9	8	7	13
5th	2	2	3	4	4	4	3	8
Males								
95th	23	25	27	28	30	27	28	30
75th	17	18	19	19	23	20	22	25
50th	13	14	15	15	18	16	16	22
25th	10	10	11	12	13	11	12	19
5th	7	6	7	7	9	6	7	14

Note. From *Skills Test Manual: Basketball for Boys and Girls* (1984). Reprinted by permission of the American Alliance for Health, Physical Education, Recreation, and Dance, 1900 Association Drive, Reston, VA 22091.

Table 8.4 Passing—Percentile Norms for Females and Males Ages 10 to College

	Age (years)							
Percentile	10	11	12	13	14	15	16-17	College
Females								
95th	36	38	43	44	46	47	48	54
75th	30	31	35	37	39	40	39	47
50th	25	27	31	32	34	35	34	42
25th	21	23	26	29	29	28	24	37
5th	7	13	20	23	24	19	18	21
Males								
95th	41	43	48	54	55	55	57	70
75th	35	36	40	43	45	48	49	58
50th	31	32	35	39	40	39	41	53
25th	25	28	30	35	35	23	25	47
5th	8	18	22	23	23	18	21	35

Note. From *Skills Test Manual: Basketball for Boys and Girls* (1984). Reprinted by permission of the American Alliance for Health, Physical Education, Recreation, and Dance, 1900 Association Drive, Reston, VA 22091.

Table 8.5 Control Dribble—Percentile Norms for Females and Males Ages 10 to College

	Age (years)							
Percentile	10	11	12	13	14	15	16-17	College
Females								
95th	10.8	10.3	8.8	8.7	8.4	8.2	8.2	7.6
75th	12.3	11.8	10.6	10.0	9.6	9.7	9.8	8.5
50th	14.3	13.2	11.9	11.0	10.7	10.7	10.7	9.3
25th	16.6	15.0	13.3	12.4	12.0	12.0	12.2	10.4
5th	21.7	20.5	19.0	17.8	18.1	15.8	15.0	13.8
Males								
95th	9.2	9.0	8.7	7.8	7.5	7.0	7.0	6.7
75th	10.4	10.1	9.5	9.0	8.5	8.1	8.1	7.3
50th	11.7	11.1	10.5	9.8	9.3	8.9	9.0	7.8
25th	13.7	12.6	11.7	10.7	10.3	10.0	10.0	8.5
5th	23.0	16.8	16.0	14.4	13.5	12.0	12.4	10.0

Note. From *Skills Test Manual: Basketball for Boys and Girls* (1984). Reprinted by permission of the American Alliance for Health, Physical Education, Recreation, and Dance, 1900 Association Drive, Reston, VA 22091.

Table 8.6 Defensive Movement—Percentile Norms for Females and Males Ages 10 to College

Percentile	10	11	12	13	14	15	16-17	College
Females								
95th	10.5	10.3	9.5	10.0	9.6	9.7	9.6	8.7
75th	11.8	11.8	11.5	11.5	11.0	11.0	11.1	10.3
50th	13.2	13.0	12.8	12.5	12.0	12.0	12.0	11.0
25th	14.6	14.3	14.1	13.6	13.2	13.4	13.2	12.0
5th	19.6	17.4	17.0	16.8	16.4	16.4	16.4	14.5
Males								
95th	10.0	9.0	8.9	8.9	8.7	7.9	7.3	8.4
75th	11.5	10.9	10.7	10.3	10.1	9.3	9.6	9.4
50th	12.7	12.0	11.9	11.4	11.3	10.3	10.3	10.3
25th	13.9	13.7	13.0	12.8	12.4	11.3	11.5	11.2
5th	18.7	17.2	17.0	16.6	15.8	14.0	15.2	12.9

Column header group: Age (years)

Note. From *Skills Test Manual: Basketball for Boys and Girls* (1984). Reprinted by permission of the American Alliance for Health, Physical Education, Recreation, and Dance, 1900 Association Drive, Reston, VA 22091.

Equipment.   Standard equipment for this item includes a standard inflated basketball, standard goal, stopwatch, and tape for marking floors.

Test/Target Dimensions.   Five floor markers (2 feet long and 1 inch wide) should be placed on the floor. For upper elementary grades 5 and 6, the markers are placed 9 feet from the backboard; for grades 7, 8, and 9 the distance should be 12 feet from the backboard; and for grades 10, 11, and 12 and college the distance should be 15 feet from the backboard. The distances for spots B, C, and D must be measured from the center of the backboard; those for spots A and E must be measured from the center of the basket. (See Figure 8.5.)

Administration.   Three trials of 60 seconds each are conducted. The first is a practice trial and the next two are recorded for scoring. The performer may stand behind any marker desig-

nated for his or her age level. On the signal *Ready, Go!*, the performer shoots, retrieves the ball, and dribbles to and shoots from another designated spot. (One foot must be behind the marker during each attempt.) A maximum of four lay-up shots may be attempted during each trial, but no two may be in succession. The performer must attempt at least one shot from each designated spot.

Violations/Penalties.   Rule infractions are penalized as follows:

- For ball-handling infractions (traveling, double dribble, etc.), the shot following the violation is scored as 0 points.
- If two lay-up shots are made in succession, the second lay-up is scored as 0 points.
- If more than four lay-ups are attempted, all excessive lay-ups are scored as 0 points.
- If the subject fails to shoot from each of the

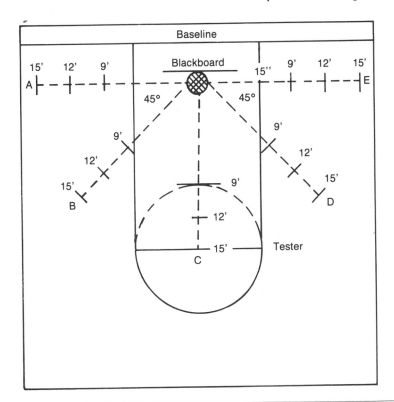

Figure 8.5 Basketball speed spot shooting. From *Skills Test Manual: Basketball for Boys and Girls* (1984). Reprinted by permission of the American Alliance for Health, Physical Education, Recreation, and Dance, 1900 Association Drive, Reston, VA 22091.

five designated spots, the trial should be repeated.

Scoring. The test administrator must record the spots from which shots are taken as well as the number of attempted lay-ups. It is recommended that the recorder use a card marked "ABCDE 1234" and draw a line through the letter corresponding to the floor spot or the number indicating a lay-up. Two points are awarded for each basket made, including lay-ups. One point is awarded for an unsuccessful shot that hits the rim from above either initially or after rebounding from the backboard. Add the total points for each legal shot for each of the two trials. The final score is the total of the two trials.

Passing

The purpose of the passing test item is to measure skill in passing and recovering the ball accurately while moving.

Equipment. Standard equipment includes an inflated basketball, stopwatch, smooth wall surface, and tape for marking targets and restraining line.

Test/Target Dimensions. Six squares of 2 feet each should be marked on the wall so that the base of the squares is either 3 or 5 feet from the floor. All adjacent squares should be 2 feet apart. A restraining line is to be marked on the floor at a distance of 8 feet from the wall.

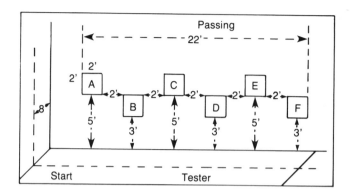

Figure 8.6 Basketball passing. From *Skills Test Manual: Basketball for Boys and Girls* (1984). Reprinted by permission of the American Alliance for Health, Physical Education, Recreation, and Dance, 1900 Association Drive, Reston, VA 22091.

Administration. A total of three trials of 30 seconds each are conducted. The first is a practice trial, and the last two are recorded for scoring. The performer stands with a ball behind the restraining line and faces the target on the far left (A). On the signal *Ready? Go!*, the performer chest passes to the first target, recovers the ball on the rebound while moving to a location behind the second target and behind the restraining line, and chest passes to Target B. This pattern continues until Target F is reached, where two chest passes are executed. The performer then passes to Target E, repeating the sequence by moving to the left. (See Figure 8.6.)

Violations/Penalties. Rule infractions are penalized as follows:

- If the subject passes from a point in front of the restraining line (foot fault), no points are awarded for the pass.
- If the subject passes to Targets B, C, D, or E twice in succession, no points are awarded for the second pass.
- If the subject fails to use the chest pass, no points are awarded for the pass.

Scoring. Each pass that hits the target or the boundary lines of the target counts 2 points. Each pass hitting the intervening spaces on the wall counts 1 point. The final score is the total of two trials. For ease in administration, an assistant should call out foot faults.

Control Dribble

The purpose of the control dribbling test item is to measure skill in handling the ball while the body is moving.

Equipment. Standard equipment includes inflated basketball, six cones, and a stopwatch.

Test/Target Dimensions. An obstacle course marked by six cones will be set up in the free throw lane of the court. (See Figure 8.7.)

Administration. Three timed trials are administered. The first is a practice trial, and the last two are scored for the record. With the ball, the performer starts on his or her nondominant hand side of Cone A. On the signal, *Ready? Go!*, the performer dribbles with the nondominant hand to the nondominant hand side of

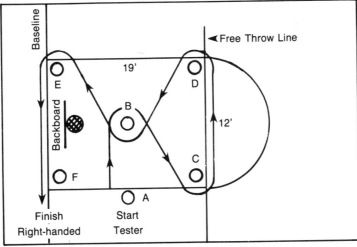

a. Right-handed control dribble.

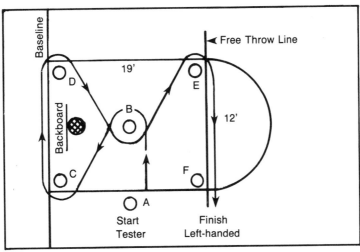

b. Left-handed control dribble.

Figure 8.7 Control dribble. From *Skills Test Manual: Basketball for Boys and Girls* (1984). Reprinted by permission of the American Alliance for Health, Physical Education, Recreation, and Dance, 1900 Association Drive, Reston, VA 22091. *Note.* 12' = 3.657 m; 19' = 5.791 m.

Cone B. The performer then proceeds to follow the course using the dominant hand, changing hands as deemed appropriate until the finish line is crossed by both feet.

Violations/Penalties. Rule infractions are penalized as follows:

- For ball-handling infractions (traveling, double dribble, etc.), stop the trial, return to start, and begin timing again.
- If either the performer or the ball fail to remain outside the cone (including dribbling the ball either inside or over the cone), stop the trial, return to start, and begin timing again.
- If the subject fails to begin at the point in the course where control was lost, stop the trial, return to start, and begin timing again.

Scoring. The score for each trial will be the elapsed time required to legally complete the course. Scores should be recorded to the nearest .10 of a second for each trial and the final score will be the sum of the two trials.

Defensive Movement

The purpose of this test item is to measure performance of basic defensive movement.

Equipment. Standard equipment includes a stopwatch, standard basketball lane, and tape for marking change-of-direction points.

Test/Target Dimensions. The test perimeters are marked by the free throw line, the boundary line behind the basket, and the rebound lane lines, which are marked into sections by a square and two lines. Only the middle line (rebound lane marker) is a target point for this test. Additional spots outside the four corners of the area should be marked with tape at Points A, B, D, and E. (See Figure 8.8.)

Administration. There are three trials to the test. The first is a practice trial, and the last two are scored for the record. The performer starts at Point A and faces away from the basket. On the signal, *Ready? Go!*, the performer slides to the left without crossing the feet and continues to Point B, touches the floor outside the lane with the left hand, executes a dropstep (see Figure 8.8), slides to Point C, and touches the floor outside the lane with the right hand. The performer continues the course as diagramed. Completion of the test occurs when both feet have crossed the finish line.

Violations/Penalties. Rule infractions are penalized as follows:

- If the performer crosses the feet during the slide or turns and runs (foot faults), stop the trial, return to start, and begin timing again.
- If the performer's hand fails to touch the floor outside the lane, stop the trial, return to start, and begin timing again.
- If the performer executes the dropstep before the hand has touched the floor, stop the trial, return to start, and begin timing again.

Scoring. The score for each trial is the elapsed time required to legally complete the course. Scores should be recorded to the nearest .10 of a second for each trial, and the sum of the two trials is the final score.

Bowling

Bowling presents a self-testing situation. Have the pupils bowl three lines and record the number of pins knocked down in each line. The teacher can also specify that certain combinations of pins that most frequently remain standing for the follow-up shot be set up to test

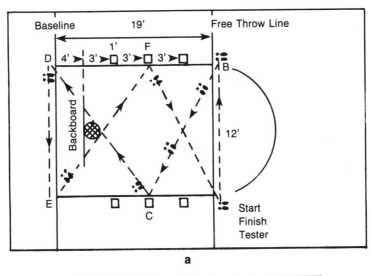

a

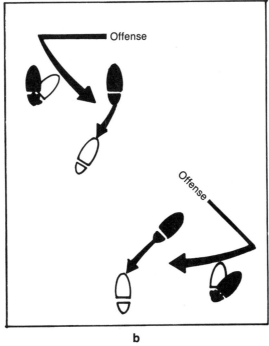

b

Figure 8.8(a) Defensive movement. **(b)** The dropstep is a basic defensive maneuver employed to stop penetration to the basket by an offensive player. It consists of changing defensive direction by moving the trail foot in the sliding motion in the direction of the offensive move. From *Skills Test Manual: Basketball for Boys and Girls* (1984). Reprinted by permission of the American Alliance for Health, Physical Education, Recreation, and Dance, 1900 Association Drive, Reston, VA 22091.

students' skill in making a spare. All class members can practice and be tested over each combination.

Canoeing

Critz (1948) developed a test to determine the general ability of a person to handle a canoe. The test is applicable for members of both sexes at most educational levels. The student paddles a canoe as fast as possible in a figure-eight path around two buoys set 525 feet (160.02 m) apart. Prior to being tested, the student should demonstrate familiarity with the appropriate paddling skills required. A class of 20 students can be tested in two 60 minute periods.

Two buoys are placed 525 feet (160.02 m) apart. The student takes a position in the stern of the canoe with a paddle; the teacher rides in the bow of the canoe to help keep it on an even keel. The canoeist begins paddling from a position behind the buoy selected as the starting point so that the canoe has full momentum when it passes the starting buoy. The pupil paddles the canoe as rapidly as possible to the other buoy and back to the starting buoy making a figure eight. Either side of the canoe may be used for paddling but the canoeist must remain paddling on the same side for the entire test. A stop watch is started as the bow passes the buoy at the starting point and continues until the figure-eight course is completed as the bow passes the same buoy where the test began. Elapsed time is the official score.

A validity coefficient of .64 was obtained by correlating test items with judges ratings of college women's stroking form and ability to handle a canoe. Test-retest reliability on successive days under similar water and wind conditions was .92. However, canoe design and construction has changed markedly since 1948, so norms need to be developed based on the age and sex of your pupils.

Diving

Torney and Clayton (1981) provide checklists for the running forward dive in the layout position, the running forward dive in the pike position, and the back dive in the layout position. The checklists are illustrated in Figures 8.9, 8.10, and 8.11. The pupil is tested on a low diving board after adequate instruction. These task analysis checklists are intended for use in formative evaluation.

Football

In 1965, AAHPER developed a test battery to assess fundamental football skills. These 10 skill tests should be used as "practice" tests because they are intended to be used by players to improve abilities in the fundamental skills of the game. Content validity is assumed. Minimum reliability of .80 for each item is reported. Percentile rank norms derived on boys 10 to 18 years of age are provided in Tables 8.7 through 8.19. Directions for the administration and scoring of each item follow:[5]

1. *Forward Pass for Distance.* The player throws a forward pass for distance from between two parallel lines 6 feet (1.828 m) apart. The player takes one or more running steps inside this zone and throws as far as possible without stepping over the second line. Players should warm up and are allowed one practice pass. The test consists of three trials or passes from inside the throwing zone. *Scoring:* The first pass is marked by inserting a stake at the point

---

[5]Adapted from the *Skills Test Manual: Football* (1965). Reprinted by permission of the American Alliance for Health, Physical Education, Recreation, and Dance, 1900 Association Drive, Reston, VA 22091.

Running Forward Dive in Layout Position

Directions: Check ✓ all items that apply to the performance of this skill. Note errors in the spaces provided.

Name _____ Name _____
         (performer)   (analyst)

Illustration of Correct Technique	Analysis of Performance	Illustration of Correct Technique	Analysis of Performance
	Starting Position		**Takeoff**
	___ The form *is* acceptable.		___ The form *is* acceptable.
	___ The form is *not* acceptable because:		___ The form is *not* acceptable because:
	___ backward lean		___ too much lean forward
	___ knees locked, body tense		___ arm and leg actions not synchronized
	___ forward lean		___ actions of body and board not synchronized
	___ (other) _____		___ feet leave board too soon
			___ feet do not rise backward and upward
	Approach		___ arm circle is reversed
	___ The form *is* acceptable.		___ (other) _____
	___ The form is *not* acceptable because:		
	___ arm swing not free		**Flight**
	___ forward lean		___ The form *is* acceptable.
	___ steps too long		___ The form is *not* acceptable because:
	___ head not erect		___ not enough height
	___ run (walk) is too rapid		___ feet raised too much
	___ (other) _____		___ partial pike is assumed
			___ legs bend at knees
	Hurdle		___ feet not raised enough
	___ The form *is* acceptable.		___ too much back arch
	___ The form is *not* acceptable because:		___ arms do not flow into position sideward
	___ too long		___ (other) _____
	___ forward lean		
	___ not high enough		**Entry**
	___ landing flat-footed		___ The form *is* acceptable.
	___ knees bend on contact with board		___ The form is *not* acceptable because:
	___ (other) _____		___ too long
			___ too far out from the board
			___ body not straight
			___ too short
			___ ears not between arms
			___ legs flop over
			___ dive is shallow
			___ arms pull to sides
			___ (other) _____

Figure 8.9 Running forward dive in layout position. From *Teaching Aquatics* (2nd ed.) (p. 229) by J.A. Torney and R.A. Clayton, 1981, Minneapolis, MN: Burgess Publishing Co. Reprinted by permission.

Running Forward Dive in Pike Position

Directions: Check ✓ all items that apply to the performance of this skill. Note errors in the spaces provided.

Name _____ Name _____
(performer)   (analyst)

Illustration of Correct Technique	Analysis of Performance
	Starting Position ___ The form *is* acceptable. ___ The form is *not* acceptable because: ___ forward lean ___ backward lean ___ body tense ___ (other) _____
	Approach ___ The form *is* acceptable. ___ The form is *not* acceptable because: ___ forward lean ___ arm swing not free ___ steps too long ___ head not erect ___ run (walk) is too rapid ___ (other) _____
	Hurdle ___ The form *is* acceptable. ___ The form is *not* acceptable because: ___ too long ___ forward lean ___ not high enough ___ arm action not synchronized with leg action ___ landing flat-footed ___ knees bend on contact with board ___ (other) _____

Illustration of Correct Technique	Analysis of Performance
	Takeoff ___ The form *is* acceptable. ___ The form is not acceptable because: ___ forward lean; takeoff is outward ___ arm circle is reversed ___ arm and leg actions not synchronized ___ body and board actions not synchronized ___ feet leave board too soon ___ head is faced downward ___ (other) _____
	Flight ___ The form *is* acceptable. ___ The form is not acceptable because: ___ not enough height ___ pike is partial ___ legs not straight ___ pike held too long ___ pike held too briefly ___ pike assumed too soon ___ feet brought up to hands ___ toes not pointed; ankles not extended ___ legs bend at knees ___ (other) _____
	Entry ___ The form *is* acceptable. ___ The form is not acceptable because: ___ too short ___ too far out ___ ears not between arms ___ too long ___ body not straight ___ legs flop over ___ dive is shallow ___ arms pulled to sides ___ (other) _____

Figure 8.10 Running forward dive in pike position. From *Teaching Aquatics* (2nd ed.) (p. 231) by J.A. Torney and R.A. Clayton, 1981, Minneapolis, MN: Burgess Publishing Co. Reprinted with permission.

Back Dive in Layout Position

Directions: Check ✓ all items that apply to the performance of this skill. Note errors in the spaces provided.

Name _____   Name _____
(performer)   (analyst)

Illustration of Correct Technique	Analysis of Performance

Starting Position
___ The form *is* acceptable.
___ The form is *not* acceptable because:
___ arms not used for balance during pivot
___ body bends forward at hips; body not erect
___ pivot on the one foot is not smooth
___ arm actions are too fast and uneven
___ (other) _____

Takeoff
___ The form *is* acceptable.
___ The form is *not* acceptable because:
___ leg and arm actions not synchronized
___ body and board actions not synchronized
___ feet lifted and returned to board before takeoff
___ backward lean is too great
___ not enough height
___ spring is outward
___ (other) _____

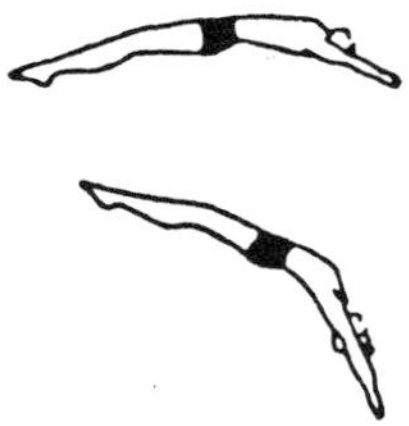

Illustration of Correct Technique	Analysis of Performance

Flight
___ The form *is* acceptable.
___ The form is not acceptable because:
___ body not stretched upward
___ backward lean
___ too much back arch
___ chest and hips not pressed upward
___ knees bend
___ body tends to twist
___ not enough height
___ head not tilted back
___ hips bend in pike
___ arms not level
___ (other) _____

Entry
___ The form *is* acceptable.
___ The form is not acceptable because:
___ too short
___ too far out from board
___ ears not between arms
___ too long
___ body not straight
___ legs flop over
___ dive is shallow
___ arms pull to sides
___ (other) _____

Figure 8.11 Back dive in layout position. From *Teaching Aquatics* (2nd ed.) (p. 233) by J.A. Torney and R.A. Clayton, 1981, Minneapolis, MN: Burgess Publishing Co. Reprinted with permission.

Table 8.7 Forward Pass for Distance—Percentile Scores Based on Age/Test Scores in Feet

Percentile	Age (years)							
	10	11	12	13	14	15	16	17-18
100th	96	105	120	150	170	180	180	180
95th	71	83	99	115	126	135	144	152
90th	68	76	92	104	118	127	135	143
85th	64	73	87	98	114	122	129	137
80th	62	70	83	95	109	118	126	133
75th	61	68	79	91	105	115	123	129
70th	59	65	77	88	102	111	120	127
65th	58	64	75	85	99	108	117	124
60th	56	62	73	83	96	105	114	121
55th	55	61	71	80	93	102	111	117
50th	53	59	68	78	91	99	108	114
45th	52	56	66	76	88	97	105	110
40th	51	54	64	73	85	94	103	107
35th	49	51	62	70	83	92	100	104
30th	47	50	60	69	80	89	97	101
25th	45	48	58	65	77	85	93	98
20th	44	45	54	63	73	81	90	94
15th	41	43	51	61	70	76	85	89
10th	38	40	45	55	64	71	79	80
5th	33	36	40	46	53	62	70	67
0	14	25	10	10	10	20	30	20

Note. Tables 8.7 through 8.19 are from *Skills Test Manual: Football* (1965). Reprinted by permission of the American Alliance for Health, Physical Education, Recreation, and Dance, 1900 Association Drive, Reston, VA 22091.

Table 8.8 Forward Pass for Distance—Percentile Scores Based on Age/Test Scores in Meters

Percentile	Age (years)							
	10	11	12	13	14	15	16	17-18
100th	29.26	32.04	36.57	45.72	51.81	54.86	54.86	54.86
95th	21.64	25.29	30.17	35.05	38.40	41.14	43.89	46.32
90th	20.72	32.16	28.04	31.69	35.96	38.70	41.14	43.58
85th	19.50	22.25	26.51	29.87	34.74	47.18	39.31	41.75
80th	18.89	21.36	25.29	28.95	33.22	35.96	38.40	40.53
75th	18.59	20.72	24.07	27.73	32.00	35.05	37.49	39.31
70th	17.98	19.81	23.46	26.82	31.08	33.83	36.56	38.70
65th	17.67	19.50	22.86	25.90	30.17	32.91	35.66	37.79

(Cont.)

Table 8.8 (Cont.)

Percentile	Age (years)							
	10	11	12	13	14	15	16	17-18
60th	17.06	18.89	22.25	25.29	29.26	32.00	34.74	36.88
55th	16.76	18.59	21.64	24.38	28.34	31.08	33.83	35.66
50th	16.14	17.98	20.72	23.77	27.73	30.17	32.91	34.74
45th	15.84	17.06	20.11	23.16	26.82	29.56	32.00	33.52
40th	15.54	16.45	19.50	22.25	25.90	28.65	31.39	32.61
35th	14.93	15.54	18.89	21.33	25.29	28.04	30.48	31.69
30th	14.32	15.24	18.28	21.03	24.38	27.12	29.56	30.78
25th	13.71	14.63	17.67	19.81	23.46	25.90	28.34	29.87
20th	13.41	13.71	16.45	19.20	22.25	24.68	27.43	28.65
15th	12.49	13.10	15.54	18.59	21.33	23.16	25.90	27.12
10th	11.58	12.19	13.71	16.76	19.50	21.64	24.07	24.38
5th	10.05	10.97	12.19	14.02	16.15	18.89	21.36	20.42
0	4.26	7.62	3.04	3.04	3.04	6.09	9.14	6.09

Table 8.9 50-Yard Dash With Football—
Percentile Scores Based on Age/Test Scores in Seconds and Tenths

Percentile	Age (years)							
	10	11	12	13	14	15	16	17-18
100th	7.3	6.8	6.2	5.5	5.5	5.5	5.5	5.0
95th	7.7	7.4	7.0	6.5	6.5	6.2	6.0	6.0
90th	7.9	7.6	7.2	6.8	6.6	6.3	6.1	6.1
85th	8.1	7.7	7.4	6.9	6.8	6.4	6.3	6.2
80th	8.2	7.8	7.5	7.0	6.9	6.5	6.4	6.3
75th	8.3	7.9	7.5	7.1	7.0	6.6	6.5	6.3
70th	8.4	8.0	7.6	7.2	7.1	6.7	6.6	6.4
65th	8.5	8.1	7.7	7.3	7.2	6.8	6.6	6.5
60th	8.6	8.2	7.8	7.4	7.2	6.9	6.7	6.6
55th	8.6	8.3	7.9	7.5	7.3	7.0	6.8	6.6
50th	8.7	8.4	8.0	7.5	7.4	7.0	6.8	6.7
45th	8.8	8.5	8.1	7.6	7.5	7.1	6.9	6.8
40th	8.9	8.6	8.1	7.7	7.6	7.2	7.0	6.8
35th	9.0	8.7	8.2	7.8	7.7	7.2	7.1	6.9
30th	9.1	8.8	8.3	8.0	7.8	7.3	7.2	7.0
25th	9.2	8.9	8.4	8.1	7.9	7.4	7.3	7.1
20th	9.3	9.1	8.5	8.2	8.1	7.5	7.4	7.2

(Cont.)

Table 8.9 (Cont.)

Percentile	Age (years)							
	10	11	12	13	14	15	16	17-18
15th	9.4	9.2	8.7	8.4	8.3	7.7	7.5	7.3
10th	9.6	9.3	9.0	8.7	8.4	8.1	7.8	7.4
5th	9.8	9.5	9.3	9.0	8.8	8.4	8.0	7.8
0	10.6	11.0	12.0	12.0	12.0	11.0	10.0	10.0

Table 8.10 Blocking—Percentile Scores Based on Age/Test Scores in Seconds and Tenths

Percentile	Age (years)							
	10	11	12	13	14	15	16	17-18
100th	6.9	5.0	5.0	5.0	5.0	5.0	5.0	5.0
95th	7.5	6.6	6.6	5.9	5.8	5.8	5.8	5.5
90th	7.7	7.1	7.1	6.5	6.2	6.2	6.1	5.7
85th	7.9	7.5	7.5	6.7	6.6	6.3	6.3	5.8
80th	8.1	8.0	7.7	6.9	6.8	6.5	6.5	6.0
75th	8.3	8.3	7.9	7.2	7.0	6.7	6.7	6.2
70th	8.5	8.6	8.1	7.4	7.1	6.9	7.0	6.3
65th	8.9	9.1	8.4	7.6	7.3	7.0	7.2	6.5
60th	9.3	9.5	8.6	7.7	7.5	7.2	7.4	6.7
55th	9.6	9.7	8.8	7.9	7.7	7.4	7.6	7.0
50th	9.8	9.9	9.0	8.1	7.8	7.5	7.8	7.2
45th	10.1	10.2	9.2	8.3	8.0	7.8	8.0	7.4
40th	10.5	10.4	9.4	8.4	8.1	7.9	8.3	7.6
35th	10.7	10.6	9.6	8.6	8.3	8.2	8.6	7.8
30th	11.0	10.9	9.7	8.9	8.5	8.3	8.8	8.0
25th	11.3	11.1	9.9	9.1	8.7	8.5	9.1	8.2
20th	11.6	11.3	10.2	9.4	9.0	8.8	9.5	8.5
15th	12.0	11.6	10.5	9.8	9.2	9.0	9.0	8.9
10th	12.8	12.0	10.9	10.2	9.5	9.4	10.6	9.4
5th	14.4	13.1	11.6	11.2	10.3	10.4	10.7	10.8
0	17.5	18.0	15.0	15.0	15.0	13.0	15.0	14.0

Table 8.11 Forward Pass for Accuracy—Percentile Scores Based on Age/Test Scores in Points

Percentile	Age (years)							
	10	11	12	13	14	15	16	17-18
100th	18	26	26	26	26	26	28	28
95th	14	19	20	21	21	21	21	22
90th	11	16	18	19	19	19	20	21
85th	10	15	17	18	18	18	18	19
80th	9	13	16	17	17	17	17	18
75th	8	12	15	16	16	16	16	18
70th	8	11	14	15	15	15	15	17
65th	6	10	13	14	14	14	15	16
60th	5	9	12	13	13	13	14	15
55th	4	8	11	13	13	13	13	15
50th	3	7	11	12	12	12	13	14
45th	2	6	10	11	11	11	12	13
40th	2	5	9	11	10	11	12	12
35th	1	5	8	10	9	9	11	12
30th	0	4	7	9	8	9	10	11
25th	0	3	6	8	8	8	9	10
20th	0	2	5	7	7	7	8	9
15th	0	1	4	5	5	6	7	8
10th	0	0	3	4	4	5	6	7
5th	0	0	1	2	2	3	4	5
0	0	0	0	0	0	0	0	0

Table 8.12 Football Punt for Distance—Percentile Scores Based on Age/Test Scores in Feet

Percentile	Age (years)							
	10	11	12	13	14	15	16	17-18
100th	87	100	115	150	160	160	160	180
95th	75	84	93	106	119	126	131	136
90th	64	77	88	98	110	119	126	128
85th	61	75	84	94	106	114	120	124
80th	58	70	79	90	103	109	114	120
75th	56	68	77	87	98	105	109	115
70th	55	66	75	83	96	102	106	110
65th	53	64	72	80	93	99	103	107
60th	51	62	70	78	90	96	100	104
55th	50	60	68	75	87	94	97	101

(Cont.)

Table 8.12 (Cont.)

Percentile	Age (years)							
	10	11	12	13	14	15	16	17-18
50th	48	57	66	73	84	91	95	98
45th	46	55	64	70	81	89	92	96
40th	45	53	61	68	78	86	90	93
35th	44	51	59	64	75	83	86	90
30th	42	48	56	63	72	79	83	86
25th	40	45	52	61	70	76	79	81
20th	38	42	50	57	66	73	74	76
15th	32	39	46	52	61	69	70	70
10th	28	34	40	44	55	62	64	64
5th	22	27	35	33	44	54	56	53
0	11	9	10	10	10	10	10	10

Table 8.13 Football Punt for Distance—Percentile Scores Based on Age/Test Scores in Meters

Percentile	Age (years)							
	10	11	12	13	14	15	16	17-18
100th	26.51	30.48	35.05	45.72	48.76	48.76	48.76	54.86
95th	22.86	25.60	28.34	32.30	36.27	38.40	39.92	41.45
90th	19.50	23.46	26.82	29.87	33.52	36.27	38.40	39.01
85th	18.59	22.86	25.60	28.65	32.30	34.74	36.57	37.79
80th	17.67	21.33	24.07	27.43	31.39	33.22	34.74	36.57
75th	17.06	20.72	23.46	26.51	29.87	32.00	33.22	35.05
70th	16.76	20.11	22.86	25.29	29.26	31.08	32.30	33.52
65th	16.15	19.50	21.94	24.38	28.34	30.17	31.39	32.61
60th	15.54	18.89	21.33	23.77	27.43	29.26	30.48	31.69
55th	15.24	18.28	20.72	22.86	26.51	28.65	29.56	30.78
50th	14.63	17.37	20.11	22.25	25.60	27.73	28.95	29.87
45th	14.02	16.76	19.50	21.33	24.68	27.12	28.04	29.26
40th	13.71	16.15	18.59	20.72	23.77	26.21	27.43	28.34
35th	13.41	15.54	17.98	19.50	22.86	25.29	26.21	27.43
30th	12.80	14.63	17.06	19.20	21.94	24.07	25.29	26.21
25th	12.19	13.71	15.84	18.59	21.33	23.16	24.07	24.68
20th	11.58	12.80	15.24	17.37	20.11	22.25	22.55	23.16
15th	9.75	11.88	14.02	15.84	18.59	21.03	21.33	21.33
10th	8.53	10.36	12.19	13.41	16.76	18.89	19.50	19.50
5th	6.70	8.22	10.66	10.05	13.41	16.45	17.06	16.15
0	3.35	2.74	3.04	3.04	3.04	3.04	3.04	3.04

Table 8.14 Ball Changing Zigzag Run—
Percentile Scores Based on Age/Test Scores in Seconds and Tenths

Percentile	Age (years)							
	10	11	12	13	14	15	16	17-18
100th	7.2	7.4	7.0	6.0	6.5	6.0	6.0	6.0
95th	9.9	7.7	7.8	8.0	8.7	7.7	7.7	8.4
90th	10.1	8.1	8.2	8.4	9.0	8.0	8.0	8.7
85th	10.3	8.6	8.5	8.7	9.2	8.3	8.4	8.8
80th	10.5	9.0	8.7	8.8	9.4	8.5	8.6	8.9
75th	10.7	9.3	8.8	9.0	9.5	8.6	8.7	9.0
70th	10.9	9.6	9.0	9.2	9.6	8.7	8.8	9.1
65th	11.1	9.8	9.1	9.3	9.7	8.8	8.9	9.2
60th	11.2	10.0	9.3	9.5	9.8	8.9	9.0	9.3
55th	11.4	10.1	9.5	9.6	9.9	9.0	9.1	9.4
50th	11.5	10.3	9.6	9.7	10.0	9.1	9.3	9.6
45th	11.6	10.5	9.8	9.8	10.1	9.2	9.4	9.7
40th	11.8	10.6	10.0	10.0	10.2	9.4	9.5	9.8
35th	11.9	10.9	10.1	10.2	10.4	9.5	9.7	9.9
30th	12.2	11.1	10.3	10.3	10.5	9.6	9.9	10.1
25th	12.5	11.3	10.5	10.3	10.7	9.9	10.1	10.3
20th	12.8	11.6	10.8	10.8	10.9	10.1	10.3	10.5
15th	13.3	12.1	11.1	11.1	11.2	10.3	10.6	10.9
10th	13.8	12.9	11.5	11.4	11.5	10.6	11.2	11.4
5th	15.8	14.2	12.3	12.1	12.0	11.5	12.2	12.1
0	24.0	15.0	19.0	20.0	14.5	20.0	17.0	15.0

Table 8.15 Catching the Forward Pass—
Percentile Scores Based on Age/Test Scores in Number Caught

Percentile	Age (years)							
	10	11	12	13	14	15	16	17-18
100th	20	20	20	20	20	20	20	20
95th	19	19	19	20	20	20	20	20
90th	17	18	19	19	19	19	19	19
85th	16	16	18	18	18	19	19	19
80th	14	15	18	17	18	18	18	18
75th	13	14	16	17	17	18	18	18
70th	12	13	16	16	16	17	17	17
65th	11	12	15	15	15	16	16	16
60th	10	12	14	15	15	16	16	16

(Cont.)

Table 8.15 (Cont.)

Percentile	10	11	12	13	14	15	16	17-18
				Age (years)				
55th	8	11	14	14	14	15	15	15
50th	7	10	13	13	14	15	15	15
45th	7	9	12	13	13	14	14	14
40th	6	8	12	12	12	13	13	13
35th	5	7	11	11	11	12	12	13
30th	5	7	10	10	10	11	11	12
25th	4	6	10	9	9	10	10	11
20th	3	5	8	8	8	9	9	10
15th	2	4	7	7	8	8	8	9
10th	1	3	6	6	6	7	6	8
5th	1	1	5	4	4	6	4	6
0	0	0	0	0	0	0	0	0

Table 8.16   Pull-Out—Percentile Scores Based on Age/Test Scores in Seconds and Tenths

Percentile	10	11	12	13	14	15	16	17-18
				Age (years)				
100th	2.5	2.2	2.2	2.2	2.2	2.0	2.0	1.8
95th	2.9	2.8	2.8	2.8	2.7	2.5	2.5	2.5
90th	3.2	3.0	3.0	2.9	2.8	2.6	2.6	2.6
85th	3.3	3.0	3.0	3.0	2.9	2.7	2.7	2.7
80th	3.4	3.1	3.1	3.0	3.0	2.8	2.9	2.8
75th	3.5	3.1	3.1	3.1	3.0	3.0	2.9	2.9
70th	3.5	3.2	3.2	3.1	3.0	3.0	3.0	2.9
65th	3.6	3.3	3.3	3.2	3.1	3.0	3.0	3.0
60th	3.6	3.3	3.3	3.2	3.1	3.1	3.1	3.0
55th	3.7	3.3	3.3	3.3	3.2	3.1	3.1	3.1
50th	3.8	3.4	3.4	3.3	3.2	3.2	3.2	3.1
45th	3.8	3.5	3.5	3.4	3.3	3.2	3.2	3.1
40th	3.9	3.6	3.5	3.4	3.3	3.3	3.3	3.2
35th	3.9	3.7	3.6	3.5	3.4	3.3	3.3	3.2
30th	4.0	3.8	3.7	3.5	3.4	3.4	3.3	3.2
25th	4.0	3.9	3.8	3.6	3.5	3.5	3.4	3.3
20th	4.1	4.0	3.9	3.7	3.5	3.6	3.5	3.4
15th	4.2	4.1	3.9	3.8	3.6	3.7	3.7	3.5
10th	4.3	4.2	4.1	3.9	3.7	3.9	3.9	3.6
5th	4.4	4.4	4.2	4.0	4.0	4.1	4.3	3.9
0	5.5	5.0	5.0	5.0	5.0	5.0	5.0	5.0

Table 8.17 Kick-Off—Percentile Scores Based on Age/Test Scores in Feet

Percentile	Age (years)							
	10	11	12	13	14	15	16	17-18
100th	88	110	120	129	140	160	160	180
95th	69	79	98	106	118	128	131	138
90th	64	72	83	97	108	120	125	129
85th	59	68	78	92	102	114	119	124
80th	58	64	74	86	97	108	114	119
75th	55	60	70	81	94	104	108	113
70th	53	58	67	78	90	100	104	108
65th	50	56	65	75	86	96	99	105
60th	47	54	64	72	84	93	97	103
55th	46	52	60	69	81	90	95	98
50th	45	50	57	67	77	87	93	95
45th	43	48	54	64	74	83	90	92
40th	40	46	52	62	71	79	87	88
35th	39	44	48	59	68	76	83	84
30th	37	42	45	56	65	72	79	79
25th	35	40	42	52	62	69	75	74
20th	32	37	38	48	58	64	70	70
15th	30	34	34	42	52	59	65	64
10th	26	30	29	36	45	50	60	57
5th	21	24	22	26	38	40	47	43
0	5	10	0	0	0	10	10	10

Table 8.18 Kick-Off—Percentile Scores Based on Age/Test Scores in Meters

Percentile	Age (years)							
	10	11	12	13	14	15	16	17-18
100th	26.82	33.52	36.57	39.31	42.67	48.76	48.76	54.86
95th	21.03	24.07	29.87	32.30	35.96	39.01	39.92	42.06
90th	19.50	21.94	25.29	29.56	32.91	36.57	38.10	39.31
85th	17.98	20.72	23.77	28.04	31.08	34.74	36.27	37.79
80th	17.67	19.50	22.55	26.21	29.56	32.91	34.74	36.27
75th	16.76	18.28	21.36	24.68	28.65	31.69	32.91	34.44
70th	16.15	17.67	20.42	23.77	27.43	30.48	31.69	32.91
65th	15.24	17.06	19.81	22.86	26.21	29.26	30.17	32.00
60th	14.32	16.45	19.50	21.94	25.60	28.34	29.56	31.39
55th	14.02	15.84	18.28	21.03	24.68	27.43	28.95	29.87

(Cont.)

Table 8.18 (Cont.)

Percentile				Age (years)				
	10	11	12	13	14	15	16	17-18
50th	13.71	15.24	17.37	20.42	23.46	26.51	28.34	28.95
45th	13.10	14.63	16.45	19.50	22.55	25.29	27.43	28.04
40th	12.19	14.02	15.84	18.89	21.64	24.07	26.51	26.82
35th	11.88	13.41	14.63	17.98	20.72	23.16	25.29	25.60
30th	11.27	12.80	13.71	17.06	19.81	21.94	24.07	24.07
25th	10.66	12.19	12.80	15.84	18.89	21.03	22.86	22.55
20th	9.75	11.27	11.58	14.63	17.67	19.50	21.33	21.33
15th	9.14	10.36	10.36	12.80	15.84	17.98	19.81	19.50
10th	7.92	9.14	8.83	10.97	13.71	15.34	18.28	17.37
5th	6.40	7.31	6.70	7.92	11.58	12.19	14.32	13.10
0	1.52	3.04	0	0	0	3.04	3.04	3.04

Table 8.19 Dodging Run—Percentile Scores Based on Age/Test Scores in Seconds and Tenths

Percentile				Age (years)				
	10	11	12	13	14	15	16	17-18
100th	21.0	18.0	18.0	17.0	16.0	16.0	16.0	16.0
95th	24.3	23.8	23.8	23.3	22.6	22.4	22.3	22.2
90th	25.8	24.6	24.6	24.2	23.9	23.5	23.3	23.2
85th	26.3	25.0	25.0	24.8	24.6	24.1	23.9	23.7
80th	26.4	25.2	25.2	24.9	24.7	24.6	24.3	24.1
75th	27.5	25.3	25.3	25.3	25.2	24.9	24.7	24.4
70th	27.8	25.8	25.8	25.7	25.2	25.2	25.0	24.7
65th	28.1	26.3	26.3	26.1	26.1	25.5	25.3	25.0
60th	28.4	26.6	26.6	26.5	26.3	25.8	25.5	25.3
55th	28.7	26.9	26.9	26.8	26.6	26.1	25.8	25.6
50th	28.9	27.4	27.3	27.2	26.9	26.4	26.1	26.0
45th	29.3	28.0	27.6	27.5	27.2	26.7	26.3	26.3
40th	29.7	28.3	27.9	27.9	27.5	27.0	26.7	26.6
35th	30.1	28.8	28.4	28.3	27.9	27.4	27.0	26.9
30th	30.5	29.2	28.8	28.7	28.3	27.8	27.3	27.2
25th	30.9	29.8	29.2	29.1	28.7	28.2	27.7	27.6
20th	31.3	30.4	29.8	29.5	29.3	28.6	28.1	28.0
15th	31.8	31.1	30.4	30.1	29.9	29.1	28.8	28.7
10th	32.7	32.0	31.3	30.8	30.7	29.8	29.6	29.2
5th	33.6	33.5	33.0	32.3	31.8	31.0	30.6	30.4
0	40.0	40.0	41.0	40.0	36.0	36.0	36.0	36.0

where the ball first hit the ground. If a succeeding pass is longer, the stake is moved to the further spot. The longest pass is then measured and recorded.

2. *Fifty-Yard Dash with Football.* The subject runs as fast as possible for 50 yards (45.72 m) carrying a football. Two trials are given with a rest in between the two trials. *Scoring:* When the starter shouts *Go!* and simultaneously swings a white cloth down with his arm, the timer starts the watch. The time is stopped when the runner crosses the finish line. The score is recorded to the nearest .10 of a second. The better score of the two trials is used as the score.

3. *Blocking.* On the signal *Go!*, the subject runs forward and executes a cross-body block against a blocking bag. The subject immediately recovers and charges toward a second bag placed 15 feet (4.57 m) directly to the right of the first bag. After cross-body blocking that bag clear to the ground, the subject scrambles to his feet and races toward the third bag. The third bag is 15 feet (4.57 m) away in the direction of the starting line, but at a 45° angle to the line from the first and second bags. (This places the third bag about 5 feet [1.524 m] from the starting line.) The subject blocks this third bag to the ground with a cross-body block and then runs across the starting line. Two trials are given. The blocking bags must be blocked clear to the ground. (See Figure 8.12 for diagram of bag placement.) *Scoring:* The time from the signal *Go!* until the subject crosses back over the line is measured to the nearest .10 second. The better of the two trials constitutes the subject's score.

4. *Forward Pass for Accuracy.* A target is painted on an 8- by 11-foot (2.438- by 3.352-m) canvas that is hung from the crossbar of the goal posts. The center circle is 2 feet (.609 m) in diameter; the middle circle is 4 feet (1.219 m) in diameter; and the outer circle is 6 feet (1.828 m) in di-

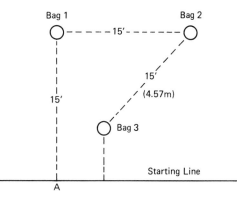

Figure 8.12 Diagram for AAHPER Football Blocking Test. From *Skills Test Manual: Football* (1965). Reprinted by permission of the American Alliance for Health, Physical Education, Recreation, and Dance, 1900 Association Drive, Reston, VA 22091.

ameter. The bottom of the outer circle is 3 feet (.914 m) from the ground. To keep the canvas taut, insert a wooden or metal bar in a channel sewn along the bottom of the canvas and then tie the channel to the goal posts. A restraining line is drawn 15 yards (13.71 m) from the target. The player takes two or three small running steps along the line, hesitates, and then throws at the target. The player may go either to the right or to the left but must stay behind the restraining line. He or she should pass the ball with good speed. Ten trials are given. *Scoring:* The target circles score 3, 2, and 1 points for the inner, middle, and outer circles respectively. Passes hitting on a line are given the higher value. The point total for the 10 trials is the score.

5. *Football Punt for Distance.* The player takes one or two steps within the 6-foot (1.828-m) kicking zone and punts the ball as far as possible. The administration and scoring of the forward punt for distance are the same as for the forward pass for distance.

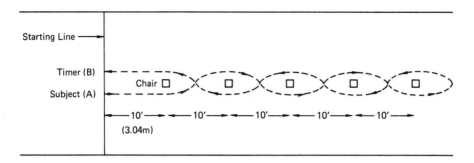

Figure 8.13 Ball Changing Zigzag Run Test. From *Skills Test Manual: Football* (1965). Reprinted by permission of the American Alliance for Health, Physical Education, Recreation, and Dance, 1900 Association Drive, Reston, VA 22091.

6. *Ball Changing Zigzag Run.* Five chairs are placed in a line, 10 feet (3.048 m) apart, and all facing away from the starting line (see Figure 8.13). The first chair is 10 feet (3.048 m) in front of the starting line. Holding a football under the right arm, the subject starts from behind the starting line on the signal *Go!* The subject runs to the right of the first chair and then changes the ball to the left arm while running to the left of the second chair. He or she continues running in and out of the chairs in this manner, changing the position of the ball to the outside arm as each chair is passed. The inside arm should be extended as in stiff-arming. The subject circles around the end chair and runs in and out of the chairs back to the starting line. The subject is not allowed to hit the chairs. Two time trials are given. *Scoring:* The time from the signal *Go!* until the subject passes back over the starting line is recorded to the nearest .10 second. The better of the two trials constitutes the subject's score.

7. *Catching the Forward Pass.* A scrimmage line is drawn with two *end* marks located 9 feet (2.743 m) to the right and to the left of the center (see Figure 8.14). At a distance of 30 feet (9.144 m) in front of these marks are *turning points*. The subject lines up on the right *end* mark facing the *turn-*

ing point 30 feet (9.144 m) directly in front of him. On the signal *Go!*, the subject runs straight ahead, cuts around the turning point, and runs to receive the pass 30 feet (9.144 m) away at the *passing point*. On the signal *Go!*, the center snaps the ball 15 feet (4.572 m) to the passer, who takes one step and then passes the ball directly over the *passing point* above head height. The passer must be able to pass the ball in a mechanical manner to the passing point without paying attention to the receiver. A similar passing point is located 30 feet (9.144 m) to the left of the left turning point. Ten trials are given to the right and 10 trials are given to the left. The player need not try to catch poorly thrown passes, but he must go around the turning point before proceeding to the passing point. *Scoring:* One point is scored for each pass caught. The sum of passes caught from both sides is recorded as the score. *Note:* The passer needs considerable practice and skill to be able to time the pass so as to enable the subject to reach the passing point in a controlled manner and catch the ball.

8. *Pull-Out.* The subject lines up in a set position halfway between two goal posts. On the signal *Go!*, he or she pulls out and runs parallel to the imaginary line of scrimmage, cuts around the right-hand goal post, and

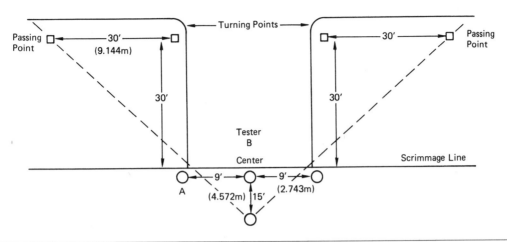

Figure 8.14 Diagram for AAHPER Football Forward Pass Catching Test. From *Skills Test Manual: Football* (1965). Reprinted by permission of the American Alliance for Health, Physical Education, Recreation, and Dance, 1900 Association Drive, Reston, VA 22091.

races straight ahead across a finish line 30 feet (9.144 m) from and parallel to the goal posts. Two time trials are given. *Scoring:* The score is the better of the two time trials, measured in seconds and tenths of seconds from the signal *Go!* until the subject crosses the finish line.

9. *Kick-Off.* A kicking tee is placed in the center of one of the lines running across the field. The ball is positioned so that it tilts slightly back toward the kicker. The player takes as long a run as desired and kicks the ball as far as possible. Three trials are given. *Scoring:* The scoring of the kick-off item is the same as for the forward pass and the punt for distance.

10. *Dodging Run.* The course is laid out as is shown in Figure 8.15. The player starts

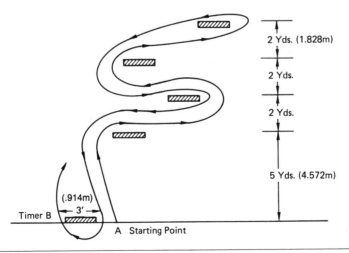

Figure 8.15 Diagram for AAHPER Dodging Run Test. From *Skills Test Manual: Football* (1965). Reprinted by permission of the American Alliance for Health, Physical Education, Recreation, and Dance, 1900 Association Drive, Reston, VA 22091.

from behind the line to the right of the first hurdle, which is on the starting line. On the signal *Go!*, he or she runs to the left of the second hurdle and follows the course as shown in the diagram. Two complete round trips constitute a run; two runs are given. The ball does not have to be changed from side to side. *Scoring:* The time is measured to the nearest .10 second. The better of the two runs is recorded as the score.

Golf

The best test of golf skill is the score an individual makes when playing 9 or 18 holes of golf. However, shorter tests may be devised. One may play only 4 or 5 holes, and if this short version includes a par 3, 4, or 5 hole, a player's golf skill may be adequately estimated.

Vanderhoff (1956) developed an *indoor golf test* that involves hitting plastic golf balls with a number 2-wood and a 5-iron. Validity coefficients of .71 and .66 were determined for the drive test and 5-iron test respectively with ratings of ability and the score on playing 6 holes of golf for college women as the criteria. The reliability correlation was .90 for the drive test and .84 for the 5-iron test.

For both tests the pupil is allowed unlimited practice swings, two or three warm-up balls, and 15 test trials with each club. The 15 shots or trials are taken at a distance of 14 feet (4.267 m) from the near edge of the target, which is divided into three zones as illustrated in Figure 8.16. Each of the three zones is 20 feet (6.096 m) long, and each ball is scored by the value of the zone in which it lands (i.e., 1, 2, or 3 points). Each shot must go under a rope 8 feet (2.438 m) high, but it must be in the air when it goes under the rope. Total the score for each club for the 15 trials. Two topped balls in succession count as one trial. Cocoa or rubber mats should be used. In the drive test,

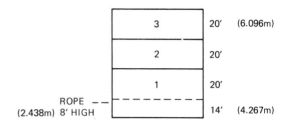

Figure 8.16   Scoring area for Vanderhoof drive and #5-iron approved shot tests. From *Beginning Golf Achievement Tests* by E.R. Vanderhoof, 1956. Master's thesis, University of Iowa, Iowa City.

the ball is placed on a plastic tee. No tee is used in the 5-iron test.

Gymnastics

A gymnastics readiness test has been developed for males and females by the United States Gymnastics Safety Association (1979). These tests are designed to promote safety in gymnastics by identifying individuals who are ready to participate in beginning-level gymnastics. The readiness tests are composed of 25 stunts for boys and 25 stunts for girls. The manual lists norms for ages 6 through 22. Learners receive a score of 1, 2, 3, or 4 points on each stunt. The total score is the sum of all stunt scores. Based on total scores, gymnasts can be classified into discrete groups (i.e., beginners, advanced beginners, and those who require remedial work to improve strength, endurance, and fundamental movements before actually beginning gymnastics instruction).

The measurement of gymnastic performance at the intermediate and advanced levels is quite complex in that routines are performed for judges. The National Federation of State High School Associations has published the *Official Boys (1985-87) and Girls (1985-86) Gymnastics Rules and Manual*. Rules for conducting meets and scoring the events of parallel bars, uneven parallel bars, vaulting, side horse, balance beam, rings, and floor exercises are covered in detail. Ten maximum points are awarded depending on the event and performance as follows:

Composition	Component parts	0.5
	Combinations and connections	2.0
	Difficulty	3.0
Execution	Execution and amplitude	4.0
	General impression	0.5
		10.0

The scoring for each event is illustrated in the manual with exact descriptions of point deductions for each fault.

Soccer

Two items that appear on a number of soccer skills tests are the soccer ball *wall volley* and the *soccer dribble* test. Directions for administering and scoring these two items are presented in the discussion of eye-foot coordination-agility in chapter 6 on "Components of Motor Performance." These two items measure the important elements of soccer performance that deal with trapping, dribbling, and overall ball control. McCabe and McArdle (1978) report validity coefficients for the test items ranging from .53 to .94 using the criterion of expert judges' ratings of playing ability for wall volley and soccer dribble skills.

The element of the soccer kick for goal can be included in the soccer dribble test with the following simple modification. The starting line for the dribbling course should be inside the semicircle 20 yards (18.28 m) from the goal line. A regulation goal on a field may be used, or the goal dimensions can be painted on a gym wall. When the player crosses the finish line

(which is also the starting line) and dribbles another 10 yards (9.14 m), he or she kicks for goal.

The *soccer kick for distance* with either foot is another suggested skill test item. The pupil kicks a stationary ball from the end line and within a lane 25 yards (12.85 m) wide. The distance the ball travels in the air is measured. Three trials are allowed with each foot. The farthest kick with each foot is recorded as the score.

Softball

The *AAHPER Softball Skills Test Manuals* (1966) offer a battery of eight items designed to measure the fundamental skills of softball for boys and girls. These eight items include (a) softball throw for distance, (b) overhand throw for accuracy, (c) underhand pitching, (d) speed throw, (e) fungo hitting, (f) base running, (g) fielding ground balls, and (h) catching fly balls. Content validity of the test items is assumed. Minimum reliability coefficients of .70 for items of accuracy and form and .80 for items scored on a distance basis are reported. The directions for administering and scoring the items are the same for both boys and girls except that the distances for the accuracy throw and underhand pitching are shorter for girls. A diagram indicating testing stations is presented in Figure 8.17. Percentile rank norms for boys and girls appear in Tables 8.20 through 8.37. Descriptions of test administration procedures follow;[6] players should go through a suitable warm-up before testing.

---

[6]Adapted from the *Skills Test Manual: Softball for Girls and Softball for Boys* (1966). Reprinted by permission of the American Alliance for Health, Physical Education, Recreation, and Dance, 1900 Association Drive, Reston, VA 22091.

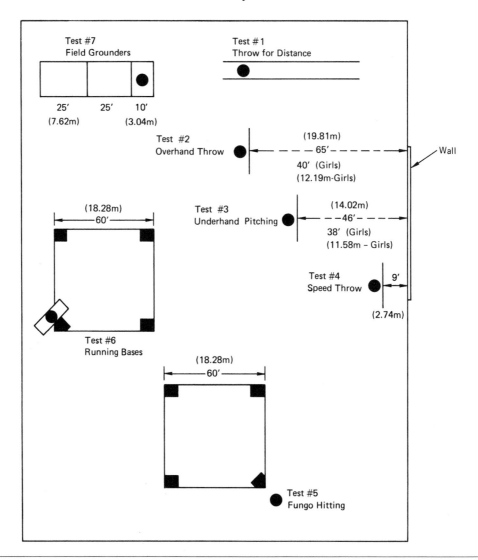

Figure 8.17 Location of softball testing stations. From *Skills Test Manual: Softball for Girls and Softball for Boys* (1966). Reprinted by permission of the American Alliance for Health, Physical Education, Recreation, and Dance, 1900 Association Drive, Reston, VA 22091.

Table 8.20 Softball Throw for Distance (Boys)—Percentile Scores Based on Age/Test Scores in Feet

				Age (years)			
Percentile	10-11	12	13	14	15	16	17-18
100th	200	208	200	230	242	247	255
95th	154	163	185	208	231	229	229
90th	144	152	175	203	205	219	222
85th	127	146	167	191	198	213	216
80th	121	140	160	184	192	208	213
75th	118	135	154	178	187	202	207
70th	114	132	150	173	182	196	204
65th	111	129	145	168	178	193	199
60th	109	125	142	163	174	190	196
55th	106	122	138	159	170	186	192
50th	103	118	135	154	167	183	188
45th	100	115	131	152	165	180	185
40th	98	113	128	148	161	174	182
35th	95	109	125	144	157	171	178
30th	92	106	122	140	154	167	173
25th	91	102	117	137	148	164	169
20th	85	98	113	133	143	159	163
15th	80	93	107	129	138	152	153
10th	72	85	101	123	133	146	147
5th	62	76	97	113	119	140	140
0	24	31	60	105	93	135	90

Note. Tables 8.20 through 8.37 are from *Skills Test Manual: Softball for Girls and Softball for Boys* (1966). Reprinted by permission of the American Alliance for Health, Physical Education, Recreation, and Dance, 1900 Association Drive, Reston, VA 22091.

Table 8.21 Softball Throw for Distance (Boys)—
Percentile Scores Based on Age/Test Scores in Meters

				Age (years)			
Percentile	10-11	12	13	14	15	16	17-18
100th	60.96	63.39	60.96	70.10	73.76	75.28	77.72
95th	46.93	49.68	56.38	63.39	70.40	69.79	69.79
90th	43.89	46.32	53.34	61.87	62.48	66.75	67.66
85th	38.70	44.50	50.90	58.21	60.35	64.92	65.83
80th	36.88	42.62	48.76	56.08	58.52	63.39	64.92
75th	35.96	41.14	46.93	54.25	56.99	61.56	63.09

(Cont.)

Table 8.21 (Cont.)

				Age (years)			
Percentile	10-11	12	13	14	15	16	17-18
70th	34.74	40.23	45.72	52.73	55.47	59.74	62.17
65th	33.83	39.31	44.19	51.20	54.25	58.82	60.65
60th	33.22	38.10	43.68	49.68	53.03	57.91	59.74
55th	32.30	37.18	42.06	48.46	51.81	56.69	58.52
50th	31.39	35.96	41.14	46.93	50.90	55.77	57.30
45th	30.48	35.05	39.92	46.32	50.29	54.86	56.38
40th	29.87	34.42	39.01	45.11	49.07	53.03	55.47
35th	28.95	33.22	38.10	43.89	47.85	52.12	54.25
30th	28.04	32.30	37.18	43.67	46.93	50.90	52.73
25th	27.73	31.08	35.66	41.75	45.11	49.98	51.51
20th	25.90	29.87	34.44	40.53	43.58	48.46	49.68
15th	24.38	28.34	32.61	39.31	42.06	46.32	46.63
10th	21.94	25.90	30.78	37.49	40.53	44.50	44.80
5th	18.89	23.16	29.56	34.44	36.27	42.67	42.67
0	7.31	9.44	18.28	32.00	28.34	41.14	27.43

Table 8.22 Overhand Throw for Accuracy (Boys)—Percentile Scores Based on Age/Test Scores in Points

				Age (years)			
Percentile	10-11	12	13	14	15	16	17-18
100th	22	22	23	25	25	27	25
95th	14	17	18	19	20	20	21
90th	12	15	16	17	17	18	19
85th	11	13	15	16	16	17	18
80th	9	12	13	15	15	16	17
75th	8	11	12	14	14	15	16
70th	8	11	12	13	13	14	15
65th	7	10	11	12	12	14	15
60th	6	9	10	11	11	13	14
55th	5	9	10	11	11	12	13
50th	5	8	9	10	10	11	13
45th	4	7	8	10	10	11	12
40th	4	6	7	9	9	10	11

(Cont.)

Table 8.22 (Cont.)

Percentile	Age (years)						
	10-11	12	13	14	15	16	17-18
35th	3	6	7	8	9	9	11
30th	3	5	6	8	8	8	10
25th	2	4	5	7	7	8	9
20th	1	3	4	6	7	7	8
15th	1	3	3	6	6	6	7
10th	0	2	2	5	5	5	6
5th	0	0	1	3	3	4	4
0	0	0	0	0	0	1	0

Table 8.23   Underhand Pitch (Boys)—Percentile Scores Based on Age/Test Scores in Points

Percentile	Age (years)						
	10-11	12	13	14	15	16	17-18
100th	18	23	21	22	24	25	25
95th	12	14	15	16	18	19	19
90th	10	12	13	15	16	17	17
85th	9	11	11	14	15	15	16
80th	8	9	10	12	14	14	15
75th	7	9	10	12	13	13	14
70th	7	8	9	11	12	12	13
65th	6	7	8	10	11	12	12
60th	6	7	8	9	10	11	12
55th	5	6	7	9	10	10	11
50th	4	6	7	8	9	9	10
45th	4	5	6	7	8	9	10
40th	3	4	5	7	7	8	9
35th	3	4	5	6	7	8	8
30th	2	3	4	6	6	7	8
25th	2	3	4	5	5	6	7
20th	1	2	3	4	4	5	6
15th	1	2	3	4	4	4	5
10th	1	1	2	3	3	3	4
5th	0	0	1	2	2	2	3
0	0	0	0	0	0	0	0

Measurement and Evaluation for Physical Educators

Table 8.24 Speed Throw (Boys)—
Percentile Scores Based on Age/Test Scores in Seconds and Tenths

| Percentile | Age (years) | | | | | | |
	10-11	12	13	14	15	16	17-18
100th	13.1	11.0	10.0	9.0	13.0	10.0	10.0
95th	16.1	15.3	14.9	13.0	13.5	12.5	12.1
90th	17.1	16.1	14.9	14.0	13.8	13.2	12.8
85th	17.6	16.8	15.7	14.6	14.2	13.7	13.2
80th	18.0	17.3	16.2	15.1	14.5	14.1	13.3
75th	18.6	17.6	16.8	15.6	14.9	14.5	13.9
70th	19.1	18.0	16.9	15.9	15.6	14.8	14.2
65th	19.7	18.4	17.3	16.3	15.9	15.1	14.5
60th	20.2	18.9	17.6	16.6	16.0	15.5	14.8
55th	20.8	19.5	17.9	17.1	16.4	15.8	14.9
50th	21.3	19.8	18.4	17.3	16.7	16.4	15.3
45th	21.8	20.4	19.1	17.7	17.1	16.6	15.6
40th	22.6	21.0	19.3	18.1	17.5	17.1	16.2
35th	23.6	21.5	19.8	18.5	17.9	17.4	16.7
30th	24.6	22.2	20.6	19.0	18.3	18.2	17.2
25th	25.7	23.1	21.2	19.5	18.9	18.8	17.6
20th	26.7	23.9	21.9	20.2	19.5	19.4	18.3
15th	28.2	25.4	23.0	21.3	20.2	19.9	18.9
10th	30.1	27.8	24.2	22.5	20.9	20.9	19.9
5th	34.7	29.5	26.4	25.1	22.2	23.0	21.2
0	43.1	36.0	29.3	28.2	24.9	25.5	26.1

Table 8.25 Fungo Hitting (Boys)—Percentile Scores Based on Age/Test Scores in Points

| Percentile | Age (years) | | | | | | |
	10-11	12	13	14	15	16	17-18
100th	40	40	39	36	40	40	40
95th	35	36	38	35	39	38	39
90th	32	33	34	35	37	36	37
85th	29	31	33	33	34	34	36
80th	27	30	31	31	33	33	35
75th	26	29	30	30	31	33	34
70th	24	28	29	29	30	32	32

(Cont.)

Table 8.25 (Cont.)

Percentile	Age (years)						
	10-11	12	13	14	15	16	17-18
65th	22	27	28	28	29	30	31
60th	21	26	27	27	28	29	30
55th	20	25	25	26	26	28	29
50th	19	23	24	24	24	26	28
45th	17	22	23	23	23	25	26
40th	16	20	21	21	21	23	25
35th	14	19	19	19	19	21	23
30th	13	17	18	18	17	19	21
25th	11	15	16	16	16	17	19
20th	10	13	15	15	14	15	17
15th	8	11	14	13	12	13	15
10th	6	10	12	12	11	11	13
5th	3	7	9	11	9	9	11
0	0	0	1	9	1	0	3

Table 8.26 Base Running (Boys)—
Percentile Scores Based on Age/Test Scores in Seconds and Tenths

Percentile	Age (years)						
	10-11	12	13	14	15	16	17-18
100th	10.1	9.6	9.4	9.7	10.0	10.0	10.0
95th	12.9	12.4	11.7	11.5	11.6	11.3	11.1
90th	13.5	12.5	12.2	11.9	11.9	11.6	11.4
85th	13.9	13.3	12.7	12.2	12.2	11.8	11.6
80th	14.1	13.5	12.9	12.5	12.4	12.0	11.8
75th	14.3	13.7	13.2	12.7	12.5	12.1	11.9
70th	14.5	13.9	13.4	12.9	12.7	12.3	12.0
65th	14.8	14.1	13.6	13.0	12.8	12.4	12.2
60th	14.9	14.3	13.8	13.1	13.0	12.5	12.3
55th	15.1	14.5	13.9	13.3	13.1	12.6	12.4
50th	15.2	14.7	14.1	13.4	13.2	12.8	12.6
45th	15.4	14.8	14.3	13.5	13.3	12.9	12.7
40th	15.6	15.0	14.5	13.7	13.5	13.0	12.8
35th	15.8	15.2	14.7	13.9	13.6	13.2	12.9

(Cont.)

Table 8.26 (Cont.)

Percentile	10-11	12	13	Age (years) 14	15	16	17-18
30th	16.0	15.4	14.9	14.1	13.7	13.3	13.0
25th	16.2	15.7	15.1	14.2	13.9	13.6	13.2
20th	16.5	15.9	15.4	14.5	14.0	13.8	13.4
15th	17.0	16.2	15.7	14.8	14.3	14.1	13.6
10th	17.4	16.5	15.9	15.2	14.5	14.4	13.9
5th	18.2	17.4	16.7	15.8	15.0	15.3	14.9
0	23.0	20.6	17.2	17.2	15.8	18.0	17.8

Table 8.27 Fielding Ground Balls (Boys)—Percentile Scores Based on Age/Test Scores in Points

Percentile	10-11	12	13	Age (years) 14	15	16	17-18
100th	20	20	20	20	20	20	20
95th	19	20	20	20	20	20	20
90th	18	19	19	19	19	20	20
85th	18	19	19	19	19	20	20
80th	17	18	18	18	18	19	19
75th	17	18	18	18	18	19	19
70th	16	17	17	17	18	19	19
65th	16	17	17	17	17	18	18
60th	15	16	16	16	16	18	18
55th	15	16	16	16	16	17	17
50th	14	15	15	15	15	17	17
45th	13	15	14	14	15	16	17
40th	13	14	14	14	14	16	16
35th	12	14	13	13	13	15	16
30th	11	13	13	12	12	14	15
25th	10	12	12	10	11	13	14
20th	9	11	11	10	10	10	12
15th	8	9	10	9	9	9	10
10th	6	8	8	8	8	9	9
5th	4	6	6	6	7	8	9
0	0	0	1	1	1	5	6

Table 8.28 Catching Fly Balls (Boys)—Percentile Scores Based on Age/Test Scores in Points

Percentile	Age (years)						
	10-11	12	13	14	15	16	17-18
100th	20	20	20	20	20	20	20
95th	20	20	20	20	20	20	20
90th	20	20	20	20	20	20	20
85th	19	19	19	19	20	20	20
80th	19	19	19	19	19	19	19
75th	19	19	19	19	19	19	19
70th	18	19	18	19	19	19	19
65th	18	18	18	18	18	19	19
60th	17	18	17	18	18	18	18
55th	17	17	17	18	17	18	18
50th	16	17	16	16	17	17	18
45th	15	16	16	16	16	16	17
40th	14	15	15	15	15	15	16
35th	12	14	14	13	14	13	15
30th	10	12	13	12	12	10	14
25th	9	10	11	10	11	10	11
20th	8	10	10	10	10	10	10
15th	7	8	9	9	9	9	10
10th	6	7	8	8	8	9	9
5th	3	5	6	7	7	8	9
0	0	0	0	0	0	0	0

Table 8.29 Softball Throw for Distance (Girls)—Percentile Scores Based on Age/Test Scores in Feet

Percentile	Age (years)						
	10-11	12	13	14	15	16	17-18
100th	120	160	160	160	200	200	200
95th	99	113	133	126	127	121	120
90th	84	104	112	117	116	109	109
85th	76	98	105	109	108	103	102
80th	71	94	98	104	103	98	97
75th	68	89	94	99	97	94	93
70th	66	85	90	95	93	91	89
65th	62	81	86	92	88	87	87
60th	60	77	83	88	85	84	84

(Cont.)

Table 8.29 (Cont.)

Percentile	Age (years)						
	10-11	12	13	14	15	16	17-18
55th	57	74	81	85	80	81	82
50th	55	70	76	82	77	79	80
45th	53	67	73	79	75	76	77
40th	50	64	70	76	72	73	74
35th	48	61	68	73	70	70	72
30th	45	58	64	69	67	67	69
25th	43	55	62	66	64	63	66
20th	41	51	60	61	61	60	63
15th	38	48	56	57	58	56	60
10th	34	43	51	52	54	51	55
5th	31	37	43	43	49	45	50
0	20	20	20	20	20	10	10

Table 8.30 Softball Throw for Distance (Girls)—
Percentile Scores Based on Age/Test Scores in Meters

Percentile	Age (years)						
	10-11	12	13	14	15	16	17-18
100th	36.57	48.76	48.76	48.76	60.96	60.96	60.96
95th	30.17	34.44	40.53	38.40	38.70	36.88	36.57
90th	25.60	31.69	34.13	35.66	35.35	33.22	33.20
85th	23.16	29.87	32.00	33.22	32.91	31.39	31.08
80th	21.64	28.65	29.87	31.69	31.39	29.87	29.56
75th	20.72	27.12	28.65	30.17	29.56	28.65	28.34
70th	20.11	25.90	27.43	28.95	28.34	27.73	27.12
65th	18.89	24.68	26.21	28.04	26.82	26.51	26.51
60th	18.28	23.46	25.29	26.82	25.90	25.60	25.60
55th	17.37	22.55	24.68	25.90	24.38	24.68	24.99
50th	16.76	21.33	23.16	24.99	23.46	24.07	24.38
45th	16.15	20.42	22.25	24.07	22.86	23.16	23.46
40th	15.24	19.50	21.33	23.16	21.94	22.25	22.55
35th	14.63	18.59	20.72	22.25	21.33	21.33	21.94
30th	13.71	17.67	19.50	21.03	20.42	20.42	21.03

(Cont.)

Table 8.30 (Cont.)

Percentile				Age (years)			
	10-11	12	13	14	15	16	17-18
25th	13.10	16.76	18.89	20.11	19.50	19.20	20.11
20th	12.49	15.54	18.28	18.59	18.59	18.28	19.20
15th	11.58	14.63	17.06	17.37	17.67	17.06	18.28
10th	10.36	13.10	15.54	15.84	16.45	15.54	16.76
5th	9.44	11.27	13.10	13.10	14.93	13.71	15.24
0	6.09	6.09	6.09	6.09	6.09	3.04	3.04

Table 8.31 Overhand Throw for Accuracy (Girls)—Percentile Scores Based on Age/Test Scores in Points

Percentile				Age (years)			
	10-11	12	13	14	15	16	17-18
100th	24	26	26	26	30	30	26
95th	17	17	18	19	19	22	20
90th	14	16	16	17	18	20	18
85th	13	14	15	15	16	18	17
80th	12	13	14	14	15	17	16
75th	11	12	13	13	14	16	15
70th	10	11	12	12	13	15	14
65th	9	10	11	11	12	13	13
60th	8	9	10	11	11	12	12
55th	7	9	9	10	11	12	11
50th	6	8	9	9	10	11	10
45th	5	7	8	9	9	10	9
40th	4	6	7	8	8	9	8
35th	4	5	6	7	8	8	7
30th	3	4	6	6	7	7	6
25th	2	4	5	5	6	6	5
20th	1	3	4	4	5	5	4
15th	1	2	3	3	3	4	3
10th	0	1	1	2	2	2	2
5th	0	0	0	1	1	1	1
0	0	0	0	0	0	0	0

Table 8.32 Underhand Pitch (Girls)—Percentile Scores Based on Age/Test Scores in Points

Percentile	Age (years)						
	10-11	12	13	14	15	16	17-18
100th	23	22	24	24	26	27	26
95th	12	14	16	17	16	19	21
90th	10	13	14	15	15	16	18
85th	8	11	12	14	13	14	17
80th	7	10	11	13	12	12	15
75th	6	9	10	12	11	12	14
70th	6	8	9	11	10	11	13
65th	5	7	9	10	9	10	12
60th	5	6	8	9	8	10	11
55th	4	6	7	8	7	9	10
50th	4	5	7	8	6	8	9
45th	3	5	6	7	6	8	9
40th	3	4	6	6	5	7	8
35th	2	4	5	5	4	6	7
30th	2	3	4	5	4	5	6
25th	1	2	4	4	3	5	5
20th	1	2	3	3	2	4	5
15th	0	1	2	3	2	3	4
10th	0	0	2	2	1	2	3
5th	0	0	1	1	0	0	2
0	0	0	0	0	0	0	0

Table 8.33 Speed Throw (Girls)—
Percentile Scores Based on Age/Test Scores in Seconds and Tenths

Percentile	Age (years)						
	10-11	12	13	14	15	16	17-18
100th	10.0	12.0	12.0	12.0	12.0	14.0	14.0
95th	20.1	13.8	13.0	13.0	15.6	15.8	15.0
90th	21.4	15.8	16.3	13.9	16.6	16.9	15.0
85th	22.8	17.7	17.8	15.3	17.6	17.6	15.6
80th	24.1	18.8	18.6	16.5	18.1	18.1	16.1
75th	25.2	19.8	19.4	17.6	18.6	18.5	17.6

(Cont.)

Table 8.33 (Cont.)

Percentile	Age (years)						
	10-11	12	13	14	15	16	17-18
70th	26.0	20.8	20.0	18.2	19.1	18.9	18.0
65th	27.0	21.6	20.6	18.7	19.6	19.4	18.5
60th	27.4	22.3	21.3	19.3	20.1	20.0	18.9
55th	28.8	23.1	21.9	19.9	20.6	20.7	19.3
50th	29.8	24.1	22.7	20.7	21.1	21.4	19.8
45th	30.9	25.2	23.4	21.1	21.7	22.2	20.3
40th	31.9	26.2	24.3	21.8	22.6	22.9	20.8
35th	33.0	27.5	25.4	22.5	23.3	23.7	21.4
30th	34.1	28.6	26.4	23.5	24.3	24.8	22.3
25th	35.9	29.8	27.5	24.6	25.4	26.1	23.3
20th	38.0	31.3	28.9	25.8	26.9	27.8	24.1
15th	41.0	33.1	30.9	27.4	28.7	30.4	25.0
10th	46.1	36.7	33.0	30.2	31.5	33.0	26.1
5th	55.2	40.8	38.5	33.5	37.4	36.9	28.9
0	105.0	66.0	52.0	50.0	50.0	52.0	40.0

Table 8.34 Fungo Hitting (Girls)—Percentile Scores Based on Age/Test Scores in Points

Percentile	Age (years)						
	10-11	12	13	14	15	16	17-18
100th	30	38	38	38	38	38	38
95th	21	28	30	31	30	30	31
90th	18	24	26	30	27	27	28
85th	15	22	23	26	25	25	26
80th	14	20	22	23	23	24	25
75th	13	18	20	21	22	22	23
70th	12	17	19	20	20	21	22
65th	12	16	18	19	19	19	20
60th	11	15	17	18	18	18	19
55th	9	14	16	17	17	17	18
50th	9	13	14	15	16	16	17
45th	8	12	13	14	15	15	16
40th	7	11	13	13	14	14	15
35th	6	10	12	12	13	13	14
30th	6	9	11	11	12	12	14

(Cont.)

Table 8.34 (Cont.)

Percentile	Age (years)						
	10-11	12	13	14	15	16	17-18
25th	5	8	10	10	11	11	13
20th	4	7	8	9	10	10	12
15th	3	5	7	8	8	9	10
10th	2	4	6	6	7	8	8
5th	0	2	4	3	4	5	6
0	0	0	0	0	0	0	0

Table 8.35 Base Running (Girls)—
Percentile Scores Based on Age/Test Scores in Seconds and Tenths

Percentile	Age (years)						
	10-11	12	13	14	15	16	17-18
100th	11.0	11.0	12.0	12.0	12.0	12.0	12.0
95th	13.1	13.4	12.6	12.7	12.9	13.2	13.6
90th	13.8	13.7	13.1	13.1	13.5	13.7	13.9
85th	14.3	14.0	13.5	13.5	13.7	14.0	14.3
80th	14.7	14.3	13.7	13.7	13.9	14.4	14.6
75th	14.9	14.5	13.9	13.8	14.1	14.6	14.8
70th	15.2	14.7	14.1	14.0	14.3	14.8	14.9
65th	15.4	14.9	14.3	14.2	14.5	14.9	15.1
60th	15.6	15.0	14.5	14.4	14.7	15.1	15.3
55th	15.8	15.2	14.7	14.5	14.9	15.3	15.5
50th	16.0	15.3	14.8	14.8	15.0	15.5	15.7
45th	16.2	15.5	15.0	14.9	15.2	15.6	15.9
40th	16.4	15.7	15.2	15.1	15.4	15.8	16.1
35th	16.7	15.8	15.4	15.3	15.5	15.9	16.3
30th	17.0	16.0	15.6	15.5	15.8	16.0	16.5
25th	17.3	16.2	16.0	15.7	16.1	16.2	16.9
20th	17.7	16.5	16.3	16.0	16.3	16.3	17.1
15th	18.2	16.9	16.6	16.4	16.7	16.4	17.6
10th	18.8	17.4	17.2	16.9	17.3	17.8	18.2
5th	19.9	18.2	18.0	17.8	18.1	18.4	19.2
0	27.0	20.0	22.0	23.0	28.0	31.0	32.0

Table 8.36 Fielding Ground Balls (Girls)—Percentile Scores Based on Age/Test Scores in Points

				Age (years)			
Percentile	10-11	12	13	14	15	16	17-18
100th	20	20	20	20	20	20	20
95th	18	20	20	20	20	20	20
90th	17	19	19	19	20	20	20
85th	16	19	19	19	19	19	19
80th	15	18	19	19	19	19	19
75th	15	18	18	18	18	19	19
70th	14	17	18	18	18	18	18
65th	13	16	17	17	18	18	18
60th	13	15	17	17	17	18	18
55th	12	15	16	17	17	17	17
50th	11	14	16	16	16	17	17
45th	10	13	15	15	16	17	17
40th	10	12	15	15	15	16	16
35th	9	10	14	14	15	16	16
30th	8	10	13	13	14	15	15
25th	8	9	12	12	13	14	14
20th	7	9	11	10	12	13	14
15th	6	8	10	10	11	12	13
10th	5	7	9	9	10	10	11
5th	3	5	8	8	9	8	9
0	0	0	0	0	0	0	0

Table 8.37 Catching Fly Balls (Girls)—Percentile Scores Based on Age/Test Scores in Points

				Age (years)			
Percentile	10-11	12	13	14	15	16	17-18
100th	15	17	19	19	20	20	20
95th	13	15	17	17	19	19	19
90th	10	13	15	16	18	19	19
85th	9	11	13	15	18	18	18
80th	9	10	12	14	17	17	17
75th	8	9	11	13	16	16	16
70th	7	8	10	12	15	15	16
65th	7	7	9	11	14	14	15
60th	6	7	8	10	13	13	15

(Cont.)

Table 8.37 (Cont.)

Percentile	Age (years)						
	10-11	12	13	14	15	16	17-18
55th	6	6	7	9	12	13	14
50th	5	6	6	9	11	12	13
45th	4	5	5	8	10	11	12
40th	4	5	5	8	9	10	11
35th	3	4	4	7	8	9	10
30th	3	3	3	6	7	8	9
25th	2	3	3	5	6	7	8
20th	2	2	2	4	5	6	7
15th	1	2	2	3	4	5	6
10th	1	1	1	2	3	4	5
5th	0	0	0	1	2	3	4
0	0	0	0	0	0	0	0

1. *Softball Throw for Distance.* A throwing line is marked off at one end of the field, and a line parallel to and 6 feet (1.82 m) from it is also marked off, thus forming a zone 6 feet (1.82 m) wide from which each of three throws is made. The player takes position in the zone, takes one or two steps, and throws the ball as far and as close to right angles to the throwing line as possible. A stake is inserted in the ground where the ball first lands. The score is the distance of the longest throw in feet or meters.

2. *Overhand Throw for Accuracy.* The subject makes 10 throws from a distance of 65 feet (19.81 m) for boys or 40 feet (12.19 m) for girls at a target with the following dimensions: three concentric circles with 1-inch (2.54-cm) lines, the center circle measuring 2 feet (.6096 m) in diameter, the next circle 4 feet (1.21 m) in diameter, and the outer circle 6 feet (1.82 m) in diameter. The bottom of the outer circle is 3 feet (.914 m) from the floor. The target may be marked on a wall or, preferably, in order to conserve softballs, on canvas against a mat hung on the wall. (This target is the same target used in the AAHPER football skills battery.) The student is given one or two practice throws prior to the 10 trials. Balls hitting the center circle count 3 points; balls hitting the second circle count 2 points; and balls hitting the outer circle count 1 point. The total points made on 10 throws is the score. Balls hitting a line are given the higher point value.

3. *Underhand Pitching.* The target is rectangular in shape, representing the strike zone. The bottom of the target is 18 inches (45.72 cm) from the floor. The target's outer lines are 42 inches (106.68 cm) and 29 inches (73.66 cm) wide. An inner rectangle is drawn 30 inches (76.2 cm) by 17 inches (43.18 cm). A 24-inch (60.96-cm) pitching line is drawn 46 feet

(14.02 m) from the target for boys and 38 feet (11.58 m) for girls. The student takes one practice pitch and then pitches 15 underhand trials to the target. He or she must keep one foot on the pitching line while delivering the ball but may take a step forward. Only legal pitches are scored. A mat behind the target helps prevent damage to the softballs. Balls hitting the center area or its boundary line count 2 points, and balls hitting the outer area count 1 point. The score is the sum of the points made with 15 pitches.

4. *Speed Throw.* Holding a softball, the student stands behind a line drawn on the floor 9 feet (2.74 m) from a smooth wall. On the signal *Go*, the student throws the ball overhand against the wall and catches the rebound. He or she repeats this as rapidly as possible until 15 hits have been made against the wall. Balls that fall between the wall and the restraining line can be retrieved, but the subject must return behind the line before continuing. If the ball gets away entirely, the student may be given one new trial. A practice trial is allowed, and two trials are then given for time. The watch is started when the first ball hits the wall and is stopped when the 15th throw hits the wall. The score is the time to the nearest .10 second on the better of the two trials.

5. *Fungo Hitting.* The student selects a bat and stands behind home plate with a ball in his or her hand. When ready, the student tosses the ball up and tries to hit a fly ball into right field. He or she then hits the next ball into left field and alternates hitting to the right and left fields until 10 balls have been hit in each direction. Each time the ball is touched by the bat counts as one trial. If a player completely misses two balls in a row, it is considered a trial; otherwise a complete miss is not counted. Regardless of where the ball goes, the next ball must

be hit to the opposite (right or left) field. Practice trials are allowed to each side. Hits to a specific side must cross the baseline between second and third or first and second base. A fly ball that goes to the proper field counts 2 points, and a ground ball counts 1 point. No score is given for a ball that lands in the wrong field. The point value for each trial is recorded and summed at the end. The maximum score is 40 points.

6. *Base Running.* The student stands holding a bat in the right-hand batter's box. On the signal to hit, the subject swings at an imaginary ball, drops the bat, and races around the bases. The bat must not be thrown or carried, and a complete swing must be taken before beginning to run. Each base must be touched in proper sequence. One practice and two timed trials are given. The watch is started on the signal *Hit* and is stopped when the runner touches home plate. The better time of the two trials to the nearest .10 second is the score. The distance from home plate to first base is 60 feet (18.28 m).

7. *Fielding Ground Balls.* A rectangular area 17 by 60 feet (5.18 m by 18.28 m) is marked off. Two lines are drawn across the area 25 feet and 50 feet (7.62 m and 15.24 m) from the front, or throwing line. This results in three areas being drawn. The subject stands in the 17- by 10-foot (5.18-m by 3.04-m) area at the end of the rectangle. The thrower stands behind the throwing line with a basket of 10 balls. On the signal to begin, the thrower begins throwing ground balls at exactly 5-second intervals into the first 17- by 25-foot (5.18- by 7.62-m) zone. The throw is made in an overhand manner with good speed. Each ball thrown must hit the ground inside the first area for at least one bounce. Some variation in direction is desirable, but the thrower should not deliberately try to make the student miss. A throw that does not land as specified

should be thrown again. The student should attempt to field each ball cleanly, hold it momentarily, and then toss it aside. The subject starts behind the 50-foot (15.24-m) line but thereafter may field the ball anywhere in back of the 25-foot (7.62-m) line. A practice trial and then 20 trials for score are given. Scoring is on a pass/fail basis. Each throw scores either 1 or 0 points. The maximum score is 20 points.

8. *Catching Fly Balls.* The subject stands at second base in the center of a 60-foot (18.28-m) square. The thrower stands in a restraining zone 5 feet (1.52 m) behind home plate and throws fly balls to the player as directed. The thrower must throw the ball over an 8-foot (2.43-m) high rope that is fastened between two standards located 5 feet (1.52 m) in front of home plate. The thrower must throw with good, regular speed. The subject must catch the ball, toss it aside, and be ready to catch the next ball. Twenty balls are thrown. The tester stands behind the player being tested and indicates to the thrower whether to throw left, right, or straight into the catching zone. At least one third of the throws should be thrown into each catching zone. Balls that are not thrown properly into the catching zone are not counted. The score is the number of balls successfully caught.

Swimming

Two test batteries using different reference standards are presented for swimming: the criterion-referenced American Red Cross progressive swimming courses, and the norm-referenced University of Kentucky Swimming Proficiency Test.

Red Cross Progressive Swimming Skills

The American Red Cross (1981) has developed a series of progressive swimming courses that are utilized in many instructional programs. A series of skills for the beginner, advanced beginner, intermediate swimmer, and advanced swimmer and for basic survival and advanced survival levels are proposed as the hierarchical instructional guides listed in Figure 8.18. These skills also form the basis for formative or summative evaluation. A work sheet used in conjunction with the swimming courses appears in Figure 8.19. In general, mastery learning utilizing the criterion-referenced standards listed in the instructor's manual are the techniques employed by the teacher.

University of Kentucky Swimming Proficiency Test

The University of Kentucky Swimming Proficiency Test was developed to measure swimming proficiency at the intermediate-advanced swimmer levels. It is proposed for summative evaluation and utilizes norm-referenced standards. The test consists of the following six items: (1) the 20-yard (18.28-m) underwater swim; (2) the 25-yard (22.86-m) crawl sprint; (3) the 5-minute swim for distance; and three 25-yard (22.86-m) swims of each of the following strokes: (4) elementary back stroke; (5) sidestroke; and (6) conventional breaststroke. Six-sigma scale scores for both sexes are available for each performance. The mean of a 6-σ scale equals .50, and the standard deviation equals 16.67 (see Tables 8.38 through 8.43). These scales were derived from the performances of students enrolled in intermediate swimming sections in the service program at the University of Kentucky. The test is administered according to the following standardized directions:[7]

---

[7]Adapted from the *University of Kentucky Swimming Proficiency Test* by the Department of Health, Physical Education, and Recreation, University of Kentucky. Reprinted by permission.

Red Cross Progressive Swimming Courses

BEGINNER SKILLS

1. Water adjustment skills
2. Hold breath—10 sec.
3. Rhythmic breathing—10 times
4. Prone float and recovery
5. Prone glide
6. Back glide and recovery
7. Survival float
8. Prone glide with kick
9. Back glide with kick
10. Beginner stroke or crawl stroke—15 yds.
11. Combined stroke on back—15 yds.
12. Leveling off and swimming
13. Jump (shallow water), swim
14. Jump (deep water), level, swim
15. Jump (deep water), level, turn over, swim on back
16. Changing directions
17. Turning over
18. Release of cramp
19. Assist nonswimmer to feet
20. Reaching and extension rescues
21. Use of PFD
22. Demonstration of artificial respiration
23. Safety information
24. Combined skills #1
25. Combined skills #2

SWIMMER SKILLS

1. Sidestroke—review/improve
2. Back crawl
3. Breaststroke—review/improve
4. Crawl stroke—review/improve
5. Surface dives—pike, tuck
6. Feet-first surface dive
7. Long shallow dive
8. 1 meter board—jumping entry
9. 1 meter board—standing dive
10. Stride jump
11. Inverted scissors kick
12. Sculling—snail and canoe
13. Open turn—front
14. Open turn—back
15. Open turn—side

16. Survival float—review
17. Survival stroke—5 min.
18. Underwater swim—20-25 ft.
19. Basic rescues
20. Artificial respiration
21. Safety information
22. Combined skills #1
23. Combined skills #2
24. Combined skills #3
25. Combined skills #4
26. Combined skills #5
27. Combined skills #6

ADVANCED BEGINNER SKILLS

1. Bobbing—deep water
2. Rhythmic breathing to side
3. Survival float—2 min.
4. Crawl stroke
5. Elementary backstroke
6. Survival stroke
7. Treading water—30-45 sec.
8. Changing positions and treading water—30 sec.
9. Stnding front dive
10. Underwater swim—3 to 4 body lengths
11. PFD—swimming
12. PFD—jumping into water
13. Artificial respiration
14. Basic rescue skills
15. Personal safety skills
16. Safety information
17. Combined skills #1
18. Combined skills #2
19. Combined skills #3

ADVANCED SWIMMER SKILLS
(Must meet prerequisites)

1. Elementary backstroke—review
2. Back crawl—review/improve
3. Breaststroke—review/improve
4. Sidestroke—both sides, both kicks
5. Crawl stroke—review/improve
6. Overarm sidestroke
7. Inverted breaststroke
8. Trudgen stroke

9. Open turns—review/improve
10. Surface dives—review/improve
11. Survival float/survival stroke—fully clothed
12. Standing dives—review/improve
13. Jumping—1 meter board—review
14. Running front dive—1 meter board
15. Combined skills #1
16. Combined skills #2
17. Combined skills #3
18. Combined skills #4
19. Combined skills #5
20. Combined skills #6
21. Combined skills #7
22. Combined skills #8

INTERMEDIATE SKILLS

1. Sidestroke—arms
2. Sidestroke—scissors kick
3. Sidestroke—coordination
4. Breaststroke—arms
5. Breaststroke—kick
6. Breaststroke—coordination
7. Crawl stroke—improve
8. Elementary backstroke—improve
9. Survival float—3 min.
10. Survival stroke—3 min.
11. Back float—1 min.
12. Sculling on back—10 yds.
13. Open turns—front and side
14. Open turn—back
15. Tread water—1 min.
16. Swim underwater—15 to 20 ft.
17. Standing front dive
18. Use of backboard—demonstration only
19. Donning PFD—deep water
20. Basic rescues
21. Artificial respiration
22. Safety information
23. Combined skills #1
24. Combined skills #2
25. Combined skills #3
26. Combined skills #4
27. Combined skills #5

Figure 8.18 Testing skills—Red Cross Progressive Swimming Courses. *Note.* The courses and skills listed are from *Swimming and Aquatics Safety.* From American Red Cross, 17th and D Streets, N.W., Washington, D.C. Reprinted with permission.

American Red Cross   WORKSHEET FOR SWIMMING COURSES

NAME OF COURSE	GROUP	DATE STARTED	DATE COMPLETED	INSTRUCTOR OR AIDE

- Skills for courses are listed on reverse side.
- Skills may be written in space provided or checked by number.
- Record activity on *Course Record— Swimming/Water Safety* (Form 5722).

GRADE "P."
PASSING
"INC."
INCOMPLETE

PARTICIPANT'S NAME	1	2	3	4	5	6	7	8	9	10	11	12	13	14	15	16	17	18	19	20	21	22	23	24	25	26	27	
1.																												
2.																												
3.																												
4.																												
5.																												
6.																												
7.																												
8.																												
9.																												
10.																												
11.																												
12.																												
13.																												
14.																												
15.																												
16.																												
17.																												
18.																												
19.																												
20.																												
21.																												
22.																												

Figure 8.19 Worksheet for swimming courses. From American Red Cross, 17th and D Streets, N.W., Washington, D.C. Reprinted with permission.

Table 8.38 Conversion of Raw Scores, Earned on a 20-Yard or 18.28-m Underwater Swim Test, Measured to .10 Second, to Six-Sigma Scores

Seconds	Men	Women	Seconds	Men	Women	Seconds	Men	Women
11.0	80	95	19.0	42	63	27.0	4	31
11.2	79	94	19.2	41	62	27.2	3	30
11.4	78	93	19.4	40	61	27.4	2	30
11.6	77	92	19.6	39	61	27.6	1	29
11.8	76	92	19.8	38	60	27.8	1	28
12.0	76	92	20.0	37	59	28.0	0	27
12.2	74	90	20.2	36	58	28.2	0	26
12.4	73	89	22.4	35	57	28.4	0	26
12.6	72	88	22.6	34	57	28.6	0	25
12.8	71	88	22.8	34	56	28.8	0	24
13.0	70	87	21.0	33	55	29.0	0	23
13.2	69	86	21.2	32	54	29.2	0	22
13.4	68	85	21.4	31	53	29.4	0	21
13.6	67	84	21.6	30	52	29.6	0	21
13.8	66	84	21.8	29	52	29.8	0	20
14.0	66	83	22.0	28	51	30.0	0	19
14.2	65	82	22.2	27	50	30.2	0	18
14.4	64	81	22.4	26	49	30.4	0	18
14.6	63	80	22.6	25	49	30.6	0	17
14.8	62	80	22.8	24	48	30.8	0	16
15.0	61	79	23.0	23	47	31.0	0	15
15.2	60	78	23.2	22	46	31.2	0	14
15.4	59	77	23.4	21	46	31.4	0	14
15.6	58	77	23.6	20	45	31.6	0	13
15.8	57	76	23.8	19	44	31.8	0	12
16.0	56	75	24.0	18	43	32.0	0	11
16.2	55	74	24.2	18	42	32.2	0	10
16.4	54	73	24.4	16	42	32.4	0	10
16.6	53	72	24.6	16	41	32.6	0	9
16.8	52	72	24.8	15	39	32.8	0	8
17.0	51	71	25.0	14	39	33.0	0	7
17.2	50	70	25.2	13	38	33.2	0	6
17.4	50	69	25.4	12	38	33.4	0	6
17.6	48	68	25.6	11	37	33.6	0	5
17.8	48	68	25.8	10	36	33.8	0	4
18.0	47	67	26.0	9	35	34.0	0	3
18.2	46	66	26.2	8	35	34.2	0	2
18.4	45	65	26.4	7	34	34.4	0	2
18.6	44	65	26.6	6	33	34.6	0	1
18.8	43	64	26.8	5	32	34.8	0	0

Note. From University of Kentucky Swimming Proficiency Test, Department of Health, Physical Education, and Recreation, University of Kentucky, Lexington, KY. Reprinted with permission.

1. *20-yard (18.28-m) Underwater Swim.* Start at the deep end of the pool. Use regulation starting commands (i.e., *Take your marks. Go!*). The swimmer dives into the water and attempts to swim the entire 20-yard (18.28-m) distance under the water. Any style of swimming is permitted. A rubber brick or other type marker is placed on the bottom approximately 20 yards (18.28 m) from the starting end. This enables the swimmer to quickly determine the finish line while underwater. *Scoring:* Record the time to the nearest .10 second. No score is given if part of the body breaks the surface before the 20-yard (18.28-m) distance is completed. Consult Table 8.38 to determine scale score for the effort.

2. *25-Yard (22.86-m) Crawl-Sprint.* Start at the shallow end of the pool and use starting boxes and the same regulation start used for the 20-yard underwater swim. Racing dives are permitted, but students who cannot execute a header are permitted to jump feet first. Encourage the student to swim as fast as possible in a straight line. *Scoring:* Record the time to the nearest .10 second. No score is granted if the distance is not completed. Consult Table 8.39 to determine scale score for the effort.

3. *5-Minute Swim for Distance.* Encourage the student to swim as far as possible in the 5-minute period allotted. Any number of strokes is allowed. Rests at interim are permitted, although the student is penalized for resting insofar as it lowers his distance score. Walking on the bottom of the pool is not permitted. The swimmer or his or her partner counts the number of lengths swum. A conventional start is used. The swimmer swims until a whistle is blown to indicate the end of the 5-minute period. *Scoring:* Convert the lengths swum to the nearest yard or meter. No score is given if the swimmer climbs out of the pool before the 5-minute period is completed or if the swimmer walks on the bottom of the pool in shallow water. Locate the scale score for this effort in Tables 8.40 or 8.41.

The gliding strokes (elementary back, side, and breaststroke) are administered in essentially the same manner. Each swimmer negotiates 25 yards (22.86 m), or one pool length, for each stroke. The swimmer's strokes are counted by a partner, with the push-off necessary to start each length counting as a stroke. The objective is to swim the distance in as few strokes as possible. The student fails the test if he or she

Table 8.39 Conversion of Raw Scores Made on the 25-Yard or 22.86-m Crawl Sprint to Six-Sigma Scale Scores

Seconds	Men	Women	Seconds	Men	Women	Seconds	Men	Women
10.0	88		19.0	44	66	28.0	1	33
10.2	87		19.2	44	65	28.2	0	33
10.4	86		19.4	43	65	28.4	0	32
10.6	85		19.6	42	64	28.6	0	31
10.8	84		19.8	41	63	28.8	0	30
11.0	83	95	20.0	40	62	29.0	0	30
11.2	82	94	20.2	39	62	29.2	0	29
11.4	81	94	20.4	38	61	29.4	0	28

(Cont.)

Table 8.39 (Cont.)

Seconds	Men	Women	Seconds	Men	Women	Seconds	Men	Women
11.6	80	93	20.6	37	60	29.6	0	28
11.8	80	92	20.8	36	60	29.8	0	27
12.0	78	92	21.0	35	59	30.0	0	26
12.2	77	91	21.2	34	58	30.2	0	25
12.4	76	90	21.4	33	57	30.4	0	25
12.6	76	89	21.6	32	57	30.6	0	24
12.8	74	89	21.8	31	56	30.8	0	23
13.0	74	88	22.0	30	55	31.0	0	22
13.2	73	87	22.2	29	54	31.2	0	22
13.4	72	86	22.4	28	54	31.4	0	21
13.6	71	86	22.6	27	53	31.6	0	20
13.8	70	85	22.8	26	52	31.8	0	20
14.0	69	84	23.0	25	52	32.0	0	19
14.2	68	84	23.2	24	51	32.2	0	18
14.4	67	83	23.4	23	50	32.4	0	17
14.6	66	82	23.6	22	49	32.6	0	17
14.8	65	81	23.8	21	49	32.8	0	16
15.0	64	81	24.0	20	48	33.0	0	15
15.2	63	80	24.2	19	47	33.2	0	14
15.4	62	79	24.4	18	46	33.4	0	14
15.6	61	78	24.6	18	46	33.6	0	13
15.8	60	78	24.8	16	45	33.8	0	12
16.0	59	77	25.0	16	44	34.0	0	12
16.2	58	76	25.2	15	44	34.2	0	11
16.4	57	76	25.4	14	42	34.4	0	10
16.6	56	75	25.6	13	42	34.6	0	9
16.8	55	74	25.8	12	41	34.8	0	9
17.0	54	73	26.0	11	41	35.0	0	8
17.2	53	73	26.2	10	40	35.2	0	7
17.4	53	72	26.4	9	39	35.4	0	6
17.6	51	72	26.6	8	38	35.6	0	6
17.8	50	70	26.8	7	38	35.8	0	5
18.0	49	70	27.0	6	37	36.0	0	4
18.2	48	69	27.2	5	36	36.2	0	4
18.4	47	68	27.4	4	36	36.4	0	3
18.6	46	68	27.6	3	35	36.6	0	2
18.8	46	67	27.8	2	34	36.8	0	1

Note. From University of Kentucky Swimming Proficiency Test, Department of Health, Physical Education, and Recreation, University of Kentucky, Lexington, KY. Reprinted with permission.

Table 8.40 Conversion of Raw Scores in Yards Made on 5-Minute Distance Swim Test to Six-Sigma Scores

Yards	Men	Women	Yards	Men	Women	Yards	Men	Women
330	99	128	250	65	85	170	31	42
328	98	126	248	64	84	168	30	41
326	98	125	246	63	83	166	29	40
324	97	125	244	62	82	164	28	39
322	96	123	242	62	81	162	27	38
320	95	122	240	61	80	160	26	37
318	94	121	238	60	79	158	26	36
316	93	120	236	59	78	156	25	35
314	92	119	234	58	76	154	24	34
312	92	118	232	57	75	152	23	33
310	91	117	230	56	74	150	22	32
308	90	116	228	56	73	148	21	31
306	89	115	226	55	72	146	20	30
304	88	114	224	54	71	144	20	29
302	87	113	222	53	70	142	19	28
300	86	112	220	52	69	140	18	26
298	86	110	218	51	68	138	17	25
296	85	110	216	50	67	136	16	24
294	84	108	214	50	66	134	15	23
292	83	107	212	49	65	132	14	22
290	82	106	210	48	64	130	14	21
288	81	105	208	47	63	128	13	20
286	80	104	206	46	62	126	12	19
284	80	103	204	45	60	124	11	18
282	79	102	202	44	60	122	10	17
280	78	101	200	44	58	120	9	16
278	77	100	198	43	58	118	8	15
276	76	99	196	42	56	116	8	14
274	75	98	194	41	55	114	7	13
272	74	97	192	40	54	112	6	12
270	74	96	190	39	53	110	5	10
268	73	95	188	38	52	108	4	10
266	72	94	186	38	51	106	3	8
264	71	92	184	37	50	104	2	7
262	70	91	182	36	49	102	2	6
260	69	90	180	35	48	100	1	5
258	68	89	178	34	47	98	0	4
256	68	88	176	33	46	96	0	3
254	67	87	174	32	45	94	0	2
252	66	86	172	32	44	92	0	1

Note. From University of Kentucky Swimming Proficiency Test, Department of Health, Physical Education, and Recreation, University of Kentucky, Lexington, KY. Reprinted with permission.

Table 8.41   Conversion of Raw Scores in Meters on 5-Minute Distance Swim Test to Six-Sigma Scores

Meters	Men	Women	Meters	Men	Women	Meters	Men	Women
301.7	99	128	228.6	65	85	155.4	31	42
299.9	98	126	226.7	64	84	153.6	30	41
298.1	98	125	224.9	63	83	151.7	29	40
296.2	97	125	223.1	62	82	149.9	28	39
294.4	96	123	221.2	62	81	148.1	27	38
292.6	95	122	219.4	61	80	146.3	26	37
290.7	94	121	217.6	60	79	144.4	26	36
288.9	93	120	215.7	59	78	142.6	25	35
287.1	92	119	213.9	58	76	140.8	24	34
285.2	92	118	212.1	57	75	138.9	23	33
283.4	91	117	210.3	56	74	137.1	22	32
281.6	90	116	208.4	56	73	135.3	21	31
279.8	89	115	206.6	55	72	133.5	20	30
277.9	88	114	204.8	54	71	131.6	20	29
276.1	87	113	202.9	53	70	129.8	19	28
274.3	86	112	201.1	52	69	128.0	18	26
272.4	86	110	199.3	51	68	126.1	17	25
270.6	85	110	197.5	50	67	124.3	16	24
268.8	84	108	195.6	50	66	122.5	15	23
267.0	83	107	193.8	49	65	120.7	14	22
265.1	82	106	192.0	48	64	118.8	14	21
263.3	81	105	190.1	47	63	117.0	13	20
261.5	80	104	188.3	46	62	115.2	12	19
259.6	80	103	186.5	45	60	113.3	11	18
257.8	79	102	184.7	44	60	111.5	10	17
256.0	78	101	182.8	44	58	109.7	9	16
254.2	77	100	181.0	43	58	107.8	8	15
252.3	76	99	179.2	42	56	106.0	8	14
250.5	75	98	177.3	41	55	104.2	7	13
248.7	74	97	175.5	40	54	102.4	6	12
246.8	74	96	173.7	39	53	100.5	5	10
245.0	73	95	171.9	38	52	98.7	4	10
243.2	72	94	170.0	38	51	96.9	3	8
241.4	71	92	168.2	37	50	95.1	2	7
239.5	70	91	166.4	36	49	93.2	2	6
237.7	69	90	164.5	35	48	91.4	1	5
235.9	68	89	162.7	34	47	86.6	0	4
234.0	68	88	163.3	33	46	87.7	0	3
232.2	67	87	159.1	32	45	85.9	0	2
230.4	66	86	157.2	32	44	84.1	0	1

Note. From University of Kentucky Swimming Proficiency Test, Department of Health, Physical Education, and Recreation, University of Kentucky, Lexington, KY. Reprinted with permission.

uses additional sculling or kicking movements or improper arm or leg movements or if he or she demonstrates insufficient coordination for proper execution of the stroke.

4. *25-Yard (22.86 m) Elementary Backstroke.* Starting in the water at the shallow end, the swimmer pushes off the wall in the gliding position of the stroke with the arms at the side of the body and the legs together. A whip or squeeze kick (both versions of the frog kick) must be used; no other kick is permitted. Arms may be raised above the shoulders in the recovery, but not above the water surface. No arm or leg motion is allowed on the push-off. The student should swim this stroke the pool's length in as few strokes as possible. *Scoring:* Record the number of strokes required to make the distance. Half or split strokes performed at the end of the length are counted as whole strokes. Consult Table 8.42 to determine the scale score for the effort.

5. *25-Yard (22.86-m) Sidestroke.* The swimmer starts in the water at the shallow end of the pool with a push-off from the wall. This glide is the normal glide for the stroke, with the lower arm extended forward in line with the body and the upper arm along the side of the body. The legs should be together, straight, and in line with the body. No arm or leg movement is permitted in the push-off. Only one leg action, the regular scissors with the top leg recovering forward, is allowed for each stroke. Inverted scissors or frog kick is forbidden. Both arms recover under the water. *Scoring:* Record the push-off plus the number of strokes required to make the distance. No score is granted for improper strokes. Again use Table 8.42 to determine the scale score for this effort.

6. *25-Yard (22.86-m) Breaststroke.* The swimmer starts in the water at the shallow end

of the pool with a push-off and glide. The glide must be executed on the surface with the body fully extended, the arms extended over the head, and the head between the arms. The face is submerged during the extended glide. The same kicking movements are employed in the 25-yard breaststroke as in the elementary backstroke except that the stroke is swum on the front. Scissors or flutter kicks are not allowed. Breath must be taken on each stroke cycle at the end of the glide. One paired kick movement and one paired arm movement should be used for each stroke cycle (a surface stroke with the arms recovering under the water). *Scoring:* Record the push-off and the number of strokes required to swim the distance. Partial strokes are counted as whole strokes. No score is granted for improper movements or improper coordination. Locate the scale score for the effort in this stroke performance in Table 8.42.

For each performance there is a scale score. The average performance for an event approximates 50 scale score points. Any performance exceeding 50 points is above average, and a score of less than 50 points is representative of below average ability on a single test item. The standard deviation is 16.67.

The scale scores can be summed to locate a composite score for all six test items. This composite, or criterion, score represents a total measurement encompassing all events. Thus a student's record of performances can be recorded. A card such as the one in Figure 8.29 is available for this purpose. This card is designed for recording the raw score performances as well as their appropriate scale scores obtained from Tables 8.38, 8.39, 8.40, 8.41, and 8.42. Although raw scores cannot be summed, the scale scores can be summed. The total of all six scale scores will locate the student's total, or criterion, score.

Table 8.42 Converting Raw Scores to Six-Sigma Scores
Performed on Three Gliding Strokes for 25 Yards or Distance

Number of strokes	Elementary backstroke		Sidestroke		Breaststroke	
	Men	Women	Men	Women	Men	Women
3	100	94	100	91	84	85
4	93	87	94	86	79	80
5	85	80	88	80	73	74
6	78	73	82	75	68	69
7	71	66	75	70	62	63
8	64	59	69	64	56	58
9	56	52	63	58	51	52
10	49	44	57	53	45	46
11	42	37	50	48	40	41
12	35	30	44	42	34	35
13	28	33	38	37	29	30
14	20	16	32	31	23	24
15	13	9	25	26	18	18
16	6	2	19	20	12	13
17	0	0	13	15	6	7
18			0	10	1	2
19			0	4	0	0
20				0		

Note. From University of Kentucky Swimming Proficiency Test, Department of Health, Physical Education, and Recreation, University of Kentucky, Lexington, KY. Reprinted with permission.

Normal scores for a criterion, or total score, are available for physical education majors. Students can determine their expected total score performances by consulting Table 8.43, which gives the performance grade.

Tennis

Three tests have been proposed to measure elements of tennis skill, including (a) the Hewitt (1966) revision of the Dyer Wallboard Test, (b) the Broer-Miller Forehand-Backhand Drive Test (1950), and (c) the Tennis Serve Test. The validity of the wallboard test was determined to be .89 and .84 with a criteria of rank order of playing ability in two advanced tennis classes in college. Test-retest reliability was .82 for beginners and an estimated .89 for advanced players (Hewitt, 1966). Validity of the forehand-backhand tests with a criterion of ratings of ability in college women was .61 for beginners and .85 for intermediate skill ability. Reliability for both groups was .80 (Broer & Miller, 1950).

Table 8.43 Conversion of Total Score to Percentage Grades and T Scores Earned by Physical Education Majors on a Six-Item Swim Test

T score	"A" Grade	Total score	T score	"B" Grade	Total score	T score	"C" Grade	Total score	T score	"D" Grade	Total score	T score	"E" Grade	Total score
77.6	98	518-525	67	89	448-455	55	79	370-379	43	69	294-301	31	59	218-223
76	97	510-517	66	88	440-447	54	78	364-369	42	68	286-293	30	58	210-217
75	96	502-509	64	87	432-439	52	77	356-363	40	67	278-285	28	57	202-209
74	95	494-501	63	86	424-431	51	76	348-353	39	66	270-277	27	56	194-201
73	94	486-493	62	85	418-423	50	75	340-347	38	65	264-269	26	55	186-193
72	93	478-485	61	84	410-417	49	74	332-339	37	64	256-263	25	54	178-185
70	92	472-477	60	83	402-409	48	73	324-331	36	63	248-255	24	53	170-177
69	91	464-471	58	82	394-401	46	72	318-323	34	62	240-247	22	52	162-169
68	90	456-463	57	81	386-393	45	71	310-317	33	61	232-239	21	51	158-161
			56	80	378-385	44	70	302-309	32	60	224-231	20	50	150-157
												19		142-149
												18		134-141
												17		126-133

Note. From University of Kentucky Swimming Proficiency Test, Department of Health, Physical Education, and Recreation, University of Kentucky, Lexington, KY. Reprinted with permission.

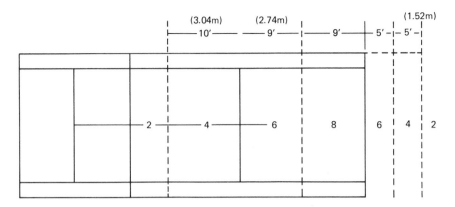

Figure 8.20 Court markings for Forehand-Backhand Drive test. From *Measurement and Evaluation in Physical Education* by M.G. Scott and E. French, 1959, Dubuque, IA: Wm. C. Brown. Reprinted with permission of Dr. M. Gladys Scott.

1. *Wallboard Volley Test.*[8] A restraining line is drawn on the floor or ground 20 feet (6.096 m) from a wall at least 10 feet (3.04 m) high. A net line 3 inches (7.62 cm) wide is painted on the wall 3 feet (.914 m) above and horizontal to the floor. The volleying area is approximately 20 feet (6.09 m) wide. A supply of extra balls should be kept in a box in a back corner (the right corner for right-handed players or left corner for left-handed players). On the signal *Go!*, the player drops a ball behind the restraining line, lets it hit the floor once, and then starts volleying it against the wall. The student continues to volley the ball until the signal *Stop!* Three 30-second trials are allowed. One point is awarded each time a ball strikes above the net line. The player may cross the restraining line to retrieve a ball, but all strokes must be taken from behind the restraining line. Every time a new ball is put into play, it

must be allowed to bounce once. Any tennis stroke may be used. After hitting the wall, the ball may bounce any number of times, or it can be returned without a bounce from behind the restraining line. Record the best score.

2. *Forehand-Backhand Drive Test.* This test is administered on a regulation tennis court marked off as shown in Figure 8.20. Two lines are drawn across the court 10 feet (3.04 m) inside the service line and 9 feet (2.74 m) outside and parallel to the service line. Two lines are drawn across the court 5 feet (1.52 m) and 10 feet (3.04 m) respectively outside and parallel to the baseline. Numbers are placed in the center of each area to indicate its scoring value. A rope is stretched 4 feet (1.21 m) above the top of the net. The player being tested stands behind the baseline, bounces the ball, hits the ball between the top of the net and the rope, and attempts to place it in the back 9 feet (2.74 m) of the opposite court. Each player is allowed 14 trials on the forehand and 14 trials on the backhand. Balls that go over the rope score one half the value of the area in which they land. Missed balls count as a trial. Net balls are taken over.

---

[8]The "Wallboard Volley Test" and "Forehand Backhand Drive Test" are from *Measurement and Evaluation in Physical Education* by M.G. Scott and E. French, 1959. Copyright 1959 by M.G. Scott. Reprinted by permission.

The total score is the sum of the points for all 28 trials.

3. *Tennis Serve Test.* The authors of this text propose the following Tennis Serve Test for use in beginners classes. The student stands behind the service line and attempts to serve the ball as in a regulation match. A rope is stretched across the court exactly 7 feet (2.13 m) above the net. The student serves 20 balls into the service court. To be scored as a good serve, the ball must be served between the rope and the net. The student's score is the number of correct serves. The teacher may calculate a test-retest reliability coefficient. An estimate of validity may also be obtained by correlating tennis serve scores against a criterion of pupils' standings in a round robin tournament.

Volleyball

The AAHPER (1969) Volleyball Skills Test consists of four items, including volleying, serving, passing, and set-ups. Content validity is claimed with minimum reliabilities of .80 for events scored on the basis of distance and .70 for events scored on the basis of accuracy and form. Percentile rank norms for boys and girls 10 to 18 years of age are presented in Tables 8.44 through 8.47. Directions for the administration and scoring of the test follow.[9]

1. *Volleying.* A solid smooth wall is needed with a 1-inch (2.54-cm) line marked on it that is 5 feet (1.52 m) long and 11 feet (3.35 m) above and parallel to the floor. Vertical lines 3 to 4 feet (.914 to 1.21 m)

---

[9]Adapted from *Skills Test Manual: Volleyball for Boys and Girls* (1969). Reprinted by permission of the American Alliance for Health, Physical Education, Recreation, and Dance, 1900 Association Drive, Reston, VA 22091.

long extend upward from each end of the line. The player with a volleyball stands facing the wall. On the signal *Go!*, the ball is tossed against the wall into the area bounded by the lines. On the rebound, the ball is then volleyed into the marked area consecutively for 1 minute. The tossed ball and each volley must strike the wall above the 11-foot (3.35-m) line and between the two vertical lines. The total number of legal volleys executed within 1 minute represents the student's score. Tosses do not count in the score.

2. *Serving.* The server (X) stands opposite the marked court in the proper serving position as shown in Figure 8.21. The server may use any legal serve to hit the ball over the net into the opposite court. For children under the age of 12, the serving line should be located 20 feet (6.09 m) from the net. The server is given 10 trials. Net balls that do or do not go over count as one trial, but no points are awarded. The score is the total number of points made as determined by where the ball lands in the opposite court. Line balls are awarded the higher score of the areas concerned.

3. *Passing.* The passer (X), who is the person being tested, stands in the center back position on the court, receives a high throw from the thrower (T), and executes a pass so that the ball goes over an 8-foot (2.43-m) high rope and onto the marked shaded area as shown in Figure 8.22. The passer is allowed 20 trials to be performed alternately to the right and to the left. If the ball touches the rope or net or does not fall in the target area, the trial counts but no points are awarded. One point is awarded for each pass going over the rope and landing on any part of the target area.

4. *Set-Up.* The set-up person (S) stands in midcourt position within the 6-foot (1.82-m) by 5-foot (1.52-m) area as shown in Figure 8.23. The set-up person receives

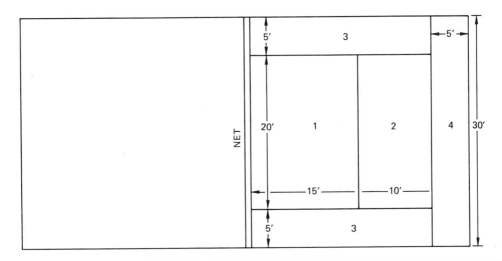

Figure 8.21 AAHPER Volleyball Serving Test. From *Skills Test Manual: Volleyball for Boys and Girls* (1969). Reprinted by permission of the American Alliance for Health, Physical Education, Recreation, and Dance, 1900 Association Drive, Reston, VA 22091.

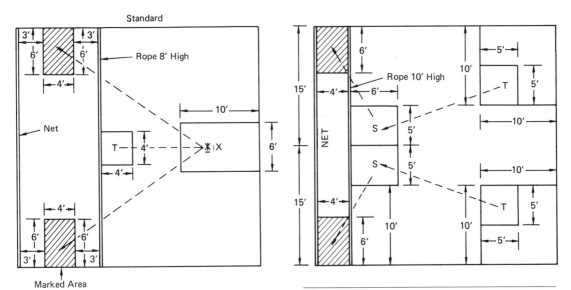

Figure 8.22 AAHPER Passing Test. From *Skills Test Manual: Volleyball for Boys and Girls* (1969). Reprinted by permission of the American Alliance for Health, Physical Education, Recreation, and Dance, 1900 Association Drive, Reston, VA 22091.

Figure 8.23 AAHPER Volleyball Set-Up Test (two stations for right and left). From *Skills Test Manual: Volleyball for Boys and Girls* (1969). Reprinted by permission of the American Alliance for Health, Physical Education, Recreation, and Dance, 1900 Association Drive, Reston, VA 22091.

a high throw from the thrower (T) and executes a set-up so that the ball goes over a 30-foot (9.14-m) rope and onto the target area. The rope is 10 feet (3.04 m) high for boys and 9 feet (2.74 m) high for girls. Two pupils may be tested simultaneously, with one setting the ball to the right and the other setting to the left. Throws from T that do not fall into the set-up position area are to be repeated. The set-up person performs 10 trials to the right and 10 trials to the left. If the ball touches the rope or the net or does not fall into the target area, the trial counts but no points are recorded. One point is scored for each set-up that goes over the rope and lands on any part of the target area, including lines.

Table 8.44 AAHPER Volleyball Test Norms

	Volleying test (boys) Percentile scores based on age/test scores in points								Volleying test (girls) Percentile scores based on age/test scores in points						
Percentile	10-11	12	13	14	15	16	17-18	Percentile	10-11	12	13	14	15	16	17-18
100th	40	42	44	50	50	50	50	100th	47	49	49	50	50	50	50
95th	24	31	35	39	42	44	45	95th	21	29	31	32	37	40	40
90th	19	28	30	36	40	41	42	90th	13	24	25	26	31	36	38
85th	17	24	28	33	36	38	42	85th	10	19	20	21	24	28	31
80th	15	22	26	31	34	36	41	80th	8	16	17	19	21	25	27
75th	13	19	24	29	32	34	40	75th	6	13	15	17	18	22	23
70th	12	18	22	27	30	33	39	70th	5	11	13	14	16	20	20
65th	11	17	21	26	29	32	37	65th	4	10	11	13	15	18	18
60th	9	16	19	24	28	30	36	60th	3	8	10	12	13	16	16
55th	8	15	18	23	27	28	34	55th	3	7	9	11	12	14	14
50th	7	13	17	21	25	26	32	50th	2	6	8	10	11	12	12
45th	6	12	15	19	24	25	29	45th	2	5	7	9	10	11	11
40th	5	11	14	18	22	23	27	40th	1	4	6	8	9	9	9
35th	4	9	12	17	20	21	24	35th	1	3	5	7	8	8	8
30th	3	8	11	15	18	19	23	30th	1	2	4	6	7	7	7
25th	3	7	9	13	17	18	20	25th	0	2	3	5	6	6	6
20th	2	6	8	11	15	16	19	20th	0	1	1	4	5	5	5
15th	1	4	7	9	13	15	17	15th	0	1	1	3	4	4	4
10th	0	3	5	7	10	12	14	10th	0	0	0	1	2	3	3
5th	0	2	3	5	6	11	11	5th	0	0	0	0	1	2	2
0	0	0	0	0	0	0	0	0	0	0	0	0	0	0	0

Note. From *Skills Test Manual: Volleyball for Boys and Girls* (1969). Reprinted by permission of the American Alliance for Health, Physical Education, Recreation, and Dance, 1900 Association Drive, Reston, VA 22091.

Table 8.45 AAHPER Volleyball Test Norms

	Serving test (boys) Percentile scores based on age/test scores in points								Serving test (girls) Percentile scores based on age/test scores in points						
Percentile	10-11	12	13	14	15	16	17-18	Percentile	10-11	12	13	14	15	16	17-18
100th	39	40	40	40	40	40	40	100th	36	38	40	40	40	40	40
95th	29	31	32	34	36	37	37	95th	24	26	26	28	30	31	32
90th	27	28	29	31	33	33	33	90th	20	22	23	26	26	26	26
85th	25	26	27	29	32	32	32	85th	18	20	20	23	23	24	24
80th	23	24	26	27	30	30	31	80th	16	18	18	21	21	22	23
75th	22	23	24	25	28	29	30	75th	15	16	17	20	20	21	21
70th	21	21	23	24	28	29	30	70th	14	15	15	18	19	20	20
65th	20	20	22	23	27	28	29	65th	13	14	14	17	17	19	19
60th	18	19	21	22	25	27	27	60th	12	13	13	15	16	18	18
55th	17	18	20	21	24	25	26	55th	11	12	12	14	15	17	17
50th	16	16	19	20	22	23	24	50th	10	11	11	13	14	16	16
45th	15	15	18	19	21	22	22	45th	9	10	10	11	13	15	15
40th	14	14	17	18	20	21	21	40th	8	9	9	10	12	14	14
35th	13	13	16	17	19	19	20	35th	7	8	8	9	11	13	14
30th	12	12	15	16	18	19	19	30th	6	6	7	8	10	13	13
25th	11	11	13	15	16	17	17	25th	5	5	5	7	9	11	11
20th	9	10	12	14	15	15	16	20th	4	4	4	6	8	10	10
15th	8	9	10	12	12	13	14	15th	2	3	3	5	6	8	9
10th	7	8	8	10	11	12	12	10th	1	1	1	3	4	7	7
5th	4	5	5	8	9	10	11	5th	0	0	0	1	2	4	4
0	0	3	3	5	6	6	7	0	0	0	0	0	0	0	0

Note. From *Skills Test Manual: Volleyball for Boys and Girls* (1969). Reprinted by permission of the American Alliance for Health, Physical Education, Recreation, and Dance, 1900 Association Drive, Reston, VA 22091.

Table 8.46 AAHPER Volleyball Test Norms

	Passing test (boys) Percentile scores based on age/test scores in points								Passing test (girls) Percentile scores based on age/test scores in points						
Percentile	10-11	12	13	14	15	16	17-18	Percentile	10-11	12	13	14	15	16	17-18
100th	19	19	19	20	20	20	20	100th	19	19	20	20	20	20	20
95th	12	14	16	17	17	17	17	95th	10	12	12	13	13	14	15
90th	10	13	14	16	16	16	16	90th	8	10	10	11	11	12	13

(Cont.)

Table 8.46 (Cont.)

	Passing test (boys) Percentile scores based on age/test scores in points								Passing test (girls) Percentile scores based on age/test scores in points						
Percentile	10-11	12	13	14	15	16	17-18	Percentile	10-11	12	13	14	15	16	17-18
85th	9	12	13	15	15	15	15	85th	7	8	9	10	10	11	12
80th	8	11	12	14	14	14	14	80th	6	7	8	9	9	10	11
75th	7	10	12	13	13	13	13	75th	5	6	7	8	8	8	9
70th	6	9	11	12	12	12	13	70th	4	6	6	7	7	8	9
65th	5	8	10	12	12	12	13	65th	3	5	5	6	6	8	8
60th	4	8	9	11	11	12	12	60th	3	4	4	6	6	7	8
55th	4	7	9	10	10	12	12	55th	2	4	4	5	5	6	7
50th	3	6	8	10	10	11	11	50th	2	3	4	5	5	6	6
45th	3	5	7	9	9	10	10	45th	1	3	3	4	4	5	6
40th	2	4	7	8	8	9	9	40th	1	2	3	4	4	4	5
35th	2	4	6	8	8	9	9	35th	0	2	2	3	3	4	4
30th	1	3	5	7	7	8	8	30th	0	1	2	3	3	3	4
25th	1	2	4	6	6	7	8	25th	0	1	1	2	2	3	3
20th	0	2	4	5	5	6	7	20th	0	0	1	1	2	2	3
15th	0	1	3	4	4	5	6	15th	0	0	0	1	1	2	2
10th	0	0	2	3	3	4	4	10th	0	0	0	0	1	1	1
5th	0	0	1	2	2	2	2	5th	0	0	0	0	0	0	0
0	0	0	0	0	0	0	0	0	0	0	0	0	0	0	0

Note. From *Skills Test Manual: Volleyball for Boys and Girls* (1969). Reprinted by permission of the American Alliance for Health, Physical Education, Recreation, and Dance, 1900 Association Drive, Reston, VA 22091.

Table 8.47 AAHPER Volleyball Test Norms

	Set-up test (boys) Percentile scores based on age/test scores in points								Set-up test (girls) Percentile scores based on age/test scores in points						
Percentile	10-11	12	13	14	15	16	17-18	Percentile	10-11	12	13	14	15	16	17-18
100th	16	18	20	20	20	20	20	100th	19	20	20	20	20	20	20
95th	10	14	16	16	16	17	17	95th	11	13	14	14	14	15	15
90th	9	12	14	15	15	15	15	90th	9	11	11	12	12	12	14
85th	8	11	13	13	13	14	15	85th	7	9	10	10	11	11	12
80th	7	10	12	12	12	13	14	80th	6	8	9	10	10	10	11

(Cont.)

Table 8.47 (Cont.)

	Set-up test (boys) Percentile scores based on age/test scores in points								Set-up test (girls) Percentile scores based on age/test scores in points						
Percentile	10-11	12	13	14	15	16	17-18	Percentile	10-11	12	13	14	15	16	17-18
75th	6	9	11	11	11	12	13	75th	5	7	8	9	9	9	10
70th	6	8	10	10	10	10	11	70th	5	6	7	8	8	8	8
65th	5	8	9	9	9	9	11	65th	4	6	7	7	7	7	7
60th	5	7	8	8	8	9	10	60th	4	5	6	6	6	7	7
55th	4	7	7	8	8	8	10	55th	3	5	5	6	6	6	6
50th	4	6	7	7	7	7	9	50th	3	4	5	5	5	6	6
45th	3	6	6	6	6	6	9	45th	2	4	4	4	4	5	5
40th	3	5	6	6	6	6	8	40th	2	3	4	4	4	5	5
35th	3	5	5	5	5	5	7	35th	2	3	3	3	3	4	4
30th	2	4	4	5	5	5	7	30th	1	2	3	3	3	3	4
25th	2	4	4	4	4	4	6	25th	1	2	2	2	2	3	3
20th	2	3	3	4	4	4	6	20th	1	2	2	2	2	2	3
15th	1	3	3	3	3	3	5	15th	0	1	1	1	1	2	2
10th	0	1	1	2	2	2	2	10th	0	0	1	1	1	1	1
5th	0	1	1	1	1	1	2	5th	0	0	0	0	0	1	1
0	0	0	0	0	0	0	1	0	0	0	0	0	0	0	0

Note. From *Skills Test Manual: Volleyball for Boys and Girls* (1969). Reprinted by permission of the American Alliance for Health, Physical Education, Recreation, and Dance, 1900 Association Drive, Reston, VA 22091.

Summary

In this chapter the authors have attempted to demonstrate that the physical educator must critically evaluate sport skills tests and test items. Older tests are not necessarily bad merely because they were developed years ago, but with advancing knowledge in measurement educators must realize that a test developed several years ago to evaluate playing ability may be inappropriate for that purpose today. However, test items from older tests may be useful to classify students into instructional groups or as practice tests or drills in beginning levels of instruction.

Physical educators are encouraged to modify test items to meet their own program objectives. They should also develop their own tests by using the techniques described earlier in chapter 5 on ''Selection and Construction of Motor Performance Tests.'' Remember, when you modify an older test you are essentially constructing a new test or test item, and the originally reported validity and reliability coefficients and norm tables will no longer apply. Hence you should conduct your own reliability and validity studies. After carefully testing about 200 students, you can establish local norms.

Problems and Exercises

1. AAHPER has developed sport skills tests for archery, football, basketball for boys and girls, softball for boys and girls, and volleyball. Sources of these tests are found in the references in this chapter. Select one of these sport skills tests and evaluate it based on the criteria for selecting a test and the principles of test construction previously presented.

2. Convert the dimensions in the skill tests in this chapter from the English to metric units of measurement if not presented as such.

3. Determine if each of the tests described in this chapter is a norm-referenced test or a criterion-referenced test. Explain your answers. If you decide that a particular test is norm referenced, how would you modify it so that it satisfies criteria for a criterion-referenced testing?

4. Indicate whether the sport skills tests in this chapter can be used for purposes of formative or summative evaluation. Why or why not?

Bibliography

American Association for Health, Physical Education, and Recreation. (1965). *Skills test manual: Football*. Washington, DC: Author.

American Association for Health, Physical Education, and Recreation. (1966). *Skills test manual: Softball for boys*. Washington, DC: Author.

American Association for Health, Physical Education, and Recreation. (1966). *Skills test manual: Softball for girls*. Washington, DC: Author.

American Association for Health, Physical Education, and Recreation. (1967). *Skills test manual: Archery*. Washington, DC: Author.

American Association for Health, Physical Education, and Recreation. (1969). *Skills test manual: Volleyball for boys and girls*. Washington, DC: Author.

American Alliance for Health, Physical Education, Recreation, and Dance. (1984). *Skills test manual: Basketball for boys and girls*. Reston, VA: Author.

American Red Cross. (1981). *Swimming and aquatics safety*. Washington, DC: Author.

Barrett, J.A. (1969). *Archery*. Pacific Palisades, CA: Goodyear.

Baumgartner, T.A., & Jackson, A.S. (1982). *Measurement for evaluation in physical education* (2nd ed.). Dubuque, IA: William C. Brown.

Broer, M.R., & Miller, D.M. (1950). Achievement tests for beginning and intermediate tennis. *Research Quarterly, 3*(3), 303-321.

Critz, M.E. (1948). *An objective test for beginning canoeists*. Unpublished master's thesis, State University of Iowa, Iowa City.

Faulkner, J.A., & Luttgens, K. (1978). Introduction to sports skills testing. In H.J. Montoye (Ed.), *An introduction to measurement in physical education* (pp. 181-194). Boston: Allyn and Bacon.

Hewitt, J.E. (1966). Revision of the Dyer backboard tennis test. *Research Quarterly, 36*(2), 153-157.

Johnson, B.L., & Nelson, J.K. (1979). *Practical measurements for evaluation in physical education* (3rd ed.). Minneapolis: Burgess.

Kerr, B., & Smoll, F.L. (1977). Variability in individual student performance implications for teachers. *Motor skills: Theory into practice, 1*(2), 75-86.

McCabe, J.F., & McArdle, W.D. (1978). Team sports skills tests. In H.J. Montoye (Ed.), *An introduction to measurement in physical education*. Boston: Allyn and Bacon.

Miller, F.A. (1951). A badminton wall volley test. *Research Quarterly, 22*(2), 208-213.

Miller, W.K. (1954). Achievement levels in basketball skills for women physical education majors. *Research Quarterly, 25*(4), 450-455.

National Federation of State High School Associations. (1985-87). In S.S. True (Ed.), *Official High School Boys Gymnastics Rules*. Kansas City, MO: Author.

National Federation of State High School Associations. (1985/86). In S.S. True (Ed.), *Official High School Girls Gymnastics Rules and Manual*. Kansas City, MO: Author.

Perry, E.L. (1969). *An investigation of field hockey skills tests for college women*. Unpublished master's thesis, Pennsylvania State University, University Park.

Schmithals, M., & French, E. (1940). Achievement tests in field hockey for college women. *Research Quarterly, 11*(3), 83-92.

Scott, M.G., Carpenter, A., French, E., & Kuhl, L. (1941). Achievement examinations in badminton. *Research Quarterly, 12*(2), 242-253.

Scott, M.G., & French, E. (1959). *Measurement and evaluation in physical education*. Dubuque, IA: William C. Brown.

Stroup, F. (1955). Game results as a criterion for validating basketball skill tests. *Research Quarterly, 26*(3), 353-357.

Torney, J.A., & Clayton, R.D. (1981). *Teaching aquatics*. Minneapolis: Burgess.

United States Gymnastics Safety Association. (1979). *Gymnastics safety manual* (2nd ed.). Pennsylvania State University Press: University Park.

Vanderhoff, E.R. (1956). *Beginning golf achievement tests*. Unpublished master's thesis, State University of Iowa, Iowa City.

Part III

Measurement in the Cognitive and Affective Domains

This section of the text deals with the use of measurement and evaluation procedures in two domains of development often neglected by professional physical educators in program settings: the cognitive and affective domains. Chapter 9 deals with techniques for constructing, using, and evaluating tests designed to estimate a particular knowledge area in the cognitive domain. A high school volleyball teacher may want to construct a test covering the rules of play, strategy, and safety considerations to be administered at the end of an instructional unit. Another teacher may desire to construct a test on physical fitness knowledge. Professionals in health spas may want to measure participants' knowledge of exercise, including how to exercise and monitor daily performance and how to use knowledge of the benefits of exercise in altering subsequent exercise activities. Every professional physical educator imparts knowledge, directly or indirectly, to program participants about the program of activities, technique of exercising, and the environment in which learning or development occurs. Calling participants' attention to cognitive outcomes sets the stage for testing for knowledge and application. The physical educator must decide when and how to measure participants' knowledge development. This decision should be guided by specific program and behavioral objectives as well as the intended use of test scores.

Chapter 10 is addressed to problems in measuring variables in the affective domain and using affective domain information in decision-making. The affective domain of development is concerned with participants' values, attitudes, sportsmanship, leadership, motivation, and personality variables. One or several of these areas can predispose an individual to exercise or to avoid exercise. The quality of physical educators' leadership and the nature of program content can have a major impact on participants' personality development and attitudes toward future exercise adherence. Today there is a great deal of discussion about the affective benefits of exercise, sports competition, fitness programs, and physical education. Unfortunately, however, most professionals do very little to monitor program participants' development in desired areas in the affective domain. Gradually, however, research in the area of mental health through exercise is increasing (Gruber, 1982; Morgan, 1983).

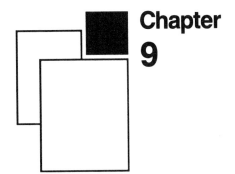

Chapter
9

Construction of
Written Knowledge Tests

A variety of different methods are available to assist physical educators in evaluating participants' cognitive knowledge. These procedures range from informal, direct observation of participants' behavior in classes to the administration of comprehensive written examinations. Each procedure has merit if it meets identified formative or summative evaluation needs. The credibility of information rests on both the validity of the measurement process and the instrument itself.

Physical educators must be familiar with the steps in constructing and evaluating a knowledge test. The steps are similar for both norm-referenced and criterion-referenced tests. For now, let us focus on constructing a *norm-referenced test*. If you follow these steps as you construct your test, the test you develop will probably provide you with useful, relevant information. If you choose to consider an existing standardized test, you must carefully examine its test manual to determine whether these steps were followed when the test was constructed. If they were not followed, the relevance and usefulness of the test are questionable and it should not be utilized. To construct a test for discrimination purposes, follow these basic steps.

1. *Plan the examination.*
   - Determine the objectives of the examination (i.e., how you intend to use the test scores).
   - Develop a table of specifications or an outline of the test.
2. *Prepare the examination.*
   - Establish content or curricular validity.
   - Determine type of items.
   - Prepare or write the items.
   - Arrange items in proper order on the test.
   - Prepare directions for administration and scoring of the test.
3. *Administer the examination.*
4. *Determine the quality of the test.*
   - Conduct item analysis (i.e., difficulty rating, item discrimination, functioning of responses).
   - Determine test validity.
   - Determine test reliability.
   - Determine test objectivity.

5. *Revise, readminister, evaluate, and then finalize the test.*
6. *Develop test norms.*

Planning the Examination

Both test content and difficulty level must conform to the intended use of the test scores. Thus the first consideration in constructing or evaluating a test is the *purpose* of the test. Do you want to measure participant achievement after a lengthy unit of instruction? Do you wish to construct a final semester or total course of study examination? What decisions must you make about participants based in part on the test scores? Again, a single test can quite possibly satisfy more than one purpose. The primary reason for testing, however, must prevail when constructing the test.

The general purposes of measurement and evaluation have been discussed in greater detail in previous chapters. They are reviewed briefly here because the purpose of the test will dictate the type of test, the difficulty level of its items or skills, and how the test is to be administered. The purposes of a test are

- to determine participants' status, progress made, or achievement level in order to determine grades or promote individuals from one grade or instructional level to another;
- to classify participants of similar ability into groups based on a particular trait or criterion;
- to select a few participants from many based on a particular criterion;
- to diagnose participants' specific strengths and weaknesses so that the most appropriate program can be developed for each individual;
- to motivate participants to work hard both in and outside of class;

- to establish or maintain minimum individual, group, and/or program standards;
- to evaluate teacher effectiveness, teaching methods, and curricular content;
- to provide a learning experience to both the participants and physical educator;
- to collect data needed for action and/or research in the schools (e.g., developing local norms); and
- to compare local program efforts with acceptable national, regional, or state standards.

Inherent in determining the purpose of a test are the concepts of process and product evaluation. *Product* evaluation usually involves a summated score (*product*) such as the number of questions answered correctly on a specified test or the summation of a number of test scores on a certain topic. We could also concern ourselves with the *process* of cognition. If a knowledge test is to be constructed to measure various levels of cognitive functioning, then we can determine the percentage of items correct in each of the basic knowledge, comprehension, application, analysis, synthesis, and evaluation dimensions of a test. The physical educator must decide which levels of cognition will provide the most effective feedback at a particular stage in learning and construct the test accordingly.

Determining Test Objectives

The steps in collecting information for decision-making involve defining and appraising program objectives, selecting an appropriate test, collecting data through testing, and comparing data against a standard to determine how effectively the objectives have been met. Objectives can be of two types. The first type involves long-term goals, such as the general goals or program objectives of a semester's physical education program. These can be stated and broken down into more specific objectives with appropriate test items selected to provide information as to how well individuals and the class as a whole met the objectives. This is an example of *summative evaluation*; that is, participants are compared with others in the program at the end of the semester for the purpose of determining student grades and promoting individuals to the next grade level. Promoting students is a crucial decision; hence tests selected and constructed for this purpose must meet high standards of validity and reliability.

The second type of objective is more specific to daily teaching and is written as a *behavioral objective*. Behavioral objectives are utilized in *formative evaluation* in order to provide day-to-day feedback to each participant. It is an individualized evaluation for individual participants or subgroups designed to diagnose strengths, weaknesses, or gaps in their knowledge base. As a teacher develops each daily

lesson plan, defines behavioral objectives for the day, and lists the specific knowledge as behavioral objectives, he or she can construct a daily appraisal instrument at the *same* time. The differences between formative and summative evaluation, criterion- or norm-referenced standards, and type of educational objectives are illustrated in Table 9.1, which is modified from the work of Baumgartner and Jackson (1982).

As stated earlier, a test may serve a number of purposes. A knowledge test in lifesaving and water safety can provide information for a physical education grade and at the same time diagnose weaknesses in important knowledge elements of water safety. These test scores may also be used to develop local norms or standards that an individual must attain to be certified as a lifeguard. These purposes can be achieved with a test of mastery or a test of discrimination.

Table 9.1 Objectives, Evaluation, and Standards: Similarities and Differences Between Formative and Summative Evaluation

	Formative	Summative
Objectives:	Specific behavioral	General goals
Evaluation:	Process or product	Process or product
Purpose:	To provide feedback to student and teacher on a day-to-day basis throughout an instructional unit	To assign grades at end of unit or course, promote participants to next grade
Time of testing:	During daily instructional periods	End of unit, semester, or course
Emphasis in evaluation:	Explicitly defined behaviors	Broader categories of behaviors or combinations of several specific behaviors
Standard:	Criterion-referenced	Generally norm-referenced, but can be criterion-referenced

Note. From Baumgartner, Ted A. and Andrew S. Jackson, *Measurement for Evaluation in Physical Education*, 2nd ed. © 1982 Wm. C. Brown Publishers, Dubuque, Iowa. All rights reserved. Reprinted by permission.

There is an interrelationship between type of test (mastery or discrimination), universe of knowledge that the test samples (all or part of it and what level of difficulty), and the reference base for decision-making (everyone who takes the test or a defined percentage of material that must be mastered).

Norm-Referenced Tests

When you develop norms or use a norm chart to determine how well an individual has performed in relation to all others tested under similar conditions, you are using norm-referenced standards and the test is known as a *test of discrimination*. The reference base for decision-making is the rank order of scores of all others who were tested. If the test scores are to be used for grading purposes, then an examinee's achievement and grade are determined after determining his or her position or rank in the distribution of scores. Test items are selected and written with optimal difficulty levels to maximize the discrimination power of the test. Keeping this last point in mind, it is important to realize that a test of discrimination may not sample all difficulty levels represented in the universe of knowledge. This issue will be discussed more fully in a later section of this chapter on item analysis.

Criterion-Referenced Tests

A criterion-referenced test may also be developed and is usually used to make decisions regarding participant mastery levels. Hence the test is called a *test of mastery*. At times it is extremely important for an individual to "master" his or her subject. For example, to ensure swimmers' safety, a certified lifeguard must pass *all* of the requirements for the certificate, not merely pass some and fail some. In order to determine proficiency, we develop a test of *mastery*. It is important to realize that examinees are given sufficient time to master the material,

or to put it another way, to pass all items or a certain percentage of items at a specified proficiency level. In this case the purpose of instruction and subsequent testing is to assess mastery rather than to discriminate among students' different ability levels. Professional standards or criteria are established to denote mastery status; thus the test of mastery is also called a *criterion-referenced test*. For example, we may require that a predetermined level of knowledge concerning lifesaving and water safety situations (e.g., 70% of the test questions answered correctly) be attained in order for certification as a lifeguard. The purpose of this test is to measure mastery of a specific proportion of the knowledge content required for certification rather than to compare the examinee's score with the rank-ordered scores of others who took the same exam. Again, the reference base in a *criterion-referenced* test is a knowledge base or universe of items from which professional standards are established.

Another evaluation decision involves the extent to which students have acquired the information in the universe of knowledge or mastered basic concepts before proceeding to more advanced levels. For example, basic definitions and concepts must be learned before an individual can use them in the higher-level mental processes of organizing, analyzing, synthesizing, and evaluating knowledge. Criterion-referenced test items are not selected on the basis of their ability to discriminate or discover differences between various levels of achievement. Instead, the items are selected because they adequately represent the universe of knowledge that is the primary reference base for measuring individuals' *achievement* levels.

You will know whether to use a norm-referenced or criterion-referenced test once you decide on the purpose of the test and how you intend to use test scores. In some cases, both types of tests can be used to achieve the same purpose. In implementing the purpose and use of test scores, the key element is what type of reference base is more important (i.e., comparing individuals' test performances or assessing individuals' mastery of subject matter in the cognitive domain).

Another decision that must be made is whether to construct your own test or to select a test from a pool of existing standardized tests. Again, this decision is made after you determine how the test scores will be used. If your purpose is to determine how well a participant or the group has achieved in terms of program objectives, the self-made test will probably be more useful than a standardized test. The use of a standardized test may lead to the problem of "testing for what has not been taught," especially if there is a gap between the content of the test and the content of the course. On the other hand, if you want to compare class or program test scores with scores from other regions of the country, you should logically select a standardized test with appropriate norm data. Statewide competency testing is being adopted in many states. Standardized tests are employed in an effort to determine how well local units meet state or national standards in teaching various subjects and to induce local schools to improve their programs when necessary. You should recognize, however, that standardized tests are usually superior to self-made tests in terms of refinement of test construction.

Developing a Table of Specifications

We must consider the test to be a sample of the information that makes up our instructional unit. We may expose our clientele to over 300 relevant knowledge facts and concepts during lectures, discussions, and assigned readings. We need to determine how well participants have both acquired these concepts and can demonstrate an ability to utilize them in concrete situations. Within a typical 40- or 50-minute testing period, asking a relevant question on every fact and concept covered in an instructional unit is obviously impossible. Hence, we must construct

a shorter test, including perhaps 75 questions, that is designed to sample the total knowledge domain. It is important for each question to be of optimal difficulty to make a contribution toward implementing the discrimination goal of the test. In order to help us adequately sample the fund of information that comprises our instructional unit, we should develop a *table of test specifications*.

The *table of specifications* is a blueprint or outline of our intended test content. Its purpose is to ensure that the test we construct is appropriate and that it tests for knowledge of what we have taught. The table of specifications guards against concentrating too many questions on certain aspects of the information fund while ignoring other important parts of the instructional material. The table of specifications should consider the goals and objectives of the instructional unit and the type of mental processes involved in learning the material and demonstrating how the acquired knowledge can be used in society. The test outline must also consider the proportion of test items that should be devoted to each of the instructional objectives. This logically should be related to the amount of time, material, and importance attached to each objective.

In testing knowledge, we are tapping some or all of the cognitive behaviors. Bloom (1956), in his taxonomy of educational objectives for the cognitive domain, lists six cognitive behaviors in ascending order. Successful demonstration of behavior at any level is dependent on achieving the levels preceding it. The six cognitive behaviors or types of mental processes with a sample question follow:

1. *Knowledge* is the recall from memory of specific information. From which line is a free throw shot in basketball?
   a. the end line
   b. the base line
   c. the restraining line
   d. the foul line

2. *Comprehension* represents the lowest level of understanding. When a player is fouled in the act of shooting,
   a. the shooter receives two free throws.
   b. the shooter throws the ball into play from out-of-bounds.
   c. the person committing the foul must leave the game.
   d. the person committing the foul is assessed two fouls.

3. *Application* is the use of ideas, rules, or procedures. A technical foul is called in basketball when
   a. a player travels with the ball at least three times during the game.
   b. a player intentionally fouls an opponent.
   c. a team calls its sixth time-out.
   d. a player enters a game more than two times.

4. *Analysis* is the process of breaking down elements, relationships, or principles. In analyzing the jump shot in basketball, which aspect contributes to the ball hanging on the rim and thereby increases the chance for a goal?
   a. effective wrist-snap and backspin on the ball at point of release
   b. keeping the elbow in to the side and in front of the shoulder when shooting
   c. bending the knees, jumping, and leaving the floor before shooting
   d. having rather flat trajectory on the ball after release

5. *Synthesis* is the process of constructing a plan of action from parts of ideas. You are playing a man-to-man defense. Your opponent is quite fast, tends to dribble with the right hand, and shoots well but only with the right hand. Your strategy should be to
   a. guard closely to prevent the opponent from shooting.
   b. keep distance between yourself and the opponent in order to neutralize speed.
   c. overguard your opponent on the right side in order to force him or her inside where you should get help from teammates.
   d. overguard your opponent on the left side, forcing him or her to the sidelines.

6. *Evaluation* is the process of making judgments about value. Which is the best statement regarding the contribution that beginning basketball makes to the physical fitness of the player?
   a. builds arm strength
   b. makes no contribution
   c. facilitates weight control
   d. effect depends on frequency and duration of play

How extensively cognitive behaviors are tapped in a test depends on the difficulty of instructional material, functional cognitive level, intellectual ability of examinees, and their background in the subject being tested. It should be pointed out that all of these cognitive behaviors can be tested with both short-answer and essay tests.

An example of a table of specifications for a basketball knowledge test for a junior high school physical education class appears in Table 9.2. The instructional objectives appear in the left-hand column, and the cognitive abilities are listed across the top of the table. Again, the test maker must determine the percentage of test content relevant for each cell of the table. This table would vary somewhat if the test was intended to measure the basketball knowledge of the junior high school varsity team. A greater percentage of the test's content would be devoted to rules, strategy, and recognition of various player formations. In addition, varsity players would probably be responsible for the higher-order cognitive skills of analysis and synthesis. Most highly skilled athletes must analyze and improve as situations develop when they perform.

Table 9.2 Specifications for a Junior High School Physical Education Class Basketball Knowledge Test

Objectives of basketball test	Percentage of total items	Cognitive behaviors					
		Knowledge	Comprehension	Application	Analysis	Synthesis	Evaluation
Basketball terminology	10	X	X	X			
History of basketball	5	X	X				
Knowledge of basketball rules	30	X	X	X			
Basketball formations: offensive and defensive	30	X	X	X			
Basketball strategy	20	X	X	X			
Safety, equipment, and conditioning	5	X	X	X			

Another table of specifications is presented in Table 9.3 for a final examination in a physical education measurement and evaluation course. Teachers should try to determine what percentages of items allocated to each objective are meant to tap the various cognitive processes. At this stage in test construction, we do not know the type or format of the test items. As we identify the concepts we wish to translate into a test item, we can at that time decide on the item's format (i.e., multiple choice, true/false, matching, etc.). The nature of the concept should play a role in determining the type of item format. Some concepts that lack a number of plausible distractors should not be presented as multiple choice items, but instead as true/false, matching, or completion items. Paying attention to this detail in item writing will help in producing items that contribute to the purpose of the test.

The importance of using a table of specifications as a primary guide to the construction of a valid test cannot be overemphasized. In the final analysis the test samples a domain of knowledge that is imparted to students through the instructional program. The relative importance of each part of the domain must be proportionally reflected in the test. Thus the table of specifications is a guarantee that learners are appropriately tested on the material that was presented to them in the instructional unit. In other words, the table of specifications is designed to enhance the content validity of the test.

Preparing the Examination

Utilizing your table of specifications as a guide, you must now establish the content or curricular validity of the test. To establish a test's content validity, you must develop appropriate test items that sample the fund of information that your students or program participants have studied.

Establishing Content or Curricular Validity

Content validity can be facilitated by using the following procedures:

1. Analyze the objectives of instruction to ensure that they are relevant to the test and are represented on the test by an appropriate number of items.
2. Identify relevant facts and concepts and write appropriate test items based on careful examination of textbooks and other reading materials assigned to the class. Determine what type of mental process may be involved in responding to each item and write each item with this in mind.
3. Examine state or local courses of study in the subject matter field.
4. Inspect previous examinations on the same subject. Textbooks quite often contain sample tests in the instructor's manual that you may wish to adopt or revise items to suit your needs.
5. Ask other experts in the subject field, such as fellow teachers, to rate your test questions and revise the test items as necessary and appropriate based on their input.
6. Consider the social relevance of the facts and concepts. (Why is it important for pupils to be tested over these concepts?)

The next step is to specifically determine the type of items that will be on the test, that is, essay or short-answer questions. Again, the purpose of the test, the nature of the concept to be tested, and the extensiveness of the material to be sampled by the test must all be considered in deciding on item format.

Preparing Test Items

Once you have identified and listed the concepts to be represented on the test, you are ready to

Table 9.3 Specifications for a Final Examination in Measurement and Evaluation

Objectives of measurement final exam	Percentage of total items	Cognitive behaviors					
		Knowledge	Comprehension	Application	Analysis	Synthesis	Evaluation
Scope and functions of measurement	5	X	X	X			
Statistics and norm development	20	X	X	X	X	X	X
Program objectives and testing purposes	5	X	X	X			
Knowledge of existing tests	15	X	X				
Criteria for evaluating and selecting tests	20	X	X	X	X	X	X
Techniques of test construction	20	X	X	X	X	X	X
Administration and scoring of tests	5	X	X	X			
Interpretation of test results	10	X	X	X	X	X	X

begin writing the test items. Item writing is an art that can be improved with practice. The first rule to remember is that the nature of the concept should dictate item format (i.e., true/false, multiple choice, matching, or completion items). The ability of a test item to test a concept or mental ability is a function of both the form of the item and the way it is applied. More than 30 years ago, Remmers and Gage (1955) proposed applying the following general principles to the formulation of test questions. These principles are still applicable today:

- Avoid obvious, trivial, or meaningless items.
- Observe the rules of rhetoric, grammar, and punctuation.
- Avoid items that have answers that nearly all experts will accept as correct.
- Avoid "trick" or "catch" items or items so phrased that the correct answer depends on a single obscure word.
- Avoid items that furnish the answers to other items because one item then becomes useless in evaluation.
- Avoid items that contain "irrelevant cues." These are items that are phrased in such a way that the correct answer can be easily guessed and does not require knowledge of the concept.
- Require all students to take the same test and permit no choice among items if you intend to compare pupils' scores with one another.

Alternate Choice Items. One type of recognition item is the *alternate choice* item. They appear on tests in the format of *true/false, yes/no, right/wrong,* or *correction of a statement.* Safrit (1986) presents the following suggestions for writing good items:

- Avoid trivial items. Items should measure meaningful concepts.
- Avoid using sentences from textbooks as questions.

- Avoid ambiguity.
- Include an equal number of questions that have true versus false answers to eliminate the tendency to answer unknown concepts as "true" when guessing because the person being tested perceives that most of the items are true statements.
- Order the items on the test in random fashion to eliminate possible cue carryover from one item to another.
- Express only a single idea in a statement.
- Avoid using negative statements unless the concept can only be presented in that manner.
- Avoid using determiners such as "sometimes," "usually," or "often" in true statements and "always," "never," or "impossible" in false statements.
- Make false statements sound plausible. They should appear equally true to the uninformed.
- Ensure that true statements are clearly true.

You should also use drawings, charts, or diagrams to assist in testing for concepts. Test questions can require the participant to analyze the material in the diagram before the correct answer can be determined. The following are some examples of alternate choice items. An item with a fault in item writing is presented first, followed by an improved version.

True/false item:

Faulty item: The correlation between scores on a basketball skill test and grades in a basketball class is high. True or False.

Problem: Ambiguity; qualitative rather than quantitative language is used. What does "high" mean?

Improved item: The correlation between scores on a basketball skill test and grades in a basketball class is at least .50. True or False.

Faulty item: The number of players on a college basketball team is restricted by NCAA rules, conference rules, and financial support on campus. True or False.

Problem: Ambiguity and presenting more than one idea to the respondent.

Improved item: The number of eligible players on a college varsity basketball team is specified by conference rules. True or False.

A number of criticisms have been raised concerning alternate choice test type items, most of which pertain to the true/false variety. One concern is that these items may be testing rote memory. This problem can be avoided if the physical educator carefully writes items that require the participant to *apply* information rather than only remembering it. Concern also exists that participants may remember false items of information. Studies have revealed this is not the case, however, because most learning material is presented in either positive or neutral terms. In addition, the examinee responding to true/false items expects a certain number of the test items to require a false response as the correct answer. Some critics are concerned that alternate choice items encourage guessing and are not highly reliable. If an equal number of correct true and false responses are on the test, we can predict in advance the average number of items guessed correctly. To compensate for such guessing, scoring procedures can be used that take guessing into account. If you write a large number of clear, meaningful test items, you can enhance test reliability; including 30 such items lends more to test reliability than only 15 items.

Multiple Choice Questions. Another type of recognition item is the *multiple choice* question. Multiple choice questions can appear in three varieties, including *correct answer, best answer*, and the *multiple answer* variety. The multiple choice question contains an introductory statement known as the *stem* and a set of *alternatives* or suggested answers. The correct alternative is known as the *answer*, and the other alternatives are known as *distractors*. Noll and Scannell (1972), Remmers and Gage (1955), and Hopkins and Stanley (1981) present excellent guidelines for use in writing multiple choice questions as well as many examples of poorly written multiple choice questions. Rules to remember for writing good multiple choice questions include the following:

* The multiple choice item should cover an important fact or concept, and the stem should clearly and distinctly identify the task posed by the item.
* The alternatives should be stated with clarity and be relevant to the stem so that all alternatives or answer choices appear plausible to the uninformed pupil.
* A multiple choice item should not have more than one acceptable answer if at all possible.
* The alternatives to the stem should come near the end of the stem.
* The best or correct answer should appear with equal frequency in each possible position of a, b, c, d, or e in order to eliminate irrelevant cues and to minimize guessing.
* Alternative answer choices should be listed in parallel form under the stem if possible.
* Alternative answer choices that can be eliminated on some basis other than the achievement being measured should not be used.
* The length of the stem and alternatives should be determined by the purpose of the item.
* The number of alternatives should be at least four, with five preferred. If this is not possible, test the concept with another type of item format.
* Words that would be repeated in each alternative should be part of the stem.
* Use ''none of the above'' and ''all of the above'' only sparingly.

The following examples of multiple choice questions are presented to demonstrate good and poor quality questions. A faulty item is presented first, followed by an improved version:

Examples of *multiple choice* questions: Select the correct answer.

Faulty item: The vessel that carries oxygenated blood from the heart to the body is called the

a. trapezius muscle.
b. forebrain.
c. patella.
d. ascending aorta.
e. descending vena cava.

Problem: Incorrect distractors should be plausibly related to the question; that is, all distractors should involve the circulatory system.

Improved item: The vessel that carries oxygenated blood from the heart to the body is called the

a. vena cava.
b. pulmonary artery.
c. femoral artery.
d. ascending aorta.
e. carotid artery.

Faulty item: When pitching baseball, we note that a fastball and a slow curve ball will fall at the same speed in a

a. any medium.
b. vacuum.
c. any relative humidity.
d. gasses.

Problem: The answer cannot be "any medium" or "any relative humidity" because the stem statement ends in "a." Similarly, the stem sentence cannot grammatically end in "a gasses." Hence this item suffers from grammatical cues that lead the respondent to the correct distractor.

Improved item: Under what medium will a pitched fastball and a slow curve ball fall at the same rate of speed?

a. any medium
b. a vacuum
c. various relative humidities
d. similar gas pressures

Problem: Do not give the correct answer for one question (e.g., #27) in the stem of another question (e.g., #6).

Examples: Item 6. The "halo" effect is most pronounced in essay examinations. The best way to minimize the "halo" effect is to

a. provide optional questions.
b. "aim" the student to the desired response.
c. read all the responses for one question before reading the other questions.
d. permit students to write their essay tests at home where they will be more at ease.

Item 27. The "halo effect" is more operative in

a. essay tests.
b. true/false tests.
c. short-answer tests.
d. multiple choice tests.

The way to improve Item 6 should be obvious.

Multiple choice questions have been criticized on the grounds that (a) the alternatives are often ambiguous; (b) participants may select a correct answer for the wrong reason or know the answer but be unable to select it; and (c) not enough relevant distractors can be written. Ambiguity can be eliminated by clearly delineating the idea in the stem and each alternative. Clarity and meaningfulness are again the hallmark. Ambiguity can be detected by asking others in your field to examine your test questions. You can also ask examinees to identify ambiguous statements; after all, they are the ones who take the test. Quite often, ambiguity can be detected through the process of item analysis, which will be presented later in this chapter. The fact that examinees may select the correct answer for a wrong reason may apply in any type of test item. Again, clarity should help reduce this fallacy in testing.

We never really know why or how examinees respond as they do or what mental process led them to select a particular answer. Relevant distractors must be written for each item. The validity of each multiple choice item depends on relevant alternatives. If relevant alternatives cannot be written, present the concept as a true/false, matching, or completion question. Although multiple choice items are more reliable than true/false questions due to their increased number of distractors, you should *not* sacrifice item validity for reliability by forcing concepts into a multiple choice format.

Matching Questions. A third type of recognition test item is the *matching* question format. Matching questions usually consist of two columns of words or phrases, with the right-hand column containing the alternatives. The student selects an alternative that goes with the word or phrase in the left-hand column. The following guidelines for preparing matching items were proposed by Noll and Scannel (1972):

1. A matching exercise should usually not contain more than 10 or 12 items.
2. Avoid one-to-one matching by using response terms to be used more than once or by having a greater number of alternative responses in the right-hand column than items in the left-hand column.
3. If the same response is used more than once, there should be only one correct choice for each phrase in the left-hand column.
4. There should be a high degree of homogeneity in every set of matching questions.
5. Arrange the terms in both lists or columns alphabetically or in some other systematic order.

Sample Matching Questions (Guidelines 1, 4, and 5 violated)

Directions: Place the letter corresponding to the correct match from the right-hand column in the space provided to the left of each statement.

_____ 1. sidestroke
_____ 2. breaststroke
_____ 3. Type II vest
_____ 4. victim in constant view
_____ 5. oxygen consumption
_____ 6. murky water
_____ 7. struggling victim
_____ 8. heaving line
_____ 9. inverted breaststroke
_____ 10. finning
_____ 11. Commodore Longfellow
_____ 12. American Red Cross
_____ 13. butterfly stroke
_____ 14. scuba diving
_____ 15. anaerobic power
_____ 16. lung capacity
_____ 17. residual volume

A. mask and snorkel
B. lungs
C. ring buoy
D. PFD
E. muscles
F. lifesaving stroke
G. World War I
H. hyperventilation
I. feet first surface dive
J. breath-holding
K. endurance swimming
L. monkey fist
M. front underwater approach
N. approach stroke
O. legs
P. front surface dive
Q. tired swimmer carry

Sample Matching Questions (Flaws Corrected)

Directions: Place the letter corresponding to the correct match from the right-hand column in the space provided to the left of each statement.

____	1. breaststroke	A.	approach stroke
____	2. heaving line	B.	feet first surface dive
____	3. murky water		
____	4. sidestroke	C.	front surface dive
____	5. struggling victim	D.	front underwater approach
____	6. Type II vest	E.	lifesaving stroke
____	7. victim in constant view	F.	mask and snorkel
		G.	monkey fist
		H.	PFD
		I.	ring buoy
		J.	tired swimmer carry

Completion Items. Another major category of test items is *recall* or *completion* items. Here the participant is expected to fill in the blank, complete a statement, list information, or write an essay to answer the question. Directions for the examinee must be straightforward to avoid ambiguous responses. Omit only *significant* words from the completion statement. Some example completion items follow:

Directions: Place the correct answer in the space provided in each question.

Faulty item: Where is the Baseball Hall of Fame?

Problem: Does "where" refer to city, county, state, school, or country? Write the item as clearly as possible to eliminate ambiguity.

Improved item: In what city in the United States is the Baseball Hall of Fame? *Cooperstown, NY*

Faulty item: In 1891, Naismith ____ _____ basketball.

Problem: Only significant terms should be left blank. Also, several different answers would be correct.

Improved item: Naismith created the game of basketball in the year ____.

Faulty item direction: List the ways in which a lifesaver can escape from the rear head hold.

Problem: The statement is too open-ended, lacks direction, and will produce a variety of answers.

Improved item direction: List the proper sequence as specified in the Lifesaving text for a lifesaver to escape from the rear head hold.

1. [take bit of air]
2. [tuck chin]
3. [submerge]
4. [place both hands at elbows of victim]
5. [thrust powerfully upward on victim's arms]

Essay Items. Hopkins and Stanley (1981), in an excellent discussion of the advantages and disadvantages of *essay testing*, concluded that most of the advantages of the essay test can also be attained by a short-answer objective test. However, if you wish to allow students the freedom to write novel, relevant responses to controversial or divergent issues, then the essay test is more effective. If language ability is important in a particular setting, then the essay test is best because it can measure the student's ability to express ideas.

The primary disadvantage of the essay examination is problems in scoring it. Grading an essay test is very time-consuming. In addition, a good deal of subjectivity enters into the scoring process; this can result in inadequate test reliability. Answers to an essay question can vary from student to student, yet they may all be correct. Student concerns over the reliability of scoring essay questions may be reduced by duplicating and distributing to the class the two or three best student answers to each question. The class then knows the standards that were applied in grading. Scores on essay questions can be skewed by several factors, including grades awarded on a previous paper, the item-to-item carryover effect, the time the papers are graded, and the "halo effect," that is, the tendency of the grader to award scores partly on the basis of a previous impression of a pupil. Quality of handwriting and grammatical and/or verbal ability can also unduly influence the scoring of essay tests.

Some suggestions for improving the construction and scoring of essay questions were offered by Wood (1961). Wood's findings indicated that in constructing essay tests the teacher should

- devote sufficient time to constructing the essay question;
- define precisely the scope and direction of the desired answers in the written question (e.g., "Discuss the essay test" may be clearer when written as "Cite the major advantages and disadvantages of the essay test, giving specific suggestions for improving the typical essay test");
- consider asking a larger number of questions requiring shorter answers rather than a small number of questions requiring lengthy answers;
- consider the time respondents will require for thinking and writing essay answers to the questions; and
- give the same examination to all the students if comparisons among student performances are to be made for grading purposes.

General guidelines for scoring essay tests include the following:

- Preparing a tentative scoring key when constructing the item, formulating extensive possible answers at the same time.

- Applying the tentative scoring key to a random assortment of answers as a preliminary check.
- Grading one question at a time for all pupils in order to reduce the "halo effect."
- Rechecking the papers graded earlier to ensure that grading standards have not shifted, especially with a large number of papers.
- Having other experts score the questions and pool the ratings to increase reliability.

Arrangement of Items

Test items that are similar in format should appear in the same place on the examination. All true/false questions should be clustered together. Similarly, matching, listing, and completion items should appear as separate subsections of the test. Test items should also be presented in ascending order of difficulty within each group of items. Thus the easier items should be presented first, followed by the items of moderate, and then high, difficulty. If all the difficult items appeared first, many participants would be discouraged at the outset and not be motivated to perform well on the remaining items. Because the purpose of achievement testing is to determine how well the examinees have learned the material, it is important to provide positive reinforcement in early stages of testing. Thus each examinee can be assured that he or she is being fairly tested and can indeed display his or her level of achievement. The first time you administer a test and have no data on item difficulty, you should randomly assign items in their order of presentation within each item format category. Alternatively, the professional who is quite experienced in writing test items may subjectively arrange the items in order of difficulty.

Preparing Directions for Administration and Scoring of Tests

Once the items are written and the general format of the test has been established, attention must be devoted to efficient test administration and scoring. If you intend to compare an examinee's test score with the scores made by other examinees on the same test, it is imperative that all individuals take the test under the same conditions. Achievement tests are usually power tests rather than speed tests; hence all students must have sufficient time to respond to all items. Test directions must be clear and specific to ensure that all examinees understand the process they must use in responding to test items. Selection of the "best" answer rather than the "correct" answer, for example, must be clearly specified and understood.

Directions for using special materials such as notes, a textbook, or a calculator in completing the test must also be specified. If special materials are permitted, all examinees must have equal access to them. The examinees should be informed where and how they should record their responses to questions. If a separate answer sheet is to be used, directions must be provided for its use. Also, directions for recording scores and/or the procedures for scoring the test should be clearly specified. All directions should be written and included in the test booklet. In this way, the same test can be administered to different persons by different physical educators. The real purpose of establishing standardized directions is to increase the reliability of measurement by controlling for measurement error due to faulty testing procedures.

In order to facilitate the scoring of short-answer (recognition) test items, the use of separate *answer sheets* and a *scoring key* is recommended by Barrow and McGee (1979) for the following reasons:

- They permit the reuse of test papers.
- They facilitate the scoring of test papers.
- They permit a mark showing the correct answer for later study of the test by students.
- They are economical in terms of time and money.
- They facilitate performing an item analysis of the test.

Answer sheets can be easily developed. Sufficient space must be provided on the answer sheet to accommodate the number of questions asked on the test. The answer sheet should also provide space for all possible responses to a test question ranging from two responses for true/false items to five responses for multiple choice items. Answer sheets can be purchased that permit both electronic machine-scoring as well as hand-scoring by using an overlay scoring pencil. (Stencil keys have the correct answers cut out.) Electronic machine scoring is extremely useful for scoring a large number of tests. Some scoring machines in computer centers can be programed to perform an item analysis at the same time. Examples of a self-made answer sheet and an answer sheet developed for electronic scoring appear in Figures 9.1 and 9.2 respectively.

Administering the Examination

After the test has been constructed, it is ready to be used to collect information about examinee achievement.

The test should be administered in an atmosphere conducive to securing good information. Appropriate heating, lighting, and ventilation of the room should be provided to ensure a comfortable testing environment. Comfortable seating should be provided, and seats should be arranged so that possible cheating is inhibited. You should read the test directions to the group and clear up any confusion concerning the process of taking the test before actual testing begins. The same test can be administered to several groups in the same course and grade level if all participants involved have been exposed to the same general fund of information. All groups should take the examination under similar conditions. Reliability of the data to be used in determining the overall quality of the test will be increased by having a large number

Answer Sheet

Student Name _____ Course Name _____ Test Form

Student Number _____ Date of Test _____ Test Number _____

Item	Possible Responses					Item	Possible Responses					Item	Possible Responses				
	a	b	c	d	e		a	b	c	d	e		a	b	c	d	e
1.	( )	( )	(x)	( )	( )	41.	( )	( )	( )	( )	( )	81.	( )	( )	( )	( )	( )
2.	(x)	( )	( )	( )	( )	42.	( )	( )	( )	( )	( )	82.	( )	( )	( )	( )	( )
3.	( )	( )	( )	(x)	( )	43.	( )	( )	( )	( )	( )	83.	( )	( )	( )	( )	( )
4.	( )	( )	( )	( )	( )	44.	( )	( )	( )	( )	( )	84.	( )	( )	( )	( )	( )
5.	( )	( )	( )	( )	( )	45.	( )	( )	( )	( )	( )	85.	( )	( )	( )	( )	( )
.						.						.					
.						.						.					
.						.						.					
40.	( )	( )	( )	( )	( )	80.	( )	( )	( )	( )	( )	120.	( )	( )	( )	( )	( )

Figure 9.1 Teacher-made answer sheet. Responses to true/false type questions can be placed in columns a or b. Numbers or letters to matching questions can be placed in column a. Responses to completion statements can be identified by item number and written on the back of the answer sheet.

of participants take the test if possible. Sufficient time should be allotted so that all participants can respond to all items.

Determining Test Quality

Was the purpose of the test realized in testing? Did the test provide information concerning differences in achievement levels? In order to answer these questions, we must determine the quality of the test. Because a test is comprised of test items, every test item should contribute to the discovery of individual differences among examinees. After all, the test score is really a summary of performance on all test items. Thus test validity and reliability can be determined and improved by utilizing internal and external methods. Internal procedures can be implemented by conducting an *item analysis*, i.e., determining the value of each item in contributing to the purpose of the test. External procedures involve validity strategies such as correlating test scores with an external criterion measure such as scores on another known valid test or with expert rankings of examinee abilities. Such procedures have been described in

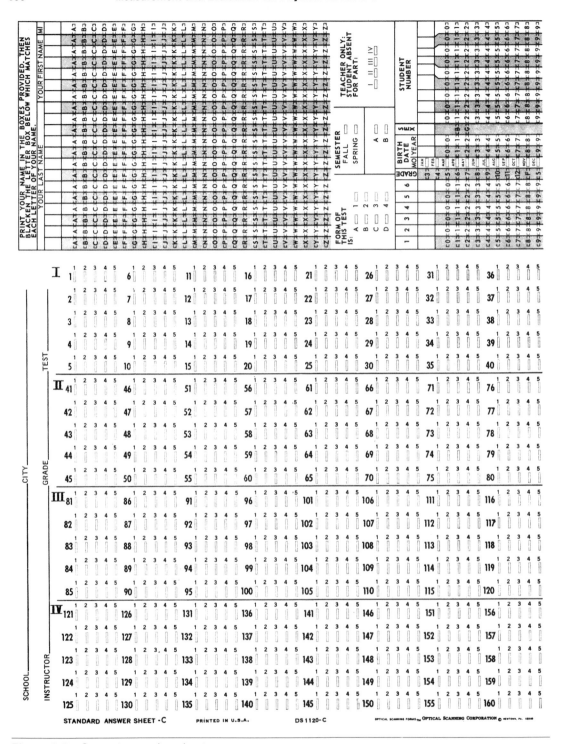

Figure 9.2 Computer scoring sheet.

detail in chapter 3 of this text. Most professionals will probably not have sufficient time to engage in external methods. The basis of any good test, however, is still the quality of each item. Thus you can and should periodically engage in the internal procedures of item analysis that have been developed to improve test quality.

Item Analysis

In conducting an item analysis, we essentially determine (a) the difficulty level of each item, (b) the index of item discrimination, and (c) the functioning of all possible responses to a test question. After this is accomplished, we can then revise the test questions and generally edit the test in order to improve test quality before it is used again. In order to conduct an item analysis, the number of correct responses to test questions is recorded at the top of each paper. This score is the number of items on the test minus the number of errors (wrong or unanswered items) on the test. The test papers or answer sheets should then be placed in rank order by score with the paper receiving the highest score on top and the paper with the lowest score on the bottom.

Item Difficulty. The *item difficulty level* is determined by dividing the number of correct responses to an item by the total number of people taking the test (N). This is the proportion of correct responses and is denoted by the letter p. Sometimes we have a large number of papers, and after ranking them from high to low on the basis of the total test score, you may divide them into two extreme groups: the highest 27% and the lowest 27%[1] (it is not necessary to do this in order to conduct an item analysis).

_____

[1]One can split papers into various proportionate groups. With small samples, the split is made in the middle (i.e., 50%). With a larger number of papers, the division can be at the top and bottom 10%, 27%, or 33%.

Sorting test papers into two extreme groups provides for a more stable analysis of item statistics because people in the middle of the group may score above or below the median on repeated applications of the test. In addition, tables of correlation values have been prepared based on a set percentage of cases in the extreme groups. These tables are not included in this text because the reader should learn to calculate his or her own item statistics. The formula for determining item difficulty for small samples becomes

$$p = \frac{\text{number of correct responses}}{N}$$

With a large number of papers, the formula becomes

$$p = \frac{p_{high} + p_{low}}{2}$$

where

$$p_H = \frac{\text{number of correct in top 27\%}}{n}$$

and

$$p_L = \frac{\text{number of correct in bottom 27\%}}{n}$$

and where p equals the proportion of correct responses in both formulas. Thus if p equals the proportion of the people who answer the item correctly, then 1 minus p is the proportion of people who answer the item incorrectly, or q.

Thus a summary of symbols so far includes the following:

p = Proportion of people who answer the item correctly.

q = $1 - p$, or the proportion of people who answer the item incorrectly.

N = Total number of test papers.

n = Number of people in top or bottom group.

p_H = Number of people answering the item correctly in the top $27\%/n$.

p_L = Number of people answering the item correctly in the lower $27\%/n$.

Item difficulty is very important in testing. There is an optimal level of difficulty for items relative to the purpose of the test and type of item format. Each test item should produce information to disclose differences among pupils. An indicator of examinee differences in test performance is called the *variance* of the test, or s^2. If there were no differences, that is, if everyone received the same test score, then there would be no variability; hence $s^2 = 0$. Thus it should follow that if everyone answers an item correctly, then the item variance is 0. Likewise, if everyone answers the item incorrectly, then the item variance is 0. These items have the same effect as adding a constant of $+1$ or -1 to everyone's score with the net effect that the test's variability remains unchanged. In other words, these items contribute nothing to the disclosure of individual differences in pupil achievement. Magnusson (1966) has shown that the item variance $= s^2 = p \times q$ (where $q = 1 - p$) and is an indication of the amount of differential information that is provided by the test item. The greatest amount of differential information is secured when $p = .50$. When this occurs, $q = 1 - p = .50$; thus $pq = .50 \times .50 = .25$. Let us apply this concept to a few items; first a small number of papers ($N = 32$) and then a large number of papers ($N = 100$) divided into the top and bottom 27% ($n = 27$ in each extreme group).

By examining the variance for each item in Table 9.4, one can readily see that Items 1 and 5 in both examples have variances equal to zero. These items make no contributions to the disclosure of individual differences through the testing process. It is also apparent that the most differential information is supplied by Item 3 in both examples. You are cautioned at this point that when working with a small number of test papers the item analysis data can fluctuate from one testing session to another. Thus do not be too quick to discard items, especially if you judge the concept being tested to be appropriate. When items show up to be consistently too hard or too easy and the tested concept is important, then editing the item or changing its format of presentation may permit the item to discriminate among the examinees' abilities. A test that is composed entirely of very easy items will produce a negatively skewed distribution of scores, whereas a test composed of all hard items will produce a positively skewed distribution of scores. Sometimes a test constructor may want this to occur, such as when the test has a special purpose. For example, if you want to *select* the top 75% of all applicants who apply to a course or program, most of the test items need to be fairly easy. On the other hand, if you can admit only 20% of the applicants to an honors program, the test items need to be quite difficult so that only this top group of people can score well. You should be aware of the fact that if a significant number of people answer all of the items correctly, you have gained no information concerning differences in achievement levels among these individuals. The same can be said if some examinees receive zeros on a test. At times you may intentionally construct items that test for *mastery* or are to be used as *criterion-referenced standards*. In these special cases, most items should be answered correctly before the examinee is allowed to proceed further in learning. This is the rationale behind programed learning: The student successfully

Table 9.4 Item Difficulty and Item Variances for Different Size Groups

	$N = 32$			$N = 100; n = 27$	
Item	Number correct top 50%	Number correct lower 50%	Item	Number correct top 27%	Number correct lower 27%
1	16	16	1	27	27
2	8	16	2	22	16
3	16	0	3	14	14
4	7	1	4	20	6
5	0	0	5	0	0

Item difficulty

$$p_1 = \frac{\text{number correct}}{N} = \frac{32}{32} = 1.00$$

$$p_2 = \frac{\text{number correct}}{N} = \frac{24}{32} = .75$$

$$p_3 = \frac{\text{number correct}}{N} = \frac{16}{32} = .50$$

$$p_4 = \frac{\text{number correct}}{N} = \frac{8}{32} = .25$$

$$p_5 = \frac{\text{number correct}}{N} = \frac{0}{32} = .00$$

Item difficulty

$$p_H = \frac{\text{number correct}}{n}, \ p_L = \frac{\text{number correct}}{n}$$

$$p_1 = \frac{p_H + p_L}{2} = \frac{1.00 + 1.00}{2} = \frac{2.00}{2} = 1.00$$

$$p_2 = \frac{p_H + p_L}{2} = \frac{.81 + .59}{2} = \frac{1.40}{2} = .70$$

$$p_3 = \frac{p_H + p_L}{2} = \frac{.518 + .518}{2} = \frac{1.036}{2} = .518$$

$$p_4 = \frac{p_H + p_L}{2} = \frac{.74 + .22}{2} = \frac{.96}{2} = .48$$

$$p_5 = \frac{p_H + p_L}{2} = \frac{0.00 + 0.00}{2} = \frac{0}{2} = .00$$

Item variance

Item	p	q	$pq = s^2$	Item	p	q	$pq = s^2$
1	1.00	.00	.00	1	1.00	.00	.00
2	.75	.25	.1875	2	.70	.30	.21
3	.50	.50	.25	3	.518	.482	.2496
4	.25	.75	.1875	4	.48	.52	.2496
5	.00	1.00	.00	5	.00	1.00	.00

passes a few self-test items before going on in the text to more difficult or newer concepts that depend on prior knowledge.

There is an optimal difficulty level for test items. It is argued that the range of item difficulties in a routine achievement test should be from 20 to 80%. This will permit both good and poor students to demonstrate their achievement levels. If you want to maximize the discrimination power of the test, at least two thirds or more of the items should have a difficulty rating of approximately 50 percent.

Index of Item Discrimination. The *index of item discrimination* tells us how well a suitably difficult item contributes to the test's effectiveness in discriminating among students of various abilities. Assuming that we have established good content or curricular validity, the total test should have some validity. Likewise, scores on each item should possess validity by agreeing with scores on the entire test. Thus an item should be answered correctly by a higher proportion of those who receive high scores on the test than of those who receive low scores on the test. When this occurs, the item is functioning in a manner consistent with the scores on the entire test. This is in effect a correlation or relationship between item scores and total test scores. This relationship can be calculated in many different ways. Test papers may be divided into different percentages of papers in the high and low groups, and a variety of correlation coefficients may be calculated. The Flanagan procedure (based on the Pearson product-moment correlation), the biserial correlation, the *phi* correlation, and the tetrachoric correlation are examples of these procedures and are illustrated in Barrow and McGee (1979) and Magnusson (1966).

A simple time-saving procedure for calculating D, the index of item discrimination, is recommended by Hopkins and Stanley (1981) as well as Noll and Scannell (1972). They indicate that the simplified procedure is highly related to the biserial correlation procedure and

will produce discrimination values of essentially the same magnitude. The simple, recommended procedure to use in determining the item discrimination index is

$$D = \frac{n_H - n_L}{N}; \text{ or } D = p_H - p_L$$

where D is the index of item discrimination; n_H is the number in the high group who answered the item correctly; n_L is the number in the low group who answered the item correctly; N is the total (similar) number in either the high or low group; p_H is the number of correct answers in the high group divided by the number of people in the high group; and p_L is the number of correct answers in the low group divided by the number of people in the low group, or where p_H or p_L is the proportion answering the item correctly in the high or low group. Again, the split into high or low groups can be at any percentage level you choose to establish. With a large number of papers, such as $N = 100$, split into the upper and lower 27%; with a small group, such as $N = 30$, split the papers into the top and bottom half. This index of discrimination has a possible range of $+1.00$ to -1.00, which is identical to the possible range for a correlation coefficient. An item answered correctly by all the high-group participants and missed by all the low-group participants would have a positive item validity of $+1.00$. The data in Table 9.5 also indicate that an item missed by all the high-group examinees and answered correctly by all those in the low group would have a negative item validity of -1.00. This latter case is unlikely because we logically expect good students to respond correctly to test items and poor students to respond incorrectly to the same items. Items with a negative index of discrimination must be carefully examined for possible flaws. If such items tap relevant concepts, the items must be edited or revised before being used again because items with a negative index of discrimination do not contribute to overall test validity.

Table 9.5 Examples of Item Discrimination Index (*D*) for Different Size Groups

Item	$N = 32$; split upper and lower 50%				Item	$N = 100$; split upper and lower 27%			
	p	*q*	*pq*	*D*		*p*	*q*	*pq*	*D*
1	1.00	.00	.00	.00[a]	1	1.00	.00	.00	.00[a]
2	.75	.25	.1872	−.50[a]	2	.70	.30	.21	.22
3	.50	.50	.25	+1.00	3	.518	.482	.2496	.00[a]
4	.25	.75	.1875	.37	4	.48	.52	.2496	.52
5	.00	1.00	.00	0.00[a]	5	.00	1.00	.00	.00[a]

$$D_1 = \frac{n_H - n_L}{N} = \frac{16 - 16}{16} = \frac{0}{16} = .00; \text{ or}$$

$$D_1 = p_H - p_L = 1.00 - 1.00 = .00$$

$$D_2 = \frac{n_H - n_L}{N} = \frac{8 - 16}{16} = \frac{-8}{16} = -.50; \text{ or}$$

$$D_2 = p_H - p_L = .50 - 1.00 = -.50$$

$$D_3 = \frac{n_H - n_L}{N} = \frac{16 - 0}{16} = \frac{16}{16} = +1.00; \text{ or}$$

$$D_3 = p_H - p_L = 1.00 - 0.00 = 1.00$$

$$D_4 = \frac{n_H - n_L}{N} = \frac{7 - 1}{16} = \frac{6}{16} = .375; \text{ or}$$

$$D_4 = p_H - p_L = .437 - .062 = .375$$

$$D_5 = \frac{n_H - n_L}{N} = \frac{0 - 0}{16} = \frac{0}{16} = 0.00; \text{ or}$$

$$D_5 = p_H - p_L = 0 - 0 = 0.00$$

$$D_1 = \frac{n_H - n_L}{N} = \frac{27 - 27}{27} = \frac{0.00}{27} = .00; \text{ or}$$

$$D_1 = p_H - p_L = 1.00 - 1.00 = 0.00$$

$$D_2 = \frac{n_H - n_L}{N} = \frac{22 - 16}{27} = \frac{6}{27} = .22; \text{ or}$$

$$D_2 = p_H - p_L = .81 - .59 = .22$$

$$D_3 = \frac{n_H - n_L}{N} = \frac{14 - 14}{27} = \frac{0}{27} = 0.00; \text{ or}$$

$$D_3 = p_H - p_L = .518 - .518 = 0.00$$

$$D_4 = \frac{n_H - n_L}{N} = \frac{20 - 6}{27} = \frac{14}{27} = .52; \text{ or}$$

$$D_4 = p_H - p_L = .74 - .22 = .52$$

$$D_5 = \frac{n_H - n_L}{N} = \frac{0 - 0}{27} = \frac{0}{27} = .00; \text{ or}$$

$$D_5 = p_H - p_L = 0 - 0 = .00$$

Note. Data are a continuation of Table 9.4.

[a]Items to be discarded or revised.

The data in Table 9.5 reveal a number of interesting points. First, Items 2, 3, and 4 in the small sample in Table 9.5 contain adequate item difficulty and allow for considerable differential information but do not always discriminate in the right direction (i.e., have a posi-tive index of item discrimination). Item 2 has negative discrimination; Item 3 has a perfect positive discrimination; and Item 4 has quite acceptable position discrimination. Thus suit-able item difficulty levels do not always guaran-tee positive discrimination; they only indicate discrimination in one direction or the other or else no discrimination, as when an equal number of people in both the top and bottom groups answer the item correctly. Item 3 in the *large sample* of Table 9.5 illustrates this last point. Secondly, Items 1 and 5 in both groups provide no differential information. Thus they do not discriminate in any direction. This occurs because everyone answered Item 1 correctly and everyone answered Item 5 incorrectly.

Generally speaking, items with an index of discrimination below .20 are considered poor items and should be rejected or improved by revision. In addition, Ebel (1965) maintains that items with an index of discrimination of .40 and above are very good items; items with an index of discrimination of .30 to .39 are reasonably good items; and items with an index of discrimination from .20 to .29 are marginal and probably need improvement.

Definite relationships exist between each item's difficulty and its maximum index of discrimination (*D* value) as well as between the mean index of item discrimination for all items and the reliability of test scores. First, the potential measurement value of an item is at a maximum when item difficulty is .50, that is, when one half of the examinees answer the item correctly. When this occurs, the maximum amount of differential information is obtained. If the item is too easy or too difficult, it will not assess individual differences very well. Secondly, assuming that you have items of suitable difficulty that discriminate in the positive direction, then as the average index of item discrimination increases in a 100-item test from .12 to .50, corresponding increases occur in the standard deviation of test scores from 5.0 to 20.4 and in the reliability of test scores from .00 to .949 (Ebel, 1965). In summary, items of 50% difficulty are needed to produce maximum differential information and to produce the higher index of discrimination. When this occurs we will have reliable test scores and can place confidence in the test's ability to disclose individual

differences in participant achievement because measurement error is decreased with improved reliability. The test now should possess improved validity.

Functioning of Responses. The last thing to check in an item analysis is the *functioning* of possible *responses* to a test question. In a true/false, yes/no, or right/wrong type of item, there are only two possible responses to the question. In a multiple choice format, there are usually four or five possible responses to the test item. Ideally, the correct response should be selected by the better participants, and the incorrect responses(s) should be selected by the poorer participants. When this happens, the various responses are functioning as intended. In other words, the correct response should have a positive index of item discrimination, and the incorrect response(s) should carry a negative index of item discrimination. In the latter case, each wrong response and/or all wrong responses added together should correlate negatively with the test scores because a greater proportion of the poorer participants selected the wrong response as compared to a small proportion of the better students who selected the incorrect response. The incorrect responses are now functioning as intended; that is, they are meaningful alternatives to the uninformed participants.

Item analysis data consisting of item difficulty, index of discrimination, and functioning of responses should be recorded on a work sheet such as that presented in Figure 9.3. This tally sheet of data (not previously presented in this chapter) contains all of the pertinent information needed to determine the quality of test items. Let Items 1 and 2 represent true/false item data and the remaining items represent multiple choice data. A heavy boxed line is drawn around the correct alternative. Item 1 is operating as intended with a difficulty rating of .60 and an item discrimination index of .67. However, Item 2 must be revised or discarded because it is

Item Analysis Tally Sheet

Test ___*Swimming*___ Number of Papers ___36___ Date ___*12/12/86*___ Grade ___*10, Sec. A*___

Item Number		(T) a	(F) b	c	d	e	Number correct answers	Proportion correct responses	Item difficulty $p = \dfrac{p_H + p_L}{2}$	Discrimination $D = p_H - p_L$	Revise or discard
1	High	17	1				17	17/18 = .94	$\dfrac{.94 + .27}{2} = .60$	.94 − .27 = .67	
	Low	5	13				5	5/18 = .27			
2	High	13	5				5	5/18 = .27	$\dfrac{.27 + .72}{2} = .499$	.27 − .72 = −.45	Yes
	Low	5	13				13	13/18 = .72			
3	High	7	2	0	8	1	8	8/18 = .44	$\dfrac{.44 + .27}{2} = .35$	.44 − .27 = −.17	Yes
	Low	2	6	3	5	2	5	5/18 = .27			
4	High	1	10	3	0	4	10	10/18 = .55	$\dfrac{.55 + .22}{2} = .38$	.55 − .22 = .33	
	Low	0	4	6	1	7	4	4/18 = .22			
5	High	3	4	5	4	2	4	4/18 = .22	$\dfrac{.22 + .33}{2} = .27$	.22 − .33 = −.11	Yes
	Low	2	6	3	5	2	6	6/18 = .33			
6	High	1	2	10	3	3	3	3/18 = .16	$\dfrac{.16 + .33}{2} = .24$	.16 − .33 = −.17	Yes
	Low	0	4	3	5	6	6	6/18 = .33			
7	High	16	1	1	0	0	16	16/18 = .88	$\dfrac{.88 + .83}{2} = .85$	.88 − .83 = .05	Yes
	Low	15	0	1	2	0	15	15/18 = .83			

Figure 9.3 Response pattern tally sheet for an item analysis.

discriminating in the wrong direction (the relationship is −.45). Inspection of the other distractors for Item 3 reveals that Option *a* would have a greater positive validity than the distractor keyed as correct. At this point the instructor should count both Options *a* and *d* as correct responses. One of these distractors, preferably Option *d*, should be revised before the test item is used again. The other Options *b*, *c*, and *e* are operating as intended. Item 4 appears to be operating properly with good item difficulty and discriminating power. Distractors *c* and *e* have the desired negative discrimination. We can see

that Item 5 does not function properly because it possesses a negative index of discrimination. Participants seem to be projecting their responses across the board. Because there is no clear-cut pattern for any distractor, the instructor should count this item either correct or incorrect for all participants. Item 6 must be carefully examined. It possesses negative validity, yet one other distractor *c* clearly appears to be operating as the correct one. Perhaps an error exists in the scoring procedure for the item. In any event, Distractor *c* is the correct one and item editing is necessary. In Item 7, the item is obviously too easy to provide for any meaningful differential information. The item should be revised or discarded before the test is used again.

After the item analysis is completed, the next step is to revise the test questions that are not contributing to the purpose of the test. The items can now be arranged into order of difficulty within type of item format, and you are now ready to administer a better test the next time.

Determine Test Validity, Reliability, and Objectivity

Once internal validity of the test has been established by item analysis techniques, total test validity, reliability, and objectivity can be determined by using external procedures. These procedures have been described in detail in chapter 3 and should be reviewed for this aspect of test construction.

Developing Norms

The final step in test construction is to develop norms if norms are desired. After you have administered the test to a number of the same type groups under similar conditions, you can derive norms. It is desirable to have over 200 cases before developing norms in order to enhance the reliability of rank ordering. Norms can be developed based on age, grade, sex, and subject taught. Norms can be prepared as percentile ranks, standard scores, T scales, or 6-σ scales. The most appropriate norms for comparing performances must be local and as specific as possible to the subject taught and grade level. Methods for constructing norms were presented in chapter 2 on statistics.

Criterion-Referenced Test Construction

The most important uses of criterion-referenced measurements are to designate examinees to mastery status and to estimate how much of the universe of knowledge was attained by the examinee. The techniques for construction and evaluation of a criterion-referenced test are similar to those for a norm-referenced test with a few exceptions worthy of discussion.

Care must be taken to guarantee the content validity of a criterion-referenced test if we want to estimate a universe of knowledge with our samples of test questions. Items of all levels of difficulty are included in the test. These items should estimate not only general knowledge but also the examinee's ability to apply, analyze, synthesize, and evaluate information. It appears that the hierarchy of cognitive function is related to item difficulty level. The validity of a criterion-referenced test necessitates using good, well-written items that represent a well-defined universe of facts or concepts defined in our table of specifications.

The intended universe of knowledge to be tested must be defined and described as clearly as possible. Otherwise we cannot claim that an item does or does not reference the intended universe, nor can we tell what a test score really estimates. In the final analysis, the quality of decisions made on the basis of test scores can be no higher than the quality of the items themselves (Brennan, 1983).

No matter how thoroughly you scrutinize items and use a table of specifications to develop content validity as a subject specialist, there is no substitute for carefully studying examinees' responses to items. Studying examinee's responses will help to eliminate future negative effects of poor items on what the test was intended to measure. After trying out your test, you can conduct an item analysis. Use the procedures previously described in this chapter for norm-referenced tests: calculate item difficulty levels, calculate the index of item discrimination, and collect information concerning the functioning of various response distractors. After you have obtained item analysis data, you can make decisions about items and how well they satisfy the purpose of the test.

This decision in part describes essential differences between norm-referenced and criterion-referenced tests and must be reflected in the content validity of each type test. The criterion-referenced test item analysis data are used to ensure that your test has sampled a defined universe of knowledge. Item difficulty information guarantees that a sufficient number of items of all levels of difficulty appears on the test. These levels of difficulty usually range from near 0 to 100%, with the majority of the items having high difficulty levels if they are correctly answered by those who received thorough instruction in the content area. This is particularly true when operating from a mastery learning mode of instruction.

The index of item discrimination will also provide useful information. The item discrimination index for the correct alternative should not be negative. In fact, the values should range from .00 to +.20 or above. The discrimination index for incorrect distractors should be negative. In summary, *the principal use of item analysis data in criterion-referenced testing is to detect flawed items*. Flaws should be corrected by rewriting the item (Brennan, 1983).

In norm-referenced testing, the purpose of the item analysis is to evaluate each item's potential for detecting differences in participants' abilities with respect to what the item estimates. A norm-referenced test also estimates a part of a knowledge universe. However, due to the dis-

crimination purpose of the test and the fact that the reference base for decision-making is a rank-ordered position in a distribution of scores, the discrimination power of the test must be maximized. To do this, quite easy or very hard items are eliminated from the test and items near a 50% difficulty are retained. Also, items that did not have an acceptable index of discrimination are revised or deleted from the test.

Criterion-referenced tests are often used to determine mastery status. In order to do this, you must establish a "cutting score," that is, the score a participant must attain on the test to demonstrate a certain level of proficiency or mastery. Mastery decisions can be used to select people for special training. For example, once an examinee masters a certain amount of material, he or she may be advanced to an honors program. Until they acquire experience in a mastery teaching situation, professionals must rely on expert judgment in setting the cutting score. After appropriate experience is acquired, they can then set more realistic mastery levels. Establishing the validity and reliability of criterion-referenced tests requires the use of carefully defined procedures. Advanced discussion of these topics is beyond the scope of this text. Interested readers are directed to Brennan (1983), Martuza (1977), Ulrich (1984), and Washburn and Safrit (1982) for more information.

Review Questions

1. What preliminary decisions should be made before constructing a test or selecting an existing standardized test?
2. What are the purposes of a test?
3. What are process evaluation and product evaluation?

4. What are the interrelationships between test purposes, process and product, formative and summative evaluation, criterion- or norm-referenced standards, and types of educational objectives described by Baumgartner and Jackson and modified in Figure 9.1?

5. In direct observation, what two types of recording information are suggested in this chapter?

6. What types of testing and examinations are suggested for use by the physical education teacher?

7. What steps should be considered in constructing a knowledge test?

8. What is a table of specifications?

9. What procedures are suggested in this chapter to facilitate content validity?

10. List the general principles for formulating test questions introduced by Remmers and Gage.

11. One type of recognition item is the alternate choice item. What are Safrit's suggestions for writing such items?

12. What are the guidelines for writing good multiple choice questions?

13. What are the advantages of using a separate answer sheet and scoring key in scoring short-answer test items?

14. What factors should be considered in the administration of a test?

15. In conducting an item analysis, what three factors does the physical education teacher essentially determine?

16. What should be the range of item difficulty level? What fraction of a test's items should have a difficulty level of 50%?

17. What does the index of item discrimination tell us? Generally speaking, what index of discrimination value should indicate a poor item?

18. In an ideal situation, what should the functioning of possible responses indicate?

19. What is the desirable number of cases to be tested before developing norms?

Problems and Exercises

1. A physical education teacher gave a 40-item written test on diving skills. Thirty-eight students took the test with the following number of correct responses to each item:

Item	Number of students answering item correctly	Item	Number of students answering item correctly
1	25	21	21
2	16	22	23
3	10	23	18
4	35	24	15
5	38	25	19
6	20	26	35
7	16	27	14

(Cont.)

Item	Number of students answering item correctly	Item	Number of students answering item correctly
8	27	28	3
9	8	29	11
10	35	30	17
11	33	31	24
12	21	32	23
13	16	33	16
14	14	34	19
15	12	35	28
16	0	36	35
17	30	37	30
18	24	38	14
19	17	39	6
20	29	40	20

What is the item difficulty level for each item? What is the variance of each item?

Answer:

Item	Item difficulty level	s^2 pq	Item	Item difficulty level	s^2 pq
1	.66	.22	21	.55	.25
2	.42	.24	22	.61	.24
3	.26	.19	23	.47	.25
4	.92	.07	24	.39	.24
5	1.00	.00	25	.50	.25
6	.53	.25	26	.92	.07
7	.42	.24	27	.37	.23
8	.71	.21	28	.08	.07
9	.21	.17	29	.29	.21
10	.92	.07	30	.45	.25
11	.87	.11	31	.63	.23
12	.55	.25	32	.61	.24
13	.42	.24	33	.42	.24
14	.37	.23	34	.50	.25
15	.32	.22	35	.74	.19
16	.00	.00	36	.92	.07
17	.79	.17	37	.79	.17
18	.63	.23	38	.37	.23
19	.45	.25	39	.16	.13
20	.76	.18	40	.53	.25

2. The physical education teacher in Problem 1 divided the students into a 50% high group and a 50% low group. In other words, the teacher took the 19 highest scores on the test and called this the high group and took the 19 lowest scores and called this the low group. The teacher then compared the number of correct responses to each item in the high group to the number of correct responses to each item in the low group with the following results:

Item	Number correct top 50%	Number correct lower 50%	Item	Number correct top 50%	Number correct lower 50%
1	15	10	21	14	7
2	9	7	22	12	11
3	5	5	23	9	9
4	18	17	24	10	5
5	19	19	25	9	10
6	15	5	26	17	18
7	10	6	27	10	4
8	17	10	28	3	0
9	8	0	29	11	0
10	18	17	30	7	10
11	17	16	31	12	12
12	17	4	32	16	7
13	9	7	33	14	2
14	7	7	34	18	1
15	12	0	35	15	13
16	0	0	36	18	17
17	18	12	37	18	12
18	15	9	38	12	2
19	7	10	39	6	0
20	15	14	40	15	5

What is the index of item discrimination for each item? If the index of discrimination is

.40 and up   = very good items;
.30 to .39   = reasonably good items;
.20 to .29   = marginal and probably need improvement;
.19 and below = eliminate the item.

What items would the physical education teacher retain, rewrite to improve, or eliminate? Has the physical education teacher constructed a fair and reasonable test to measure the students' knowledge of diving skills?

3. The physical education teacher in Problem 1 found that Items 1 and 24 were marginal in discrimination and decided to rewrite these two items. The teacher examined the Response Pattern Tally Sheet for Item Analysis and found the following results for Items 1 and 24:

Response Pattern Tally Sheet for Item Analysis

Test <u>Knowledge Diving Skills</u>   Number of papers <u>38</u>   Date <u>1/3/77</u>   Grade <u>11</u>

Item		Multiple choice number of answers a b c d e					Number correct answers	Proportion correct answers	Item difficulty	Discrimination	Revise or discard
1	High	1	15	1	0 1		15	.79	.66	.26	revise
	Low	2	10	4	0 2		10	.53			
24	High	3	0 0	10	5		10	.53	.39	.26	revise
	Low	0	2 1	5	5		5	.26			

What evaluation can the teacher make in order to improve Items 1 and 24 as multiple choice items?

Answer: Item 1 stem could be reworded to make it more difficult because the item difficulty indicates that both the high and low group answer the question correctly. Distractor "d" definitely needs to be rewritten because no one responded to "d." The teacher would try to rewrite distractor "d" to pull more low responses toward "d."

Item 24 appears to have a fair difficulty rating. Distractor "e" needs to be rewritten because it appears to be confusing in light of the fact that 5 students in the high group and 5 students in the low group selected this incorrect answer. Likewise, distractor "a" needs to be rewritten because no one in the low group selected it, whereas 3 students in the high group selected this incorrect answer.

4. A physical education supervisor in a large school system developed a physical education concept test for ninth-grade students. The teacher applied her newly constructed 20-item multiple choice test to 200 ninth-grade students. The teacher decided to take the highest 27% and the lowest 27% of the scores to run an item analysis and tabulated the following results:

Item		\multicolumn{5}{c}{Number answers multiple choice}
		a	b	c	d	e
1	High	3	48	1	1	1
	Low	15	3	12	15	9
2	High	5	2	1	2	44
	Low	8	10	10	20	6
3	High	2	45	2	2	3
	Low	7	10	17	15	5
4	High	2	5	40	5	2
	Low	4	14	6	28	2
5	High	3	0	1	48	2
	Low	31	9	4	0	10
6	High	40	3	4	3	4
	Low	35	10	4	2	3
7	High	50	1	0	3	0
	Low	2	2	6	40	4
8	High	2	1	1	3	47
	Low	8	2	2	30	12
9	High	2	5	40	5	2
	Low	4	20	7	18	5
10	High	0	54	0	0	0
	Low	25	6	20	3	0
11	High	0	4	0	50	0
	Low	2	40	2	8	2
12	High	38	3	5	4	4
	Low	2	4	18	15	15

(Cont.)

13	High	1	3	3	4	43
	Low	0	1	9	32	12

14	High	4	6	35	6	3
	Low	2	12	16	12	2

15	High	1	1	0	52	0
	Low	8	8	18	12	8

16	High	4	4	2	3	41
	Low	15	16	10	7	6

17	High	2	42	6	2	2
	Low	4	4	34	6	6

18	High	47	1	1	2	3
	Low	8	12	8	16	10

19	High	3	2	47	1	1
	Low	16	12	16	6	4

20	High	0	0	0	3	51
	Low	2	2	2	45	3

   a. What is the item difficulty level for each item?
   b. What is the variance of each item?
   c. What is the index of item discrimination of each item?
   d. As a whole, would you say the test is fair and reasonable? What items need revising or elimination?

5. List the current subject and activities that you teach. What are your daily, weekly, or grading period objectives? Indicate which objectives can be met by utilizing formative and summative evaluation techniques.

6. Describe how you can establish and implement both criterion-referenced and norm-referenced standards.

7. Develop a table of specifications for a volleyball knowledge test.

8. Write some essay questions to cover the objectives listed in your volleyball knowledge test table of specifications. Do they meet the established standards set for writing essay questions?

9. Write a number of true/false, multiple choice, and matching type test questions for the same volleyball area. Do they meet the established standards for writing short-answer questions?

10. Administer a short-answer test to a class. Conduct an item analysis. Are all items sufficiently difficult? Do they provide information about differences in pupil achievement? Do all possible responses function as intended?

11. Set up an item analysis summary table and record the data from Question 10 on it.

Bibliography

Barrow, H.M., & McGee, R. (1979). *A practical approach to measurement in physical education* (3rd ed.). Philadelphia: Lea and Febiger.

Baumgartner, T.A., & Jackson, A.S. (1982). *Measurement for evaluation in physical education* (2nd ed.). Dubuque, IA: William C. Brown.

Bloom, B.S. (Ed.). (1956). *Taxonomy of educational objectives: Handbook I cognitive domain.* New York: David McKay.

Brennan, R.L. (1983). Some statistical procedures for domain-referenced testing. In L.D. Hensley & W.B. East (Eds.), *Proceedings of the fourth measurement and evaluation symposium* (pp. 60-130). Cedar Falls, IA: University of Northern Iowa and the American Alliance for Health, Physical Education, Recreation, and Dance.

Ebel, R.L. (1965). *Measuring educational achievement.* Englewood Cliffs, NJ: Prentice-Hall.

Gruber, J.J. (1982). Physical activity and emotional health. In H.M. Eckert (Ed.), *The academy papers number 16—Synthesizing and transmitting knowledge: Research and its applications* (pp. 49-58). Reston, VA: American Academy of Physical Education and the American Alliance for Health, Physical Education, Recreation, and Dance.

Hopkins, K.D., & Stanley, J.C. (1981). *Educational and psychological measurement and evaluation* (6th ed.). Englewood Cliffs, NJ: Prentice-Hall.

Magnusson, D. (1966). *Test theory.* Reading, MA: Addison-Wesley.

Martuza, V.R. (1977). *Applying norm-referenced and criterion-referenced measurement in education.* Boston: Allyn and Bacon.

Morgan, W.P. (1983). Physical activity and mental health. In H.M. Eckert & H.J. Montoye (Eds.), *The academy papers number 17—Exercise and health* (pp. 132-145). Champaign, IL: The American Academy of Physical Education and Human Kinetics Publishers.

Noll, V.H., & Scannell, D.P. (1972). *Introduction to educational measurement* (3rd ed.). Boston: Houghton Mifflin.

Remmers, H.H., & Gage, N.L. (1955). *Educational measurement and evaluation* (rev. ed.). New York: Harper and Brothers.

Safrit, M.J. (1986). *Introduction to measurement in physical education and exercise science.* St. Louis: Times Mirror/Mosby College Publishing.

Ulrich, D.A. (1984). The reliability of classification decisions made with the objectives-based motor skill assessment instrument. *Adapted Physical Activity Quarterly,* **1**(1), 52-60.

Washburn, R.A., & Safrit, M.J. (1982). Physical performance tests in job selection: A model for empirical validation. *Research Quarterly for Exercise and Sport,* **55**(3), 267-270.

Wood, D.A. (1961). *Test construction.* Columbus, OH: Charles E. Merrill.

Chapter

10

Measurement in the Affective Domain

The affective domain of development is concerned with people's values, attitudes, interests, and their related personal-social behaviors. Indeed, personal-social development has long been one of the general objectives of physical education (Stoner, 1982). Affective goals are presented as concomitant learnings, those things that Ebel (1972) claims are difficult to teach but yet are learned as instruction in more tangible elements takes place. The affective goals linger on to become part of our personality and influence us to behave in certain ways.

We have all heard coaches and sports writers proclaim that the "character" and "sportsmanship" we develop on the playing field will help steer us through life's future journey. Unfortunately, however, affective objectives are developed and learning outcomes are evaluated only rarely in school physical education and athletic programs. Despite a lack of formalized teaching strategies designed to develop affective learnings, nearly all fitness and psychomotor objectives involve an affective component. If a child is taught physical fitness activities but will participate only if forced to do so, an important affective goal was not achieved.

The reader should realize that affective goals and objectives are important outcomes wherever physical educators practice their profession. Clients seek fitness experiences not only in schools and colleges but also in health spas, employee fitness programs, cardiac rehabilitation programs, and programs for senior citizens. Most of the measuring instruments for the affective domain described in this chapter have been used in a school setting. Some have been used on varsity sport teams, and others have been used by researchers to investigate the contributions of physical activity to the development of emotional health. Affective domain measuring instruments are also used to monitor improvement in patients who seek treatment for anxiety and depression in a mental health setting where exercise is one of the treatment modalities (Gruber, 1982; Morgan, 1984).

Several of the instruments described in this chapter are fairly old. They are presented as example instruments and because more appropriate inventories have not yet been developed for use in physical education or sport. This does not mean that all of the older inventories are now obsolete. Each instrument, old or new, must be carefully evaluated to determine if it meets our measurement need. After the purpose of testing and the use to be made of test data are determined, we are in a position to evaluate any instrument. Do not use an old or a new instrument simply because it is the only one available. The instrument you use must be relevant to your purpose for testing.

We can illustrate the question of whether to use an "old" versus a "new" inventory with an example. Suppose we want to measure aggression in competitive situations. A new inventory (Wall & Gruber, 1986) failed to discriminate among levels of agression in women basketball players being stimulated by the rigors of competition. However, the much older procedure of merely recording overtly aggressive acts and their provoking situational stimuli does provide needed information concerning aggressive behavior during competition. In another example, we may want to determine whether either the new or old instrument designed to estimate sportsmanship assesses current sportsmanship behaviors indigenous to a specific sport. What is acceptable sportsmanship in golf may be unacceptable in football. This implies a need for sport-specific measuring instruments, a topic discussed later in this chapter. Any measuring instrument can be updated and revised by the professional. Some revision of items and/or vocabulary may be necessary to enhance an instrument's content validity to meet specific needs.

Philosophy, Purposes, and Use of Affective Measures

Values, appreciations, attitudes, and self-realization are the components of our feelings and emotions. These affective dispositions are important outcomes of all human experience, including what happens today in the gymnasium or on the athletic field. If we subscribe to the proposition that physical educators, like other teachers, are interested in students' affective development, then we must set realistic, obtainable affective objectives for our students. After all, measurement is a process of collecting information that relates to attainable objectives.

Stoner (1982) indicates that affective objectives should be uniquely appropriate to physical activity and to the physical education setting. Affective objectives may *not* be needed for every unit of instruction. The following physical education experiences appear to lend themselves to affective development:

- Learning and following the rules required for many games and sports helps to develop knowledge and attitudes relating to accepting adverse decisions.
- Group activities such as team sports, group games, and creative movement experiences serve as a convenient laboratory for developing cooperation, leadership, and followership.
- Movement activities require the student to become familiar with the body and its capabilities and limitations and thus provide a basis for the development of self-concepts relating to body image.
- Physical education promotes the development of positive attitudes toward physical activity as a way of life.
- Physical education and fitness activities can teach students the value of perseverance under trying circumstances.

At issue is whether physical educators should engage in affective evaluation. Mood (1982) claims that we should not. His position is based on the following questions and observations:

- How many tasks must the teacher take on? Physical educators have more than enough to do in teaching motor skills without delving into the affective domain.

- Why should physical educators spend more time with affective learning than other classroom teachers spend? Can we really teach someone to have a positive attitude toward something?
- The availability of measuring instruments for the affective domain is questionable, and the reliability of affective measures continues to be a problem. (More will be said about instrument problems and their susceptibility to faked responses later in this chapter.)

Mood recommends that affective concerns be removed from our primary physical education objectives because of the above reasons.

An advocate for affective evaluation in physical education is Griffin (1982), who quite aptly presents a rationale for such objectives. He states that the affective learning that results from experiences such as shooting a basketball cleanly through a hoop, swimming a mile without stopping for the first time, or being valued as a member of a class team are important. These are feelings and appreciations that shape students' attitudes—attitudes that motivate them to return to the court or pool on their *own* time. In contrast, the affective learning that results from being ridiculed by classmates for dropping a fly ball, failing a physical fitness test in front of the whole class, or being picked last for teams day after day is learning that encourages students to avoid further participation in sport and physical activity. Hence, in both of these examples students received input, organized it, evaluated it, and responded to it by placing a value on their physical education experiences. According to Krathwohl, Bloom, and Masia (1964), these physical education learning experiences are in the affective domain.

Krathwohl developed a taxonomy of educational objectives dealing with the affective domain. The domain is ordered on a continuum from a base level where an individual is aware of a value construct up to a persuasive outlook that influences a person's actions. Kirkendall (1972) provided the following example of how the affective taxonomy can be applied to physical education where the teacher is interested in developing students' sense of "fair play."[1]

1. *Receiving*
   - *Awareness.* The student develops an awareness that there is such a thing as fair play.
   - *Willingness to receive.* The student appreciates observing activities where honesty is demonstrated by others.
   - *Controlled or selected attention.* The student begins looking for situations in which respect for others and fair play occur.

2. *Responding*
   - *Acquiescence in responding.* The student observes all the rules of the game at the request or threat of the teacher.
   - *Willingness to respond.* The student sometimes calls rule violations on himself or herself but does so mainly to please the teacher.
   - *Satisfaction in response.* The student becomes emotionally involved and begins to get some personal pleasure out of being honest.

3. *Valuing*
   - *Acceptance of a value.* The student accepts that honesty and fair play in sports are good and desirable.
   - *Preference for a value.* The student calls rule violations on himself or herself without any prompting because he or she strongly feels this is the right thing to do.

---

[1]Condensed from "Physical Education Effects in the Affective Domain" by D.R. Kirkendall, 1972, in the *75th Proceedings of the National College Physical Education Association for Men* (pp. 147-151), New Orleans, LA.

- *Commitment (conviction).* The student clearly values "fair play" and demonstrates this not only by his or her own actions but by trying to convince others that this is the way to enjoy the game.

4. *Organization*
   - *Conceptualization of a value.* The student sees how the concept of honesty and fair play can be used in other aspects of life.
   - *Organization of a value system.* The student places the sense of "fairness" into his or her total value system.

5. *Characterization by a value or value complex*
   - *Generalized set.* The student becomes consistent in all aspects of his or her life in the display of "honesty."

This hierarchy of a developing value construct can be applied to many of the other desirable affective behaviors we claim are inherent in physical education, sports, and games. Once we recognize their existence, define them, and plan and teach for students to acquire and display these desirable affective behaviors, we can determine how well the learner has acquired and utilized the values taught.

The main question appears to be how physical educators can take responsibility for the affective learning that always occurs in physical education classes to ensure that most of what students learn about themselves contributes positively to their human development. The teacher who states some objectives within the affective domain has some obligation to assess whether those objectives have been met. Measurement techniques for the affective domain fall into two categories: those that are applied to the group and those that are applied to individuals (McGee, 1982).

Affective Measurements for Groups

Information relative to class status in an affective variable may be used in several ways. The discovery of *interests* or preferences for certain physical education activities should help us to develop and offer classes in which people voluntarily enroll. Evaluation of the class, the conditions of teaching, and the role of the teacher can also provide helpful information for improving instruction. Certain measures appropriate for groups can be used to help *classify* students into more effective team patterns and/or for competitive experiences. Affective measurements can also help to assess group needs. Do class members cooperate well with one another? Does the class as a whole need to improve in areas of sportsmanship? Another use for group measurements is in the area of research. Professional teachers should be able to conduct on-site research. For example, a teacher may use group measures to study whether the body image scores of class members improve along with improvements in their physical fitness and motor skills. Group measurements can also be used to identify students who are ready for leadership training or experiences.

In order to secure data relevant to purpose, class members should respond to affective questionnaires in an atmosphere of anonymity. Certain data should never be used as input for an individual's grade in physical education because other members of the class can markedly influence one individual's grade. An estimate of an individual's personal distance or peer status, for example, is obtained from other class members.

Affective Measurements for Individuals

Affective measures are particularly useful for identifying individual strengths and weaknesses in the affective domain. After individual needs have been identified, appropriate programmatic action can be undertaken. For example, daily observation of behavior based on certain affective measurement criteria can help to identify the socially rejected or unpopular child. Some children are rejected because they lack adequate play skills. Placement into a remedial skills program may provide them with the play skills valued by their peers. The improvement in motor performance may also be accompanied by a better body image and self-concept. The teacher may also use information from sociometric instruments to structure the membership of squads to foster integration into a social group. Affective measures can also identify the child with problems that inhibit achievement or that interfere with the achievement of other students in the class. If necessary, *referral* of the pupil to appropriate school specialists may help alleviate the problem. In addition, daily class observations can identify the child who consistently displays a lack of respect for established regulations or who behaves in socially unacceptable ways. Keeping anecdotal records can help when we work with the child, parents, and school guidance personnel in problem solving. A sympathetic ear and counsel can be offered to students who occasionally experience adverse affective feelings in class.

Information from the affective domain is sometimes used in determining the child's grade. This should be done only if the school's grading policy dictates it and should be recorded as a "citizenship" or "conduct" grade and be kept separate from grades assigned for proficiency in the acquisition of physical skills. Affective domain data should be used to determine a student's specific physical education grade only in situations where the student's performance in physical skills is hindered by inappropriate behaviors. An overly anxious student will perform poorly on skills requiring intense concentration or cognition. A reduction in anxiety should enhance skill performance. The effort the student expends in learning to control anxiety should be rewarded in the total grade. In addition, students become aware of the importance of certain affective goals when they know those goals are part of the grading system.

In other situations physical educators may be teaching children who are emotionally disturbed. A principal objective of physical education for this population is to reduce inappropriate behaviors (crying, pushing, hitting, acting out hostility, etc.) in class. This objective is made known to the children, and they are rewarded when a reduction of inappropriate behaviors is observed. Continued progress is reflected as part of the input for each child's physical education grade. We must now decide whether to use norm-referenced or criterion-referenced standards in decision-making. Perhaps affective domain objectives should be set on an individual basis and viewed in a mastery learning context. This approach would certainly be more meaningful if the teacher had to award a grade for achievement in the affective domain. Remember, in emotionally disturbed populations, the parent and child receive a grade report concerning the child's *behavior*, not his or her skill performance. Reports to parents can also include written descriptive appraisals of the child's progress in the affective area.

As teachers, we must be wary of setting leadership as an objective for the class unless we are skillful in ensuring that every student in class has an opportunity to learn and practice leadership skills. Teachers can award grades for leadership only if each student has received adequate leadership experiences and opportunities. To be most effective, feedback relative to proficiency in leadership skills should be given as soon as possible after behavior is rated.

Considerations in Affective Measurement

Measuring aspects of the affective domain involves several problems and considerations regardless of how the data are collected. These problems are discussed by Stanley and Hopkins (1972) and are summarized here.[2] First, a fundamental difference exists between a physical fitness, psychomotor, or cognitive item score versus an affective item score. In the former, we are usually interested in a person's *maximal* performance or what the person can do on the test item, whereas an affective score should measure the person's *typical* response or what the person does or feels under *ordinary* circumstances. Obviously, one of the uses of an affective measurement is to identify persons who deviate markedly from the norm. Secondly, the correct response to an affective statement depends on the person being questioned, whereas the correct response to a cognitive question is the same for everyone.

For example, two people may differ in their appreciation of distance running, but to receive credit for a correct response the same two people must know that a field goal in basketball is worth 2 points. In other words, there is rarely, if ever, a "correct" response or a "right" or "wrong" answer to an affective statement. Thirdly, the situational factors of the examiner and the assessment environment may influence the results of an affective measurement. If the respondents perceive that the examiner is in a position to make crucial decisions that will affect them, and if the respondents do not understand the use to be made of the data, the affective measurements may produce invalid results.

Fourth, the cultural background of the student will shape his or her response as well as acceptance of what constitutes appropriate behavior. Fifth, human beings tend to put their best foot forward when they know they are being rated. As a result, affective measurements are not likely to obtain the respondent's typical score. Sixth, most affective measures are unstable. This is probably due to day-to-day variations in respondents' dispositions as well as the instability of what is being measured. For example, a student's attitude toward a basketball class may change due to a new teacher who introduces a grueling running program as punishment for improper class behavior.

The most serious problems encountered in affective measurements tend to involve (a) the susceptibility of items to faked responses, (b) self-deception, (c) semantics, and (d) criterion inadequacy (Stanley & Hopkins, 1972). Because affective measures do not usually lend themselves to intrinsically right or wrong responses, the respondent can easily *fake* the response. Respondents are often motivated to project what they perceive to be the socially acceptable answer instead of their true feelings. A number of self-report inventories have been constructed that include a distortion scale that identifies individuals with a tendency to fake their responses. However, responses to affective measures can be falsified no matter how well the measures are constructed. As a result, the faked scores lack validity and the purpose for administering the instrument cannot be achieved. In order to increase the validity of affective measures, respondents should be provided with some type of anonymity. In this way examiners can reduce respondents' incentive to be untruthful.

Another problem with affective measures lies in the tendency of the respondent to indulge in *self-deception*. People want to *like* what they see when engaging in introspection and may therefore idealize their responses to affective

---

[2]Paraphrased from J.C. Stanley and K.D. Hopkins, *Educational and Psychological Measurement and Evaluation*, © 1972, pp. 282-301. Adapted by permission of Prentice-Hall, Inc., Englewood Cliffs, NJ.

measurement items. If a respondent really believes that he or she is a great athlete when in fact he or she is not, responses to particular items will convey this distortion, and the respondent's projected behavior when at play will probably be influenced by this belief. Self-deceptions and their related manifestations are usually indicative of some personality problem. Students who exhibit aspects of self-deception should be referred to appropriate school psychologists.

Semantics is another problem in affective measurements. Responses to affective measurement items usually convey a difference in degree such as "often," "seldom," "frequently," and "most of the time." Unfortunately, however, there is considerable variation in the connotative meanings various people attach to these words. "Often" may mean most of the time to one person and about one third of the time to another person. The meaning people attach to terms such as "acceptable" and "unacceptable" in response to a particular item or situation will vary among different age groups and cultures. What do we really mean when we use terms such as "interesting" or "easily"? How interesting is "interesting"? How easy is "easily"? The validity of affective measures is reduced to the extent that words do not have uniform meaning across all respondents. Uniform meaning can be increased when constructing instruments by carefully and exactly defining each descriptive category and exhorting the respondent to use a particular category in such a way that the category definition corresponds to the actual feeling, belief, or practice of the respondent.

Criterion inadequacy is another serious problem in affective measurement. Identifying and obtaining a criterion measure to correlate with scores on an affective measuring device is extremely difficult. This fact, coupled with respondents' incentive to fake responses to emotionally sensitive questions, makes instru-ment validation extremely difficult. One can, however, utilize techniques to develop internal validity by identifying the traits or constructs that are being measured by the items on the measuring instrument. Factor analysis is the correlational research tool that identifies the factors that are being estimated by certain items. Once identified, each factor is given a psychological name, such as "anxiety" or "dependence." The name is also referred to as a "construct." Thus the construct validity of an instrument can be developed through factor analysis. We then know what dimension of an affective instrument, such as an attitude scale, is being measured by each item.

An excellent example of the application of factor analysis to the multidimensional area of values in physical activity is provided by Kenyon (1968a, b), who identified six constructs in his model. The second validity step is the identification of an external criterion measure. As stated previously, this is a difficult process. However, the problem must be solved before we can use scores in any predictive fashion. Due to the many problems mentioned, extreme caution must be used in interpreting scores obtained on affective measuring devices. Information from a variety of sources as well as repeated measures must be obtained before crucial decisions are made about the student.

Types of Inventories

Several appraisal instruments have been constructed to measure certain aspects of personal-social behavior, attitudes, and adjustment in physical education. We can subjectively classify these instruments into seven general types of inventories that purport to measure interest, attitude, sportsmanship, leadership, social development, behavior, and personality.

Interest Inventories

Interest inventories are usually self-report instruments in which the individual expresses his or her likes and dislikes for certain activities, situations, or programs. Interest inventories are often used as a basis for establishing programs and program content in recreational settings. Students generally participate in intramural sports or elect a particular activity from the physical education offerings based on their liking for a particular sport. Their interest or lack of interest in a particular activity may be influenced by past experience, peer pressure, teacher or parent stimulation, and other cultural factors. An expressed interest may reflect a student's attitude toward certain forms of activity. A person who values physical activity from an aesthetic point of view, for example, will probably express a preference for dance as opposed to football.

Attitude Inventories

Attitude inventories are usually self-report instruments in which the student is asked to reveal his or her state of mind or feelings about specific objects, events, people, activities, social institutions, and so forth. An individual's attitude or basic feeling about physical activity is believed to be a primary motivating force affecting the degree of future participation in a selected physical activity. Hence we should try to identify individuals with negative points of view toward class activities in order to deter them from dropping the class. Certain class routines or the nature of the exercise program might be changed in order to accommodate participants' attitudes and desires.

Sportsmanship Inventories

Sportsmanship inventories are self-reports or reports made by others concerning the degree to which an individual abides by the rules, accepts victory or defeat graciously, and is willing to make personal sacrifices for the good of the group. Sportsmanship is often viewed as the "character" a participant displays in game situations. The teacher may apply a sportsmanship rating scale during the first fun class periods. Type and frequency of inappropriate sportsmanship behaviors observed can then be discussed with the class. Ratings of behavior can be obtained several weeks later in an attempt to identify progress made.

Leadership Inventories

Leadership inventories are reports made by members of a group in which they are asked to identify individuals in the group who are or are likely to be the class leaders. This is a difficult identification to make unless all group members are given an equal opportunity to function as a leader. To provide equal opportunities, the teacher can assign specific leadership duties to each person in class during the course of the semester or school year. Progress in acquiring leadership skills can then be rated and discussed with each class member.

Social Development Inventories

Instruments designed to measure aspects of social development may take the form of self-reports, ratings by teachers, and ratings by the peer group. One type of instrument attempts to assess the degree to which a student has adjusted to the social environment of the class and school. Other instruments can give an indication of an individual's degree of acceptance by peers (peer status or popularity). Unpopular students or students who appear to be socially isolated can be identified and helped. The teacher can introduce activities into the curriculum that require a high level of social interaction during instruction and practice.

Behavior Ratings

Behavior ratings are made by the teacher after observing the student over a period of time. Behavior ratings are usually confined to the content of a particular instrument. Traits that are measured by a number of instruments include acting out, withdrawal, disturbed peer relations, immaturity, loyalty, self-control, leadership, sociability, conforming to class procedures, and cooperation. The validity, reliability, and objectivity of behavior ratings are open to question. Quite often the child's rating is a function of the "halo effect," that is, the tendency of a teacher to give a higher rating to students that he or she likes than to students the teacher dislikes. In addition, not all students have an equal opportunity to display the behavior being rated in similar situations.

Personality Inventories

Personality inventories are largely paper and pencil self-report instruments in which the respondent is presented with a series of questions describing typical behavioral patterns. An individual's score consists of the number of questions answered in a direction that supposedly displays the behavioral trait being measured. Some personality inventories are designed to measure only one trait, such as anxiety. Other inventories attempt to measure as many as 16 personality traits. The study and evaluation of human personality are exceedingly complex phenomena beyond the scope of the typical physical educator's professional training. Hence, it is strongly recommended that the assessment and interpretation of personality traits be left to qualified school psychologists.

Modes of Measurement

Information in the affective domain is usually collected in one of three ways: (a) teacher ratings

of observed student behavior, (b) student self-ratings or self-reports, and (c) student ratings of other students in the group. The same instrument could quite possibly be used by both teachers and students. If this approach is used, information concerning a particular behavior can be obtained from three different points of view. Indeed, when crucial decisions about students are to be made, information must be obtained from a variety of sources.

The relevance of this tactic is vividly illustrated by the findings of a number of studies. Jackson and Lahaderne (1967) found that teachers were poor predictors of their students' affective responses. In the area of social adjustment, Cowell (1958) found that the relationship between teacher ratings of social adjustment and student ratings of other students' social adjustment was only .50. This may indicate that either different behaviors were being rated or that the behavior was being interpreted differently by the teachers and the students. More recently, Noland and Gruber (1978) demonstrated that the scores obtained by two different sets of teachers on a problem identification checklist were independent. In other words, the objectivity or reliability between scorers was quite low. This occurred in a school setting in which the teachers had constant supervision over the students for more than a month before the ratings were made. If different sources of information reflect inconsistent findings, the problem of planning educational programs becomes one of pooling and synthesizing information from a variety of sources. It is imperative that self-report data be reliable so that evaluators can place confidence in it. Gruber (1977) reported that the test-retest reliabilities of personality trait inventory scores on a highly refined self-report instrument were low in three different samples of students. Thus students are inconsistent in reporting their own responses to questions on a personality inventory. Certainly repeated observations must be made to ensure some consistency in reporting behavior. The crucial questions still remain:

Which data are more influential in decision-making, the teacher's or the pupils', and why?

The many problems encountered in obtaining affective measurements may underlie the lack of relevance and consistency of affective data. These problems will be discussed in a latter portion of this chapter.

Types of Scales

Data representing aspects of the affective domain can be obtained from various types of scales. Procedures such as Likert Scales, the semantic differential, rating scales, and questionnaires appear to be used quite frequently in physical education and sport. Hence we will briefly describe and present a few sample items for each of these techniques.

Likert Scales

One of the most widely used techniques for attitude measurement is the Likert Scale in which a statement is usually followed by a five-response continuum on which the respondent is to indicate the degree of affect or intensity of his or her feeling about the statement. The following is an example of a typical positive attitude item: "The best way to become more socially desirable is to participate in group physical activities."

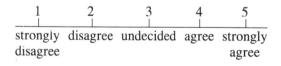

The subject selects the response on the continuum that best describes his or her reaction to the statement. Attitude scales sometimes present both positively and negatively worded statements. The following is an example of a

negatively worded statement: "There are better ways of getting to know people than through games and sports."

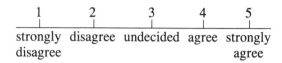

Care must be taken in scoring Likert Scales to ensure that the point value for the negative statement scale is reversed by subtracting the score on a negatively worded statement from the total number of categories plus 1 in order to avoid obtaining a zero on any single question; that is, 5 minus 5 equals 0, whereas 6 minus 5 equals 1. After the negatively worded scores have been converted, the total scale or subscale score can be totaled.

It should be mentioned that fewer or more than five categories can be used. With younger children, two categories such as yes/no, like/dislike, like me/not like me, or present/absent are often used as two-dimensional response choices. Guilford (1954) demonstrated that reliability increases as the number of response choices increases, with the greatest reliability found at around seven categories.

Semantic Differential

A technique that may become increasingly useful in physical education attitude measurement is the semantic differential developed by Osgood, Suci, and Tannenbaum (1957). Semantic differential instruments have become popular because they allow attitudes to be assessed with a very short instrument that requires little time to administer and score. Attitudes toward concepts such as exercise or physical fitness are measured and portrayed in three dimensions of meaning that Osgood calls "semantic space." The dimensions or factors are evaluation (good/bad), potency (strong/weak), and activity (fast/slow).

Each dimension or factor has a series of bipolar pairs of adjectives that the respondent considers. A minimum of three adjective pairs is needed for each factor, and nine pairs are needed to measure all three factors. Care must be taken to ensure that the instrument's vocabulary and concepts are suitable to the age level, reading comprehension, and culture of the people responding. It is most important that the concepts presented are valid in the educational world of the child and that suitable adjective pairs are developed that will permit a projection of actual feelings that people hold. Some concepts that can be projected in physical education include exercise, team sports, swimming, the teacher or coach, playmates, physical education class, and athletics. Remember, the concepts selected should provide meaningful feedback to the teacher about the instructional atmosphere and possible problems in modifying student behavior.

A good example of a semantic differential applied in physical education is provided by Baumgartner and Jackson (1982) and illustrated in Figure 10.1. A response to the first adjective pair (pleasant/unpleasant) in Figure 10.1

Physical Education Class

pleasant		unpleasant	(Evaluation)
relaxed		tense	(Activity)
passive		active	(Activity)
unsuccessful		successful	(Evaluation)
delicate		rugged	(Potency)
fast		slow	(Activity)
good		bad	(Evaluation)
weak		strong	(Potency)
lazy		busy	(Activity)
masculine		feminine	(Potency)
heavy		light	(Potency)
unfair		fair	(Evaluation)

Figure 10.1 Example of a semantic differential scale. From Baumgartner, Ted A., and Andrew S. Jackson, *Measurement for Evaluation in Physical Education*, 2nd ed. © 1982 William C. Brown Publishers, Dubuque, Iowa. All rights reserved. Reprinted by permission.

can be checked at 1 of 7 points. Hence this scale provides for seven categories. As previously indicated, in order to arrive at a total score for all 12 adjective pairs, the score must be reversed for the adjective pair in which the least desirable (i.e., negative) adjective appears on the left. Responses to the scale depicted in Figure 10.1 are likely to vary from class to class, especially if one class is taking archery and the other is taking aerobics. Differences in teaching methods, teacher personalities, teaching materials, and instructional atmosphere can all cause different responses to the concepts presented. Therein lies one of the primary values of this type of assessment.

Rating Scales

Rating scales differ from Likert Scales only in that instead of using a standard set of response categories for each statement presented rating scales use descriptive terms for each response category of the statement. The following example items pertaining to affective traits illustrate how a rating scale is presented.

The value of a separate descriptive term for each response category lies in focusing on specific behavior boundaries when making a rating. This method should also increase the reliability and objectivity of the scale because all raters will hopefully be rating the same dimensions of behavior.

Questionnaires

The questionnaire format involves presenting a set of self-report questions either through the mail, to a captive audience such as all students in a class, or by a trained interviewer asking the questions of most individuals in a particular locale. The questions usually begin with background data such as date of birth, sex, number of years of school completed, marital status, mode of residence, and so forth. The next set of questions solicits the specific information needed based on how the investigator intends to use the information, including questions on the respondent's opinions, interests, and values. Responses can be registered in a variety of ways ranging from a one-word response, a brief state-

Rating Scales

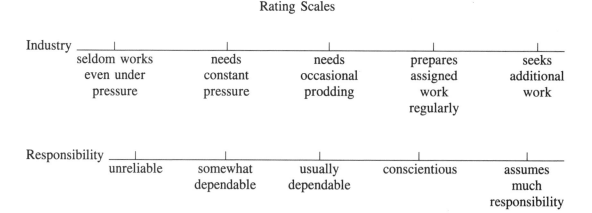

ment, or indicating an appropriate category on a rating scale. Questionnaires are frequently used in physical education and recreation to survey student interests and needs in order to provide more effective instructional and recreational programs.

Questionnaires suffer from many of the usual limitations of self-report inventories. Inadequate sampling procedures or surveying only a certain segment of the population can inject bias into any generalizations based on questionnaire results. Under what conditions and at what time of day did the respondent complete the questionnaire? Did all respondents use similar care and thought in responding to the questions? Some respondents may send back unusable or illegible answer sheets. If the topic being surveyed is a particularly sensitive area, such as sexual attitudes and behavior, the anonymity of respondents must be guaranteed to minimize distortion of responses. In any event, the validity of data depends on respondent anonymity, adequate sampling, careful directions to respondents as to when and how to make responses, and effective follow-up procedures. Follow-up procedures are essential in order to increase the number of respondents needed to fulfill sampling requirements.

Examples of Affective Instruments

Many instruments and techniques have been developed to collect information relative to the many aspects of the affective domain. Only a few examples of interest to physical educators will be presented in this chapter. Information concerning additional data collection techniques

can be found in the bibliography at the end of this chapter.

Anecdotal Record

The anecdotal record is a written statement of the various types of behavior exhibited by a student and observed by the teacher. Usually, the teacher describes the behavior that deviates markedly from the norm for that pupil. The purpose of the anecdotal record is to record information that cannot be obtained using other instruments. The teacher records what is actually seen or heard and must take care to ensure that the interpretation of behavior is not influenced by "halo effect." To use anecdotal records effectively, one should (a) observe behavior, (b) record observations, (c) analyze and interpret anecdotes, and (d) use the information. The most important element is using the information. Based on the type of information recorded, the pupil may be referred to a specialist for further diagnosis. Anecdotal records also provide fruitful input for case conferences with other teachers or parents about a student's progress. Anecdotal records should be consulted periodically and should be made part of the student's cumulative record to permit changes in behavior over time to be noted. An example of an anecdotal record that can be used in physical education presented by Meyers and Blesh (1962) is illustrated in Figure 10.2.

Class Behavior Checklist

Dexter (1957) developed a class behavior checklist to be completed by the student. Although this checklist was developed as a self-appraisal of behavior for high school girls in a physical education class, it can be easily adapted for use with boys. The teacher can also use the same

Anecdotal Record

Name _____

Directions: In the space provided, record observations that bear on the individual's physical, mental, and social development under the respective headings of technical, associated, and concomitant learnings. *Do not evaluate, but describe.* Avoid vague words such as "good," "strong," "shy," etc. Enter statements of what happened or what you saw, such as "Did three push-ups and couldn't do any more," "Cried and started fighting when he was called out." *Date and sign each entry.*

                                                    Date   Signature

Technical Learning:

Associated Learning:

Concomitant Learning:

Figure 10.2   Anecdotal record for physical education.

checklist. In this way, class behavior can be scrutinized from the point of view of both the teacher and student. When used in this way, both the differences and agreed deviations from acceptable behavior can form the basis for counseling. Validity and reliability of the checklist illustrated in Figure 10.3 have not been determined.

Teachers can run their own reliability check. It should be emphasized at this point that teachers should be encouraged to define the class behaviors they expect from their students. Once this is accomplished, the teacher can develop his or her own checklist. The checklist provides an opportunity to periodically record behavior.

Sport and Behavior

A number of the learning outcomes sometimes presented under the rubric of "sportsmanship" or "character education" that is supposed to be developed as one participates in physical educa-

tion and athletics are the basis for the Cowell (1957) *Social Outcomes of Sports Check List* that is illustrated in Figure 10.4. This checklist is intended for use with high school boys but can also be used with girls. This device provides for a self-analysis of the extent to which a student has attained certain behavioral goals. No data are available relative to the validity or reliability of the Cowell instrument.

Sportsmanship Attitude Scale

Johnson (1969) devised a sportsmanship attitude scale for use with both junior high school boys and girls. The scale illustrated in Figure 10.5 is designed to detect attitudes and changes in attitudes and is to be used as material for class discussion. Alternate form reliability is reported as .856, and test-retest reliability for Forms A and B respectively are .812 and .863. The content for the instrument is based on football, basketball, and baseball situations.

Class Behavior Checklist

Name _____ Date _____

Directions: Read each statement and think how well it describes your behavior. Put a check in the column that tells most nearly what statement is correct for you.

Always	Often	Seldom	Never	*Self-Direction*

_____　1. I work diligently even though I am not supervised.

_____　2. I practice to improve the skills I use with least success.

_____　3. I follow carefully directions that have been given me.

_____　4. I willingly accept constructive criticism and try to correct faults.

_____　5. I play games as cheerfully as I can.

_____　6. I appraise my progress in each of my endeavors to learn.

Social Adjustment

_____　1. I am considerate of the rights of others.

_____　2. I am courteous.

_____　3. I am cooperative in group activities.

_____　4. I accept gladly responsibility assigned to me by a squad leader.

_____　5. I accept disappointment without being unnecessarily disturbed.

_____　6. I expect from the members of my group only the consideration to which I am entitled.

(Cont.)

Class Behavior Checklist (Cont.)

Participation

_____ 1. I am prompt in reporting for each class.

_____ 2. I dislike being absent from class.

_____ 3. I ask to be excused from an activity only when it is necessary.

_____ 4. I do the best I can regardless of the activity in which I am participating.

_____ 5. I give full attention to all instructions that are given in class.

_____ 6. I encourage others with whom I am participating in an activity.

Care of Equipment and Facilities

_____ 1. I use equipment as I am supposed to use it.

_____ 2. I return each piece of equipment to its proper place after using it.

_____ 3. I avoid making my dressing area untidy.

_____ 4. I arrange my clothes neatly in my locker.

Personal Attractiveness

_____ 1. I am particular about my personal appearance.

_____ 2. I take a shower after I have participated in any vigorous activity.

_____ 3. I wear clean clothes in physical education.

_____ 4. I dress appropriately for each activity.

_____ 5. I bathe regularly even during my menstrual period.

Figure 10.3 Class behavior checklist. From *Teachers Guide to Physical Education for Girls* (p. 318) by G. Dexter, 1957, Sacramento, CA: California State Department of Education. Copyright by California State Department of Education. Reprinted by permission.

Cowell Social Outcomes of Sports Check Sheet

To what extent did I learn:	(1) Not at all	(2) Very little	(3) Somewhat	(4) A great deal	(5) A very great deal
1. To sacrifice my own personal "whims" or desires for the good of the group or team?					
2. To test myself—to see if I could "take it," endure hardship, and "keep trying" to do my best even under adversity?					
3. To overcome awkwardness and self-consciousness?					
4. To recognize that the group can achieve where the individual alone cannot?					
5. That each team member has a unique or special contribution to make in the position he plays?					
6. To share difficult undertakings with my "buddies" (teammates) because of struggling together for a goal?					
7. To respect the skill and ability of my opponents and be tolerant of their success?					
8. To make friendships with boys from other schools and to maintain good guest/host relationships in interschool games?					
9. To feel that the school team helped to break up "cliques" and factions in the school by developing common loyalty and community of interests?					
10. To consider and practice correct health and training routine such as proper eating, sleeping, avoidance of tobacco, etc.?					
11. To "take turns" and to "share"?					
12. To develop physical strength, endurance, and a better-looking body?					
13. To be loyal and not "let my buddy, the coach, team, or school down"?					
14. To give more than I get—not for myself but for an ideal or for one's school, town, or country?					
15. To develop a sense of humor and even be able to laugh at myself occasionally?					
16. To think and act "on the spot" in the heat of a game?					
17. To understand the strategy—the "why" of the best methods of attack and defense in games?					
18. To understand and appreciate the possibilities and limitations of the human body with respect to skill, speed, endurance, and quickness of reactions?					
19. That in sports there is no discrimination against talent? It is performance and conduct and not the color of one's skin or social standing that matters.					
20. That nothing worthwhile is accomplished without hard work, application, and the "will to succeed"?					

Figure 10.4 Cowell Social Outcomes of Sports: An Evaluation Check-Sheet. From "Our function is still education," by C.C. Cowell, 1957, *The Physical Educator*, March, pp. 6-7. Copyright 1957 by Phi Epsilon Kappa Fraternity. Reprinted by permission.

Johnson Sportsmanship Attitude Scale

Directions: This booklet contains several statements describing events that happen in sports and games. Read each statement carefully and decide whether you approve or disapprove of the action taken by the person. Circle the *one* response category that tells the way you feel. Please complete every item.

Example: A pitcher in a baseball game threw a fast ball at the batter to scare him.

~~Strongly approve~~   Approve   Disapprove   Strongly disapprove

(If you strongly approve of this action by the pitcher, you would circle the first response category as shown.)

The four responses can appear either after each item or an answer sheet can be used.

The Scales: Form A

1. After a basketball player was called by the official for traveling, he slammed the basketball onto the floor.

2. A baseball player was called out as he slid into home plate. He jumped up and down on the plate and screamed at the official.

3. After a personal foul was called against a basketball player, he shook his fist in the official's face.

4. A basketball coach talked very loudly in order to annoy an opponent who was attempting to make a very important free throw shot.

5. After a baseball game the coach of the losing team went up to the umpire and demanded to know how much money had been paid to "throw" the game.

6. A basketball coach led the spectators in jeering at the official who made calls against his team.

7. After two men were put out on a double play attempt, a baseball coach told the players in his dugout to boo the umpire's decision.

8. As the basketball coach left the gymnasium after the game, he shouted at the officials, "You lost me the game! I never saw such lousy officiating in my life."

9. A basketball coach put sand on the gym floor to force the opponents into traveling penalties.

10. A football coach left the bench to change the position of a marker dropped by an official to indicate where the ball went out of bounds.

11. During the first half of a football game a touchdown was called back. At halftime the football coach went into the official's dressing room and cursed the officials.

(Cont.)

Johnson Sportsmanship Attitude Scale (Cont.)

12. A football player was taken out of the game for unsportsmanlike conduct. The player changed jerseys, and the coach sent him back into the game.

13. Following a closely played basketball game, the coach of the losing team cursed his boys for not winning.

14. After a baseball game the losing team's coach yelled at spectators to "Go get the ump!"

15. A baseball coach permitted players to use profanity loud enough for the entire park to hear when the players did not like a decision.

16. The basketball coach drank alcoholic beverages while supervising his basketball team on a trip.

17. A college football player was disqualified for misconduct. While on the way to the sideline, the player attacked the official.

18. During a timeout in a basketball game, the clock was accidentally left running. The coach whose team was behind ran over to the scoring table and struck the timekeeper.

19. After a basketball player was knocked into a wall, his coach rushed onto the court and hit the player who had fouled.

20. After a baseball player had been removed from the game, the coach met him at the sidelines and hit him.

21. After a runner was called out at first base, the baseball coach went onto the field and wrestled the umpire down to the ground.

Form B

1. During a basketball game the B team coach sat on the bench and called loudly to the officials telling them who to watch for fouls.

2. Repeated complaints and griping came from the football players on the bench toward the officials when fouls were called on their team, and the coach did nothing to stop this action.

3. After a basketball game the hometown coach made fun of the visiting team's playing ability.

4. A football coach took time out and came onto the playing field and accused referees of cheating his team.

5. During a football game a player made an error that resulted in a touchdown for the opponents. The coach ran onto the field and bawled out the player in front of the fans.

6. After a questionable foul was called against a football player, his coach went onto the field and refused to leave when the referee told him to do so.

7. During a basketball game the coach of the losing team yelled that the officials had been "paid off" by the opposing team.

(Cont.)

Johnson Sportsmanship Attitude Scale (Cont.)

8. A baseball coach acted as referee for an important game and called in favor of his team.

9. A basketball coach installed a light to blind the opponents when they were shooting at a goal.

10. After a third baseman caught a ball which put a player out, the opposing coach cursed the third baseman.

11. A football coach used profane language during workouts and in conversation with the boys.

12. A baseball coach cursed loudly after a runner was called out on first base.

13. After a football game a player attacked the official who had taken him out of the game. The coach covered up for the player and said the player had not done such a thing.

Figure 10.5 Johnson Sportsmanship Attitude Scale. From "Construction of a Sportsmanship Attitude Scale" by M.L. Johnson, 1969, *Research Quarterly*, **40**(2), 312-316. Copyright 1969 by American Alliance for Health, Physical Education, Recreation and Dance. Reprinted by permission.

Leadership

The development of leadership traits is considered one of the goals of sports participation. Leadership can only be defined by the items that appear on an appraisal instrument. Leadership assessment should not be attempted until all students have interacted with one another in the group for a rather long period of time. The time span must be sufficiently long to allow each student an opportunity to perform in a leadership role. The teacher should assign leaders to squads within a class on a rotating basis. In the final analysis, the teacher should define those qualities of leadership that should be developed in a physical education class and then devise a situation-specific rating scale for each quality. A leadership scale developed by Johnson and Nelson (1979) to identify athletic leaders among boys and girls in junior high school through college is illustrated in Figure 10.6. Students write the name of their choices in the blanks labeled A and B on the questionnaire. These authors report reliability coefficients of .96 for ninth-grade football players and .78 for college basketball players.

Modified Nelson Sports Leadership Questionnaire

A. _____
B. _____
1. If you were on a trip and had a choice of the players you would share the hotel room with, who would they be?

A. _____
B. _____
2. Who are the most popular members of the team?

A. _____
B. _____
3. Who are the best scholars on the team?

A. _____
B. _____
4. Which players know the most about the sport in terms of strategy, rules, etc.?

(Cont.)

Modified Nelson Sports Leadership Questionnaire (Cont.)

A. _____
B. _____   5. If the coach were not present for a workout, which athletes would be the most likely to take charge of the practice?

A. _____
B. _____   6. Which players would you listen to first if the team appeared to be disorganized during a crucial game?

A. _____
B. _____   7. When the team is behind in a close match and there is still a chance to win, who is the most likely teammate to score the winning points?

A. _____
B. _____   8. Of all of your teammates, who exhibits the most poise during crucial parts of the match?

A. _____
B. _____   9. Who are the most valuable players on the team?

A. _____
B. _____   10. Who are the players who play "most for the team"?

A. _____
B. _____   11. Who are the most consistent point makers for the team?

A. _____
B. _____   12. Who are the most respected performers on the team?

A. _____
B. _____   13. Which teammates have the most overall ability?

A. _____
B. _____   14. Which teammates train the hardest to improve their performance off season?

A. _____
B. _____   15. Who are the most likable players on the team?

A. _____
B. _____   16. Which players have most favorably influenced you?

A. _____
B. _____   17. Which players have actually helped you the most?

A. _____
B. _____   18. Which teammates do you think would make the best coaches?

A. _____
B. _____   19. Which teammates do you most often look to for leadership?

A. _____
B. _____   20. Who are the hardest workers during regular practice hours?

Figure 10.6   Modified Nelson Sports Leadership Questionnaire. From *Practical Measurements for Evaluation* (3rd ed.) (p. 394) by B.L. Johnson and J.K. Nelson, 1979, Minneapolis, MN: Burgess. Copyright by Burgess Publishing Company. Reprinted by permission.

Social Development

Social development has long been cited as one of the goals of physical education. As students interact and exhibit play skills to one another, they are simultaneously exhibiting the extent to which they have adapted to the behavioral standards of the school, class, and peer group. Usually, selected aspects of behavior in a social group are presented in the form of a rating scale that is completed by teachers and pupils or both. A few rating scales have been developed specifically in junior and senior high school physical education class settings. Three such devices are the Cowell Social Behavior Trend Index that is completed by teachers, the Cowell Personal Distance Ballot, and a Who's Who in My Group instrument (Cowell, 1958). The latter two devices are measures of what is usually referred to as "peer status," "degree of group integration," "social acceptance," or "popularity" within a group.

Cowell Social Behavior Trend Index. The *Cowell Social Behavior Trend Index* presents 10 behavioral trends from a positive (Form A) and negative (Form B) point of view. Three teachers who have been observing the students for some time complete Form A illustrated in Figure 10.7. Three weeks later the teachers complete Form B that appears in Figure 10.8. The student's score is the algebraic sum of the score from both forms. Cowell (1958) reported a validity coefficient of .824 with teachers' ratings of the "best" and "worst" socially adjusted boys. The alternate form reliability is .82.

Cowell Personal Distance Ballot. The Cowell Personal Distance Ballot depicted in Figure 10.9 is a quick, simple way to determine the extent of belonging to or being accepted as

a member of one's own social group. Validity of the ballot is indicated by a correlation of .90 with guidance office ratings and .844 with the who's who in my group score. Reliability coefficients of .91, .88, and .93 are also reported by Cowell (1958).

In another article, Cowell and Ismail (1962) summarized the research into the relationships between social and physical factors. They concluded that boys who score high on physical measures are likely to have leadership potential, to be quite popular with their peers, and to be well adjusted socially. In addition, those participating in team sports are likely to be more accepted in the group than those engaged in individual physical activities.

Attitude Scales

Attitude usually reflects one's degree of feeling, appreciation, or concern about a particular concept. A person's attitude toward participating in physical activities is believed to be an underlying dimension of his or her motivation for participation. In other words, if one enjoys exercising and values exercise for a particular purpose, that person will likely participate in a physical activity program in the future. Several attitude scales developed for use in physical education appear in the literature. Most consider attitude towards physical activity to be unidimensional. Some are specific to particular situations such as "the gym class," "athletic participation," "physical fitness," and "sportsmanship." Sources for locating these attitude inventories appear in the bibliography at the end of this chapter.

Kenyon (1968a, b) employed factor analysis to a large number of items believed to measure several hypothesized attitude dimensions. The results of the factor analysis confirmed that six

Cowell Social Behavior Trend Index (Form A)

Behavior Trends	Descriptive of the student			
	Markedly (+3)	Somewhat (+2)	Only slightly (+1)	Not at all (+0)
1. Enters heartily and with enjoyment into the spirit of social intercourse				
2. Frank, talkative, and sociable; does not stand on ceremony				
3. Self-confident and self-reliant, tends to take success for granted, strong initiative, prefers to lead				
4. Quick and decisive in movement; pronounced or excessive energy output				
5. Prefers group activities, work or play; not easily satisfied with individual projects				
6. Adaptable to new situations, makes adjustments readily, welcomes change				
7. Is self-composed, seldom shows signs of embarrassment				
8. Tends to elation of spirits, seldom gloomy or moody				
9. Seeks a broad range of friendships, not selective or exclusive in games and the like				
10. Hearty and cordial, even to strangers; forms acquaintanceships very easily				

_____   Date _____ Grade _____
Last name   First name

_____   School _____ Age _____
Describer

Instruction: Think carefully of the student's behavior in group situations and check each behavior trend according to its degree of descriptiveness.

Figure 10.7 Cowell Social Behavior Trend Index (Form A). From "Validating an Index of Social Adjustment for High School Use" by C.C. Cowell, 1958, *Research Quarterly*, **29**(1), pp. 7-18. Copyright 1958 by the American Alliance for Health, Physical Education, Recreation and Dance. Reprinted by permission.

Cowell Social Behavior Trend Index (Form B)

Behavior Trends	Descriptive of the student			
	Markedly (−3)	Somewhat (−2)	Only slightly (−1)	Not at all (−0)
1. Somewhat prudish, awkward, easily embarrassed in his social contacts				
2. Secretive, seclusive, not inclined to talk unless spoken to				
3. Lacking in self-confidence and initiative, a follower				
4. Slow in movement, deliberative or perhaps indecisive; energy output moderate or deficient				
5. Prefers to work and play alone, tends to avoid group activities				
6. Shrinks from making new adjustments, prefers the habitual to the stress of reorganization required by the new				
7. Is self-conscious, easily embarrassed, timid or "bashful"				
8. Tends to depression, frequently gloomy or moody				
9. Shows preference for a narrow range of intimate friends and tends to exclude others from his association				
10. Reserved and distant except to intimate friends, does not form acquaintanceships readily				

Figure 10.8 Cowell Social Behavior Trend Index (Form B). From "Validating an Index of Social Adjustment for High School Use" by C.C. Cowell, 1958, *Research Quarterly*, **29**(1), pp. 7-18. Copyright 1958 by the American Alliance for Health, Physical Education, Recreation and Dance. Reprinted by permission.

different constructs were being measured. Kenyon therefore developed a multidimensional scale for college men and another for college women. The men's scale consists of 59 items, and the women's scale has 54 items. Scoring is on a seven-point Likert-type scale ranging from "very strongly disagree" to "very strongly agree."

Construct validity for Kenyon's Attitude Toward Physical Activity Scale has been demon-

strated. The six constructs or attitude dimensions and their reported reliabilities are as follows:

1. *Social Experience:* .70 to .72 for men and .68 to .72 for women
2. *Health and Fitness:* .79 for men and .83 for women
3. *Pursuit of Vertigo:* .88 to .89 for men and .89 for women

Confidential Personal Distance Ballot

What to do!	I would be willing to accept him:						
If you had full power to treat each student in this squad as you feel, just how would you consider him? Every student should be checked in some *one* column. Circle your own name and be sure you check every student in *one* column only.	Into my family as a brother	As a very close "pal" or "chum"	As a member of my "gang" or club	On my street as a "next-door neigh-bor"	Into my class at uni-versity	Into my uni-versity	Into my city
	1	2	3	4	5	6	7
1.							
2.							
3.							
4.							
5.							
6.							
7.							
8.							
9.							
10.							
11.							
12.							
13.							
14.							

Figure 10.9 Confidential Personal Distance Ballot. From "Validating an Index of Social Adjustment for high school use" by C.C. Cowell, 1958, *Research Quarterly*, **29**(1), pp. 7-18. Copyright 1958 by the American Alliance for Health, Physical Education, Recreation and Dance. Reprinted by permission.

4. *Aesthetic Experience:* .82 for men and .87 for women
5. *Catharsis:* .77 for men and .79 for women
6. *Ascetic Experience:* .81 for men and .74 to .78 for women

A small portion of Kenyon's Attitude Toward Physical Activity Scale appears next. The first four items for each dimension of the men's and women's scales are presented as examples of items used to measure attitude constructs. The complete scale with directions for administration and scoring are available from Kenyon.[3]

Dimension 1: Physical activity as a social experience. Physical educators maintain that physical activity meets certain social needs. Individuals who score high on this factor would value physical activities "whose primary purpose is to provide a medium for social intercourse, i.e., to meet new people and to perpetrate existing relationships."

Men

It is important that everyone belong to at least one group that plays games together.

I like to engage in socially oriented physical activities.

Colleges should sponsor many more physical activities of a social nature.

I enjoy sports mostly because they give me a chance to meet new people.

Women

The best way to become more socially desirable is to participate in group physical activities.

I like to engage in socially oriented physical activities.

Colleges should sponsor many more physical activities of a social nature.

I enjoy sports mostly because they give me a chance to meet new people.

Dimension 2: Physical activity for health and fitness. The importance of physical activity for maintaining health and fitness is generally recognized. Individuals who score high on this factor would value physical activity for its "contribution to the improvement of one's health and fitness."

Men

Of all physical activities, those whose purpose is primarily to develop physical fitness would not be my first choice.

I would usually choose strenuous physical activity over light physical activity if given the choice.

A large part of our daily lives must be committed to vigorous exercise.

Being strong and highly fit is not the most important thing in my life.

Women

Physical education programs should stress vigorous exercise since it contributes most to physical fitness.

The need for much higher levels of physical fitness has been established beyond all doubt.

Of all physical activities, those whose purpose is primarily to develop physical fitness would not be my first choice.

If given a choice, I sometimes would choose strenuous rather than light physical activity.

---

[3]From "Six Scales for Assessing Attitude Toward Physical Activity" by G.S. Kenyon, 1968, *Research Quarterly,* **39**(3), pp. 566-574. Copyright 1968 by American Alliance for Health, Physical Education, Recreation and Dance. Reprinted by permission. Further details and summary of studies using scales are available from G.S. Kenyon, University of Lethbridge, Lethbridge, Alberta T1K 3M4.

Dimension 3: Physical activity as the pursuit of vertigo. The pursuit of vertigo is considered to be an important factor for participation in "those physical experiences providing, at some risk to the participant, an element of thrill through the medium of speed, acceleration, sudden change of direction, or exposure to dangerous situations, with the participant usually remaining in control."

Men

I would prefer quiet activities like swimming or tossing a ball around rather than activities such as automobile or speedboat racing.

The risk of injury would be well worth it when you consider the thrills that come from engaging in such activities as mountain climbing and bobsledding.

Among the best physical activities are those that represent a personal challenge, such as skiing, mountain climbing, or heavy weather sailing.

Frequent participation in dangerous sports and physical activities is all right for other people, but ordinarily they are not for me.

Women

I would prefer quiet activities like swimming or golf rather than activities such as water skiing or sailboat racing.

Among the best physical activities are those that represent a personal challenge, such as skiing, mountain climbing, or heavy weather sailing.

Frequent participation in dangerous sports and physical activities is all right for other people, but ordinarily they are not for me.

The least desirable physical activities are those providing a sense of danger and risk of injury, such as skiing on steep slopes, mountain climbing, or parachute jumping.

Dimension 4: Physical activity as an aesthetic experience. Many people believe that some forms of physical activity are generally pleasing to watch. People that score high on this factor perceive physical activity as having "aesthetic value" for the individual; that is, activities are conceived as possessing beauty or certain artistic qualities.

Men

Among desirable forms of physical activity are those that show the beauty and form of human movement, such as modern dance and water ballet.

The degree of beauty and grace of movement found in sports is sometimes less than claimed.

Physical education programs should place a little more emphasis upon the beauty found in human motion.

I am not in the least interested in those physical activities whose sole purpose is to depict human motion as something beautiful.

Women

The most important value of physical activity is the beauty found in skilled movement.

Among the most desirable forms of physical activity are those that present the beauty of human movement, such as modern dance and water ballet.

I am not particularly interested in those physical activities whose sole purpose is to depict human motion as something beautiful.

Physical education programs should place much more emphasis upon the beauty found in human motion.

Dimension 5: Physical activity as catharsis. Many people believe that physical activity can provide a release from frustration created by the pressures of modern living. Catharsis involves "physical activity perceived as providing a release of tension precipitated by frustration through some vicarious means." The validity of the catharsis factor has not been fully established. A negative relationship was reported between catharsis scores and preference for "physical activity for recreation and relaxation."

Men

A happy life does not require regular participation in physical activity.

Almost the only satisfactory way to relieve severe emotional strain is through some form of physical activity.

There are better ways of relieving the pressures of today's living than having to engage in or watch physical activity.

For a healthy mind in a healthy body, the only place to begin is through participation in sports and physical activities every day.

Women

Almost the only satisfactory way to relieve severe emotional strain is through some form of physical activity.

There are better ways of relieving the pressures of today's living than having to engage in or watch physical activity.

For a healthy mind in a healthy body, the only place to begin is through participation in sports and physical activities every day.

Practically the only way to relieve frustrations and pent-up emotions is through some form of physical activity.

Dimension 6: Physical activity as an ascetic experience. Individuals who score high on this

scale value the type of dedication and self-discipline required for championship level performance. Such physical activity involves long, strenuous, and often painful training and stiff competition that demands deferment of many gratifications.

Men

I would gladly put in the necessary years of daily hard training for the chance to try out for the U.S. Olympic Team.

I prefer those sports that require very hard training and involve intense competition, such as interscholastic and intercollegiate athletics.

I would get by far the most satisfaction from games requiring long and careful preparation and involving stiff competition against a strong opposition.

A sport is sometimes spoiled if allowed to become too highly organized and keenly competitive.

Women

I would gladly put up with the necessary hard training for the chance to try out for the United States Women's Olympic Team.

The years of strenuous daily training necessary to prepare for today's international competition is asking a lot of today's young women.

I would get by far the most satisfaction from games requiring long and careful preparation and involving stiff competition against a strong opposition.

A sport is sometimes spoiled if allowed to become too highly organized and keenly competitive.

Kenyon (1968c) also developed a physical activity attitude scale for use in secondary schools. In addition, Simon and Smoll (1974) developed the Children's Attitude Toward Physical Activity Inventory for use on fourth-, fifth-, and sixth-grade children. This scale is a semantic differential inventory modeled after the Kenyon adult scale with internal consistency coefficients ranging from .72 to .89. The six dimensions measure attitudes toward physical activity

1. as a social experience,
2. for health and fitness,
3. as a thrill that involves some risk,
4. as the beauty in human movement,
5. for the release of tension, and
6. as long and hard training.

Another children's instrument is the Children's Attitudes Towards Female Involvement in Sport inventory (Selby & Lewko, 1976). This Likert-style questionnaire was developed to assess attitudes of grade and junior high school children toward women's participation in sport. Twenty items were found to have a test-retest reliability of .81. The following is an example item from this scale: "Only boys, not girls, should try to become a famous sports player."

The Physical Estimation and Attraction Scale is an attitude scale designed to explain motivation toward physical activity (Sonstroem, 1978). The scale consists of 100 items to which the student responds either *true* or *false* as it pertains to him or her. Thirty-three of the items measure *physical estimation*; 56 measure *physical attraction*; and 11 are neutral. The estimation items ask the student to affirm or deny statements about his or her own physical characteristics, fitness, athletic ability, or potential skill in motor performance. Examples of this type of item include the following:

- My body is strong and muscular compared to other boys my age.
- I am in better physical condition than most boys my age.
- I am better coordinated than most people I know.

- If I wanted, I could become an excellent tennis player.

The attraction items ask students to affirm or deny their personal interests in or likes for certain forms of physical activity. Examples of attraction items follow:

- Sports provide me with a welcome escape from present day life.
- Most sports require too much time and energy to be worthwhile.
- Exercise relieves me of emotional strain.
- I would prefer to listen to a concert than to watch a gymnastics match.

Validity and reliability studies were conducted on boys in Grades 8 through 12. Coefficients of internal consistency of .87 and .89 and stability coefficients of .92 and .94 are reported for the estimation and attraction scales respectively. Factorial validity of the scale has been established. The estimation scale is related to self-concept. Hence the scale may be used to help identify students who have low self-esteem about their physical capabilities. The scales are also related to self-reports of height, weight, athletic experiences, participation in sports activities, and various motor performance tests (Sonstroem, 1974).

Self-Perception

Measures of self-perception usually attempt to secure information about a person's self-concept or how one views oneself. Devices have been developed to measure body image, body cathexis (i.e., the amount of psychological energy attached to the body), and a more global self-esteem. Self-perception is a constant force in everyday living because the value one places on oneself may be the prime determiner of one's behavior. Changes in body weight, fitness, strength, stature, skill, and ability can affect the body image element of self-concept (Harris,

1973; Gruber, 1986). These references also provide the reader with two excellent sources summarizing the literature on self-concept, body image, and physical attributes.

A simple, easily scored instrument that is available for use in elementary and junior high schools is the 58-item Coopersmith Self-Esteem Inventory (Coopersmith, 1967). Sample items for each subscale of the school form version appear in Figure 10.10. Coopersmith reported test-retest reliability following a 5-week interval to be .88. In addition, Noland and Gruber (1978) found a test-retest reliability over a 2-week period to be .74 and a concurrent validity of −.70 with the anxiety second-order factor of the *Children's Personality Questionnaire*, indicating that children who view themselves more favorably tend to have lower anxiety.

Self-Esteem Inventory

Please print:

Name _____ Age _____

School _____ Sex: M _____ F _____

Grade _____ Date _____

Directions: On the next pages, you will find a list of statements about feelings. If a statement describes how you usually feel, put an X in the column "Like me." If the statement does not describe how you usually feel, put an X in the column "Unlike me." There are no right or wrong answers.

Like me	Unlike me	
		General self
☐	☐	I often wish I were someone else.
☐	☐	I'm pretty happy.
		Social self
☐	☐	I'm popular with kids my own age.
☐	☐	I don't like to be with other people.
		Home-parents
☐	☐	I get upset easily at home.
☐	☐	My parents expect too much of me.
		School-academic
☐	☐	I'm proud of my school work.
☐	☐	I often get discouraged in school.
		Lie scale
☐	☐	I never worry about anything.
☐	☐	I like everyone I know.

Figure 10.10 Coopersmith Self-Esteem Inventory (sample items from The School Form). Reproduced by special permission of the publisher, Consulting Psychologist Press, Inc., from the Self-Esteem Inventory (School Form) by Stanley Coopersmith, PhD. Copyright 1981.

Martinek and Zaichkowsky (1977) developed a nonverbal self-concept scale for children that requires little or no reading ability and can be administered to non-English-speaking groups. The scale consists of 25 items that measure attributes of appropriate behavior and intellectual, social, and physical aspects of a child's self-concept. The items are portrayed by a pair of cartoon pictures. Each pair of pictures shows a bipolar representation of that item to facilitate a forced-choice response by the examinee. Each set of pictures shows a boy or girl in a different situation. For example, one of the pictures shows a child who is happy, and the other picture shows the child sad. The child being tested is asked to identify which picture is more like himself or herself. Coefficients of internal consistency ranged from .75 to .92 for Grades 1 through 4.

Coaching and Teaching Behavior

Weber (1977) designed the *Teacher Competency Questionnaire* to gather responses on the degree of importance assigned to various professional competencies that a female high school physical education teacher might be expected to possess. Content validity was established by a panel of judges. The 89-item instrument has a test-retest reliability of .99. This questionnaire may be useful in identifying the role of the teacher and in determining role expectations held for the teacher by various groups of university and public school personnel involved in the teacher education process. Responses to items on a five-point Likert Scale reflect the degree of importance attached to each expectation. Sample items from the scale include the following:

- Help students to evaluate own performance.
- Help students to develop positive self-concepts.
- Utilize latest research findings regarding the exceptional student.

- Apply appropriate techniques for group instruction.
- Demonstrate knowledge of current trends in facility planning.
- Apply the principles of the psychology of coaching.
- Maintain a normal range of self-control and emotional stability under stress.
- Cooperate with other professionals in program planning.
- Effectively utilize various types of instructional aids.
- Teach and apply concepts of safety for accident prevention.

Overt coaching behaviors can be assessed by means of the *Coaching Behavior Assessment System* (Smith, Smoll, & Hunt, 1977). This technique permits the direct observation and coding of a coach's behavior during practices and games. The *CBAS* assesses two major classes of behaviors: reactive behaviors and spontaneous behaviors. *Reactive* behaviors are the coach's responses to immediately preceding player or team behaviors. *Spontaneous* behaviors are initiated by the coach and are not responses to immediately preceding events. The behaviors are listed as follows:

Reactive Behaviors (responses to player or team behavior)
1. Desirable performances
   - Positive Reinforcement (R)
   - Nonreinforcement (NR)
2. Player or team mistakes/errors
   - Mistake-Contingent Encouragement (EM)
   - Mistake-Contingent Technical Instruction (TIM)
   - Punishment (P)
   - Punitive (TIM + P)
   - Ignoring Mistakes (IM)
3. Misbehaviors
   - Keeping Control (KC)

Spontaneous Behaviors

1. Game related

   - General Technical Instruction (TIG)
   - General Encouragement (EG)
   - Organization (O)

2. Game irrelevant

   - General Communication (GC)

Consistency of scoring the CBAS was obtained by computing the percentage of behaviors scored identically by 24 observers on two administrations. The average consistency percentage was 96.4. Average interrater reliability was .88.

Sport Situation-Specific Trends in Affective Measurements

A review of the completed research in sport personality reveals much confusion due to contradictory findings of different studies. Differences in the results of these studies can be due to the use of different or inappropriate measuring instruments, different study procedures, or inappropriate statistical methods. After describing methodological problems involved in sport personality assessment, both Smith (1970) and Kroll (1970) indicated that there is a need to depart from the traditional ways of applying psychological theories to problems in physical education and sport. One approach proposes that the stable trait characteristics of a person interact with specific situations and that each can influence the other. Thus momentary environmental situations play a role in influencing observed behavior. This seems to call for the development of situation-specific measuring instruments, an approach that appears particularly suitable to sport and athletic situations. Rushall (1978) maintains that situation-specific measurements are the most viable and effective approach because these inventories take into account the conceptual structure underlying assessing a person's behavior in a specific environment. A few early attempts to develop sport-specific measuring instruments were presented earlier in this chapter, including the Cowell Social Outcome of Sports Checklist; the Johnson Sportsmanship Attitude Scale for football, basketball, and baseball situations; the Kenyon Physical Activity Attitude Scales; and the Nelson Sports Leadership Questionnaire.

Another recent trend is the differentiation between *trait* and *state* measures and the construction and validation of trait and state inventories for the specific sport environment. Anxiety and aggression inventories are examples. *Trait anxiety* is a relatively stable general personality trait that predisposes an individual to perceive certain situations as threatening and to respond to these situations with varying levels of state anxiety. *State anxiety*, then, is how one feels at that point in time when a perception of threat or danger is experienced in a specific situation, such as prior to an athletic contest when the athlete's reputation is at stake and the outcome of the contest is uncertain.

In an extensive series of sequential studies, Martens (1977) constructed the *Sport Competition Anxiety Test* to assess competitive trait anxiety. This instrument possesses both construct and concurrent validity. The Sport Competition Anxiety Test is a better predictor of state anxiety than of general trait anxiety, and its ability to predict anxiety states improves as the time to compete nears. Two forms of the 15-item Sport Competition Anxiety Test exist, one for adults 15 years and older (Form A) and another for children ages 10 through 14 years (Form C). Example items from Form A to which the respondent indicates degree of affect on a Likert-type scale include the following:

- Competing against others is socially enjoyable.
- Before I compete I feel uneasy.

- Before I compete I worry about not performing well.
- I am a good sportsman when I compete.
- When I compete I worry about making mistakes.

To fill the need for a Competitive State Anxiety Inventory, Martens (1977) proposed a 10-item instrument possessing construct validity. Gruber and Beauchamp (1979) have found this Competitive State Anxiety Inventory to be quite relevant for detecting changes in the anxiety states of university women varsity basketball players. The changes in anxiety states were a function of winning or losing the game and the importance of the contest to the women. Fifteen of 16 coefficients of internal consistency ranged from .74 to .94. Sample items from the Competitive State Anxiety Inventory to which the respondent indicates intensity of feeling at that particular moment on a Likert Scale include the following:

- I feel at ease.
- I feel nervous.
- I feel comfortable.
- I am tense.
- I feel secure.

Bredemeier (1978) developed an *Athletic Aggression Inventory* comprised of 100 items that measure identified factors of *instrumental* or *reactive* aggression. This trait inventory instrument has been applied in at least 14 different sport groups in attempts to determine if levels of aggression change over time in the same sport or to determine if aggression levels are similar from one sport to another. In an effort to assess aggression before and after an athletic event, Wall and Gruber (1986) developed a 28-item short form of the Bredemeier inventory. The 28 items measure the individual's disposition for hostility, anger, and frustration toward opponents and the self.

Another trend in the development of sport situation-specific instruments is the attempt to identify the sources and cognitive interpretations of elements that predispose individuals to respond in certain ways to items on a questionnaire. Kroll (1982) identified sources of competitive athletic stress factors in athletes and coaches; in athletes, some of the factors include somatic complaints, fear of failure, feelings of inadequacy, loss of control, and guilt.

Thus it appears that the development of sport situation-specific measuring instruments is a step toward increasing the relevance of measurements in the affective domain. More relevant measures will add to the credibility of utilizing affective domain data as input for grading or counseling students about their feelings, attitudes, and displayed behavior in sport and physical activity. The teacher or coach must carefully define the affective domain objective of interest, determine what decision is to be made based in part on test data, select a valid measuring instrument, and apply it according to standardized directions. In the final analysis, the data collected are only as good as the instrument itself and the procedures employed during testing. If a valid instrument does not exist, the teacher should construct his or her own test or modify an existing one. Seek the counsel of specialists in test construction at a local university when developing a test.

Review Questions

1. What are the areas of concern in the affective domain?
2. What is Kirkendall's hierarchy of a developing value construct for fair play?
3. What are the general categories of instruments constructed to measure in the affective domain?
4. What three ways is information usually collected in the affective domain?
5. What are the types of rating scales?

6. What problems and considerations are involved in measuring aspects of the affective domain?

7. For what general purposes or reasons do teachers collect information in the affective domain?

8. What types of affective instruments are listed in this chapter?

Problems and Exercises

1. List some of the values you believe to be inherent in competitive sports. Select one value and apply the taxonomy of the affective domain to it.

2. As a class project, define the traits of behavior that you all feel define or underlie the construct of sportsmanship. Present the items in the form of a rating scale.

3. Determine the reliability of the sportsmanship rating scale that the class has developed.

4. Assume that you are the director of intramural sports in a large high school of 2,000 students. Develop an interest inventory to determine what activities you should provide the students.

5. Write some statements that express your likes or dislikes for physical education. Present the statements in the form of a Likert Scale. Are your statements sampling the same attitude dimension?

6. Take the semantic differential scale illustrated in Figure 10.1 of this chapter and apply it to both a boys and a girls physical education class. Is there a difference in mean scores? Now apply it to different activity classes.

7. The validity and reliability of the *Cowell Social Behavior Trend Index* and the *Cowell Personal Distance Ballot* were determined 20 years ago. Compute these coefficients again. Are there any differences? Why?

Bibliography

Baumgartner, T.A., & Jackson, A.S. (1982). *Measurement for evaluation in physical education* (2nd ed.). Dubuque, IA: William C. Brown.

Bredemeier, B.J. (1978, May). *The assessment of reactive and instrumental aggression.* Paper presented at the annual meeting of the North American Society for Psychology of Sport and Physical Activity, Tallahassee, FL.

Coopersmith, S. (1967). *The antecedents of self-esteem.* San Francisco: W.H. Freeman.

Cowell, C.C. (1957). Our function is still education. *The Physical Educator,* **14**(1), 6-7.

Cowell, C.C. (1958). Validating an index of social adjustment for high school use. *Research Quarterly,* **29**(1), 7-18.

Cowell, C.C., & Ismail, A.H. (1962). Relationships between selected social and physical factors. *Research Quarterly, 33*(1), 40-43.

Dexter, G. (1957). *Teachers guide to physical education for girls in high school.* Sacramento: California Department of Education.

Ebel, R.L. (1972). What are schools for? *Phi Delta Kappan, 54,* 3-7.

Griffin, P.S. (1982). Second thoughts on affective evaluation. *Journal of Physical Education, Recreation, and Dance, 53*(2), 25-86.

Gruber, J.J. (1978). Comments on the reliability of a personality questionnaire used in physical education and sports research. *International Journal of Sport Psychology, 9,* 111-118.

Gruber, J.J. (1982). Physical activity and emotional health. In H. Eckert (Ed.), *The academy papers number 16—Synthesizing and transmitting knowledge: Research and its application* (pp. 49-58). Reston, VA: American Academy of Physical Education and the American Alliance for Health, Physical Education, Recreation, and Dance.

Gruber, J.J., & Beauchamp, D. (1979). Relevancy of the competitive state anxiety inventory in a sport environment. *Research Quarterly, 50*(2), 207-214.

Gruber, J.J. (1986). Physical activity and self-esteem development in children: A meta-analysis. In G.A. Stull & H.M. Eckert (Eds.), *Effects of physical activity on children: A special tribute to Mabel Lee* (pp. 30-48). The American Academy of Physical Education Papers No. 19. Champaign, IL: Human Kinetics.

Guilford, J.P. (1954). *Psychometric methods* (2nd ed.). New York: McGraw-Hill.

Harris, D.V. (1973). *Involvement in sport: A somatopsychic rationale for physical activity.* Philadelphia: Lea & Febiger.

Hopkins, K.D., & Stanley, J.C. (1981). *Educational and psychological measurement and evaluation* (6th ed.). Englewood Cliffs, NJ: Prentice-Hall.

Jackson, P.W., & Lahaderne, H.M. (1967). Scholastic success and attitude toward school in a population of sixth graders. *Journal of Educational Psychology, 58*(1), 15-18.

Johnson, M.L. (1969). Construction of a sportsmanship attitude scale. *Research Quarterly, 40*(2), 312-316.

Johnson, B.L., & Nelson, J.K. (1979). *Practical measurements for evaluation in physical education* (3rd ed.). Minneapolis: Burgess.

Kenyon, G.S. (1968a). A conceptual model for characterizing physical activity. *Research Quarterly, 39*(1), 96-105.

Kenyon, G.S. (1968b). Six scales for assessing attitude toward physical activity. *Research Quarterly, 39*(3), 566-574.

Kenyon, G.S. (1968c). *Values held for physical activity by selected urban secondary school students in Canada, Australia, England, and the United States.* Washington, DC: United States Office of Education.

Kirkendall, D.R. (1972). Physical education effects in the affective domain. In *75th Proceedings of the National College Physical Education Association for Men* (pp. 147-151). New Orleans, LA.

Krathwohl, D.R., Bloom, B.S., & Masia, B.B. (1964). *Taxonomy of educational objectives: The classification of educational goals. Handbook II: Affective domain.* New York: David McKay.

Kroll, W.P. (1970). Current strategies and problems in personality assessment of athletes. In L.E. Smith (Ed.), *Psychology of motor learning.* Chicago: Athletic Institute.

Kroll, W.P. (1982). Competitive athletic stress factors in athletes and coaches. In L.D. Zaichkowsky & W.E. Sime (Eds.), *Stress management for sport.* Reston, VA: The American Alliance for Health, Physical Education, Recreation, and Dance.

McGee, R. (1982). Uses and abuses of affective measurement. *Journal of Physical Education, Recreation, and Dance, 53*(2), 21-22.

Martens, R. (1977). *Sport competition anxiety test.* Champaign, IL: Human Kinetics.

Martinek, T.J., & Zaichkowsky, L.E. (1977). *Manual for the Martinek-Zaichkowsky self-concept scale for children.* Jacksonville, IL: Psychologists and Educators.

Meyers, C.R., & Blesh, T.E. (1962). *Measurement in physical education*. New York, NY: Ronald.

Mood, D. (1982). Evaluation in the affective domain? No! *Journal of Physical Education, Recreation, and Dance, 53*(2), 18-20.

Morgan, W.P. (1984, April). *Affective beneficence of vigorous physical activity.* Paper presented at the National Institute of Mental Health State-of-the-Art Workshop on Coping with Mental Stress: The Potential and Limits of Exercise Intervention, Washington, DC.

Noland, M.P., & Gruber, J.J. (1978). Self-perception, personality, and behavior in emotionally disturbed school children. *Behavioral Disorders, 4*(1), 6-12.

Osgood, C.E., Suci, G.J., & Tannenbaum, P.H. (1957). *The measurement of meaning*. Urbana: University of Illinois Press.

Rushall, B.S. (1978). Environment specific behavior inventories: Developmental procedures. *International Journal of Sport Psychology, 9*, 97-110.

Selby, R., & Lewko, J.H. (1976). Children's attitudes toward females in sport: Their relationship with sex, grade, and sports participation. *Research Quarterly, 47*(3), 453-463.

Simon, J.A., & Smoll, F.S. (1974). An instrument for assessing children's attitudes toward physical activity. *Research Quarterly, 45*(4), 407-415.

Smith, L.E. (1970). Personality and performance research. *Quest, 13*, 74-83.

Smith, R.E., Smoll, F.S., & Hunt, E. (1977). A system for the behavioral assessment of athletic coaches. *Research Quarterly, 48*(2), 401-407.

Sonstroem, R.J. (1974). Attitude testing examining certain psychological correlates of physical activity. *Research Quarterly, 45*(2), 93-103.

Sonstroem, R.J. (1978). Physical estimation and attraction scale: Rationale and research. *Medicine and Science in Sports, 10*(2), 97-102.

Stanley, J.C., & Hopkins, K.D. (1972). *Educational and psychological measurement and evaluation*. Englewood Cliffs, NJ: Prentice-Hall.

Stoner, L.J. (1982). Evaluation in the affective domain? Yes! *Journal of Physical Education, Recreation, and Dance, 53*(2), 16-17.

Wall, B.R., & Gruber, J.J. (1986). Relevancy of athletic aggression inventory for use in women's intercollegiate basketball: A pilot investigation. *International Journal of Sport Psychology*, in press.

Weber, M. (1977). Physical education teacher role identification. *Research Quarterly, 48*, 445-451.

Part IV

Application of Measurements in Evaluation

In chapter 1, the importance of utilizing evaluation in the planning and operation of physical education programs was emphasized. It was stated that evaluation procedures can and should be used in making decisions about the appropriate program for individuals and/or groups. As a knowledgeable physical educator, you should approach program planning with a definite pattern of decision-making. You should first establish general goals for your programs. These general goals provide the guidelines for assessing participants' entry-level performance levels. Initial behavioral and performance objectives also need to be established. Decisions need to be made about what to test, what tests to employ, and how to use the test results. This information, once obtained, will help you to establish priorities and specific objectives for each participant and/or the total class.

After the specific objectives have been set, you must select the best activities for the program to achieve the objectives. Periodically retesting participants on the same tests will yield information on their progress during their participation in the program. By comparing periodic test results with previous test results, the instructor will be able to determine whether each participant's performance level has improved, leveled, or regressed. Periodic measurement of participants' progress also helps in determining whether the program and its objectives are adequate or should be changed. This process allows for the continuous modification of the program and/or its objectives.

Now that all the tools necessary for conducting evaluation have been introduced, we will illustrate how measurements can be applied in various physical education settings. Chapter 11 deals with the actual administration of the evaluation program. Chapter 12 presents some solutions to the perennial problem of marking and grading in school physical education, and chapters 13 through 16 present example evaluation programs in a variety of physical education settings. After studying these examples, you should be prepared to apply your own measurement and evaluation program when given that opportunity.

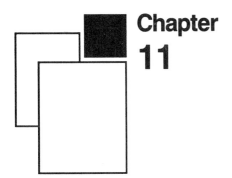

Chapter

11

Administration of the Evaluation Program

Three general concerns must be addressed in applying a measurement and evaluation program. First, relevant behaviors must be selected for assessment. For example, one might think that assessing speed is important when attempting to evaluate individuals' cardiovascular fitness, but this is not true. This problem of selecting irrelevant behaviors can primarily be overcome by being knowledgeable about the field in which you evaluate.

The second general concern in evaluation is that after relevant and important behaviors are identified, appropriate and adequate tests or measures must be chosen to assess them. The selection of appropriate tests has been the major focus of this text up to this point.

Finally, you may choose appropriate behaviors for assessment and may select proper tests for measuring these behaviors but then inadequately administer the tests. If tests are inadequately administered, then the test scores obtained are invalid and the entire evaluation process becomes useless. Thus the proper administration of tests is the third and equally important aspect of applying measurements in evaluation. All physical educators must realize that careless or "sloppy" administration of tests

will result in unreliable and invalid measures, regardless of how valid or reliable the tests may be.

After briefly considering the first two concerns of evaluation indicated above, this chapter considers some critical areas of concern involved in the actual administration of tests. At the end of the chapter, the administrative concerns of evaluating both teacher effectiveness and program effectiveness are introduced.

Administering Motor Performance Tests

Whenever a test is administered, great care must be taken if the test is to yield meaningful results. Time spent preparing for the administration of a test will yield great dividends in terms of time saved later and the quality of measurements obtained. If certain procedural steps are followed, you will have some assurance that the testing is being conducted smoothly, accurately, and for good reasons. Even more importantly, you will be obtaining valid test scores, which must always be our ultimate goal when administering tests.

Determining the Purpose and Use of Measurement

This first step in evaluation is the most important and a prerequisite to everything else, including the selection of the test(s) we wish to administer. For anyone to administer a test without knowing why it is being given is unthinkable, but each of us can probably relate an experience where this has occurred. What happens more commonly, however, is that a test is selected first and *then* the purpose of measurement is determined. Determining the purpose or purposes of measurement, however, must precede test selection. Indeed, the purpose must be the primary consideration in determining *what* to test or measure. What we are trying to measure will then guide us in our test selection. The results of measurement and evaluation activities should justify the time these activities take away from the rest of an instructional program. Some possible purposes of measurement were discussed in chapter 1, including classification, measuring achievement, selection, diagnosis, motivation, improving instruction, maintenance of standards, and research. It is recommended that you return to that chapter and review these purposes. Finally, we should mention again that a test can serve more than one purpose at any one time. For example, we may be testing for purposes of classification and diagnosis simultaneously.

Selecting Relevant Tests

After determining why and what you need to measure, you are ready to select or construct the best test(s) possible utilizing the criteria for test selection and construction presented in chapter 3. These criteria include a test's validity, reliability, objectivity, economy, ease of admin-

istration, developmental value, interest, norms, and duplicate forms.

In addition, these criteria must be considered in terms of conditions unique to each testing situation, including the number of students to be tested, available facilities and equipment, time available for testing, and preparation time of testers. Above all, the unique purpose(s) for a particular testing effort must be kept in mind.

Knowing the Test

Before any other preparations for actually administering a test are made, it is paramount for you to be completely familiar with every detail of the test. Many of these details would have been considered during the selection of the test, but all details of administering the test may not have been taken into account.

First, you should review the directions for the test very thoroughly. Before attempting to administer any test, you need to answer the following questions:

1. What are the exact directions to be given to the person taking the test? Often these directions will or should be written out.
2. What are the exact scoring requirements? For example, does a ball that hits on the line count or not? What are the exact dimensions of a target area? Is one allowed to take a run toward the line before jumping?
3. What units of measurement are to be used? Will measurements be made to the nearest inch or foot? Are scores to be recorded in inches or feet and inches?
4. How many trials are allowed? Does the best trial or the sum of all trials constitute the score? Is a practice trial allowed? If a participant's performance is interfered with, is he or she given an extra trial?

In checking this list of questions, think of yourself as the referee in a sport contest who must know every detail of every rule. Nothing can be left to guesswork or chance in administering a test.

Surveying Facilities and Equipment

You must determine what space is required to administer any test. Although space requirements should have been determined before the test was selected, it is important to remain aware of space and facility requirements throughout the planning process. If sufficient space or facilities are not available, you may need to reconsider the test(s) you have selected or constructed. In addition, facilities should be checked for the location of testing stations.

You should also make a list of all the materials and equipment needed for each test to be administered. Making a materials and equipment list will help prevent embarrassing shortages on testing day. Also check to ensure that all necessary equipment and materials are available and in good working condition. Timing the 100-meter dash is difficult without an accurate, working stopwatch!

Gathering Testing Materials

All necessary materials should be gathered before the day of testing. Equipment should be checked to be sure it is in good working condition. Imagine the embarrassment and frustration that would result if participants ran a 3,000-meter race for time only to discover after the race that the stopwatch was not working or had not been wound! All equipment should be checked for accuracy. It may be necessary to calibrate equipment such as scales, dynamometers, and watches. *If your equipment is inaccurate, the scores obtained from the equipment are bound to be unreliable and invalid and therefore useless.*

Preparing Testing Stations

Equipment and testing stations must be placed to ensure a smooth flow of traffic. A determi-

nation will first need to be made as to whether each test can be administered to a group or if it must be administered individually. If multiple testing stations are to be used, the number of individuals to be tested at each station during a period of time must also be determined. You must also know the type of leadership necessary for each test or item. Are testing assistants, recorders, and/or scorers needed?

If different stations are used for each test, the flow of subjects from one station to the next must be steady. Ensure that in going from station to station subjects do not interfere with the performance of others. Either a written diagram or simple verbal directions should be planned to allow subjects to proceed readily through the various stations. The time required for each item or station should also be determined. More than one station for the same item may be needed.

The order in which items are administered may be very important in some physical performance tests. In some situations the sequential order of test items can alter the results obtained. For example, scheduling consecutive test items that tire the same muscle groups is most unwise. Also, plan to administer endurance types of tests on separate days or at the end of testing periods.

A few other items, when planned for in advance, will greatly facilitate the testing process. All trials for one test item, for instance, should be administered in succession unless the event is too fatiguing. For example, if the standing long jump calls for three trials, one person should perform all three trials before the next person begins. Also, a demonstration should be conducted for each new group of subjects coming to a station. This approach is better than providing demonstrations for all items to the entire class or group. In addition, some activity should be provided for subjects who finish the testing early. This will help to prevent potential discipline problems. However, this activity should not be of a type or in a place that will distract other subjects who have not finished testing. In many tests, special markings need to be made on the walls or floor. These must be determined and marked before the actual testing. Usually special tapes or water-soluble paints must be used for marking areas.

Preparing Score Cards or Sheets

Score cards and sheets that are easy to read and understand must be prepared. Items on the score sheet or card should be arranged in a logical sequence in order to minimize recording errors. If possible, the items should appear on the score sheet in the same order that they are to be administered. The general format of the sheet should facilitate accuracy and neatness. For example, sufficient space must be provided for and between recordings if they are to be neatly written.

If possible, the same person should score all students on the same item, especially when ratings are involved. Likewise, it may be advantageous to have one scorer for each group. With older clientele and for some tests, however, each person might be allowed to record his or her own scores. In some situations a paired partner system could be functional. These are decisions that you must make in advance of actually administering the test.

Training Testers

If help will be needed to administer the test, the helpers must be prepared well in advance of the actual testing. Directions and procedures must be standardized; otherwise the same test may be administered differently by different testers. The test instructions should be brief and easily understood, and, whenever possible, they should include demonstrations and/or a preliminary test. Above all, the same instructions must be given to everyone who takes the test.

All testers should be acquainted beforehand with the testing equipment. They should practice using it and should be aware of any peculiarities associated with it. The testers should also actually practice administering the items or tests for which they will be responsible. They should rehearse exactly what they will do on test day. Questions will arise in these practice sessions that otherwise would not come out until test day.

Preparing Persons to be Tested

It is wise to determine in advance who is to be at each testing station. Also, everyone should be informed of the rotation scheme before actual testing begins in order to avoid confusion. If the individuals who are taking the test need to make any special preparations for the test in advance, they will obviously need to be informed in advance. For example, if an exhausting cardiovascular endurance test is to be given, subjects should be informed in advance so that they can get adequate rest and not overeat beforehand. Often you may choose to demonstrate a test several days in advance of the test administration so that the participants may practice it. In any case, examinees should always be told in advance why a test is to be administered. They should be informed of the purpose of the test and what use will be made of their test scores. Also, provision must be made for those who are absent the day of the test.

As previously stated, on many physical performance tests, warm-up activities immediately before performing the test will increase the reliability and validity of the test. Therefore, warm-up activities are highly recommended. Warm-up activities that are highly related to the specific test to be given are preferred to general calisthenics. In some situations, practice trials may serve as the warm-up activity; in other situations, exercises for specific muscle groups may be appropriate.

A decision must be made as to how much external motivation is to be given to the individuals to be tested. Typically, the test itself will provide adequate motivation, but in some testing situations subjects may need additional encouragement. However, caution must be used in providing external motivation in testing situations. First, if the testing is to be fair, all persons being tested should receive the same encouragement. Second, some individuals' performances are impaired when too much "hype" is given.

Administering the Tests

If close attention has been paid to the details above, the actual testing session should proceed smoothly and trouble-free. The importance of advance planning cannot be overemphasized. Without thorough planning, chaos, embarrassment, and wasted time can easily result. With sufficient planning, a testing session can be a meaningful educational experience for all concerned. Furthermore, much of what has been presented simply involves being careful and using common sense. If you utilize good judgment and constantly remind yourself that tests must be properly administered to be of any value, then and only then will you be successful.

To have an *evaluation* program rather than merely a *testing* program, something must be done with the test scores. Test results must be analyzed and the findings used.

Analyzing and Using Test Results

After the scores are obtained from testing, the descriptive parameters presented in chapter 2 should first be determined. You will probably want to determine at least the mean and the standard deviation for each test item. This will give a good description of the group's performance. A comparison between a particular class and city, state, or national norms may be made. Is this class's performance average, above average, or below average? Does this result indicate that a modification in program is required? Perhaps a comparison can be made between a class's present performance and its earlier performance. The issue then becomes a question of whether there has been improvement. If not, why not? Finally, decisions need to be made about the accomplishment of instructional objectives. Have program objectives been sufficiently accomplished to leave the program as is, or does it need to be changed? Were the objectives realistic, or do they need to be reexamined and possibly revised? You may want to review the model presented in chapter 1.

You may want to compare each person's performance with his or her peers' performances. This can best be done by determining a standard score (i.e., percentile, z-score, T score, 6-σ, or whatever) for each person. By comparing participants' scores, future instruction can be individualized to address each person's specific strengths and weaknesses. Along these same lines, participants can be counseled into activities most appropriate to their needs and abilities.

Each participant should be given his or her test results as soon as possible after the test in order to maximize learning and/or motivation. The results should be expressed simply, clearly, and concisely in a manner compatible with the understanding of the group involved and with the purpose served in presenting the results. This implies giving the basic facts in condensed form so that the outstanding points for emphasis will be evident. Individual profiles can be quite effective. An example of one profile sheet is presented in Figure 11.1. Through the proper presentation of results participants can be motivated to improve their performance.

Participants who need special attention must be identified. A good test will help you do this. This special attention may be provided by you, or it may require the services of professionals in other areas. In any event, it is the physical educator's responsibility to see that the special attention is in fact received.

Administering Written Tests

So far this chapter has been focused on the administration of physical performance tests

Individual Performance Profile

Name _____

Date _____

Percentile scores	Chin-ups		Standing broad jump		50-yard dash		Basketball goals		9-minute run test		
	Initial	Final	Initial	Final	Initial	Final	Initial	Final	Initial	Final	
100											Excellent
90											
80											Good
70											
60											Above average
50											Average
40											Below average
30											
20											Poor
10											
0											Needs improvement

Comments:

Figure 11.1 Sample performance profile sheet.

simply because numerous difficulties surround the administration of physical performance tests that are not present when administering written tests. For example, the only equipment and facilities needed for administering a written test are the test and answer sheet, a pencil, and an adequate room with desks.

Although the administration of written tests is not a complicated procedure, several guidelines should be followed to ensure that valid and reliable scores are obtained. Many of the following guidelines are similar to the steps for administering motor performance tests, but some are specific to written tests:

1. Know the test. As with motor performance tests, the administrator of the test must know everything about it, including the exact directions.
2. Strictly adhere to the time limits of the test if there are time limits.
3. Maintain a testing environment that is conducive to taking the test. Try to use a classroom with desks for testing if at all possible. Ensure that lighting and ventilation are provided. Eliminate noise and visual distractions.
4. Ensure that each examinee has a usable pencil and that spares are available.
5. Post signs on doors to indicate that testing is in progress to prevent unnecessary interruptions.
6. Try to separate examinees so that they are not tempted to ''copy'' or ''borrow'' information from each other.
7. Conduct a pretest orientation session for the examinees to inform them about the general nature of the test, its purposes, and the use to be made of their scores.
8. Maintain a relaxed manner without being cool or aloof.
9. Never leave the room during the examination.

Classifying Physical Activity Participants

Throughout this text we have suggested that some system of classifying physical activity participants is desirable. Classification is usually defined as the placement of participants into homogeneous (similar) groups or heterogeneous (differing) groups based on some common trait or ability. The general purposes of utilizing some type of classification technique include the following:

- *To create a more effective learning atmosphere.* Classification of program participants into groups of similar ability levels means that instructors need to prepare for only one general ability level within a group. Participants feel more comfortable if they know that they are receiving instruction in a setting in which their classmates' abilities are similar to their own.
- *To provide an atmosphere conducive to motivating individuals for participation and performance.* People enjoy participating with other individuals of similar abilities and/or ages.
- *To make activities more adaptable to meeting individual participants' interests, needs, and abilities.* Activity instruction becomes more individualized when participants are classified into homogeneous groups.
- *To provide a better basis for evaluating individual and group performances.* Participants in classified groups recognize that their performances are being compared to those of other participants similar to them in terms of body size and other relevant criteria.
- *To improve competitive atmosphere.* A better competitive atmosphere is developed with equated teams. No one enjoys competing when teams are unevenly matched.
- *To increase safety in competitive sports.* This is why we have weight categories in boxing, wrestling, and football.

Methods of Classifying Participants

Several methods are recommended in the literature for practitioners to use in classifying participants. You must decide which methods best suit your program goals.

Medical Examination. A medical examination is recommended as the first type of classification to be employed by the physical educator. Based on the results of an examination by a physician, each participant is placed into one of three categories that authorize (a) unlimited participation in all physical activity and athletic programs, (b) somewhat restricted activity, or (c) restricted activity. The latter two categories require close cooperation between appropriate medical, institutional, and physical education experts to diagnose and prescribe appropriate adapted physical education activities.

Gender. Although the recent trend to provide coeducational instruction in physical education is appropriate, there may be some activities such as tackle football and wrestling that should not be offered on a coeducational basis. Certainly strength, speed, power, and other physical ability norm charts should provide for gender differences.

Interest. Participants classify themselves or select activities of interest to them in elective programs of physical activity.

Age or Grade Level. Age or grade level appear to be the most commonly employed classification criterion because it is administratively convenient for school authorities to schedule people into classes based on age or grade. In physical education, however, age or grade level tells the teacher nothing about the pupils' motor abilities. In fitness clubs, persons usually prefer to participate with those of similar age.

Functional Ability. Functional ability is the most specific and logical classification technique to employ after the medical examination. If one is involved in swimming instruction, one or more swimming skill tests can identify the beginner, intermediate, and advanced swimmers. Note that age or grade cannot provide an instructor with information about swimming ability.

Physical Maturity. In the 1920s, Neilson and Cozens found that two general factors account for successful motor performance, namely, a "body size" factor and a "participation" (skill) factor. This substantiated the notion that "structure permits function." As a result, Neilson and

Cozens and McCloy developed easy-to-use age, height, and weight indices. These indices are to be taken as indicators of physical maturity. Directions for use of these devices appear in Clarke (1976), Meyers and Blesh (1962), and Mood (1980). The classification indices are as follows:

1. Neilson-Cozens Classification Index for High School Boys

    $$(20 \times age) + 5.55 \ (height) + (weight)$$

2. McCloy Classification Index I for High School Boys

    $$(20 \times age) + (6 \times height) + (weight)$$

3. McCloy Index II for College Men

    $$(6 \times height) + (weight)$$

4. McCloy Index III for Elementary School Boys

    $$(10 \times age) + (height)$$

A correlation of .98 between the McCloy Index I and the Neilson-Cozens Index is reported in the references previously cited. Thus either scheme can be used. McCloy and Young (1954) reported a correlation of .82 between the Index I and success in track and field events. Indeed, these indices appear to be quite useful for classifying boys and girls into groups of different body size for instruction and participation in events that are heavily dependent on muscular strength, endurance, speed, and power.

It is also logical to consider physical maturity and body structure in constructing norm charts. Thus a boy or girl will compare his or her performance against the performance of children of similar body size. The AAHPERD norm charts utilizing percentile ranks for each age group illustrate this principle and appear in the chapter on fitness testing (chapter 7). When examining the AAHPERD norm charts, note that only age is taken into account as the differentiating variable in growth and development. In studying the motor performances of over 7,600 boys and girls ages 10 through 18, Espenschade (1983) found that height and weight added very little additional information to the relationship between age and motor performance. Thus age is recommended for use in the future as a quick classifier of the physical maturity of children. It should be emphasized at this point that using age, height, and weight in combination is *not* correct, but it does save time to use age alone and secure essentially the same results. You must also be aware that maturity and body structure vary within the same age group, and you must also take into account the negative relationship between body weight and performance in certain items.

In summary, classifying participants by physical maturity for instructional purposes only means that participants will be of similar size. You may still need to use a functional skill test to determine ability groupings within a group.

Methods for Choosing Teams

The following practical scheme is proposed for choosing teams in physical education classes and for intramural competition.

Choosing Teams by Secret Ballot. One rather unusual method of selecting teams starts with the election of captains. By secret ballot, each student in the class is asked to nominate two class members who they believe would make the best captains. These votes are then tabulated, and the four individuals receiving the most votes become the captains. To start team selection, each captain is allowed to choose one teammate, and these persons become cocaptains. Usually, these selections are made from the class roster before school or during a conference period.

Subsequently, it is the duty of the captains (with the aid of the teacher) to divide the rest of the class into four teams of equal strength.

Captains do not know which team will be theirs until every class member has been assigned. The teams are then assigned to the captains and co-captains by means of a drawing.

Because the captains do not know which of the four teams will eventually be assigned to them, they strive to ensure that all teams are equally balanced. When the teams have been equalized to the greatest degree possible and all four captains agree that they would be satisfied with any one team, the drawing is made. No class member may act as a captain twice within the same semester, and because new teams may be selected every six weeks or so, many pupils receive leadership experience through being a captain.

Choosing Teams by Height. Line the class up according to height and have them count off by fours. All number ones, number twos, number threes, and number fours constitute four separate teams. Each team selects its own captain and cocaptain. On rare occasions, one team may be much superior to any of the others, and thus the teacher may need to make some adjustments.

Skill Test Scores (Functional Basis). Administer a skill test to all participants. Rank participants on the basis of their test scores and assign them to teams.

Example: 30 players; 5 basketball teams.

	Team A	Team B	Team C	Team D	Team E
Players' ranks	1	2	3	4	5
	10	9	8	7	6
	11	12	13	14	15
	20	19	18	17	16
	21	22	23	24	25
	30	29	28	27	26

Compute the mean for each group and, if all are the same, you have teams of equal strength on the basis of the skill test scores. You can also have the various vertical teams or squads compete in actual play and have the horizontal squads work on skills and drilling.

Record of Time Allotment in Class

Class: 9ᵗʰ GRADE/MR. ALLEN   Date: 1/9   Time: 2:00-2:40

Teacher Talk (Demonstration and Instruction)	Management	Active Learning
3:06	1:17	6:18
1:08	1:24	5:20
4:30	0:46	3:50
2:06	0:40	4:25
12:00	2:50	19:13
	1:00	
	0:20	
	8:47	

Duration recording was used here to classify physical education class time into three categories. A clock or stopwatch is used to record the duration of each instance of the three categories. The time is jotted down as the next sequence begins. These data could be expressed as a percentage of the total class time, which in this case was 40 minutes. You will notice that an undue amount of time was spent in management and "teacher talk," and that not quite half of the class time was spent in active learning. These data show a situation that badly needs to be changed, especially in the large amount of time devoted to management.

Figure 11.2 Sample duration-recording format. From Daryl Siedentop (1983), *Developing Teaching Skills in Physical Education* (p. 270) (2nd ed.). Palo Alto, CA: Mayfield.

Evaluating Teacher Effectiveness

In the last few years, a great deal of interest has been shown in attempting to evaluate how effectively teachers teach. Unfortunately, however, no excellent devices have been developed to accomplish such a worthy goal. If caution is practiced, however, some useful tools can be applied that give some indication of teaching skill. The cautions to be practiced are given after two possible teacher evaluation tools are presented.

One means of assessing teacher effectiveness is to have peers or supervisors observe the act of teaching. When this is done a specified method should be incorporated if meaningful information is to be acquired. A guide for what is to be observed should be developed. Siedentop (1976) developed several such devices, including the duration-recording device presented in Figure 11.2.

A commonly used method, particularly at the college level, for giving some indication of how effectively a teacher performs is the student evaluation of teaching forms. One such form that was developed by Noble and Cox (1983) has been shown to have acceptable reliability and some validity (see Table 11.1).

Caution must be exercised when utilizing instruments such as those just presented. Solid validity has not been established for these types of instruments. Therefore, they should be used primarily for the purpose of providing some feedback to a teacher to help improve his or her teaching skills. Although it is frequently done, using these assessments as the primary means for determining merit raises, reappointments, and promotions is a highly questionable practice. Results from such instruments should be considered as only one source of information along with other sources, such as analysis of course content, in making such important decisions.

Table 11.1 Lifetime Sports Course Evaluation Form

Your thoughtful answers to these questions will provide helpful information to your instructor.

Part I. Describe your instructor in terms of the following items by blackening a number between "1" and "5" on the answer sheet provided. Use this code:

1 = Rarely or never   4 = Quite often
2 = Seldom   5 = Almost always
3 = Sometimes

The instructor

1. put material across in an interesting way.
2. seemed enthusiastic about the subject matter.
3. effectively demonstrated the skills needed.
4. planned activities so that the whole class could participate maximally.
5. explained course material clearly, and explanations were to the point.
6. provided individual instruction when needed.
7. made presentations that were dry and dull.
8. seemed to enjoy teaching.
9. had knowledge beyond the textbook or readings.
10. clearly stated the objectives of the course.
11. introduced and explained the skills effectively.
12. encouraged students to express themselves freely and openly.
13. spoke with expressiveness and variety in tone of voice.
14. made it seem that what he or she was teaching was worthwhile.
15. answered students' questions in a way that demonstrated his or her expertise.
16. made it clear how each topic fit into the course.
17. gave me feedback on performance that was clear and meaningful.
18. used different kinds of explanations or demonstrations if students were having trouble understanding.

(Cont.)

Table 11.1 (Cont.)

Part II. The next eight questions ask you to describe yourself. Use the following code:

1 = Definitely false
2 = More false than true
3 = In between
4 = More true than false
5 = Definitely true

19. I now possess the skills necessary to participate successfully in this activity on my own.
20. I understand the fundamentals sufficiently so that I will be able to improve my skills with further practice.
21. I believe I could teach the fundamentals of this activity to others.
22. During this term, I participated in this activity more than was required by the course.
23. I intend to participate in this activity after I leave college.
24. The skills I acquired in this course have made me more self-confident.
25. If the opportunity arose, I would welcome a chance to take another course from this instructor.
26. Overall, I gained more from this course than from the average course I have taken at this institution.

Note. From "Development of a Form to Survey Student Reactions on Instructional Effectiveness of Lifetime Sport Classes" by L. Noble and R. Cox, 1983, *Research Quarterly for Exercise and Sport,* **54**(3), p. 248. Reprinted by permission of the American Alliance for Health, Physical Education, Recreation and Dance, 1900 Association Drive, Reston, VA 22091.

Overall Program Evaluation

The overall evaluation of physical education programs is an area of evaluation that has not received a great deal of attention. However, some instruments have been developed. The state of Kansas has developed such an instrument that is presented in its entirety on pages 367-371. This instrument is not presented as a final answer in evaluating the physical education program, but its application could certainly provide valuable feedback to teachers and/or administrators.

Review Questions

1. What procedural steps should be considered in the administration of a test?
2. What two basic descriptive parameters are you most likely to calculate in order to analyze test results?
3. What is the value of comparing your class test results with norms?
4. What questions can be answered if a comparison is made between your class's present performance and its earlier performance?
5. What descriptive tools should be used when comparing students' scores with one another?
6. What purposes are served in presenting test results to our students?
7. How should test results be fed back to students?
8. What precautions need to be exercised in the application of teacher effectiveness forms?

Self-Evaluation of Elementary Physical Education Programs

To assist schools as well as school districts in determining areas of strength or weakness within the total physical education program, the following self-evaluation checklist is divided into six separate sections, including philosophy and principles; organization and administration; personnel; curriculum; facilities, equipment, and supplies; and evaluation. This will aid in determining priorities for program improvements.

Evaluation Scale

The evaluator should read each statement carefully and determine the degree of compliance according to the evaluation scale.

0 = Compliance lacking; provisions missing or not functioning.
1 = Compliance very limited in provisions or functioning.
2 = Compliance limited or partial; adequacy of provisions or functioning questionable.
3 = Compliance adequate regarding provisions or functioning.
4 = Compliance complete; provisions extensive; functioning excellent.

Self-evaluation scale
(Circle one)

Philosophy

1. The school district has a clearly written statement of the philosophy and objectives upon which the physical education program is based   0   1   2   3   4

2. The school district has a curricular structure in place that reflects a scope and sequence and/or competency program   0   1   2   3   4

3. Physical education is conceived as an integral part of the total educational effort of the school district and is directed toward the achievement of sound educational objectives   0   1   2   3   4

4. The characteristics and needs of the students are considered when activities within the program are determined   0   1   2   3   4

5. The staff recognizes and conscientiously utilizes the biological, social, and psychological foundations of physical education in planning and teaching   0   1   2   3   4

6. The school seeks the cooperation of outside agencies, public and private, in an outgoing development of the program   0   1   2   3   4

Possible score = 24. Self-evaluation score = _____

(Cont.)

Self-Evaluation of Elementary Physical Education Programs (Cont.)

Self-evaluation scale
(Circle one)

Organization

1. All students are enrolled in and participate in physical education classes 0   1   2   3   4

2. Adapted physical education activities are provided as needed 0   1   2   3   4

3. District/school policy provides for exclusion from the physical education class 0   1   2   3   4

4. Activities within the program are progressively sequential from grade to grade or level to level, according to the readiness level of the student 0   1   2   3   4

5. The program is planned according to
   A. the readiness level of the student 0   1   2   3   4
   B. the time available.. 0   1   2   3   4
   C. the facilities and equipment available.................... 0   1   2   3   4
   D. the nature of the activities.............................. 0   1   2   3   4

6. Enrollment in physical education classes is limited to
   no limit   = 0
   35 pupils per teacher = 1
   30 pupils per teacher = 2
   25 pupils per teacher = 3
   20 pupils per teacher = 4................................. 0   1   2   3   4

7. The time allotted for the physical education program is
   1 day per week only = 0
   2 days per week   = 1
   3 days per week   = 2
   4 days per week   = 3
   5 days per week   = 4 0   1   2   3   4

8. The method of grading and reporting to parents coincides with the method used in the other areas of the total educational program... 0   1   2   3   4

9. A written accident policy is in existence 0   1   2   3   4

Possible score = 48. Self-evaluation score = _____

Self-evaluation scale
(Circle one)

Personnel

1. All physical education teachers are properly certified 0   1   2   3   4

2. The physical education staff promotes its program both in the school and the community................................ 0   1   2   3   4

(Cont.)

Self-Evaluation of Elementary Physical Education Programs (Cont.)

3. The professional physical education staff all have a major degree in physical education 0   1   2   3   4

4. Members of the physical education staff strive for professional growth by attending and participating in workshops, clinics, and other inservice experiences 0   1   2   3   4

5. The staff are all members of KAHPERD* and AAHPERD** professional associations and maintain a current library of professional materials... 0   1   2   3   4

*Kansas Association of Health, Physical Education, Recreation and Dance
**American Alliance of Health, Physical Education, Recreation and Dance

Possible score = 20. Self-evaluation score = _____

Self-evaluation scale
(Circle one)

Curriculum

1. The physical education curriculum consists of the following areas: (.5 point each; round total half points up)
   A. Games of low and high organization
   B. Body mechanics
   C. Rhythms and dance
   D. Aquatics
   E. Gymnastics
   F. Physical fitness
   G. Perceptual motor activities
   H. Movement education
   I. Manipulative skills.................................... 0   1   2   3   4

2. The program for each grade level is structured around the needs of the individual 0   1   2   3   4

3. The curriculum provides specific opportunities for the student to develop physically, socially, and emotionally 0   1   2   3   4

4. The curriculum is adapted to serve the needs of the exceptional child... 0   1   2   3   4

5. The curriculum provides opportunities for the students to develop both leadership and followership qualities 0   1   2   3   4

6. The program includes opportunities for students to participate in coeducational activities 0   1   2   3   4

7. The school is making continuous efforts to upgrade its program by striving for
   A. daily instructional program in physical education 0   1   2   3   4
   B. adequate facilities and equipment 0   1   2   3   4

Possible score = 32. Self-evaluation score = _____

(Cont.)

Self-Evaluation of Elementary Physical Education Programs (Cont.)

Self-evaluation scale
(Circle one)

Facilities, Equipment, and Supplies

1. Indoor and outdoor facilities are designed for use by both the school and the community 0   1   2   3   4

2. There is sufficient outdoor instructional space to accommodate current as well as projected student enrollment 0   1   2   3   4

3. An indoor facility with adequate space for maximum pupil load is provided 0   1   2   3   4

4. A budget exists for the purchase of physical education equipment and materials 0   1   2   3   4

5. Equipment is purchased for specific use in the physical education program 0   1   2   3   4

6. An equipment inspection program exists on a regular basis to ensure the safety of the student 0   1   2   3   4

7. Outdoor and indoor facilities are inspected by instructional and maintenance staff to eliminate hazards to students 0   1   2   3   4

Possible score = 28. Self-evaluation score = _____

Self-evaluation scale
(Circle one)

Evaluation

1. An evaluation program is implemented on a regular basis 0   1   2   3   4

2. Program revisions are made as indicated by the evaluation 0   1   2   3   4

3. Pupils are evaluated in accordance with the cognitive, psycho-motor, and affective domains 0   1   2   3   4

4. Pupils are evaluated annually using one of the following instruments:
AAHPERD/PCFF — Fitness Test
AAHPERD — Health-Related Fitness Exam
AAU — Fitness Test
Other — Standardized Test 0   1   2   3   4

Possible score = 16. Self-evaluation score = _____

Summary of Actual Points		**Rating Scale**
		for Total Points
Philosophy (24)	_____	Very Poor . . . 0-102
Organization (48)	_____	Poor 103-119
Personnel (20)	_____	Fair 120-137
Curriculum (32)	_____	Good 138-154
Facilities, Equipment & Supplies (28)	_____	Excellent 155-168
Evaluation (16)	_____	
Total	_____	

Note. From *Physical Education Program Self-Evaluation Model for Elementary Schools* by G. Christensen, 1984, Kansas State Department of Education. Reprinted by permission.

Bibliography

Barrow, H.M., & McGee, R. (1979). *A practical approach to measurement in physical education* (3rd ed.). Philadelphia: Lea and Febiger.

Baumgartner, T.A., & Jackson, A.S. (1982). *Measurement for evaluation in physical education* (2nd ed.). Dubuque, IA: William C. Brown.

Bloom, B.S., Englehart, M.D., Furst, E.J., Hill, W.H., & Krathwohl, D.R. (Eds.). (1956). *A taxonomy of educational objectives: Handbook I, the cognitive domain*. New York: David McKay.

Bloom, B.S., Hastings, J.T., & Madaus, G.F. (1971). *Handbook on formative and summative evaluation of student learning*. New York: McGraw-Hill.

Christensen, G. (1984). *Physical education program self-evaluation model for elementary schools*. Topeka, KS: Kansas State Department of Education.

Clarke, H.H. (1976). *Application of measurement to health and physical education* (5th ed.). Englewood Cliffs, NJ: Prentice-Hall.

Colvin, W.W., & Roundy, E.S. (1976). An instrument for the student evaluation of teaching effectiveness in physical education activity classes. *Research Quarterly, 47*, 296-298.

Espenschade, A.A. (1963). Restudy of relationships between physical performance of school children and age, height, and weight. *Research Quarterly, 34*(2), 144-153.

Feldman, K.A. (1976a). Grades and college students' evaluations of their courses and teachers. *Research in Higher Education, 4*, 69-111.

Feldman, K.A. (1976b). The superior college teacher from the student's view. *Research in Higher Education, 5*, 243-288.

Feldman, K.A. (1977). Consistency and variability among college students in rating their teachers and courses: A review and analysis. *Research in Higher Education, 6*, 223-274.

Feldman, K.A. (1978). Course characteristics and college students' ratings of their teachers: What we know and what we don't. *Research in Higher Education, 9*, 199-242.

Frey, P.W. (1978). A two-dimensional analysis of student ratings of instruction. *Research in Higher Education, 9*, 69-91.

Hoyt, D.P. (1973). Measurement of instructional effectiveness. *Research in Higher Education, 1*, 367-378.

Johnson, B.L., & Nelson, J.K. (1979). *Practical measurements for evaluation in physical education* (3rd ed.). Minneapolis: Burgess.

Larson, L.A., & Yocom, R.D. (1951). *Measurement and evaluation in physical, health, and recreation education*. St. Louis: C.V. Mosby.

Mathews, D.K. (1978). *Measurement in physical education* (5th ed.). Philadelphia: W.B. Saunders.

McCloy, C.H. (1932). *The measurement of athletic power*. New York: Barnes & Co.

McCloy, C.H., & Young, N.D. (1954). *Tests and measurements in health and physical education*. New York: Appleton-Century-Crofts.

Meyers, C.R., & Blesh, T.E. (1962). *Measurement in physical education*. New York: Ronald Press.

Mood, D.P. (1980). *Numbers in motion*. Palo Alto, CA: Mayfield.

Neilson, N.P., & Cozens, F.W. (1934). *Achievement scales in physical education activities*. Sacramento, CA: State Department of Education.

Noble, L., & Cox, R. (1983). Development of a form to survey student reactions on instructional effectiveness of lifetime sport classes. *Research Quarterly for Exercise and Sport, 54*(3), 247-254.

Safrit, M.J. (1977). Criterion-referenced measurement: Applications in physical education. *Motor Skills: Theory into Practice, 2*, 21-35.

Safrit, M.J. (1981). *Evaluation in physical education* (2nd ed.). Englewood Cliffs, NJ: Prentice-Hall.

Siedentop, D. (1976). *Developing teaching skills in physical education*. Boston: Houghton Mifflin.

Chapter 12

Grading

Several times throughout this text, formative evaluation has been contrasted to summative evaluation. In formative evaluation, test results are given to participants (feedback) daily or several times each day with the express purpose of improving their performance. Summative evaluation is the assessment of an individual's overall accomplishments at the end of an instructional unit. The authors' position throughout has been that formative evaluation is the more valuable procedure in physical education programs. However, summative evaluation can also be of considerable value when it is conducted seriously and carefully.

The most commonly used summative evaluations are grades that are assigned in school settings. Grading is an area that often causes teachers (especially beginning teachers) a great deal of anguish. There are numerous arguments for and against assigning grades to students in physical education classes. Some of the usual arguments for grading are that (a) grades give students and parents a definite idea of the progress the students are making; (b) grades motivate students to improve performance; and (c) performance is graded in all other subjects

in school, so performance in physical education should be graded also. On the other side of the issue, opponents of grading performance in physical education argue that (a) students who receive low grades will be negatively motivated and thus less inclined to voluntarily participate in physical activity later in life; (b) the fear of poor grades takes the enjoyment out of physical activity; and (c) there is no really "fair" way to grade in physical education. To grade or not to grade is a decision you may have to make, although in most school systems the decision will be made for you. Nevertheless, if the decision is made to assign grades, then you must be able to do so fairly and in a way that can be logically and educationally justified.

Criteria for a Grading System

In order for a grading system to be considered adequate, it should meet the following three criteria: (a) it should have a purpose; (b) it should be fair to all students; and (c) it should be clearly explained and understood.

The purpose or purposes for assigning grades should be known and evident; that is, there must be a reason why you are assigning grades. Remmers, Gage, and Rummel (1965) noted the following common purposes of grading/marking systems:

- Information for parents on pupil status or progress
- Promotion and graduation
- Motivation of school work
- Guidance of learning
- Guidance of educational and vocational planning
- Guidance of personal development
- Honors
- Participation in many school activities
- Reports and recommendations to future employers
- Data for curriculum studies
- Reports to a school the pupil may attend later (p. 288)

Although you would not expect to have all of these purposes for all grading situations, more than one purpose would likely be appropriate in most situations.

Whatever grading system is chosen, it must be fair to all students. Physical educators are often perplexed by the problem of how to evaluate the progress of all students fairly because usually there is a great range of ability among students in almost any class; very highly skilled students are often in the same class as the very poorly skilled. Some people believe that students' levels of ability at the end of a grading period should be the sole determining factor in the assignment of grades. This approach seems grossly unfair because it gives a great advantage to the student who began the unit or grading period at a high level. Furthermore, this approach makes no attempt to evaluate the achievement that took place *during* the grading period because entry-level abilities are ignored. Physical educators, however, must be interested

in what has been learned or achieved during the grading period.

Because we are most likely to be interested in achievement, a common proposal is for each student to be graded based on his or her improvement during the course of instruction. However, if this is done without considering students' initial ability levels, the student who began at a high level is greatly penalized because he or she will not have as much room for improvement as an unskilled classmate. For example, the student who can initially run the 100-meter dash in 12 seconds will certainly have more difficulty improving his or her time by .5 second than the student who initially ran the dash in 16 seconds.

What, then, do you do? The authors suggest that you classify students at the beginning of a unit or grading period on the basis of their present ability. This classification may involve an objective test, rating scale, checklist, subjective judgment, or combination of these. At the end of the unit or grading period, each student's performance can then be judged within that group. Of course, classifying students does not necessarily mean that they must be physically divided into groups. Although breaking a class into groups may often be advantageous for instructional purposes, classification can also be only a conceptual division for grading purposes.

An extreme approach would be to allow each student to be classified conceptually and to then make decisions about grades on that basis. This would, of course, make the grading process totally subjective and could leave you, the teacher, open to considerable criticism. One grading system that approaches this scheme is contract grading. Contract grading is discussed more fully later in this chapter.

Your grading system should not be clouded by mystery. All grades and grading systems must be clearly understood by the students and/or their parents. A grade is an evaluation of the student. Thus if the grade is to have any educational impact, the student and/or parent should understand the rationale used to determine it.

No grading system is foolproof. Whatever grading system is used will have some problems associated with it. Any grading scheme is, in fact, subjective and must be defended by the teacher using it. Thus you must take care to select a grading system on sound educational bases that are compatible with your philosophy. Then, above all, use good judgment in applying it. Remember that there is no substitute for judgment in measurement and evaluation. You must ask questions such as, Is this attribute an important objective of physical education? Do all students have an equal chance to demonstrate proficiency in the attributes? Should attitude be a part of the grade and, if so, how can attitude be measured?

Standards for Grades

Assigning grades ultimately means that a teacher decides the standards by which students' performances are to be judged. In chapter 1, two main types of standards were introduced: norm-referenced and criterion-referenced. These standards are also relevant to grading systems. If a teacher assigns grades on the basis of norm-referenced standards, then the standard for various grades is determined from the performance of some defined group. On a push-ups test, for example, a teacher might state that a student must score above the 90th percentile rank to receive an A, between the 70th and 90th percentile ranks for a B, between the 40th and 70th percentile ranks for a C, and so forth. Another teacher who uses criterion-referenced standards to assign grades might state that a student must do 60 or more push-ups to receive an A, between 50 and 59 push-ups for a B, between 40 and 49 push-ups for a C, and so forth. The choice between a criterion- or norm-referenced approach to grading is a crucial philosophical decision that each teacher must make.

A norm-referenced approach is utilized to discriminate among individuals. An individual's performance is compared to the performances of other individuals in order to determine how the individual performs in relation to the group. Therefore, scores or grades in a norm-referenced system are expected to vary; otherwise comparisons among individuals cannot be made. On the other hand, a criterion-referenced approach is utilized to allocate individuals to mastery levels. The estimation of mastery levels (grades) for individuals reflects the proportion of a specific domain that the individual has mastered. The allocation of individuals to mastery levels is based on set levels of mastery being accomplished by an individual. Therefore, the primary focus in a criterion-referenced approach is on the mastery level of an individual, whereas the primary focus of a norm-referenced approach is how far an individual deviates from the group mean.

Advocates of the criterion-referenced approach to grading argue that professional teachers should know what students must accomplish or master and that therefore it is their duty to set definite levels of mastery or accomplishments for different grades. Opponents of the criterion-referenced approach favoring a norm-referenced approach argue that in many motor performance areas we do not know what levels of performance should be expected in a criterion-referenced approach and that therefore it is more appropriate and fair to allow the performance of the group to determine the levels of expectation. Norm-referenced advocates also suggest that the criterion-referenced advocate probably determines the mastery levels that he or she uses by determining the average level of performance for the population to be graded. The criterion-referenced advocate might counter by stating that the average performance for groups of students varies and that therefore a norm-referenced grading scheme is unfair because it changes over time. Another criticism sometimes leveled against a criterion-referenced approach to grading is that different levels of ability cannot be taken into account. This criticism can, of course, be answered by suggesting that different sets of mastery expectations need to be developed for different ability groups.

The arguments presented above are all valid. What, then, is a teacher to do? One solution is to use some aspects of both approaches. For some activities, particularly activities such as swimming that involve the safety of participants, a criterion-referenced approach should be used to ensure that definite and permanent standards are established. For other activities in which the levels of expectation are truly unknown, a norm-referenced approach appears to be reasonable. In many other activities and in assigning grades at the end of a unit, each teacher must decide which approach to use in accordance with his or her educational philosophy. Whatever standards are used, students' grades should never be determined by other members of the class or team. (If a student is an "A" player on a losing team, should he or she get a D because the team ended up in last place?) Teachers' standards should be consistent from class to class and semester to semester. The performance required for a certain grade should be the same from class to class and teacher to teacher.

Types of Grades

Grades or marks are reported in numerous ways. Some of these ways have been discussed earlier and are grouped here with brief comments for comparison.

- *Actual scores received on tests* (e.g., a numeral such as 85, 55, or 70). This type of reporting is typically not recommended because there is no way to determine what the numerals mean. If literal terms of measurement are attached, this method is improved (e.g., 85 cm or 55 correct). This is still quite inadequate, however, because no indication is given regarding the quality of performance.

- *Percentages* (e.g., 65 percent, 90 percent, and so forth). Percentages are often used to grade written tests and represent the percentage of items the student completed correctly. This method of marking or grading has the distinct advantage that most people understand percentages. In most physical performance scores, however, percentages are not realistic. For example, when someone performs 12 chin-ups, it is not possible to convert this to a percentage.

- *Standard scores* (e.g., T scores, 6-σ, and percentile ranks). Standard scores are perhaps the most preferred marks to be used if we assume that a norm-referenced approach to grading is desired. If a criterion-referenced approach is desired, then standard scores are not appropriate. The preferred standard scores to use when reporting performance grades are percentile ranks because students and/or parents are more likely to understand them. One other definite advantage to using standard scores is that they do not involve measurement units; that is, a percentile rank of 70 means the same for any test whether it is a written exam, speed in a dash, or pounds lifted in a bench press.

- *Letter grades* (e.g., A, B, C, D, and F). Letter grades are probably the most common form used for reporting a qualitative judgment of student performance. Qualitative descriptors are generally given along with letter grade classifications of performance. Those frequently found are

A = Outstanding or Excellent;
B = Above Average or Good;
C = Average or Acceptable;
D = Below Average or Poor; and
F = Failing or Unsatisfactory.

A numerical standard is usually attached to each letter grade. The type of numerical standard used depends on whether the teacher chooses a criterion-referenced or norm-referenced standard. Examples of each are given in the next section. The main disadvantage of using letter grades is that the small number of grade categories used reduces information about the student's performance and may not be as exact or accurate as desired. To help overcome this problem, pluses (+) and minuses (−) are often attached to letter grades to provide further classifications of performance.

- *Dichotomies* (e.g., Pass/Fail, Satisfactory/ Unsatisfactory, Credit/No Credit). The same discussion about letter grades also applies to dichotomous grades. Dichotomous grading systems provide only two classifications of performance, which often is not as descriptive or accurate as desired. However, these dichotomous types of grades are well suited to a criterion-referenced grading system because the question may be whether a student has or has not mastered the material.

Grading Systems

Countless different grading systems are used by teachers. Only a few of the more common systems are presented here as examples, with brief discussions of the advantages and disadvantages of each. In each case it is assumed that the letter grades A, B, C, D, and F are to eventually be used in reporting grades to students and/or parents.

Gaps in Distribution Method

A distribution of test scores usually has gaps where no scores occur. Some teachers use these gaps to determine their students' grades. For example, in Table 12.1 two distributions of test scores were attained by two different classes of 30 students each. The teacher might likely assign grades as indicated. In Class A, there were clear gaps in the distribution, whereas in Class

Table 12.1 Distribution of Test Scores for Two Classes

Class A	Assigned grade	Class B	Assigned grade
95	A	88	A
95		88	
94		88	
93		87	
92		87	
85	B	85	B
84		85	
83		85	
82		84	
77	C	81	C
77		80	
77		79	
76		78	
76		77	
76		76	
74		76	
74		76	
68	D	75	D
67		75	
67		74	
66		73	
66		72	
		71	
		70	
52	F	69	F
51			
48			

B gaps were not as evident. As can be seen, the grading scale is considerably different for the two classes. This is the primary objection to this method of assigning grades; that is, there are *no* standards. Students' grades are totally dependent on the completely unreliable and invalid "gaps" that may happen to occur. Although this norm-referenced approach to grading is frequently used by some teachers, you are strongly urged to *avoid its use*. There appears to be no good rationale for this system except that it is easy to use.

Percentage Method

A frequently used scale for grades, particularly in colleges, is one that assigns a grade of A when students get 90% or more items correct on a test, B when they get 80 to 89%, C when they get 70 to 79%, D when they get 60 to 69%, and F if they get less than 60% correct. In high schools, the grading scale is often A for 95% or more correct, B for 88-94%, C for 78-87%, D for 70-77%, and F for below 69% correct. Of course, other percentages can also be used.

This method of assigning grades is clearly an example of a criterion-referenced approach to grading. In physical performance activities, the set percentages would refer to the percentage of tasks that a student has mastered, whereas on written tests the percentages refer to the percentage of items answered correctly.

If a teacher is committed to a criterion-referenced approach to grading, this method is satisfactory. However, the standards (percentages) set for each grade must be carefully considered because the difficulty of different tests or sets of tasks can greatly vary. For example, a 60% score on one test may actually represent a better performance than an 85% score on another test because the first test may be much more difficult than the second. This possibility is why norm-referenced advocates maintain that you should look at the average performance for the group and then determine your standards. Advocates of the criterion-referenced approach

argue that the percentage standards should be set after careful thought based on knowledge and experience instead of setting them because the standards are convenient or commonly used. Unfortunately, too many teachers utilize set percentages strictly out of tradition and/or convenience.

Point Accumulation Method

The point accumulation method, like the percentage method, is a criterion-referenced approach. Points are assigned to various tasks and/or tests in an instructional unit, and then standards for point totals are set. The following example is a grading scale used by a teacher of an American Red Cross Water Safety Instructor's Course. As you will observe this method is actually another form of the percentage method. Thus the comments on the percentage method also apply to the point accumulation method.

Task	Points	Grading scale	
Performance of		A	482-535
selected skills	90	B	428-481
Exam I	50	C	375-427
Exam II	50	D	321-374
Final exam	100		
Lesson Plan I	20		
Lesson Plan II	30		
Teaching I	40		
Teaching II	60		
Game	20		
Attendance and			
preparation	75		
Total possible			
points =	535		

Contract Grading

Another criterion-referenced approach to grading that has been successfully used by some physical education teachers is contract grading. In this system, the teacher and each student *agree* on exactly what the student must do to earn a particular grade. For example, on a fitness unit, a student and his teacher may agree that if the student can perform 10 chin-ups, do 40 sit-ups in a minute, run the mile in less than 6 minutes, read three professional articles on fitness, and write a four-page report on the benefits of physical activity, then he or she will receive an A. To receive a B, the student must be able to perform 8 chin-ups, do 30 sit-ups in a minute, run the mile in less than 7 minutes, and read three articles on fitness. The teacher and student also agree on standards for the other letter grades. The contract is then signed by both the teacher and student. A true contract system of grading means that the teacher must negotiate standards for grades with each student. Contract grading has been sharply and justifiably criticized because a student's grade will largely depend on how well he or she can negotiate. Furthermore, contract grading is terribly time-consuming, particularly in physical education settings where there is typically a very large number of students with whom the teacher would have to negotiate.

To alleviate some of these problems in the ''pure'' contract approach, some teachers have adopted a modified contract system whereby the same contract is negotiated with an entire class and then all students are held to the same standards. Another modified contract system sometimes found is where the teacher alone sets various standards for different students depending upon their capabilities. This system is at least a serious effort to individualize learning expectations with a criterion-referenced approach.

Normal Curve Method

A commonly used and sound norm-referenced approach to grading is the normal curve method. In this method, the normal distribution, which was extensively explained in chapter 2, provides the basis for assigning grades. Examples of two different grade distributions using the normal distribution are given in Table 12.2. In Example 1, the teacher has decided that over the long term, 7% of the students should earn As, 18%

Table 12.2 Grade Distributions Using the Normal Curve

Grade	z-score	T score	Percentile rank
Example 1			
7% A =	1.48 and above	64.8 and above	93 and above
18% B =	0.67 to 1.48	56.7 to 64.8	75 to 92
50% C =	−0.67 to 0.67	43.3 to 56.7	26 to 74
18% D =	−1.48 to −0.67	35.2 to 43.3	8 to 25
7% F =	−1.48 and below	35.2 and below	7 and below
Example 2			
10% A =	1.28 and above	62.8 and above	90 and above
30% B =	0.25 to 1.28	52.5 to 62.8	60 to 89
40% C =	−0.84 to 0.25	41.6 to 52.5	21 to 59
15% D =	−1.65 to −0.84	33.5 to 41.6	6 to 20
5% F =	−1.65 and below	33.5 and below	5 and below

should earn Bs, 50% should earn Cs, 18% should earn Ds, and 7% earn Fs. In Example 2, another teacher has decided to use different percentages. This method can be applied to classifications or subgroups of a class that were determined for grading purposes, as was suggested earlier in this chapter. However, caution must be used with this method. It should be rigidly applied only if standardized tests are used and only if the students' grades are based on their performance as compared to normative data compiled by the teacher or from local, state, or national norms. To apply the normal curve to each class independently excludes the possibility of having a class with an unusual number of high or low achievers. In other words, we are assuming that the abilities of the students in each class are normally distributed and are forcing the percentages of assigned grades. The normal curve method is excellent for applying a norm-referenced approach to grading if the cautions outlined are observed.

Regardless of the method used to determine a grade, the final decision is subjective. As stated earlier, you should allow reasonableness and good judgment to prevail and be sure that you have a sound justification for whatever grading system you employ.

Determining Grade Components

When grades are assigned at the end of a unit or grading period, a decision must be made concerning what factors should be considered in determining students' grades. A rather simple but compelling guideline is that the grade should reflect a summation of how well a student accomplished the objectives for that unit. Typically, various components of the unit will be weighted for grading purposes. For example, the following weighting was used in a lifetime sports class at a university:

50% attendance
20% final written exam
20% written homework assignments
10% skills test improvement

Obviously, the instructor believed that attendance was a very important objective for the course insofar as one half of the grade was based on it. This emphasis on attendance could be debated if the overall goal of the course is for the student to learn the skill. As we know, attendance alone does not ensure learning or mastery.

In elementary and secondary schools, a great deal of weight (sometimes as much as 50%) is frequently given to how appropriately students dress for activity. Such a practice should be questioned unless 50% of the importance of the course or 50% of the instruction deals with proper dress. These two examples are given to emphasize that each part of a grade must be weighted in terms of its importance to instructional objectives and the resultant time spent on it in instruction. Examples of how this is done are shown in Table 12.3.

In Example A, general objectives and their proportionate importance for a particular grading period are given. The grades earned by a student for each objective and the means for determining this student's composite grade are also given. Examples B and C give similar information.

In Example B, also notice that the final grade was determined by finding the weighted average of T scores. The procedure of averaging component T scores or percentage scores is preferred for accuracy purposes. When we average only letter grades, as we did in Example A, we are dealing with a scale that has only five discrete categories, which reduces accuracy because these discrete categories typically represent a range of possible scores (e.g., A = 58 and above, B = 50-58, etc.). Example C alleviates some of the problem of using grades by providing 15 categories. The advantage of using letter grade categories to indicate an average is

Table 12.3 Final Grade Determinations

Example A: Assume A = 5 points, B = 4 points, C = 3 points, D = 2 points, F = 1 point

Objective	Percentage of importance	Student grade	Points
Organic development	30%	B (4)	$0.3 \times 4 = 1.2$
Neuromuscular development	30%	A (5)	$0.3 \times 5 = 1.5$
Intellectual development	20%	D (2)	$0.2 \times 2 = 0.4$
Social-emotional development	20%	B (4)	$0.2 \times 4 = 0.8$
			Final grade = 3.9 = B

Example B: Assume A = T score 63 and above, B = 52-62, C = 47-51, D = 33-40, F = below 40

Factor	Weight	Student T score	Points
Skill achievement	3	58	$3 \times 58 = 174$
Fitness improvement	2	65	$2 \times 65 = 130$
Knowledge	1	50	$1 \times 50 = 50$
Attitude	1	48	$1 \times 48 = 48$
	7		Final grade = 402/7 = 57.4 = B

Example C: Assume we have the following grading scale:

Excellent	Good	Fair	Poor	Failing
A+ = 5.3	B+ = 4.3	C+ = 3.3	D+ = 2.3	F+ = 1.3
A = 5.0	B = 4.0	C = 3.0	D = 2.0	F = 1.0
A− = 4.7	B− = 3.7	C− = 2.7	D− = 1.7	F− = 0.7

Objective	Weighting	Grade	Points
Performance, skill	2	4.3	8.6
Knowledge of rules, etc.	1	2.7	2.7
Attitude (personal-social)	1	4.0	4.0
Posture and physique improvement	1	4.0	4.0
	5		19.3
			Final grade = 19.3/5 = 3.8
			= Good = B−

that they are more easily understood by students and their parents.

Reporting Grades

The means by which grades are reported to students and parents are critically important. A grade report typically carries only one composite grade. As was just illustrated, however, this grade is generally a composite of the scores or grades achieved for various instructional objectives or tests. Therefore, simply placing a composite letter grade on a report card is not sufficient, especially because many parents do not understand the nature of physical education and may not appreciate the progress their children have made. Thus it is suggested that a supplemental letter be sent to parents informing them of the grading system used in terms of your objectives and of the progress their children have made. An example of such a letter is presented in Figure 12.1. As the letter suggests, personal conferences between parents and the teacher should also be encouraged.

Cumulative Physical Education Records

In physical education we typically deal with students for only 1 to 4 years and have no knowledge about their prior performance. Nor do we typically pass information about students on to teachers who have the students after us. This need not be the case. A longitudinal account of each student's record of sport participation, specific strengths and weaknesses, and test scores in areas of physical fitness, skill, and knowledge should be maintained. These records can be of great assistance in helping students to achieve the objectives of physical education. Such records also allow programs for classes and individuals to be more soundly planned. One word of caution is necessary: Care must be taken not to categorize a student rigidly as "good" or "poor" and assume that he or she must stay in that category. The "halo" effect and its counterpart, the "devil" effect, must be guarded against.

Review Questions

1. What arguments are usually given for assigning grades in physical education courses?
2. What arguments are usually given for not assigning grades in physical education courses?
3. Why would we not grade on the final ability level of each student at the end of a grading period?
4. Why would we not grade on the improvement of each student during a grading period?
5. What methods and ideas are suggested in this chapter for assigning a grade for each student at the end of a grading period?
6. What is contract grading?

Wonder City High School
Department of Health and Physical Education

Dear Mr. and Mrs. _____:

This letter is to acquaint you with our new form for reporting your child's progress in physical education. The school report card will indicate a grade for physical education. Actually, this grade is a summary of progress in the four general goals of our physical education program. This letter will describe each of these areas and indicate how your child has progressed in each.

I. *Organic Development*
    This generally includes muscular strength, endurance, power, speed, and agility. (30% of the total grade is allotted here.)
    Partial grade _____

II. *Neuromuscular Skills*
    This area is concerned with developing a well-coordinated body that can perform complex motor skills such as throwing and catching, pivoting and shooting a basketball, and batting in baseball. Finally, these complex skills are put together into recreational game skills such as golf, tennis, swimming, basketball, baseball, etc. (30% of the total grade is allotted here.)
    Partial grade _____

III. *Interpretive and Intellectual Development*
    This area evaluates your child's knowledge of the rules of games, game strategy, and techniques and also his or her knowledge of the effects and benefits of physical activity to the individual. (20% of the total grade is allotted here.)
    Partial grade _____

IV. *Personal-Social Development*
    This area deals with the extent to which your child exhibits traits of good sportsmanship and leadership and the extent to which she or he cooperates with fellow students in their assigned class duties. Also included here is an appraisal of conforming to established class procedures, personal cleanliness, health habits, and knowledge and practice of safety habits in and around the gymnasium. (20% of the total grade is allotted here.)
    Partial grade _____
    Total grade _____

General Comments:

Sincerely yours,
John Doe
Physical Education Teacher

P.S. Please feel free to discuss your child's progress with me. Call and we can arrange an appointment.

Figure 12.1 Sample parents' letter indicating child's progress in physical education.

Problems and Exercises

1. A physical education teacher developed the following grading scale for a gymnastics unit:

Excellent	Good	Fair	Poor	Failing
A+ =10.0	B+ =8.0	C+ =6.0	D+ =4.0	F+ =2.0
A = 9.5	B =7.5	C =5.5	D =3.5	F =1.5
A− = 9.0	B− =7.0	C− =5.0	D− =3.0	F− =1.0

Objective	Weighting
Performance-skill	4
Knowledge of rules	2
Attitude (personal-social)	1

A student was assigned a subjective grade on performance-skill of 7.5. On a test on knowledge of rules, the student attained a grade of 4.0. The teacher subjectively graded the student's attitude at 9.0. What would be the student's final grade for the gymnastics unit?

Answer: B−

2. An elementary school physical education teacher developed the following grading procedure for determining a final grade for the year: A = 5 points, B = 4, C = 3, D = 2, and F = 1 point. The teacher also decided to test and measure organic development with a grading weight of 40% importance; neuromuscular development, 40% of grade; intellectual development, 10% of grade; and social-emotional development, 10% of grade. The teacher applied standardized tests in each of these areas at the beginning, middle, and end of the year. The teacher also decided to assign a grade of A to any test score that was 1.28 standard z-scores above the normal, B to any score between .25 to 1.28 standard z-scores, C to any score between −.84 to .25 standard z-scores, D to any score between −1.65 to −.84 standard z-scores, and F to any score below −1.65 standard z-scores. The teacher decided to average the z-scores of each student in each area to get a final grade. One of the students secured the following average standard z-score in each area:

Objective area	Average z-score
Organic development	−0.19
Neuromuscular development	0.56
Intellectual development	0.23
Social-emotional development	0.04

What is the student's final grade for the year?

3. A physical education teacher gave a national standardized written test on the basic concepts of physical education. The standardized test had a mean of 40 and a standard deviation of 5. The teacher decided on the following scale for determining grades:

T score	Grade
62.8 and above	A
52.5 to 62.8	B
41.6 to 52.5	C
33.5 to 41.6	D
Below 33.5	F

The teacher applied the test to 20 students with the following results:

Student	Score	Student	Score
S1	48	S11	31
S2	43	S12	35
S3	47	S13	38
S4	45	S14	41
S5	45	S15	37
S6	48	S16	39
S7	45	S17	43
S8	40	S18	40
S9	41	S19	30
S10	33	S20	49

(Cont.)

What grade was assigned to each student?

Answer: A: S1, S3, S6, S7, and S20
       B: S2, S4, S5, and S17
       C: S8, S9, S12, S13, S14, S15, S16, and S18
       D: S10 and S11
       F: S19

4. A physical education teacher gave a local standardized test on archery. The test mean was 110 with a standard deviation of 6. The teacher decided on the following scale for determining grades:

z-score	Grade
1.48 and above	A
0.67 to 1.48	B
−0.67 to 0.67	C
−1.48 to −0.67	D
Below −1.48	F

The teacher applied the test to 20 students with the following results:

Student	Score	Student	Score
S1	100	S11	114
S2	95	S12	111
S3	100	S13	112
S4	102	S14	109
S5	103	S15	106
S6	118	S16	106
S7	117	S17	105
S8	115	S18	103
S9	114	S19	110
S10	112	S20	102

What grade was assigned to each student?

Bibliography

Barrow, H.M., & McGee, R. (1979). *A practical approach to measurement in physical education* (3rd ed.). Philadelphia: Lea & Febiger.

Baumgartner, T.A., & Jackson, A.S. (1982). *Measurement for evaluation in physical education* (2nd ed.). Dubuque, IA: William C. Brown.

Bloom, B.S., Englehart, M.D., Furst, E.J., Hill, W.H., & Krathwohl, D.R. (Eds.). (1956). *A taxonomy of educational objectives: Handbook I, the cognitive domain*. New York: David McKay.

Bloom, B.S., Hastings, J.T., & Madaus, G.F. (1971). *Handbook on formative and summative evaluation of student learning*. New York: McGraw-Hill.

Hanson, D.L. (1967). Grading in physical education. *Journal of Health, Physical Education, and Recreation*, **38**, 37.

Johnson, B.L., & Nelson, J.K. (1979). *Practical measurements for evaluation in physical education* (3rd ed.). Minneapolis: Burgess.

Karmel, L.J. (1970). *Measurement and evaluation in the schools*. London: Macmillan.

Larson, L.A., & Yocom, R.D. (1951). *Measurement and evaluation in physical, health, and recreation education*. St. Louis: C.V. Mosby.

Mathews, D.K. (1978). *Measurement in physical education* (5th ed.). Philadelphia: W.B. Saunders.

Remmers, H.H., Gage, N.L., & Rummel, J.F. (1965). *A practical introduction to measurement and evaluation* (2nd ed.). New York: Harper & Row.

Safrit, M.J. (1977). Criterion-referenced measurement: Applications in physical education. *Motor Skills: Theory into Practice*, **2**, 21-35.

Safrit, M.J. (1981). *Evaluation in physical education* (2nd ed.). Englewood Cliffs, NJ: Prentice-Hall.

Singer, R. (1967). Grading in physical education. *Journal of Health, Physical Education, and Recreation*, **38**, 38-39.

Solley, W.H. (1967). Grading in physical education. *Journal of Health, Physical Education, and Recreation*, **38**, 35-36.

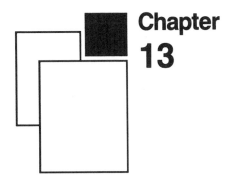

Chapter
13

Evaluation
of Special Populations

A hierarchy of motor development testing for special populations is presented in this chapter. This hierarchy suggests a nonclassification approach to testing special populations. The hierarchical approach is presented to assist physical educators in the process of deciding what to test and what tests are good indicators of the components to be measured. Tests are presented for each level of motor development. The tests presented by no means include all the tests that may be used to test the components presented. Supplemental tests are referenced, and suggested readings are listed at the end of the chapter for readers who desire additional information.

Although the terms *impaired*, *disabled*, and *handicapped* are often used interchangeably, each of these terms has a specific and different meaning. Some individuals with impairments that result in specific disabilities do not consider themselves to be handicapped. The American Association for Health, Physical Education, and Recreation (AAHPER) established the following definitions of these terms in 1973:

- *Impaired* refers to individuals who have identifiable organic or functional conditions; that is, some part of the person's body or portion of an anatomical structure is actu-

ally missing, or one or more parts of the body do not function properly or adequately.
- *Disabled* refers to individuals with impairments that limit or restrict their ability to perform certain skills, jobs, tasks, or activities.
- *Handicapped* refers to individuals with impairments or disabilities that adversely affect their psychological, emotional, or social functioning level.

Instructors who work with impaired, disabled, and/or handicapped individuals must understand and utilize these terms in their correct meanings. In fact, proper understanding and usage of these terms can result in fewer individuals being designated as ''handicapped'' and can help to minimize the limitations posed by certain of their disabilities. Conversely, misunderstanding and misuse of these terms can result in overemphasizing individuals' disabilities and can cause individuals who may be able to overcome their disabilities to be unduly classified as ''handicapped.'' Practitioners' misunderstanding or misuse of these terms can thus impede the ability of individuals with special needs to achieve their full potential level of development.

As an example, suppose that an individual whose lower left arm has been amputated at the elbow enrolls in an advanced handball course. According to our definition, this person is impaired because a part of the body is actually missing. A disability resulting from this impairment would be the individual's being unable to execute a left-hand return shot simply because he has no left hand. The instructor accordingly informs this individual that handball might not be his sport. By attempting to dissuade the individual from enrolling in the course, however, the instructor is unduly handicapping the individual. To prove his point, the instructor suggests that they play a game of handball to see if the individual is suited for the course. To assist the impaired individual in the game, the instructor decides to return and serve the ball to the right-hand side. The instructor quickly realizes that this strategy is losing the game, so he starts serving and returning the ball to the back left corner. Much to the instructor's surprise, the participant rotates counterclockwise, runs quickly to the back left corner, and returns each shot with a backhand movement of the right hand. The instructor loses the game.

It just so happens that this impaired individual is a nationally ranked handball player and was also an all-state player in baseball and basketball. This athlete has an impairment and resulting disabilities but does not consider himself to be handicapped. The instructor never won a single game of handball against this "impaired" individual. Instructors who work with impaired, disabled, and/or handicapped individuals should stress what they *can* do, not what they cannot do.

Nonclassification in Special Population Testing

Instructors can determine the strengths and weaknesses of an impaired, disabled, and/or handicapped individual through motor development testing. In the measurement and evaluation process, what is important is not to classify a participant as "neurologically impaired," "sensory impaired," "mentally retarded," or "learning disabled," but rather to determine the participant's *present physical functioning level*. This noncategorical approach will assist an instructor in program development and in the decision-making process of screening individuals for placement in the least restrictive physical functioning environment. A *least restrictive environment* is an environment that affords maximum physical functioning, participation, and development for an individual while at the same time accommodating the individual's particular impairments, disabilities, and/or handicaps. The least restrictive environment thus provides each individual with the greatest possibility for success rather than failure in physical activity and development programs.

Public Law 94-142 (U.S. 94th Congress, 1975) established guidelines for providing direct services to special populations, including classroom instruction, physical education, home instruction, and instruction in hospitals and institutions. What do these guidelines mean for physical educators in a school setting? First, impaired individuals must be tested for levels of physical functioning, and test results must be recorded. If the individual is performing below expectations for his or her age level, a least restrictive environment must be chosen and an individualized physical activity program must be prepared. The evaluation of test results assists in determining goals and behavioral objectives for each individual. These goals and behavioral objectives in turn facilitate the direction, development, and recording of an individualized physical activity program.

Periodic retesting and comparing retest results with established goals and behavioral objectives provide accountability for the program and input and directions for future goals, objectives, and programming. Evaluation of the test results allows for screening each individual into the least restrictive physical functioning environment. The test results may indicate that an impaired individual should be placed in (a) a regular physical education class with no modification, (b) a regular physical education class with modifications or a teaching aid to assist, (c) an adapted physical education class where identified goals and objectives can be accomplished in a closed environment in small groups, or (d) referral of the individual to support services such as physical therapy or occupational therapy.

Knowledgeable instructors working with impaired individuals will approach the problem of screening, setting goals and behavioral objectives, and program development with a definite, coherent decision-making process. They will first try to determine each participant's present motor development level. This requires decisions to be made about what to test and what tests to employ. The following is a hierarchy of the components of motor development testing previously presented in Figure 6.1, chapter 6. Here the hierarchy is presented in reverse order:

Basic Functioning Level (Basic motor development)
- Reflex testing
- Sensory input and motor response testing

Intermediate Functioning Level (Physical fitness)
- Muscular strength testing
- Muscular endurance testing
- Cardiovascular endurance testing
- Power testing
- Flexibility testing

High Functioning Level (Advanced motor development)
- Speed testing
- Coordination testing
- Agility testing

The knowledgeable physical educator may use this hierarchical approach to

- determine each participant's present physical functioning level through testing and evaluating;
- use the information gathered to establish the least restrictive environment and appropriate priorities, long-range goals, and short-term objectives for a program;
- choose and apply physical activities that can be expected to approach the long-range goals and achieve the short-term objectives; and
- periodically retest and evaluate the effects of the applied program.

The interplay between levels and components of motor development is delicately balanced. This hierarchical approach helps the instructor to make decisions about what to test and what tests are good indicators of the components to be measured. The hierarchy presented is for guidance purposes only and may be changed to meet the instructor's specific purposes and needs. Keep in mind that nothing can take the place of your professional judgment in evaluation. The hierarchy is presented to assist you in your decision-making processes.

Basic Motor Development Testing

The components of testing basic motor development include reflex testing and sensory motor testing.

Reflex Testing

Reflex testing and evaluation are not the responsibility of adapted physical educators, recreational therapists, or instructors who conduct physical activity programs for the impaired.

Responsibility for reflex testing is usually assigned to a physical or occupational therapist. However, any individual who conducts a physical activity program for the impaired should be aware of a few important reflexes and the influence that each may have on motor performance. A reflex that is developmentally delayed, does not integrate, and/or inhibits motor response may be considered an impairment. The instructor must understand that a reflex impairment will limit or restrict a participant in performing certain motor skills or physical activities. A lack of understanding of reflex responses could cause an instructor to overemphasize physical disabilities brought about by the reflex impairment and overestimate the severity of an individual's handicapping conditions. The following are a few examples of reflexes that will influence motor performance if impairment is present.

Tonic Labyrinthine Reflex (TLR). When the whole body is in the prone position, there is increased trunk flexion; when in the supine position, there is increased trunk extension. This reflex should appear in the first 4 weeks after birth and should be inhibited by the age of 4 months. Any lack of inhibition of this brain stem reflex will interfere with forward or backward rolls, swimming prone or supine, sitting upright in a chair, and attaining an upright position (Fiorentino, 1972).

Asymmetrical Tonic Neck Reflex (ATNR). When the head is rotated to the right, the right arm and leg extend while the left arm and leg flex. When the head is rotated to the left, the left arm and leg extend while the right arm and leg flex. This reflex should appear in the first 4 weeks after birth and should be inhibited by the 7th month. Any lack of inhibition of this brain stem reflex will interfere with agility turns right or left, most catching and throwing activities, and proper breathing in the crawl stroke in swimming (Fiorentino, 1972).

Grasp Reflex. When an object is placed in the hand, an automatic grasping of the object occurs. This reflex should appear in the first 4 weeks after birth and should be fully integrated by 6 months of age. Any lack of integration of this spinal reflex will affect voluntary release of the grasp. Difficulty in executing the grasp-then-release response is present in many individuals who have cerebral palsy. Impairment of this reflex will interfere with throwing and catching activities and any physical activity that requires manual manipulation of an object (Banus, Kent, Norton, Sukiennicki, & Beckel, 1979).

Equilibrium Reflexes. Equilibrium reflexes allow for segmental rotation in turning the head, then the trunk and shoulders, and then the pelvic region. The head can turn without the whole body turning in the same direction. These reflexes allow the head to be righted when the whole body or trunk moves toward an off-postural alignment. This reflex should appear at about 6 months of age and continue throughout life. Any developmental delay in this midbrain reflex will interfere with neuromuscular responses to gravity, body movement, and any airborne activities (Fiorentino, 1972).

Protective Extension Reflex. When the sensation of falling occurs, both arms extend for protection. This reflex should appear around 6 months of age and continue throughout life. Any developmental delay in this reflex will interfere with breaking a fall and performing many gymnastic skills (Fiorentino, 1972).

Cortical Equilibrium Reflex. When in a quadrupedal, sitting, or kneeling position, balance is lost, the head will attempt to right itself, and the limbs on the side opposite from the fall will abduct and extend while the limbs on the side of the fall will protect the body. When in a standing position, balance is lost and hopping or shuffling with the feet will occur to regain balance. These reflexes should appear at about 8 to 15 months of age and continue throughout life. Any developmental delay in this cortical reflex will interfere with agility activities and balance activities (Fiorentino, 1972).

It must be stressed that these examples of reflexes do not cover the complete field of reflex testing and represent only a small sample of the field of reflex testing. Other sources of information about reflex testing are presented in the selected references and bibliography at the end of the chapter. We should emphasize again that the physical educator will probably not actually conduct reflex testing, but he or she should be aware of the selected reflexes described in this section because impairments in any of these reflexes can influence motor performance.

Sensory Motor Testing

The sense organs are designed to transduce force, energy, pressure, and so forth into undistorted neural impulses called *afferents*. These impulses then travel via the central nervous system to the brain-mind complex. The brain-mind complex transforms these impulses into sensations and initiates its own neural impulses, called *efferents*, to various muscle groups. The various muscle groups respond to produce force, energy, and pressure, which again travel through the sense organs. This is not simply a loop process but rather a spiral process with constant adjustments being made throughout life. The sensory, brain-mind complex (perceptual), and motor response systems interact to secure knowledge for human beings about their interaction with the environment.

One of the difficult problems in sensory-motor testing is determining the cause of a distorted message. If a sense organ has a malfunction, a distorted afferent impulse is produced. For example, the major function of the eye is to change visual electromagnetic energy (i.e., light) into undistorted neural impulses that carry coded images of our environment. These coded impulses are sent to the brain-mind com-

plex, which transforms these impulses into sensation. The brain-mind complex then initiates efferent neural impulses to the various muscle groups for responses to the perceived environmental situation. If an individual has any visual impairment, such as refractive errors or structural anomalies of the eye, then a distorted coded impulse is sent to a perfectly functional brain-mind complex, which interprets these distorted impulses and then initiates efferent impulses that usually produce distorted motor performance, thus indicating an impairment. If an individual has a malfunction in the brain-mind complex, the same results would occur. Regardless of the origin of the impairment, an instructor who works with impaired individuals must be aware of the various motor responses that may occur when testing in the sensory-motor area. This awareness will allow the instructor to refer an impaired individual to a specialist for appropriate therapy. If and when an impairment has been appropriately diagnosed, this awareness will enable the instructor to adapt a physical activity program to meet the special needs of each participant.

The components that are usually tested in the sensory-motor area include the following:

Tactile Discrimination. Tactile discrimination involves the sense of touch, pressure, and temperature. Tests involve identifying various surfaces, textures, object shapes, pressures, locations of pressure, sensations of pain, sensations of various temperatures, differentiations of two or more simultaneously applied stimuli, and tactile fusion frequencies.

Kinesthetic Discrimination. Kinesthetic discrimination involves the sense of muscle force, tendon stretching, and joint position. Tests involve describing limb position, muscular and limb adjustment to balance situations, and various force and weight discrimination tasks.

Auditory Discrimination. Auditory discrimination involves the sense of hearing. Formal tests are performed by a licensed otolaryngologist (medical doctor) or speech and hearing therapist. Tests involve discriminating frequencies (pitch), intensities (decibel measure), and sound direction. Informal tests involve, without the aid of vision, facing and tracking a sound source and, with vision, keeping time to a cadence or rhythmic beat. Observation of an apparent hearing problem is also an informal test for discriminating sound intensity.

Visual Discrimination. Visual discrimination involves the sense of vision. Formal tests are performed by a licensed ophthalmologist (medical doctor) or an optometrist (an individual that performs eye examinations only). Tests involve focusing, accommodation, and refraction. Informal testing involves fixation, release, ocular alignment, convergence, divergence, and visual tracking. Observation of an apparent visual problem is also an informal test of vision.

Balance. Balance involves interaction of the sensations of tactile, kinesthetic, and visual discrimination along with the vestibular system.

The vestibular system, which is located in the inner ear, is designed to detect linear and angular changes in motion. It is connected to oculomotor control by introducing angular acceleration and eliciting a gyronystagmus (eye flick) response. Tests involve static balance responses in quadruped, sitting, kneeling, and standing positions with and without the aid of vision. Tests also involve dynamic balance responses to movement, such as walking a balance beam, hopping, and jumping-landing activities. There are four basic conditions in testing balance: static medium/static individual (e.g., stork stand), static medium/dynamic individual (e.g., walking a balance beam), dynamic medium/static individual (e.g., standing on a tiltboard), and dynamic medium/dynamic individual (e.g., jumping on a trampoline) (Figure 13.1).

Body Awareness. Body awareness involves the sensations of tactile, kinesthetic, auditory, and visual discrimination. *Body part awareness* tests involve knowing the names of various body parts and where they are located (Figure 13.2). *Body side awareness* (laterality) tests involve

Figure 13.1 Balance—static medium—static individual student attempting to extend right leg and left arm.

knowing the right and left body parts. Tests may also include knowing the top, bottom, front, and back of body segments. *Space awareness* (directionality) tests involve knowing the right, left, front, back, top, and bottom of objects in space (Figures 13.3A and 13.3B). *Tempo awareness* tests involve measuring the ability to move the body and body segments in rhythm to various beats.

Gross and Fine Motor Control. Gross and fine motor control involve the sensations of tactile, kinesthetic, auditory, and visual discrimination in various motor control situations. Tests of fine motor control involve manual dexterity skills and ocular motor control. Tests of gross motor control involve moving various segments of the body using large muscle groups.

Reflex and sensory-motor testing assist an instructor in evaluating the motor development

Figure 13.2 Body segment and body part awareness—student touching left ear.

Figure 13.3 Space awareness—student touching head of self, then other.

level of an individual at the basic motor level. A listing of sensory-motor tests, the components measured by each test, and an address for correspondence and additional information is provided at the end of this chapter. In the next section we move to an intermediate level of motor development—physical fitness testing.

Physical Fitness Testing

The degree of an impairment and the resulting disabilities along with the age of an individual will assist an instructor in determining what test or tests are most appropriate for evaluating the individual's physical fitness.

Components of Physical Fitness

As discussed earlier, the components of physical fitness are muscular strength, muscular endurance, cardiorespiratory endurance, power, and flexibility. The strength component is the primary essential element for human movement; without strength, no movement can be made. An individual might be diagnosed as lacking balance skill, for example, but the lack of balance skill might be due to a lack of strength. Inadequate strength can restrict performance of many physical activities.

The endurance component is also essential for human movement; without endurance, the individual's capacity for sustained movement progressively decreases. There are two basic types of endurance: muscular endurance, which involves sustained strength activities, and cardiorespiratory endurance, which involves heart rate and breathing efficiency before, during, and after sustained movement. The person who fatigues easily when performing sustained physical movement lacks endurance.

The power component involves force (weight), distance, and time. The product of a force times the distance through which the force moves divided by the time expended in doing the physical act equals power. An individual that can move a greater weight through a given vertical distance in less time has more power than an individual who moves less weight through the same distance in more time. Power is essential for performing many physical activities and is useful in securing and maintaining a source of livelihood. The flexibility component involves the individual's ability to move the segments of the body through a desirable range of motion. The lack of flexibility adversely affects an individual's ability to perform physically and puts undesirable strain on muscles, ligaments, and tendons of the body when performing physical activities.

Selected Norm Tables

Many of the tests presented elsewhere in this text may be used in testing and subsequent evaluation of the strength, endurance, power, and flexibility of impaired individuals. When testing impaired individuals, keep in mind that the norms, where presented, are for "normal" individuals. These norms may be a useful guide in establishing the least restrictive environment for impaired participants. After all, one would not want to place an impaired participant who scores in the lower percentile on most of the tests in a mainstream situation.

In this section, norm tables for children 6 to 9 years of age are provided through the courtesy of the Adapted Physical Education Section of the Department of Physical Education, Dance, and Leisure Studies at Kansas State University for six physical fitness test items: standing long jump, bent-knee sit-ups, hamstring stretch, flexed-arm hang, 400-yard run-walk, and stair running. These tables are presented for within-group comparison standards for children already classified as normal (Nor), learning disabled (LD), mildly retarded (educable retarded, or ER), and moderately retarded (trainable retarded, or TR). These norm tables should not be used for classification or diagnosis but only as motivational standards for previously classified individuals. They may be useful in determining a least restrictive physical activity environment for impaired individuals, especially when compared to "normal" norms.

Comparing the test results of a participant or a group of participants to the following norms will allow a physical educator to determine the strengths and weaknesses of each participant, establish more realistic and individualized long-range goals and short-term behavioral objectives, and develop a program of physical activities to meet established objectives and goals.

Standing Long Jump. Specific directions for this test are given in chapter 7. Briefly, the participant stands with the feet several inches apart and toes just behind the take-off line. Before jumping, the participant swings the arms backwards and bends the knees then jumps as far forward as possible by extending the knees and swinging the arms forward. Three trials are allowed and the longest jump from take-off line to the nearest heel (or other body part touching the floor) is recorded in feet and inches. Examine Tables 13.1 to 13.4 for norms.

Bent-Knee Sit-Ups. Specific directions for this test are given in chapter 7. Briefly, the participant lies on the back with the knees bent at less than 90°, clasps his fingers behind the neck, and using the abdominal muscles, curls up to touch the elbows to the knees while a partner holds the feet to the surface. The number of completed sit-ups in 60 seconds is recorded. Examine Tables 13.5 to 13.8 for norms.

Table 13.1 Norms for Standing Long Jump (Measured to Nearest Inch) for 6-Year-Old Males (M) and Females (F)

Percentile	Normal		LD		ER		TR	
	M	F	M	F	M	F	M	F
100	63	57	59	57	55	53	30	26
90	59	53	55	50	49	47	25	23
80	54	48	53	47	46	45	18	19
70	51	46	50	45	44	42	16	17
60	47	43	47	43	40	39	14	15
50	42	41	45	39	38	37	12	12
40	38	38	37	35	35	33	9	9
30	35	33	34	31	30	28	6	5
20	30	29	30	28	26	25	4	3
10	25	25	23	23	23	22	1	2
0	21	19	20	17	19	18	0	0
N	78	70	61	58	61	52	68	57

Table 13.2 Norms for Standing Long Jump (Measured to Nearest Inch) for 7-Year-Old Males (M) and Females (F)

Percentile	Normal		LD		ER		TR	
	M	F	M	F	M	F	M	F
100	67	66	64	61	56	54	39	32
90	61	61	62	59	50	46	30	26
80	59	59	60	56	48	45	20	20
70	54	56	54	51	45	43	16	15
60	49	50	49	49	41	40	15	13
50	43	43	44	46	39	38	14	12
40	36	37	41	41	35	34	8	8
30	34	34	37	36	29	29	6	4
20	29	28	29	31	26	25	4	2
10	27	27	24	26	24	23	2	2
0	22	23	19	21	21	19	0	0
N	73	73	78	56	61	52	68	58

Table 13.3 Norms for Standing Long Jump (Measured to Nearest Inch) for 8-Year-Old Males (M) and Females (F)

Percentile	Normal		LD		ER		TR	
	M	F	M	F	M	F	M	F
100	69	71	66	64	62	57	40	39
90	64	63	63	60	56	53	32	30
80	60	59	61	58	53	51	25	24
70	56	57	56	53	50	48	21	20
60	54	54	52	51	45	42	17	16
50	46	43	44	46	41	40	18	14
40	43	42	40	42	35	35	15	12
30	38	39	37	36	30	30	13	11
20	36	35	34	34	27	29	9	8
10	34	30	28	26	25	25	5	6
0	24	26	22	20	22	21	2	2
N	83	88	82	61	61	52	68	58

Table 13.4 Norms for Standing Long Jump (Measured to Nearest Inch) for 9-Year-Old Males (M) and Females (F)

Percentile	Normal		LD		ER		TR	
	M	F	M	F	M	F	M	F
100	73	72	69	66	66	66	51	49
90	86	64	66	64	60	59	43	39
80	65	62	63	62	58	57	38	37
70	62	60	59	57	54	53	35	32
60	57	57	55	51	50	48	31	26
50	52	50	51	45	45	44	29	22
40	47	47	45	40	37	37	20	19
30	43	42	39	35	33	34	17	14
20	39	38	36	33	28	29	12	10
10	37	36	33	29	26	26	6	5
0	33	31	27	24	23	23	3	2
N	76	76	105	51	61	52	68	58

Table 13.5 Norms for Bent-Knee Sit-Ups (Number Correctly Done) for 6-Year-Old Males (M) and Females (F)

Percentile	Normal		LD		ER		TR	
	M	F	M	F	M	F	M	F
100	47	35	46	34	44	39	20	16
90	42	32	42	30	39	36	16	15
80	34	29	38	24	32	29	14	14
70	32	27	34	22	30	28	11	10
60	29	25	32	20	27	25	9	9
50	21	21	22	14	20	19	5	4
40	19	19	19	12	19	16	4	3
30	15	18	17	10	17	14	3	3
20	8	14	8	4	10	8	1	0
10	5	6	4	2	4	3	0	0
0	2	2	2	1	2	2	0	0
N	78	70	61	58	61	52	68	58

Table 13.6   Norms for Bent-Knee Sit-Ups (Number Correctly Done) for 7-Year-Old Males (M) and Females (F)

Percentile	Normal		LD		ER		TR	
	M	F	M	F	M	F	M	F
100	51	44	42	22	47	40	22	18
90	48	41	36	19	44	38	19	17
80	43	39	28	17	39	34	17	16
70	40	36	26	15	36	32	14	14
60	37	34	23	13	32	29	11	10
50	27	26	14	7	22	20	7	5
40	25	24	12	6	20	19	6	4
30	22	21	9	5	18	16	5	3
20	12	14	5	2	14	11	4	1
10	9	9	3	1	8	6	0	0
0	3	5	1	0	4	1	0	0
N	73	73	78	56	61	52	68	58

Table 13.7   Norms for Bent-Knee Sit-Ups (Number Correctly Done) for 8-Year-Old Males (M) and Females (F)

Percentile	Normal		LD		ER		TR	
	M	F	M	F	M	F	M	F
100	55	45	44	39	48	44	24	20
90	50	43	40	33	45	38	20	17
80	47	39	36	27	40	30	19	16
70	45	36	33	25	37	29	17	15
60	42	34	28	22	33	26	16	14
50	31	24	14	13	22	20	11	10
40	29	22	12	12	20	18	9	8
30	27	19	11	10	17	16	7	7
20	19	12	4	3	11	8	4	3
10	10	7	2	1	8	5	3	3
0	6	3	1	0	4	2	1	1
N	83	88	82	61	61	52	68	58

Table 13.8 Norms for Bent-Knee Sit-Ups (Number Correctly Done) for 9-Year-Old Males (M) and Females (F)

Percentile	Normal		LD		ER		TR	
	M	F	M	F	M	F	M	F
100	61	59	49	39	47	44	30	25
90	58	55	45	36	44	40	27	23
80	52	50	43	31	40	36	25	22
70	49	46	40	28	37	34	23	20
60	45	43	36	25	34	31	19	16
50	34	33	25	15	23	22	12	10
40	32	30	23	14	21	20	11	8
30	29	26	20	12	19	18	10	6
20	23	20	12	7	14	12	9	5
10	15	12	8	4	9	6	7	4
0	8	5	5	2	5	3	2	1
N	76	76	105	51	61	52	68	58

Hamstring Stretch. The hamstring stretch is an indicator of the flexibility of the back and hamstring muscles. The participant sits on the floor with the legs fully extended and the heels approximately 6 inches apart. A yardstick is placed between the participant's legs with the 20-inch mark even with his or her heels. Keeping the knees straight, the participant bends forward and reaches down the yardstick as far as possible without bouncing. Three attempts are allowed. Record the farthest point reached by the participant's fingers. Measure to the nearest .10 inch. The fingers of both hands must be held together. No turning of the shoulder or trunk is allowed to get one hand further down the yardstick. Examine Tables 13.9 to 13.12 for norms.

Flexed-Arm Hang. Specific directions for this test are given in chapter 7. Briefly, the participant grasps a horizontal bar using an overhand grip to raise the body off the floor to a position where the chin is above the bar and elbows are flexed. The participant holds this position as long as possible; the recorded score is the length of time in seconds that the participant maintains the proper hanging position. Examine Tables 13.13 to 13.16 for norms.

400-Yard Run-Walk. The 400-yard run-walk is an indicator of cardiorespiratory endurance. A track, paved area, or football field may be used and should be marked for 400 yards. A stopwatch should be used for the timing element. Each participant runs or walks or uses a combination of running, walking, and resting to complete the 400 yards as quickly as possible. Keep in mind that walking and resting are permitted but should be minimized because the idea is to complete the distance in the shortest possible time. Record the time in minutes and seconds to the nearest second. Examine Tables 13.17 to 13.20 for norms.

Table 13.9 Norms for Hamstring Stretch (Measured to Nearest .10 Inch) for 6-Year-Old Males (M) and Females (F)

Percentile	Normal		LD		ER		TR	
	M	F	M	F	M	F	M	F
100	26.5	27.8	27.4	27.5	28.5	28.5	28.8	28.3
90	24.7	26.2	25.7	26.5	27.3	27.5	27.5	27.0
80	23.2	24.3	24.5	25.3	26.0	26.3	26.0	26.0
70	21.5	23.0	23.0	24.1	24.9	25.3	24.7	24.5
60	21.0	22.2	22.3	22.5	23.5	24.1	23.5	23.3
50	20.5	21.4	21.4	21.6	22.3	22.3	22.5	22.8
40	19.0	20.6	19.7	20.0	21.0	21.0	21.3	21.3
30	17.3	19.0	18.0	18.4	19.5	19.7	19.7	20.0
20	15.7	17.2	16.0	16.7	18.2	18.6	18.5	18.3
10	14.3	15.6	14.5	15.0	16.5	17.3	16.9	16.8
0	13.0	13.4	13.0	13.5	15.3	15.8	15.5	15.3
N	76	71	63	59	60	56	60	57

Table 13.10 Norms for Hamstring Stretch (Measured to Nearest .10 Inch) for 7-Year-Old Males (M) and Females (F)

Percentile	Normal		LD		ER		TR	
	M	F	M	F	M	F	M	F
100	26.8	27.1	29.0	28.1	28.7	27.9	30.5	27.0
90	25.5	25.9	27.0	26.4	27.4	26.5	28.5	25.8
80	24.1	24.9	25.1	24.7	25.5	25.3	26.6	24.6
70	22.9	23.5	23.4	23.1	24.2	23.5	24.8	23.4
60	21.4	22.0	21.5	21.4	22.4	22.1	22.9	22.5
50	20.1	21.1	19.7	19.7	20.8	20.6	21.0	21.0
40	18.6	19.6	18.6	18.4	19.4	19.4	19.5	19.5
30	17.1	18.0	17.1	17.2	18.3	18.2	17.9	18.0
20	15.5	16.4	15.8	16.0	16.7	16.7	16.4	16.5
10	13.8	15.0	14.5	14.7	15.6	15.4	14.6	15.2
0	12.5	13.5	13.2	13.4	14.0	14.1	13.0	13.5
N	72	73	78	58	60	52	66	59

Table 13.11 Norms for Hamstring Stretch (Measured to Nearest .10 Inch) for 8-Year-Old Males (M) and Females (F)

Percentile	Normal		LD		ER		TR	
	M	F	M	F	M	F	M	F
100	26.5	28.8	29.5	28.8	27.0	29.0	27.5	28.5
90	25.7	27.6	27.9	27.8	25.9	27.5	26.2	27.0
80	24.9	26.4	26.6	27.0	24.5	26.0	25.0	25.8
70	24.0	25.1	24.7	26.3	23.7	24.8	23.7	24.3
60	23.1	23.6	23.3	25.2	22.5	23.4	22.3	22.9
50	22.3	22.6	21.5	24.3	21.5	22.0	21.0	21.5
40	20.3	20.5	19.9	22.2	19.9	20.5	19.3	20.1
30	18.3	18.5	18.5	20.0	18.1	18.6	17.7	18.7
20	16.4	16.5	16.7	18.0	16.5	16.9	15.7	17.5
10	14.0	14.4	15.2	15.9	14.7	15.0	14.2	15.9
0	12.2	12.3	13.5	13.8	13.0	13.5	12.5	14.5
N	82	86	80	60	61	53	67	57

Table 13.12 Norms for Hamstring Stretch (Measured to Nearest .10 Inch) for 9-Year-Old Males (M) and Females (F)

Percentile	Normal		LD		ER		TR	
	M	F	M	F	M	F	M	F
100	26.7	28.0	27.0	28.0	28.0	28.5	29.6	28.2
90	25.9	26.9	26.2	26.4	26.5	27.0	28.0	26.9
80	25.0	25.6	25.2	25.0	25.2	25.3	26.5	25.7
70	24.2	24.4	24.3	23.5	23.5	23.9	24.6	24.2
60	23.6	23.3	23.4	22.1	22.3	22.3	22.9	22.8
50	22.8	22.1	22.5	20.6	20.5	20.8	21.2	21.5
40	20.5	20.2	20.7	19.4	19.0	19.2	19.4	20.4
30	18.4	18.1	18.9	17.8	17.9	18.1	17.8	19.1
20	16.3	16.3	17.0	16.5	16.7	16.7	16.0	17.8
10	14.1	14.4	15.3	15.0	15.3	15.4	14.2	16.7
0	11.9	12.5	13.5	13.6	14.0	14.0	12.5	15.5
N	75	76	102	53	60	50	67	58

Table 13.13 Norms for Flexed-Arm Hang (Measured to Nearest .10 Second) for 6-Year-Old Males (M) and Females (F)

Percentile	Normal M	Normal F	LD M	LD F	ER M	ER F	TR M	TR F
100	26.4	33.5	19.9	16.9	18.7	15.5	4.2	1.8
90	23.6	28.9	17.7	15.0	16.5	13.8	3.0	1.5
80	20.2	25.8	15.4	13.3	14.3	12.0	2.2	1.0
70	18.3	23.3	14.0	12.1	13.1	10.8	2.0	0
60	16.3	20.1	12.7	10.9	11.8	9.5	1.9	0
50	8.4	10.4	6.4	6.4	5.2	5.0	0	0
40	7.6	9.1	5.6	5.7	4.5	4.2	0	0
30	6.3	8.5	4.7	4.9	3.7	3.4	0	0
20	2.2	2.7	.9	2.9	2.1	1.8	0	0
10	1.0	1.0	0	1.1	0	0	0	0
0	0	0	0	0	0	0	0	0
N	76	71	63	59	60	56	60	57

Table 13.14 Norms for Flexed-Arm Hang (Measured to Nearest .10 Second) for 7-Year-Old Males (M) and Females (F)

Percentile	Normal M	Normal F	LD M	LD F	ER M	ER F	TR M	TR F
100	28.3	21.7	25.0	29.0	19.2	16.5	9.3	9.0
90	25.6	19.7	22.2	26.1	18.6	15.7	8.2	7.9
80	22.2	17.8	19.3	23.5	17.9	14.8	7.5	7.0
70	20.2	16.0	16.8	19.5	14.7	12.9	5.3	4.9
60	18.1	14.1	13.9	15.4	11.0	11.1	3.2	2.7
50	10.1	8.2	7.9	7.3	8.0	7.9	1.0	.5
40	9.0	7.8	6.7	5.6	6.9	6.7	0	0
30	8.2	7.0	5.1	3.7	5.6	5.5	0	0
20	4.1	3.5	2.3	0	3.1	2.9	0	0
10	2.2	1.6	1.1	0	1.0	1.0	0	0
0	0	0	0	0	0	0	0	0
N	72	73	78	58	60	52	66	59

Table 13.15 Norms for Flexed-Arm Hang (Measured to Nearest .10 Second) for 8-Year-Old Males (M) and Females (F)

Percentile	Normal		LD		ER		TR	
	M	F	M	F	M	F	M	F
100	28.5	29.2	19.9	25.4	23.6	23.8	8.1	5.2
90	25.8	26.9	18.3	22.7	21.1	21.6	7.5	4.8
80	22.9	23.8	16.5	19.6	18.2	18.9	6.7	4.3
70	20.2	20.9	13.8	17.1	16.0	16.6	4.8	3.3
60	17.3	17.9	11.0	14.3	13.9	14.0	3.1	2.1
50	11.7	11.6	5.5	8.6	9.2	9.1	0	0
40	10.9	10.5	4.3	6.7	8.0	7.8	0	0
30	9.9	9.6	3.2	5.9	6.9	6.9	0	0
20	6.1	5.5	.7	3.1	4.7	4.2	0	0
10	3.2	2.9	0	1.9	2.6	2.0	0	0
0	1.1	1.0	0	0	0	0	0	0
N	82	82	80	60	61	53	67	57

Table 13.16 Norms for Flexed-Arm Hang (Measured to Nearest .10 Second) for 9-Year-Old Males (M) and Females (F)

Percentile	Normal		LD		ER		TR	
	M	F	M	F	M	F	M	F
100	25.6	25.2	30.0	26.4	25.3	21.0	14.3	9.2
90	23.5	23.1	26.9	23.5	22.7	19.1	13.0	8.3
80	21.1	20.8	23.5	19.8	19.8	16.9	11.2	7.8
70	19.0	18.9	21.0	17.2	17.7	15.3	8.7	5.9
60	16.8	16.8	17.9	14.2	14.5	12.9	5.6	4.0
50	12.1	12.0	11.1	6.6	8.9	8.4	0	0
40	10.9	10.9	8.2	4.2	7.9	7.2	0	0
30	9.6	10.0	4.9	3.5	6.6	5.2	0	0
20	7.0	7.6	2.1	0	3.4	1.0	0	0
10	3.6	3.5	1.0	0	.9	0	0	0
0	1.0	1.0	0	0	0	0	0	0
N	75	76	102	53	60	50	67	58

Table 13.17 Norms for 400-Yard Run-Walk (in Minutes-Seconds)
for 6-Year-Old Males (M) and Females (F)

Percentile	Normal		LD		ER		TR	
	M	F	M	F	M	F	M	F
100	1-44	1-44	2-00	2-05	1-54	1-56	2-14	2-36
90	1-48	1-47	2-04	2-10	2-00	2-02	2-28	2-57
80	1-50	1-50	2-09	2-16	2-04	2-07	2-38	3-18
70	1-51	1-53	2-14	2-20	2-10	2-12	2-52	3-37
60	1-54	1-57	2-18	2-24	2-14	2-15	3-03	3-50
50	2-02	2-04	2-21	2-28	2-17	2-18	3-13	4-00
40	2-10	2-06	2-30	2-36	2-25	2-30	3-39	4-21
30	2-17	2-14	2-42	2-44	2-37	2-40	3-56	4-31
20	2-26	2-21	2-51	2-51	2-47	2-50	4-06	4-44
10	2-42	2-41	2-58	3-00	2-59	3-00	4-19	4-59
0	2-52	2-56	3-02	3-08	3-05	3-06	4-42	5-11
N	80	72	60	57	60	53	67	57

Table 13.18 Norms for 400-Yard Run-Walk (in Minutes-Seconds)
for 7-Year-Old Males (M) and Females (F)

Percentile	Normal		LD		ER		TR	
	M	F	M	F	M	F	M	F
100	1-39	1-40	1-58	2-00	1-49	1-50	1-54	2-00
90	1-42	1-45	2-00	2-04	1-56	1-58	2-12	2-28
80	1-44	1-49	2-03	2-11	2-02	2-05	2-43	2-48
70	1-48	1-51	2-07	2-18	2-05	2-06	2-30	2-40
60	1-53	1-55	2-13	2-22	2-09	2-10	3-16	2-30
50	1-58	2-01	2-24	2-29	2-12	2-15	3-00	3-12
40	2-02	2-05	2-27	2-32	2-17	2-18	3-30	3-40
30	2-07	2-11	2-40	2-42	2-21	2-22	3-44	4-08
20	2-15	2-20	2-48	2-50	2-28	2-30	3-58	4-28
10	2-29	2-38	2-51	2-55	2-40	2-48	4-24	4-56
0	2-41	2-49	2-56	2-59	3-00	3-04	4-40	5-06
N	70	72	76	55	62	52	68	58

Table 13.19 Norms for 400-Yard Run-Walk (in Minutes-Seconds)
for 8-Year-Old Males (M) and Females (F)

Percentile	Normal		LD		ER		TR	
	M	F	M	F	M	F	M	F
100	1-35	1-42	1-50	1-56	1-47	1-50	1-50	1-58
90	1-38	1-45	1-55	2-02	1-52	1-56	2-00	2-24
80	1-41	1-48	2-00	2-07	1-56	2-00	2-30	2-36
70	1-44	1-51	2-04	2-12	1-59	2-05	2-48	2-48
60	1-48	1-54	2-10	2-18	2-04	2-09	2-51	3-00
50	1-50	1-58	2-20	2-25	2-08	2-15	3-00	3-08
40	2-00	2-03	2-24	2-30	2-13	2-24	3-24	3-30
30	2-05	2-10	2-27	2-38	2-17	2-30	3-30	4-00
20	2-09	2-14	2-35	2-44	2-28	2-40	3-42	4-30
10	2-25	2-28	2-38	2-46	2-38	2-48	4-20	4-36
0	2-35	2-39	2-44	2-50	2-54	2-59	4-32	4-42
N	82	87	80	63	62	51	67	57

Table 13.20 Norms for 400-Yard Run-Walk (in Minutes-Seconds)
for 9-Year-Old Males (M) and Females (F)

Percentile	Normal		LD		ER		TR	
	M	F	M	F	M	F	M	F
100	1-29	1-35	1-45	1-50	1-43	1-48	1-39	1-48
90	1-31	1-31	1-50	1-56	1-48	1-52	2-00	2-18
80	1-33	1-38	1-56	2-02	1-52	1-57	2-28	2-34
70	1-36	1-43	2-00	2-06	1-55	2-02	2-36	2-42
60	1-38	1-48	2-03	2-11	1-58	2-05	2-49	2-55
50	1-42	1-50	2-06	2-15	2-01	2-07	3-00	3-00
40	1-54	2-01	2-14	2-22	2-07	2-12	3-18	3-18
30	2-06	2-08	2-20	2-29	2-13	2-21	3-24	3-55
20	2-14	2-15	2-28	2-35	2-26	2-31	3-30	4-30
10	2-26	2-30	2-33	2-37	2-38	2-43	4-00	4-48
0	2-30	2-36	2-38	2-44	2-50	2-55	4-24	5-00
N	80	79	101	53	62	54	69	57

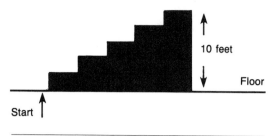

10 feet

Floor

Start

Figure 13.4 Stair running measurements.

Stair Running. The stair running test is an indicator of whole body power. Weigh each participant to the nearest pound, preferably but not necessarily in gym clothes without shoes. Measure 10 feet vertically on the stairs.

A participant starts on the floor in a standing position with the toes of both shoes touching the bottom of the first step. When a participant starts the movement of either foot to run up the stairs, a stopwatch is started. Each participant is to run as fast as possible. The watch is stopped when a participant's trunk section (not the head) passes by the 10-foot mark. More than one step on the stairs may be taken at a time if the participant can do so. Measure the time to the nearest .10 second. Use the formula

$$\text{Power} = \frac{\text{Weight} \times \text{Vertical Distance}}{\text{Time}}$$

to calculate the whole body power of each participant. For example, suppose we have two participants, one weighing 63 pounds and the other 111 pounds. The 63-pound participant ran the 10-foot vertical distance in 2.5 seconds, and so did the 111-pound participant. What is the whole body power of each participant?

63-pound participant:

$$\text{Power} = \frac{63 \text{ lbs} \times 10 \text{ feet}}{2.5 \text{ seconds}}$$

$$= 121 \text{ foot lbs/second}$$

111-pound participant:

$$\text{Power} = \frac{111 \text{ lbs} \times 10 \text{ feet}}{2.5 \text{ seconds}}$$

$$= 444 \text{ foot lbs/second}$$

As you can see, the 111-pound participant has more than three times the whole body power of the 63-pound participant. No suitable norms have been established for this test. However, you can compare test-retest results to evaluate the progress of each participant in the power component. Be sure to use the same flight of stairs for test-retest situations. More information about physical fitness tests and testing procedures for special populations is available from the list of resources provided in Appendix 13.A at the end of this chapter.

Testing of Severely Impaired Individuals

Testing severely or multiply impaired individuals in the components of strength, endurance, and flexibility may be accomplished by subdividing the whole body into its most appropriate segments. These major body segments include the following:

1. Head/neck
2. Upper arm
3. Lower arm
4. Hand
5. Total arm (2-4 inclusive)
6. Trunk/head
7. Upper leg
8. Lower leg
9. Foot
10. Total leg (7-9 inclusive)

Examination of Figure 13.5, "Major Segments of the Body," will give you a better understanding of where each segment begins and ends. We often forget that each body segment

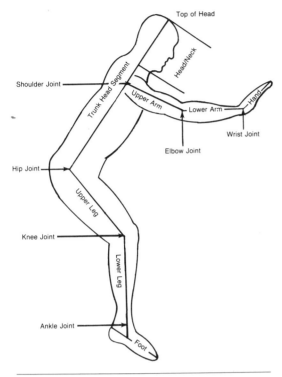

Top of Head

Shoulder Joint

Head/Neck

Trunk Head Segment

Upper Arm

Lower Arm

Hand

Wrist Joint

Elbow Joint

Hip Joint

Upper Leg

Knee Joint

Lower Leg

Ankle Joint

Foot

Figure 13.5 Major segments of the body.

has weight and that to move a body segment requires strength. To move and hold a body segment in a static position against the pull of gravity for a period of time requires muscular endurance. To move a body segment around its joint center through its range of motion is a test of flexibility.

In order to test an individual, you can place the whole body in one of four basic positions, then move each segment or segments in such a manner that you test for strength, endurance, and flexibility. One of the problems in movement of a segment is to ensure that little help is acquired from other segments that would add to the effective movement of the segment under test. Placing the whole body in one of the four basic positions assists in isolating the segment being tested and minimizes the effects of un-

wanted movement or muscular assistance from other segments of the body. The four basic body positions for testing muscular strength, muscular endurance, and flexibility include the following:

- Lying on back (face up).
- Lying on stomach (face down).
- Lying on left side (right side up).
- Lying on right side (left side up).

Each test will be described by giving the whole body position, segment or segments being tested, the starting position of the segment(s), the required movement of a specific segment, and what you are testing (e.g., strength, can move or cannot move; endurance, weight of limb multiplied by the time held; flexibility, range of motion and major muscles tested). Equipment needed is a testing table or floor with mat and a goniometer for measuring range of motion in degrees. Complete instructions for testing severely impaired individuals appear in Appendix 13.B at the end of this chapter.

Advanced Motor Development Testing

Moving with speed, coordination, and agility requires a delicately balanced interplay of all the motor components previously discussed in this chapter. It is the highest physical functioning level to be tested.

Speed Testing

Average speed is defined as the total distance covered divided by the time it took to cover the distance. Thus

$$\text{Average Speed} = \frac{\text{Distance}}{\text{Time}}$$

The distance most often run for speed is the 50-yard dash. However, many instructors have a participant run the 100-yard dash as a test of speed. Suppose we have a normal 14-year-old participant who runs the 50-yard dash in 7.1 seconds and a 14-year-old trainable retardate who runs 50 yards in 10.6 seconds. The normal 14-year-old's average speed is

$$\frac{50 \text{ yards}}{7.1 \text{ seconds}} = 7.0 \text{ yards/second}$$

whereas the 14-year-old trainable retardate's average speed is

$$\frac{50 \text{ yards}}{10.6 \text{ seconds}} = 4.7 \text{ yards/second}$$

When administering the 50-yard dash for average speed the participant should run on a smooth, solid surface. The participant starts be-hind the starting line in a standing set position. The commands *set* and then *go* are given. The starter drops a raised hand on the *go* command. A timer starts a stopwatch when he or she sees the hand drop and stops the watch when the participant passes through the finish line. Time is measured to the nearest .10 second. The average speed is recorded for each participant using the following formula:

$$\text{Average Speed} = \frac{50 \text{ yards}}{\text{Time (to nearest .10 second)}}$$

Round the average speed to the nearest .10 yard per second as in the following example:

$$\frac{50 \text{ yards}}{9.7 \text{ seconds}} = 5.1546392 \text{ yards/second}$$

$$= 5.2 \text{ yards/second}$$

Examine Tables 13.21 to 13.24 for norms.

Table 13.21 Norms for Average Speed in 50-Yard Dash (to Nearest .10 Yard/Second) for 6-Year-Old Males (M) and Females (F)

Percentile	Normal M	Normal F	LD M	LD F	ER M	ER F	TR M	TR F
100	5.0	5.3	4.8	4.8	4.8	4.7	4.4	3.6
90	4.8	4.9	4.5	4.5	4.6	4.6	4.0	3.4
80	4.5	4.5	4.3	4.3	4.4	4.2	3.7	3.1
70	4.3	4.2	4.2	4.1	4.2	4.0	3.6	3.0
60	4.2	4.1	3.8	3.8	3.9	3.7	3.3	2.9
50	4.0	4.0	3.6	3.5	3.7	3.5	3.0	2.7
40	3.8	3.7	3.1	3.1	3.4	3.1	2.8	2.4
30	3.7	3.6	2.9	2.7	2.9	2.8	2.4	2.2
20	3.5	3.4	2.6	2.5	2.6	2.3	2.0	1.6
10	3.3	2.9	2.3	2.0	2.2	1.9	1.7	1.5
0	2.0	1.8	1.8	1.6	1.8	1.5	1.0	0.8
N	76	71	63	59	60	56	60	57

Table 13.22 Norms for Average Speed in 50-Yard Dash (to Nearest .10 Yard/Second) for 7-Year-Old Males (M) and Females (F)

Percentile	Normal		LD		ER		TR	
	M	F	M	F	M	F	M	F
100	6.0	6.0	5.9	5.8	5.0	4.9	4.8	4.3
90	5.6	5.3	5.6	5.5	4.8	4.7	4.2	3.6
80	5.2	4.9	5.3	5.2	4.6	4.6	3.5	3.5
70	5.0	4.7	4.8	4.8	4.4	4.2	3.3	3.4
60	4.7	4.4	4.6	4.4	4.1	4.0	3.1	3.0
50	4.4	4.2	4.3	4.1	3.9	3.8	2.9	2.9
40	4.2	4.1	4.0	3.8	3.8	3.4	2.7	2.7
30	4.0	3.9	3.8	3.4	3.2	3.1	2.5	2.2
20	3.8	3.6	3.5	2.8	2.7	2.6	2.2	2.0
10	3.5	3.1	3.3	2.4	2.3	2.2	2.1	1.7
0	3.2	2.0	3.0	2.0	1.9	1.8	1.2	1.0
N	72	73	78	58	60	52	66	59

Table 13.23 Norms for Average Speed in 50-Yard Dash (to Nearest .10 Yard/Second) for 8-Year-Old Males (M) and Females (F)

Percentile	Normal		LD		ER		TR	
	M	F	M	F	M	F	M	F
100	6.4	6.2	6.2	6.0	5.0	5.2	5.0	4.5
90	6.0	5.7	5.9	5.7	4.8	5.0	4.3	3.8
80	5.6	5.3	5.7	5.6	4.6	4.7	4.0	3.3
70	5.4	5.1	5.4	5.3	4.5	4.5	3.8	3.1
60	5.1	5.0	5.2	5.0	4.3	4.2	3.6	3.0
50	5.0	4.9	4.9	4.7	4.1	4.0	3.5	2.8
40	4.8	4.6	4.5	4.3	3.7	3.6	3.3	2.6
30	4.6	4.4	4.2	4.1	3.3	3.3	2.9	2.4
20	4.2	4.3	3.8	3.6	2.8	2.7	2.8	2.1
10	3.9	3.5	3.5	3.1	2.4	2.3	2.5	1.9
0	3.3	2.1	3.0	2.0	2.0	1.9	0.8	1.0
N	82	86	80	60	61	53	67	57

Table 13.24 Norms for Average Speed in 50-Yard Dash (to Nearest .10 Yard/Second) for 9-Year-Old Males (M) and Females (F)

Percentile	Normal M	Normal F	LD M	LD F	ER M	ER F	TR M	TR F
100	6.5	6.4	6.3	6.2	5.9	5.8	5.3	5.9
90	6.4	6.3	6.2	6.0	5.6	5.5	5.0	4.3
80	6.2	6.1	6.1	5.9	5.3	4.9	4.3	4.0
70	6.1	6.0	5.8	5.7	5.0	4.7	4.2	3.7
60	6.0	5.8	5.4	5.5	4.6	4.5	4.0	3.6
50	5.9	5.6	5.2	5.3	4.4	4.2	3.8	3.2
40	5.6	5.4	4.9	4.9	4.2	3.8	3.6	3.1
30	5.5	5.2	4.7	4.6	4.0	3.4	3.4	2.9
20	5.4	5.0	4.4	4.2	3.7	3.1	3.2	2.4
10	5.1	4.8	4.2	3.9	3.5	2.7	2.7	1.9
0	4.2	3.5	3.9	3.5	3.3	2.3	1.0	1.0
N	75	76	102	53	60	50	67	58

Coordination Testing

Coordination may be defined as the harmonious interplay of muscle groups during a motor performance that provides some indication of skill. Two tests will be presented. One test is for hand-eye coordination, and the other is for foot-eye coordination. Hand-eye coordination is the ability to use both the visual system and one or both hands to perform a skill. Foot-eye coordination is usually determined by evaluating a participant's ability to contact a stationary or moving ball with the foot. If a participant has none of the motor impairments previously mentioned in this chapter but still fails to perform the skill successfully, the evaluator should consult the task analysis checklist provided for clues about what component of the skill is not being performed properly.

Hand-Eye Coordination.[1] The following hand-eye coordination items represent appropriate tests for participants 7 or more years of age. If a participant fails after three trials, the evaluator may use the task analysis checklist provided to determine what components of the task are not being performed properly. Additional trials may be used for the task analysis procedure.

Catching
Purpose. This test measures the learner's ability to catch a ball.

Materials. Standard equipment for the catching test includes a 9-1/2-inch playground ball, a tennis ball, a 10-foot measuring tape, and marking tape.

Procedure. Place two pieces of marking tape on the floor 10 feet apart. The evaluator stands on one piece of tape with the ball in hand. The learner stands on the other piece of tape to catch the ball.

---

[1]The hand-eye coordination and foot-eye coordination tasks are from *Adapted Physical Education Manual* by J. Pyfer and R. Johnson, 1982, Topeka, KS: Special Education Division, State of Kansas Department of Education. Reprinted by permission.

Task 1. The learner is to catch with both hands a 9-1/2-inch playground ball that is lobbed from a distance of 10 feet 4 out of 5 times.

Task 2. The learner is to catch with the preferred hand a tennis ball that is lobbed from a distance of 10 feet 4 out of 5 times.

Scoring. Record the number of catches the learner completed successfully; 4 catches out of 5 throws in a row is considered acceptable. If a learner catches fewer than four balls thrown in a row, tends to trap the ball between the hands and body, or turns the head or closes the eyes, use the following task analysis to determine where the learner is having difficulty:

Task analysis of two-handed catch:

- Arms are bent at the elbows and held relaxed at side or in front of the body while waiting to receive the ball.
- Hands are cupped together with the thumbs or little fingers in opposition (depending upon height of thrown ball).
- Hands clasp toward each other as contact is made with the ball.
- Arms give upon contact with the ball to absorb force at completion of catch (elbows come to rest at sides of the body).
- Eyes follow the ball from point of release to final contact.

Task analysis of one-handed catch:

- Preferred arm is held extended in front of the body while waiting to receive the ball.
- Preferred hand is held cupped with palm upward.
- Hand clasps the ball as contact is made.
- Arm gives upon contact with the ball to absorb force at completion of catch.
- Eyes follow the ball from point of release to final contact.

Throwing

Purpose. The purpose of the throwing test is to measure the learner's ability to use a crossed pattern throwing movement.

Materials. A tennis ball is the only required equipment.

Procedure. Have the learner stand approximately 25 feet from a wall and throw the ball at the wall five times. The evaluator stands off to the side of the learner and slightly ahead to observe the learner's eyes and throwing movement.

Task. The learner can throw a tennis ball with the preferred hand using an alternate arm-leg pattern.

Scoring. Observe the child's tendency to use the correct throwing method (see following task analysis).

Task analysis of throw:

- Arm swings backward in preparation for throw.
- Upper arm and elbow of the throwing arm move forward horizontally as the arm extends.
- Body weight is initially on the rear foot.
- As forward motion of the arm begins, the trunk rotates through the hips, spine, and shoulders.
- Throwing shoulder rotates to a position in line with the target.
- As the trunk rotates, weight is completely shifted with a step on the foot that is on the nonthrowing side of the body.
- Eyes fixate on the wall directly in front of the body throughout the preparatory and throwing motion.

Foot-Eye Coordination.

Purpose. The foot-eye coordination test measures the learner's ability to kick a ball.

Materials. Equipment includes a standard soccer ball, a 10-foot measuring tape, and marking tape.

Procedure. Place two pieces of marking tape on the floor 10 feet apart. For the first task, the evaluator should place the ball down on one of the pieces of marking tape and then stand approximately 10 feet beyond the other tape mark. The learner is instructed to stand on one piece of marking tape. The evaluator stands on the second piece of marking tape and rolls the ball to the learner. The learner is instructed to kick the rolling ball back to the evaluator.

Task 1. The learner can kick a stationary soccer ball using a toe or instep contact (3 out of 5 times).

Task 2. The learner can kick a rolling soccer ball rolled at a medium speed from a distance of 10 feet away to a person standing 10 feet in front of the learner (3 out of 5 times).

Scoring. Record the number of kicks the learner completed correctly; 3 out of 5 kicks is considered acceptable. If a learner kicks fewer than three balls, use the task analysis to determine where the child is having difficulty.

Task analysis of kick:

- During the backswing and prior to contact, the knee of the kicking foot is bent.
- Contact with the foot is in the center of the ball.
- Contact with the ball is made with the toe or instep.
- When contact is made with the ball, the knee of the kicking leg is completely extended.
- As contact is made with the ball, the arm on the kicking side tends to swing from a forward to a backward position.
- As contact is made with the ball, the arm on the nonkicking side tends to move from a backward or sideward position to a forward position.
- The trunk bends at the waist during the follow-through.
- The support leg bends when contact with the ball is made with the opposite foot.
- After contact is made with the ball, the kicking foot swings forward in an arc.

Agility Testing

Agility is the ability to change whole body directions and body segment directions quickly and accurately in a coordinated manner. The ability to perform with agility in sports or recreational activities is the highest level of motor development. The following norm tables are provided through the courtesy of the Adapted Physical Education Section of the Department of Physical Education, Dance, and Leisure Studies at Kansas State University.

Agility Run. The agility run is an indicator of the ability to rapidly move the body and alter directions in a coordinated manner. Four cones are placed 5 feet apart in a straight line. The instructor demonstrates the test and explains that on the command *go* the participant is to run as fast as possible in a zigzag pattern around the cones, starting on the right side of the first cone. Examine Tables 13.25 to 13.28 for norms. Scoring is based on the total number of cones passed in 20 seconds. For a complete run down and back, the participant receives a total of 8 points. Repeat the run until 20 seconds have elapsed. Use a stopwatch or wristwatch with a sweep second hand to keep time. When testing trainable retardates, the instructor may allow an individual who knows how to run the zigzag pattern to run in front of the retardate. Some retarded participants have great difficulty understanding the pattern but may be rather agile. Use your professional judgment in this matter.

More information about testing speed, coordination, and agility is provided in a listing of recommended tests in Appendix 13.2 at the end of this chapter.

Table 13.25 Norms for Agility Run (Number of Cones Passed in 20 Seconds) for 6-Year-Old Males (M) and Females (F)

Percentile	Normal		LD		ER		TR	
	M	F	M	F	M	F	M	F
100	28	27	25	26	20	20	8	7
90	26	25	24	24	18	19	7	6
80	22	23	22	23	17	17	6	6
70	20	22	21	21	15	16	6	6
60	19	20	19	20	14	14	5	5
50	18	18	18	18	12	13	4	4
40	17	16	16	16	11	11	3	3
30	15	15	15	15	9	10	2	2
20	13	13	13	13	8	8	0	0
10	12	11	12	12	6	7	0	0
0	10	10	10	10	5	5	0	0
N	84	75	65	59	63	53	69	57

Table 13.26 Norms for Agility Run (Number of Cones Passed in 20 Seconds) for 7-Year-Old Males (M) and Females (F)

Percentile	Normal		LD		ER		TR	
	M	F	M	F	M	F	M	F
100	28	28	26	24	22	23	8	8
90	27	27	24	23	21	22	7	6
80	24	24	22	22	20	20	6	6
70	23	23	21	20	18	19	6	6
60	21	21	19	19	17	17	5	5
50	19	19	17	18	16	16	4	4
40	17	17	16	16	14	14	3	3
30	16	15	14	15	12	12	2	2
20	14	14	13	13	11	10	1	1
10	13	11	12	12	9	9	0	0
0	11	10	10	10	7	7	0	0
N	72	75	77	55	63	51	63	55

Table 13.27   Norms for Agility Run (Number of Cones Passed in 20 Seconds) for 8-Year-Old Males (M) and Females (F)

Percentile	Normal		LD		ER		TR	
	M	F	M	F	M	F	M	F
100	31	30	27	25	27	26	10	9
90	29	28	26	24	26	25	8	8
80	28	26	25	22	23	23	8	7
70	25	25	23	21	21	21	7	7
60	23	22	22	19	19	20	6	6
50	21	20	21	18	17	18	5	5
40	20	19	19	16	15	16	4	3
30	19	17	17	15	13	14	2	2
20	17	16	15	13	12	12	1	1
10	16	14	13	12	12	11	0	0
0	15	13	11	10	8	8	0	0
N	85	85	83	60	60	53	69	57

Table 13.28   Norms for Agility Run (Number of Cones Passed in 20 Seconds) for 9-Year-Old Males (M) and Females (F)

Percentile	Normal		LD		ER		TR	
	M	F	M	F	M	F	M	F
100	31	31	28	28	30	29	12	11
90	30	29	26	26	28	28	10	9
80	28	27	25	24	26	25	9	8
70	26	24	24	22	23	23	8	7
60	25	22	22	20	21	21	6	6
50	23	20	21	18	19	19	5	5
40	22	19	19	17	17	17	4	4
30	20	18	17	15	16	15	3	2
20	19	17	16	14	15	14	1	1
10	17	17	14	13	14	14	0	0
0	16	15	12	11	11	10	0	0
N	80	79	103	55	60	50	65	57

Review Questions

1. An individual may have an impairment with resulting disabilities but not consider himself or herself to be handicapped. Explain.
2. What implications does Public Law 94-142 have for the physical educator in a school setting?
3. Write down from memory the hierarchy of motor development testing presented in this chapter.
4. List the least restrictive environments presented in this chapter.
5. Name from memory the reflexes described in this chapter.
6. What disabilities affecting physical skills or motor performance would result from the impairment of each reflex?
7. What is involved in (a) tactile discrimination testing, (b) kinesthetic discrimination testing, (c) auditory discrimination testing, (d) visual discrimination testing, (e) balance testing, (f) body awareness testing, and (g) gross and fine motor testing?
8. What is the major function of the sense organs?
9. What are the major functions of the brain-mind complex?
10. What is the major function of the motor response system?
11. What tests are presented in this chapter as good indicators of (a) muscular strength and endurance, (b) cardiorespiratory endurance, (c) flexibility, (d) coordination, and (e) agility?
12. (a) What is power? (b) What test is presented in this chapter for measuring power?
13. (a) What is average speed? (b) What test is presented in this chapter for measuring average speed?
14. Explain the method presented in this chapter for testing severely and/or multiply impaired individuals in the components of strength, endurance, and flexibility.

Problems and Exercises

1. Ten members of a wheelchair basketball team were measured for power. The coach found a football stadium that has a ramp with a 15-foot vertical distance. Each participant wheeled up the ramp as fast as possible and was timed with a stopwatch. The weight of each wheelchair and player was added to determine the total weight being moved the vertical distance. The following results were obtained:

Player	Total weight (lbs)	Time (seconds)
P1	186	7.0
P2	202	7.9
P3	175	6.7

(Cont.)

Player	Total weight (lbs)	Time (seconds)
P4	179	7.3
P5	192	7.6
P6	239	9.0
P7	232	9.2
P8	218	8.3
P9	212	8.7
P10	194	7.2

What is the power rating for each player?
Answer:
P1 = 399 foot lbs/second; P2 = 384 foot lbs/second;
P3 = 392 foot lbs/second; P4 = 368 foot lbs/second;
P5 = 379 foot lbs/second; P6 = 398 foot lbs/second;
P7 = 378 foot lbs/second; P8 = 394 foot lbs/second;
P9 = 366 foot lbs/second; P10 = 404 foot lbs/second.

2. The coach in Problem 1 developed a weight-training program for increasing upper body muscular strength and endurance. He applied this program for 2-1/2 months and then tested his athletes once again for power with the following results:

Player	Total weight (lbs)	Time (seconds)
P1	186	5.6
P2	205	5.7
P3	185	4.6
P4	185	5.6
P5	194	6.3
P6	235	6.6
P7	227	6.7
P8	223	7.6
P9	217	6.6
P10	197	5.4

(a) Did the weight-training program assist in increasing the power of each athlete? (b) What is the new power rating for each athlete?

3. (a) What is the mean, variance, and standard deviation of the power-testing in Problem 1? (b) What is the mean, variance and standard deviation in Problem 2? (c) Which power testing session had the greatest variability?

Answer:
(a) $\overline{X}$ (1st power test) = 386.2 foot lbs/second, σ_x^2 = 157.76 foot² lbs²/second², σ_x = 12.56 foot lbs/second.
(b) $\overline{Y}$ (2nd power test) = 512 foot lbs/second, σ_y^2 = 1923.2 foot² lbs²/second², σ_y = 43.85 foot lbs/second.
(c) The second power testing has the greatest variability because σ_y = 43.85 foot lbs/second is larger than σ_x = 12.56 foot lbs/second.

4. The coach working with the wheelchair basketball players had each athlete sprint the 50-yard dash 2 days after the second power testing session. Each was timed in an all-out sprint for 50 yards with the following results:

Player	Time (seconds)
P1	7.1
P2	6.9
P3	6.8
P4	7.0
P5	7.4
P6	7.0
P7	6.9
P8	7.5
P9	7.2
P10	6.8

What is the average speed of each athlete?

5. (a) Calculate a Pearson r between the average speed and the second power rating. (b) Plot the average speed on the X-axis and the power rating on the Y-axis. Draw a graphic representation of the paired scores. (c) Develop a predictive equation from the paired scores. Plot the line of best fit on the graph.
Answers:
(a) r = .912, indicating a rather high positive rating.
(b)

Player	X (yards/second)	Y (foot lbs/second)
P1	7.0	498
P2	7.2	539
P3	7.4	603

(Cont.)

Player	X (yards/second)	Y (foot lbs/second)
P4	7.1	496
P5	6.8	462
P6	7.1	534
P7	7.2	508
P8	6.7	440
P9	6.9	493
P10	7.4	547

(c) $Y = -759.83 + 179.6371(x)$

6. Three new prospects joined the wheelchair basketball team. The coach timed them for the 50-yard dash and calculated each one's average speed with the following results: Prospect 1 = 6.9 yards/second; Prospect 2 = 6.7 yards/second; and Prospect 3 = 6.5 yards/second. (a) Using the predictive equation developed in Problem 5, what would be each prospect's predictive power rating? Later the coach actually measured each prospect's power with the following results: Prospect 1 = 485 foot lbs/second; Prospect 2 = 445 foot lbs/second; and Prospect 3 = 400 foot lbs/second. (b) What is the deviation of each prospect's acutal power rating from the predictive power rating? (c) Would you consider the predictive equation to be a good, fair, or poor predictor of power?

7. An evaluation team in an elementary school setting had already classified four students as follows: Student 1 = female, moderately retarded (TR), 7 years of age; Student 2 = male, learning disabled (LD), 9 years of age; Student 3 = male, mildly retarded (ER), 8 years of age; Student 4 = female, moderately retarded (TR), 6 years of age. These four individuals were sent to an adapted physical education specialist for screening each into the least restrictive physical functioning environment. The specialist and physical education teacher at the school determined the following criteria for placing students in different types of least restrictive environments:

A. To be placed in a regular physical education class with no modifications, the student must be in the 70th percentile or above using "normal" norms in at least 90% of the norm-referenced tests performed. The student must pass all criterion-referenced tasks performed. The student must be emotionally and socially able to handle a regular physical education class. Consultation with parents for their approval of placement is necessary.

B. To be placed in a regular physical education class with modifications or an aid to assist, the student must be in the 40th to 69th percentile or above using "normal" norms in at least 90% of the norm-referenced tests performed. The student must pass 50% of the tasks in the criterion-referenced test performed. The student must be emotionally and socially able to handle this learning environment. Consultation with parents is required for their approval of the placement.

C. To be placed in an adapted physical education class in a closed environment in a small group, the student will not qualify for the standards set in A and B above. Consultation with parents is required for their approval of the placement.

D. To be referred to support services, the student should be at or below the 10th percentile rating for all "within group" norm-referenced tests performed. The student fails to pass any criterion-referenced tests. Consultation with parents is required for their approval of the referral because they must finance such services. The school nurse should be present when consulting with parents.

The adapted physical education specialist tested each student in the norm-referenced tests of standing long jump, bent-knee sit-ups, hamstring stretch, flexed-arm hang, 400-yard run-walk, 50-yard dash, and agility run. The criterion-referenced tests of hand-eye coordination and foot-eye coordination were applied. The following test results were obtained for each student:

Student 1. Female, moderately retarded (TR), 7 years of age.

Standing long jump	15	inches
Bent-knee sit-ups	16	correctly done in 60 seconds
Hamstring stretch	21	inches
Flexed-arm hang	0	seconds
400-yard run-walk	3-15	minutes-seconds
50-yard dash	3.0	yards/second average speed
Agility run	4	number of cones passed in 20 seconds

Eye-hand coordination:
   Catching, Task 1: Successfully caught a 9-1/2-inch playground ball 4 out of 5 times. *pass*
   Catching, Task 2: Caught tennis ball 1 out of 5 times. *fail*; does not use the preferred hand in a cupped, palm-up position. Arm does not give on contact.

Throwing:
  (a) Arm does not swing backward in preparation for throw. *fail*
  (b) Arm does not fully extend in throw. *fail*
  (c) Body weight too much on forward foot. *fail*
  (d) Fair rotation of hips. *pass*
  (e) Fair shoulder rotation. *pass*
  (f) Cross pattern not present. *fail*
  (g) Watched tester rather than fixating in direction of throw. *fail*
Failed 5 out of 7 tasks. *fail*

Eye-foot coordination:
  Kicking stationary ball, Task 1: Kicked soccer ball 3 out of 5 times with toe contact. *pass*
  Kicking rolling ball, Task 2: Scored 1 out of 5 times. Difficulty in tracking. *fail*

Task analysis:
  (a) Keeps kicking leg straight, does not bend.
  (b) Contacts ball a little high up from center.
  (e) Lacks arm movement.
  (g) Keeps trunk too straight.
  (h) Support leg does not bend when contact is made with ball.
  (i) Very little follow-through with kicking leg.

Comments: She has a tendency to pout or quit when she cannot perform a task as well as others. Wants her own way when in a social situation, as reported by her teacher.

Student 2. Male, learning disabled (LD), 9 years of age.

Standing long jump	65	inches
Bent-knee sit-ups	44	correctly done in 60 seconds
Hamstring stretch	25.0	inches
Flexed-arm hang	23.5	seconds
400-yard run-walk	1-35	minutes-seconds
50-yard dash	6.2	yards/second average speed
Agility run	28	number of cones passed in 20 seconds

Eye-hand coordination:
  Catching, Task 1: Successfully caught a 9-1/2-inch playground ball 5 out of 5 times. *pass*
  Catching, Task 2: Caught tennis ball 5 out of 5 times. *pass*
  Throwing: Passed all 7 task analysis criteria.

Eye-foot coordination:
  Kicking stationary ball, Task 1: Successfully kicked ball 5 out of 5 times with instep of foot. *pass*

Kicking rolling ball, Task 2: Successfully kicked rolling ball 5 out of 5 times with instep of foot. *pass*
Comments: Student is well adjusted socially and emotionally, as reported by teacher and school psychologist. Gets along well with other students and has an excellent personality. Has a specific learning disability in math concepts. Is receiving special help for this problem.

Student 3. Male, mildly retarded (ER), 8 years of age.

Standing long jump	46	inches
Bent-knee sit-ups	33	correctly done in 60 seconds
Hamstring stretch	21.5	inches
Flexed-arm hang	9.2	seconds
400-yard run-walk	1-56	minutes-seconds
50-yard dash	5.0	yards/second average speed
Agility run	26	number of cones passed in 20 seconds

Eye-hand coordination:
  Catching, Task 1: Successfully caught a 9-1/2-inch playground ball 4 out of 5 times. *pass*
  Catching, Task 2: Caught tennis ball 4 out of 5 times. *pass*
  Throwing: Passed 6 of the 7 tasks. Had difficulty with (f); did not shift weight completely to foot on non-throwing side. *pass*
Eye-foot coordination:
  Kicking stationary ball, Task 1: Successfully kicked ball 5 out of 5 times with toe contact. *pass*
  Kicking rolling ball, Task 2: Successfully kicked rolling ball 4 out of 5 times with toe contact. *pass*
  Comments: He has a quick temper but may be controlled if prompt disciplinary action is taken, as reported by school psychologist. Flares up with other students occasionally but not often. If told to apologize for this fault, will do so, as reported by his teacher.

Student 4. Female, moderately retarded (TR), 6 years of age.

Standing long jump	0	inches
Bent-knee sit-ups	0	correctly done in 60 seconds
Hamstring stretch	12	inches
Flexed-arm hang	0	seconds
400-yard run-walk	did not complete	minutes-seconds
50-yard dash w/assistance	.5	yards/second average speed
Agility run	0	number of cones passed in 20 seconds

Eye-hand coordination:

Catching, Task 1 and Task 2: Unsuccessful; would not respond to catching with either both or one hand. Attention span quite short.

Throwing: Failed all 7 tasks. Would just hold the ball but not attempt to throw it. Had difficulty in release of ball.

Eye-foot coordination:

Kicking stationary ball, Task 1, and kicking a rolling ball, Task 2: Unsuccessful. Suspect lack of inhibition of symmetrical tonic neck reflex because when head was flexed to look at ball, there was elbow flexion in both arms and both legs were extended.

Comments: Recommend reflex testing by a physical therapist. Believe equilibrium reflex impairment present. Consult parents.

A. For each norm-referenced test performed on each of these students, give the percentile rating each student would receive when (a) compared to normal students and (b) when compared to their own "within group" norms. (c) Based on the standards established, what would be the recommended least restrictive physical functioning environment for each student?

Answers:

Student 1

	(a) Normal Percentile	(b) TR Percentile
Standing long jump	Below 0	70
Bent-knee sit-ups	Between 20-30	80
Hamstring stretch	50	50
Flexed-arm hang	0	Between 0-40
400-yard run-walk	Below 0	Near 50
50-yard dash	10	60
Agility run	Below 0	50

She passed only 2 of the tasks in the criterion-referenced tests and failed all others.

(c) It would be recommended that she be placed into an adapted physical education class. She met none of the standards to be mainstreamed into a regular physical education class. She would not be recommended for referral services because she did not score at the 10 or below percentile within her own group (TR) and passed two of the tasks in the criterion-referenced test.

	(a) Normal Percentile	(b) LD Percentile
Standing long jump	80	Near 90
Bent-knee sit-ups	Near 60	Between 80-90
Hamstring stretch	80	Near 80
Flexed-arm hang	90	80
400-yard run-walk	Above 70	100
50-yard dash	80	90
Agility run	80	100

He passed all of the criterion-referenced tests.
(c) 90% of 7 norm-referenced tests is $.9 \times 7 = 6.3 = 6$ norm-referenced tests that had to be passed at or above the 70th percentile rating for normal students to qualify for placement in a regular physical education class with no modifications. Student 2 met this requirement. The only percentile rank that did not meet the 70th percentile rating was the bent-knee sit-up rating; all others did. All tasks in criterion-referenced tests were passed. He is well adjusted socially and emotionally. It is recommended that he be placed in a regular physical education class with no modifications.

Student 3

	(a) Normal Percentile	(b) ER Percentile
Standing long jump	50	Near 60
Bent-knee sit-ups	Near 50	60
Hamstring stretch	Between 40-50	50
Flexed-arm hang	Between 20-30	50
400-yard run-walk	Between 40-50	80
50-yard dash	50	100
Agility run	Near 70	90

Student passed all criterion-referenced tests.
(c) He passed 6 of the 7 norm-referenced tests for normal students at a rating of 40 to 69 or above percentile points. He passed all tasks in the criterion-referenced tests, which surpasses the 50% standard established for placement in a regular physical education class with modifications or a teaching aide. Due to his quick temper, it is recommended that he be

placed in a regular physical education class with an aide to assist the regular physical education teacher.

Student 4

	(a) Normal Percentile	(b) TR Percentile
Standing long jump	Below 0	0
Bent-knee sit-ups	Below 0	Can't evaluate; probably 0
Hamstring stretch	Below 0	Below 0
Flexed-arm hang	0	Can't evaluate; probably 0
400-yard run-walk	Below 0	Below 0
50-yard dash	Below 0	Below 0
Agility run	Below 0	Can't evaluate; probably 0

This student should be referred to support services. The adapted physical education specialist suspects reflex impairment and possible brain damage. Referral to a physical therapist for reflex testing as well as a neurologist for diagnosis and treatment of possible nervous system impairments would be recommended. Consultation with parents with school nurse present is absolutely necessary. Hopefully, after work with a physical therapist on a one-to-one basis, this child can be placed into an adapted physical education class.

8. Examine more carefully the test results and percentile ratings of Student 1, who will be placed in an adapted physical education class. (a) Identify her strengths and weaknesses. (b) Develop and write long-range goals for this student. (c) Take one of the goals and develop and write measurable objectives for attaining that goal.

9. A Special Olympics coach is training twelve 14- and 15-year-old moderately retarded individuals, including both males and females. She ran a test in the 50-yard dash and the standing long jump with the following results:

Subject	Sex	Age	50-yard dash (seconds)	Standing long jump (inches)
S1	F	14	9.5	66
S2	F	14	9.7	54

(Cont.)

Subject	Sex	Age	50-yard dash (seconds)	Standing long jump (inches)
S3	F	14	9.9	46
S4	F	15	8.2	65
S5	F	15	9.1	50
S6	F	15	9.7	42
S7	M	14	6.9	76
S8	M	14	7.5	64
S9	M	14	8.0	60
S10	M	15	7.0	80
S11	M	15	7.4	73
S12	M	15	7.8	67

(a) Calculate an $\overline{X}$ and σ for each event.
(b) Calculate a T score for each subject in each event.
(c) Calculate a Spearman rank-order correlation coefficient.
(d) What relationship exists between the 50-yard dash and the standing long jump results? What is the co-efficient of determination? What is the coefficient of nondetermination?

Answers:
(a) $\overline{X}$ 50-yard dash = 8.4 seconds; σ 50-yard dash = 1.1 seconds.
   $\overline{Y}$ SLJ = 61.9 inches; σ SLJ = 11.4 inches.

(b) Subject	T score (50-yard dash)	T score (standing long jump)
S1	40	54
S2	38	43
S3	36	36
S4	52	53
S5	44	40
S6	38	33
S7	66	62
S8	58	52
S9	54	48
S10	63	66
S11	59	60
S12	55	54

(c) *rho* = .85
(d) Coefficient of determination = .7225 and coefficient of nondetermination = .2775.

10. A severely multiply impaired individual is a member of the local YMCA. He wanted to improve his physical fitness and asked the physical activity instructor if this were possible. The instructor told him that it was possible but that he must be tested for his present physical functioning level. The instructor used the test presented in Appendix 13.B (at the end of this chapter) for testing severely multiply impaired individuals with the following results:

Position and movement	Strength Pass	Fail	Endurance Hold Time time (seconds)	held	Flexibility Range degrees	Record range	Comments
1. Back lying (face up)							
A. Left hand							Cannot innervate
Wrist flexion		✓	180	0	0-90	0	
Wrist extension		✓	180	0	0-70	0	
B. Right hand							
Wrist flexion	✓		180	100	0-90	45	
Wrist extension	✓		180	95	0-70	60	
C. Left lower arm							Cannot innervate
Elbow flexion		✓	180	0	0-160	0	
D. Right lower arm							
Elbow flexion	✓		180	40	0-160	160	
E. Left total arm							Cannot innervate
Shoulder flexion		✓	90	0	0-180	0	
F. Right total arm							
Shoulder flexion	✓		90	50	0-180	180	
G. Head/neck							
Neck flexion	✓		180	95	0-70	60	
H. Trunk/head							
Trunk flexion	✓		20	3	0-100	100	
I. Left total leg							
Hip flexion	✓		30	10	0-125	116	
J. Right total leg							
Hip flexion	✓		30	12	0-125	115	
K. Left foot (standing)							Change of whole body position
Plantar flexion	✓		10	6	0-45	25	
L. Right foot (standing)							Change of whole body position
Plantar flexion	✓		10	8	0-45	30	
2. Stomach lying (face down)							
A. Left total arm							Cannot innervate
Shoulder extension		✓	90	0	0-50	0	
B. Right total arm							
Shoulder extension	✓		90	10	0-50	35	

(Cont.)

Position and movement	Strength Pass Fail	Endurance Hold Time time held (seconds)	Flexibility Range degrees	Record range	Comments
C. Head/neck					
Neck extension	✔	180 50	0-25	15	
D. Trunk/head					
Trunk extension	✔	20 0	0-50	5	
E. Left total leg					
Hip extension	✔	30 5	0-15	6	
F. Right total leg					
Hip extension	✔	30 4	0-15	5	
G. Left lower leg					
Knee flexion	✔	110 85	0-130	130	
H. Right lower leg					
Knee flexion	✔	110 90	0-130	130	
3. Right side lying (left side up)					
A. Trunk/head					
Trunk abduction	✔	10 0	0-30	1	
B. Left total leg					
Hip abduction	✔	30 0	0-45	3	
C. Right total leg					
Hip adduction	✔	30 0	0-25	3	
D. Head/neck					
Adduct to abduct	✔	180 110	0-130	120	
4. Left side lying (right side up)					
A. Trunk/head					
Trunk abduction	✔	10 0	0-30	3	
B. Right total leg					
Hip abduction	✔	30 0	0-45	5	
C. Left total leg					
Hip adduction	✔	30 0	0-25	5	
D. Head/neck					
Adduct to abduct	✔	180 130	0-130	125	

The subject weighs 135 pounds. (a) Calculate the weight of each segment. (b) Calculate the desired endurance for each position by taking the body segment(s) weight times the desired hold time. (c) Calculate the actual endurance for each position by taking the body segment(s) weight times the actual time held by the subject. Compare the actual time held to the desired time. (d) What flexibility problems need to be improved? (e) What major muscles need to be improved? To help find the solutions to these problems, carefully examine Appendix 13.B.

Appendix 13.A
Tests for Special Populations

The following resources are recommended for information in physical fitness testing, sensory motor testing, and testing for speed, coordination, and agility.

Components measured: arm strength, abdominal strength, leg strength, endurance, eye-foot coordination, eye-hand coordination, gross body coordination, balance, and posture orientation.

Physical Fitness Tests

AAHPER Youth Fitness Test Adaptation for the Blind. American Alliance for Health, Physical Education, Recreation, and Dance, 1900 Association Drive, Reston, VA 22091. Components measured: arm and shoulder power, abdominal endurance, leg power, cardiorespiratory endurance, and speed-and-agility.

Motor Fitness Testing Manual for the Moderately Mentally Retarded by Leon Johnson and Ben Londeree. American Alliance for Health, Physical Education, and Recreation, 1900 Association Drive, Reston, VA 22091. Components measured: arm and shoulder endurance, abdominal endurance, leg strength, cardiorespiratory endurance, flexibility, speed, height, weight, hopping, skipping, tumbling progression, and target throwing.

Physical Fitness for the Mentally Retarded. Metropolitan Toronto Association for Retarded Children, 186 Beverley Street, Toronto, Canada. Components measured: muscular endurance of shoulder and arms, flexibility of back, leg power, abdominal endurance, flexibility of hamstrings, cardiorespiratory endurance, and physique.

Project Active. Township of Ocean School District, Dow Avenue, Oakhurst, NJ 07755.

Sensory-Motor Tests

Denver Developmental Screening. University of Colorado Medical Center, Denver, CO 80220. Components measured: fine motor, gross motor, and language; also identifies developmental delay.

Direct Pressure Test of Tactile Discrimination. Taylor, N. (1972). A stereognostic test for screening tactile sensations. *The American Journal of Occupational Therapy,* **16**(5). Component measured: tactile discrimination.

Frostig Developmental Test of Visual Perception. Consulting Psychologist Press, 577 College Avenue, Palo Alto, CA 94360. Components measured: eye-motor coordination, figure ground, constancy of shape, perception of position in space, and perception of spatial relations.

Perceptual Motor Survey. Matthew Sullivan, Physical Education Consultant, Special School District, Saint Louis County, 12100 Clayton Road, Town and Country, MO 63125. Components measured: static and dynamic balance, awareness of self, and spatial orientation.

Purdue Perceptual Motor Survey. Charles E. Merrill Publishing Company, 130 Alum Creek Drive, Columbus, OH 43216. Components measured: balance, posture, body image, perceptual motor matching, ocular control, and form perception.

Quick Neurological Screening Test. Academic Therapy Publications, 20 Commercial Boulevard, Novato, CA 94949. Components measured: large and small muscle control, motor planning and sequencing, sense of rate and rhythm, spatial organization, visual and auditory perceptual skills, balance and cerebella vestibular function, and disorders of attention.

Southern California Sensory Integration Tests. Western Psychological Services, 13081 Wilshire Boulevard, Los Angeles, CA 90025. Components measured: figure ground, position in space, design copying, kinesthesia, manual form perception, tactile discrimination, midline crossing, bilateral motor control, right-left discrimination, and standing balance.

Speed, Coordination, and Agility Tests

Bruininks-Osteretsky Test of Motor Proficiency. AGS American Guidance Service, Publishers Building, Circle Pines, MN 55014. Components measured: running speed and agility, balance, bilateral coordination, strength, upper-limb coordination, response speed, visual-motor control, upper-limb speed, and dexterity.

Lincoln-Osteretsky Motor Development Scale. AGS American Guidance Service, Publishers Building, Circle Pines, MN 55014. Components measured: static coordination, dynamic manual coordination, general coordination, motor speed, simultaneous movement, and synkinesia.

Appendix 13.B
Combined Testing of Severely Impaired Individuals

Instructions for testing severely impaired individuals include: the whole body position, segments being tested, starting position of the segment(s), required movement of a specific segment, and fitness component being tested (e.g., strength, endurance, flexibility).

I. Lying on back (face up), arms at sides, feet together, legs extended (straight).
    A. Left Hand
        1. Palm of hand up (back of hand resting on mat, fingers extended straight). This is the starting position, or 0°.
            a. Wrist flexion (move hand up then down). Keep fingers extended straight.
                1. Strength. Have the student move the hand up from starting position (keeping fingers extended) as far as possible, then back to the starting position. Any movement from the starting position is a pass situation.
                2. Endurance. Have the student move the hand up from the starting position to approximately 45° (keeping fingers extended) and hold this position for 180 seconds. Record the number of seconds.
                3. Flexibility (wrist flexion). Have the student move the hand up from the starting position (0°), keeping the fingers extended as far as possible. Range will vary

from starting position 0° to maximum position 90°. Record range. Major muscles tested include flexors carpi radialis and carpi ulnaris.
        2. Palm of hand down (palm of hand resting on mat, fingers extended straight). This is the starting position (0°).
            a. Wrist extension (move hand up then down). Keep fingers extended straight.
                1. Strength. Have the student move the hand up from starting position (keeping fingers extended) as far as possible, then back to the starting position. Any movement from the starting position is a pass situation.
                2. Endurance. Have the student move the hand up from the starting position to approximately 35° (keeping fingers extended) and hold this position for 180 seconds. Record the number of seconds.
                3. Flexibility (wrist extension). Have the student move the hand up from the starting position (0°) keeping fingers extended as far as possible. Range will vary from 0° to 70°. Record range. Major muscles tested include extensors carpi radialis longus, carpi radialis brevis, and carpi ulnaris.

B. Right Hand (Follow same procedures that are used for left hand.)
C. Left Lower Arm
  1. Hand, lower arm, and upper arm lying on mat. Lower arm supinated (palm of hand up). This is the starting position (0°).
    a. Elbow flexion (move lower arm up then down). Keep lower arm supinated. Keep upper arm in contact with the mat in all the tests.
      1. Strength. Have the student move the lower arm up from the starting position as far as possible (keeping the upper arm in contact with the mat), then back to the starting position. Any movement from the starting position (0°) is a pass situation.
      2. Endurance. Have the student move the lower arm up from the starting position (0°) to approximately 45° and hold this position for 180 seconds. Record the number of seconds.
      3. Flexibility (elbow flexion). Have the student move the lower arm up from the starting position (0°) as far as possible. Range will vary from 0° to (145°-160°). Record range. Major muscles tested: biceps brachii and brachialis.
D. Right Lower Arm (Follow same procedures that are used for left lower arm.)
E. Left Total Arm
  1. Hand, lower arm, and upper arm lying on mat. Lower arm pronated (palm of hand down). This is the starting position (0°).
    a. Shoulder flexion (move total arm up, then down). Keep the total arm (hand, lower arm, and upper arm) straight in all the tests.
      1. Strength. Have the student move the total arm up from the starting position (0°) as far as possible, keeping the total arm straight even to above the head if possible. Any movement from the starting position (0°) is a pass situation.
      2. Endurance. Have the student move the total arm up from the starting position (0°) to approximately 45° and hold this position for 90 seconds. Record the number of seconds.
      3. Flexibility (shoulder flexion). Have the student move the total arm up from the starting position (0°) as far as possible above the head. Range will vary from 0° to 180°. Record range. Major muscles tested: deltoid anterior.
F. Right Total Arm (Follow same procedures that are used for left total arm.)
G. Head/Neck
  1. Back of head resting on mat. This is the starting position (0°).
    a. Neck flexion (move head up and then down). Keep shoulders on mat in each test.
      1. Strength. Have the student move the head up from starting position (0°) as far as possible, keeping both shoulders in contact with the mat, then back to the starting position. Any movement from the starting position (0°) is a pass situation.

2. Endurance. Have the student move the head up from the starting position (0°) to approximately 30° and hold this position for 180 seconds. Record the number of seconds.

3. Flexibility (neck flexion). Have the student move the head up from the starting position (0°) as far as possible. Keep both shoulders on the mat. Range will vary from 0° to (60°-70°). Record range. Major muscles tested: sternocleidomastoideus.

H. Trunk/Head
   1. Back of trunk and head resting on mat. Arms folded across chest. Legs in bent-knee sit-up position. This is the starting position (0°).
      a. Trunk flexion (curl trunk up, then down).
         1. Strength. Have the student curl trunk up from the starting position (0°) as far as possible, then back to the starting position. Any movement from the starting position (0°) is a pass situation.
         2. Endurance. Have the student curl trunk up from starting position (0°) to approximately 45° and hold this position for 20 seconds. Record the number of seconds.
         3. Flexibility (trunk flexion). Have the student curl the trunk up from the starting position (0°) as far as possible. Range will vary from 0° to (90°-100°). Record the range. Major muscles tested: rectus abdominis.

I. Left Total Leg
   1. Back of upper leg, lower leg, and foot (heel) resting on mat. Arms folded across chest. This is the starting position (0°).
      a. Hip flexion (lift total leg up, then down).
         1. Strength. Have the student lift total leg up from starting position (0°) as far as possible, then back to the starting position. Be sure to keep total leg extended (straight; do not bend at knee joint). Any movement from the starting position (0°) is a pass situation.
         2. Endurance. Have the student lift total leg up from the starting position (0°) to approximately 45° and hold this position for 30 seconds. Be sure to keep the total leg extended (straight; do not bend at knee joint). Record the number of seconds.
         3. Flexibility (hip flexion). Note that in this test the student should flex the knee joint (bend lower leg toward upper leg). Have the student lift the lower leg toward the trunk as far as possible. Range 0° to (115°-125°). Record range. Major muscles tested: psoas major and iliacus.

J. Right Total Leg (Follow same procedures that are used for left total leg.)

K. Left Foot
   1. This test is done in the standing position (total body supported by foot) with the heel and toes touching the floor. This is the starting position (0°). Note that the right foot does not touch the floor.
      a. Plantar flexion (up on tiptoe). Move heel up off floor, then

back down. Keep knee straight.
1. Strength. Have the student move the heel up from the starting position (0°) as far as possible. (The student may need assistance in keeping balance; just support the student without lifting the student upward). Any movement from the starting position (0°) is a pass situation.
2. Endurance. Have the student move the heel up from the starting position (0°) to approximately 20° and hold this position for 10 seconds. Record the number of seconds. (Instructor may assist student in balance but should not lift the student upward.)
3. Flexibility (plantar flexion). Have the student move the heel up from starting position (0°) as far as possible. (Instructor may assist in balance.) Range will vary from 0° to (40°-45°). Record range. Major muscles tested: gastrocnemius and soleus.
L. Right Foot (Follow same procedures used for left foot.)

II. Lying on stomach (face down), arms at side, feet together, legs extended (straight).
A. Left Total Arm
1. Back of hand, lower arm, upper arm, and right side of face lying on mat. This is the starting position (0°).
a. Shoulder extension. Move the total arm up, then down. Keep the total arm straight.
1. Strength. Have the student move the total arm up from the starting position as far as possible. Any movement

from the starting position (0°) is a pass situation.
2. Endurance. Have the student move the total arm up from the starting position (0°) to approximately 25° and hold this position for 90 seconds.
3. Flexibility (shoulder extension). Have the student move the total arm (keeping total arm straight) up from the starting position (0°) as far as possible. Range will vary from 0° to 50°. Record range. Major muscles tested: latissimus dorsi and teres major.
B. Right Total Arm (Follow same procedures that are used for left total arm, except that left side of face is lying on mat.)
C. Head/Neck
1. Chin resting on mat, hands placed in small of back. This is the starting position (0°).
a. Neck extension: Move the head up, then down.
1. Strength. Have the student move the head up from the starting position as far as possible. Any movement from the starting position (0°) is a pass situation.
2. Endurance. Have the student move the head up from the starting position (0°) to approximately 10° and hold this position for 180 seconds. Record the number of seconds.
3. Flexibility (neck extension). Have the student move the head up from the starting position (0°) as far as possible. (Stabilize upper thoracic area and scapulae). Range will

vary from 0° to (20°-25°). Record range. Major muscles tested: trapezius, semispinalis capitis, splenius capitis, and splenius cervicis.

D. Trunk/Head
  1. Chin resting on mat, hands placed in small of back. This is the starting position (0°).
    a. Trunk extension. Stabilize pelvis. Student extends thoracic and lumbar spine (upper part of trunk, shoulders, and head) up, then down.
      1. Strength. Have the student move the head and upper part of trunk plus shoulders up as far as possible from starting position (0°). Any movement from the starting position of the shoulders and upper trunk is a pass situation.
      2. Endurance. Have the student move the head and upper part of trunk plus shoulders up to approximately 20° and hold this position for 20 seconds. Record the number of seconds.
      3. Flexibility (trunk extension). Have the student move the head, upper trunk, and shoulders up from the starting position (0°) as far as possible. Range will vary from 0° to (45°-50°). Record range. Major muscles tested: iliocostalis thoracis, longissimus thoracis, spinalis thoracis, and iliocostalis lumborum.

E. Left Total Leg
  1. Side of face resting on mat (right or left), hands placed in small of back, and legs straight resting on mat. This is the starting position (0°).
    a. Hip extension beyond midline. Stabilize pelvis. Student extends total leg upward, then down. Keep total leg straight, do not bend at knee.
      1. Strength. Have the student move total leg up from the starting position as far as possible and then back down. Keep total leg straight throughout move. Any movement from the starting position is a pass situation.
      2. Endurance. Have the student move the total leg up from the starting position to approximately 5° and hold this position for 30 seconds. Record the number of seconds.
      3. Flexibility (hip extension beyond midline). Have the student move the total leg up from the starting position (0°) as far as possible. Be sure to stabilize the pelvis and keep total leg straight. Range will vary from 0° to (10°-15°). Record range. Major muscles tested: gluteus maximus, semitendinosus, semimembranosus, and biceps femoris.

F. Right Total Leg (Follow the same procedures that are used for left total leg.)

G. Left Lower Leg
  1. Side of face resting on mat (right or left), hands placed at sides, and legs straight resting on mat. This is the starting position (0°).
    a. Knee flexion. Have the student move the lower leg up toward the upper leg, then back down.
      1. Strength. Have the student move the lower leg up from

the starting position as far as possible. Any movement from the starting position (0°) is a pass situation.

2. Endurance. Have the student move the lower leg up from the starting position (0°) to approximately 45° and hold this position for 110 seconds. Record the number of seconds.

3. Flexibility (knee flexion). Have the student move the lower leg up to and as close to the upper leg as possible. Range will vary from 0° to (120°-130°). Record range. Major muscles tested: biceps femoris, semitendinosus, and semimembranosus.

H. Right Lower Leg (Follow the same procedures that are used for the left lower leg.)

III. Lying on right side, left side up, arms folded across chest, left leg resting on right leg, both legs extended (straight).

A. Trunk/Head

1. Right side of head/trunk and right total leg resting on mat with left leg resting on top of right leg. Arms folded across chest. Both legs extended and trunk straight. This is the starting position (0°).

   a. Trunk abduction left: Move the trunk up to the left. Must support legs above and below knees. Do not allow student to use arms to assist in motion.

      1. Strength. Have the student move the trunk/head segment up from the starting position as far as possible. Be sure to support student's legs. Do not allow arms to assist.

Any movement from the starting position (0°) is a pass situation.

2. Endurance. Have the student move the trunk/head segment up to the left from the starting position (0°) to approximately 15° and hold this position for 10 seconds. Record the number of seconds.

3. Flexibility. Have the student move the trunk/head up as far as possible to the left. Support student's legs. Range will vary from 0° to (20°-30°). Major muscles tested: external oblique and rectus abdominis.

B. Left Total Leg

1. Left leg resting on right leg. Both legs extended (straight). This is the starting position (0°).

   a. Lift total leg abduction or hip abduction. Move the left total leg up away from right total leg.

      1. Strength. Have the student move the left total leg up from starting position as far as possible. Any movement from the starting position (0°) is a pass situation.

      2. Endurance. Have the student move the left total leg up from starting position (0°) to approximately 20° and hold this position for 30 seconds. Record the number of seconds.

      3. Flexibility (left total leg abduction or hip abduction). Have the student move the left total leg up from the starting position (0°) as far as possible. Range will vary from 0° to 45°. Record

range. Major muscles tested: gluteus medius.

C. Right Total Leg
  1. Right total leg resting on mat. Left total leg supported in approximately 25° of abduction. This is the starting position (0° right total leg).
     a. Right total leg adduction (hip adduction). Move the right total leg (keep straight) up to the left total leg. You must support the student's left total leg so that right leg can be moved up to it.
        1. Strength. Have the student move the right total leg up to the left total leg (keep both legs straight and support left leg). Any movement from starting position is a pass situation.
        2. Endurance. Have the student move the right total leg up to the left total leg and hold for 30 seconds. Record the number of seconds.
        3. Flexibility. Have the student move the right total leg up as near to or touching the left total leg. Range will vary from 0° to 25°. Record range. Major muscles tested: adductor magnus, adductor brevis, adductor longus, pectineus, and gracilis.

D. Head/Neck
  1. Head resting as far to right (near right shoulder) without forcing. This is the starting position (0°).
     a. Head adduct to abduction. Bring head from right starting position to near the left shoulder.
        1. Strength. Have the student move the head from the starting position as far as possible

(near the left shoulder). Any movement from starting position is a pass situation.

        2. Endurance. Have the student move the head to the center position (approximately 60° to 70° from starting position). Hold this position for 180 seconds. Record seconds.
        3. Flexibility. Have the student move the head from the starting position (0°) to approximately 120° (or near left shoulder). Range will vary from 0° to (120°-130°). Record range. Major muscles tested: sternocleidomastoideus and trapezius.

IV. Lying on left side, right side up. (Follow the same procedures that are used for lying on right side left side up. Sides now change; where instructions say left, you test right, etc.).

It should be obvious from reading the descriptions of the movements and observation of the Recording Sheet (Figure 13.B.1) that you can measure all three factors (i.e., strength, endurance, and flexibility) at the same phase. Flexibility and strength can be measured at the same time, then back to a hold position for each segment(s) to determine how long the participant held that segment(s) as a measure of endurance.

The approximate weight of each segment can be calculated using the values presented in Table 13.B.1. As an example of how to use Table 13.B.1 to estimate body segment weight, suppose we have a 12-year-old male who weighs 85 pounds and a 7-year-old female who weighs 52 pounds. For our male and female, each body segment weight is determined by multiplying the decimal fraction ratio by the whole body weight (Table 13.B.2).

Recording Sheet

		Strength		Endurance Hold time (seconds)	Time held (seconds)	Flexibility Range degrees	Record range
	Position and movement	Pass	Fail				
I.	Back lying (face up)						
	A. Left hand						
	Wrist flexion			180		0-90	
	Wrist extension			180		0-70	
	B. Right hand						
	Wrist flexion			180		0-90	
	Wrist extension			180		0-70	
	C. Left lower arm						
	Elbow flexion			180		0-160	
	D. Right lower arm						
	Elbow flexion			180		0-160	
	E. Left total arm						
	Shoulder flexion			90		0-180	
	F. Right total arm						
	Shoulder flexion			90		0-180	
	G. Head/neck						
	Neck flexion			180		0-70	
	H. Trunk/head						
	Trunk flexion			20		0-100	
	I. Left total leg						
	Hip flexion			30		0-125	
	J. Right total leg						
	Hip flexion			30		0-125	
*	K. Left foot (standing)						
	Plantar flexion			10		0-45	
*	L. Right foot (standing)						
	Plantar flexion			10		0-45	
II.	Stomach lying (face down)						
	A. Left total arm						
	Shoulder extension			90		0-50	
	B. Right total arm						
	Shoulder extension			90		0-50	
	C. Head/neck						
	Neck extension			180		0-25	
	D. Trunk/head						
	Trunk extension			20		0-50	

(Cont.)

Position and movement	Strength Pass	Strength Fail	Endurance Hold time (seconds)	Endurance Time held (seconds)	Flexibility Range degrees	Flexibility Record range
E. Left total leg						
Hip extension			30		0-15	
F. Right total leg						
Hip extension			30		0-15	
G. Left lower leg						
Knee flexion			110		0-130	
H. Right lower leg						
Knee flexion			110		0-130	
III. Right side lying (left side up)						
A. Trunk/head						
Trunk abduction			10		0-30	
B. Left total leg						
Hip abduction			30		0-45	
C. Right total leg						
Hip adduction			30		0-25	
D. Head/neck						
Adduct to abduct			180		0-130	
IV. Left side lying (right side up) *Pass*						
A. Trunk/head						
Trunk abduction			10		0-30	
B. Right total leg						
Hip abduction			30		0-45	
C. Left total leg						
Hip adduction			30		0-25	
D. Head/neck			180		0-130	
Adduct to abduct			180		0-130	

*Note change of whole body position.

Figure 13.B.1 Recording sheet for testing segment movements.

Now in your strength test you can see how much approximate weight is actually being lifted

Table 13.B.1 Decimal Fraction Ratio of Segment Weight to Whole Body Weight

Segment	Male	Female
Head/neck	.081	.081
Head/trunk	.536	.540
Upper arm	.0262	.0234
Lower arm	.0176	.0208
Hand	.0103	.0089
Upper leg	.114	.113
Lower leg	.0451	.0444
Foot	.0188	.0195

Note. From ''An approach to finding the centers of gravity of the segments of the living body'' by R.E. Johnson and S. Musgrave, 1976. Unpublished paper, University of Kentucky, Lexington, KY.

for each body segment. In endurance, taking the weight times the time held gives a better factor for endurance. *Keep in mind that if more than one segment is involved in a movement, then the sum of all the segment weights equals the total weight moved.* Consider the following example: Trunk flexion for the 85-lb male; 2(2.2 lbs + 1.5 lbs + .9 lbs) + 45.6 lbs = total weight being lifted, which is equal to 54.8 lbs. If he held the trunk flexion at 45° for the full 20 seconds, then endurance = 54.8 lbs × 20 seconds = 1096 lb seconds. Most individuals have two hands, two lower arms, two upper arms, and one head/trunk. So our formula for trunk flexion, i.e., total weight = 2(upper arm weight + lower arm weight + hand weight) + head/trunk weight is correct. Suppose our 85-lb male has the total left arm amputated. Our new formula then would be total weight = weight of right hand + weight of right lower arm + weight of right upper arm + weight of head/trunk = .9 lbs + 1.5 lbs + 2.2 lbs + 45.6 lbs = 50.2 lbs. If held for 10 seconds, the endurance would be 502 lb seconds.

Table 13.B.2 Example of Decimal Fraction Ratio Usage with Males and Females

Segment	Male	Female
Head/neck	.081 × 85 lbs = 6.9 lbs	.081 × 52 lbs = 4.2 lbs
Head/trunk	.536 × 85 lbs = 45.6 lbs	.540 × 52 lbs = 28.1 lbs
Upper arm	.0262 × 85 lbs = 2.2 lbs	.0234 × 52 lbs = 1.2 lbs
Lower arm	.0176 × 85 lbs = 1.5 lbs	.0208 × 52 lbs = 1.1 lbs
Hand	.0103 × 85 lbs = .9 lbs	.0089 × 52 lbs = .5 lbs
Upper leg	.114 × 85 lbs = 9.7 lbs	.113 × 52 lbs = 5.9 lbs
Lower leg	.0451 × 85 lbs = 3.8 lbs	.0444 × 52 lbs = 2.3 lbs
Foot	.0188 × 85 lbs = 1.6 lbs	.0195 × 52 lbs = 1.0 lbs

Selected References

The following references are recommended if further information is desired:

Reflex Testing

Banus, B.S., Kent, C., Norton, Y., Sukiennicki, D., & Beckel, M. (1979). *The developmental therapist* (2nd ed.). Thorofare, NJ: Charles B. Slack.

Bobath, B., & Bobath, K. (1975). *Motor development in the different types of cerebral palsy.* London: International Ideas.

Crowe, S.C., Auxter, D., & Pyfer, J. (1981). *Adapted physical education and recreation* (4th ed.). St. Louis: C.V. Mosby.

Fiorentino, M.R. (1972). *Reflex testing methods for evaluating CNS development.* Springfield, IL: Charles C. Thomas.

Seaman, J.A., & Depauw, K.P. (1982). *The new adapted physical education.* Palo Alto, CA: Mayfield.

Sensory Motor Testing

Crowe, W.C., Auxter, D., & Pyfer, J. (1981). *Adapted physical education and recreation* (4th ed.). St. Louis: C.V. Mosby.

Kalakian, L., & Eichstaedt, C. (1982). *Developmental adapted physical education.* Minneapolis: Burgess.

Pyfer, J., & Johnson, R. (1982). *Adapted physical education manual.* Topeka, KS: Division of Special Education, Kansas State Department of Education.

Seaman, J., & DePauw, K. (1982). *The new adapted physical education.* Palo Alto, CA: Mayfield.

Sherrill, C. (1976). *Adapted physical education and recreation.* Dubuque, IA: William C. Brown.

Bibliography

American Alliance for Health, Physical Education, and Recreation & Bureau of Education. (1973). *Guidelines for professional preparation programs for personnel involved in physical education and recreation for the handicapped.* Washington, DC: Author.

American Red Cross. (1977). *Adapted aquatics.* Garden City, NJ: Doubleday.

Ayers, A. (1973). *Sensory integration and learning disorders.* Los Angeles: Western Psychological Services.

Daniels, L., & Worthingham, C. (1972). *Muscle testing techniques of manual examination* (3rd ed.). Philadelphia: W.B. Saunders.

Hoppenfeld, S. (1976). *Physical examination of the spine and extremities.* Norwalk: Appleton-Century-Crofts.

Kephart, N. (1971). *The slow learner in the classroom* (2nd ed.). Columbus, OH: Charles E. Merrill.

Montessori, M. (1964). *The Montessori method.* Cambridge, MA: Bentley.

Piaget, J. (1970). *The development of the concept of space in the child.* New York: International University Press.

U.S. 94th Congress. (1975). Public Law 94-142. Washington, DC: Author.

Winnick, J.P., & Short, F.X. (1984). *Physical fitness testing of the disabled: Project Unique.* Champaign, IL: Human Kinetics.

Wiseman, D. (1982). *A practical approach to adapted physical education.* Reading, PA: Addison Wesley.

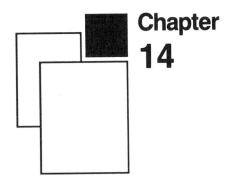

Chapter 14

Evaluation Programs in Preschools and Elementary Schools

Preschool and elementary school children move for the pure joy of movement. Their lives center around physical movement. These children must have sufficient movement opportunities to ensure adequate physical growth, physical development, motor development, and motor fitness. A well-developed, organized, and applied preschool or elementary school physical education program will help to meet children's movement needs.

Teachers who work with preschool or elementary school children should involve their students in a well-developed physical education program. Physical education programs for preschool or elementary school children must provide for individual differences in students and allow each participant to work at his or her own level of ability. Early identification of individual differences and ability levels may be accomplished through testing, measuring, and evaluating.

The tests presented in this chapter will assist the elementary physical educator in identifying ability levels and recognizing individual differ-

ences. Evaluation of the test results will help to identify the motor development and motor fitness levels of each child. After ability levels have been identified, goals and behavioral objectives can be established for both the group as a whole and each individual participant. When the goals and behavioral objectives have been established, a more realistic program of physical activities can be developed and applied to meet individual differences and strive toward goals and behavioral objectives.

Presented in this chapter are a checklist for motor movement patterns for young children and a norm-referenced basic motor ability test with 11 subtests. An example is provided later in the chapter of how this norm-referenced test can be used to establish group goals and behavioral objectives along with individual goals and behavioral objectives for an elementary school class of 10-year-old students. This example shows how to identify levels of ability and design appropriate programs to attain the goals and objectives. The tests presented in this chapter by no means include all the tests that may be used to test preschool or elementary children. Supplemental tests are referenced, and addresses for correspondence are provided in the appendix to this chapter for readers who desire additional information.

Check Sheet for Motor Movement Patterns

The first test presented is a check sheet that requires the subjective evaluation of children by observing them perform various physical activities during the school day. Based on these observations, the teacher will make decisions concerning each child's needs for help. The teacher observes and evaluates fine (small) motor movements that require hand and finger dexterity, eye movements, and gross (large) motor movements in which the child performs various physical activities that require movement of the arms, legs, and whole body.

This test is designed to help the teacher intensify his or her powers of observation and subsequent evaluation of preschool and early elementary school children and to improve the

teacher's ability to make decisions regarding students' needs for help. Finger-hand dexterity, motor control of the eyes, and gross motor movements are areas in which permanent or temporary physical impairments could adversely affect a child's present and future physical performance, self-image, and acceptance among his or her peer group.

The test items are presented in the Motor Movement Check Sheet in Figure 14.1. The movement elements in each area are listed from simple to more complex tasks. The tester (teacher) should observe and evaluate each element in the order listed. Children who receive a rating of "inadequate" or "cannot do" in any item should be considered in need of help for that particular item. When a need has been identified, the teacher can more realistically establish behavioral objectives, design a program of activities for improvement, apply the program, and then reevaluate the results after a period of program participation to determine whether the objectives are being accomplished. If a child continues to have difficulty performing a particular item, the teacher might recommend that the child be evaluated by a specialist such as an ophthalmologist, neurologist, or orthopedist.

Motor Movement Check Sheet

Name _____ Age _____ Sex _____

School _____ Teacher _____ Date _____

Finger/hand dexterity	Adequate	Inadequate	Cannot do

1. Finger to palm (both hands). Palmar grasp (i.e., picking up objects such as an eraser, pencil, book, etc.).

2. Fingers to thumb (both hands). Pincer grasp (i.e., picking up objects such as an eraser, pencil, book, etc.).

3. Turns single pages of a book (both hands).

(Cont.)

Motor Movement Check Sheet (Cont.)

4. Catches rolling ball with palms.

5. Catches rolling ball with fingers.

6. Catches bouncing ball with palms.

7. Catches bouncing ball with fingers.

8. Catches thrown airborne ball with palms.

9. Catches thrown airborne ball with fingers.

Eye movement

1. Focusing (both eyes contract).

2. Fixation (both eyes together on a target).

3. Release (both eyes together from a target).

4. Ocular pursuit (both eyes following a target).

5. Accommodation (seeing near and far target).

6. Peripheral (seeing a target out of corner of eyes).

Gross motor movement

1. Crawling (prone—on stomach).

    a. Homologous (arms move together; legs move together).

(Cont.)

Motor Movement Check Sheet (Cont.)

b. Homolateral (arms and leg of same side move together).

c. Cross-pattern (arm and leg of opposite sides move together).

2. Creeping (hands and knees on all fours).

a. Homologous (hands move together; knees move together).

b. Homolateral (hand and knee of same side move together).

c. Cross-pattern (hand and knee of opposite sides move together).

3. Walking

a. Homologous (body falls forward as a whole).

b. Homolateral (hand and knee of same side move together, ''toddling'').

c. Cross-pattern (hand and knee of opposite sides move together).

4. Running

a. Homolateral (hand and knee of same side move together ''awkwardly'').

b. Out-of-sync (hand and knee of opposite sides not in good cross-pattern; ''uncoordinated'').

Figure 14.1 Motor Movement Pattern Check Sheet.

No special material or equipment is needed to administer the Motor Movement Pattern Check Sheet. Observe two or three children each day as they perform various physical activities in the classroom, recess, or physical education class. Subjectively evaluate each child and place a check mark in the appropriate column for each activity on the check sheet.

Diagnostic Motor Ability Test

The Arnheim and Sinclair (1979) Basic Motor Ability Test (BMAT)[1] is a diagnostic motor ability test designed to help the practitioner evaluate motor response through a battery of 11 subtests designed to measure strength, coordination, large-muscle control, static balance, agility, fine-motor control, and flexibility.

A child can be tested in approximately 15 to 20 minutes. Norms were established by testing 1,563 children from various ethnic, cultural, social, and economic groups. The retest reliability for the entire test was .93. Face validity was assumed.

Subtest 1: Bead-Stringing

Purpose. The purpose of the bead-stringing subtest is to test bilateral eye-hand coordination and dexterity.

Equipment. Materials required for the test include a stopwatch, the 1/2-inch beads supplied with the Stanford-Binet test set, and an 18-inch round shoelace with a 3/4-inch plastic tip and a knot tied at the end.

Procedure. Place the beads and shoelace before the child. Demonstrate the task by putting two beads on the lace one at a time while explaining to the child that speed is essential. The beads merely need to be on the lace, and time should not be wasted by pulling the beads all the way down to the knot. Time limit for this test is 40 seconds.

Scoring. Record the total number of beads strung in the 40-second period.

Subtest 2: Target Throwing

Purpose. The purpose of the target throwing test is to test an individual's eye-hand coordination associated with throwing.

Equipment. Equipment for the test includes a wastepaper basket 14 inches high with an opening 13 inches in diameter and twenty 4- by 5-inch beanbags.

Procedure. A wastepaper basket is placed a minimum of 1 foot away from all surrounding structures to prevent the tossed beanbags from hitting the target after rebounding off an adjacent surface. Five successive throwing lines are marked on the floor. The throwing lines range from 3 to 15 feet from the target, with 3-foot intervals separating the marks. The tester demonstrates the test by throwing two bags at the wastepaper basket while explaining to the child that the beanbags landing inside the basket have a value of 2 points and bags that hit the basket but fail to drop inside it have a value of 1 point. No points are scored if the bag rebounds off the floor and strikes the basket. The child is then told to score as many points as possible by first throwing (either underhand or overhand) two beanbags with the preferred hand and then two beanbags with the other hand from each of the five testing lines. The wastebasket should be weighted down by a heavy object such as a textbook to prevent excessive movement resulting from the tossed beanbags.

---

[1]Directions for the Basic Motor Ability Test (BMAT) are from *The Clumsy Child* (2nd ed.) by D.D. Arnheim and W.A. Sinclair, 1979, St. Louis: C.V. Mosby. Copyright 1979 by D.D. Arnheim and W.A. Sinclair. Reprinted by permission. Norm tables for the BMAT are located in Appendix 14.A at the end of the chapter.

Subtest 3: Marble Transfer

Purpose. The purpose of the marble transfer subtest is to test finger dexterity and speed of hand movement crossing from one side of the body to the other.

Equipment. Equipment for the test includes 30 regular-size marbles, a table, a chair, and a transfer board consisting of two 8-ounce margarine containers 4 inches in diameter attached to and positioned on the board 12 inches apart.

Procedure. The children are seated at a table with the transfer board placed directly in front of them. The tester demonstrates the test twice while explaining that the test is taken in two parts, the first part with the preferred hand and the second part with the other hand. The test consists of reaching into the nearest container, picking up a single marble, and transferring it across the midline of the body to the opposite container. Time limit for the test is 20 seconds for each hand.

Scoring. Record the total number of marbles transferred in the allotted time by each hand and then record the cumulative score by adding together the number of marbles transferred by each hand.

Subtest 4: Back and Hamstring Stretch

Purpose. The purpose of the back and hamstring stretch subtest is to measure the flexibility of the back and the hamstring muscles.

Equipment. A 3-meter rule or yardstick is the only equipment needed.

Procedure. The children sit on the floor with their legs fully extended and heels approximately 6 inches apart. A 3-meter rule or yardstick is placed between the children's legs with the 30-centimeter or 20-inch mark in line with their heels. Keeping their knees straight, they bend forward and reach or slide with their fingers down the rule as far as possible and hold for a count of 3 (see Figure 14.2). Three attempts are allowed.

Scoring. Record the farthest point reached by each child's fingertips in the three attempts. Measure to the nearest centimeter or 1/8 inch.

Subtest 5: Standing Long Jump

Purpose. The purpose of the standing long jump subtest is to test the strength and power in the thigh and lower leg muscles.

Equipment. Necessary equipment includes

Figure 14.2 Back and hamstring stretch.

Figure 14.3 Standing long jump.

a 3-meter rule or yardstick and a nonslippery surface for taking off and landing.

Procedure. First the tester demonstrates while explaining to the children that they are to jump by swinging the arms back, bending the knees, and swinging the arms forward and extending the legs at the moment of takeoff (see Figure 14.3). A maximum of three trials is allowed.

Scoring. Measurement is made from the body part nearest the takeoff point, with the longest jump of the three trials recorded in centimeters or inches.

Subtest 6: Face Down to Standing

Purpose. The purpose of this subtest is to test speed and agility in changing from a prone to a standing position.

Equipment. A 4- by 6-foot mat or carpeted surface and a stopwatch are the only equipment needed.

Procedure. The tester demonstrates twice while explaining to the children that they are to start in a front-lying position with their foreheads touching the mat and their feet at the base of the wall. (The feet do not have to touch the wall after the test has begun.) On the command *go*, they stand to a fully erect position with their knees straight. When erect they reach directly back and touch with one hand above a mark on the wall that is approximately head level. They repeat this cycle as many times as possible within the allotted time limit of 20 seconds (see Figure 14.4a, b).

Scoring. Record the number of times the child is able to touch above the mark within the allotted time.

Subtest 7: Static Balance

Purpose. The purpose of this subtest is to measure static balance with the eyes open and with the eyes closed.

Equipment. Equipment for this subtest includes a blindfold, a stopwatch, and a 2- by 4-inch balance board with an actual width of 1-3/4 inches.

Procedure. The tester demonstrates the test on the board, explaining to the child that first the preferred foot and then the other foot will be tested. While the child is balancing (with shoes on), the hands must be kept on the hips with the nonsupporting foot hooked behind the knee of the support leg (see Figure 14.5). First the child is given one trial for each foot on the board with the eyes open, and then the test is repeated with the eyes closed or blindfolded. There is a time limit of 10 seconds per trial.

Scoring. Record the total number of seconds the child maintains a balanced position, first with the eyes open and then with the eyes closed for both the right foot and the left foot. Record the cumulative score for the left and right feet and their total by adding the scores obtained with the eyes both open and closed.

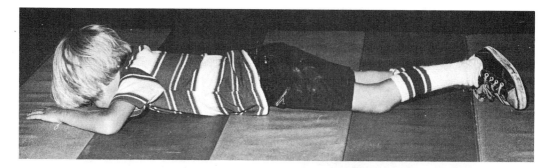

Figure 14.4   Face down to standing.

Subtest 8:
Basketball Throw for Distance

Purpose. The purpose of the basketball throw for distance subtest is to measure arm and shoulder girdle explosive strength.

Equipment. A basketball and 50-foot tape measure are the only equipment needed.

Procedure. The examiner demonstrates twice while explaining that the children are to assume a seated position with both their backs and their heads resting against the wall. Using a two-hand chest pass, the children propel the ball in a horizontal direction as far as possible. A maximum of three trials is allowed. To ensure that the ball is being projected solely by the muscles in the arms and shoulders, the child's head, shoulders, and buttocks must remain in contact with the wall during the throwing process.

Scoring. The longest throw of the three trials is recorded in centimeters or inches.

Subtest 9: Ball-Striking

Purpose. The purpose of the ball-striking subtest is to test coordination associated with striking.

Equipment. Equipment for this test includes two Nerf balls, one 3 inches and the other 10 inches in diameter, and a target consisting of four vertical lines 1 inch wide and 8 feet high that are connected at the top by a horizontal line 1 inch wide. The vertical lines that are used to designate target areas are separated by 2-foot intervals. The target could be marked on any wall with sufficient surface area.

Procedure. Children 4 to 6 years of age stand behind a restraining line 3 feet from the wall and are tested with a Nerf ball 10 inches

Figure 14.5 Static balance.

in diameter. Children 7 to 9 years of age stand behind a restraining line 3 feet from the wall and are tested with a Nerf ball 3 inches in diameter. Children 10 to 12 years of age stand

behind a restraining line 6 feet from the wall and are tested with a Nerf ball 3 inches in diameter. The tester assumes a sideways position in relation to the wall and demonstrates a waist-level horizontal swing while explaining the following point system to the children: One point is awarded if hand contact is made with the Nerf ball; 4 additional points are awarded if the Nerf ball after being struck lands in the target area designated by the two middle vertical lines and the 8-foot high horizontal line; 2 points are awarded if the Nerf ball lands below the 8-foot high horizontal line and between either of the two middle vertical lines and one of the two outer lines. The Nerf ball is positioned and dropped by the tester from a point vertically equal to the child's height and horizontally equal to the length of the child's arm measured from the center of the hand. The children are allowed two practice tries with each arm.

Scoring. Record the scores for both the right and left sides by adding the points earned in five swings with each arm. If a Nerf ball lands on a target line, the larger score is awarded. Record the cumulative total by adding the scores obtained from each side.

Subtest 10: Target Kicking

Purpose. The purpose of the target kicking subtest is to test eye-foot coordination.

Equipment. Equipment for the target kicking subtest includes a rubber playground ball 10 inches in diameter and a target consisting of four vertical lines 1 inch wide and 8 feet high that are connected together at the top by a horizontal line 1 inch wide. The vertical lines are separated by 2-foot intervals. The target used in Subtest 9 (ball-striking) could also be used in this subtest.

Procedure. Children 4 to 6 years of age stand behind a restraining line 10 feet from the target. Children 7 to 9 years of age stand behind a restraining line 15 feet from the target.

Children 10 to 12 years of age stand behind a restraining line 20 feet from the target. The tester demonstrates by kicking two balls at the target while explaining the scoring procedure to the children. Four points are awarded if the ball lands (either on the fly or on a rebound from the floor) below the horizontal line and between the middle two vertical lines, and 2 points are awarded if the ball lands below the horizontal line and between either of the middle two lines and one of the two outer lines. The children are then told to place the ball in a stationary position behind the restraining line and kick five times with each foot.

Scoring. Record the scores for both the right and the left foot by adding the number of points earned in 5 kicks with each foot. If the ball lands on a target line, the larger score is awarded. Record the cumulative total by adding the scores obtained from each foot.

Subtest 11: Agility Run

Purpose. The purpose of the agility run subtest is to measure ability to rapidly move the body and alter direction.

Equipment. Equipment for the agility run includes four cones or chairs and a stopwatch.

Procedure. The cones are placed 5 feet apart in a straight line. The examiner demonstrates the test and explains that on the command *go* the child is to run as fast as possible in a zigzag pattern around the cones, starting on the right side of the first cone (see Figure 14.6). The time limit is 20 seconds.

Scoring. Scoring is based on the total number of cones that are passed in 20 seconds. For a complete run down and back, the child would receive a total of 8 points. Tables 14.A.1 through 14.A.18 located in Appendix 14.A at the end of this chapter provide normative values for boys and girls aged 4 to 12 years.

Figure 14.6 Agility run.

Additional Preschool and Elementary School Tests

The importance of providing a wide variety of movement experiences for preschool and elementary school children has been widely acknowledged by parents, teachers, supervisors, and administrators. Ideally, such experiences are provided through well-planned physical education programs taught by trained elementary physical education specialists. In recent years, however, budgetary constraints have reduced the number of elementary physical education specialists in many school districts and in some cases have eliminated them entirely. In such situations, classroom teachers, either alone or in conjunction with specialists, provide the physical education program for the children. Regardless of who has responsibility for organizing a physical movement program, the physical activities presented must serve the purpose of improving each child's physical functioning level. We have stressed throughout this book that current physical functioning level may be determined through testing and evaluation. The following list of selected tests is by no means comprehensive; the tests listed were selected to help elementary physical educators to determine the current physical functioning level of the children under their supervision. Mailing addresses for more information about these tests are provided in Appendix 14.B at the end of this chapter.

- The Growth Chart: The First Year of Life produced by the Fireside Publishing Company can be used to evaluate motor development, language vocalization, social responses, and cultural routines. This instrument can be used by trained or untrained personnel and requires minimal materials and equipment. Criterion-referenced tests with measurable objectives are provided.
- The Bruininks-Oseretsky Test of Motor Proficiency produced by the American Guidance Service can be used to evaluate running speed and agility, balance, bilateral coordination, strength, upper limb coordination, response speed, visual motor control, upper limb speed, and dexterity. A testing

kit is provided that includes easy-to-use test materials that have been specially selected for their appeal to young children. Instructions for administering and scoring the test are clear and precise.
- The Movement Pattern Checklist produced by the University of Illinois can be used to evaluate basic movement patterns. This instrument can be used by both trained or untrained personnel. Materials and equipment are held to a minimum.
- The Purdue Perceptual-Motor Survey produced by the Charles E. Merrill Publishing Company can be used to evaluate perceptual motor patterns. Instructions for administering and scoring the survey are clear and precise. Some special equipment must be used.
- The Physical Ability Rating Scale produced by the University of Iowa can be used to evaluate basic physical functions. This test can be used by trained or untrained personnel. Some special materials and equipment must be used.
- The Hughes Basic Gross Motor Assessment produced by the Denver Public Schools Office of Special Education can be used to evaluate gross motor development. This test can be used by trained or untrained personnel. Some special inexpensive materials must be used.

Most of the tests presented in chapter 13 may also be used with preschool and early elementary school children.

Measurement and Evaluation in Program Development

In this section, the development of a fitness program for 10-year-old elementary school children is presented as an example of how measurement and evaluation can be used to enhance program development. Although fitness activities are only one part of a total elementary physical education program, we may use fitness activities as an example to illustrate the decision-making process for setting program goals and objectives and then evaluating the extent to which these goals and objectives have been accomplished as the basis for future program development. The decision-making processes presented here illustrate procedures the elementary physical educator can employ to determine children's ability levels and to develop programs that account for individual and group differences and needs. In addition, testing, measuring, recording, and evaluating data enable the educator to establish accountability for his or her decisions.

What should an instructor test? The answer to this question is the starting point for the decision-making process necessary for program development. What factors of physical fitness and physical skill are necessary and important for 10-year-old elementary school children? Most fifth-grade students enjoy competition and want to do better than others in both physical fitness and physical skills. Fifth graders vary widely in their physical abilities and skills. They like to be an important member of the peer group. With these points in mind, suppose that we decided to test the following factors on twenty-five 10-year-old elementary school children: (a) muscular strength, (b) muscular endurance, (c) cardiorespiratory endurance, (d) eye-hand coordination, (e) eye-foot coordination, and (f) agility.

What tests are good indicators of the factors to be measured? First, each test must be valid and reliable, should have appropriate normative data, and must be economical and easy to administer. To meet these criteria, the following tests were chosen:

- *Sit-Ups.* A sit-ups test will be used as an indication of abdominal strength and endur-

ance. Normative data from the AAHPERD Health-Related Physical Fitness Tests will be used.
- *Standing Long Jump.* A standing long jump test will be used as an indication of muscular strength and power in the thigh and lower leg muscles. Normative data from the Arnheim and Sinclair Basic Motor Ability Test (BMAT) will be used.
- *Basketball Throw.* A basketball throw test will be used as an indicator of arm and shoulder girdle muscular strength. Normative data from the Arnheim and Sinclair BMAT will be used.
- *9-Minute Run.* A 9-minute run test will be used as an indication of cardiorespiratory endurance. Normative data from the AAHPERD Health-Related Physical Fitness Tests will be used.
- *Target Throwing.* A target throwing test will be used as an indication of eye-hand coordination. Normative data from the Arnheim and Sinclair BMAT will be used.
- *Target Kicking.* A target kicking test will be used as an indicator of eye-foot coordination. Normative data from the Arnheim and Sinclair BMAT will be used.
- *Agility Run.* An agility run test will be used as an indicator of whole body agility. Normative data from the Arnheim and Sinclair BMAT will be used.

The testing should be conducted on two different days to minimize fatigue. On the first day the students will complete the target throwing, standing long jump, and 9-minute run test items. On the second day they will do the basketball throw, agility run, target kicking, and sit-ups. The raw scores on each test for each student will be recorded. We will compare the raw scores to the appropriate norms and record a percentile rank for each student in each test. The mean values will be evaluated and recorded for each test for both boys and girls and will be compared to the 50th percentile (P50) score in the normative data. Any mean value that falls below the normative P50 score will be considered a weak area, and any mean value at or above the normative P50 score will be considered a strength area. Students at or below the 20th percentile rank in any test will be considered to have serious problems needing special attention in those factors that the test results indicate.

The data we record and evaluate will allow us to establish goals and behavioral objectives for the class as a group and for each individual participant. Raw scores and percentiles recorded for the twenty-five 10-year-old fifth graders are listed in Tables 14.1-14.3. The goals and behavioral objectives we establish will determine the physical activities for the program and will also help us to select appropriate teaching methods, skills, strategies, equipment, and materials. We decided to establish the following group goal and behavioral objectives:

- *Group Goal:* To improve the average muscular strength, muscular endurance, cardiorespiratory endurance, eye-hand coordination, eye-foot coordination, and agility of the class.
- *Group Behavioral Objective 1:* In weak areas where the group's mean value in a test falls below the P50 score from the appropriate norm, to improve these mean values to at least the P50 score.
- *Group Behavioral Objective 2:* In strong areas where the group's mean value for a test is at or above the P50 score from the appropriate norm, to improve that mean value.

We decided to establish the following individual goal and behavioral objectives:

- *Individual Goal:* To improve each class member's muscular strength, muscular endurance, cardiorespiratory endurance, eye-hand coordination, eye-foot coordination, and agility.

- *Individual Behavioral Objective 1:* Have each student increase his or her starting (entry level) percentile rank in each test.
- *Individual Behavioral Objective 2:* Have each student whose entry-level percentile rank is 20 or below increase that rank by at least 15 percentile rank points.

We have now established attainable direction and observable outcomes for both the class as a whole and each individual participant.

Table 14.1 presents the raw score for each child in each event with a calculated mean score ($\overline{X}$ = females; $\overline{Y}$ = males) at the bottom of each test column. Comparing the P50 score from Table 14.2 to the mean value in Table 14.1 for each test, we find that our fifth-grade students as a whole have weak areas. Females scored below average in sit-ups (P50 = 32; $\overline{X}$ = 29.9), the basketball throw (P50 = 175; $\overline{X}$ = 171), the 9-minute run (P50 = 1460; $\overline{X}$ = 1267.5), and target kicking total (P50 = 18; $\overline{X}$ = 16.9). Males were below average in the basketball throw (P50 = 189; $\overline{Y}$ = 186) and the 9-minute run (P50 = 1690; $\overline{Y}$ = 1553).

Similarly, the class as a whole was near average or slightly above average on the following items: for females, the standing long jump (P50 = 55; $\overline{X}$ = 54.9), target throwing total (P50 = 18; $\overline{X}$ = 18.5), and the agility run (P50 = 21; $\overline{X}$ = 21.4); for males, sit-ups (P50 = 34; $\overline{Y}$ = 33), target kicking total (P50 = 16; $\overline{Y}$ = 16.8), the standing long jump (P50 = 58; $\overline{Y}$ = 59), target throwing total (P50 = 20; $\overline{Y}$ = 19.9), and the agility run (P50 = 24; $\overline{Y}$ = 25.2).

The comparison of the norm P50 score with the group means indicated that our fifth-grade class was lacking most in cardiorespiratory endurance. We decided to start each class session with 10 to 15 minutes of continuous movement to music as a warm-up and as an initial effort to increase the group's cardiorespiratory endurance. We further decided to build a program of activities that would address a weak area

Table 14.1 Fitness Test Battery Raw Scores for 10-Year-Old Females and Males

Student	Sit-ups	Standing long jump (inches)	Basketball throw (inches)	9-minute run (yards)	Target throwing			Target kicking			Agility run
					RH	LH	Total	RF	LF	Total	
Females											
S1	29	55	172	1230	10	8	18	10	8	18	23
S2	29	54	169	1290	8	10	18	8	8	16	21
S3	34	58	175	1230	12	6	18	10	8	18	21
S4	32	58	175	1290	11	11	22	8	10	18	23
S5	37	54	172	1375	10	7	17	8	6	14	20
S6	19	49	154	1100	8	6	14	5	6	11	19
S7	34	60	175	1290	11	11	22	10	8	18	21
S8	26	54	169	1230	10	7	17	10	8	18	19
S9	32	55	172	1375	10	8	18	8	6	14	23
S10	34	58	182	1375	12	11	23	12	12	24	26
S11	34	58	191	1375	11	11	22	12	8	20	23
S12	19	46	146	1050	6	7	13	6	8	14	18
ΣX	359	659	2052	15210	119	103	222	107	96	203	257
$\overline{X}$	29.9	54.9	171	1267.5	9.9	8.6	18.5	8.9	8.0	16.9	21.4
Percentile	40	50	40	25	50	50	50	45	70	45	50
Males											
S13	29	54	176	1536	11	7	18	8	6	14	24
S14	36	63	196	1600	12	8	20	12	10	22	27
S15	34	58	182	1563	12	8	20	10	6	16	24
S16	34	56	182	1563	11	8	19	8	6	14	24
S17	36	62	189	1563	13	8	21	12	10	22	26
S18	31	58	176	1420	11	7	18	6	6	12	24
S19	29	53	176	1420	10	7	17	6	4	10	24
S20	34	56	182	1420	12	8	20	10	6	16	24
S21	34	62	182	1420	12	8	20	10	6	16	26
S22	34	63	196	1600	14	9	23	12	10	24	26
S23	31	63	196	1536	12	9	21	10	6	16	26
S24	36	63	196	1859	14	9	23	10	8	18	27
S25	31	56	189	1690	11	8	19	8	10	18	26
ΣY	429	767	2418	20190	155	104	259	122	94	218	328
$\overline{Y}$	33	59	186	1553	11.9	8	19.9	9.4	7.2	16.8	25.2
Percentile	50	50	45	30	50	50	50	50	60	50	55

Note. RH = right hand; LH = left hand; RF = right foot; LF = left foot.

and then a strong area in alternating order. An outline of our program follows:

A. Developing muscular strength
   1. Continuous movement to music (10-15 minutes)
   2. Basic gymnastics
      A. Mat and floor activities
         1. Basic body positions
         2. Stunts
            a. Inch worm
            b. Bear walk, etc.
      B. Tumbling
         1. Rolls
         2. Stands
         3. Balance activities
         4. Low vaulting box
      C. Scooter board activities
         1. Prone activities
         2. Kneeling activities
         3. Races and scooter soccer

Table 14.2 50th Percentile (P50) Score From Norm Tables for 10-Year-Old Males and Females

Test Item	P50 Score Males	Females
Sit-ups	34	32
Standing long jump (inches)	58	55
Basketball throw (inches)	189	175
9-minute run (yards)	1690	1460
Target throwing		
Right hand	12	10
Left hand	8	8
Total	20	18
Target kicking		
Right foot	10	10
Left foot	6	8
Total	16	18
Agility run	24	21

Table 14.3 Percentiles for Twenty-Five 10-Year-Old Female and Male Fifth Graders

Student	Sit-ups	Standing long jump	Basketball throw	9-minute run	Target throwing RH	LH	Total	Target kicking RF	LF	Total	Agility run
Females											
S1	40	50	40	20*	50	50	50	50	50	50	60
S2	40	40	30	30	20*	60	50	40	40	40	50
S3	60	60	50	20*	70	20*	50	50	50	50	50
S4	50	60	50	30	60	60	60	40	70	50	60
S5	70	40	40	40	50	40	40	40	30	30	40
S6	10*	20*	20*	10*	20*	20*	20*	10*	10*	10*	30
S7	60	70	50	30	60	60	60	50	50	50	50
S8	30	40	30	20*	50	40	40	50	50	50	30
S9	50	50	40	40	50	50	50	40	30	30	60
S10	60	60	60	40	70	70	70	80	80	80	70
S11	60	60	70	40	60	60	60	70	70	70	60
S12	10*	10*	10*	10*	10*	40	10*	10*	40	10*	10*

(Cont.)

Table 14.3 (Cont.)

Student	Sit-ups	Standing long jump	Basketball throw	9-minute run	Target throwing			Target kicking			Agility run
					RH	LH	Total	RF	LF	Total	
Males											
S13	30	30	30	30	40	30	30	40	40	40	40
S14	60	70	60	40	50	50	50	70	70	70	70
S15	50	50	40	30	50	50	50	50	50	50	50
S16	50	40	40	30	40	40	40	40	40	40	50
S17	60	60	50	30	60	60	60	70	70	70	60
S18	40	50	30	20*	30	30	30	20*	20*	20*	50
S19	30	20*	30	20*	20*	20*	20*	20*	10*	10*	40
S20	50	40	40	20*	50	50	50	50	50	50	50
S21	50	60	40	20*	50	50	50	60	50	50	60
S22	50	70	60	40	70	70	70	70	70	70	60
S23	40	70	60	30	50	70	60	50	50	50	60
S24	60	70	60	70	70	70	70	60	60	60	70
S25	40	40	50	50	40	40	40	40	70	60	60

Note. * = need special attention.

B. Coordination (ball-handling skills)
  1. Continuous movement to music (10-15 minutes)
  2. Ball skills
     a. Basic
     b. Intermediate
     c. Advanced
C. Jumping and standing
  1. Continuous movement to music (10-15 minutes)
  2. Jumping activities
     a. Jumping in place
     b. Jumping on the move
     c. Jumping over apparatus
D. Rhythmic activities
  1. Introductory activities
     a. Scatter formation
     b. Partner formations
     c. Basic ways of moving
  2. Mimetics in rhythms
     a. Walking

  b. Running
  c. Galloping
  3. Phrasing
     a. Time
     b. Weight
     c. Space
     d. Flow
E. Developing muscular endurance
  1. Continuous movement to music (10-15 minutes)
  2. Bench work
  3. Rope climbing
  4. Chinning bars
F. Speed and fun
  1. Continuous movement to music (10-15 minutes)
  2. Group games
     a. Speed games
     b. Agility games
  3. Novelty relays
G. Primary play days

As pointed out earlier, children of this age enjoy competition and want to be important members of the group. Play days are different from the annual field day. In play day, the children in the class participate in teams of perhaps five members rather than as individuals. Emphasis is upon group participation rather than the achievement of a few. Play day items include the following:

1. Obstacle course. Conduct like the agility run test. Add number of cones passed by all members of the team.
2. Standing long jump. Add team members' longest jumps.
3. High jump. Add team members' best heights.
4. Sit-ups. Add team members' numbers completed.
5. Basketball throw. Add team members' best distances.
6. Target throwing. Add team members' total numbers completed.
7. Target kicking. Add team members' total numbers completed.
8. 9-minute run. Add team members' distances covered.

This competition will take several days to complete. Team scores should be posted each day. *Use the results of the play days as retest situations to see if your goals and measurable objectives are being attained.*

Table 14.3 presents the percentile rank for each student in each test compared to the norms. Those students who scored in the 20th percentile rank or below will be considered to have special problems requiring special attention. For example, Student 12 (S12) needs special help in all the basic factors tested, including muscular strength, muscular endurance, cardiorespiratory endurance, eye-hand coordination, eye-foot coordination, and agility. Similarly, Student 6 (S6) needs special help to improve strength, endurance, and coordination. As the program is conducted, those students who need special attention to improve in their weak areas will be helped by adapting the physical activities so that the students can be challenged but not frustrated. They will participate in the regular program but will receive special attention from the teacher when necessary.

Decisions about the programs of activities will be based on the play day results. Are the group goal and behavioral objectives being met? On the average, has the class as a whole improved, leveled, or regressed in each test? Are the individual goal and behavioral objectives being met? Has each individual improved, leveled, or regressed in each test? The current test results indicate the current level of the class and each individual participant. Comparing the current test results to the past test results allows us to determine whether we are attaining our goals and behavioral objectives. If necessary, we then redesign the program to meet the needs of the students. Continuous cycles of modification of the program and/or goals and behavioral objectives will be established to improve the functioning level of each participant. This process of testing, measuring, and evaluating allows for dynamic program development and application, but even more importantly, it provides for accountability in program development and application.

Review Questions

1. What is the purpose of the Arnheim and Sinclair Basic Motor Ability Test (BMAT)?
2. What is the difference between a pincer

grasp and a palmar grasp (see Figure 14.1)?
3. Define the following terms: (a) homologous, (b) homolateral, and (c) cross-pattern movement.
4. Define the following terms: (a) ocular fixation, (b) ocular release, (c) ocular pursuit, (d) ocular accommodation, and (e) ocular peripheral.
5. Why should we be concerned with basic

motor development in preschool and early elementary school children?
6. Of what value are the normative data presented in this chapter?
7. What factors does each subtest in the BMAT measure?
8. What factors does each test measure in the AAHPERD Health-Related Physical Fitness Test?

Problems and Exercises

1. A 4-year-old female student was given the Arnheim and Sinclair Basic Motor Ability Test (BMAT) with the following results:

Subtest 1: Bead-stringing ___6___
Subtest 2: Target throwing RH ___6___ LH ___5___
Total ___11___
Subtest 3: Marble transfer RH ___12___ LH ___10___
Total ___22___
Subtest 4: Back and hamstring stretch ___23___ inches
Subtest 5: Standing long jump ___35___ inches
Subtest 6: Face down to standing ___3___
Subtest 7: Static balance
RS (eyes open) ___6___ LS (eyes open) ___6___
RS (eyes closed) ___2___ LS (eyes closed) ___1___
Total right side ___8___ Total left side ___7___
Total right and left sides ___15___
Subtest 8: Basketball throw ___47___ inches
Subtest 9: Ball-striking RH ___9___ LH ___3___
Total ___12___
Subtest 10: Target kicking RF ___14___ LF ___10___
Total ___24___
Subtest 11: Agility run ___14___

What are the (a) percentile ranking of the preschooler for each subtest and (b) mean percentile ranking over all the subtests? (Note: Use Final Total Score for each subtest in calculating the mean.)

Answers: (a) Bead-stringing ___60___; Target throwing RH ___70___, LH ___70___, Total ___70___; Marble transfer RH ___70___, LH ___60___, Total ___60___; Back and hamstring stretch ___70___ inches; Standing long jump ___50___ inches; Face down to standing ___30___; Static balance RS (eyes open) ___60___, RS (eyes closed) ___50___, Total right side ___50___; LS (eyes open) ___60___, LS (eyes closed) ___40___, Total left side ___40___; Total right and left sides ___40___; Basketball throw ___30___; Ball-striking

RH __70__ , LH __35__ , Total __50__ ; Target kicking
RF __80__ , LF __70__ , Total __70__ ; Agility run __60__ .
(b) 53.6.

2. A 4-year-old male preschool student was given the Arnheim and Sinclair BMAT with the following results:

Subtest 1:   Bead-stringing __4__
Subtest 2:   Target throwing RH __5__ LH __6__
             Total __11__
Subtest 3:   Marble transfer RH __8__ LH __12__
             Total __20__
Subtest 4:   Back and hamstring stretch __22__ inches
Subtest 5:   Standing long jump __39__ inches
Subtest 6:   Face down to standing __5__
Subtest 7:   Static balance
             RS (eyes open) __6__   LS (eyes open)__8__
             RS (eyes closed) __2__   LS (eyes closed) __3__
             Total right side __8__   Total left side __11__
             Total right and left sides __19__
Subtest 8:   Basketball throw __75__ inches
Subtest 9:   Ball-striking RH __3__ LH __14__
             Total __17__
Subtest 10: Target kicking RF __8__ LF __16__
             Total __24__
Subtest 11: Agility run __10__

What are the (a) percentile ranking of the preschooler for each subtest and (b) mean percentile ranking over all the subtests? (Note: Use Final Total Score for each subtest in calculating the mean.)

3. Ten 8-year-old early elementary school children were tested using the Arnheim and Sinclair BMAT with the following results:

Raw Scores of Ten 8-Year-Old Children (BMAT)

Subject	Sex	Bead stringing	Target throwing			Marble transfer		
			RH	LH	Total	RH	LH	Total
1	F	13	11	7	18	19	18	37
2	F	16	13	8	21	22	22	44
3	F	6	9	6	15	11	13	24
4	F	9	10	6	16	16	13	29
5	F	15	10	7	17	19	13	32
6	M	11	10	7	17	16	15	31
7	M	8	11	8	19	13	12	25
8	M	18	13	8	22	21	20	41
9	M	11	9	7	16	15	14	29
10	M	9	9	6	15	17	12	29

Subject	Sex	RS (eyes open)	RS (eyes closed)	RS total	Static balance LS (eyes open)	LS (eyes closed)	LS total	Total right and left sides
1	F	9	3	12	8	4	12	24
2	F	10	5	15	10	3	13	28
3	F	9	3	12	9	3	12	24
4	F	10	4	14	10	3	13	27
5	F	9	3	12	9	3	12	24
6	M	10	4	14	10	3	13	27
7	M	9	3	12	9	3	12	24
8	M	10	6	16	10	6	16	32
9	M	10	4	14	9	4	13	27
10	M	9	3	12	9	3	12	24

Subject	Sex	Basketball throw (inches)	Ball-striking RH	LH	Total	Target kicking RF	LF	Total	Agility run
1	F	117	10	10	20	14	8	22	21
2	F	163	16	15	31	18	17	35	30
3	F	116	4	3	7	8	8	16	18
4	F	157	10	10	20	10	8	18	19
5	F	156	10	6	16	14	14	28	26
6	M	123	10	6	16	12	10	22	20
7	M	112	9	6	15	14	8	22	21
8	M	134	16	14	30	16	12	28	27
9	M	123	10	5	15	12	10	22	20
10	M	85	4	3	7	8	8	16	17

(a) Determine a percentile rank for each subject in each factor.

(b) Calculate a $\overline{X}$ and σ of the raw scores for each column.

(c) Calculate a T score for each subject in each subtest. Use the total score in target throwing, marble transfer, ball-striking, and target kicking to calculate the T score. Use the Right and Left Sides Total in the static balance subtest to calculate the T score.

(d) Calculate a $\overline{X}$ T score for each subject and then rank the students in descending order.

(e) Calculate a rank order correlation coefficient between raw scores in bead stringing and the marble transfer total.

Answers:
(a) Percentile ranks

Subject	Bead stringing	Target throwing RH	LH	Total	Marble transfer RH	LH	Total	Back and hamstring stretch
1	70	60	60	60	80	80	80	70
2	90	90	70	80	90	90	90	80
3	20	40	20	30	20	40	30	40
4	50	50	20	40	70	40	50	70
5	80	50	60	50	80	40	70	90
6	60	60	60	60	60	60	60	60
7	40	70	70	70	40	40	40	40
8	100	90	80	80	100	90	90	90
9	60	40	60	50	50	50	50	80
10	50	40	50	40	70	40	50	60

Subject	Standing long jump	Face down to standing	Static balance RS (eyes open)	RS (eyes closed)	RS total	LS (eyes open)	LS (eyes closed)	LS total	Total right and left sides
1	60	60	60	50	50	40	80	60	50
2	90	90	100	90	90	100	70	80	80
3	30	20	60	50	50	60	80	60	50
4	50	60	100	70	70	100	80	80	70
5	80	60	60	50	50	60	80	60	50
6	70	30	100	70	70	100	80	80	70
7	60	50	60	60	60	60	60	60	60
8	100	80	100	90	90	100	100	100	100
9	60	80	70	70	70	60	90	80	70
10	20	50	60	60	60	60	80	60	60

Subject	Basketball throw	Ball-striking RH	LH	Total	Target kicking RF	LF	Total	Agility run
1	50	70	70	70	80	60	60	60
2	90	90	90	90	100	100	100	100
3	50	30	25	30	20	60	20	30
4	80	70	70	70	40	60	40	50

(Cont.)

Subject	Basketball throw	Ball-striking			Target kicking			Agility run
		RH	LH	Total	RF	LF	Total	
5	80	70	45	55	80	80	80	80
6	60	50	50	50	50	60	50	40
7	50	40	50	40	70	40	50	50
8	70	90	90	90	100	80	80	80
9	60	50	30	40	50	60	50	40
10	20	20	20	20	20	20	20	10

(b) Subtest $\overline{X}$s and σs:

	Beads	Target throw			Marble transfer			Back and hamstring stretch (inches)
		RH	LH	Total	RH	LH	Total	
$\overline{X}$	11.6	10.5	7.0	17.6	16.9	15.2	32.1	20.6
σ	3.6	1.4	.8	2.3	3.3	3.4	6.3	1.4

	Standing long jump (inches)	Face down to standing	Static balance						Total right and left sides
			RS (eyes open)	RS (eyes closed)	RS total	LS (eyes open)	LS (eyes closed)	LS total	
$\overline{X}$	53.7	5.7	9.5	3.8	13.3	9.3	3.5	12.8	26.1
σ	9.6	1.4	.5	1.0	1.4	.6	.9	1.2	2.5

	Basketball throw (inches)	Ball-striking			Target kicking			Agility run
		RH	LH	Total	RF	LF	Total	
$\overline{X}$	128.6	9.9	7.8	17.7	12.6	10.3	22.9	21.9
σ	23.0	3.8	4.0	7.7	3.1	3.0	5.7	4.1

(c) Subtest T scores: (Found on page 465).

Subject	Bead stringing	Target throwing	Marble transfer	Back and hamstring stretch	Standing long jump
1	54	52	58	53	51
2	62	65	69	56	59
3	34	39	37	39	36
4	43	43	45	49	44
5	59	47	50	64	57
6	48	47	48	46	52
7	40	56	39	31	52
8	68	69	64	62	67
9	48	43	45	58	51
10	43	39	45	46	32

Face down to standing	Static balance	Basketball throw	Ball-striking	Target kicking	Agility run	$\overline{X}$-T
52	42	45	53	48	48	50.5
66	58	65	67	71	70	64.4
31	42	45	36	38	40	37.9
52	54	62	53	41	43	48.1
52	42	62	48	59	60	54.5
38	54	48	48	48	45	47.5
45	42	42	46	48	48	45.0
59	74	52	66	59	62	63.6
59	54	48	46	48	45	49.5
45	42	31	36	38	38	39.5

(Cont.)

(d) Subject	$\overline{X}$-T score	Rank in descending order
1	50.5	1. Subject 2 64.4 F
2	64.4	2. Subject 8 63.6 M
3	37.9	3. Subject 5 54.5 F
4	48.1	4. Subject 1 50.5 F
5	54.5	5. Subject 9 49.5 M
6	47.5	6. Subject 4 48.1 F
7	45.0	7. Subject 6 47.5 M
8	63.6	8. Subject 7 45.0 M
9	49.5	9. Subject 10 39.5 M
10	39.5	10. Subject 3 37.9 F

(e) *rho* = .957

4. Ten 6-year-old early elementary school children were tested on the AAHPERD Health-Related Physical Fitness Test with the following results:

Raw Score on Ten 6-Year-Old Children (AAHPERD)

Subject	Sex	Mile run	Triceps and subscapula	Triceps	Sit-ups	Sit and reach
1	F	11:24	12	9	28	30
2	F	15:27	16	14	14	23
3	F	13:48	15	9	21	27
4	F	12:46	13	8	24	27
5	F	8:02	9	6	40	34
6	M	8:06	7	5	47	37
7	M	15:10	20	12	15	16
8	M	12:29	12	8	21	26
9	M	11:33	11	6	22	27
10	M	13:20	13	8	18	24

(a) Determine a percentile rank for each subject in each factor.
(b) Calculate a $\overline{X}$ and σ of the raw scores for each column.
(c) Calculate a T score for each subject in each factor.
(d) Calculate a $\overline{X}$ T score for each subject and then rank the students in descending order.
(e) Calculate a Pearson correlation coefficient between triceps plus subscapular and triceps.

Bibliography

American Alliance for Health, Physical Education, Recreation and Dance. (1980). *Health-related physical fitness manual*. Reston, VA: Author.

Arnheim, D., & Sinclair, W. (1979). *The clumsy child* (2nd ed.). St. Louis: C.V. Mosby.

Cochran, N., Wilkinson, L., & Turlow, J. (1981). *Learning on the move (An activity guide for preschool parents and teachers)*. Dubuque, IA: Kendall-Hunt Publishing Company.

Gallallahue, D. (1982). *Developmental movement experiences for children*. New York: John Wiley and Sons.

Graham, G., Hale, S., McEwen, T., & Parker, M. (1980). *Children moving: A reflective approach to teaching physical education*. Palo Alto, CA: Mayfield.

Logsdon, B., Barrett, K., Broer, M., McGee, R., Ammons, M., Halverson, L., & Roberton, M. (1984). *Physical education for children*. Philadelphia: Lea and Febiger.

Roberton, M.A., & Halverson, L. (1984). *Developing children—Their changing movement: A guide for teachers*. Philadelphia: Lea and Febiger.

Appendix 14.A
Norm Tables for the Basic Motor Ability Test

Note. Tables 14.A.1 to 14.A.18 of the Basic Motor Ability Test (BMAT) are from *The Clumsy Child* (2nd Ed.) by D.D. Arnheim and W.A. Sinclair, 1979, St. Louis: C.V. Mosby. Copyright 1979 by D.D. Arnheim and W.A. Sinclair. Reprinted by permission.

Table 14.A.1   BMAT Male Age 4 Years

Percentile	Bead stringing	Target throwing			Marble transfer			Back and hamstring stretch	
		RH	LH	Total	RH	LH	Total	Inches	Cm
100	10	8	7	15	14	12	26	26-1/2	67
90	9	7	6	13	13	12	25	24	61
80	8	6	6	12	11	12	23	23-1/2	60
70	7	6	4	10	10	9	19	23	58
60	6	5	4	9	9	9	18	22-3/8	57
50	5	4	4	8	9	8	17	22	56
40	4	3	3	6	8	8	16	18-1/2	47
30	3	3	3	6	6	6	12	16-3/8	42
20	2	3	3	6	5	4	9	16	41
10	1	3	2	5	4	3	7	15-1/4	39

Percentile	Standing long jump		Face down to standing	Static balance						Right and left total
				Right side			Left side			
	Inches	Cm		Eyes open	Eyes closed	Total	Eyes open	Eyes closed	Total	
100	51-1/4	130	7	8	4	12	8	3	11	23
90	45-3/4	116	6	8	3	11	7	2	9	20
80	40-1/8	102	5	8	2	10	7	2	9	19
70	39	99	4	8	2	10	7	2	9	19
60	38-1/8	97	4	8	2	10	7	1	8	18
50	35	89	3	7	2	9	7	1	8	17
40	27	69	3	7	1	8	6	1	7	15
30	23-7/8	61	3	7	1	8	5	1	6	14
20	20	51	2	6	1	7	3	1	4	11
10	16-1/2	42	2	4	1	5	3	1	4	9

(Cont.)

Table 14.A.1 (Cont.)

Percentile	Basketball throw Inches	Cm	Ball striking RH	LH	Total	Target kicking RF	LF	Total	Agility run
100	98	249	17	16	33	16	16	32	18
90	86	218	15	14	29	16	14	30	17
80	80	203	10	10	20	14	14	28	15
70	75	190	8	6	14	12	12	24	14
60	71	180	5	4	9	12	10	22	14
50	67	170	4	4	8	10	10	20	12
40	57	144	4	3	7	10	8	18	10
30	46	117	3	2	5	8	8	16	9
20	39	99	3	2	5	8	6	14	7
10	31	78	1	1	2	6	6	12	6

Table 14.A.2   BMAT Female Age 4 Years

Percentile	Bead stringing	Target throwing RH	LH	Total	Marble transfer RH	LH	Total	Back and hamstring stretch Inches	Cm
100	11	8	8	16	15	15	30	16-1/2	67
90	9	7	7	14	14	13	27	25	64
80	8	7	6	13	13	12	25	23-3/4	60
70	7	6	5	11	12	12	24	23	58
60	6	6	4	10	11	11	22	22-3/8	57
50	5	5	4	9	9	8	17	22-1/4	57
40	4	4	3	7	8	7	15	18-5/8	47
30	3	4	3	7	6	6	12	16-3/8	42
20	2	3	3	6	6	6	12	16-1/4	41
10	1	3	3	6	5	5	10	15	38

Percentile	Standing long jump Inches	Cm	Face down to standing	Static balance Right side Eyes open	Eyes closed	Total	Left side Eyes open	Eyes closed	Total	Right and left total
100	50-3/4	129	7	8	4	12	8	3	11	23
90	45-1/4	115	6	8	3	11	7	3	10	21

(Cont.)

Table 14.A.2 (Cont.)

Percentile	Standing long jump Inches	Standing long jump Cm	Face down to standing	Right side Eyes open	Right side Eyes closed	Right side Total	Left side Eyes open	Left side Eyes closed	Left side Total	Right and left total
						Static balance				
80	43	109	6	7	3	10	7	2	9	19
70	40-1/8	102	5	7	3	10	7	2	9	19
60	38-1/8	97	5	6	3	9	6	2	8	17
50	35	89	4	6	2	8	6	2	8	16
40	29-3/8	75	4	6	2	8	6	1	7	15
30	24	51	3	4	2	6	5	1	6	12
20	20-1/2	52	2	4	1	5	4	1	5	10
10	16-7/8	43	2	3	1	4	3	1	4	8

Percentile	Basketball throw Inches	Basketball throw Cm	Ball striking RH	Ball striking LH	Ball striking Total	Target kicking RF	Target kicking LF	Target kicking Total	Agility run
100	99	251	18	15	33	16	14	30	19
90	91	231	17	14	31	16	12	28	18
80	84	213	10	9	19	14	12	26	16
70	76	193	9	9	18	14	10	24	15
60	71	180	7	5	12	12	10	22	14
50	68	173	5	4	9	10	10	20	12
40	58	147	4	4	8	8	8	16	10
30	47	119	3	2	5	6	8	14	9
20	40	101	1	2	3	6	6	12	8
10	31	79	1	1	2	6	6	12	7

Table 14.A.3 BMAT Male Age 5 Years

Percentile	Bead stringing	Target throwing RH	Target throwing LH	Target throwing Total	Marble transfer RH	Marble transfer LH	Marble transfer Total	Back and hamstring stretch Inches	Back and hamstring stretch Cm
100	12	10	8	18	15	16	31	26-1/2	67
90	10	9	7	16	14	14	28	23-3/4	60
80	9	8	7	15	13	14	27	23-1/8	59

(Cont.)

Table 14.A.3 (Cont.)

Percentile	Bead stringing	Target throwing			Marble transfer			Back and hamstring stretch	
		RH	LH	Total	RH	LH	Total	Inches	Cm
70	8	8	6	14	12	12	24	22-1/4	57
60	7	7	6	13	11	10	21	22	56
50	6	7	5	12	10	10	20	21-1/4	54
40	5	6	5	11	8	9	17	18-3/8	47
30	4	6	4	10	7	7	14	16-1/4	41
20	3	5	3	8	6	6	12	15-7/8	40
10	2	4	3	7	5	5	10	11	36

| Percentile | Standing long jump | | Face down to standing | Static balance | | | | | | Right and left total |
| | | | | Right side | | | Left side | | | |
	Inches	Cm		Eyes open	Eyes closed	Total	Eyes open	Eyes closed	Total	
100	54-3/4	139	8	10	4	14	9	3	12	26
90	47-1/4	120	7	9	3	12	9	2	11	23
80	45	114	6	9	3	12	8	2	10	22
70	43-1/8	110	6	9	3	12	8	2	10	22
60	39	99	5	8	3	11	8	2	10	21
50	38-1/4	97	4	8	2	10	8	1	9	19
40	34-7/8	89	4	8	2	10	7	2	9	19
30	27-5/8	70	3	8	1	9	7	1	8	17
20	25-1/8	64	3	6	1	7	5	1	6	13
10	22	56	2	4	1	5	3	1	4	9

| Percentile | Basketball throw | | Ball striking | | | Target kicking | | | Agility run |
	Inches	Cm	RH	LH	Total	RF	LF	Total	
100	117	297	19	18	37	18	16	34	22
90	100	254	17	16	33	16	16	32	21
80	96	244	12	14	26	16	14	30	19
70	92	234	12	10	22	14	12	26	18
60	87	221	10	8	18	12	12	24	17
50	81	206	8	8	16	12	10	22	16
40	69	175	6	6	12	10	10	20	11
30	60	152	4	4	8	10	8	18	11
20	54	137	4	2	6	10	6	16	10
10	47	119	2	2	4	8	6	14	9

Table 14.A.4   BMAT Female Age 5 Years

Percentile	Bead stringing	Target throwing			Marble transfer			Back and hamstring stretch	
		RH	LH	Total	RH	LH	Total	Inches	Cm
100	13	10	9	19	16	15	31	26-1/2	67
90	11	9	8	17	15	14	29	24	61
80	9	8	7	15	14	13	27	23-1/4	59
70	8	8	6	14	13	12	25	22-1/4	57
60	7	7	5	12	12	12	24	22	56
50	6	7	5	12	11	11	22	21-7/8	56
40	5	6	5	11	9	9	18	19	48
30	4	6	4	10	8	8	16	17-1/4	44
20	3	5	3	8	7	8	15	16-1/8	41
10	2	4	3	7	6	5	11	14-1/4	36

| Percentile | Standing long jump | | Face down to standing | Static balance | | | | | | Right and left total |
| | | | | Right side | | | Left side | | | |
	Inches	Cm		Eyes open	Eyes closed	Total	Eyes open	Eyes closed	Total	
100	53-1/8	135	8	9	4	13	9	4	13	26
90	46	117	7	9	3	12	9	3	12	24
80	44-3/4	114	6	9	2	11	8	2	10	21
70	43	109	6	8	2	10	8	2	10	20
60	39-1/8	99	5	8	2	10	8	1	9	19
50	37-3/8	95	4	7	2	9	7	1	8	17
40	34	86	4	7	2	9	6	1	7	16
30	26-1/8	66	4	6	2	8	6	1	7	15
20	25	64	3	6	1	7	5	1	6	13
10	22-1/2	57	2	4	1	5	4	1	5	10

| Percentile | Basketball throw | | Ball striking | | | Target kicking | | | Agility run |
	Inches	Cm	RH	LH	Total	RF	LF	Total	
100	117	297	20	19	39	18	16	34	23
90	110	279	18	17	35	16	14	30	22
80	105	267	14	13	27	14	12	26	20
70	95	241	12	12	24	14	12	26	18

(Cont.)

Table 14.A.4 (Cont.)

Percentile	Basketball throw Inches	Cm	Ball striking RH	LH	Total	Target kicking RF	LF	Total	Agility run
60	91	231	8	7	15	14	10	24	17
50	82	208	8	7	15	12	10	22	16
40	67	170	6	5	11	12	8	20	12
30	55	140	3	2	5	10	8	18	12
20	53	135	3	1	4	8	8	16	11
10	51	130	2	1	3	8	6	14	9

Table 14.A.5 BMAT Male Age 6 Years

Percentile	Bead stringing	Target throwing RH	LH	Total	Marble transfer RH	LH	Total	Back and hamstring stretch Inches	Cm
100	13	10	10	20	19	18	37	26	66
90	12	9	8	17	18	17	35	23	58
80	10	9	8	17	15	13	28	22-1/4	57
70	9	8	7	15	14	13	27	22	56
60	8	8	6	14	13	12	25	21-5/8	55
50	7	8	5	13	11	10	21	20	51
40	6	7	4	11	8	7	15	18	46
30	5	7	4	11	7	7	14	16	41
20	4	6	3	9	7	6	13	15-3/8	39
10	3	5	3	8	5	5	10	13-3/8	34

Percentile	Standing long jump Inches	Cm	Face down to standing	Static balance Right side Eyes open	Eyes closed	Total	Left side Eyes open	Eyes closed	Total	Right and left total
100	61-3/8	156	8	10	6	16	9	6	15	29
90	55-7/8	142	7	10	4	14	9	4	13	27
80	53-1/8	135	7	10	3	13	9	3	12	25
70	50-1/4	128	6	9	3	12	9	3	12	24
60	45	114	6	9	3	12	9	2	11	23

(Cont.)

Table 14.A.5 (Cont.)

Percentile	Standing long jump Inches	Standing long jump Cm	Face down to standing	Right side Eyes open	Right side Eyes closed	Right side Total	Static balance Left side Eyes open	Static balance Left side Eyes closed	Static balance Left side Total	Right and left total
50	40-7/8	104	4	8	3	11	8	2	10	21
40	35	89	4	8	3	11	8	2	10	21
30	30	76	3	8	2	10	8	1	9	19
20	26-3/4	68	3	6	2	8	4	2	6	14
10	25-1/4	64	2	6	1	7	4	1	5	12

Percentile	Basketball throw Inches	Basketball throw Cm	Ball striking RH	Ball striking LH	Ball striking Total	Target kicking RF	Target kicking LF	Target kicking Total	Agility run
100	135	343	21	19	40	20	18	38	27
90	125	318	19	19	38	18	16	34	26
80	117	297	17	16	33	18	14	32	23
70	108	274	15	15	30	16	14	30	19
60	100	254	13	12	25	16	14	30	18
50	89	226	11	10	21	14	12	26	17
40	79	201	8	8	16	14	10	24	16
30	65	165	7	5	12	12	10	22	15
20	57	145	5	4	9	10	8	18	13
10	54	137	3	2	5	10	8	18	12

Table 14.A.6   BMAT Female Age 6 Years

Percentile	Bead stringing	Target throwing RH	Target throwing LH	Target throwing Total	Marble transfer RH	Marble transfer LH	Marble transfer Total	Back and hamstring stretch Inches	Back and hamstring stretch Cm
100	15	10	10	20	19	18	37	26	66
90	13	9	9	18	18	17	35	23-1/4	59
80	12	9	7	16	16	16	32	22	56
70	10	8	7	15	14	14	28	22	56
60	9	8	6	14	13	12	25	21-7/8	56
50	8	7	6	13	11	11	22	21-1/8	54

(Cont.)

Table 14.A.6 (Cont.)

Percentile	Bead stringing	Target throwing			Marble transfer			Back and hamstring stretch	
		RH	LH	Total	RH	LH	Total	Inches	Cm
40	7	7	5	12	10	10	20	19	48
30	6	6	5	11	9	9	18	17	43
20	5	5	5	10	8	8	16	16	41
10	4	4	5	9	6	6	12	14	36

| Percentile | Standing long jump | | Face down to standing | Static balance | | | | | | Right and left total |
| | | | | Right side | | | Left side | | | |
	Inches	Cm		Eyes open	Eyes closed	Total	Eyes open	Eyes closed	Total	
100	57-1/8	145	8	10	5	15	10	6	16	30
90	53-1/8	135	7	10	3	13	9	2	11	25
80	52	132	7	9	3	12	9	2	11	23
70	47-7/8	122	6	9	3	12	9	2	11	23
60	42	107	6	8	3	11	8	2	10	21
50	39-3/8	100	5	8	3	11	8	2	10	21
40	35	89	4	7	3	10	7	2	9	19
30	30-1/8	77	3	7	2	9	7	1	8	17
20	28-1/2	72	3	6	2	8	5	1	6	14
10	25	64	2	4	1	5	4	1	5	10

| Percentile | Basketball throw | | Ball striking | | | Target kicking | | | Agility run |
	Inches	Cm	RH	LH	Total	RF	LF	Total	
100	124	345	21	20	41	20	18	38	27
90	115	292	19	18	37	18	18	36	26
80	109	277	17	15	32	16	14	34	24
70	103	262	14	13	27	16	14	30	20
60	94	239	12	10	22	14	14	28	19
50	87	221	10	9	19	14	10	24	18
40	75	191	8	7	15	12	10	22	15
30	67	170	5	4	9	12	8	20	13
20	60	152	3	3	6	10	8	18	12
10	55	140	3	1	4	8	8	16	11

Table 14.A.7 BMAT Male Age 7 Years

Percentile	Bead stringing	Target throwing			Marble transfer			Back and hamstring stretch	
		RH	LH	Total	RH	LH	Total	Inches	Cm
100	15	12	10	22	20	21	41	25	64
90	14	12	8	20	19	20	39	22-3/8	57
80	12	11	7	18	18	16	34	21-3/4	55
70	11	10	7	17	16	16	32	21-1/2	55
60	10	9	6	15	14	13	27	21-1/2	55
50	9	9	5	14	13	12	25	19-5/8	50
40	7	8	5	13	11	10	21	18-1/4	46
30	6	7	5	12	10	10	20	16-1/4	41
20	5	6	5	11	9	8	17	15-1/4	39
10	3	6	5	11	8	7	15	12-1/8	31

| Percentile | Standing long jump | | Face down to standing | Static balance | | | | | | Right and left total |
| | | | | Right side | | | Left side | | | |
	Inches	Cm		Eyes open	Eyes closed	Total	Eyes open	Eyes closed	Total	
100	67-1/4	171	9	10	7	17	9	6	15	32
90	59	150	8	10	5	15	9	5	14	29
80	58	147	7	10	5	15	9	5	14	29
70	53-3/8	136	6	9	4	13	9	4	13	26
60	50-1/8	127	6	9	3	12	9	3	13	24
50	45-1/4	115	5	8	3	11	9	2	11	22
40	36-3/4	93	4	8	3	11	8	2	10	21
30	33-3/4	86	4	7	3	10	8	2	10	20
20	28-1/8	71	3	6	2	8	5	1	6	14
10	27	69	3	3	2	5	5	1	6	11

| Percentile | Basketball throw | | Ball striking | | | Target kicking | | | Agility run |
	Inches	Cm	RH	LH	Total	RF	LF	Total	
100	144	366	16	16	32	16	14	30	30
90	128	325	14	12	26	16	12	28	29
80	121	307	10	11	21	14	12	26	25
70	115	292	10	8	18	12	10	22	21
60	108	274	8	6	14	10	10	20	21

(Cont.)

Table 14.A.7 (Cont.)

Percentile	Basketball throw Inches	Cm	Ball striking RH	LH	Total	Target kicking RF	LF	Total	Agility run
50	98	249	8	6	14	10	8	18	19
40	81	206	6	5	11	10	6	16	18
30	70	178	4	4	8	8	6	14	17
20	61	155	4	3	7	8	6	14	16
10	59	150	1	1	2	6	6	12	14

Table 14.A.8 BMAT Female Age 7 Years

Percentile	Bead stringing	Target throwing RH	LH	Total	Marble transfer RH	LH	Total	Back and hamstring stretch Inches	Cm
100	17	12	9	21	21	21	42	25-3/8	64
90	15	10	8	18	20	20	40	22-7/8	58
80	13	9	8	17	18	17	35	22	56
70	12	9	7	16	16	15	31	21-3/4	55
60	11	8	7	15	14	13	27	21-3/8	54
50	9	8	6	14	13	13	26	20	51
40	8	7	6	13	12	12	24	19-1/8	49
30	7	6	6	12	11	10	21	16-3/4	43
20	6	6	6	12	10	10	20	16	41
10	5	5	5	10	8	8	16	13-3/8	34

Percentile	Standing long jump Inches	Cm	Face down to standing	Static balance Right side Eyes open	Eyes closed	Total	Left side Eyes open	Eyes closed	Total	Right and left total
100	65-3/8	166	8	10	5	15	10	6	16	31
90	59	150	7	9	4	13	9	4	13	26
80	57-1/8	145	7	9	4	13	9	3	12	25
70	54-7/8	139	6	8	4	12	9	3	12	24
60	49	124	6	8	3	11	8	2	10	21

(Cont.)

Table 14.A.8 (Cont.)

Percentile	Standing long jump Inches	Cm	Face down to standing	Right side Eyes open	Eyes closed	Total	Static balance Left side Eyes open	Eyes closed	Total	Right and left total
50	43-3/4	111	5	8	3	11	8	2	10	21
40	37-1/8	94	5	8	2	10	8	2	10	20
30	34	86	4	7	2	9	7	2	9	18
20	28-3/8	72	4	7	1	8	6	1	7	15
10	27-1/4	69	3	5	1	6	5	1	6	12

Percentile	Basketball throw Inches	Cm	Ball striking RH	LH	Total	Target kicking RF	LF	Total	Agility run
100	150	381	16	15	31	16	16	32	29
90	128	325	14	13	27	16	14	30	28
80	126	320	13	10	23	14	10	24	26
70	119	302	9	8	17	14	8	22	20
60	102	259	7	7	14	12	8	20	20
50	97	246	6	6	12	10	8	18	19
40	93	236	6	5	11	10	8	18	18
30	89	226	3	3	6	8	6	14	17
20	75	191	2	1	3	6	6	12	16
10	60	152	1	1	2	6	4	10	14

Table 14.A.9 BMAT Male Age 8 Years

Percentile	Bead stringing	Target throwing RH	LH	Total	Marble transfer RH	LH	Total	Back and hamstring stretch Inches	Cm
100	17	14	10	24	21	22	43	24	61
90	15	13	9	22	20	21	41	22-1/4	57
80	13	12	8	21	19	18	37	21-3/4	55
70	12	11	8	19	17	15	32	21	53
60	11	10	7	17	16	15	31	20	51

(Cont.)

Table 14.A.9 (Cont.)

| Percentile | Bead stringing | Target throwing | | | Marble transfer | | | Back and hamstring stretch | |
		RH	LH	Total	RH	LH	Total	Inches	Cm
50	9	10	6	16	15	14	29	19-1/4	49
40	8	9	6	15	13	12	25	18	46
30	6	9	6	15	11	10	21	16	41
20	6	8	6	14	10	10	20	15-1/4	39
10	4	8	6	14	9	8	17	10-1/2	27

| Percentile | Standing long jump | | Face down to standing | Static balance | | | | | | Right and left total |
| | | | | Right side | | | Left side | | | |
	Inches	Cm		Eyes open	Eyes closed	Total	Eyes open	Eyes closed	Total	
100	68-1/8	173	9	10	7	17	10	6	16	33
90	63-3/8	161	8	10	6	16	10	4	14	30
80	59-3/8	151	7	10	5	15	10	3	13	28
70	56	142	7	10	4	14	10	3	13	27
60	55-1/4	140	6	9	3	12	9	3	12	24
50	48-3/4	124	5	9	2	11	9	3	12	23
40	43-1/4	110	5	8	2	10	8	3	11	22
30	39-1/8	99	4	8	2	10	8	2	10	20
20	36-7/8	94	4	6	1	7	5	2	7	14
10	35	89	3	5	1	6	4	1	5	11

| Percentile | Basketball throw | | Ball striking | | | Target kicking | | | Agility run |
	Inches	Cm	RH	LH	Total	RF	LF	Total	
100	155	394	18	18	36	16	16	32	30
90	143	363	16	14	30	16	14	30	29
80	137	348	16	12	28	16	12	28	27
70	134	340	15	12	27	14	12	26	26
60	123	312	12	12	24	14	10	24	23
50	112	284	10	6	16	12	10	22	21
40	99	251	9	6	15	12	8	20	20
30	89	226	6	6	12	10	8	18	19
20	85	216	4	3	7	8	8	16	19
10	80	203	2	2	4	8	6	14	17

Table 14.A.10   BMAT Female Age 8 Years

Percentile	Bead stringing	Target throwing			Marble transfer			Back and hamstring stretch	
		RH	LH	Total	RH	LH	Total	Inches	Cm
100	19	14	12	26	23	23	46	24-1/2	62
90	16	13	10	23	22	22	44	22-1/2	57
80	15	12	9	21	19	18	37	21-3/8	54
70	13	12	8	20	16	16	32	21	53
60	12	11	7	18	15	15	30	20-7/8	53
50	9	10	7	17	15	14	29	20	51
40	8	9	7	16	13	13	26	19	48
30	8	8	7	15	12	12	24	17-1/4	44
20	6	7	6	13	11	12	23	15-7/8	40
10	5	7	5	12	10	9	19	12	30

| Percentile | Standing long jump | | Face down to standing | Static balance | | | | | | Right and left total |
| | | | | Right side | | | Left side | | | |
	Inches	Cm		Eyes open	Eyes closed	Total	Eyes open	Eyes closed	Total	
100	70-7/8	180	9	10	7	17	10	6	16	33
90	62-1/8	158	8	10	5	15	10	4	14	29
80	59-1/8	150	7	10	5	15	10	3	13	28
70	56-1/8	143	7	10	4	14	10	3	13	27
60	55	140	6	9	4	13	9	3	12	25
50	47-1/2	121	6	9	3	12	9	3	12	24
40	44	112	5	8	3	11	8	3	11	22
30	40-1/8	102	4	8	2	10	7	3	10	20
20	36	91	3	6	1	7	6	1	7	14
10	29-3/8	75	3	5	1	6	5	1	6	12

| Percentile | Basketball throw | | Ball striking | | | Target kicking | | | Agility run |
	Inches	Cm	RH	LH	Total	RF	LF	Total	
100	171	434	19	17	36	18	16	34	29
90	163	414	16	15	31	16	16	32	28
80	157	399	13	12	25	14	14	28	26
70	137	348	10	10	20	14	10	24	23
60	126	320	9	8	17	14	8	22	21

(Cont.)

Table 14.A.10 (Cont.)

Percentile	Basketball throw Inches	Cm	Ball striking RH	LH	Total	Target kicking RF	LF	Total	Agility run
50	117	297	8	7	15	12	8	20	19
40	107	272	5	5	10	10	8	18	19
30	98	249	4	4	8	10	8	18	18
20	86	218	3	2	5	8	8	16	17
10	71	180	2	2	4	8	6	14	17

Table 14.A.11 BMAT Male Age 9 Years

Percentile	Bead stringing	Target throwing RH	LH	Total	Marble transfer RH	LH	Total	Back and hamstring stretch Inches	Cm
100	19	14	11	25	23	22	45	24	61
90	16	13	10	23	22	21	43	22	59
80	14	13	9	22	20	20	40	21	53
70	13	13	8	21	17	16	33	20-1/2	52
60	12	12	8	20	16	16	32	20	51
50	10	11	8	19	15	13	28	19	48
40	8	11	7	18	14	13	27	16-1/2	42
30	7	10	7	17	12	11	23	15-3/8	39
20	6	9	7	16	12	10	22	15	38
10	5	8	7	15	11	9	20	10	25

Percentile	Standing long jump Inches	Cm	Face down to standing	Static balance Right side Eyes open	Eyes closed	Total	Left side Eyes open	Eyes closed	Total	Right and left total
100	72-3/4	185	10	10	8	18	10	8	18	36
90	67	170	9	10	6	16	10	5	15	31
80	65	165	8	10	4	14	9	4	13	27
70	60-1/8	153	8	10	4	14	9	3	12	26
60	57-1/8	145	6	10	3	13	8	3	11	24

(Cont.)

Table 14.A.11 (Cont.)

Percentile	Standing long jump Inches	Standing long jump Cm	Face down to standing	Right side Eyes open	Right side Eyes closed	Right side Total	Static balance Left side Eyes open	Static balance Left side Eyes closed	Static balance Left side Total	Right and left total
50	51	130	5	9	3	12	8	2	10	22
40	47-1/8	120	4	8	2	10	7	2	9	19
30	40-1/4	102	3	7	2	9	7	2	9	18
20	39	99	3	6	2	8	5	1	6	14
10	38	97	3	5	1	6	4	1	5	11

Percentile	Basketball throw Inches	Basketball throw Cm	Ball striking RH	Ball striking LH	Ball striking Total	Target kicking RF	Target kicking LF	Target kicking Total	Agility run
100	223	566	20	18	38	18	18	36	31
90	205	521	18	18	36	16	16	32	30
80	196	498	16	14	30	16	14	30	28
70	184	467	13	10	23	14	12	26	26
60	177	450	12	10	22	14	10	24	24
50	156	396	12	8	20	14	8	22	23
40	140	356	10	8	18	12	8	20	22
30	122	310	8	8	16	10	6	16	21
20	120	305	7	5	12	10	6	16	20
10	116	295	3	2	5	8	5	13	18

Table 14.A.12　BMAT Female Age 9 Years

Percentile	Bead stringing	Target throwing RH	Target throwing LH	Target throwing Total	Marble transfer RH	Marble transfer LH	Marble transfer Total	Back and hamstring stretch Inches	Back and hamstring stretch Cm
100	20	14	10	24	24	23	47	26	66
90	18	13	10	23	22	22	44	24	61
80	17	12	10	22	19	19	38	22-1/2	57
70	14	11	9	20	17	17	34	21-1/4	54
60	13	11	7	18	16	16	32	21	53

(Cont.)

Table 14.A.12 (Cont.)

Percentile	Bead stringing	Target throwing			Marble transfer			Back and hamstring stretch	
		RH	LH	Total	RH	LH	Total	Inches	Cm
50	10	10	6	16	16	15	31	20-3/8	52
40	9	10	6	16	14	13	27	16-1/4	41
30	8	9	6	15	13	12	25	16	41
20	7	8	6	14	12	12	24	14	36
10	6	7	5	12	11	10	21	11	28

| Percentile | Standing long jump | | Face down to standing | Static balance | | | | | | Right and left total |
| | | | | Right side | | | Left side | | | |
	Inches	Cm		Eyes open	Eyes closed	Total	Eyes open	Eyes closed	Total	
100	70-1/8	178	10	10	9	19	10	8	18	37
90	63-7/8	162	9	10	7	17	10	6	16	33
80	61	155	8	10	6	16	9	6	15	31
70	59-3/8	151	7	9	5	14	9	3	12	26
60	56-3/4	144	7	9	3	12	9	3	12	24
50	51-1/4	130	6	9	2	11	9	2	11	22
40	46-1/8	117	5	8	2	10	8	2	10	20
30	41	104	5	8	1	9	8	1	9	18
20	38-1/8	97	4	7	1	8	6	1	7	15
10	37	94	4	5	1	6	6	1	7	13

| Percentile | Basketball throw | | Ball striking | | | Target kicking | | | Agility run |
	Inches	Cm	RH	LH	Total	RF	LF	Total	
100	206	523	20	18	38	18	18	36	30
90	186	472	18	17	35	16	16	32	29
80	178	452	16	16	32	16	12	28	27
70	171	434	13	12	25	16	12	28	24
60	160	406	11	10	21	16	10	26	22
50	148	376	8	7	15	14	10	24	20
40	141	358	6	6	12	12	10	22	19
30	130	330	5	4	9	12	10	22	18
20	118	300	4	3	7	10	10	20	18
10	107	272	3	2	5	10	8	18	17

Table 14.A.13 BMAT Male Age 10 Years

Percentile	Bead stringing	Target throwing			Marble transfer			Back and hamstring stretch	
		RH	LH	Total	RH	LH	Total	Inches	Cm
100	20	15	12	27	23	24	47	24-3/8	62
90	17	14	11	25	22	23	45	23	58
80	15	14	10	24	20	20	40	21	53
70	14	14	9	23	18	17	35	20-1/2	52
60	13	13	8	21	17	15	32	20	51
50	10	12	8	20	16	14	30	19	48
40	9	11	8	19	13	13	26	16	41
30	8	11	7	18	12	13	25	15-1/8	38
20	7	10	7	17	11	11	22	14-7/8	38
10	5	9	7	16	10	10	20	10-1/2	27

Percentile	Standing long jump		Face down to standing	Static balance							Right and left total
				Right side			Left side			
	Inches	Cm		Eyes open	Eyes closed	Total	Eyes open	Eyes closed	Total	
100	75-5/8	192	10	10	8	18	10	8	18	36
90	69-1/4	176	8	10	7	17	10	4	14	31
80	66-3/8	169	8	10	4	14	9	3	12	26
70	63	160	7	9	4	13	9	3	12	25
60	61-7/8	157	6	9	3	12	9	2	11	23
50	58-1/4	148	6	10	3	13	9	2	11	24
40	56	142	5	9	3	12	9	1	10	22
30	54-1/8	137	4	8	2	10	8	1	9	19
20	52-7/8	134	4	6	1	7	5	1	6	13
10	48	122	3	4	1	5	4	1	5	10

Percentile	Basketball throw		Ball striking			Target kicking			Agility run
	Inches	Cm	RH	LH	Total	RF	LF	Total	
100	248	630	18	17	35	14	14	28	33
90	225	572	17	15	32	14	12	26	32
80	215	546	16	15	31	12	12	24	30
70	205	521	15	14	29	12	10	22	27

(Cont.)

Table 14.A.13 (Cont.)

Percentile	Basketball throw Inches	Cm	Ball striking RH	LH	Total	Target kicking RF	LF	Total	Agility run
60	196	493	14	14	28	10	8	18	26
50	189	480	12	10	22	10	6	16	24
40	182	462	12	8	20	8	6	14	24
30	176	447	10	8	18	8	6	14	23
20	167	424	5	3	8	6	6	12	21
10	156	396	3	3	6	6	4	10	19

Table 14.A.14 BMAT Female Age 10 Years

Percentile	Bead stringing	Target throwing RH	LH	Total	Marble transfer RH	LH	Total	Back and hamstring stretch Inches	Cm
100	21	15	13	28	24	24	48	24-7/8	63
90	19	14	12	26	23	22	45	23-7/8	61
80	16	13	11	24	20	18	38	22	56
70	15	12	11	23	18	17	35	21	53
60	14	11	11	22	17	16	33	20-3/8	52
50	11	10	8	18	17	16	33	20-1/8	51
40	10	10	7	17	15	14	29	17	43
30	9	9	7	16	13	13	26	16-1/2	42
20	8	8	6	14	12	12	24	15-1/2	39
10	7	7	6	13	11	11	22	11-3/4	30

Percentile	Standing long jump Inches	Cm	Face down to standing	Static balance Right side Eyes open	Eyes closed	Total	Left side Eyes open	Eyes closed	Total	Right and left total
100	75-1/2	192	10	10	7	17	10	6	16	33
90	65-1/8	165	9	10	6	16	10	5	15	31
80	62	157	8	10	4	14	10	3	13	27
70	60	153	7	9	4	13	9	4	13	26
60	58-3/8	148	6	9	4	13	9	3	12	25

(Cont.)

Table 14.A.14 (Cont.)

| | Standing long jump | | | Static balance | | | | | | | |
| | | | | | Right side | | | Left side | | | |
Percentile	Inches	Cm	Face down to standing	Eyes open	Eyes closed	Total	Eyes open	Eyes closed	Total	Right and left total
50	55-1/8	140	5	9	2	11	9	3	12	23
40	54-7/8	139	4	9	1	10	9	1	10	20
30	52-1/2	133	4	8	1	9	8	1	9	18
20	49-3/8	125	4	5	1	6	5	1	6	12
10	46	117	3	4	1	5	4	1	5	10

| | Basketball throw | | Ball striking | | | Target kicking | | | Agility run |
Percentile	Inches	Cm	RH	LH	Total	RF	LF	Total	
100	239	607	18	17	35	16	14	30	30
90	215	516	17	17	34	14	14	28	29
80	198	503	16	15	31	12	12	24	28
70	191	485	14	13	27	12	8	20	26
60	182	462	12	11	23	12	8	20	23
50	175	445	12	9	21	10	8	18	21
40	172	437	9	9	18	8	8	16	20
30	169	429	7	6	13	8	6	14	19
20	154	391	5	5	10	8	6	14	19
10	116	371	3	3	6	6	6	12	18

Table 14.A.15 BMAT Male Age 11 Years

| | Bead stringing | Target throwing | | | Marble transfer | | | Back and hamstring stretch | |
Percentile		RH	LH	Total	RH	LH	Total	Inches	Cm
100	21	15	14	29	26	25	51	24-1/2	62
90	18	15	10	25	25	24	49	23	58
80	15	14	10	24	22	21	33	22-1/8	56
70	15	14	9	23	20	18	38	21-1/2	55
60	14	13	9	22	19	18	37	21-1/4	54

(Cont.)

Table 14.A.15 (Cont.)

Percentile	Bead stringing	Target throwing			Marble transfer			Back and hamstring stretch	
		RH	LH	Total	RH	LH	Total	Inches	Cm
50	11	12	9	21	18	16	34	19-1/2	50
40	10	12	8	20	16	16	32	18	46
30	9	11	8	19	14	13	27	16-3/8	42
20	7	11	8	19	13	13	26	15-1/4	39
10	6	10	8	18	12	11	23	11-3/8	29

| Percentile | Standing long jump | | Face down to standing | Static balance | | | | | | Right and left total |
| | | | | Right side | | | Left side | | | |
	Inches	Cm		Eyes open	Eyes closed	Total	Eyes open	Eyes closed	Total	
100	81-1/2	207	11	10	8	18	10	7	17	35
90	73-1/8	186	9	10	6	16	10	3	13	29
80	69	175	8	10	5	15	10	3	13	28
70	64-3/8	163	7	10	4	14	10	3	13	27
60	64	163	6	10	2	12	10	2	12	24
50	62	157	5	9	2	11	9	2	11	22
40	61	155	4	9	2	11	8	2	10	21
30	58-1/8	148	4	8	2	10	8	2	10	20
20	55-3/4	142	3	6	2	8	5	2	7	15
10	52	132	3	4	2	6	4	2	6	12

| Percentile | Basketball throw | | Ball striking | | | Target kicking | | | Agility run |
	Inches	Cm	RH	LH	Total	RF	LF	Total	
100	278	706	17	17	34	16	14	30	35
90	250	635	16	15	31	14	12	26	33
80	233	566	16	14	30	14	10	24	30
70	217	551	15	14	29	14	10	24	28
60	213	541	15	14	29	12	10	22	27
50	210	533	14	13	27	12	8	20	26
40	205	521	12	10	22	10	8	18	25
30	198	500	8	8	16	8	8	16	23
20	185	470	6	3	9	8	6	14	22
10	176	447	3	2	5	6	6	12	22

Table 14.A.16 BMAT Female Age 11 Years

Percentile	Bead stringing	Target throwing			Marble transfer			Back and hamstring stretch	
		RH	LH	Total	RH	LH	Total	Inches	Cm
100	22	15	13	28	25	25	50	25-1/4	64
90	21	14	12	26	24	24	48	23-1/2	60
80	17	13	11	24	22	20	42	22-1/4	57
70	16	13	10	23	20	20	40	21	53
60	15	12	9	21	18	17	35	20	51
50	12	11	9	20	17	17	34	19-7/8	50
40	10	10	8	18	15	16	31	17-5/8	45
30	9	9	8	17	13	13	26	17-3/8	44
20	8	8	7	15	13	12	25	16	41
10	7	7	7	14	11	10	21	12-1/2	32

Percentile	Standing long jump		Face down to standing	Static balance						Right and left total
				Right side			Left side			
	Inches	Cm		Eyes open	Eyes closed	Total	Eyes open	Eyes closed	Total	
100	81-1/8	206	9	10	8	18	10	7	17	35
90	70	178	8	10	5	15	10	4	14	29
80	65-3/4	167	8	9	5	14	9	4	13	27
70	64-1/8	163	7	9	4	13	9	3	12	25
60	60-1/8	153	7	8	4	12	8	4	12	24
50	60-1/2	151	6	8	3	11	8	2	10	21
40	57	145	5	8	3	11	7	2	9	20
30	54-1/8	137	4	8	1	9	7	2	9	18
20	52	132	3	6	1	7	6	1	7	14
10	48-1/8	122	3	5	1	6	5	1	6	12

Percentile	Basketball throw		Ball striking			Target kicking			Agility run
	Inches	Cm	RH	LH	Total	RF	LF	Total	
100	255	648	16	15	31	14	14	28	32
90	220	559	16	14	30	14	12	26	31
80	201	511	15	13	28	14	12	26	29
70	198	503	14	12	26	14	10	24	27

(Cont.)

Table 14.A.16 (Cont.)

Percentile	Basketball throw Inches	Cm	Ball striking RH	LH	Total	Target kicking RF	LF	Total	Agility run
60	194	493	13	11	24	12	10	22	24
50	190	483	11	9	20	12	8	20	23
40	186	472	10	9	19	10	8	18	21
30	181	460	8	7	15	8	8	16	21
20	171	434	6	6	12	8	8	16	20
10	161	417	3	2	5	8	6	14	19

Table 14.A.17 BMAT Male Age 12 Years

Percentile	Bead stringing	Target throwing RH	LH	Total	Marble transfer RH	LH	Total	Back and hamstring stretch Inches	Cm
100	22	16	15	31	25	25	50	24-3/4	63
90	19	15	12	27	24	24	48	23	58
80	16	15	11	26	22	22	44	22-3/8	57
70	15	15	10	25	21	21	42	22	56
60	14	14	10	24	20	18	38	21-3/4	55
50	12	13	10	23	18	17	35	20-3/8	52
40	11	13	9	22	17	16	33	17-1/2	44
30	10	13	8	21	16	15	31	16	41
20	8	12	8	20	15	13	28	15-3/4	40
10	6	12	8	20	14	13	27	11	28

Percentile	Standing long jump Inches	Cm	Face down to standing	Static balance Right side Eyes open	Eyes closed	Total	Static balance Left side Eyes open	Eyes closed	Total	Right and left total
100	87	221	12	10	8	18	10	8	18	36
90	77-1/4	196	9	10	5	15	10	4	14	29
80	72	183	8	10	4	14	9	4	13	27
70	69	175	7	9	4	13	9	4	13	26

(Cont.)

Table 14.A.17 (Cont.)

| | Standing long jump | | Face down | Static balance | | | | | | | Right and |
| | | | | Right side | | | Left side | | | | |
Percentile	Inches	Cm	to standing	Eyes open	Eyes closed	Total	Eyes open	Eyes closed	Total		left total
60	68	173	6	9	3	12	9	2	11		23
50	66-1/8	168	5	8	3	11	8	2	10		21
40	65	165	4	7	3	10	7	3	10		20
30	62-1/4	158	4	7	2	9	7	1	8		17
20	60	152	3	5	2	7	5	1	6		13
10	57-7/8	147	3	4	1	5	5	1	6		11

| | Basketball throw | | Ball striking | | | Target kicking | | | Agility |
Percentile	Inches	Cm	RH	LH	Total	RF	LF	Total	run
100	308	782	20	19	39	18	18	36	37
90	273	693	19	17	36	18	16	34	35
80	255	647	18	16	34	16	16	32	31
70	244	620	15	13	28	16	14	30	29
60	241	612	14	12	26	16	12	28	28
50	234	594	12	10	22	14	12	26	27
40	230	584	10	9	19	14	10	24	25
30	219	556	7	5	12	12	8	20	25
20	212	538	5	4	9	10	8	18	24
10	201	511	3	2	5	8	6	14	23

Table 14.A.18 BMAT Female Age 12 Years

| | Bead | Target throwing | | | Marble transfer | | | Back and hamstring stretch | |
Percentile	stringing	RH	LH	Total	RH	LH	Total	Inches	Cm
100	22	16	14	30	26	25	51	25	64
90	20	15	12	27	25	24	49	24	61
80	18	14	11	25	22	21	43	22-1/4	57
70	16	13	11	24	21	21	42	21-1/8	54
60	14	12	10	22	18	17	35	21	53

(Cont.)

Table 14.A.18 (Cont.)

Percentile	Bead stringing	Target throwing			Marble transfer			Back and hamstring stretch	
		RH	LH	Total	RH	LH	Total	Inches	Cm
50	13	12	8	20	17	17	34	20-1/2	51
40	11	11	7	18	16	16	32	17-5/8	45
30	10	10	7	17	14	12	26	17-1/2	44
20	9	10	7	17	13	12	25	16-1/4	41
10	8	8	7	15	12	11	23	12	30

| Percentile | Standing long jump | | Face down to standing | Static balance | | | | | | Right and left total |
| | | | | Right side | | | Left side | | | |
	Inches	Cm		Eyes open	Eyes closed	Total	Eyes open	Eyes closed	Total	
100	81-1/2	207	9	10	7	17	10	5	15	32
90	72-1/4	184	8	10	4	14	10	4	14	28
80	69-3/8	176	7	10	3	13	9	4	13	26
70	66	168	7	9	3	12	9	3	12	24
60	64-1/4	163	6	9	3	12	9	2	11	23
50	63-3/8	161	6	8	3	11	8	2	10	21
40	60-1/8	153	5	8	2	10	8	1	9	19
30	58	147	5	7	1	8	7	1	8	16
20	54-7/8	139	4	6	1	7	6	1	7	14
10	52-1/2	133	3	5	1	6	5	1	6	12

| Percentile | Basketball throw | | Ball striking | | | Target kicking | | | Agility run |
	Inches	Cm	RH	LH	Total	RF	LF	Total	
100	282	716	17	15	32	18	16	34	34
90	248	630	16	14	30	14	14	28	32
80	238	605	14	12	26	14	12	26	29
70	227	577	13	11	24	12	12	24	27
60	221	561	11	9	20	12	10	22	26
50	217	551	10	8	18	10	10	20	24
40	210	533	9	7	16	10	8	18	22
30	200	508	6	5	11	10	6	16	20
20	191	485	5	4	9	8	6	14	20
10	183	465	4	2	6	8	4	12	19

Appendix 14.B
Selected Motor Tests
for Preschool and Elementary School Children

For information, write to the addresses listed.

Bruininks-Osteretsky Test of Motor Proficiency
American Guidance Service
Circle Pines, MN 55014

Growth Chart: The First Year of Life
Fireside Publishing Company
Simon and Schuster
1230 Ave. of the Americas
New York, NY 10020

Hughes Basic Gross Motor Assessment
Office of Special Education
Denver Public Schools
Denver, CO 80203

Movement Pattern Checklist
Department of Physical Education
University of Illinois
Urbana, IL 61801

Physical Ability Rating Scale
University Hospital School
Iowa City, IA 52240

Purdue Perceptual-Motor Survey
Charles E. Merrill Publishing Company
1300 Alum Creek Drive
Columbus, OH 43216

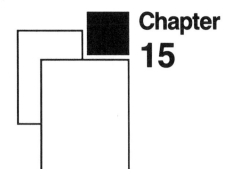

Chapter

15

Example Evaluation Programs for Secondary Physical Education and Competitive Athletics

Numerous evaluation programs could be used in secondary schools and competitive athletics. The exact nature of any evaluation program will depend upon the activity program itself, its goals and objectives, and the philosophy of the teacher or coach and the institution. The evaluation programs outlined in this chapter should be viewed only as examples.

Evaluation Program for Ninth-Grade Physical Education

Ninth-grade physical education is the secondary school level selected for this example evaluation program. For 14- and 15-year-old students, the physical activities offered and the tests subsequently used will be at the intermediate and advanced levels of motor development. Thus emphasis is placed on skill development in life-

time sports that require relatively high degrees of speed, agility, and coordination.

Our example physical education program is assumed to be completely coeducational. We will further assume that the school year consists of 32 weeks of instruction and that the physical education class will meet for three 50-minute periods per week. The following activities will be taught for the durations indicated:

- Archery (4 weeks)
- Gymnastics (6 weeks)
- Swimming (6 weeks)
- Badminton (5 weeks)
- Basketball (4 weeks)
- Golf (6 weeks)

Before the start of the school year, students will be required to have a health appraisal by a physician in order to identify those students needing special programs, as well as to protect the teacher and school against possible law suits.

Programs will be modified for students with special needs.

During the first week of school, the AAHPERD Health-Related Youth Fitness Test will be administered to all students. The 9-minute run-walk will be used as the cardiorespiratory endurance test in place of the 600-yard run-walk. Based on the results of this test, an individual fitness program will be planned for each student.

The goal of every participant will be to improve his or her percentile rank on all items. For example, students who score at the 25th percentile rank or below will have the goal of improving their percentile rank by 15 points. Anyone who starts out at the 95th percentile rank or above will attempt to maintain this status.

The individual fitness programs will emphasize improvement in the area or areas in which the person has the lowest rating. For example, if a student scored above the 50th percentile rank on all items except the upper body strength and endurance item (chin-ups), in which the student scored at the 20th percentile rank, then he or she will be put on a weight-training circuit consisting of the bench press, biceps lift, military press, and triceps extension.

Ten to 15 minutes at the beginning of each class period will be spent on fitness. This time will be spent primarily on educating the student about proper ways of becoming fit. Each student will be encouraged to conduct his or her own personal fitness program outside of class. Roll can be taken during this time. Testing of weak areas will be repeated every 6 weeks, and students' fitness programs will be adjusted according to the results. Each student will keep his or her own profile chart. The teacher will also keep copies of these profile charts.

The results of the fitness tests will also be used in identifying students who will need special attention in the activities planned for the year. For example, the student who cannot do a single chin-up will need to use a lightweight bow in archery.

For grading purposes, students will be classified according to sex and pretest results for each activity. There will be three initial ability categories for each sex in each activity: the top one third, middle one third, and bottom one third. These will be the norm-referenced groups to be used for determining grades on the posttests. Grades will be determined solely on the basis of physical performance and written tests. The weight of each test and activity will be indicated later. An anecdotal record on each student will be kept in order to identify students who may be having special problems. These records, however, will not be used in determining student grades. In general, the following distribution of grades will be used for each of the six units:

- A—10%
- B—25%
- C—45%
- D—15%
- F—5%

The following is an outline of the tests to be used:

Archery

- *Pretest.* The AAHPER Archery Skills Tests (see chapter 8) will be administered in order to classify students into three groups for each sex and to identify the problems of individual students. This classification will be used for posttest grading. This test will be repeated at least once every third class period.
- *Posttest.* The AAHPER will also be used for the posttest. Posttest results will count for 50% of a student's grade.
- *Written test.* A test on archery rules, safety, and technique will be given. A student's score on this test will count 50% of his or her grade.

Badminton

- *Pretest.* A rating scale similar to the one described on page 213 will be used while observing students playing during the first week of instruction. Students will be classified into three groups within each sex for instruction and posttest grading purposes. The pretest results will be used to identify individuals' specific problems.
- *Posttest.* At the conclusion of the program, a round robin tournament will be played within each group, and for this tournament the same rating scales will be applied. Each student's rating scale score for the tournament will count 60% of his or her grade.
- *Written tests.* A test on badminton rules, strategy, and technique will be given. A student's score on this test will count 40% of his or her grade.

Gymnastics

- *Pretest.* On the basis of the fitness test, students who are identified as lacking sufficient strength will be placed in appropriate activities. For example, a student who cannot do one push-up could not be expected to perform dive-and-rolls or dips on the parallel bars or any other skills requiring strength in the triceps. For each apparatus or tumbling item, students will perform progressive stunts until they reach a point where they can no longer perform. This point will be determined subjectively by the teacher. This progression testing will be applied continuously throughout the unit. Three classifications of students within each sex will be formed for posttest evaluation.
- *Posttest.* For the posttest, each student will develop a routine of three to five stunts for at least three apparatus or exercise items.

Performance will be judged much the same as a gymnastics meet. However, difficulty of the stunts will count in relation to the group in which the student started the instructional unit. This will count as 70% of the student's grade.
- *Written test.* A written test will be given on spotting and performance technique and judging rules. A student's score on this test will count 30% of his or her grade.

Basketball

- *Pretest.* During initial drills, students will be rated on their skills in dribbling, passing, defending, and shooting. These pretest ratings will provide the direction of instruction for each individual throughout the remainder of the unit. Students will also be classified into three different ability groups for each sex for posttest grading purposes.
- *Posttest.* Students' skills will again be rated during game playing conditions. The teacher will compare these ratings within classification to determine each student's posttest score. The posttest score will constitute 40% of the grade.
- *Written test.* A written test on the various offenses and defenses, technique, and rules will be given for the other 60% of the grade.

Swimming

- *Pretest.* Because swimming instruction is offered in this school, students will be classified into the Red Cross categories from Nonswimmer to Lifesaver. Programs for each category will be planned. Rating sheets such as the one given in chapter 8 will be completed for each stroke.

- *Posttest.* An achievement test for high school swimming will be given within each classification group. A student's score on this test will constitute 60% of his or her grade.
- *Written test.* A written test on water safety and skill technique will be given for 40% of the grade.

Golf

- *Pretest.* Students will be required to play nine holes of golf and turn in a verified score. Each student's handicap will be established. Also, the golf rating scale presented in chapter 8 will be applied to each student in order to provide feedback in instruction and to classify students into four ability groups without regard to sex.
- *Posttest.* For the posttest, students will again be required to play nine holes, and the rating scale will again be applied. Handicapped scores for the nine holes will count 30% of each student's grade. Another 30% of each student's grade will be determined from the rating scale score within his or her classification group.
- *Written test.* A written test on club selection, rules, and golf etiquette will be given for the remaining 40% of the grade.

Evaluation Programs in Competitive Athletics

Testing for classification and selection in sport requires knowledge of the physical factors that are essential for good performance in that sport. Once these factors have been identified, the coach must select those tests that are good indicators of the factors selected. He or she then applies each test and evaluates the results. The final decision for classification and selection must involve actual competitive situations for the sport as well as tests for physical sport skill factors. Tests are evaluation tools that a coach can use to improve his or her decision-making processes.

Coaches of athletic teams have always been engaged in the evaluation of their team members and potential team members. Although in many cases this evaluation has been informal and completely subjective, many coaches have formalized their evaluation procedures and made excellent use of objective tests and measures. Examples of these formalized procedures are presented here for the sports of basketball, football, volleyball, and track and field.

Basketball

A new basketball coach in a consolidated rural high school had 75 prospects try out for the team. The coach wanted to evaluate the prospects to select 15 members of a varsity "A" team. The coach knew that basketball is a sport that requires the ability to pass, dribble, make baskets, jump vertically, change whole body direction quickly and accurately in a coordinated manner, and respond quickly to various defensive and offensive situations. The coach also knew that basketball is a game that requires cardiorespiratory endurance.

The coach decided to use the speed pass (SP) to test passing and recovery ability, the jump and reach (JR) to test vertical jumping ability, the zigzag dribble (ZD) to test whole body agility and dribbling ability, spot shooting (SS) to test shooting ability, and the 12-minute run (12M) to test cardiorespiratory endurance.

The coach decided to test the 75 participants using these tests with the help of assistant coaches. In addition, they decided to (a) calculate a T score for each participant in each test, (b) calculate a mean T score for each participant, and (c) use the mean T scores to rank the participants into five squads of 15 participants each. Squad A will be composed of the top-ranked 15 participants, Squad B the next 15, Squad C the next 15, and so forth.

The coach decided to have the squads scrimmage against each other for the next two weeks of tryouts. Each participant was allowed equal time of play during the scrimmages. Statistics were kept on the scrimmages using the following game situation tests: number of defensive rebounds (DR), number of offensive rebounds (OR), number of assists, (Ast), field goal percent (FGP), free throw percentage (FTP), and comments. The coach once again decided to (a) calculate a T score for each participant in each game situation test, (b) calculate a mean T score for each participant, and (c) use the mean T scores to rank the participants into two new squads of 15 participants each. The new Squad A will consist of the top-ranked 15 participants, and the new Squad B will consist of the next 15 participants. The remaining partici-

pants will be encouraged to participate in an intramural basketball program.

The head coach then decided to look at the A Squad and determine who will be the starting players and what position will be assigned to each participant. The coach decided to evaluate the results of all the tests given and rank the top 15 participants among themselves. The following results were recorded along with the coach's evaluative comments and rationale:

Player	Comments
P1	A bit young, good height, good rebound (Forward) *Starter*
P2	*Definite starter*, good height (Center)
P3	*Definite starter*, good height, aggressive (Forward)
P4	Good height, very young, hard worker (Center) 2nd team
P5	Good passer, good assists, aggressive (Guard) *Starter*
P6	Good team player, aggressive (Forward) 2nd team

Rank Order of Players: Squad A

Player	Age	Ht	SP	JR	ZD	SS	12M	DR	OR	Ast	FGP	FTP
P1	16	6-7	7	5	11	5	14	2	1	11	5	3
P2	17	6-5	3	1	2	4	4	1	2	5	4	5
P3	17	6-3	2	2	1	3	2	3	4	3	1	1
P4	15	6-3	12	15	14	13	15	8	8	14	11	12
P5	17	6-1	1	3	4	1	1	5	3	2	6	6
P6	15	6-0	8	6	6	7	10	10	11	13	9	7
P7	16	6-0	6	7	8	10	9	9	7	4	7	8
P8	16	6-0	4	4	3	2	5	4	5	1	2	2
P9	15	5-11	15	13	13	14	13	11	10	8	10	10
P10	17	5-11	5	8	7	6	3	6	6	6	3	4
P11	16	5-11	11	11	9	8	8	7	9	9	13	14
P12	16	5-10	14	14	12	15	12	13	12	12	14	13
P13	16	5-10	9	9	10	9	7	12	13	7	8	9
P14	15	5-10	13	12	15	12	11	14	15	15	15	15
P15	15	5-9	10	10	5	11	6	15	14	10	12	11

P7 Good team player, lacks aggressiveness (Forward) 2nd team

P8 Good outside shooter, good assists (Guard) *Starter*

P9 Good in assist, young (Forward) 3rd team

P10 Intelligent, good all around (Guard) *6th man*

P11 Younger player, shows promise (Guard) 2nd team

P12 Young, needs work in all factors (Forward) 3rd team

P13 Good shooter, shows promise, young (Guard) 2nd team

P14 Young, needs aggression, spirit (Guard) 3rd team

P15 Good dribbler, short, may grow (Guard) 3rd team

The coach's logic in making decisions about starters and positions for starters from testing and measurement results follows.

Player 1: 16 years old, 6 feet 7 inches in height, ranks ranged from 14 to 1 in testing. Decided to start him instead of Player 10 at forward because we need the height under the boards. He is an excellent rebounder. He is a junior and will most likely be the nucleus of the team next year as a senior. Need to give him lots of game experience this year for development.

Player 2: 17 years old, 6 feet 5 inches in height, ranked in the top 5 in all-test rating. Senior, one of the best rebounders on team, has experience, excellent height, best jumper on team.

Player 3: 17 years old, 6 feet 3 inches in height, ranked in the top 5 in all-test rating. Senior, best shooter on the team, has experience, good height. Was not placed at center because Player 2 has 3 inches of height on him. Can play center or guard if needed.

Player 5: 17 years old, 6 feet 1 inch in height, ranked in top 6 in all-test rating. Senior, best conditioned athlete we have, good at as-

sisting, fair shooter, has experience, quick hands.

Player 8: 16 years old, 6 feet 0 inches in height, ranked in top 5 in all-test rating. Junior, excellent shooter, good ball handler, limited experience, shows great promise.

Player 10: 17 years old, 5 feet 11 inches in height, ranks ranged from 1 to 8 when tested but does not have the height of Player 1. Intelligent player so would be a good sixth man for explaining and implementing strategic changes to other players during the game.

Football[1]

During the first week of fall practice at Kansas State University, each football player's height and weight are measured, and a battery of the following eight tests is administered:

1. Power clean. Maximum weight for one repetition.
2. Bench press. Maximum weight for one repetition.
3. Power ratio. Bench press plus power clean divided by body weight.
4. Vertical jump. Athlete stands near the wall tape measure with strong side facing tape. Extended hand and reach is recorded. Athlete's middle finger is dipped in blue chalk. Athlete jumps vertically with a 2-foot takeoff and touches the tape at peak of jump. No step is allowed.
5. 40-yard dash for time.
6. 40s percentage. The average time of eight consecutive 40-yard dashes is divided by a single best 40-yard time previously recorded.

---

[1]Materials for the football section were provided by Russell Reiderer, Strength Coach, Kansas State University Football Team, Manhattan, KS.

7. 1.5-mile run for time.
8. 880-yard run for time.

All players are given the position goals sheet presented in Table 15.1 the spring and/or year before the current testing year. The goals represent the minimum standards that must be attained for each playing position. Players are not cut from the team solely on the basis of the established goals; rather, the primary purposes of these tests are to provide player motivation and *initial* screening of players for team selection.

Volleyball[2]

An excellent example of a coach developing a test battery for use in selecting team members is the work of Donald Shondell at Ball State University. After several years of study and research, Shondell devised a six-item volleyball test battery consisting of the following items:

1. *30-yard dash*
   Scoring. Each player performs two trials for the record. The player's score is the sum of two trials, measured to the nearest .10 second.
2. *Basketball toss*
   Procedure. The subject, on knees on mat, uses a two-hand chest pass to toss the ball straight ahead into the scoring area. If the player does not pass the ball correctly, a foul is recorded and the player repeats until the toss is executed correctly.
   Scoring. Each player receives two practice tosses and performs three trials for the record. The player's score is the sum of three trials measured to the nearest one half foot.

[2]Materials for the volleyball section were provided by Don Shondell, Ball State University, Muncie, IN.

Table 15.1 Football Testing Team Goals

Position	Standard
Offensive and defensive backs	
Bench press	300 and above
Power clean	255 and above
Power ratio	2.85 and above
Vertical jump	28 inches and above
1-1/2-mile run	9:15 and below
880-yard run	2:25 and below
40s percentage	100% to 93 = good
	92% to 89 = average
	88% and below = poor
40s	4.7 or better
Offensive and defensive line	
Bench press	340 and above
Power clean	285 and above
Power ratio	2.65 and above
Vertical jump	26 inches and above
1-1/2-mile run	10:30 and below
880-yard run	2:45 and below
40s percentage	100% to 93 = good
	92% to 89 = average
	88% and below = poor
40s	5.1 or better
Tight ends and linebackers	
Bench press	325 and above
Power clean	270 and above
Power ratio	2.75 and above
Vertical jump	28 inches and above
1-1/2-mile run	9:45 and below
880-yard run	2:30 and below
40s percentage	100% to 93 = good
	92% to 89 = average
	88% and below = poor
40s	4.85 or better

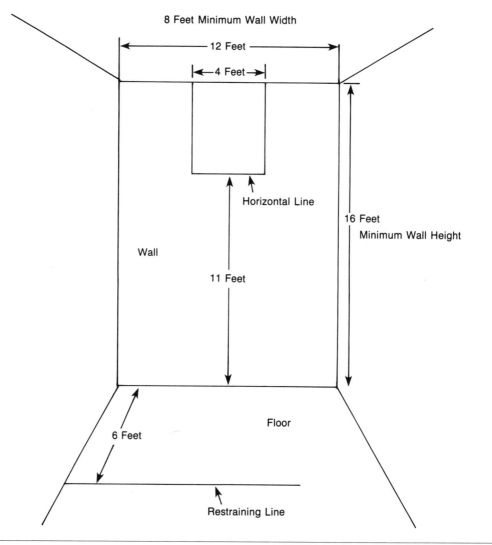

Figure 15.1   Wall Pass and Catch.

3. *Wall pass and catch*

Facilities. This test requires a flat, unobstructed wall space at least 16 feet high and 8 feet wide. A horizontal line, 11 feet from the floor and 4 feet wide, is marked on the wall. Vertical lines extend upward from each end of the line. A restraining line is marked on the floor parallel to the wall so that the farthest edge of the line is 6 feet from the wall (see Figure 15.1).

Procedure. The subject stands behind the restraining line with the volleyball in hands. The judge stands to the side of the player. On the signal *ready, go* from the head timer, the player tosses the ball against the wall into the scoring area using a two-hand overhead toss. As the ball rebounds from the wall, it is *caught* with two hands and rethrown into the scoring area. This sequence is continued for 30 seconds. Dur-

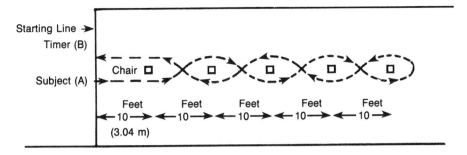

Figure 15.2 Zigzag Dodge Run course.

ing the test, the ball must be clearly caught and thrown using two hands, and the player must stand behind the restraining line with both feet on the floor.

Scoring. Each player receives one 15-second practice trial and two 30-second trials for the record. One point is scored each time a rebounding ball is legally caught and passed into the scoring area from behind the restraining line. The player's score is the sum of two 30-second trials.

4. *Vertical jump.* Same procedures and scoring as football test, Item 4, p. 498.
5. *Zigzag dodge run*
   Facilities. This test requires a gym floor marked off as in Figure 15.2.
   Procedure. The player starts from behind and within the starting lane. On the command *ready, go*, the player passes to the right of Chair 1, to the left of Chair 2, and continues to follow indicated path. The circuit should be completed two times to complete the trial. The chairs should not be moved. If the chairs are displaced, the trial must be repeated after a 2-minute rest period.
   Scoring. Each player receives one practice trial and two trials for the record. The player's score is the total elapsed time for the two trials measured to the nearest .10 second. A rest of at least 2 minutes should be given between trials.

6. Record weight to the nearest half pound.

This six-item battery had a multiple correlation coefficient of .732 with the criterion of experts' (X_e) ratings of player abilities and a standard error of estimate on the predicted score of 4.471. The regression equation for the battery is

X_e = (.272) basketball toss
  + (−3.984) 30-yard dash + (.281) wall catch
  + (−.375) zigzag run
  + (−.210) jump and reach
  + (−.051) weight + 47.031 (constant)

Shondell also found that a four-item battery consisting of the basketball toss, 30-yard dash, zigzag run, and wall catch had a multiple correlation coefficient of .708 with the criterion of experts' ratings and a standard error of estimate on the predicted score of 4.618. The regression equation for the four-item test battery is

X_e = (.196) basketball toss
  + (−2.991) 30-yard dash + (.253) wall catch
  + (−.387) zigzag run + 26.303 (constant)

Track and Field

In track and field, measurement and evaluation play a direct role in team selection. The athletes who sprint the fastest times are selected as sprinters, those who jump the highest or longest distances are selected as jumpers, and those who throw the greatest distance are selected as throwers. In other words, one of the best evaluations a track and field coach can make is to conduct time and field trials for an event. The results of the trials will help you as a coach in selecting the best prospect for an event.

Each time an athlete competes in a track or field event is a test and measurement situation. Track and field is a time and distance sport. All running events are measured in time, and all field events are measured in distance. What times or distances represent a quality high school performance (QHP), a recruitable high school performance (RHP), and a nationally ranking performance (NRP)? Examples of high school

boys' and girls' performance tables are presented in Tables 15.2 and 15.3 respectively. Keep in mind that performances may depend on locale; performances from state to state may vary slightly from those listed.

Factors for the Developing Track and Field Prospect

The factors that are important for developing an individual's potential in track or field include power, muscular strength, anthropometric measurements, motor coordination, speed, aerobic strength, and anaerobic power. Standards for selecting elite track and field athletes are presented in Table 15.4. The standards presented are for jumpers, throwers, sprinters, and runners for the above mentioned factors.

Table 15.2 High School Boys' Performance Table

Event	QHP FAT	QHP (HH[a])	RHP FAT	RHP (HH[a])	NRP FAT	NRP (HH[a])
100 meters	10.90	(10.7)	10.60	(10.4)	10.50	(10.3)
200 meters	21.90	(21.7)	21.40	(21.2)	21.00	(20.8)
400 meters	48.60	(48.4)	47.80	(47.6)	47.20	(47.0)
800 meters	1:55.30	(1:55.1)	1:53.00	(1:52.8)	1:51.50	(1:51.3)
1600 meters	4:19.70	(4:19.5)	4:14.20	(4:14.0)	4:12.50	(4:12.3)
3200 meters	9:28.20	(9:28.0)	9:10.20	(9:10.0)	9:04.00	(9:03.8)
110-meter hurdles	14.60	(14.4)	14.20	(14.0)	14.00	(13.8)
300-meter inter. hurdles	38.80	(38.6)	37.80	(37.6)	37.40	(37.2)
High jump (feet-inches)	6-7		7-0		7-1	
Long jump (feet-inches)	22-6		24-0		24-6	
Triple jump (feet-inches)	45-0		48-0		49-0	
Shot put (feet-inches)	54-0		60-0		62-6	
Discus (feet-inches)	162-0		175-0		184-0	
Javelin (feet-inches)	190-0		210-0		215-0	
Pole vault (feet-inches)	14-6		15-6		16-4	

Note. QHP = Quality High School Performance; RHP = Recruitable High School Performance; NRP = Nationally Ranking Performance (high school); FAT = fully automatic timing; HH = hand-held timing. Data compiled by Steve Miller, Kansas State University Head Track Coach, and Craig McVey, Kansas State University Assistant Track Coach in September 1984.

[a]HH marks include .24 conversion from FAT and rounded up to next .10 second.

Table 15.3 High School Girls' Performance Table

Event	QHP		RHP		NRP	
	FAT	(HH[a])	FAT	(HH[a])	FAT	(HH[a])
100 meters	12.50	(12.3)	12.20	(12.0)	11.95	(11.7)
200 meters	25.60	(25.4)	24.60	(24.4)	24.30	(24.1)
400 meters	57.50	(57.3)	56.20	(56.0)	55.10	(54.9)
800 meters	2:14.50	(2:14.3)	2:13.00	(2:12.8)	2:10.50	(2:10.3)
1600 meters	5:10.50	(5:10.3)	5:04.20	(5:04.0)	4:57.00	(4:56.8)
3200 meters	11:15.00	(14:14.8)	10:50.00	(10:49.8)	10:39.00	(10.38.8)
110-meter hurdles	14.80	(14.6)	14.20	(14.0)	13.95	(13.7)
300-meter inter. hurdles	45.60	(45.4)	44.50	(44.3)	43.50	(43.3)
High jump (feet-inches)	5-6		5-9		5-11	
Long jump (feet-inches)	17-2		19-0		19-6	
Triple jump (feet-inches)	33-6		36-5		38-0	
Shot put (feet-inches)	40-0		48-0		49-0	
Discus (feet-inches)	130-0		145-0		150-0	
Javelin (feet-inches)	130-0		140-0		150-0	

Note. QHP = Quality High School Performance; RHP = Recruitable High School Performance; NRP = Nationally Ranking Performance (high school); FAT = fully automatic timing; HH = hand-held timing. Data compiled by Steve Miller, Kansas State University Head Track Coach, and Craig McVey, Kansas State University Assistant Track Coach in September 1984.
[a]HH marks include .24 conversion from FAT and rounded up to next .10 second.

Table 15.4 Selection Factors for Elite Track and Field Athletes

Factor	Jumpers	Throwers	Sprinters	Runners
Power				
Jump and reach	20'' W	18'' W	20'' W	14'' W
	30'' M	26'' M	26'' M	20'' M
Standing long jump	8' W	7' W	7'6'' W	6'6'' W
	9' M	8' M	8'6'' M	7'6'' M
Overhead shot		4 K 38''		
Two-hand throw		12# 43''		
5 double leg bounds	36' W	36' W	34' W	
	40' M	40' M	38' M	
Standing triple jump	25' W	24' W	24' W	20' W
	29' M	27' M	27' M	24' M

(Cont.)

Table 15.4 (Cont.)

Factor	Jumpers	Throwers	Sprinters	Runners
Strength				
Bench press	Body wt W 1.5 body wt M	1.25 body wt W 2.0 body wt M	Body wt W 1.5 body wt M	Body wt-M.D. W Body wt-M.D. M .75 body wt DW .85 body wt DM
Squat	1.5 body wt W 1.75 body wt M	1.75 body wt W 2.0 body wt M	1.5 body wt W 1.75 body wt M	1.25 body wt W 1.50 body wt M
Snatch	.65 body wt W .75 body wt M	.85 body wt W 1.0 body wt M		
Anthropometric				
Height	(H.J.) 5'10" W 6'2" M	5'8"-5'10" W 6'-6'5" M		Slightly built for distance Meso-ecto for middle distance
Weight		160-190 W 200-250 M		110-125 W 140-160 M
% body fat	10-13% W 6.5-9% M	15-21% W 12-15% M	11-14% W 5-8% M	5-9% W 1-5% M
Other				
Motor coordination	Ability to transfer force to vertical lift	Softball throw 200' W 250' M	Stride cadence 4.2-4.5/sec	
Speed	6.4 50 yds W 5.8 50 yds M 30'/sec W 31.5'/sec M	6.9 50 yds W 6.2 50 yds M	6.3 50 yds W 5.6 50 yds M 30'/sec W 31.5'/sec M	7.0 50 yds W 6.2 50 yds M 27'/sec 800 W 30'/sec 800 M 26'/sec 1500 W 29'/sec 1500 M
Aerobic strength			6 min/mile (55 ml/kg/min) MW	60 ml/kg/min W 64 ml/kg/min M
Anaerobic power			Recommend 2 × 40 sec power run (no norms as yet)	2 × 60 sec with 3 min recovery 820 yds W 930 yds M
Self image	Strong support from parents and friends . . . Coach should observe athlete's ability to deal with social situations, note reactions to peer pressure, etc. . . . especially with female athletes.			

Note. M = men; W = women. From Ken Foreman (1982), *Coaching Track and Field Techniques*, 4th edition, Wm. C. Brown Company Publishers.

Task Analysis as a Measurement

All track and field events lend themselves quite well to the technique of task analysis. As an example, let's consider the task of pole vaulting and analyze the complete execution of the pole vault using the task analysis technique. Most track coaches agree that the elements of the pole vault are the plant, take-off, ride-rock-back, pull, and cast-off. Task analyses for each element follow:

Approach
- The hand grip is measured from the tip of the pole to the top hand (preferred hand, usually the right hand for most vaulters).
- The hand grip should be approximately 2 feet below the vaulting height.
- The nonpreferred hand (left hand in most vaulters) is placed about 18 to 28 inches below the preferred hand.
- The distance between hands remains constant throughout the vault.
- The elbow of the preferred arm is held vertically and relaxed, and the nonpreferred elbow is held away from the body with the forearm parallel to the ground and relaxed.
- The shoulders should be held square to the front.
- The pole should be carried so that the tip is held at head height.
- The tip of the pole should be pointing directly down the runway from starting to pole planting.
- Rhythmical sprinting action is maintained throughout the approach. (Look for any break in sprinting.)
- The facial, neck, shoulder, and arm muscles remain relaxed throughout the approach. (Look for any tense contractions.)

Pole Plant
- Within three or four strides away from the plant, the vaulter swings the pole sideways

and over the head with a short hooking action, keeping the shoulders square to the run.
- At the planting of the pole, both arms are extended.
- The vaulter looks at the planting box, not the crossbar.

Take-Off
- The take-off foot should be planted on the runway below the top hand grip or at least between the hands.
- The pole should be directly overhead.
- The vaulter springs lightly off the ground.
- The take-off leg should be extended.
- The lead leg should be brought forward and upward.
- The nonpreferred arm (usually the left) should be flexed at the elbow.
- The preferred arm (usually the right) has full shoulder flexion and elbow extension at take-off.

Ride-Rock-Back
- The vaulter delays any movement and rides up and into pole.
- When back is parallel with the ground, the vaulter brings knees to elbows.
- The head should be held up with eyes looking at crossbar.

Pull
- When hips are between the hand grips, the vaulter pulls with the arms through the hips to keep the feet going upward.
- The nonpreferred (usually left) leg should be moved quickly under the preferred (usually right) leg to turn the trunk toward the crossbar.
- Look for a handstand position at the top of the pull.

Cast-Off
- Start pushing downward on the pole with preferred hand (usually right); hips must be higher than shoulders.

- Legs drop over the crossbar together.
- Vaulter brings heels upward and throws preferred arm up and backward to clear the crossbar.

To use the task analysis method, a coach observes a prospective athlete performing the task to see what is and what is not being performed correctly according to the standards established in the task analysis. It is best for the coach to observe one phase of a task at a time rather than to try to observe and analyze the task as a whole. When observing a prospective pole vaulter, for example, the coach should first look at the approach and the sequential elements for the approach listed in the task analysis before he or she looks at the pole plant, take-off, and remaining elements. This allows the coach to focus on the elements contained in that phase of the task analysis. Improper execution of the approach will adversely affect the pole plant, which will adversely affect the take-off, and so forth.

Advantages of Videotapes and Films

A method that greatly enhances observation is to videotape or film an athlete's performance of a complete task. Each phase of a task can then be observed repeatedly by simply replaying the tape or film. The coach and athlete can replay the videotape or film to analyze any one phase of the task by comparing what appears in the recorded results to the criteria of the task analysis. Videotaping or filming will also allow the prospective athlete to conduct the task analysis on his or her own performance and thus receive immediate feedback on what he or she should do to improve.

Review Questions

1. Outline the procedures used to develop the example ninth-grade physical education evaluation program presented in this chapter.
2. What physical factors are important for developing potential in basketball?
3. What tests are good indicators of the physical factors for basketball?
4. What is the value of keeping statistics in scrimmage sessions in basketball?
5. What are the primary purposes of the eight-item football test presented in this chapter?
6. What six elements comprised the volleyball test battery presented in this chapter?
7. What constitutes a Quality High School Performance (QHP) in the 100-, 200-, 400-, 800-, 1600-, 3200-, and 110-meter hurdles, 300-meter intermediate hurdles, and the high jump, long jump, triple jump, shot put, discus throw, javelin throw, and pole vault for both males and females?
8. What constitutes a Recruitable High School Performance (RHP) for each track and field event for both boys and girls?
9. What constitutes a Nationally Ranking Performance (NRP) for high school track and field for each event for both boys and girls?
10. What physical factors are important for developing potential in track and field?
11. What tests are presented in this chapter as good indicators of the factors important for developing potential in track and field?
12. What are the skill components of a pole vault?
13. Of what value is recording an individual's performance of a sport skill or event on videotape or film?

Problems and Exercises

1. Calculate the average speed for the hand-held timing for 100-, 200-, 400-, 800-, 1600-, and 110-meter hurdles for a Quality High School Performance (QHP) in meters/second. Take these average speeds and calculate the equivalent time for the 100-yard dash, 220-yard dash, 440-yard dash, 880-yard dash, mile, and 120-yard hurdles.
   Answers: 100-yard dash in 9.8 seconds; 220-yard dash in 21.8 seconds; 440-yard dash in 48.7 seconds; 880-yard dash in 1:55.8 seconds; mile in 4 minutes, 21 seconds; 120-yard high hurdles in 14.4 seconds.

2. (a) Calculate a rank-order correlation coefficient from the following results in a basketball testing session:

Prospect	Jump and reach	12-minute run
P1	5	14
P2	1	4
P3	2	2
P4	15	15
P5	3	1
P6	6	10
P7	7	9
P8	4	5
P9	13	13
P10	8	3
P11	11	8
P12	14	12
P13	9	7
P14	12	11
P15	10	6

   (b) What does this coefficient imply?

Bibliography

Bowerman, W. (1974). *Coaching track and field*. Boston: Houghton Mifflin.

Foreman, K. (1982). *Coaching track and field techniques* (4th ed.). Dubuque, IA: William C. Brown.

Powell, J. (1973). *Track and field fundamentals for teacher and coach* (3rd ed.). Champaign, IL: Stipes.

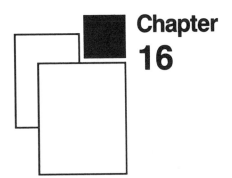

Chapter
16

Evaluation Programs
in Nonschool Settings

An increasing number of physical educators are securing employment in the growing health and physical fitness industry. Programs of activities are being conducted by public and private recreational centers, commercial health spas, hospitals and wellness centers, colleges and universities, businesses and industries, senior citizen centers, and municipal governments for employees in high-stress occupations. Recently, legislation was passed by one state legislature providing public employees access to financial support for their health and fitness programs (Haydon, Murray, & Edwards, 1986). Program directors must be specifically trained to develop individualized exercise prescriptions based on valid testing in order to protect program participants from injury as well as improve their fitness levels in a pleasant atmosphere. This chapter first discusses some general guidelines for managing effective testing programs and then provides some examples of using evaluation procedures in specific types of programs.

General Guidelines

Program directors of physical fitness programs in nonschool settings must be familiar with several important aspects of fitness programs. The guidelines presented here include discussions on (a) the purpose and program of activities, (b) informed consent, (c) medical examination and exercise testing, (d) pretesting, (e) exercise prescription, (f) participant monitoring, and (g) posttesting and client consultation.

Purpose and Program of Activities

Each agency—public, private, industrial, or commercial—should have a statement of purpose of its program and a description of the type of fitness services the agency is *qualified* to offer participants. Most agency programs claim to promote health and fitness by improving cardiovascular fitness, reducing body fat, and toning up the muscles. A few agencies may concentrate solely on bodybuilding and strength training. The statement of purpose and detailed program of activities are what appeal to the potential client. These activities must be professionally sound and capable of being translated into specific behavioral objectives for each participant. The fitness activities must also lend themselves to careful performance evaluation so that the participant can readily see the benefits of exercise. In the various agency programs that are part of the exercise and fitness business, you will find people of all ages, body types, and levels of health and fitness in your classes. Hence individual differences must be recognized and addressed through effective testing and the development of individual exercise prescriptions.

Informed Consent

Some agencies require participants to sign a statement of informed consent in which the purpose of the program, all activities, and testing are carefully described. If any of the test data are to be used in any way other than to provide direct feedback to each participant, the agency supervisor must have each participant's permission to do so. Any hazards or risks that the exercise program might pose to the participant must be fully described. In some cases, the statement of informed consent will include a waiver of lawsuit clause. Here the participant signs a statement indicating that he or she and his or her heirs will not hold the agency director or staff responsible for injuries incurred in the fitness program and will not bring suit for damages. The extent to which program liability waivers protect the agency and staff are discussed by Kaiser (1984). All physical educators should be advised to seek legal counsel about legal liability relative to all phases of fitness program management. More and more lawsuits are appearing in court resulting from failure to provide adequate standards of care

to protect clients (Alexender & Alexender, 1970; *Trial*, 1982), problems arising from unauthorized use of test data (Clement, 1983), and failure to take due precaution to protect those clients who may suffer from coronary heart disease (Herbert & Herbert, 1984).

Medical Examination and Exercise Testing

Because clients in fitness centers vary in age and degree of cardiovascular health, the health status of every participant must be determined before any testing occurs. The activity director may be held legally liable if he or she does not have medical clearance for exercise for each participant. The American College of Sports Medicine (1986) has established guidelines for evaluating participant health status prior to exercise testing. These guidelines insist on preliminary medical evaluation to screen individuals for participation in graded exercise testing and exercise programs. Age, health status, and previous physical activity history are critical determining factors. The exercise leader and program director should become familiar with the ACSM (1986) guidelines and their implications for graded exercise testing and prescription.

Pretesting

After medical clearance is secured, the participant should be pretested. Based on these test results, an exercise prescription is written for each person. Tests that might be utilized include estimates of body weight, percent body fat, oxygen consumption per kilogram body weight, strength, flexibility, and so forth. The age and fitness needs of each participant will determine the tests to be used. Keep the testing as simple as possible and try to avoid tests that require expensive high-tech equipment. Field tests are recommended wherever possible. The mode of pretesting (and posttesting) should be similar to the mode of training prescribed when evaluating program effects.

Physical fitness professionals must again be reminded of the potentially serious consequences of making a "false positive" or "false negative" decision based on test data. Both types of false decision can lead to legal difficulties depending on the seriousness of the decision's impact on the participant. If, for example, you do not utilize appropriate testing procedures and you declare a high-risk, coronary-prone individual to be ready for vigorous exercise (a false negative decision), you have placed the participant in a hazardous situation. A false positive decision in which you indicate a participant has a heart problem when in fact he or she does not may lead to the risk of psychological trauma as well as an unduly conservative exercise prescription. If you do err, it is better to make a false positive decision than a false negative decision because the repercussions are far less costly.

Exercise Prescription

The exercise prescription must take into account the mode, intensity, frequency, duration, and progression of exercise. The American College of Sports Medicine (1986) suggests the following guidelines be followed in prescribing cardiorespiratory exercise programs for *healthy* adults.

- *Mode:* Rhythmical aerobic activities that can be maintained for a prolonged period of time that involve large muscle groups. Cycling, swimming, hiking, jogging, rope skipping, skating, and dancing are examples.
- *Intensity:* 65% to 90% of maximum heart rate or 50% to 85% of maximum oxygen uptake (functional capacity).
- *Frequency:* At least 3 to 5 days a week.
- *Duration:* 15 to 60 minutes of continuous or discontinuous (walk-jog) aerobic exercise; duration is dependent on intensity.

- *Rate of progression:* The exercise prescription is adjusted as the participant achieves desired conditioning effects.

Participant Monitoring

Periodically throughout the program, the client is given another exercise test. Based on this test data, the program is adjusted up or down in intensity and duration in order to maximize fitness benefits within the exercise limitations of each person. Quite often this frequent testing is conducted by each client in the form of self-testing. Every day that they jog, they put themselves to the test so to speak. Also, if participants go through a par course or a fitness trail, each activity area is a form of self-testing.

Posttesting and Client Consultation

After the program ends, each person is tested again. The results of these final tests can be compared to initial test results and individually interpreted for each participant. Then an individualized exercise prescription can be given to all participants so that they may continue to exercise on their own in an environment of their choice. Many participants will continue to exercise in a group at a health club or spa, whereas others will choose to exercise alone. This is our ultimate goal: to keep participants exercising after we have educated them in a professionally sound program that is based on tests, measurements, and careful evaluation.

Specific Program Examples

Several program examples of implementing evaluation procedures in specific nonschool programs are provided in this part of the chapter. The examples selected represent programs in which a physical educator might be employed.

These include programs for (a) coronary rehabilitation, (b) healthy adults, (c) law enforcement and fire department personnel, and (d) older adults and retired citizens.

Coronary Rehabilitation Programs

Thorough medical evaluations may disclose symptoms of coronary heart disease in some clients. Extreme care must be taken during graded exercise testing (see Figure 16.1) to ensure the safety of these participants. Indeed, special training and certification are essential for the exercise test specialist, exercise leader, and program director working with such clients (ACSM, 1986). A physician must be present or in an adjacent area during testing. Personnel present during the testing must be able to perform cardiopulmonary resuscitation and be familiar with the use of defibrilating equipment. The following fitness testing program components for adults have been recommended by Pollock, Wilmore, and Fox (1984):

- *Cardiorespiratory component. At rest:* heart rate, blood pressure, electrocardiogram. *During exercise:* symptom-limited graded exercise test with heart rate and blood pressure measurements, electrocardiogram monitoring, and assessment of aerobic work capacity. A treadmill, bicycle ergometer, or step test is the mode of exercise.
- *Body composition:* measurement of percent body fat and percent lean mass by underwater weighing if possible; anthropometric determination of percent body fat (skinfolds, girth measures, height, and weight).
- *Blood measures:* serum cholesterol, triglycerides, glucose, and high-density lipoprotein levels.
- *Muscular strength and endurance:* maximum bench press and bent-leg sit-ups for 1 minute (this component may be contraindicated for hypertensive and high-risk persons).
- *Flexibility:* sit-and-reach test.

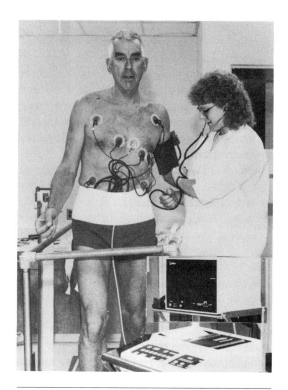

Figure 16.1 A graded exercise stress test with electrocardiograph monitoring. Test results are used partly as a basis for diagnosis of heart disease as well as an exercise prescription.

Upon completion of the graded exercise test, an exercise prescription is prepared and approved by the supervising physician. Activities are conducted on an individual or group basis depending on severity of heart disease and need for close supervision. Careful monitoring of patients during activity sessions is essential. The graded exercise test is repeated frequently to adjust the exercise prescription. More detailed descriptions of clinical exercise testing appear in Jones and Campbell (1984) and Ellestad (1986).

Programs for Healthy Adults

This section deals with programs for healthy postcollege and middle-aged adults. Like all participants, these individuals should receive medical clearance prior to pretesting and exercise prescription. All individuals in this category should be asymptomatic of coronary heart disease and other medical problems such as severe diabetes, inflammation of the alimentary canal, and orthopedic problems. The components of a fitness testing program would include muscle strength, muscular endurance, desirable body composition, cardiovascular endurance, agility, and flexibility. Based on an aerobic fitness assessment, each participant should be classified into either a low, average, or high fitness category. The intensity and duration of aerobic activity prescribed depend on this assessment. The following testing program may be used for healthy adults:

- *Strength:* one repetition of maximum bench press.
- *Muscular endurance:* push-ups and bent-knee sit-ups for 1 minute.
- *Percent body fat:* underwater weighing; skinfolds or other anthropometric measures described in chapter 7.
- *Cardiovascular endurance:* the estimate of aerobic work capacity may be gathered from a bicycle ergometer or treadmill exercise test if this equipment is available and one is trained to use it. In the absence of laboratory equipment, field tests such as the Åstrand step test or Cooper's 12-minute walk, run, cycle, or swim test may be used. Field tests should not be used as diagnostic tools; best results from field tests are obtained after participants have had a few training sessions and have learned how to pace themselves.
- *Agility:* the AAHPERD shuttle run fitness test items described in chapter 7 may be used.
- *Flexibility:* the sit-and-reach test described in chapter 7 may be used.

After pretesting is completed, the participant begins a prescribed program. The program can

be conducted on an individual or group basis with individual differences taken into account to determine intensity of work. The exercise leader must use sound professional judgment and not allow participants to overtrain who are not physically ready to do so. Doing too much too soon discourages continued participation and is one of the primary reasons that participants drop out of a program. The components of the physical fitness program would consist of the following:

1. Warm-up (stretching, low level calisthenics, walking 5 to 10 minutes)
2. Muscular fitness (calisthenics, weight-training on Universal equipment if available for 10 to 15 minutes)
3. Aerobics (fast walk, jog, swim, bicycle, cross-country skiing, or vigorous games for 20 to 25 minutes)
4. Cool-down (walking, stretching, or flexibility activities, 5 to 10 minutes)

The time for each component may be adjusted depending on the specific purpose of the fitness program for special occupational groups. The fitness program should be conducted in the following manner (Heyward, 1984; Pollock, Wilmore, & Fox, 1984):

- *Frequency:* 3 to 5 days per week
- *Intensity:* 60 to 90% of maximum heart rate reserve or 50 to 80% of maximum oxygen uptake
- *Duration:* 15 to 60 minutes of continuous activity
- *Mode of activity:* run, jog, swim, cycle, endurance sports, and dance
- *Initial level of fitness:* high = higher work load; low = lower work load

Programs for Law Enforcement and Fire Department Personnel

A good deal of attention is currently being paid to the physical fitness level and preparedness for duty in police (Price, Pollock, Guttman, & Kent, 1978) and fire departments (Ross & Gallagher, 1984). Both of these occupations involve high stress levels with workers performing duty in a rather sedentary way. Police spend a lot of duty time riding in a squad car, and fire fighters wait for emergency calls in the fire station. Yet both police officers and fire fighters must maintain sufficient aerobic power and muscular endurance to perform their duties when called upon to do so. Hence their fitness programs should focus on strength and muscular endurance activities.

Donato and Pounds (1985) conducted a 20-week fitness program for police recruits in police academy training. The program was designed to improve cardiovascular endurance, muscle power, muscular endurance, agility, and percent body fat of the male and female recruits. Test items included running time on a treadmill, pull-ups, push-ups, sit-ups, standing broad jump, shuttle run, and percent body fat measured by underwater weighing. After participating in the fitness program, the entire recruit class demonstrated statistically significant improvements in all of the fitness capacity tests.

A follow-up test conducted 7 months after training ended revealed that dramatic decreases in fitness had occurred. On the average, all individuals had lost 79% of the fitness they had gained, indicating the need for an ongoing fitness program for officers during their police career. In another study on police officers ranging in age from 28 to 49 years, Donato (1984) demonstrated the effects of a circuit weight-training program on selected fitness components. The officers significantly improved their performance on maximum oxygen uptake in ml/kg • min^{-1}, work pulse, push-ups, sit-ups, lean body weight, percent body fat, and flexibility. There is currently a need for police departments to adopt normative data so that reasonable fitness standards can be set for officers (Collingwood, 1984).

Programs for Older Adults and Retired Citizens

America is aging. The average life expectancy of Americans has jumped from 48 to 73 years since 1900. Today, 11% of Americans are 65 years or older, and by the year 2030 a projected 18% of the population will be over 65 years of age (Ostrow, 1984). Older adults are more diverse than similar, and there is greater variability in biological and behavioral functioning among older adults than among younger adults. Older adults become increasingly inactive as time passes, but this is more of a culturally rather than a biologically motivated life-style. Old people are expected to "sit back" and enjoy their last years. However, sufficient data exist to indicate that older adults can lead vigorous lives and participate in carefully planned physical fitness programs. Such programs delay biological and emotional degeneration and improve the quality of life. Older individuals require programs of activities designed to improve the following fitness components (Ostrow, 1984; Piscopo, 1985):

- *Cardiorespiratory efficiency.* Improvement in oxygen uptake is essential with endurance activities of low intensity and long duration (e.g., hiking, walking, walk-jog, swimming). Deep breathing exercises are also essential.
- *Muscular strength and endurance.* Push-ups, sit-ups, and light weight work are needed to improve muscular strength and endurance.
- *Flexibility.* Activities designed to increase the range of motion around the joints of the body are necessary and should be included in the warm-up phase of the program.
- *Balance.* Because older adults experience many falls that result in serious injury, activities to develop balance are essential.
- *Neuromuscular coordination.* Activities are

needed to improve coordination, reaction time, and movement time.

- *Visual-motor.* Activities are needed to enhance visual acuity.
- *Perception.* Perception, neuromuscular coordination, and visual-motor skills may be enhanced through a series of perceptual-motor activities similar to those found in elementary school programs.

Review Questions

1. What is informed consent? What content should be included in an informed consent statement? Why is a statement of informed consent necessary?
2. Identify the differences in fitness components found in programs for senior citizens, police officers, young adults attending a health spa, and patients involved in a cardiac rehabilitation program.
3. List the steps involved in exercise testing.
4. What are the essential components of an exercise prescription? Can these components be monitored with testing? If so, how?

Bibliography

Alexender, R.H., & Alexander, K. (1970). *Teachers and torts: Liability for pupil injury.* Middletown, KY: Maxwell.

American College of Sports Medicine. (1986). *Guidelines for exercise testing and prescription* (3rd ed.). Philadelphia: Lea & Febiger.

Clement, A. (1983). Testing and the courts. In L.D. Hensley & W.B. East (Eds.), *Proceedings of the Fourth Measurement and Evaluation Symposium* (pp. 159-167). Cedar Falls, IA: University of Northern Iowa and the American Alliance for Health, Physical Education, Recreation, and Dance.

Collingwood, T.R. (1984). Police fitness: Why is it still an issue? *Athletic Business,* **8**(5), 24-29.

Donato, J.W., & Pounds, R.A. (1985). Successful physical fitness programs require long-term commitment. *Law and Order*, October, 48-52.

Donato, J.W. (1984). *The effects of a nine week circuit weight training program on selected physical fitness capacities of metropolitan police officers.* Unpublished master's research project, University of Kentucky, Department of Health, Physical Education, and Recreation, Lexington.

Ellestad, M.H. (1986). *Stress testing, principles and practice* (3rd ed.). Philadelphia: F.A. Davis Co.

Haydon, D.F., Murray, T.D., & Edwards, T.L. (1986). Texas Employee Health and Fitness Program. *Journal of Physical Education, Recreation and Dance,* **57**(8), 28-32.

Heyward, V.H. (1984). *Designs for fitness: A guide to physical fitness appraisal and exercise prescription.* Minneapolis: Burgess.

Herbert, D.L., & Herbert, W.G. (1984). *Legal aspects of preventative and rehabilitative exercise programs.* Kenton, OH: Professional and Executive Reports and Publication.

Jones, N.L., & Campbell, E.J.M. (1984). *Clinical exercise testing* (2nd ed.). Philadelphia: W.B. Saunders.

Kaiser, R.A. (1984). Program liability waivers; do they protect the agency and staff? *Journal of Physical Education, Recreation, and Dance,* **55**(6), 54-56.

Ostrow, A.C. (1984). *Physical activity and the older adult.* Princeton, NJ: Princeton Book Company.

Piscopo, J. (1985). Prescriptive exercise for older adults. *Journal of Physical Education, Recreation, and Dance,* **56**(8), 65-69.

Pollock, M.L., Wilmore, J.H., & Fox, S.M. (1984). *Exercise in health and disease: Evaluation and prescription for prevention and rehabilitation*. Philadelphia: W.B. Saunders.

Price, C.S., Pollock, M.L., Guttman, L.R., & Kent, D.A. (1978). *Physical fitness programs for law enforcement officers: A manual for police administrators* (Stock No. 027-000-00671-6). Washington, DC: United States Government Printing Office.

Recreational Torts. (1982, February). *Trial—The National Legal Magazine, 18*(2).

Ross, M.L., & Gallagher, R.M. (1984). Getting firefighters fit. *Athletic Business, 8*(7), 28-30.

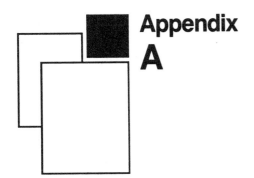

Appendix A

Metric and English Conversion Factors

Meters × 3.28 = feet
Meters × 39.37 = inches
Meters × 1.09 = yards
Feet × 30.48 = centimeters
Feet × .3048 = meters
Centimeters × .3937 = inches
Inches × 2.54 = centimeters
Kilometers × .6214 = miles
Miles × 1.609 = Kilometers
Meters/hour × .0006 = miles/hour
Meters/hour × .0547 = feet/second
Meters/minute × .0373 = miles/hour
Meters/second × 196.85 = feet/minute
Meters/second × 2.2369 = miles/hour
Miles/hour × 44.704 = centimeters/second
Miles/hour × 1.609 = kilometers/hour
Meters/second^2 × 3.28 = feet/second^2
Feet/second^2 × .3048 = meters/second^2
Kilograms × 2.2 = pounds

Grams × .0353 = ounces
Pounds × .4536 = kilograms
Ounces × 28.3495 = grams
Meter squared × 10.7584 = feet squared
Inch squared × 6.4516 = centimeters squared
Temperature
F° = 1.8 (Celsius) + 32
$$C° = \frac{\text{Fahrenheit} - 32}{1.8}$$
Time (same in Metric and English)
1 hour = 60 minutes
1 minute = 60 seconds
1 kilosecond = 1000 seconds
1 second = 10 deciseconds
1 second = 100 centiseconds
1 second = 1000 milliseconds
Absolute Units of Force
Newtons × .2248 = pounds
Pounds × 4.448 = Newtons

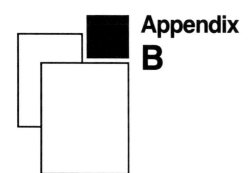

Appendix
B

Algebraic Derivation of the Calculating Variance Formula

The following is the algebraic derivation of the calculating variance formula from the definitional variance formula.

The definitional variance formula is

$$\sigma^2 = \frac{\sum_{i=1}^{N} (X_i - \overline{X})^2}{N}$$

By squaring the quantity inside the parentheses, we have

$$\sigma^2 = \frac{\sum_{i=1}^{N} (X_i^2 - 2X_i\overline{X} + \overline{X}^2)}{N}$$

Taking the $\sum_{i=1}^{N}$ inside the parentheses gives us

$$\sigma^2 = \frac{\sum_{i=1}^{N} X_i^2 - 2\overline{X}\sum_{i=1}^{N} X_i + \sum_{i=1}^{N} \overline{X}^2}{N}$$

Because

$$\overline{X} = \frac{\sum_{i=1}^{N} X_i}{N}$$

and

$$\sum_{i=1}^{N} \overline{X}^2 = N\overline{X}^2 = N\left(\frac{\sum_{i=1}^{N} X_i}{N}\right)^2$$

we now have

$$\sigma^2 = \frac{\sum_{i=1}^{N} X_i^2 - 2 \dfrac{\sum_{i=1}^{N} X_i \sum_{i=1}^{N} X_i}{N} + \dfrac{\left(\sum_{i=1}^{N} X_i\right)^2}{N}}{N}$$

$$= \frac{\sum_{i=1}^{N} X_i^2 - 2 \dfrac{\left(\sum_{i=1}^{N} X_i\right)^2}{N} + \dfrac{\left(\sum_{i=1}^{N} X_i\right)^2}{N}}{N}$$

(Cont.)

519

$$= \frac{\sum\limits_{i=1}^{N} X_i^2 - \dfrac{\left(\sum\limits_{i=1}^{N} X_i\right)^2}{N}}{N}$$

$$= \frac{N\left(\sum\limits_{i=1}^{N} X_i^2\right) - \left(\sum\limits_{i=1}^{N} X_i\right)^2}{N^2}$$

which is the computational variance formula.

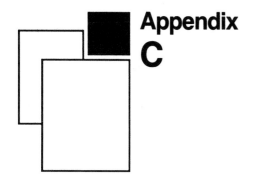

Programmable Hand-Held Calculators

Many hand-held calculators today can, using ungrouped data, automatically calculate the mean, variance, standard deviation, linear correlation coefficient, slope of a predictive equation, *y*-intercept of a predictive equation, predict a *y*-score for a given *x*-score, and predict an *x*-score for a given *y*-score. These hand-held calculators are also programmable. They may be programmed to perform the functions necessary to calculate a *z*-score, T score, and 6-σ-score. These calculators are reasonable in price, ranging from around $30 to $60.

The steps presented here are general in nature and are not instructions for any given calculator. The owner's manual should be consulted for precise instructions.

Basic Statistics

Press Mean Button is usually symbolized by $\overline{X}$ or mean, and the mean is automatically displayed.

Press Variance Button is usually symbolized by σ^2 or Var, and the variance is automatically displayed.

Press Standard Deviation Button is usually symbolized by σ or *SD*, and the standard deviation is automatically displayed.

General Procedures for Determining the Mean, Variance, and Standard Deviation

Example problem: What are the mean, variance, and standard deviation of 16, 20, 24, 28, and 32 push-ups?

Press	Display	Comments
16	16	Number 16
$\Sigma+$	1	Put into sum 1 number entered
20	20	Number 20
$\Sigma+$	2	Put into sum 2 numbers entered
24	24	Number 24
$\Sigma+$	3	Put into sum 3 numbers entered

28	28	Number 28
Σ+	4	Put into sum 4 numbers entered
32	32	Number 32
Σ+	5	Put into sum 5 numbers entered
Mean	18	Mean automatically calculated and displayed
Variance	80	Variance automatically calculated and displayed
$\gamma\bar{x}$	8.94427	Standard deviation. Extracts square root of 80 previously displayed for the variance.

Note of Caution. Read your owner's manual carefully to determine if the variance button or the standard deviation button automatically calculates the desired value using N for descriptive statistics.

Linear Correlation Coefficient

Press Correlation Button is usually symbolized by r or *corr*, and the correlation coefficient is automatically displayed.

Press Slope Button is usually symbolized by b, *slope*, or m, and the slope of the predictive equation is automatically displayed.

Press Intercept Button is usually symbolized by a, *y-cept*, *incept*, or b, and the y-intercept of the predictive equation is automatically displayed.

Press Predict Y Button is usually symbolized by Y' or Y, and a predicted y-score will be displayed for a given x-score.

Press Predict X Button is usually symbolized by X' or X, and a predicted x-score will be displayed for a given y-score.

General Procedures for Determining the Correlation, Slope, and Intercept of Paired Scores

Example problem: What are the correlation coefficient, slope, and y-intercept of the following paired scores?

Subject No.	X (Chins)	Y (Push-ups)
1	5	20
2	2	19
3	12	35
4	8	17
5	1	12

Press	Display	Comment
5	5	Number 5
X⇌Y	0	Enter into X
20	20	Number 20
Σ+	1	Enter into Y 1 paired numbers entered
2	2	Number 2
X⇌Y	6	Enter into X (6 display not important)
19	19	Number 19
Σ+	2	Enter into Y 2 paired numbers entered
12	12	Number 12
X⇌Y	3	Enter into X (3 display not important)

35	35	Number 35
Σ+	3	Enter into Y 3 paired numbers entered
8	8	Number 8
X⇌Y	13	Enter into X (13 display not important)
17	17	Number 17
Σ+	4	Enter into Y 4 paired numbers entered
1	1	Number 1
X⇌Y	9	Enter into X (9 display not important)
12	12	Number 12
Σ+	5	Enter into Y 5 paired numbers entered
Correlation	.8317	Correlation coefficient automatically calculated and displayed
Slope	1.5911	Slope of predictive equation automatically calculated and displayed
Intercept	11.6896	Y-intercept of predictive equation automatically calculated and displayed

Programmable Mode

Press Learn Mode Button is usually symbolized by learn or LRN, and this enables the calculator to learn a program that will be punched in by you.

Press Run Stop Button is usually symbolized by R-S or R/S, and this instructs the calculator to run the already punched-in steps of a program and then stop.

Press Reset Button is usually symbolized by reset or RST, and this instructs the calculator to go back to the start of the program and get ready to run the program again.

General Procedures for Programming to Calculate a z-Score and T Score

Example problem:

Subject	X (Chins)	
1	5	
2	2	$\overline{X} = 5.6$
3	12	$\sigma = 4.03$
4	8	
5	1	

(a) What is the z-score for each subject?
(b) What is the T score for each subject?

Remember,

$$z\text{-score} = \frac{X - \overline{X}}{\sigma}$$

and

$$T \text{ score} = 10(z) + 50$$

$$\text{Programmable } z = \frac{RCL1 - RCL2}{RCL3}$$

and

$$T \text{ score} = 10(\text{Programmable } z) + 50$$

Button RCL usually means recall a position. For example, RCL1 means recall Position 1 and what is stored in Position 1. To record a number in RCL1, we can say 5 store 1 or 5 STO1, and the number 5 will be stored in Position 1 to be recalled when RCL1 is activated. With this in mind, let us program to get a z-score and T score.

Press	Display	Comment
LRN	00 00	Enter learn mode; calculator now programmable.
RCL	01 00	Step 1 Recall 1
1	02 000	Step 2
−	03 00	Step 3 Minus
RCL	04 00	Step 4 Recall 2
2	05 00	Step 5
=	06 00	Step 6 Equal
÷	07 00	Step 7 Divided By
RCL	08 00	Step 8 Recall 3
3	09 00	Step 9
=	10 00	Step 10 Equal
R/S	11 00	Step 11 Run Stop answer to z-score
X	12 00	Step 12 Multiply display in Step 11 z-score
10	14 00	Step 14 By 10
+	15 00	Step 15 Add
50	17 00	Step 17 50
=	18 00	Step 18 Equal
R/S	19 00	Run Stop answer to T score
RST	20 00	Reset back to run program again
LRN	0	Exit learn mode
RST	0.	Reset for first calculation

We have now programmed to get a z-score on our first run stop and a T score on our second run stop provided we store the correct numbers in the correct recall positions. Let's find the z-score and T score for Subject 1.

Press	Display	Comment
5	5	This says take the number 5 and store it into recall 1, which is the score (number of chins) for Subject 1. Our formula $$z = \frac{RCL1 - RCL2}{RCL3}$$ now becomes $$z = \frac{5 - RCL2}{RCL3}$$
STO		
1		
5.6	5.6	This says take the mean of the data $\overline{X} = 5.6$ and store it into Recall 2. Our formula $$z = \frac{5 - RCL2}{RCL3}$$ now becomes $$z = \frac{5 - 5.6}{RCL3}$$
STO	5.6	
2	5.6	
4.03	4.03	This says take the standard deviation of the data $\sigma = 4.03$ and store it into Recall 3. Our formula $$z = \frac{5 - 5.6}{RCL3}$$ now becomes $$z = \frac{5 - 5.6}{4.03}$$ the z-score for Subject 1.
STO	4.03	
3	4.03	
RCL1	5	To be sure the score 5 of Subject 1 is stored in Recall 1
RCL2	5.6	To be sure the $\overline{X} = 5.6$ is stored in Recall 2
RCL3	4.03	To be sure the $\sigma = 4.03$ is stored in Recall 3

You are now ready to run your programs.

Press	Display	Comment
R/S	−0.1488	Calculator performs program to the first run stop, and this is Subject 1's z-score.
R/S	48.5111	Calculator performs program after first run stop, and this is Subject 1's T score.

To get the z- and T scores of Subject 2

Press	Display	Comment
2	2	This says take the number 2 and store it into Recall 1, which is the number of chins Subject 2 performed. This automatically removes the number 5 put into this position for Subject 1 and places the number 2 into Recall 1.
STO	2	
1	2	

The mean and standard deviation are already

placed into Recall 2 and Recall 3, so we do not need to change these values.

Press	Display	Comment
R/S	−.8993	Subject 2's z-score
R/S	41.006	Subject 2's T score
12	12	
STO	12	
1	12	
R/S	1.5988	Subject 3's z-score
R/S	65.988	Subject 3's T score
8	8	
STO	8	
1	8	
R/S	.599	Subject 4's z-score
R/S	55.99	Subject 4's T score
1	1	
STO	1	
1	1	
R/S	−1.1491	Subject 5's z-score
R/S	38.508	Subject 5's T score

Once again we must stress that the steps and programs presented in this appendix are general in nature. The owner's manual should be consulted for precise instructions.

Appendix D

The Computer in Physical Education

The potential for computer use in the area of physical education is enormous. Using a computer for lab work, classroom and sport instruction, and record-keeping is no longer considered unusual. You will almost certainly be confronted with the need to use a computer in your career as a physical educator.

A computer can store large amounts of data, process information, and produce output with speed and precision. Taking over boring and repetitive tasks, giving precision and accuracy to laborious mathematical processes, grading exams, analyzing movement patterns, individualizing instruction and exercise programs, and quickly referencing information are just a few examples of how the computer can be helpful to the physical educator. The efficiency of the computer's operations and the accuracy of its work, however, are determined by the person giving it instructions. In other words, a computer can be a wonderful tool for virtually any task as long as the user is knowledgeable about what he or she is doing and what the computer

is doing. Thus gaining a familiarity with computers and the high-tech world is recommended as a part of the physical education student's preparation in college.

The best way to overcome any apprehension about computers and avoid frustration in attempting to use one is to take an introductory course in computer science. Most colleges and universities offer an introductory computer course designed for the novice. The introductory course provides the opportunity to learn how the computer works, what are some of its many applications, and what one basically needs to know to use one. Gaining computer literacy gives the student the ability to participate in discussions and decision-making regarding the use of computers without feeling ignorant. Knowing how a computer works and seeing some of its applications are helpful in foreseeing practical applications in one's own work environment.

Physical educators should also establish some proficiency in at least one computer language in order to be able to program a computer to perform specific tasks. Currently, the most widely used language in physical education is BASIC. Other languages (i.e., Pascal,

The programs and text for Appendix D were written by Randy Kirkendall.

527

Fortran, and Assembler) are used simply because they are more adequate for certain types of programming. Following are two examples of programs written in BASIC that might be used in physical education.

Program 1: Determining Mean, Standard Deviation, z-Score, and T Score

This program written in BASIC will take a group of scores and figure the mean and standard deviation for the group. It will also figure a z-score and a T score for any one score.

Here is how the program would be typed into the computer:

```
100 Print "HOW MANY SCORES WILL
    YOU ENTER?"
110 INPUT NUMSCORES
120 FOR I = 1 TO NUMSCORES
130 PRINT "ENTER SCORE"
140 INPUT SCORE
150 TOTAL = TOTAL + SCORE
160 SUMSQUARES = SUMSQUARES +
    SCORE**2
170 NEXT I
180 MEAN = TOTAL/NUMSCORES
190 STANDDEV = SQR
    ((NUMSCORES*SUMSQUARES −
    TOTAL**2)/NUMSCORES**2)
200 PRINT "THE MEAN:", MEAN
210 PRINT "THE STANDARD
    DEVIATION:", STANDDEV
220 PRINT "DO YOU WISH A Z-SCORE
    AND A T SCORE?(Y/N)"
230 INPUT ANSWER$
240 WHILE ANSWER$ = "Y"
250 PRINT "ENTER THE SCORE"
260 INPUT ONESCORE
270 ZSCORE = (ONESCORE − MEAN)/
    STANDDEV
```

```
280 TSCORE = 10*ZSCORE + 50
290 PRINT "THE SCORE:", ONESCORE
300 PRINT "THE Z-SCORE:", ZSCORE
310 PRINT "THE T SCORE:", TSCORE
320 PRINT "DO YOU WISH ANOTHER
    Z-SCORE AND T SCORE?(Y/N)"
330 INPUT ANSWER$
340 WEND
350 STOP
360 END
```

The following is a description of what the program is telling the computer to do. All variables are italicized.

100 PRINT "HOW MANY SCORES WILL YOU ENTER?"

The print statement will print on the screen exactly what is contained in the quotation marks. This print statement asks a question requiring the user to type in an answer.

110 INPUT *NUMSCORES*

The input statement reads what the user has typed in and assigns that to the variable in the input statement. In this case NUMSCORES is the variable, and it would be assigned whatever value the user typed in (the total number of scores).

120 FOR I = 1 TO *NUMSCORES*
130 PRINT "ENTER SCORE"
140 INPUT *SCORE*
150 *TOTAL = TOTAL + SCORE*
160 *SUMSQUARES = SUMSQUARES =*
    SCORE**2
170 NEXT I

The instructions in lines 120-170 are called a FOR LOOP. The variable I is set equal to 1. Then lines 130-160 are executed (carried out). When the computer gets to line 170, the variable I is incremented by 1 and then lines 130-160 are executed again. This whole process will continue until the variable I becomes greater than the variable NUMSCORES. The computer will then go on to line 180. In this case the FOR LOOP is used for summation. The variable TOTAL will become equal to the sum of all the scores, and the variable SUMSQUARES will become equal to the sum of all the scores after they have been squared. SCORE**2 means "square the variable SCORE."

180 *MEAN = TOTAL/NUMSCORES*

The variable MEAN is assigned the value derived by dividing the variable TOTAL by the variable NUMSCORES.

190 *STANDDEV = SQR ((NUMSCORES*SUMSQUARES − TOTAL**2)/ NUMSCORES**2)*

The variable STANDDEV (standard deviation) is assigned the value of the equation on the right of the equals sign. The asterisk stands for multiplication, and the operations in parentheses are done first. The SQR outside of the parentheses means take the square root of the final value on the inside of the parentheses.

200 PRINT "THE MEAN:", *MEAN*

This print statement will print two things. It will print exactly what appears inside the quotation marks, followed by the value of the variable MEAN.

210 PRINT "THE STANDARD DEVIATION:", *STANDDEV*

220 PRINT "DO YOU WISH A Z-SCORE AND A T SCORE?(Y/N)"

The response by the user will be either Y for yes or N for no.

230 INPUT *ANSWER$*

Variables in BASIC that are to contain characters (i.e., Y,N) must be followed by a dollar sign so that the computer knows the variable is for characters.

240 WHILE *ANSWER$* = "Y"
250 PRINT "ENTER THE SCORE"
260 INPUT *ONESCORE*
270 *ZSCORE = (ONESCORE = MEAN)/ STANDDEV*
280 *TSCORE = 10*ZSCORE + 50*
290 PRINT "THE SCORE:", *ONESCORE*
300 PRINT "THE Z-SCORE:", *ZSCORE*
310 PRINT "THE T SCORE:", *TSCORE*
320 PRINT "DO YOU WISH ANOTHER Z-SCORE AND T SCORE?(Y/N)"
330 INPUT *ANSWER$*
340 WEND

Lines 240-340 are called a WHILE LOOP. Lines 250-330 will be executed repeatedly as long as the variable ANSWER$ contains the character Y. The computer will check the variable ANSWER$ every time before executing lines 250-330. If the variable ANSWER$ contains anything besides Y (i.e., N), then lines 250-330 will not be executed and the computer will go on to line 350.

350 STOP
360 END

STOP tells the computer to stop executing the program, and END tells the computer this is the end of the program.

The following is an example of what would appear on the computer screen if the scores 55, 89, 93, 64, 86 were used for this program. The responses typed in by the user are italicized.

HOW MANY SCORES WILL YOU ENTER?
5
ENTER SCORE
55
ENTER SCORE

89
ENTER SCORE
93
ENTER SCORE
64
ENTER SCORE
86
THE MEAN: 77.4
THE STANDARD DEVIATION: 15.05457
DO YOU WISH A Z-SCORE AND A T SCORE?(Y/N)
Y
ENTER THE SCORE
55
THE SCORE: 55
THE Z-SCORE: −1.487921
THE T SCORE: 35.12079
DO YOU WISH ANOTHER Z-SCORE AND T SCORE?(Y/N)
N

Program 2: Determining Body Composition

The next program is for determining body composition from data collected by the underwater weighing technique. Using a short program such as this one saves time and gives correct results every time.

```
100 PRINT "ENTER THE PERSON'S
    DRY WEIGHT IN KILOGRAMS"
110 INPUT DRYWT
120 PRINT "ENTER THE PERSON'S
    UNDERWATER WEIGHT IN
    KILOGRAMS"
130 INPUT WATERWT
140 PRINT "ENTER THE PERSON'S
    RESIDUAL VOLUME IN LITERS"
150 INPUT RESIDVOL
160 PRINT "ENTER THE CORRECTED
    WATER DENSITY IN GRAMS/
    MILLILITER"
170 INPUT WATERDENSE
180 BODYDENSE = DRYWT/((DRYWT
    − WATERWT)/WATERDENSE −
    RESIDVOL)
190 PERCENTFAT = (495/BODYDENSE)
    − 450
200 PERCENTLEAN = 100 −
    PERCENTFAT
210 FATWT = (PERCENTFAT/100)
    *DRYWT
220 LEANWT =
    (PERCENTLEAN/100)*DRYWT
230 PRINT "DRY WEIGHT(KG):",
    DRYWT
240 PRINT "UNDERWATER WEIGHT
    (KG):", WATERWT
250 PRINT "RESIDUAL VOLUME(L):",
    RESIDVOL
260 PRINT "WATER DENSITY
    (G/ML):", WATERDENSE
270 PRINT "BODY DENSITY (G/ML):",
    BODYDENSE
280 PRINT "PERCENTAGE OF FAT
    TISSUE:", PERCENTFAT
290 PRINT "PERCENTAGE OF LEAN
    TISSUE:", PERCENTLEAN
300 PRINT "AMOUNT OF FAT WEIGHT
    (KG):", FATWT
310 PRINT "AMOUNT OF LEAN
    WEIGHT (KG):", LEANWT
320 STOP
330 END
```

The following is an example of the screen display when using this program:

ENTER THE PERSON'S DRY WEIGHT IN KILOGRAMS
81.6
ENTER THE PERSON'S UNDERWATER

WEIGHT IN KILOGRAMS
3.6
ENTER THE PERSON'S RESIDUAL
VOLUME IN LITERS
1.3
ENTER THE CORRECTED WATER
DENSITY IN GRAMS/MILLILITER
.997
DRY WEIGHT (KG): 81.6

UNDERWATER WEIGHT (KG): 3.6
RESIDUAL VOLUME (L): 1.3
WATER DENSITY (G/ML): .997
BODY DENSITY (G/ML): 1.06064
PERCENTAGE OF FAT TISSUE: 16.69946
PERCENTAGE OF LEAN TISSUE: 83.30055
AMOUNT OF FAT WEIGHT (KG): 13.62676
AMOUNT OF LEAN WEIGHT (KG):
67.97325

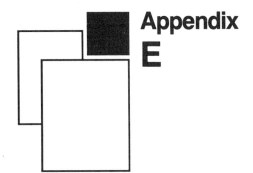

Analysis of Variance in Determining an Intraclass Correlation Coefficient

As presented in chapter 5, the variability among any group of scores may be characterized as $\sigma_{os}^2 = \sigma_t^2 + \sigma_e^2$ where σ_{os}^2 = total variance for observed scores, σ_t^2 = true score variance, and σ_e^2 = error score variance. It was further stated that

$$\text{Reliability} = \frac{\sigma_t^2}{\sigma_{os}^2} = \frac{\sigma_{os}^2 - \sigma_e^2}{\sigma_{os}^2}$$

or that reliability is the relative proportion of total variance that is true score variance. The Pearson product-moment correlation coefficient was presented as one means of estimating this reliability. However, we saw the inadequacy of this technique when more than two trials of a test are administered, which is frequently the case in motor performance tests. In order to determine an appropriate reliability coefficient for multi-trialed tests, an estimate of the variance components indicated above must be found. They are found by analysis of variance techniques that allow the determination of an intraclass correlation coefficient. For demonstrating the techniques desired, a simple example prob-

lem will be presented. Assume that four students performed the maximum number of chins that they could on three different occasions. The hypothetical results are presented in Table E.1.

From chapter 4, we know that the variance for the entire group of 12 scores would be

$$\sigma_x^2 = \frac{\sum(X - \overline{X})^2}{N}$$

However, because the use of analysis of variance requires the assumption of inference, we would use

$$s_x^2 = \frac{\sum(X - \overline{X})^2}{N - 1}$$

Furthermore, we first want to determine the total amount of *variation* present among scores, not the average variation or variance. Therefore, we find $\sum(X - \overline{X})^2$, which is the total sum of squares, denoted by SST. Thus

$$\text{SST} = \sum(X - \overline{X})^2 = \sum X^2 - \frac{(\sum X)^2}{N}$$

Table E.1 Three Trials of Chins for Four Students

Student	Trial 1 score	Trial 2 score	Trial 3 score	Total student score	Mean student score
A	9	8	9	26	8.67
B	1	2	3	6	2.00
C	3	2	2	7	2.33
D	5	5	3	13	4.33
Trial totals	18	17	17	52	
Trial means	4.5	4.25	4.25	4.33	

which, for our example is

$$\text{SST} = 316 - \frac{(52)^2}{12} = 316 - \frac{2704}{12}$$

$$= 316 - 225.33 = 90.67$$

Now our problem is to find the sum of squares for the true scores and the sum of squares for the error scores. If our scores were perfectly reliable, there would be no variation from trial to trial for each student. In order to determine the amount of trial to trial variation for each student, we find the sum of the squared differences between each trial score for a student and his or her mean score. For example, Student B's variation would be $(1 - 2)^2 + (2 - 2)^2 + (3 - 2)^2 = 1 + 0 + 1 = 2$. Symbolically, we could write this as

$$\sum (X_B - \overline{X}_B)^2 = \sum X_B{}^2 - \frac{T_B{}^2}{n}$$

$$= (1^2 + 2^2 + 3^2) - \frac{(6)^2}{3}$$

$$= (1 + 4 + 9) - \frac{36}{3}$$

$$= 14 - 12 = 2$$

where T_B = total score for Student B and n = number of trials.

For Student A, we would have

$$\sum (X_A - \overline{X}_A)^2 = \sum X_A{}^2 - \frac{T_A{}^2}{n}$$

$$= (81 + 64 + 81) - \frac{(26)^2}{3}$$

$$= 226 - \frac{676}{3}$$

$$= 226 - 225.33 = .67$$

Similarly, for Student C we would have

$$\sum X_C{}^2 - \frac{T_C{}^2}{n} = 17 - \frac{49}{3} = 17 - 16.33 = .67$$

and for Student D we would have

$$\sum X_D{}^2 - \frac{T_D{}^2}{n} = 59 - \frac{169}{3}$$

$$= 59 - 56.33 = 2.67$$

Therefore, the total error variation, called the sum of squares error (SSE), is equal to the sum of the individual variations. In our example,

$$\text{SSE} = 2 + .67 + .67 + 2.67 = 6.01$$

This procedure condensed will result in a general formula for finding SSE, which is much easier to use than separately finding the variation for each student. The condensed formula is

$$SSE = \sum X^2 - \frac{\sum\limits_{i}^{k} T_i^2}{n}$$

where T_i = the total score for Student i, k = number of students, and n = number of trials.

Just to see that this works the same for our example, if we use this condensed procedure, we find

$$SSE = \sum X^2 - \frac{\sum\limits_{i}^{k} T_i^2}{n}$$

$$= 316 - \frac{(676 + 36 + 49 + 169)}{3}$$

$$= 316 - \frac{930}{3} = 316 - 310 = 6$$

which, within rounding, is the same as before.

We would expect students, on the average, to differ in how well they perform. An estimate of this among student variation is defined as

$$SSA = n \sum\limits_{j=1}^{P} (\overline{X}_j - \overline{X})^2$$

where $\overline{X}$ represents the overall mean or the mean of all scores, $\overline{X}_j$ represents the mean score for a particular student, P represents the number of students, and n represents the number of trials. For our example,

$$SSA = 3[(8.67 - 4.33)^2 + (2 - 4.33)^2$$
$$+ (2.33 - 4.33)^2 + (4.33 - 4.33)^2]$$
$$= 3 (18.84 + 5.43 + 4 + 0)$$
$$= 3(28.27) = 84.81$$

A simpler formula to use for SSA is:

$$SSA = \frac{\sum\limits_{i}^{k} T_i^2}{n} - \frac{(\sum X)^2}{nk}$$

where the symbols represent the same as before. Using this formula for the example problem, we find:

$$SSA = \frac{930}{3} - \frac{2704}{3 \cdot 4} = 310 - 225.33 = 84.67$$

which is the same, within rounding, as before. Notice that for our example, we have found

$$SST = 90.67$$
$$SSE = 6$$
$$SSA = 84.67$$

In fact, SST = SSA + SSE.

In order to determine intraclass correlation, we must use variances instead of variations. These variance estimates are called mean squares. In order to find the variance among the students' scores (MSA), we divide the sum of squares among SSA by one less than the number of students, or $k - 1$. Thus

$$MSA = \frac{SSA}{k - 1}$$

For the error score, we divide the error sum of squares (SSE) by one less than the number of trials, or $n - 1$. Thus

$$MSE = \frac{SSE}{n - 1}$$

In statistics, these divisors are called the *degrees of freedom* for each variation component and denoted as *df*. For our example,

$$MSA = \frac{SSA}{k - 1} = \frac{84.67}{4 - 1} = \frac{84.67}{3} = 28.22$$

and

$$MSE = \frac{SSE}{n - 1} = \frac{6}{3 - 1} = \frac{6}{2} = 3.00$$

At first glance, we might think that MSA would be a likely candidate for estimating true score variance. However, MSA cannot be used as an estimate of true score variance because it contains measurement error. This is because in the calculation of SSA, the actual observed scores are used, which of course contain measurement error as well as the true score. Thus, MSA is considered to be the total or obtained score variance in which we are interested, and to find an actual estimate of the true score variance we must subtract the error score variance estimate from the among student variance estimates. In other words,

$$\text{Estimated } \sigma_t^2 = \text{MSA} - \text{MSE}$$

Because MSA is considered to be the total or obtained score variance in which we are interested and reliability is defined as

$$\frac{\sigma_t^2}{\sigma_{os}^2} = \frac{\sigma_{os}^2 - \sigma_t^2}{\sigma_{os}^2}$$

our reliability estimate, called intraclass correlation and symbolized by R, is defined as

$$R = \frac{\text{MSA} - \text{MSE}}{\text{MSA}}$$

In our example,

$$R = \frac{28.22 - 3.00}{28.22} = \frac{25.22}{28.22} = .89$$

It should be noted that this coefficient is the estimated reliability for total scores. If one wishes to determine the reliability of some other number of trials, then the appropriate formula to use is

$$R = \frac{\text{MSA} - \text{MSE}}{\text{MSA} + (\frac{n}{n'} - 1)\text{MSE}}$$

where n' is the desired number of trials for which a reliability estimate is needed.

In our example, if we wanted to determine the reliability for a single trial, then $n' = 1$ and

$$R = \frac{25.22}{28.22 + (\frac{3}{1} - 1)3}$$

$$= \frac{25.22}{28.22 + 6} = \frac{25.22}{34.22} = .74$$

We can see that our original formula given for total score is a special case of this present formula because the original case $n = n'$ and

$$\left(\frac{n}{n'} - 1\right) = 0$$

All of the procedures introduced thus far are summarized in Table E.2.

It must be emphasized that the procedures described here have assumed that no trend across trials exists. More specifically, it has been assumed that there is not a significant difference among trial means. For our example, we saw that the trial means were: $\overline{X}_1 = 4.5$, $\overline{X}_2 = 4.25$, and $\overline{X}_3 = 4.25$, which subjectively would indicate that no trial to trial trend exists.

The technique for objectively determining the existence of trend requires the application of an inferential statistical procedure called *two-way analysis of variance*. This method will not be presented here. Rather, it is suggested that at this point in your studies you always determine the means of each trial and if there subjectively appears to be a trend present, use the trials where stability appears to be present in the determination of intraclass correlation and the subsequent use of the test.

Table E.2 Analysis of Variance and Intraclass Correlation

Sources of variation	Sum of squares	Degrees of freedom	Mean squares
Among students	SSA	$k - 1$	$\text{MSA} = \dfrac{\text{SSA}}{k - 1}$
Error	SSE	$n - 1$	$\text{MSE} = \dfrac{\text{SSE}}{n - 1}$

$$\text{SSA} = \frac{\sum\limits^{k} T_i^2}{n} - \frac{(\sum X)^2}{nk}$$

$$\text{SSE} = \sum X^2 - \frac{\sum\limits^{k} T_i^2}{n}$$

where n = number of trials, k = number of students, and T_i = total score for student i.

$$\text{Intraclass correlation } R = \frac{\text{MSA} - \text{MSE}}{\text{MSA} + \left(\dfrac{n}{n'} - 1\right)\text{MSE}}$$

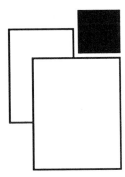

Glossary

Abduction. Moving away from the midline of the body.

Achievement. Accomplishment of an individual beyond a defined starting point.

Adduction. Moving toward the midline of the body.

Agility. The ability to change whole body and body segment directions quickly and accurately in a coordinated manner.

Anthropometry. Body measurements.

Assessment. The process of determining the value or worth of a particular thing.

Auditory discrimination. The process of discerning differences in sound through the sense of hearing.

Balance. Sensory-perceptual-neuromuscular response to motion or gravity.

Battery. Series of tests or test items.

Behavioral objective. A statement that is measurable and observable and that describes a standard of excellence expected of a participant.

Central tendency. The tendency of a group of scores to concentrate toward the middle.

Concurrent validity. The degree to which a developed test correlates to an established standard.

Construct validity. How well a construct or structure describes an ability or phenomenon.

Content validity. The degree to which the items on a test actually measure the content they purport to measure. Sometimes called "face" or "logical validity."

Correlation coefficient. The mathematically computed degree of relationship or agreement between variables.

Criterion. A standard for judging the worth of something for a specific purpose at a certain time.

Criterion-referenced test. A test that has written or stated standards determined by the evaluator.

Data. Facts or scores that are used as sources of information.

Deviation score. The result of subtracting the mean from a score in a data set.

Distribution. Any group of scores.

Dynamometer. An instrument used as an indicator of static muscular strength.

Evaluation. The process of assessing the worth of collected data. It includes testing and measurement and is utilized in the decision-making process.

Extension. Movement of a body segment that

increases the angle of measure around a joint.

Flexibility. Range of movement around a joint.

Flexion. Movement of a body segment that decreases the angle of measure around a joint.

Formative evaluation. The process of judging accomplishment or lack of accomplishment at the developmental stages of learning. It is characterized by frequent and immediate feedback to each participant.

Goal. A general statement concerning desired accomplishments.

Goniometer. An instrument that measures flexibility.

Hierarchy. Placement of activities in an ordered fashion in which one task precedes a more complex task.

Interval measurement. Measurement that reflects equal differences between the numbers assigned, which reflects equal amounts of the attributes measured. The zero point of the interval scale can be placed arbitrarily and does not indicate absence of the property measured.

Item analysis. An analysis of the items on a knowledge test. It assists in determining the value of each item in contributing to the purpose of the test.

Item difficulty. The difficulty level of an item in a knowledge test; determined by dividing the number of correct responses to an item by the total number responses to the same item.

Item discrimination index. How well an item on a knowledge test discriminates among participants taking the test.

Kinesthetic discrimination. Sense of muscle force, tendon stretching, and joint position.

Least restrictive environment. Educational environment that least restricts an impaired person's learning ability.

Mainstreaming. Placement of an impaired individual into a normal situation with or without aid.

Mastery test. A test of proficiency that mea-

sures how well a participant has mastered requirements and content of instruction.

Mean. The arithmetic average of a set of scores.

Median. The middle point in an ordered distribution.

Mode. The most frequently occurring score in a set of scores.

Motor fitness. Includes physical fitness plus the functioning level of an individual's balance, speed, coordination, and agility.

Motor development. Includes physical fitness, motor fitness, plus the functioning level of an individual's reflexes, sensory input, perception, and motor responses.

Nominal measurement. The process of grouping objects into classes that have the same attributes.

Norms. Performance standards recently derived and based on a large number of scores.

Norm-referenced standards. Judgment of a performance as related to standards established by a large sample of a well-defined group.

Objective measurement. The process of collecting a score that is meaningful and observable in an impartial manner.

Objectivity. The degree of agreement among testers.

Ordinal measurement. Measurement that can detect differing degrees or amounts of an attribute.

Parameter. A measurable characteristic of a population.

Percentile rank of a score. The percentage of scores that are equal to or less than that score.

Physical fitness. The functioning level of an individual's muscular strength, muscular endurance, cardiovascular endurance, power, and flexibility.

Population. Any group of people or objects with a common characteristic. A population is to be defined by an investigator.

Posttest results. Data gathered after the application of a program.

Power. The product of force times distance (work) divided by time.

Predictive validity. The degree of ability to predict a performance test score on one measure from that of another measure.

Pretest results. Data gathered before the application of a program.

Range. The largest score in a distribution minus the smallest score. A measure of variability.

Rank order. Scores placed in order, either from high to low or from low to high.

Rating scale. Response to a statement using a standard set of response categories. Rating scales are descriptive terms for each category of the statement. A rating scale measures performance subjectively.

Ratio measurement. Measurement that has all the properties of an interval scale, and in addition an absolute zero point exists on the scale.

Reliability. The degree to which a test measures whatever it measures consistently.

Sample. Any subgroup of a population.

Sampling. The process of selecting a limited number of cases from a particular population.

Self-image. How a person views himself or herself.

Six-sigma score. A standard score with a mean of 50 and a standard deviation of 16.67.

Stadiometer. Instrument for measuring height.

Skinfold calipers. A measuring instrument to determine the thickness of subcutaneous fat tissue.

Speed. Distance divided by time.

Sphygmomanometer. Instrument used for indirect measurement of blood pressure.

Spirometer. Equipment for measuring lung capacity.

Standard deviation. The positive square root of the variance. A linear measure of variability about the mean of a set of scores.

Standard error of measurement. The amount of error one would expect in an individual score.

Standard score. The position of a subject's raw score relative to the mean and standard deviation of the set of raw scores. Transforms a set of raw scores to an arbitrary scale usually called z, T, or 6-σ-scores.

Standardized test. A test with standard procedures of measurement, validity, and reliability.

Statistic. A measurable characteristic of a sample.

Summative evaluation. Evaluation that takes place at the end of a unit of instruction.

Tactile discrimination. Differentiating among sensations of touch, pressure, and temperature.

Task analysis. Identifying required behaviors of a task for analysis.

Tensiometer. An instrument for measuring the pulling force on a cable. An indicator of static muscular strength.

T score. A standard score with a mean of 50 and a standard deviation of 10.

Validity. The degree to which a test measures what it purports to measure.

Variance. A measure of variability. It is the average of the sum of the squared deviations about the mean.

Visual discrimination. The act of recognizing differences in visual sensations.

z-score. A standard score with a mean of 0 and a standard deviation of 1.

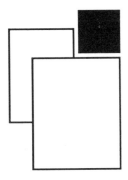

Author Index

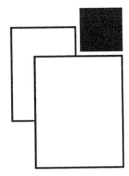

Subject Index

U

United States Gymnastics Safety Association, 279
Universe of abilities, 81-82
University of Kentucky Swim Test, 260, 263-267, 269-270

V

Validity
  defined, 53, 67
  concurrent, 56-57, 92-93
  construct, 55-56, 93
  content, 54, 290
  criterion-related, 56-57
  curricular, 290
  external, 92-93
  factors affecting, 57-58

  internal, 92-93
  predictive, 57
  rating, 57
Variability, 14, 24, 26-29
  of skill, 86-88
Variance, 27-28
Volleyball Skill Tests, 272-277

W

Writing
  behavioral objectives, 76-79
  goals, 73-76

Z

z-score, 29-31